THE

COMPLETE LETTERS

OF

Lady Mary Wortley Montagu

VOLUME I

1708-1720

Lady Mary Wortley Montagu
From a painting by Jonathan Richardson, senior

THE
COMPLETE LETTERS
OF
Lady Mary
Wortley Montagu

EDITED BY

ROBERT HALSBAND

VOLUME I

1708–1720

OXFORD

AT THE CLARENDON PRESS

1965

Oxford University Press, Ely House, London W. 1

GLASGOW NEW YORK TORONTO MELBOURNE WELLINGTON
CAPE TOWN SALISBURY IBADAN NAIROBI LUSAKA ADDIS ABABA
BOMBAY CALCUTTA MADRAS KARACHI LAHORE DACCA
KUALA LUMPUR HONG KONG

PRINTED IN GREAT BRITAIN
AT THE UNIVERSITY PRESS, OXFORD
BY VIVIAN RIDLER
PRINTER TO THE UNIVERSITY

PREFACE

LADY MARY WORTLEY MONTAGU owes her cumbersome name to her father, whose peerage gave her the courtesy title, and to her husband, who sometimes called himself Wortley but usually Wortley Montagu. In her own day her intellectual prominence and her connexion with Alexander Pope and his circle earned for her the equivocal distinction of being recognized in print as *the* Lady Mary. Merely notorious during her lifetime, she became famous in 1763, the year after her death, when her Turkish Embassy Letters were published. Edward Gibbon exclaimed over their fire, their ease, their knowledge of Europe and Asia; Dr. Johnson read them for sheer enjoyment; Voltaire trumpeted their excellence throughout Europe; and Tobias Smollett announced to England that they were unequalled by any letter-writer of any sex, age, or nation. With these letters Lady Mary won her first renown as a great writer.

Forty years later, an edition of her letters and works was published that showed a wider range of her art; it included the vivacious letters of her girlhood, the grave correspondence of her courtship, the brilliant gossip-letters to her sister, and the leisurely, diversified series to her daughter from her Continental retirement. Successive editions further expanded her *œuvre* until the most recent, in 1861, which printed an extensive selection, almost entirely from the Wortley Manuscripts.[1]

The present edition can be called 'complete'—if that word is interpreted in human terms: it includes almost every letter by Lady Mary uncovered after a search of almost three decades, and it prints the complete text of each letter. The 1861 edition was not only selective; it bowdlerized and

---

1 Additional extracts from the Wortley MSS, mainly to Wortley, are printed in *Lady Mary Wortley Montagu and Her Times*, 1907, by George Paston [Emily Morse Symonds].

took other editorial liberties no longer tolerable. It printed, often in emasculated or 'corrected' versions, about 470 letters by Lady Mary. The present edition prints about 900 letters by her. Among these are four entirely new correspondences—with Philippa Mundy, a girlhood friend, with Francesco Algarotti, writer and savant, with Chiara Bragadin Michiel, a Venetian patrician, and with James Stuart Mackenzie, brother of the 3rd Earl of Bute. In addition there are printed here about 100 letters (entire or in part) written to Lady Mary, most of them from Wortley, and others by such literary and political figures as Montesquieu, Fielding, Edward Young, and Lord Hervey.[1] It may be rash to claim that this edition contains the 'complete letters' of Lady Mary, for impish Fate may at any time reveal new ones after these are published. Still, that risk may be taken in view of the fact that the edition prints the full text of every one of Lady Mary's letters known some two hundred years after her death.

The question may well be asked, why Lady Mary's letters deserve such thorough and careful publication in a scholarly edition extending to three volumes.[2] Are they of sufficient literary and intellectual value? Such an unlikely champion as Thomas Carlyle thought that she deserved to be remembered as 'the first Englishwoman who combined the knowledge of classical and modern literature with a penetrating judgment and correct taste.'[3] Since her own day literary critics have praised her style. Walter Bagehot, in 1862, claimed for her the highest merit of letter-writing: 'she is concise without being affected. . . . She said what she had to say in words that were always graphic and always sufficiently good, but she avoided curious felicity. Her expressions seemed choice, but not chosen.'[4] Early in our century Lytton Strachey considered the most conspicuous quality of her letters to be 'a certain outspoken clarity. . . . She is always absolutely frank and absolutely sensible; yet she manages never to be heavy.'

1 The letters from Pope are excluded mainly because they were impeccably edited in 1956 from the manuscripts (in the Pierpont Morgan Library) by George Sherburn in his edition of Pope's Correspondence.

2 Volumes ii and iii (with complete index) will be published shortly.

3 'Lady Mary Wortley Montagu' (1820), Works, 1903-4, xxx. 77.

4 Literary Studies, ed. R. H. Hutton, 1895, ii. 255.

Preface

Her wit has that quality which is the best of all preservatives against dullness—it goes straight to the point.'[1]

Aside from their literary excellence, Lady Mary's letters deal with many aspects of eighteenth-century life and culture, and are frequently drawn upon by scholars in other disciplines. The political historian, for example, turns to them for the parliamentary election campaigns that preceded and followed the accession of George the First; the diplomatic historian, for her comments on the courts of Europe and Constantinople; the musicologist, for her description of Viennese opera in 1716; the art historian, for her judgement of European painters and of Consul Smith of Venice; the medical historian, for her pioneering of smallpox inoculation in England; and the social historian, for her analysis of religion, customs, and morality in Ottoman Turkey, and for her keen-eyed observations during a long lifetime in England and on the Continent. Her letters, with these rich ramifications, deserve the most conscientious treatment and presentation. At the same time, footnotes and other apparatus have been arranged in such a way that they can easily be disregarded by the general reader—who, since the first publication of Lady Mary's letters, has read them simply for enjoyment.

In editing them I have been helped by many friends, collectors, scholars, and librarians. Specific acknowledgements appear in the third volume, but here I should like particularly to thank Columbia University, for various privileges; the Earl of Harrowby, for his truly noble generosity; the late George Sherburn and D. Nichol Smith, for advice and encouragement; Miss Isobel Grundy, for zeal and acuteness far beyond her duties; and my wife, finally, for unflagging and inspiring encouragement. Like my biography of Lady Mary, this edition is dedicated to her.

R. H.

New York City
March 1965

1 *Characters and Commentaries*, 1933, p. 24. The most extended and recent critique is my essay 'Lady Mary Wortley Montagu as Letter-Writer' in *PMLA* (Pub. of the Mod. Lang. Assoc. of America), June 1965, pp. 155–63.

ix

CONTENTS

LIST OF PLATES

INTRODUCTION TO VOLUME I

IN this first volume of Lady Mary's letters there are three extended correspondences. The longest, with Wortley, spans their protracted courtship (1710–12) and the early years of their married life until, at the beginning of 1715, she joined him in London to take advantage of the prosperity that George the First's accession brought to the Whigs. Many of Wortley's letters, either in whole or part, have been dovetailed with hers in order to clarify their arguments. The main themes of their courtship are finance (her dowry and his settlement), meetings at friends' houses and social functions, their future life together (love, solitude, and economy), his jealousy and her denials, her father's choice of a husband and her defiance, and their plans for an elopement—which they achieved after a succession of scenes worthy of sentimental comedy.

This phase of their correspondence gives way, after their marriage, to her letters in 'a proper matrimonial stile'[1]— where she expresses herself as a submissive and affectionate wife, and after the birth of their son the next year, a solicitous mother. She now applies herself to such practical matters as house-renting, servants, and the price of meat. But it is inconceivable that she should dwindle into domesticity; she also delivers strenuous advice to Wortley about his parliamentary election, and canvasses their friends to find where he can stand most securely and economically. Seen in its entire perspective her correspondence with him ranges over a wide field from a tremulous beginning as a romantic girl to a bustling conclusion as the wife of the Ambassador to Turkey.

Her correspondence with Philippa Mundy, a young lady

---

[1] Printed below, pp. 168 ff.

her own age, extends to twenty-four letters, from 1711 to 1714; they are printed here for the first time.[1] They show how she regarded her courtship when confiding in an intimate friend. And then, after her marriage, from her store of matronly wisdom she advises Philippa about *her* courtship. These new letters are important enough for their contrapuntal design to those she sent Wortley; in their own right they are a fresh, vivacious addition to her works.

The Turkish Embassy Letters[2] are distinctive in being a compilation and in being addressed to various correspondents. Aside from the complicated problem of their composition and their relationship to actual letters, they are brilliant virtuoso letters in which she exploited her rich opportunities when she visited the courts of Western Europe, rode across the frozen, war-ravaged plains of Hungary, basked in the exotic splendour of Turkey, and sailed along the classical shores of the Mediterranean. Besides their distinction as literature, the Embassy Letters are biographically significant since they show how much she had developed in literary skill and intellectual sophistication. Finally, these letters contributed greatly to the exchange of ideas between Islamic Turkey and Christian Europe. By virtue of their clear-sighted observation, their expansive tolerance, and their candid sympathy for an alien culture, they are Lady Mary's valid credential for a place in the European 'Enlightenment'.

THE TURKISH EMBASSY LETTERS

Lady Mary's Turkish Embassy Letters, fifty-two in number, exist almost entirely in her own autograph as copied by her into two small albums.[3] They are not the actual letters she sent to her friends and relations; they are, instead, a compilation of pseudo-letters, dated, and addressed to people either named or nameless. Although they are clearly an accurate record of her experiences and observations during her two-year sojourn abroad, we may still wonder to what extent they are based on real letters. Are they perhaps a travel-memoir

---

[1] Below, pp. 106 ff.
[2] Printed below, pp. 248 ff.

[3] H MS 253, 254. (For list of abbreviations, see p. xxi below).

in the form of letters (a literary genre popular since the Renaissance)?

According to her granddaughter, she extracted these letters from a journal which she wrote during the Embassy.[1] In fact, only two long episodes—her day-by-day record of the dangerous journey across the plains of Hungary and her voyage through the Mediterranean—show signs of having had such a source. She turned elsewhere to compile her collection—most logically, to the full and interesting letters she was sending to her friends and relations. In her own albums she labelled the collection 'Copys of Letters'.

Among the Wortley Manuscripts is a document written by her, and endorsed by Wortley as 'Heads of L. M.'s Letters From Turky'.[2] In it she had jotted down the initials of correspondents with brief summaries of the letters she sent to them between 1 April 1717 and 1 March 1718.[3] From this period only one of her actual letters survived in manuscript, sent to Mrs. Hewet in April 1717;[4] and it matches its summary in the 'Heads'. Yet none of its personal and homely contents can be found in the Embassy Letters. As a conscious literary artist Lady Mary carefully selected what she included. But among the 'Heads' is another which provides a link with the Embassy Letters—the summary[5] of a letter to the Abbé Antonio Conti, a cosmopolitan savant living at the time in Paris. That she sent a letter to Conti (in French) dealing with precisely the topics of her summary we know through a curious circumstance: Conti was so proud of the witty letters he received from her that he showed them to his friends in Paris, and one of them, Antoine-Robert Pérelle (1695–1735), then described that very letter in his diary:

> . . . I have seen Master Kownte [*sic*]. Il m' a montré une Lettre de Mylady Marie; je n'ai gueres vu tant d'exactitude avec tant de vivacité.

---

[1] Stuart, p. 83; the journal was destroyed by LM's daughter (p. 64).

[2] W MS vii. 124–5; printed below, pp. 344–6, 352–3, 370, 374, 379.

[3] In the 'Heads' there are seventeen letters (some probably long ones) listed for 1 April 1717, but LM may have meant that she sent them off on that day (see below, p. 346, n. 6); and there is a gap of five months without any letters listed, which may merely mean that the list is incomplete.

[4] Below, pp. 308–9.

[5] See below, p. 315, n. 4.

Elle luy fait le Recit de son Voyage de Constantinople, ou elle est Ambassadrice d'Angletere. Elle parle de Peuples qu'elle a vu sur son Chemin qui de crainte de se tromper honorent Mahomet et Jesus Christ. Ils vont les vendredis aux Mosquées et les Dimanches a la Messe, et ils disent qu'apres leur mort ils scauront quel est le Veritable Prophete.¹ Elle y parle des Monts Hemus et Rhodope² et du fleuve Hebrus et cite a ce propos les fameux vers du 4e livre des Georgiques.³ On voit dans toute cette lettre un esprit indifferent, degagé de prejugé, et consequemment tres tolerant. Elle se moque des differentes sectes des Turcs et les Compare avec Les Lutheriens, Les Calvinistes, et les Romanistes. . . . Dans sa lettre elle paroist aimer fort la Verité et surtout a dire librement son sentiment.⁴

What this demonstrates is that Lady Mary's actual letter to Conti expatiated on the topics she listed in her 'Heads' for that letter, but she then distributed the topics among different Embassy Letters addressed to Conti, Pope, and the Princess of Wales.

Further proof, if necessary, that the Embassy ones came from actual letters can be found in the 'Heads'. Two letters listed there, instead of having their summaries set down, bear the simple notation 'Copyd at length'; and, in fact, these two letters were copied by an amanuensis into the albums. It would thus seem that in the main Lady Mary compiled her Embassy Letters from actual letters which she 'edited' by transposing sections and otherwise manipulating them to achieve a more artistic collection. The two letters 'Copyd at length', along with a third in the hand of the same copyist, she evidently considered suitable enough to be included *in toto*.⁵ Besides, in the course of her correspondence with her sister Lady Mar and with Pope she promised to

---

¹ This topic is dealt with in the Embassy Letter dated 1 April [1717] addressed to Conti (p. 319 below).

² These mountains and the River Hebrus are mentioned in the Embassy Letter dated 1 April [1717] addressed to the Princess of Wales (p. 311 below).

³ The Hebrus is mentioned and the quotation from Virgil's *Georgics* copied in the Embassy Letter dated 1 April [1717] addressed to Alexander Pope

(p. 330 below).

⁴ MS Fr. 14708, f. 42, Bibliothèque Nationale. Part of this passage is published, without identification of LM, in the article by E. R. Briggs, 'L'Incrédulité et la pensée anglaise en France au début du dix-huitième siècle' in *Revue d'histoire littéraire de la France*, xli, 1934, pp. 497–538.

⁵ See below, pp. 365–7, 371–3, 396–403.

keep copies of her letters.[1] The Embassy Letters are those copies, rearranged and 'edited'.

It is certain that she intended them to be published, though not in her lifetime. In 1724 she loaned the albums to Mary Astell (1668–1731), the feminist and pamphleteer, who then wrote an exuberant preface in the blank pages at the end of the second volume.[2] Lady Mary kept the albums with her when she left England in 1739; and on her way home twenty-two years later, while delayed by bad weather in Rotterdam, she met an English clergyman there and presented the albums to him with the inscription: 'These 2 Volumes are given to the R[everen]d Benjamin Sowden, minister at Rotterdam, to be dispos'd of as he thinks proper. This is the will and design of M. Wortley Montagu, Dec. 11, 1761.' In May 1763, less than a year after her death, the letters were published without her family's permission from an imperfect copy of the manuscript.[3] This text was the basis of all editions of the Embassy Letters until 1861, when the albums themselves were first used.

PREVIOUS EDITIONS

1763

Letters Of the Right Honourable Lady M——y W——y M——e: Written, during her Travels in Europe, Asia and Africa, To Persons of Distinction, Men of Letters, &c. in different Parts of Europe. Which Contain, Among other Curious Relations, Accounts of the Policy and Manners of the Turks; Drawn from Sources that have been inaccessible to other Travellers. In Three Volumes. London: Printed for T. Becket and P. A. De Hondt, in the Strand. MDCCLXIII.

This unauthorized edition is based on a copy of her Embassy Letters MS.[4] It contains many verbal variants, none of them significant. John Cleland (1709–89) has been credited with being the editor,[5] though no proof of it exists.

---

[1] See below, p. 379, and Pope, *Corr.* i. 470.

[2] Printed below, pp. 466–8.

[3] For the story of their publication, see Halsband, *LM*, pp. 278–9, 287–9.

[4] The manuscript used as printer's copy for the 1763 edition is now in the Hampstead Public Library; it was among the papers of William Beattie, who was a friend of Andrew Becket, son and partner of the printer of that edition.

[5] John Nichols, *Lit. Anecdotes of the 18th Century*, 1812–15, viii. 412; also 1803, i. 24–25; 1861, i. 84.

1767

An Additional Volume To The Letters Of the Right Honourable Lady M——y W——y M——e: . . . . London: Printed for T. Becket and P. A. De Hondt, in the Strand. MDCCLXVII.

Published as a supplementary volume to the 1763 edition (and concluding with a table of contents for all four volumes), this contains five spurious letters.[1] No manuscript source for these five letters has ever been found; and internal factual evidence as well as literary style makes it practically certain that the letters are spurious. The editor of Lady Mary's letters in 1861 was also convinced of this, and firmly stated so.[2] But since he also reprinted these letters, careless anthologists have used them as samples of Lady Mary's epistolary art. The volume also contains some verse and two authentic prose pieces by Lady Mary which had previously been printed: a letter to the Abbé Conti[3] and an essay refuting a maxim of La Rochefoucauld.[4] This may be why Lady Mary's daughter was convinced that the volume published in 1767 must be 'genuine' after 'turning over half a dozen pages';[5] the pages were probably from the authentic, but previously printed, letter to Conti.

The circumstances of this publication are, like those of the 1763 one, mysterious. One account, by a reviewer whose testimony is of some value, states that the spurious letters were the result of a wager that Lady Mary's style could be imitated.[6] Their author, another version goes, was John Cleland.[7] Whoever the perpetrator, they should not be included in the canon of Lady Mary's letters.

1803

The Works of the Right Honourable Lady Mary Wortley Montagu, Including Her Correspondence, Poems, and Essays. Published, by Permission, from Her Genuine Papers. In Five Volumes. [ed. James Dallaway] London: Printed for Richard Phillips, No. 71, St. Paul's Churchyard. 1803.

This edition, the first one sanctioned by Lady Mary's family,[8] contains a brief, inaccurate biographical sketch by the editor; and, besides reprinting the Embassy Letters, gives for the first time selections from other important series of her letters—to Anne Wortley, to Edward Wortley Montagu, to her sister

---

[1] Four listed below on pp. 245, 293, 371, 443; the fifth on ii. 202.
[2] i. 15–16.
[3] Printed below, pp. 374–8.
[4] *Annual Register for 1763*, pp. 204–9; 1861, ii. 421–8.
[5] Stuart, 82–83.

[6] *Monthly Review*, 1784, p. 575; Benjamin C. Nangle, *The Monthly Review First Series 1749–1789*, 1934, pp. 28, 108.
[7] *Gentleman's Mag.*, 1803, p. 1043.
[8] For the strange story of its publication, see Halsband, *LM*, pp. 289–90.

Lady Mar, and (from her sojourn on the Continent) to her husband and to their daughter the Countess of Bute.

1805

[The same as 1803, except] The Fifth Edition . . . 1805. Lady Mary's letters to Mrs. Frances Hewet were printed here for the first time, at the end of volume v.

1837

The Letters and Works of Lady Mary Wortley Montagu. Edited by Her Great Grandson Lord Wharncliffe.[1] In Three Volumes. London: Richard Bentley, New Burlington Street, Publisher in Ordinary to His Majesty. 1837.

The important additions here are the 'Introductory Anecdotes' by Lady Mary's granddaughter Lady Louisa Stuart, and important series of letters to Lady Pomfret, to Lady Oxford, and to Sir James and Lady Frances Steuart (first printed privately in 1818).

1861

The Letters and Works of Lady Mary Wortley Montagu. Edited by Her Great-Grandson Lord Wharncliffe. Third Edition, With Additions and Corrections Derived from the Original Manuscripts, Illustrative Notes, and a New Memoir By W. Moy Thomas. In Two Volumes. London: Henry G. Bohn, York Street, Covent Garden. MDCCCLXI.

Thomas replaced Dallaway's memoir with one by himself; and without adding any new correspondences enlarged those from the Wortley MSS. By his transcription from MSS whenever possible, particularly of the Embassy Letters, he produced for the first time an edition worthy of her literary rank.

MANUSCRIPT OWNERS

Lady Mary's letters and papers are, for the most part, among the Wortley MSS now owned by the Earl of Harrowby. Their descent can easily be traced. At her death all of Lady Mary's papers were inherited by her only daughter, the Countess of Bute, who left them to her eldest son. Since he, the 1st Marquess of Bute, left all his 'Manuscript papers whatsoever' to his second wife, the Wortley MSS then descended to their only son, Lord Dudley Coutts Stuart; and he in turn left them to his sister Frances, wife of the 2nd Earl of

---

[1] James Archibald Stuart-Wortley-Mackenzie (1776–1845), 1st Baron.

Harrowby. Several groups of Lady Mary's letters still remain among Lord Bute's papers; and a miscellaneous collection of her letters and documents, owned by the Earl of Wharncliffe (another descendant), is now deposited in the Sheffield Public Library.

In addition, the following own letters printed in this volume: the Society of Antiquaries, Newcastle upon Tyne (1), the Editor (1), Anthony Massingberd-Mundy (24), the Pierpont Morgan Library (1), the Duke of Newcastle (1), the Earl Stanhope (1), the Duke of Sutherland (1), Robert H. Taylor (1), Sir Eustace F. Tickell (1), Yale University (1).

EDITORIAL PRINCIPLES

Manuscript Sources

In general I have used a literal transcription, changing only what I thought might impede smooth reading.[1] My specific principles are as follows: exact spelling and numerals are retained; most abbreviations (including the ampersand) are expanded—except in addresses and endorsements, where transcription is exact; raised letters are lowered; punctuation is adjusted when required,[2] with a full stop always at the end of a sentence; capital letters are retained,[3] and added (if necessary) for persons, places, book-titles, and at the beginning of sentences; apostrophes are added for possessives and deleted in plurals; long passages are usually lightened by paragraphing; square brackets [ ] indicate editorial interpolations, and angle brackets ⟨ ⟩ doubtful readings.

Printed Sources

Texts are reprinted literally, though obvious misprints are silently corrected, and new paragraphs sometimes indicated.

[1] My rationale is set forth in my article 'Editing the Letters of Letter-Writers', in *Studies in Bibliography*, xi, 1958, pp. 25–37.

[2] Since most of my transcriptions have been made from microfilm or photocopies, exact reproduction of punctuation, even if desirable, would not be possible.

[3] In eighteenth-century handwriting it is not always certain whether the writer intended a capital or not.

SHORT TITLES AND OTHER ABBREVIATIONS

All dates in England before 1752 are given in Old Style (o.s.) and on the Continent in New Style (n.s.), eleven days later.

All references to Lady Mary's published letters and works are cited by the dates of the editions (described above, pp. xvii–xix).

The following standard biographical works and peerages have been used but will not be cited unless for a particular reason: ENGLISH—Collins; *DNB*; G. E. Cokayne, *Complete Baronetage*, 1900–9; GEC *Peerage*; FRENCH—F.-A. A. de La Chenaye-Desbois, *Dictionnaire de la noblesse*, 3rd ed., 1863–76; J. C. F. Hoefer, *Nouvelle Biographie générale*, 1853–70; H. Jougla de Morenas, *Grand Armorial de France*, 1934–49; J. F. Michaud, *Biographie universelle ancienne et moderne*, [1870–3]; GERMAN—*ADB*; C. von Wurzbach, *Biographisches Lexikon*, 1856–91.

Standard encyclopaedias likewise have been used but will not generally be cited.

ADB	*Allgemeine Deutsche Biographie*, 1875–1912.
Add MS	Additional Manuscripts, British Museum.
Collins	Arthur Collins, *Peerage of England*, ed. Sir Egerton Brydges, 1812.
DNB	*Dictionary of National Biography*.
Dumont	Jean Dumont, *A New Voyage to the Levant*, 4th ed., 1705.
Eg MS	Egerton Manuscripts, British Museum.
Encycl. of Islam	*The Encyclopaedia of Islam*, new ed., volume i (A–B), 1960; (C–Z), 1913–36.
GEC *Peerage*	G. E. Cokayne, *The Complete Peerage*, ed. V. Gibbs *et al.*, 1910–59.
H MS	Harrowby Manuscripts Trust, Sandon Hall, Stafford.
Halsband, *LM*	Robert Halsband, *The Life of Lady Mary Wortley Montagu*, 1956.
Hill	Aaron Hill, *A Full and Just Account of the Present State of the Ottoman Empire*, 1709.
HMC	Historical Manuscripts Commission Reports.

Isenburg	W. K. von Isenburg, *Stammtafeln zur Geschichte der europäischen Staaten*, revised ed., 1958–61.
LM	Lady Mary (Pierrepont) Wortley Montagu.
M/M	Massingberd-Mundy Manuscripts, on deposit in the Lincoln Record Office.
MS	Manuscript *or* Manuscripts.
Nugent	Thomas Nugent, *The Grand Tour*, 3rd ed., 1778.
OED	*Oxford English Dictionary.*
P.C.C.	Prerogative Court of Canterbury (wills), Somerset House.
Pöllnitz	Karl Ludwig Pöllnitz, *Lettres et mémoires*, 3rd ed., 1737.
Pope, *Corr.*	Alexander Pope, *Correspondence*, ed. G. Sherburn, 1956.
PRO	Public Record Office, London.
SP	State Papers, Public Record Office.
Stuart	Lady Louisa Stuart, 'Introductory Anecdotes', in vol. i of LM's *Letters and Works*, 1861.
Tickell MS	Owned by Sir Eustace F. Tickell.
W	Edward Wortley Montagu.
W MS	Wortley Manuscripts (vols. i–viii: Harrowby MS, vols. 74–81).
Wentworth Papers	*Wentworth Papers 1705–1739*, ed. J. J. Cartwright, 1883.
Wh MS	Wharncliffe Muniments, on deposit in the Sheffield Central Library.

INDEX OF CORRESPONDENTS AND LETTERS IN VOLUME I

LETTERS previously unpublished are indicated by an asterisk (*). Letters previously published either in full or in extracts (×) are indicated by the date of their first publication among LM's letters (1763, 1803, 1805, 1861) and in these two biographies: 1907, George Paston [Emily Morse Symonds], *Lady Mary Wortley Montagu and Her Times*; and 1956, Halsband, *LM.*

Whether or not previously published, the great majority of letters are printed here from the original manuscripts.

To Anne Wortley[1] [*c. 25 Aug. 1708*][2]

I am convince't, however dear you are to me, Mrs. Anne Wortley, I am no longer of anny concern to you; therefore I shall only trouble you with an insignificant Story, when I tell you, I have bin very near leaveing this changeable World, but now by the Doctor's assistance and heaven's blessing, am in a condition of being as impertinently troublesome to you as formerly. A sore throat, which plague'd me for a long while, brought me at last to such a weakness, you had a fair chance for being ⟨released from me⟩,[3] but God has not yet decre⟨ed you⟩ so much happyness, thô I mus⟨t s⟩ay this, you have omitted nothing to make your self so easy, haveing strove to kill me by Neglect, but Destiny triumphs over all your efforts; I am yet in the land of the liveing, and still Your

M.P.[4]

Text W MS iv. 136–7   *Address* To Mrs Anne Wortley Montague at Peterborrough[5] in Huntingtonshire by way of London. care   *Post-mark* TUXFORD AV 27

To [6] Lady —— [*1708*]

Having (like other undeserving people) a vast opinion of my own merits, and some small faith in your sincerity, I

[1] The 2nd da. of the Hon. Sidney Wortley (1650–1727), M.P. and coalmine owner. He was 2nd son of Edward Montagu, 1st Earl of Sandwich, but had changed his name by the terms of the will of Sir Francis Wortley, whose natural daughter he had married (Jos. Hunter, *South Yorkshire*, 1831, ii. 319).

[2] The year is speculative. In 1709 the two young ladies were carrying on a busy correspondence to which this letter does not belong.

[3] Restored from 1861, i. 158. A postscript is also torn away.

[4] Lady Mary Pierrepont (1689–1762), eldest da. of Evelyn Pierrepont, 1st Marquess of Dorchester, and of Lady Mary Feilding (*c.* 1668–92), da. of 3rd Earl of Denbigh.

[5] Sidney Wortley was M.P. for Peterborough 1698–1710.

[6] Since Dallaway (1803) is the only source for this letter, its accuracy is highly doubtful.

believed it impossible you should forget me, and therefore very impudently expected a long letter from you this morning; but Heaven, which you know delights in abasing the proud, has, I find, decreed no such thing; and notwithstanding my vanity and your vows, I begin to fancy myself forgotten; and this epistle comes, in humble manner, to kiss your hands, and petition for the scanty alms of one little visit, though never so short: pray Madam, for God's sake, have pity on a poor prisoner—one little visit—so may God send you a fine husband, continuance of beauty, etc.; but if you deny my request, and make a jest of my tenderness (which between friends, I do think a little upon the ridiculous), I do vow never to——; but I had better not vow, for I shall certainly love you, do what you will—though I beg you would not tell some certain people of that fond expression, who will infallibly advise you to follow the abominable maxims, of no answer, ill-treatment, and so forth, not considering that such conduct is full as base as beating a poor wretch who has his hands tied; and mercy to the distressed is a mark of divine goodness. Upon which godly consideration I hope you will afford a small visit to your disconsolate

M. Pierrepont.

Text 1803, i. 107–8

To Anne Wortley 9 *March 1709*[1]

Ash Wednesday, 1709.

This comes to inquire after your health in the first place; and if there be any hopes of the recovery of my diamond? If not, I must content myself with reckoning it one of the mortifications proper to this devout time, and it may serve for a motive of humiliation. Is not this the right temper with which we ought to bear losses which ——?

Text 1803, i. 108–9

[1] Dallaway's dates are unreliable, but in the absence of other evidence they are repeated here.

To Anne Wortley 2 *May* [*1709*]

May 2nd

I hope, my dear Mrs. Wortley, that you are so just to me, to beleive I could not leave the Town without Seeing you, but very much against my own Inclination. I am now at Thorsby.[1] Our Journey has been very bad, but in my Opinion the worst part of it was going from you. I hope you intend to be kinder to me this Summer than you was the last. There needs nothing to keep up the remembrance of you in my Heart, but I would not think of you, and think you forget me.

Farewell, my Dear. My Letter should be longer, if it was possible to make it so without Repetition, but I have allready told you I love you, and implor'd you not to forget me, which (as I hope to breathe) is all I have to say.

Text W MS iv. 138–9   *Address* To Mrs Anne Wortley Montague in great Queen street near Lincoln's inn Feilds London   *Postmark* MA 4 TUXFORD

To Anne Wortley *21 July 1709*

July 21, 1709.

How often (my dear Mrs. Wortley,) must I assure you that your letters are ever agreeable, and, beyond expression, welcome to me? Depend upon it, that I reckon the correspondence you favour me with, too great a happiness to neglect it; there is no dangers of your fault, I rather fear to grow troublesome by my acknowledgments. I will not believe you flatter me, I will look upon what you say as an obliging mark of your partiality. How happy must I think

1 Thoresby House, near Nottingham, was the main seat of LM's father, Evelyn Pierrepont (*c.* 1665–1726), 5th Earl of Kingston, 1st Marquess of Dorchester, later 1st Duke of Kingston-upon-Hull. It was a large formal mansion designed by William Talman and built about 1683 for the 4th Earl of Kingston. An exhaustive account of it, with illustrations, is given in John Harris's articles in *Architectural History* iv, 1961, pp. 11–19; vi, 1963, pp. 103–5.

myself when I fancy your friendship to me even great enough
to overpower your judgment? I am afraid this is one of the
pleasures of the imagination,[1] and I cannot be so very successful in so earnest and important a wish. This letter is
excessively dull. Do you know it is from my vast desire of
pleasing you, as there is nothing more frequent than for the
voice to faulter when people sing before judges, or, as those
arguments are always worst where the orator is in a passion.
Believe me, I could scribble three sheets to —— (I must not
name), but to twenty people, that have not so great a share
of my esteem, and whose friendship is not so absolutely
necessary for my happiness, but am quite at a loss to you.
I will not commend your letters (let them deserve never so
much), because I will shew you 'tis possible for me to forbear
what I have a mind to, when I know 'tis your desire I should
do so. My dear, dear, adieu! I am entirely your's, and wish
nothing more than that it may be some time or other in my
power to convince you that there is nobody dearer than yourself to

M. Pierrepont.

I am horridly ashamed of this letter, pray Heaven you
may not think it too inconsiderable to be laughed at—that
may be.

Text 1803, i. 109–10

From Anne Wortley [*c. 3 Aug. 1709*]

Dear Lady Mary grows very coole. If I could write a hunderdth
part as well as You I should dispatch the post as often as I do the coachman to St. Jam's, but as it is, if you will exchange pearl for Glase,
I shall think mine well bestow'd. I am just come into the country
where I have met with nothing but what you have in perfection,
and could I have any part of your imagination, I should write per-
petualy. I am now in the room with an humble Servant of yourn[2]

---

[1] In her letter of 17 July 1709, Anne
Wortley had referred to LM as 'the
auther of the pleasure of the imagination' (W MS iv. 126).

[2] Her brother Edward Wortley
Montagu, who probably dictated the
arguments she set forth. Born in 1678,
he was the second but eldest surviving

who is arguing so hotly about marrige that I cant goe on with my Letter. Would be very glad to bring you into the argument, being sure you would soon convince us in what desturbs so many. Every body seeks happyness but tho every body has a deferent tast, yet all persue money, which make people chouse great wigs, because there neighbourgh swets in it tha dare not be easie out of the fashion; but you have dar'd to have wit joyn'd with beauty, a thing so much out of fashion that we fly after you with as much invitertness [*sic*] as you often see the birds do when one superior com's near them. If you could give me a resept how to divert you I would try to practice, but find it imposible to be pleas'd with my self or any thing I doe. Send me word what books to read, etc. In hast,

A. Wortley

Direct to me at Pet[erborou]gh in Northamtonshire.

Text W MS iv. 132–3   *Address* To the Rt Honble the Lady Mary Peirrepoint at Thorsby Notinghamshire   Tuxford bag

To Anne Wortley *8 Aug. 1709*

August 8th, 1709.

I shall run mad—with what heart can people write, when they believe their letters will never be received? I have already writ you a very long scrawl, but it seems it never came to your hands; I cannot bear to be accused of coldness by one whom I shall love all my life. This will, perhaps, miscarry as the last did; how unfortunate am I if it does! You will think I forget you, who are never out of my thoughts. You will fancy me stupid enough to neglect your letters, when they are the only pleasures of my solitude; in short, you will call me ungrateful and insensible, when I esteem you as I ought, in esteeming you above all the world. If I am

son of Sidney Wortley. He attended Westminster School under Dr. Busby, and matriculated at Trinity College, Cambridge, in 1693, without taking a degree. He was admitted to the Middle Temple 1693, and called to the Bar 1699. He made the Grand Tour 1700–3. In 1705 he was elected M.P. for Huntingdon, a borough controlled by his father, and held the seat until 1713. In 1706 he was admitted to the Inner Temple. Among his close friends were Joseph Addison, who had travelled with him on part of his Grand Tour, and Richard Steele, who in 1710 dedicated to him the second volume of the collected *Tatler* papers.

not quite so unhappy as I imagine, and you do receive this, let me know it as soon as you can; for till then I shall be in terrible uneasiness; and let me beg you for the future, if you do not receive letters very constantly from me, imagine the post-boy killed—imagine the mail burnt—or some other strange accident; you can imagine nothing so impossible as that I forget you, my dear Mrs. Wortley.

I know no pretence I have to your good opinion but my hearty desiring it; I wish I had that imagination you talk of, to render me a fitter correspondent for you, who can write so well on every thing. I am now so much alone, I have leisure to pass whole days in reading,[1] but am not at all proper for so delicate an employment as chusing you books. Your own fancy will better direct you. My study at present is nothing but dictionaries and grammars.[2] I am trying whether it be possible to learn without a master; I am not certain (and dare hardly hope) I shall make any great progress; but I find the study so diverting, I am not only easy, but pleased with the solitude that indulges it. I forget there is such a place as London, and wish for no company but your's. You see, my dear, in making my pleasures consist of these unfashionable diversions, I am not of the number who cannot be easy out of the mode. I believe more follies are committed out of complaisance to the world, than in following our own inclinations—Nature is seldom in the wrong, custom always; it is with some regret I follow it in all the impertinencies of dress; the compliance is so trivial, it comforts me: but I am amazed to see it consulted even in the most important occasions of our lives; and that people of good sense in other things can make their happiness consist in the opinions of others, and sacrifice every thing in the desire of appearing in fashion. I call all people who fall in love with furniture, clothes, and equipage, of this number; and I look

---

[1] A French visitor at Thoresby thirty years later described the library as the largest and handsomest apartment in the house, and as containing a great number of Greek, Latin, English, and French authors in the best editions (Hélène Monod-Cassidy, *Un Voyageur-Philosophe au XVIIIe siècle: l'abbé Jean-Bernard Le Blanc*, 1941, pp. 266–7).

[2] In 1741 LM told Joseph Spence that in order to learn Latin she had got hold of a dictionary and a grammar, and secretly studied them for two years to learn the language. But she also told Spence that she had begun to study at thirteen [1702], and that W had encouraged her to undertake it (Eg MS 2234, f. 247).

upon them as no less in the wrong than when they were five years old, and doated on shells, pebbles, and hobby-horses.

I believe you will expect this letter to be dated from the other world, for sure I am you never heard an inhabitant of this talk so before. I suppose you expect, too, I should conclude with begging pardon for this extreme tedious and very nonsensical letter—quite contrary, I think you will be obliged to me for it. I could not better shew my great concern for your reproaching me with a neglect I knew myself innocent of, than proving myself mad in three pages.

My sister[1] says a great deal about Mrs. K[atherine][2] but besides my having forgot it, the paper is at an end.

Text 1803, i. 111–14

From Anne Wortley[3] *15* [*Aug.*] *1709*

15nth 1709

It is as imposible for my Dearest Lady Mary to utter a thought that can seem dull as to put on a look that is not beatiful. Want of wit is a fault that those who envy you most woud not be able to find in your kind Compliments. To me they seem perfect, since repeated asurance of your kindness forbid me to question their Sincerity. [*Passage omitted*] I wish the most happy person now in being, whom I have often dicoverd to be so, in spight of your art to hide it, may be as able to make this reflection at the Notingham Race,[4] as I that am not subdued by so strong a pashion of that sort (for Hinchingbrook Air, from whence I am just come, has not so kind an influence upon all as on L[ord] S[andwich]).[5] Such pashions as those where there is an

[1] Of LM's two sisters, Lady Evelyn Pierrepont (1691–1727) had lived since 1699 with their aunt Lady Cheyne; hence LM means her other sister, Lady Frances (1690–1761).

[2] Probably Anne Wortley's sister Catherine (d. 1761), who m. (1728) John Orme of Northamptonshire, later a naval captain (*London Eve. Post*, 31 Aug.–3 Sept. 1728).

[3] Copied by her from W's draft (W MS i. 86–87).

[4] The races, held each summer, drew an 'Illustrious Company. . . . Nor is the

Appearance of the Ladies to be omitted, as fine and without Comparison more Bright and Gay' (Daniel Defoe, *A Tour thro' Great Britain*, 1726, ed. 1927, ii. 553).

[5] Hinchingbrooke, near Huntingdon, had been in the Montagu family since 1627, and was owned by Edward Montagu (1670–1729), 3rd Earl of Sandwich, nephew of Sidney Wortley, to whom it was heavily mortgaged. At various times Lord Sandwich lived at Wortley Hall under restraint (Vict. Co. Hist. *Huntingdonshire*, ii, 1932, p. 34).

7

object like Lady Mary leave no room for Cool reflections, and I wish
he may not be so far overcome by his fears for the future as to forget
what a favourite he is of fortune in the present possesion of so great
a bliss. You'll want to know how this Race comes into my head. This
country, out of which many go thither, affords no other tittle Tattle at
this time, beside that yesterday as I was talking of it with Mrs.
Sherrad[1] she said Lady Mary would be well diverted for Nicolini
would be there.[2] One that was by said there would be much better
diversion there, looking upon me as if he insinuated you would have
pleasures less imaginary than those Nicolini can afford.

When that Race is over and your thoughts are free again, I should
be glad to hear you have bin well entertain'd. Every one but your self
will be, I am very sure. The sight of you is a satisfaction I envy 'em
heartyly. There is not a man among 'em that woud not be contented
to be any thing but the man I have nam'd, to enjoy the prosperous
gale that one of them does. I will be sure to conceal your Letter, not
for the faults you say you are asham'd of, but to give no pangs to him
or any other by discovering your kind assurance that none is Dearer
to You than my self, which woud make the Dullest Letter that ever
was writ subscribd by Lady Mary, more valuable than all I ever
Received. Don't think so long a Letter as thise is inexcuseable from so
fond an admirer of charming Lady Mary as

A. W.

Text W MS iv. 134–5   *Address* To the Rt Honble the Lady Mary
Peirripoint at Thorsby Notinghamshire Tuxford bag   *Postmark*
AV 19 PTERBURGH

From Anne Wortley[3] [*19 Aug. 1709*]

fryday, aug'st the 20th[4]

Dear Lady Mary will pardon my vanity; I could not forbear reading to a Cambridge Docter[5] that was with me, a few of those lines
that did not make me happy till this week. Where you talk of turning
over Dictionaries and Grammars, he stop'd me, and said, the reason
why you had more wit than any Man was that your mind had never

---

[1] Lucy Sherard (1685–1751), da. of
2nd Baron Sherard of Leitrim, m. (1713)
2nd Duke of Rutland.

[2] Nicolini (Nicolo Grimaldi, 1673–
1732), the famous *castrato* singer, had
arrived in England in the late autumn of

1708 (Grove, *Dict. of Music*, ed. Eric
Blom, 1954).

[3] From W's draft (W MS i. 90–91).

[4] Either Friday, 19 or 26 Aug. 1709.

[5] An obvious reference to W, whose
draft reads 'a friend'.

bin encumber'd with those tedious Authors; that Cowley never submitted to the Rules of Grammar and therefore excell'd all of his own time in learning as well as wit;[1] that with out 'em you would read with pleasure in 2 or 3 months, but if you persisted in the use of 'em you would throw away your Latin after a year or 2 and the Commonwealth of Letters have reason to mourn, whereas if I could prevail with you it would be bound to thank me for a brighter ornament than any it can boast of. It is not because I am bublick [*sic*] spirited that I cou'd not delay telling you what I believed might make you succeed in your attempt, nor can I positively affirm it proceeds from fondness but rather admiration. [*Passage omitted*]

You may remember you once told me it was as easiy to write kindly to a hobby horse as a woman, nay, or a man. I should know tow how Diverting a Scene it is (I have forgot where I met with it but you can tell) to make a plowman find himself on a throne and fancy he's an Emperour. However, tis a Cheat so pleasing I can't helpe indulging it, and to keep off the evil day of being undeceived, shall remain with truth and pashion, Yours,

A. Wortley.

Our family is gone to Lord Manchester's[2] to dine, so pray direct to Hichingbrook where we shall Stay a fortnight.

Text W MS iv. 128–9   *Address* To the Rt Honble the Lady Mary Peirripoint at Thorsby Notingamshire Tuxford bag

To Anne Wortley *21 Aug. 1709*

Aug. 21, 1709.

I am infinitely obliged to you, my dear Mrs. Wortley, for the wit, beauty and other fine qualities, you so generously bestow upon me. Next to receiving them from Heaven, you are the person from whom I would chuse to receive gifts and graces; I am very well satisfied to owe them to your own delicacy of imagination, which represents to you the idea

---

[1] In his essay 'Of My Self' (1668) Abraham Cowley writes that as a boy at school 'I was . . . so much an Enemy to all Constraint, that my Masters could never prevail on me, by any Persuasions or Encouragements, to learn without Book the common Rules of Grammar' (*Complete Works*, ed. A. B. Grosart, 1881, ii. 339).

[2] Charles Montagu (*c.* 1662–1722), 4th Earl, later 1st Duke of Manchester, diplomatist and distant relation of the Wortleys. He lived at Kimbolton Castle in Huntingdonshire.

of a fine lady, and you have good nature enough to fancy I am she. All this is mighty well, but you do not stop there, imagination is boundless. After giving me imaginary wit and beauty, you give me imaginary passions, and you tell me I'm in love; if I am, 'tis a perfect sin of ignorance, for I don't so much as know the man's name: I have been studying these three hours, and cannot guess who you mean. I passed the days of Nottingham races [at]¹ Thorsby, without seeing or even wishing to see one of the sex. Now if I am in love, I have very hard fortune to conceal it so industriously from my own knowledge, and yet discover it so much to other people. 'Tis against all form to have such a passion as that, without giving one sigh for the matter. Pray tell me the name of him I love, that I may (according to the laudable custom of lovers) sigh to the woods and groves hereabouts, and teach it to the echo. You see, being I am in love, I am willing to be so in order and rule; I have been turning over God knows how many books to look for precedents. Recommend an example to me; and, above all, let me know whether 'tis most proper to walk in the woods, encreasing the winds with my sighs, or to sit by a purling stream, swelling the rivulet with my tears; may be, both may do well in their turns:—but to be a minute serious, what do you mean by this reproach of inconstancy? I confess you give me several good qualities I have not, and I am ready to thank you for them, but then you must not take away those few I have. No, I will never exchange them; take back the beauty and wit you bestow upon me, leave me my own mediocrity of agreeableness and genius, but leave me also my sincerity, my constancy, and my plain dealing; 'tis all I have to recommend me to the esteem either of others or myself. How should I despise myself if I could think I was capable of either inconstancy or deceit? I know not how I may appear to other people, nor how much my face may belie my heart, but I know that I never was or can be guilty of dissimulation or inconstancy—you will think this vain, but 'tis all that I pique myself upon. Tell me you believe me and repent of your harsh censure. Tell it me in pity to my uneasiness, for you are one of those few people about whose good opinion

¹ The text has 'into' here.

I am in pain. I have always took so little care to please the generality of the world, that I am never mortified or delighted by its reports, which is a piece of stoicism born with me; but I cannot be one minute easy while you think ill of Your faithful

M. P.

This letter is a good deal grave, and, like other grave things, dull; but I won't ask pardon for what I can't help.

Text 1803, i. 124–7

To Anne Wortley *21 Aug. 1709*

Aug. 21, 1709.

When I said it cost nothing to write tenderly, I believe I spoke of another sex; I am sure not of myself; 'tis not in my power (I would to God it was) to hide a kindness where I have one, or dissemble it where I have none. I cannot help answering your letter this minute, and telling you I infinitely love you, though, it may be, you'll call the one impertinence, and the other dissimulation; but you may think what you please of me, I must eternally think the same things of you.

I hope my dear Mrs. Wortley's shewing my letter is in the same strain as her compliments, all meant for raillery, and I am not to take it as a thing really so; but I'll give you as serious an answer as if 'twas all true.———

When Mr. Cowley and other people, (for I know several have learnt after the same manner,) were in places where they had opportunity of being learned by word of mouth, I don't see any violent necessity of printed rules; but being where, from the top of the house to the bottom, not a creature in it understands so much as even good English, without the help of a dictionary or inspiration I know no way of attaining to any language. Despairing of the last, I am forced to make use of the other, though I do verily believe I shall return to London the same ignorant soul I went from it; but the study is a present amusement. I must own I have vanity enough to fancy, if I had any body with me, without much trouble perhaps I might read.

11

What do you mean by complaining I never write to you in the quiet situation of mind I do to other people? My dear, people never write calmly, but when they write indifferently. That I should ever do so to you, I take to be entirely impossible; I must be always very much pleased or in very great affliction: as you tell me of your friendship, or unkindly doubt mine. I can never allow even prudence and sincerity to have any thing to do with one another, at least I have always found it so in myself, who being devoted to the one, had never the least tincture of the other. What I am now doing, is a very good proof of what I say, 'tis a plain undesigning truth—your friendship is the only happiness of my life; and whenever I lose it, I have nothing to do but to take one of my garters and search for a convenient beam. You see how absolutely necessary it is for me to preserve it. Prudence is at the very time saying to me, are you mad; you won't send this dull, tedious, insipid, long letter to Mrs. Wortley, will you? 'tis the direct way to tire out her patience; if she serves you as you deserve, she will first laugh very heartily, then tear the letter, and never answer it, purely to avoid the plague of such another: will her good-nature for ever resist her judgment?—I hearken to these counsels, I allow 'em to be good, and then—I act quite contrary: no consideration can hinder me from telling you, my dear, dear Mrs. Wortley, no body ever was so entirely, so faithfully yours, as

M. P.

I put in your lovers, for I don't allow it possible for a man to be so sincere as I am; if there was such a thing, though, you would find it; I submit therefore to your judgment.

I had forgot to tell you that I writ a long letter, directed to Peterborough, last post; I hope you'll have it:—you see I forgot your judgment, to depend upon your goodness.

Text 1803, i. 117–20

From Anne Wortley¹ [3] *Sept.* [*1709*]

Saturday, Sept.

There cannot be a stronger proofe of inconstancy than your severity
to me for using the word. Whoever shou'd read over those inestimable
kind things you writ just before, and see this cruel repremand come
immediately after it, wou'd bewail the incertainty of human happyness. A change like this is not to be meet with in Tragedy. If it is any
where, the Poet can't but be condemn'd for going out of nature by all
but my self. I had infallibly rav'd ere now, if this letter had not gon
round by Peterborough, and met the other on the rhoad, in which
your indignation seams a little abated. This I had the good fortune
to open first, so that I escap'd the fright that your present anger wou'd
have given me, and viewing a pashion I knew half extinguish'd, I had
only the displeasure of seeing how soon you cou'd be offend'd at me,
and how easie your affection was to be lost, which I allways knew was
hard to be obtain'd. I heartyly wish those plains of Notingam that have
given me all this pain, may be turn'd by some earthquake into Mountains and rocks, that none of its rivulets may ever receive the tears,
nor its brees's the Sighs of a lover. Nay, let 'em be wholley inaccesable
both to man and beast. But how can my Dearest Lady Mary think it
so wild (tho an unhappy) thought in me to mention that race? You
may eaisily recollect how either I or an another rallid you upon one
you met last year in that field or—,where you din'd together after the
diversion was over. Well, henceforward I have done with all Jealous
tricks. I did not imagine I could have paid so dearly for this, tho I had
heard they seldom give quiet and securitity [*sic*] but commonly dis-
crating [distracting *draft*] pain.

Was it posible to hear of this race and be without the apprehension
of a rival in your favour? Did I write a word of it that you Could
take gravley acording to the letter? Or, if you did, how cou'd you
be angrey unless you were before dispos'd to it? Were I less punish'd
than I am by your correction I should enlarge on what is very obvious
to one inclin'd [to] make remarks; say your being out of humour cou'd
not be for any thing but your absence from that Dear Race; say that
every thing I write is so dull that it can't have your attention unless it
be true, but henceforward I will not dare to speak, no, nor so much as
think any thing of my Dearest Lady Mary in a laughing way, nor
will I ever presume to meddle with so high a subject as your pity to
any of the other sex, which you outshine so far, but shall be satisfied

¹ W's draft of this letter (W MS i. 88–89) lacks the postscript.

13

if I'm admitted into your lower entertainments. If I have the same
rank among your admirers, that your Grammars and dictionaries have
among your books; if I serve only to assist you in procuring pleasures
without the least hopes of being ever able to give 'em, let me send you
what stories I collect, which you will sure to make diverting; choose
your Ribbons and heads on which you will bestow the power of
Enchanting. I will be contented never to soar above transmitting to
you the best rueles I hear for gaining Languages, which, tho it can't
raise a Genius alredy so high, yet may very much enlarge your
dominions by adding all that can posibly disobey you—the ignorant
who are taught to believe that learning is wit. Make what you will of
me; tis enough that you own me to be yours.

A. Wortley

P.S. If you have any more queries about Latin you must send 'em
quick, for a week hence I shall be alone. Lest I should be less able
in Solitude to bear the thoughts of your being angry, a very little
letter to tell me you are not wou'd be kind.—Servis to Lady F[rances].
Servis from us.

Text W MS iv. 130–31   *Address* To the Rt Honble The Lady Mary
Pierrepoint at Thorsby Notingamshire Tuxford bagg

To Anne Wortley 5 *Sept. 1709*

Sept. 5, 1709.

My dear Mrs. Wortley, as she has the entire power of
raising, can also, with a word, calm my passions. The kindness of your last recompenses me for the injustice of your
former letter; but you cannot sure be angry at my little
resentment. You have read that a man who, with patience,
hears himself called heretic, can never be esteemed a good
Christian. To be capable of preferring the despicable wretch
you mention[1] to Mr. Wortley, is as ridiculous, if not as
criminal, as forsaking the Deity to worship a calf. Don't
tell me any body ever had so mean an opinion of my inclinations; 'tis among the number of those things I would forget.
My tenderness is always built upon my esteem, and when the
foundation perishes, it falls: I must own, I think it is so
with every body—but enough of this: you tell me it was

---

[1] No 'wretch' is named in any of Anne Wortley's surviving letters.

meant for raillery—was not the kindness meant so too? I fear I am too apt to think what is amusement designed in earnest —no matter, 'tis for my repose to be deceived, and I will believe whatever you tell me.

I should be very glad to be informed of a right method, or whether there is such a thing alone, but am afraid to ask the question. It may be reasonably called presumption in a girl to have her thoughts that way. You are the only creature that I have made my confidante in that case: I'll assure you, I call it the greatest secret of my life. Adieu, my dear, the post stays, my next shall be longer.

M. P.

Text 1803, i. 127–8

To Mrs. Frances Hewet[1] [*Sept. 1709*]

Ten thousand thanks to you for Mdd de Noijer's letters;[2] I wish Signor Roselli[3] may be as diverting to you as She has been to me. The storys are very extraordinary; I know not whether she has not added a few Agrements of Invention to 'em. However there is some truth; in perticular I have been told the history of the fair unfortunate Mdd de Barbeseiux by people who could not be suspected of Romance-ing.[4] Don't you think the Court of England would furnish stories as entertaining? Say nothing of my Malice, but I can't help secretly wishing Mdd de Noijer would turn her thoughts a little that way; I fancy she would succeed better than the

[1] Frances Bettenson (1668–1756), da. of Richard Bettenson and granddaughter of Viscount Wimbledon, m. (1689) Thomas Hewet, whose family seat was Shireoaks, near Worksop, Notts. (John Holland, *Hist., Antiquities and Description of Worksop*, 1826, p. 176; W. Bazeley, 'Some Records of . . . the Selwyns,' *Trans. of Bristol and Glos. Archaeol. Soc.*, 1876, p. 262).

[2] *Lettres historiques et galantes* by Anne Marguerite Petit du Noyer, (1704).

[3] *L'Infortuné napolitain, ou les aventures et mémoires du Signor Rosselly* by the Abbé J. Olivier, 1704 (Cat. of Bibliothèque Nationale). LM's library in 1739 contained a copy listed as 'Vie de Rozelli' (Wh MS 135).

[4] In this episode M. de Barbesieux's young and pretty wife is mistreated by him because he suspects her fidelity; and when he tries to do away with her a servant dilutes the poison and she merely falls sick (Lettre xii).

Authoresse of the memoirs of the New Attalantis.[1] I'm sure
I like her method much better, which has (I think) exactly
hit that difficult path between the gay and the severe, and
is neither too loose nor affectedly Prude.

I take an Interest in Mr. Selwin's successe (in a battle
like that I think it may be calld so, to come off alive).[2]
I should be so sensible of any Affliction could touch you or
Mrs. Selwin I may very well rejoyce when you have no
Occasion for any.

Adieu, madame. This post has brought me nothing but
Compliments, without one bit of news. Heard I the last that
Lord Stair is mortally wounded;[3] you can tell me whether
I am to believe it or no. Excuse my dullness and be so good
never to open a Letter of mine but in one of those minutes
when you are entirely alone, weary of ev'ry thing and in-
quiete to think what you shall do next. All people who live
in the Country must have of those minutes, and I know so
well what they are, I believe even my letters may be welcom
when they are to take them off of your hands.

Text Lady Charnwood, *Call Back Yesterday*, 1937, pp. 113–14;
J. Netherclift, *Autograph Letters*, 1838 (facsimile fragm.)   *Address*
Mrs. Huet. To be left at Mrs. Smiths at Worksop[4]   *End.* [*from the
coll. of William Upcott (1779–1845)*]

To Mrs. Frances Hewet [*Oct. 1709*]

I suppose my dear Mrs. Hewet has by this time resolved
never to think more on so insensible and ungrateful a

[1] The notorious *roman à clef* by
Mary de la Rivière Manley, *Secret
Memoirs and Manners of Several Per-
sons of Quality, of Both Sexes, From the
New Atlantis*, vol. i, May 1709.

[2] Mrs. Hewet's sister Albinia (d.
1738) was widow of Major-General
William Selwyn; and their eldest son
John (b. 1688), captain in the First
Foot Guards, served under Marl-
borough (Bazeley; Charles Dalton,
George the First's Army 1714–1727,
1910–12, i. 186, 218). The battle of
Malplaquet, fought on 31 Aug., was

won by England and her allies but at
a terrible cost in lives.

[3] John Dalrymple (1673–1747), 2nd
Earl of Stair. He took a prominent part
in the campaign, and at Malplaquet led
the Scots Greys without harm to himself. His regiment charged the French
household cavalry three times to break
through that hitherto invincible corps
(Archibald K. Murray, *History of the
Scottish Regiments in the British Army*,
1862, p. 27).

[4] Sotheby Catalogue, 16 March 1937,
lot 506.

creature, that could be so long in returning thanks for such a letter, and has repented of past favours. I cannot blame your resentment, appearances are so much against me; and yet I am not so much to blame as you imagine. You expressed a desire of seeing the second part of the Atalantis.[1] I had just then sent to London for it, and did not question having it last Saturday. I hoped that a book you had a mind to see might atone for the nothingness of my letter, and was resolved not to send one without the other; but like an unfortunate projector as I am, my designs are always followed by disappointment. Saturday came, and no book; God forgive me, I had certainly wished the lady who was to send it me hanged, but for the hopes it was come by the Nottingham carrier, and then I should have it on Monday; but, after waiting Monday and Tuesday, I find it is not come at all. Now, madam, I do not question your forgiveness, and hope that when I do not write to Mrs. Hewet, there is some unavoidable cause for my silence. Your news and your book very much diverted me; it is an old, but very pleasant Spanish novel.

When we leave this place I am not able to tell you. I have no reason to wish it but, since I cannot see you, that it may be in my power to write you more entertaining letters. I had some last post told me that Lady Essex Saville was going to be married to Lord Londsdale.[2] I won't swear to the truth of it, for people make no conscience of what they write into the country, and think any thing good enough for poor us. There is another story that I had from a hand I dare depend upon. The Duke of Grafton and Dr. Garth ran a foot-match in the Mall of 200 yards, and the latter, to his immortal glory, beat.[3] I pray God you mayn't have heard this already. I am promised a cargo of lampoons from the Bath, and if

---

[1] The second volume of *The New Atlantis* was announced for publication on 20 Oct. but the (Whig) government attempted to suppress it because of its Tory bias (P. B. Anderson, 'Mistress Delarivière Manley's Biography,' *Mod. Phil.*, xxxiii, 1936, p. 274).

[2] This gossip was incorrect. Lady Essex Saville, da. of 2nd Marquess of Halifax, died at an early age unmarried,

as did Richard Lowther (1692–1713), 2nd Viscount Lonsdale.

[3] Charles Fitzroy (1683–1757), 2nd Duke of Grafton, and Dr. Samuel Garth (1661–1719), physician, poet, and wit. This story may be based on a foot-race in St. James's Park in 1682 between the 1st Duke of Grafton and the Earl of Thanet (*Cal. of State Papers Dom. 1682*, 1932, p. 591).

they come safe you shall share them with me. My dear, dear Mrs. Hewet, could I contribute any way to your diversion, it would be the height of my ambition.

Text 1805, v. 237–9[1]

To Mrs. Frances Hewet *12 Nov.* [*1709*]

Nov. 12.

You have not then received my letter? Well! I shall run mad. I can suffer any thing rather than that you should continue to think me ungrateful. I think 'tis the last of pains to be thought criminal, where one most desires to please, as I am sure it is always my wish to dear Mrs. Hewet.

I am very glad you have the second part of the New Atalantis; if you have read it, will you be so good as to send it me, and in return I promise to get you the key to it. I know I can. But do you know what has happened to the unfortunate authoress? People are offended at the liberty she uses in her memoirs, and she is taken into custody.[2] Miserable is the fate of writers; if they are agreeable, they are offensive; and if dull, they starve. I lament the loss of the other parts which we should have had; and have five hundred arguments at my fingers' ends to prove the ridiculousness of those creatures that think it worth while to take notice of what is only designed for diversion. After this, who will dare to give the history of Angella?[3] I was in hopes her faint essay would have provoked some better pen to give more elegant and secret memoirs; but now she will serve as a scarecrow to frighten people from attempting any thing but heavy panegyric; and we shall be teized with nothing but heroic poems, with names at length, and false characters, so daubed with flattery, that they are the severest kind of

[1] MS letter sold at Sotheby's on 23 April 1934, lot 155.

[2] On 29 Oct. Mrs. Manley was taken into custody, but released on bail a week later. She was tried the following Feb. and discharged (Luttrell, *Hist.* *Relation*, 1857, vi. 505, 508, 546).

[3] Angela is the capital city (London) on the Isle of Atlantis. Undaunted, Mrs. Manley brought out two additional volumes of *The New Atlantis* in 1710.

lampoons, for they both scandalise the writer and the subject, like that vile paper the Tatler.[1]

I believe, madam, you will think I have dwelt too long on this business; but I am in a violent passion about it. My dear Mrs. Hewet, is it impossible you should come here? I would not ask it if I had a coach to wait upon you: but I am not born to have any thing I have a mind to. All the news I know is, that Mrs. Reeves is married to Colonel Sydney[2] (if you know neither of them I'll send you their pictures at full length); and that giddy rake Cresswell[3], to a fortune of 2000 l. a year. I send you the Bath lampoons—Corinna is Lady Manchester,[4] and the other lady is Mrs. Cartwright,[5] who they say has pawned her diamond necklace, to buy Valentine a snuff-box. These wars make men so violent scarce, that these good ladies take up with the shadows of them. This is the sum total of all the news I know, and you see I am willing to divert you all in my power. I fancy the ill spelling of the lampoons will make you laugh more than the verses; indeed I am ashamed for her who wrote them. As soon as possible, be pleased to send me the second part of the Atalantis, etc.

Text 1805, v. 239–42

To Mrs. Frances Hewet [*Nov. 1709*]

Till this minute I was in hopes of waiting on dear Mrs. Hewet before we left the country, which made me defer writing, but now positive orders oblige us to go to-morrow, and the horses must rest to-day, so that this paper must give

[1] In *Tatler* No. 92 (10 Nov. 1709) Steele criticizes the prevalence of libels, and the denigration of great men. He objects to 'the strange delight men take in reading lampoons and scandal, with which the age abounds'; but he is also against false or exaggerated praise. Mrs. Manley assumed that the paper was directed against her writings (Rich. Steele, *Corr.*, ed. R. Blanchard, 1941, p. 30).

[2] Mary Reeve, da. of Sir Robert Reeve, m. the Hon. Thomas Sydney, brother of 20th Earl of Leicester. At her mother's death in July 1709 she had inherited £24,000 (*Wentworth Papers*, p. 95).

[3] Not identified.

[4] Dodington Greville (1672–1721), da. of 4th Baron Brooke, m. (1691) 4th Earl, later 1st Duke of Manchester.

[5] Not identified.

you thanks for me, for all the many favours which could not have been bestowed on one who could have had a more quick and lasting sense of them. When I am in London, I will certainly send you all that passes, though I fancy you have it from people better both at writing and intelligence.

Mrs. C[olyear] whose character you desire to know, is a lady who has made a great noise in the world; but I never thought she would come to make such a figure in it. The lord she has snapt[1] made a lampoon on her last winter. For my part, I never heard her speak in my life. She is generally thought handsome. If Miss Selwyn (as I wish she may) supplies her place, there will be one much handsomer.[2] Amidst the hurry of taking such a journey to-morrow, I am sure you will forgive my letter's being no longer: you know people can never leave your company, or writing to you, without regret. Write to me where to direct to you, and direct to me in Arlington street,[3] near St. James's, London.

Text 1805, v. 248–9

To Mrs. Frances Hewet [*13 Feb. 1710*]

I hope my Dear Mrs. Hewet does not beleive I follow my Inclination when I am 2 or 3 posts before I return thanks for her most Agreable Letters, but in this busy Town there is very little time at one's own Disposal.

My greatest pleasure is Mrs. Selwin's;[4] I come from thence just now, and I beleive am the only Young Woman in Town that am in my own house at ten a Clock to Night.

---

[1] Elizabeth (d. 1768), da. of Lt.-Gen. Walter Colyear, m. Lionel Cranfield (1688–1765) 10th Earl, later 1st Duke of Dorset. Their marriage, in Jan. 1709, was not made public until Nov. (Luttrell, vi. 516). Her marriage disqualified her as Maid of Honour to the Queen, at £300 a year, though she is still listed in 1710 (J. Chamberlayne, *Magnae Britanniae Notitia*, p. 541).

[2] Margaret Selwyn, da. of Albinia

and William Selwyn, and hence Mrs. Hewet's niece, did not win the appointment.

[3] Lord Dorchester's town house was on the west side of Arlington Street, adjoining the Green Park; his neighbours on either side were Lord Stair and Lord Guildford (*Wentworth Papers*, p. 168).

[4] Mrs. Hewet's sister Albinia lived in London.

This is the Night of Count Turrucca's Ball,[1] to which he has invited a few barefac'd, and the whole Town en Masque. I suppose you'l have a description of the Ball from some who were at it; I can only give it at 2nd hand and will therefore say nothing of it.

I have begun to learn Italian and am much mortify'd I cannot do it of a Signor of Monsieur Rasingade's recommendation,[2] but tis allwais the Fate of Women to obey and my papa has promis'd me to Mr. Cassotti.[3] I am afraid I shall never understand it as well as you do, but Laissons cela, and talk of something more Entertaining—

Next to the great ball, what makes the most noise is the marriage of an old Maid that lives in this street, without a portion To a Man of £7,000 per Annum and they say £40,000 in ready money. Her Equipage and Liverys outshine any body's in Town. He has presented her with £3,000 in Jewells and never was man more smitten with these Charms, that [had] lain invisible this forty year. But with all this Glory, never Bride had fewer Envyers; the dear Beast of a Man is so filthy, frightful, odious and detestable I would turn away such a footman for fear of spoiling my Dinner while he waited at Table. They was marry'd friday and came to church en Parade Sunday. I happen'd to sit in the pue with them and had the honnour of seeing Mrs. Bride fall fast asleep in the middle of the Sermon and snore very comfortably, which made several women in the Church think the bridegroom not quite so ugly as they did before. Envious people say 'twas all counterfeited to oblige him, but I beleive that's scandal, for she's so devout, I dare swear nothing but downright necessity could make her miss one Word of the

---

[1] João Gomes da Silva (1671–1738), Conde de Tarouca, minister plenipotentiary to the Netherlands, was in London for the purpose of persuading England to include Portugal in peace negotiations (with France and Spain) to end the War of the Spanish Succession (F. Hausmann, *Repertorium der diplomatischen Vertreter*, 1936–50, i. 430; *Encyclopedia e diccionario internacional*). There was much talk of his 'Splendid Ball and entertainment' on 13 Feb. 1710; and two years later he gave a ball at the Hague that made 'as great a noise' (*Wentworth Papers*, pp. 109, 308).

[2] Perhaps Alexander Rasigade, a Frenchman who after serving under King William in Flanders became naturalized in 1702 (*Pub. of Huguenot Soc. of London*, xxvii, 1923, p. 16).

[3] LM studied Italian with, probably, Ludovico Casotti. Her library in 1739 contained his *Italian Grammar* and *Prediche morali* (Wh MS 135).

Sermon. He proffesses to have marry'd her for the devotion, patience, meeknesse and other Christian virtues he observ'd in her, his first Wife (who has left no Children) being very handsome and so good natur'd to have ventur'd her own Salvation to secure his. He has marry'd this, to have a Compannion in that paradise where his first Lady has given him a Title. I beleive I have given you too much of this Couple, but they are not to be comprehended in few words.

My dear Mrs. Hewet, remember me and beleive nothing can put you out of my head.

Text MS owned by Mr. Robert H. Taylor *Address* To Mrs. Hewet at Chireoaks near Worksop Nottinghamshire *Postmark* FE 14

To Mrs. Frances Hewet [*c. 27 March 1710*]

'Tis so long since I had a letter from dear Mrs. Hewet, I should think her no longer in the land of the living, if Mr. Resingade[1] did not assure me he was happier than I, and had heard of your health from your own hand, which makes me fancy that my last miscarried, and perhaps you are blaming me at the same time that you are thinking me neglectful of you. Apropos of Mr. Resingade—we are grown such good friends, I assure you, that we write Italian letters to each other, and I have the pleasure of talking to him of madame Hewet. He told me he would send you the two *tomes* of madame de Nöyer's Memoirs.[2] I fancy you will find yourself disappointed in them, for they are horridly grave and insipid; and instead of the gallantry you might expect, they are full of dull morals. I was last Thursday at the new Opera, and saw Nicolini strangle a lion with great gallantry.[3] But he represented nakedness so naturally, I was surprised to see those ladies stare at him without any confusion, that

[1] Mentioned on previous page.
[2] Anne Marguerite Petit du Noyer's *Mémoires* (1710)
[3] Nicolini (see above, p. 8) won his greatest success in London as the hero of Francesco Mancini's *Idaspe fedele,* first produced on Thursday, 23 March 1710, at the Queen's Theatre, Haymarket (*London Stage 1660–1800*, Part 2, ed. E. L. Avery, 1960, p. 216), in which he subdued and killed a sham lion. His performance was ridiculed by Addison in the *Spectator* of 15 March 1711.

pretend to be so violently shocked at a poor *double entendre* or two in a comedy, which convinced me that those prudes who would cry fie! fie! at the word *naked*, have no scruples about the thing.

The marriage of Lord Willoughby goes on,[1] and he swears he will bring the lady down to Nottingham races. How far it may be true, I cannot tell. By what fine gentlemen say, you know it is not easy to guess at what they mean. The lady has made an acquaintance with me after the manner of Pyramus and Thisbe, I mean over a wall three yards high, which separates our garden from Lady Guildford's.[2] The young ladies had found out a way to pull out two or three bricks, and so climb up and hang their chins over the wall, where we, mounted on chairs, used to have many *belles conversations à la dérobé* for fear of the old mother. This trade continued several days, but fortune seldom permits long pleasures. By long standing on the wall the bricks loosened, and one fatal morning down drops Miss Nelly[3], and to compleat the misfortune, she fell into a little sink, and bruised her poor —— self to that terrible degree, she is forced to have surgeons' plaisters, and God knows what, which discovered the whole intrigue; and their mamma forbade them ever to visit us, but by the door. Since that time, all our communications have been made in a vulgar manner, visiting in coaches, etc. etc. which took away half the pleasure. You know danger gives a *haut goût* to every thing. This is our secret history—pray let it be so still—but I hope all the world will know that I am most entirely yours,

M. P.

Text 1805, v. 229–31

[1] Peregrine Bertie (1686–1742), Lord Willoughby de Eresby, later 2nd Duke of Ancaster, was engaged in Dec. 1709 to the third da. of Sir John Brownlow, but *c*. July 1710 she d. of smallpox (*Wentworth Papers*, pp. 99, 137).

[2] Alice (1684–1727), da. of Sir John Brownlow, m. (1703) 2nd Baron Guild-ford. She lived in Arlington Street together with her sisters and her widowed mother Alice (d. 1721), da. Richard Sherard, who m. (1676) Sir John Brownlow.

[3] Eleanor Brownlow (1691-1730), m. (1712) her cousin Sir John Brownlow, later Viscount Tyrconnel.

To Wortley [*28 March 1710*]

Perhaps you'l be surprizd at this Letter. I have had manny debates with my selfe before I could resolve on it. I know it is not Acting in Form, but I do not look upon you as I do upon the rest of the world, and by what I do for you, you are not to judge my manner of acting with others. You are Brother to a Woman I tenderly lov'd.[1] My protestations of freindship are not like other people's. I never speak but what I mean, and when I say I love, it is for ever. I had that real concern for Mrs. Wortley I look with some regard on every one that is related to her. This and my long Acquaintance with you may in some measure excuse what I am now doing.

I am surprizd at one of the Tatlers you sent me.[2] Is it possible to have any sort of Esteem for a person one beleives capable of having such triffling Inclinations? Mr. Bickerstaff has very wrong notions of our sex. I can say there are some of us that dispises charms of show, and all the pageantry of Greatnesse, perhaps with more ease than any of the Philosophers. In contemning the world they seem to take pains to contemn it. We dispise it, without takeing the pains to read lessons of Morrality to make us do it. At least I know I have allwaies look'd upon it with contempt without being at the Expence of one serious refflection to oblige me to it. I carry the matter yet farther. Was I to chuse of £2,000 a year or twenty thousand, the first would be my choice. There is something of an unavoidable embarras in makeing what is calld a great figure in the world, [that] takes off from the happynesse of Life. I hate the noise and hurry inseparable from great Estates and Titles, and look upon both as blessings that ought only to be given to Fools, for tis only to them that they are blessings.

The pritty Fellows you speak of, I own entertain me sometimes, but is it impossible to be diverted with what one dispises? I can laugh at a puppet shew, at the same time I know there is nothing in it worth my attention or regard. General

---

[1] Anne Wortley had died since the previous autumn.

[2] No. 143 (9 March 1710), by Steele.

Notions are generally wrong. Ignorance and Folly are thought the best foundations for Virtue, as if not knowing what a Good Wife is was necessary to make one so. I confesse that can never be my way of reasoning. As I allwaies forgive an Injury when I think it not done out of malice. I can never think my selfe oblig'd by what is done without design. Give me leave to say it (I know it sounds Vain): I know how to make a Man of sense happy, but then that man must resolve to contribute something towards it himselfe. I have so much Esteem for you I should be very sorry to hear you was unhappy, but for the world I would not be the Instrument of makeing you so, which (of the humour you are) is hardly to be avoided if I am your Wife. You distrust me. I can neither be easy nor lov'd where I am distrusted, nor do I beleive your passion for me is what you pretend it; at least I'm sure, was I in love I could not talk as you do.

Few Women would have spoke so plainly as I have done, but to dissemble ⟨is⟩ among the things I never do. I take more pains to approve my conduct to my selfe than to the world, and would not have to accuse my selfe of a minute's deceit. I wish I lov'd you enough to devote my selfe to be for Ever miserable for the pleasure of a day or two's happynesse. I cannot resolve upon it—You must think otherwise of me or not at all.

I don't injoin you to burn this Letter. I know you will.[1] Tis the first I ever writ to one of your sex and shall be the last. You must never expect another. I resolve against all correspondance of this kind. My resolutions are seldom made and never broken.

Text W MS i. 276–7   *Address* To Mr. Edward Wortley Mountague at Wortley near Sheffeild Yorkshire   *Postmark* MR ⟨?⟩   *End. by W on copy*   From M. P. 28 March 1. to Wortley.[2]

[1] Not only did W not burn the letter; he made a careful copy (W MS i. 278–9).

[2] W's frequent endorsements are not always explicit or accurate: he sometimes repeats LM's date, or gives the date he received the letter or a date of no apparent relevance.

From Wortley *8 April* [*1710*]

'In the Humour You are'—'If I am distrusted'—that is in other words, if you Love me—if You have any Apprehension of Losing me. My Dearest Lady M[ary], you had wrong'd me had you taken me to be of another Humour, had you thought otherwise of me or believ'd I coud Think Otherwise of you. Do you Imagine any one that is able to set a just Value on You can under a Passion be less uneasy or insecure? I appeal even to your Experience, which to my great Grief is so much less than mine, whether any one that Loves is free from Fear. [*Passage omitted*] It requires an uncommon greatness of Mind to chose to be reduc'd to less than a third part of your present Attendance, your Apartments, your Table, and be quite stript of what glitters more than all the rest of those Ornaments that are no part of You, the Train of Admirers. Did I to gain You quit the same Proportion of my small Trappings, I own my happiness woud not arise from a selfe denial, and therefore you will think me ungenerous in recommending it to you. It woud be the highest improvement of that Model of life I always took to be the best. I coud almost come up to the Rules you laid down when you said your letter shoud have bin dated from another world.[1] I ever believ'd the compleatest Plan of Felicity that we are acquainted with, was to enjoy one woman friend, one Man, and to think it of little moment whether those that were made use of to fill up some idle hours were Princes or Peasants, wise or foolish, but rather to seek the Lower as less likely to work any change in a mind thoroughly satisfi'd that knew no want nor so much as a wish. Had I you, I shoud have at one view before me all the Charms of either sex met together. I shoud enjoy a perpetual succession of new Pleasures, a constant Variety in One. This is far beyond what I thought sufficient to make life Happy. [*Passage omitted*]
8 April

Text W MS i. 82–85 (draft)   *End. by W* To M. P. 8 April

To [Wortley] [*April 1710*]

I can't account for my fears that you do not love me but from a dispondence in my temper which disposes me this moment to dispeare of ever seeing you againe. If I were to

[1] A reference to her letter of 8 Aug. 1709 to Anne Wortley.

finde myself described in any writings I shud believe the author had strain'd a carrictor beyond nature, and yet there appears no extravagance to me, since I consider you come the neerest my notion of a fine gentleman of any I ever saw. . . .

Text Excerpt in Sotheby Catalogue for 27–29 Feb. 1896, lot 224 (3 pp., folio, from [William] Upcott collection).

To Wortley *17 April 1710*

Dear Sir,

I ask pardon for my presumption, but the occation that happen'd makes me take this liberty. My Lady Mary gave orders to write to let you know she received your two letters this day. The very time you went away she went to Acton[1] and is very ill of the measles, and is very sory she could not write sooner, for she had not conveniency; but as soon as she comes to London she does designe to see you. Betty tooke a great deal of troble goeing often to Acton to see for a letter, but Lady Mary could gett no conveniency to write. She gives her love and respects to you, but if it is not expressed as is proper you'l excuse it as from whence it comes insteed of my Lady.

Lady Mary desires you to direct your letter for Betty Laskey at the Bunch of Grapes and Queen's head in Knights Bridge. She had not time when Betty gave her the letters to read them. She signs her name to this for I shewed it her.
Aprill 17th 1710   M. P.[2]

Text W MS i. 234–5   *End. by W* M. P. 17 April. Signed.   *End. by Steele* Ap. 18th 1710. This is left to-night with Me to send to you. I send You no news because I beleive this will employ you better. Your most Obedient Servant, Richd Steele

[1] LM's father maintained a house in Acton, then a country village, about 8 miles west of St. Paul's.

[2] LM denied sending this letter (see below, p. 37).

From Wortley 20 *April* [1710]

20 April.

Tho last night I was perfectly well till I saw the letter sign'd by you, I am this morning downright sick. Had there bin any such thing as Sympathy that is occasion'd by Griefe, I shou'd have bin sensible of it when you first fell ill. I had griev'd at your Illness, tho I had bin sure you hated me. An Aversion may possibly be remov'd, but the loss of you woud be irretrievable; there has not yet bin, there never will be, another L.M. You see how far a man's passion carries ⟨his⟩ reflexions. It makes him uneasy because the ⟨wor⟩st may possibly happen from the least dangerous Distempers. I take yours to be so, and think a thousand to one that I hear of your recovery when I hear of you next. I am not the least concern'd to fancy your Colour may receive some Alteration. I shoud be overjoy'd to hear your Beauty was very much impair'd, cou'd I be pleas'd with any thing that wou'd give you displeasure, for it woud lessen the number of your Admirers, but even the loss of a feature, nay of your Eyes themselves, wou'd not make you seem less beautifull to —— [*Passage omitted*]

Text W MS ii. 392–3 (draft)   *End. by W* 20 Apr. Letter sign'd.

From Wortley [22 *April 1710*]

Saturday, 7 at night.

When your health will allow you I hope you will not fail to inform me of all I want to know. In the meantime I intreat you not to let another day pass as this has done, but send one line to let me know you do not grow worse. This is the third of those to which I want an answer.

Text W MS i. 71–72   *Address* To the Rt Honble the Lady Mary Pierrepont.

From Wortley [*c.* 23 *April 1710*]

I had just now the ill news from Betty [Laskey] that not only your servants and your sister, but my Lord knew of my addresses to you.

I am afraid he has mention'd it to a neighbour of his, who is intimate with a near Relation of mine and was drawing a Conveyance, which woud have mended my Circumstances very much. ⟨I⟩ suspect they may have heard it or suspected it either from my Lord or some other because that matter stands still whereas it shoud have bin ended at my coming to town. I beg you will use all the caution imaginable that our correspondence may be secret if possible till you and I agree it shoud not. Otherwise I not only suffer in my fortune but may be renderd incapable of having you. This I know, that relation of mine woud agree to nothing which he thought woud facilitate such a design. But if this business were finish'd, I shoud be in no want of his assistance. Pray let this particular be a secret kept by your selfe only. Since your sister[1] knows of my writing to you, what if I enclos'd to her and sent by the post when I write to you? For Betty's going is, I doubt, remarkable. The hearing of your better state of Health makes me cheerful under this ⟨?⟩.

Text W MS i. 78–79   *End. by W* her being better in 1710. The Ill consequence of its being known I write to her.

To Wortley [*25 April 1710*]

I have this minute receivd your 2 Letters. I know not how to direct to you, whether to London or the country, or if in the country to Durham or Wortley. Tis very likely you'l never receive this. I hazard a great deal if it falls into other hands, and I write for all that—

I wish with all my soul I thought as you do. I endeavor to convince my selfe by your Arguments, and am sorry my reason is so obstinate not to be deluded into an Opinion that tis impossible a Man can esteem a Woman. I suppose I should then be very easy at your thoughts of me. I should thank you for the wit and Beauty you give me and not be angry at the follys and weaknesses, but to my Infinite affliction I can beleive neither one nor tother. One part of my Character is not so good nor th'other so bad as you fancy it. Should we ever live together you would be disapointed both ways; you would find an easy equality of temper you

[1] Lady Frances Pierrepont.

do not expect, and a thousand faults you do not imagine.
You think if you marry'd me I should be passionately fond
of you one month and of some body else the next. Neither
would happen. I can esteem, I can be a freind, but I don't
know whether I can Love. Expect all that is complaisant and
easy, but never what is fond in me. You Judge very wrong
of my Heart when you suppose me capable of veiws of
Interest, and that any thing could oblige me to flatter any
body. Was I the most indigent Creature in the world I
should answer you as I do now, without adding or deminish-
ing. I am incapable of Art, and 'tis because I will not be
capable of it. Could I deceive one minute, I should never
regain my own good Opinion, and who could bear to live
with one they despis'd?

If you can resolve to live with a Companion that will have
all the deference due to your superiority of good sense, and
that your proposals can be agreable to those on whom I
depend—I have nothing to say against them.

As to travelling, tis what I should doe with great pleasure,
and could easily quit London upon your account, but a
retirement in the country is not so disagreable to me, as I
know a few months would make it tiresome to you. Where
people are ty'd for Life, tis their mutual Interest not to grow
weary of one Another. If I had all the personal charms that
I want, a Face is too slight a foundation for happynesse.
You would be soon tir'd with seeing every day the same
thing, where you saw nothing else. You would have leisure
to remark all the defects, which would encrease in proportion as the novelty lessend, which is allwaies a great charm.
I should have the displeasure of seeing a coldnesse, which
tho' I could not reasonably blame you for, being involuntary,
yet it would render me uneasy, and the more because I know
a Love may be reviv'd which Absence, Inconstancy, or even
Infidelity has extinguish'd, but there is no returning from
a degout given by Satiety.

I should not chuse to live in a croud. I could be very well
pleasd to be in London without makeing a great Figure or
seeing above 8 or 9 agreable people. Apartments, Table
etc. are things that never come into my head. But [I] will
never think of any thing without the consent of my Family,

and advise you not to fancy a happynesse in entire solitude, which you would find only Fancy.

Make no an⟨swer t⟩o this. If you can like me on my own terms, tis not to me you must make your proposals.[1] If not, to what purpose is our Correspondance?

However, preserve me your Freindship, which I think of with a great deal of pleasure and some Vanity. If ever you see me marry'd, I flatter my selfe you'l see a Conduct you would not be sorry your Wife should Imitate.

Text W MS i. 261–3   *Address* To Mr. Edward Wortley Mountague at the Deanery of Durham[2] care   *Postmark* AP 25

From Wortley [*c. 28 April 1710*]

When I first read your letter I thought it best to make you no answer as you desire. So little was I pleas'd with it that I read it but once at the time I receiv'd it, and laid it by with a resolution to look on it no more, but being ill to day and bound to stay within, I saw it and coud not help opening it again. I find there are words as if you left me quite at liberty to break off; not as if you did it, which I thought before. You did not take me right. I think one shoud carefully avoid deceiving a person one may possibly pass all one's life with, and when I said I cou'd not determine I told you true, that I thought you and yet think you as valuable to any but my selfe as ever I did, so far was I from having a lower opinion of you. That I have more reason than any other to esteem you I can by no means admit. Nor is it in my power to make you uneasy. That you care very little whether we differ or not is visible in every line you write. Coud any woman write with so much wit and be so much upon her guard with one she was afraid of losing? I own I have endeavourd to express as little concern as I coud, but you see an air of sincerity in all I tell you. Does any thing of that appear in yours? However, my present intention is not to take the leave you give me of breaking off, but when you absolutely

[1] In an autobiographical romance, written probably in the summer of 1710, LM recounts her meeting with W and the beginning of his courtship, ending with his formal request to her father, 'and the Lawyers were appointed to meet on both sides according to Custom' (W MS vii. 196–9). Most of this is printed in George Paston [E. M. Symonds], *Lady Mary Wortley Montagu and Her Times*, 1907, pp. 4–5, 7–8, 21–22, 28–30.

[2] W's uncle the Hon. John Montagu, D.D. (1655?–1728), had been Dean of Durham since 1699 (*DNB*).

31

forbid me to write or leave off answering, then I will consider what to do. It is possible I may wait till you send a letter of mine back unopen'd: the most proper ceremony of parting for good and all. I do not yet desire to see this, and therefore must let you know thus much of my temper, that whoever treats me roughly is less belov'd by me for it. I dont say the first day or week, but when I have leisure to reflect and see it is best not to run a hazard of suffering more.

I am sick and write this to shew I have not yet given over conversing with you. I cant answer for't that when I am well I shall think exactly as I do now.

Text W MS i. 1

To Wortley [*c. 3 May 1710*]

At this minute I am so ill my selfe, your Letter is come in very good time if you have a mind I should say any thing soft to you. I have kept my Chamber this 5 days, and have so much compassion for people that are sick, I am very likly to forget you are ill natur'd, and only remember that you are sick and talk with a great deal of tendernesse. But I hope there is no occassion for this. You are now very well, and if I am to take your word for't, your thoughts very much alter'd—I will take no notice of this but write as if they were not, and answer your last letter tho' perhaps by this time you have forgot you ever writ it.

You seem to reproach me with being upon my guard. What would I give this reproach was Just? I have been foolishly otherwise. I agree with you that you have lesse reason than any one else to esteem me. No other knows so manny of my weaknesses, and I cannot blame you for thinking of me as I do of my selfe. I could wish—impossibillitys— that I could be what you seem to reproach me with, or you what I could wish you—This Letter will be astonishingly silly, but there are several excuses for it. I am not well, there is musick in the next room that I hear whither I will or no, and—this must be my last letter. If only my own Resolution design'd it so, neither you nor I would have any reason to beleive it; tho' once I told you my resolutions were never broken (and I remember I thought so at that time), yet I

have broke 2 or 3 every day since, a punishment due to the
vanity of that Expression. There is now a greater bar to our
Correspondance; if I am well I leave this place the 28th [*sic*]
of this month, and then twill be utterly impossible to send a
letter to, or receive one from you. 'Tis now a hazard and will
be then a certainty of discovery. A letter comeing to my
Maid will be suspected, and I beg you to beleive me that
I speak perfect truth, that even an Attempt of that kind
would ruin me.

If you wait till I se⟨nd⟩ you a Letter back unopend you
will wait very long. I have not courrage to do it, nor is it
in my power to be rough. The softnesse of my temper is the
most unfortunate part of my Composition. Nobody can be
throughly unhappy that wants it, and I think you very
happy that know not what it is.

You say you do not yet think to break off. If you do not,
'tis only to my Family you must speak. I can now hear no
more from you, nor can I make you any other Answer than
what they are pleasd to direct. If you do not agree with them,
or if (which is most likely) you have resolvd not to try, do
not think of me otherwise than as of one who where ever ill
fortune conducts her, will preserve an Esteem for you and
some unavailing good wishes, which are very sincere tho’
very insignificant.

I say nothing of my Letters; I ⟨?⟩ you will burn them.
Adeiu, do not think of returning an Answer except you
would have it fall into the Hands of my Relations on purpose
to make me miserable. Once more Adeiu. I would not have
you persist in your causelesse suspicions, but what remedy
can I give to ’em?

Text W MS i. 296–7　　*Address* To Mr Edward Wortley Mountague
End. by W Ans. to 5. From P.

To Wortley [*c. 4 May 1710*]

Tho’ I have reason to fear my Reputation of Sincerity is
very low with you, yet I am unwilling to give you any real
Cause to suspect my want of it. When I writ my last, I

beleivd twas to bid you Adeiu, thinking we begun our Journey next Thursday. I have Just now receivd a letter that
tells me a Lady is falln dangerously ill of the small pox over
against our House,[1] and I am to stay here till all danger of
Infection is over.

Tis a prodigious while since we have seen one another,
and I beleive I am the only body who thinks the better of
people for being Absent. My Fancy represents to me only
what is pleasing in them. I don't see, and I forget the
occassions they give me to dislike 'em.

I only writ this to prevent your imagining my last an
Artifice, should you accidentally hear we was not yet come
to Town, being sensible how often you give me the honnour
of having more invention than I'm capable of. You need not
trouble your selfe with answering it—since I beleive it is
a trouble. Besides I know if you do write, twill be scrupules,
suspicions and cross questions. I am alone ⟨and⟩ not very
well, and any thing that vexes me now vexes me too much.
Therefore don't send an ill naturd Letter.

Text W MS i. 193–4   *Address* To Mr Edward Wortley Mountague
End. by W Ans. to 5. From P. 2d Answ. to 5.

To Wortley [5 *May 1710*]

Your Indiscretion has given me so much trouble, I would
willingly get rid of it at the prize of my Fever's returning.
You employd the foolishest and most improper messenger
upon Earth.[2] She has prattled all she knows, and all she
suppos'd, which goes a great deal farther. Tis not her
custom to make secrets of names. Every thing is known but
my Innocence, which is never to be cleard. I could Justifye
my selfe in part by showing your Letters. I could not resolve
to do what I thought not right, and burn't them to prevent
their being seen, which was otherwise unavoidable.

How unhappy am I! I think I have been scrupulously

---

[1] At Lady Guildford's (see above,
p. 23, n. 2) the Miss Brownlow engaged
to marry Lord Willoughby died in 1710
of smallpox (*Wentworth Papers*, p. 137).
[2] Betty Laskey, the messenger in the
letter of 17 April.

just to my Duty. I cannot so much as call to mind an Expression I have cause to blame my selfe for, but I am not the lesse unfortunate. All commerce of this kind between men and women is like that of the Boys and Frogs in L'Estrange's Fables.—Tis play to you, but tis death to us—and if we had the wit of the frogs, we should allwaies make that answer.[1]

I am mighty happy in Mr. St[eele] and his wife knowing this affair.[2] He over a bottle and she over a tea table has (I don't question) said manny witty things upon this Occassion. My answers have not (by great good fortune) passd their hands. On 2nd thoughts I half wish they had. To be sure, they do you Justice in supposeing I would answer them, and perhaps me the injustice in supposeing them other than they was, without Authority for it. I find tis in your power to exclude me the Town. If I was as fond of it as you think me, I should be very angry at the cause of my going into a frightful solitude[3] instead of returning to London, where my Family is now perswaded I have behav'd my selfe very ill. Were I dispos'd to tell the whole story, it would do me no good. They have reason to beleive my vanity or worse has been more the cause of this busynesse than any honnourable design you had on me.

Your last letter (which came safe to me by miracle) I don't understand a word of, nor what Letter you speak of. I writ you one to the Deanery of Durham. It had no name to it, and was in the same hand as the first. I fear you never receiv'd it. I know of no other.

My sicknesse was more dangerous than you think it. I have ⟨no⟩t liv'd very long in the world, but ⟨begin⟩ to be weary of it, and in the ⟨situation⟩ I am in, am very sorry I'm recov⟨ered.⟩

[1] 'A Company of Waggish *Boys* were watching of *Frogs* at the Side of a Pond, and still as any of 'em put up their Heads, they'd be pelting them down again with Stones. Children (says one of the Frogs) you never consider, that *though this may be Play to you, 'tis Death to us*' (Roger L'Estrange, *Fables of Æsop and other Eminent Mythologists*, 8th ed., 1738, p. 423).

[2] Steele had endorsed the letter of 17 April.

[3] At West Dean, near Salisbury, Wiltshire, a manor which Lord Dorchester had inherited from his mother Elizabeth Pierrepont (1639–99), da. of Sir John Evelyn (Richard C. Hoare, *History of Modern Wilts.*, 1822–44, V, i. 23).

[Postscripts] By an indiscreet resentment to the foolish creature you employd, do not expose me to her tongue.

Make no attempts of writeing. Either think of me no more, or think in the way you ought.

Text W MS i. 246–7   *Address* To Mr Edward Wortley Mountague at Mr Knaptons a Glasse Shop in Queens street near Lincolns inn feild London   *End. by W* May 5.

From Wortley [*5 May 1710*]

The letter you sent into the Country came this evening.[1] It is in every part of it a Contradiction to the Compliment you make me and proves that no one is superior to you in good sense. However, I heartily thank you for it as well as for your saying you can bring your selfe to be easy and Complaisant. I wish you had bin able to stop there and forbear telling me you cou'd be nothing more. Had you, immediatly after you said you might be easy, gone to the mention of settlements, I might only have taken you to be very prudent and still have hop'd for something above easiness and Complaisance. But to say there cou'd be nothing more and then be so exact about the method of proposing, I refer it to yourselfe whether this does not look as if you were studying how to put yourselfe in the road to happiness and not preparing to enter upon the Possession of it. *[Passage omitted]* The satiety you speak of never happens where there is not a want of understanding on the side of t'other. A very small share of Reason with a great deal of kindness will secure a Passion longer than the perfection of it with your sort of Return. If you say a man is not satiated when he has got rid of such an Attachment, I will not say he is, nor quarrel with you about a word, but this I must beg leave to say, that I had much rather be cur'd, and that I shoud be much longer in curing by what you call satiety than such a Coldness as yours. If you woud keep a man a slave for a long time that you dont value, I can't say you are in the wrong or that he woud be less serviceable to you than if you did value him. But for my part I can have no such Ambition. I shoud be sorry to be ti'd to one to whom I coud take my selfe to be superiour, or whom I coud live with as if I had any power. For this reason, as much as I desir'd to have you, I would not think of it without first letting you know all I knew my selfe of my temper, that if it did not suit with yours it might give you no trouble. Most others woud have first secur'd you and then seem'd surpriz'd you should not be satisfid in any

1 LM's letter of 25 April.

place or Company that pleas'd them most. That I have chose rather to love you than govern you will, I hope, give me some title to that Friendship you promise me.

I am not sure a retirement woud agree with me better than with others, but a man shoud never run the hazard of hearing one he loves find fault with a Place where she may not only have as much as she pleases of his Company, but know she has his heart wholly to herselfe.

Text W MS i. 48–49 (draft) *End. by W* To M. P. May 5. Abt being easy and Complaisant. Answer to that of 25 Apr.

From Wortley [*6 May 1710*]

Saturday Morning 7 a Clock.

I am the less troubled at your letter because I know I deserve none of the Reproches in it. Before I went out of town you know I never sent Betty [Laskey] but with Answers to what she had brought from You. She has told me many times since I came that you orderd her to be very frequently at Acton. The letter which now you disown orders me expressly to direct my letters to her. Had you thought her going to you improper, as I do assure you I always did, you woud rather have told me to what friend of yours I might enclose. But you say you know nothing of this letter in another hand, and I am sorry for it because it is more favourable than any of the rest. The first of those that are yours tells me my temper and yours cant agree. That I had yesterday from Durham says I can never please you, and that which came, as I was going to bed, by the Pennypost accuses me of very great faults and of Folly. While I take the sense of your letters to be such, I shoud be altogether as indiscreet as you make me if I made any proposals. If I mistake the meaning of 'em I hope you will give your selfe the trouble of explaining. [*Passage omitted*]

Whether you resolve to take or refuse me it is necessary some things shoud be cleard up between us. If you dont like sending to me under a Cover directed to Mr. St[eele] in Bury street,[1] pray send to me at Mr. Goodwin's[2] a Bookseller at the Queen's head, over against St. Dunstan's Church, Fleet street. The penny-post letter had bin open'd and seald up again; it might possibly be by some of my father's servants, for the Postman by mistake carri'd it to his House instead of my Lodging. Those that open'd it, if it was done here and they can possibly ghess

---

[1] The Steeles had lived in Bury Street, St. James's, since 1707 (Rich. Steele, *Corr.*, ed. R. Blanchard, 1941, p. 210).

[2] Timothy Goodwin (d. 1720) (H. R. Plomer, *Dict. of Printers . . . 1668–1725*, 1922, iii. 129–30).

whence it came, may do me a great prejudice, but that I don't value, but will never own they did open it by publishing what was in it.

By misfortune I read your letter as I was going to bed. You may imagine I had little sleep and hope you will pardon any inconsistencies or other faults you find in what I write. I shall not wonder if you think it as senseless as you did the other you don't understand a word of. I hope you will not forget to say how I may write to you. I am going to find her out since you say she is an improper messenger, and will take that from her I gave her yesterday unless she can convey both this and that in some better manner than she did the others.

Text W MS i. 26–27 (draft)   *End. by W* May. Abt the letter signed in April. Abt another sent from Durham. writ before going abroad. Answer to that of 5 May.

To Wortley [*c. 6 May 1710*]

Your conduct is more surprizeing every day than other. —How could you think of employing that creature?[1] I beg'd you not to write again. I told you what would inevitably happen. You might have beleiv'd me. To finish your discretion you come to Acton that your name may be known. She has impos'd upon you a thousand ways. I suppose she writ the letter you speak of; I knew nothing of it. You have heard, I dare swear, 50 lies from her own mouth. I beleive I may venture to afirm she never told you a word of truth. She has made every thing public to every servant in the house. Imagine the pritty pickle I am in.—

I'm so discompos'd I know not what I write. That I gave you no directions to any body was because I would not (as I think, as I told you) keep any private correspondance. You accuse me in your last of want of generosity. Tis a fault I never found in my selfe. I thought nothing so generous as telling the truth, and would not buy any thing at the price of a deceit.—

I know not whether you can make me happy; you have convinc'd me you can make me Miserable. Nothing is more dreadful than to live uneasy with people one must live with and lose the good opinion of those that command one.—I have said enough to you—too much—Happy only in my

[1] Betty Laskey.

38

Innocence and something of a temper that can bear misfortunes with patience tho' I don't deserve 'em.

Your last letter is excessively obliging, and I have a great deal of reason to be pleas'd with it. I find it is not enough to act generously; one should leave it in no body's power to act otherwise.

I read over again your last letter. I find you think very ill of me, but my passion is abated, and upon cooler consideration I begin to think you in the right. Yet there is something you wrong me in. Could you suppose I would willingly expose you to any inconvenience upon my account? —Would I do that?—Forgive every thing that is peevish in these 2 last letters. I writ that you receiv'd last and great part of this in a distraction. I knew not what I did. If my Indiscretion (for I am now convinc'd I was indiscreet) has occasion'd you any trouble pardon it; be so just to beleive it was not design'd. I was born ⟨to⟩ be unfortunate, and shall complain of my destiny without complaining of you. Forgive and forget me, and tis all I have require⟨d⟩.

Tis none of your fault your letters were not seen, and my answering known where it is of the highest importance it should be conceald.—I hope tis yet a secret. If you have any remaining regard for me, oblige that wench to silence; tis not anger must do it.

Text W MS i. 195–6   *Address* To Mr Edward Wortley Mountague at Mr Goodwins a Bookseller at the Queens Head over against St Dunstans Church in Fleet street London

To Wortley [7 *May 1710*]

Sunday night

Till this minute I had not opertunity of receiving your last letter, and twas a wonder I ever did. Had it falln into any body's hand but one, I had never seen it. I was walking in the Garden and expecting nothing lesse, when it was brought me by one that I did not know knew any thing of the matter, and was surpriz'd they should do me such a hazardous peice of service without my requiring it, or expecting any reward for it. I had not seen them till that evening since Betty's comeing.

What you say about my Sister[1] is altogether impossible. Since this unlucky busynesse, she is a spie on my Actions and leaves me not a minute's time to my selfe. While I am writeing I fear a surprize every minute.—When your last was given me, I gave one to be sent that I had ready writ about me. If you look upon it as an Answer to what I have just now receiv'd, you think me the unjustest thing alive; it was to that which was dated Satterday morning, 7.

I hope you are mistaken. I dare Swear nothing will be said by the person you mention, but the Indiscretion of your messenger has told it to so manny, it is a chance if any body is ignorant of it. Perhaps this may be open'd or intercepted, perhaps my last never came to you. I shall be mightily disquieted about it. If you have received it, you may direct 2 or 3 lines for me, by the penny post, as if it came from an unknown hand. Say any stuff, tis no matter what; I shall know my letters came safe. But do not write me word so. If you had allwaies made use of the post, things would not have been as they are. —There is no recalling the past.—If any body is so much mistaken as to fear you have more regard for me than they wish, methinks tis easy to convince them. 'Tis but promising to think of me no more, keep your word, and the busynesse is done. If you have reason to complain of me for prejudicing your affairs undesignedly, you may t⟨hank⟩ me for willingly telling you the way to set them right again.

[*Postscript*] How to send this I cant imagine. The person [who] gave me yours I may probably not see this ten days, and can never be seen to speak to without Suspicion. If you write again, your Letters will certainly be stop'd and I shall never see them. I hope you would not do that Injury to a person that never design'd you one in her Life.

Text W MS i. 166–7   *Address* To Mr Edward Wortley Mou⟨ntagu⟩ with Care   *End. by W* This seems an answer to that abt the Ill Consequence. To say any Stuffe.

To Mrs. Frances Hewet [*June 1710*]

I would have writ long ago to dear Mrs. Hewet, but I waited for the good news of saying when I might hope to

[1] Lady Frances Pierrepont.

see you, which I now despair of for this long time. We go, next week, into Wiltshire, which will be quite a new world to us. I was about eight years old when I left it, and have intirely forgot every thing in it.[1] I am sorry we shall not see you, though I am still in hopes we shall return into Nottinghamshire the latter end of the year; but all that is supposals, and I have no ground to believe it, but that I wish it very much. You can expect no news from one who has nothing at present in her head but packing up, and the ideas that naturally come upon going to a place, I may almost say I never saw, so perfectly have I forgotten it.

Be so good when you see Mrs. Levenz[2] to ask her if she received my letter; if she did not, I am sure I must suffer very much in her opinion, and appear very ungrateful, after her inquiry when I was sick. Mrs. Hewet should never talk of being rivalled; there is no such thing as not liking her, or liking any body else better. It is a provoking thing to think so many tedious years as we have passed at Thoresby, we should always be asunder so many dirty miles, and the first summer you come nearer, I am tossed to the other side of the world, where I do not know so much as one creature, and am afraid I shall not meet with such agreeable neighbours as in Nottinghamshire. But destiny must be followed, and I own, was I to choose mine, it should never be to stay perpetually in the same place. I should even prefer little storms to an eternal calm; and though I am displeased not to see you, I am not sorry to see a new part of the kingdom.

My dear Mrs. Hewet, preserve me your friendship wherever my fortune carries me, and believe that I am equally in all places yours,

M. P.

Continue your direction to Arlington street.

Text 1805, v. 246–8

[1] After the death of LM's mother in 1692 (PR 538, Diocesan Rec. Office, Notts. Co. Council), the Pierrepont children lived with their grandmother Elizabeth Pierrepont at West Dean until her death in 1699. In her will (Eg MS 3517, ff. 153–65) she left bequests to a Mrs. Dupont—probably the children's French governess—and to two nurses.

[2] Probably Ann Buck who m. (1693) William Levinz (1671–1732), M.P. for Notts. 1710–22 (J. Foster, *Alumni Oxon. 1500–1714*, iii. 905).

To Anne Justice[1] [*June 1710*]

Ay, ay, as you say my dear, men are vile inconstant toads
[. . . . *a description of a mansion in Wiltshire*].

Text Sotheby Catalogues for 25–26 June 1829 (lot 195) and 18–19
July 1904 (lot 98).

To Anne Justice [*c. 5 July 1710*]

Yes, yes, my dear, Here is Woods and Shades and Groves
in abundance; you are in the right on't. Tis not the place,
but the solitude of the place that is intollerable. Tis a horrid
thing to see nothing but trees in a wood, and to walk by a
purling stream to ogle the Gudgeons in it.

I'm glad you continue your Inclinations to reading; tis
the most improving and most pleasant of all Employments,
and helps to wear away manny melancholy hours.

I hear from some Nottinghamshire people that Mrs.
B[anks] is not at all concern'd at the breaking off her match.[2]
I wonder at her courage if she is not, and at her prudence in
dissembling it if she is. Prudent people are very happy; tis
an exceeding fine thing, that's certain, but I was born with-
out it, and shall retain to my day of Death the Humour of
saying what I think. Therefore you may beleive me when
I protest I am much mortifyd at not seeing the North this
Year, for a hundred and fifty reasons; amongst the rest
I should have been heartily glad to have seen My Lord
Holdernesse.[3]

[1] Anne Justice (1691–1773), da. of
William Justice, an attorney, m. (Jan.
1712) Jonas Thompson (1680–1739), an
attorney and Lord Mayor of York 1731
(Skaife MS, Archives of the City of
York; her will: vol. 117, f. 213, Prerog.
Court of York).

[2] Mary Banks (1690–1726), da. of
Joseph Banks, attorney and land agent,
m. (1717) Sir Francis Whichcote of
Aswarby. She lived at Scofton near
Worksop, not far from Thoresby. In

the summer of 1710 negotiations for her
marriage to George Vane were broken
off (*Letters and Papers of the Banks
Family . . . 1704–1760*, ed. J. W. F. Hill,
Lincoln Record Soc., xlv, 1952, p. xv).
Two of her letters to LM are W MS iv.
116–18.

[3] Robert Darcy (1681–1722), 3rd
Earl of Holdernesse, owned Hornby
Castle in Bedale, Yorks. For LM's high
opinion of him, see below, p. 232.

In this Hidious Country tis not the fashion to visit, and the few Neighbours there are, keep as far from one Another as ever they can. The Diversion here is walking, which indeed are very pritty all about the house,[1] but then you may walk 2 mile without meeting a living creature but a few straggling cows. We have been here near this month and seen but one visiter, and her I never desird to see again, for I never saw such a Monster ⟨in⟩ my Life.

I am very sorry for your sore Eyes. By this time I hope all's over and you can see as well as ever. Adeiu, my dear. When you drink tea with Mrs. B[anks] drink my health and do me the Justice to beleive I wish my selfe with you.

Text MS owned by Lord Stanhope, Chevening   *Address* To Mrs Anne Justice at Mr Justices upon the pavement at York by way of London   *Postmark* IY 7

To Gilbert Burnet[2] *20 July 1710*[3]

To My Lord Bishop of Salisbury

My Lord,

Your hours are so well employ'd, I hardly dare offer you this Triffle to look over, but then so well am I acquainted with that sweetnesse of temper which accompanys your Learning, I dare even assure my Selfe of a Pardon. You have allready forgiven me greater Impertinencies, and con-descended yet farther in giving me Instructions and bestow-ing some of your Minutes in teaching me.[4] This Surprizing Humillity has all the Effect it ought to have on my Heart; I am sensible of the Gratitude I owe to so much Goodnesse, and how much I am ever bound to be your servant.

[1] The house at West Dean 'stood in a grove of elm trees at the top of a suc-cession of terraces and formal gardens facing west in which direction lay the park, well timbered and adorned with canals in the Dutch manner, fed from a large fish pond which, with its over-hanging bank of yew, formed a pro-minent feature of the ornamental grounds' (Edith Olivier, *Wiltshire*, 1951, pp. 254–5).

[2] The famous Bishop (1643–1715).

As a Whig politician he was associated with LM's father, and his diocesan seat at Salisbury was close to West Dean.

[3] Date (missing in MS) in 1803, i. 133.

[4] Many years later she recalled Burnet's kindness: 'I knew him in my very early Youth, and his condescention in directing a Girl in her studies is an Obligation I can never forget' (letter of 14 July [1758] to Lady Bute).

Here is the Work of one Week of my solitude.[1] By the manny faults in it, Your Lordship will easily beleive I spent no more time upon it. It was hardly finish'd when I was oblig'd to begin my Journey, and I had not leisure to write it over again. You have it here without any Corrections, with all its blots and Errors. I endeavor'd at no Beauty of Style but to keep as Litterally as I could to the Sense of the Author. My only intention in presenting it is to ask your Lordship whither I have understood Epictetus.[2] The 4th Chapter perticularly I am afraid I have mistaken. Piety and greatnesse of Soul sets you above all misfortunes that can happen to your Selfe, and the Calumnys of False Tongues, but that same Piety which renders what happens to your selfe Indifferent to you, yet softens the natural Compassion in your Temper to the Greatest Degree of Tendernesse, for the Interests of the Church and the Liberty and welfare of your Country. The Steps that are now made towards the destruction of both, the Apparent Danger we are in, the Manifest Growth of Injustice, Oppression, and Hypocrisie,[3] cannot do otherwise than give your Lordship those Hours of Sorrow, which, did not your Fortitude of Soul and Refflections from Religion and Philosophy shorten, would add to the National Misfortunes by injureing the health of so great a supporter of our sinking Libertys.

I ought to ask pardon for this Digression; it is more proper for me in this place to say something to excuse an Addresse that looks so very presumeing. My Sex is usually forbid studys of this Nature, and Folly reckon'd so much our proper Sphere, we are sooner pardon'd any excesses of that, than the least pretentions to reading or good Sense. We are permitted no Books but such as tend to the weakening and Effeminateing the Mind, our Natural Deffects are every way indulg'd, and tis look'd upon as in a degree Criminal to improve our Reason, or fancy we have any. We are taught to place all our Art in adorning our Outward Forms, and permitted, without reproach, to carry that

---

[1] Her work was a translation, from a Latin version, of the *Enchiridion* of Epictetus.

[2] The Bishop corrected her transla-tion very carefully, but only the first 36 of the 79 sections (H MS, vol. 252; printed 1837; 1861, ii. 391–412).

[3] See below, p. 50, n. 2.

Custom even to Extravagancy, while our Minds are entirely neglected, and by disuse of Refflections, fill'd with nothing but the Triffling objects our Eyes are daily entertain'd with. This Custom, so long establish'd and industriously upheld, makes it even ridiculous to go out of the common road, and forces one to find as manny Excuses, as if it was a thing altogether criminal not to play the fool in Consort with other Women of Quality, whose Birth and Leisure only serve to render them the most uselesse and most worthlesse part of the creation.

There is hardly a character in the World more Despicable or more liable to universal ridicule than that of a Learned Woman. Them words imply, according to the receiv'd sense, a tatling, impertinent, vain, and Conceited Creature. I beleive no body will deny that Learning may have this Effect, but it must be a very superficial degree of it. Erasmus was certainly a Man of great Learning and good sense, and he seems to have my Opinion of it when he says, Fœmina qui vere sapit, non videtur sibi sapere; contra, quæ cum nihil sapiat sibi videtur sapere, ea demum bis stulta est.[1] The Abbé Bellegarde gives a right reason for Women's talking over much. They know nothing, and every outward Object strikes their Imagination and produces a multitude of thoughts, which if they knew more, they would know not worth their thinking of.[2] I am not now arguing for an Equality for the 2 Sexes; I do not doubt God and Nature has thrown us into an Inferior Rank. We are a lower part of the Creation; we owe Obedience and Submission to the Superior Sex; and any Woman who suffers her Vanity and folly to deny this, Rebells against the Law of the Creator and indisputable Order of Nature. But There is a worse Effect than this, which

---

[1] 'A woman who is truly wise does does not think herself so; on the contrary, when a woman who knows nothing thinks herself wise, she is indeed twice a fool' (Erasmus, 'Colloquia Familiaria Abbatis et Eruditae,' *Opera Omnia*, Leyden, 1703, i. col. 745).

[2] 'That which makes Women talk so much, is their want of understanding; this Maxim seems a Paradox, and yet 'tis very true; as they are very shallow and empty, whatever strikes their Senses, takes up their Capacities, and becomes the Subject of their Discourse; whatever they see or hear, their Pleasures and Pains, their Domestick Affairs, their Intrigues, their Quarrels, are inexhaustible Topics, and provided you only talk fiddle-faddle, they are never at a loss in Conversation' (Jean Baptiste Bellegarde, *Reflexions upon Ridicule*, transl. 1706, p. 126).

follows the Carelesse Education given to Women of Quality, its being so easy for any Man of Sense, that finds it either his Interest or his Pleasure, to corrupt them. The common Method is to begin by attacking their Religion. They bring them a thousand fallacious Arguments their excessive ignorance hinders them from refuteing; and, I speak now from my own knowledge and Conversation amongst them, there are more Atheists amongst the fine Ladys than the Loosest sort of Rakes, and The same Ignorance that generally works out into Excesse of Superstition, exposes them to the Snares of any who have a fancy to carry them to tother extream.

I have made my Excuses allready too long, and will conclude in the Words of Erasmus, Vulgus sentit quod Lingua Latina non convenit fœminis, quia parum facit ad tuendum illarum Pudicitiam, quoniam rarum et insolitum est fœminam scire Latinam; Attamen Consuetudo omnium malarum rerum magistra. Decorum est fœminam in Germania nata[m] discere Gallice, ut loquatur cum his qui sciunt Gallice. Cur igitur habetur indecoram discere Latine, ut quotidie confabuletur cum tot auctoribus tam facundis, tam eruditis, tam sapientibus, tam fidis consultoribus? Certe mihi quantulumcunque cerebri est, malim in bonis studiis consumere, quam in precibus sine mente dictis, in pernoctibus conviviis, in exhauriendis capacibus pateris.[1]

I have tir'd your Lordship and too long[2] delayed to subscribe myself your Lordship's

Most respectful and obliged

M. Pierrepont.

Text W MS v. 4–7 (perhaps a draft)

[1] 'The common opinion is that the Latin language is not suitable for the ladies because it does too little toward the preservation of their modesty, just because it is a rare and unusual thing for a woman to know Latin; however custom is the mistress of all evil things. It is proper for a woman born in Germany to learn French so that she can talk with those who know French. Why then is it considered indecorous if she learns Latin so that she can converse daily with so many eloquent, learned and wise authors and trustworthy counsellors? Certainly, however little brains I have, I had rather employ them in liberal studies than in prayers uttered without attention, in nightlong feasting and in drinking down full glasses' (the Latin adapted by LM from the same passage in Erasmus as p. 45, n. 1).

[2] The text from here to the end, missing in MS, is supplied from 1803, i. 139.

To Wortley *20* [*July 1710*]

Thursday 20th

I receiv'd 2 letters from you this Afternoon. The first
I open'd was dated Satterday noon, and pleas'd me so well
I wish I had not open'd the second, writ from Hartford-
bridge,[1] which seems out of Humour with me. How can you
be so? Perhaps I am to blame, but is there nothing to be
forgiven to a Woman's fears? I own I am a coward; I
tremble at every thing. Forgive me; if I injure your fortune
any way, I do not deserve you should. You speak of losing
£20,000. Lose nothing for me. I set you free from any
engagement you may think your selfe under. Tis too generous that you take me with nothing; I can never deserve even
that Sacrifice. You shall not however have to reproach your
selfe or me that I have lessen'd your fortune. You do not
know how much I think my selfe oblig'd for what you have
allready done. I would make you any return in my power.
I beg you sincerely if you find that the disobliging your
F[ather] will be of consequence to you, and that it is unavoidable if you do it, leave me.[2] I shall blame nothing but
my own fears, that to silly nicetys sacrifice'd all my happynesse. Perhaps that understanding you complement me with,
should we come to be better acquainted, you would find
your selfe deceiv'd in, and the silly woman appear in manny
instances. But I am honest; I would do right. I am naturally
generous, tho' I have no Opertunitys of shewing it, and I
could never forgive my selfe (of all Mankind) an injury to
you.

I can not answer that part of your Letter which regar⟨ds⟩
Mr. —. There is no judging what fools are capable of, ⟨and⟩
in what manner he will behave himselfe upon any Occasion.
As to my F[ather], tis just the same thing how I do it; he

---

[1] Hartford Bridge, a hamlet near
Basingstoke in Hampshire, and about
half way between London and Dean.

[2] 'The marriages between landed
families in the eighteenth century . . .
involved hard bargaining in which the
size of the bride's fortune was carefully
matched against the income which the
bridegroom's father was prepared to
settle on him' (H. J. Habakkuk in
Studies in Social History, ed. J. H.
Plumb, 1955, p. 158).

will never see me more, and he will give me nothing, let me
do it in what way I will. Your next Letter shall guide me.
I once more entreat you to do nothing but entirely with
your own consent. Put me out of the case, and think what
is best of your selfe. After that point is settle'd, consider me
a little. Think if you can allwaies speak after the manner you
do in your Satterday's Letter. Were you allways to be so kind
to me, I should allways think my selfe happy. Should you
ever be uneasy with me, should you ever give me reason to
think you repented, there would be nothing more unhappy
than me.

Text W MS i. 290–1   *End. by* *W* M. P. 20 Oct. [*sic*] from Dean.

From Wortley [*28 July 1710*]

Had I a month or ⟨six weeks⟩ longer to consider, we shoud be
much more likely to come together. Shoud we be of a mind now, we
may both alter before I come back. I must go in the first place to the
Spaw.[1] Those waters (I know by having tried) are the quickest method
of recovering an Appetite. The want of one is my present indisposition, tho I must pretend some greater to excuse my going away. The
sooner you tell me your mind, the more you will oblige me. For if
you let me go on Friday,[2] I shall have a friend for my Companion,
otherwise I shall go without any. I will write at least once a day while
I stay and hope you will write as often unless you can at once say that
which will fix me. If I engage at all at present it must either be upon
a bargain I am to know just now or to have you without any. But to
pretend I may comply with what your family shall demand is what I
cannot come up to. I judge by your way of writing that your match is
to go on unless I break it. If I ghess right, I am unhappy in having so
little time for so weighty an affair, but it is not my fault. I beg you will
alter nothing upon what I write now but let your treaty go on or
continue as it is till I say more. If nothing hinders my return to
England before the winter or in the winter, I shall be fully dispos'd
to close with you if the terms can be agreed between us and I have no

---

[1] Spa, the health resort in Belgium.
[2] On 29 July Steele wrote to his wife
that he was staying in town that night
'having businesse of Consequence with
Mr. Montague who goes out of Town
tomorrow in order to take a Voyage'
(Steele, *Corr.*, ed. R. Blanchard, 1941,
p. 262–3).

fresh ground of Complaint. But I dont know whether I can say any thing to be depended on before I go.[1] I will not excuse the plain dealing of this letter. I am mistaken if you dont find a good deal of passion, thô I avoided to mention it.

Tuesday afternoon. I propos'd to write early in the morning, but I slept ill, rose late, and found those that carri'd me out as soon as I was out of bed.

Text W MS i. 28–29   *Address* To the Rt Honble the Lady Mary Pierrepont. Care and Speed. *End. by* [*?*] received ⟨*?*⟩ight

To Mrs. Frances Hewet [*c. 2 Aug. 1710*]

Most of the Neighbours hereabouts have been to see me, But they are very few, and few of them few that are supportable, none agreable. This part of the world is so different from Nottinghamshire, I can hardly perswade my selfe tis the same Kingdom. The Men here are all Silvios, no Mirtillos; if they could express themselves so well, they would all say like him:

> Mille nimphe darai per una fera,
> Che de Melampo mio cacciata fosse;
> Godasi queste gjoie
> Chi n'ha di me più gusto, io non le sento.[2]

Tho they can't say it in Italian verse they often speak to that purpose in English prose over a Bottle, insensible of other pleasures than Hunting and drinking, the consequence of which is the poor female part of their family being seldom permitted a Coach, or, at best, but a couple of starv'd Jades to drag a dirty Chariot, their Lords and masters having no

---

[1] W's draft (W MS i. 92–93), dated 28 July, ends here.

[2] In Guarini's *Il Pastor Fido* (1590), Mirtillo is the passionate lover, Silvio the passionate hunter, and Melampo one of the latter's dogs. The passage quoted by LM, from Act I, Scene i, is translated thus by Richard Fanshawe (1648, p. 10):

> . . . I take more joy
> In one beast caught by my Melampo far,
> Than in the love of all the Nymphs that are.
> Keep they these joyes unto themselves alone
> That find a soul in them; for I find none.

Occasion for such a Machine, the morning spent among Hounds and the nights with as Beastly compannions, with what liquor they can get in this country, which is not very famous for good drink. If this Mannagement of theirs did not hinder me the companny of my she Neighbour I should not regret the Absence of Pastor Fidos, being of the opinion of Silvia in Tasso:

> Altri segua i diletti de l'amore
> Se pur v'è ne l'amor alcun diletto.[1]

I would fain perswade you to practise your Italian; I fear I shall forget to speak it for want of somebody to speak it to. Amongst the rest of the advantages I should have in your Conversation (if I was so happy to be with you) I would endeavor to improve in that polite language.

I find you are very busy about politicks; we are the same here, perticularly in the pulpits where the parsons would fain become as famous as Sacheverel and are very sorry they shant have the Honnour of being tryd too.[2] For my part I content my selfe in my humble sphere, am passive in all disputes, and endeavor to study my Italian in peace and quietnesse. But people mistake very much in placing peace in woods and Shades; I beleive solitude puts folks out of Humour and makes em disposd to quarrel, or there would not be so manny violent disputes about Religion and Liberty by Creatures that never understood the first, nor have, or are like ever to have, a tast of the Latter. Damnd to the stint of thirty pound a year.[3]

Text MS now owned by the Editor   *Address* To Mrs Hewet at Chireoaks near Worksop Nottinghamshire By way of London. *Postmark* AV 4

[1] From Tasso's *Aminta* (1573), I. i. 9–10; as translated by John Dancer (1660, p. 6):
Let others follow love's delight for me,
If that in love any delight there be.
[2] Henry Sacheverell (1674?–1724), the High Church Tory preacher, had been tried for his seditious sermons in Feb. 1710; and although found technically guilty (in March) and forbidden to preach for three years he enjoyed a comfortable martyrdom and fame.
[3] As noted by John Chamberlayne (*Magnae Britanniae Notitia*, 1710, p. 160): 'Such has been the unhappy Condition of the *English* Clergy . . . till it pleas'd the Queen who now reigns . . . to take the same into Her Princely Consideration; and having in the first place remitted all the Arrears of Tenths due from small Livings not exceeding 30 l. *per Annum*. . . .'

From Wortley [*10 Aug. 1710*]

Harwich, Aug.

Tho the treaty I fear is quite broke off, I am no longer able to forbear acquainting you that I cant lay the blame of its miscarriage on my
selfe. The offers I made were very advantageous according to the
common way of reckoning, such as I am sure any man without knowing the Persons and taking 'em to be equal as they ought to be suppos'd, will not believe to have bin rejected. I dont at all wonder it
shoud be thought no rules ought to [be] observ'd in your case. I know
too high a rate cant be set upon you. All I am worth woud be as far
short of your merit as what I offerd.[1] But if nothing like a proportion
between the money and the land is to be observ'd, what woud be the
Consequence? I must give away all I have and be undone without the
pleasure of paying you your due, and I certainly woud give all were
I to be insur'd you woud be bound to live with me, and yet be easy.
Some are vain enough to think they are every way equal to you. With
them it is that you shoud be treated for and I know very well what
you please will be granted you. But I that know how great the danger
is of seeing all your charms lost to me by your being out of humour,
cannot so readily agree to make my selfe uncapable of any satisfaction
in case I shoud have none from you.

What makes me excuse my selfe the more is that we differd chiefly
about taking from me what was not to be given to you. Had the demand
bin for yourselfe, perhaps I coud not have withstood it. It was for a
larger settlement on an heir.[2] Now, I dont know any man that woud
give £500 out of his pocket that his heir yet unborn and that is sure
to have enough whatever he proves to be, may have £1,000 a year
added to his fortune after the father's death, and yet whoever settles
£1,000 a year of his own after his death, parts with at least £10,000.
Is it not strange that a man without being in love shoud part with as
much of his estate as is really worth £10,000 for what no one that
thinks woud value at £500, and for what the Lady values yet less?
I dont name the sum we talk'd of in a letter, but the same way of

[1] In July 1710, when Steele dedicated the second volume of the collected
Tatlers to W, his preface paid tribute
to their friendship, and added his
wishes for W's future happiness, hoping
'that you may ever think, as I know
you now do, that you have a much
larger Fortune than you want'.

[2] W had drawn up elaborate notes
and calculations on entail and marriage

settlements (W MS vii. 130–4, 258–65),
and these served Steele for *Tatler* papers
on 18 July and 12 Sept. 1710 condemn-
ing mercenary marriages. Steele used W's
ideas in both papers, with passages verbatim in the second (Richmond P. Bond,
'Mr. Bickerstaff and Mr. Wortley'
in *Classical Mediaeval and Renaissance
Studies in Honor of B. L. Ullman*, ed.
C. Henderson, jr., 1964, ii. 491–504).

reasoning will hold in any sum. This Demand of so much from me and so little, I think nothing, for you troubled me the more because it might be altogether at your own desire. You may imagine I have bin desirous to know whether it was or not and whether it will be insisted upon.

But after I had so long obey'd your command of not writing, which was very severe for a time, I resolv'd to stay till I was got thus far of my journey, least an answer shoud have in it any forbidding or favourable expressions. Such as pleas'd might have oblig'd me to give up my selfe and all I have without any further reflection; the other might have bin insupportable. I shall now have your answer (if you send one) at such a distance that even your kindness cou'd not destroy me on a sudden, and for your Anger, that may be spent or your Aversion cease before I see you again. Now that I shall reason better than I coud do if I were near you, it will be generous in you to tell me, not wittily as you have always done, but plainly, your mind. This I make no doubt will either hasten or delay my return, for at this instant I admire you as much as ever.

If all things besides a settlement were adjusted I coud consent to refer that to any impartial body, but I fear we differ in Points of greater moment.

Some men have parted with their fortunes to gain women, others have di'd with despair for the loss of 'em, but such Passions have always bin raisd by a strong belief of a return. The least proofe of your being partial to me woud, I am sure, have put me wholly in your power, for I only hope I am not. I woud give a great deal to be satisfi'd I am not, tho the greatest mark of distinction you have shewn me is your allowing a treaty, which amounts to no more than this, that you may think my faults as supportable as those of other pretenders that have the same fortune, which cannot be very numerous. But admitting this to be a proofe of Esteem or even Friendship, no man ever undid himselfe to gain or to continue a Friendship or di'd for the loss of it.

Shoud you write to me it woud not be a greater Compliment. Every woman wou'd write instead of dressing for any lover she had not resolv'd to strike out of her list, that coud persuade herselfe she did it halfe so well as you. I know that when you write you shine out in all your beauty.

It is well for you the Packet boat wont wait for me else I don't [know] when I shoud have given over. I can only add that letters are left for me at Mr. Goodwin's, the Bookseller, or Mr. Steele's. My going abroad is known to few.

Ha⟨rwich⟩

Text W MS i. 19–21   *Address* To Lady Mary   *End. by W* From Harwich. 10. Aug.

To Wortley [*20 Aug. 1710*]

I never thought to hear from you more.—Tis impossible to tell you my Surprize.—What would you have me say? There is a great deal of generosity and good nature in your Letter, but I know not how to answer it.—

I will shew you a Confidence that will convince you I am at least very sincere in my Freindship. I am told my Brother is going to marry a great Fortune.[1] Ten thousand pounds is to be settled on me, without its being possible to be recalld by any one.[2] A single woman may live very well on that money. The dispute I have at present with my selfe is whither I will or will not marry at all. Now in my opinion you are very much obligd to me that it is a dispute. I should not hesitate upon manny proposalls. Was I sure that you would live after a way agreable to me, I should not be long in makeing my Answer. But if instead of travelling, the fancy should take you to confine me to the Country, I could bear Solitude, but perhaps not when it was for Life, and I had much rather be my own mistrisse as long as I live. If you realy intend to travel, as it is the thing upon Earth I should most wish, I should prefer that manner of living to any other; and with the utmost Sincerity I confess I should chuse you before any Match could be offerd me.

I think I have said a thing so favourable I ought to be asham'd of it. If you expect Passion I am utterly unacquainted with any. It may be a fault of my temper. Tis a stupidity I could never justifye, but I do not know I was in my Life ever touch'd with any. I have no Notion of a

---

[1] On 12 May 1711 LM's only brother, William Pierrepont (1692–1713), Earl of Kingston, m. Rachel Baynton (1695–1722), natural da. of John Hall of Bradford, Wilts., whose vast estates she inherited (HMC *MSS of House of Lords, 1712–14,* ed. M. F. Bond, New Series, vol. x, 1953, pp. 66–67; Jos. Foster, *Collectanea Genealogica,* 1883, i. 17–19).

[2] On 25 Jan. 1711 LM's father introduced in the House of Lords the Marquess of Dorchester Estate Act, which provided that he raise £8,000 for his daughters (HMC *MSS of House of Lords, 1710–12,* ed. M. F. Bond, New Series, vol. ix, 1949, p. 95). Probably LM and Lady Frances were to share this since their sister Lady Evelyn had been left £12,000 by their grandmother Elizabeth Pierrepont.

Transport of Anger, Love, or any other. I here tell you the plain state of my Heart, and more than I shall ever think it worth my while to tell another. I beleive if I could disemble I should please you better, but you must have some Esteem for a Woman that will not disemble tho' to please.

I think I have said enough, and as much as ought to be expected. Flights of Passion I neither know how to feel or to counterfeit. I have no hand in the makeing of Settlements. My present Duty is to obey my Father. I shall so far obey blindly as not to accept where he refuses, tho' perhaps I might refuse where he would accept. If you think tolerably of me, you think I would not marry where I hated. As for the rest, my Father may do some things disagreable to my Inclinations, but passive Obedience is a doctrine should allwaies be receivd among wives and daughters. That principle makes me cautious who I set for my Master. I ought, and I hope I should, obey a severe one, but severity is never so terrible as where it meets with a temper not made to resist. I have a Softnesse that would make me perfectly wretched.

My Letter is allready very long. Adeiu, Sir. If you think me worth your takeing, it can be on no other terms than those of my Father. If not, I wish you all the happynesse immaginable, and that your future Wife (whoever she is to be) may not be one of those Ladies so very free of their Expressions of tendernesse, at best withering, generally false. You would like her manner better than you do mine, till Time convinc'd you of your Mistake, but I rather chuse to wish you a Happynesse more lasting.

You did very ri⟨ght⟩ in directing to that Maid. Any other way it would have miscarry'd. It is not from Severity I beg you to write no more. I should think your Correspondance a pleasure if it was Among the number of the permitted. But you know it is forbidden, and I am in pain when I do any thing that must be a Secret.

You conclude yours with something about power. I know none that I have, or if that was possible would I use it to your prejudice.

Text W MS i. 190–2   *Address* To Mr Edward Wortley Mountague

To Wortley [*c. 22 Aug. 1710*]

Reading over your Letter as fast as ever I could, and answering it with the same ridiculous precipitation, I find, one part of it escapd my sight, and the other I mistook in several places. Yours was dated the 10th of Aug.; it came not hither till the 20th. You say something of a pacquet boat etc. makes me uncertain whither you'l receive my Letter and fretts me heartily.

Kindnesse, you say, would be your destruction. In my opinion this is something contradictory to some other Expressions. People talk of Being in Love just as widows do of Affliction. Mr. Steele has observd in one of his Plays, the most passionate amongst them has allwaies calmnesse enough to drive a hard Bargain with the Upholders.[1] I never knew a Lover that would not willingly secure his Interest as well as his mistresse, or if one must be abandonnd had not the prudence (amongst all his distractions) to consider, A woman was but a Woman, and money was a thing of more real merit than the whole sex put together. Your Letter is to tell me you should think your selfe undone if you marryd me, but if I would be so tender to confesse I should break my heart if you did not, then you'd consider whether you would or no, but yet you hop'd you should not. I take this to be the right Interpretation of: Even your kindnesse cant destroy me of a sudden, I hope I am not in your power, I would give a good deal to be satisfy'd etc.

As to writeing, that any woman would do that, [that] thought she writ well, now I say, no woman of common good sense would. At best, tis but doing a silly thing well, and I think tis much better not to do a silly thing at all. You compare it to dressing. Suppose the comparison Just, perhaps the Spanish dresse would become my face very well, yet the whole Town would condemn me for the highest Extravagance if I went to Court in't, tho' it improv'd me to

[1] Mr. Sable, an undertaker, says: '. . . I never yet could meet with a sorrowful Relict, but was herself enough to make a hard Bargain with me' (*The Funeral: or, Grief A-la-mode*, 1701, Act I; ed. 1758, p. 15).

a Miracle. There are a thousand things not ill in themselves which custom makes unfit to be done.

This is to convince you I am so far from Aplauding my own conduct, my conscience flys in my face every time I think on't. The generallity of the world have a great Indulgence to their own Follies. Without being a jot wiser than my Neighbours I have the peculiar misfortune to know and condemn all the wrong things I do.

You beg to know whether I would not be out of humour. The expression is modest enough, but that is not what you mean in saying I could be easy. I have allready said I should not be out of humour. But you would have me say I am violently in Love. That is, finding you think better of me than you desire, you would have me give you a just cause to contemn me. I doubt much whither there is a creature in the world humble enough to do that. I should not think you more unreasonable if you was in love with my Face and ask'd me to disfigure it to make you easy. I have heard of some Nuns that made use of that Expedient to secure their own happynesse, but amongst all the popish Saints and Martyrs I never read of one whose charity was sublime enough to make themselves deformd or ridiculous to restore their Lovers to peace and quietnesse. In short, If nothing can content you but dispiseing me heartily, I am Afraid I shall be allwaies so barbarous to wish you may esteem me as long [as] you live.

Text W MS i. 274–5   *Address* To Mr Edward Wortley Mountague   *End. by W* Ans. to that of 10 Aug.

To Wortley [*Sept. 1710*]

I cannot imagine the reason of your silence, and I am perpetually thinking of it without being able to guesse from whence it should probably proceed. You must think I'm uneasy concerning the Successe of my letters, and I cannot perswade my selfe you are ill naturd enough to delight in it. You orderd me to direct to Mr. Goodwin. He must know where to send them. Who should stop them? I use all imaginable care they should go safe from hence and I am sure they do. Am I to say you use me ill, or to be sorry for your illnesse, or have you forgot me so entirely you no longer remember there is such a creature in the World?—

I am torn with variety of Imaginations, and not one pleaseing one. I conjure you to write; I beg it of you, and promise to teize you no longer upon the least intimation of being troublesome. Tis impossible to expresse the pain I write in, when I neither know whether you'l receive my letter nor into whose hands it may fall.

I have not heard from you since yours of the 10th of Aug., and have writ several times.

Text W MS i. 232–3   *Address* Pray send this wth care to Mr Edward Wortley Mountague wherever he is. *End. by W* 2nd Ans. to that of 10 Aug.

To Wortley [*4 Oct. 1710*]

Yours of the 10th of August I receivd the 20th and answerd it immediately. There was some things in mine requir'd a speedy answer. I have waited for it with the utmost impatience. Tis now the 4th of Oct. After writeing several times I hear nothing from you. My unquietnesse forces me upon directing to Mr. St[eele]. I fear the other direction is false.

This letter may never go to you or may be opend by 50 people.

Text W MS i. 230–1   *Address* To Edward Wortley Mountague [*struck out*] To Mr Edward Wortly Mountague [*in another hand*] *End. by W* 4 Oct. 3d Ans. to that of 10 Aug.

From Wortley *24 Oct.* [*1710*]

I was no sooner got into Holland, but I resolv'd to have a Truce (if it were possible) with business, Politicks and Love, and therefore

desir'd Mr. St[eele], who took care of all my letters, to keep 'em till
I sent for 'em.[1] Four of yours I found in his hands; two that he takes
to have bin of the same hand or paper (by what mistake I cant ghess)
he sent beyond sea and I must wait for 'em. It is misfortune that I
want em for they might have explaind or confirmd some one of these.
No two of 'em seem to have bin writ while you was of the same mind.
In some or one of 'em you say a great deal more, in others I think
somewhat less, than I deserve. I am at a loss to know why you are at
so much pains to assure me I must never expect any thing of Passion
from you, for you are incapable of it. I dont believe I ever said it was
due to me, and I am sorry to hear from you the Constant saying of a
woman that woud marry, or is marri'd to one man and has a passion
for another. A man always uses this discourse after he has marri'd
one he does not care for; a woman often says so beforehand that a
disappointment may not make a breach. Your assurances of this calmness of temper are the more remarkable because they are not very
credible. I know very well your Wit and Beauty must give you many
admirers and you'll say how can you be troubled for the loss of any
one. You know it to be true that the most admir'd have generally had
their share of Concern.

But you dont stop at these protestations you give me of your indifference. You tell me after, I must never expect to please another, and
hope I shall not have one of those that are free of their kind expressions. I readily grant you I am without all those qualities that give
you so much power and yet I deny that I ought to be excluded from
pretending to the favour of some. The opportunities that are gaind by
Money or Artifice or Chance many times set a man above those that
have all the charms that Nature can bestow, and this you cant but have
observ'd. If you know me to be uncapable of having success anywhere,
I desire to hear no proofs but woud willingly enjoy the pleasure of
thinking it is in the power of Fortune to favour me. I hope we shall
meddle no more with this subject.

Your declaring against the Country (another Refuge of some
women) was for ought I know meant to break off quite. You know
I dont care for the town and can not oblige myselfe to be there for a
time. Nor is my estate sufficient for two families. It is full enough for
my selfe, but I fear you woud think it too straight if we liv'd together,
much more if we liv'd asunder. It is less than you take it to be, for
I resolve never to spend so much as I receive.

You shew me pretty plainly you have strong reasons against taking
me, tho you may have some reasons for it. I can assure you, it is the

[1] W had returned to London by 19   Irish wine' (*Journal to Stella*, ed. H.
Oct., when he spent the evening with   Williams, 1948, p. 65).
Swift and Addison 'over a bottle of

most rash thing you can do to meddle with me unless you are pretty secure we shall live as well together as it is possible. I am one of those that coud not bear to live with you unless I were treated as well as ever any man was. I shoud choose to let our disagreeing be made publick rather than feel the burthen of it at home. The difficulties that are certainly of your own raising seem great; those made (as you are pleas'd to say) by others, I am not yet able to get over. If I can judge right, the time for disposing of yourselfe is not yet come. You will have offers which you will be glad to accept of; you throw yourselfe away unless you wait till they are made. Your Comparison of the Widows' making a hard bargain with the Upholder I hope I dont deserve, I am sure not of you. You are as much mistaken in saying a woman does not write on such occasions. I have heard from good hands that many have writ and have writ to declare that Passion which you are not the least acquainted with. I yield to you so far as to own it has not yet happend to myselfe. I dare say I never hinted to you I desird any such thing, but you suppose I do, only for an occasion of assuring me you dont value me overmuch. Your Comparison of the Spanish dress is not, I think, well appli'd. I agree a woman woud not go to Court in one, but woud certainly find out the means to be seen in it by the man she woud marry if she thought that woud secure him. You are out too in your Spanish story, for a young man did mangle his face that it might not charm any more.

I think I have given full answers to all I saw in 4 letters. I only think I have, for I was more out of humour on reading em than I have bin this two or 3 months, and dont care to open 'em again. Because I cannot see any thing of yours with Indifference, I don't oppose your proposition of Corresponding no more. So that I agree with you in one thing, tho indeed for a contrary reason.

[Passage omitted]

London, 24 Oct'ber

Since I writ what is in the other sheet I have had your letter. I am infinitely oblig'd to you for it and will ever be grateful for all your Favours. I am sorry I writ it all and yet how can I avoid sending it? How wretched am I! It is now not possible to have any reliefe but from Absence and Time. Tell me only what I shall say to your Father; by that I shall know you have had my letter.

In few days I go out of town for a month. Lest I shoud be gone before you write, direct to me at Mr. Goodwin's over against St. Dunstan's Church.

Another time be sure to chuse one far superiour to me or you will not be able long to undergo the Drudgery of pleasing him and will repent you ever thought of him.

You speak of Gaiety and a desire to please many; dont mistake. A woman is never pursu'd long, unless for her money, till she has given Possession or very strong hopes. Why will you be thought to have gone so far with several? One with a very small share of your Beauty or wit can draw as many and as deserving, even as yours are, after her whenever she pleases; nay, take most of your own from you if she will seem more fond of 'em and is a new woman.

Tuesday night.

Text W MS i. 34–36   *Address* To Lady Mary Pierpoint.   *End.* *by W* To direct to me at Mr Goodwins.

To Wortley [?*c. 26 Oct. 1710*][1]

I resolvd not to answer your Letter when I first read it, since I beleiv'd that the most agreable way of answering it.—After I had made this resolution it came into my Head that according to your way of interpreting things you would fancy I was so transported with going to London I could think of nothing else. Rather than you should have the least appearance of reason for such a thought, I write in an Inn after the most fateiguing day's journey that ever I passd in my Life. The sense of your Letter I take to be this: Madam, you are the greatest Coquet I ever knew, and withall very silly. The only happynesse you propose to your selfe with a Husband is in Jilting him most abundantly. You must stay till my Lord Hide is a widower,[2] or Heaven raises up another Mr. Popham.[3] For my part, I know all your tricks. I beleive you are in love with me, but dont flatter your selfe—think

---

[1] This is a particularly difficult letter to date, its topics being the ones that the lovers continually discussed. If the date is correct, LM is returning to London from West Dean, in the autumn of 1710.

[2] Henry Hyde (1672–1753), later 2nd Earl of Rochester and 4th Earl of Clarendon, m. (1692) Jane Leveson-Gower (1670–1725), a famous beauty. One of her reputed lovers was Matthew Prior, the poet and diplomatist (V. Biddulph, *Kitty, Duchess of Queensberry*,

1935, p. 10). For LM's repeated comments on Lady Hyde's infidelities, see [*c.* 20 March 1725] and 1 March [1754]

[3] In 1688 the wife of Alexander Popham of Burton, Glos., confessed on her deathbed that her last four children had been fathered by a neighbour; and they were illegitimated the next year (HMC *12th Report, Part VI: MSS of the House of Lords, 1689–90,* 1889, pp. 133–4).

not of me, for I shall never change my opinion of you.—
This is the exact miniature of your Letter.

Now to shew your mistake, tho' plain dealing has been
very unfortunate to me, I will persist in it, and tell you the
sort of Life I should chuse to lead. The softnesse of my
temper gives me a mortal aversion to crouds and disputes,
place and attendance, and could one chuse the place of one's
birth, I would be a farmer's daughter. Them admirers you
speak of—wretches that are won by being well dress'd and
lost by a patch misplac'd, I have ever contemnd so much,
I have often given God thanks there was nothing in me to
attract 'em. This is cutting off at once all the Town pleasures;
'tis therefore no wonder 'tis indifferent to me. Nay, I had
rather be out on't than in't. My schemes are a little Romantic. Was I to follow entirely my own Inclinations it would be
to travel, my first and cheifest wish. If I had a Compannion, it
should be one (now am I going to make you a picture after
my own heart) that I very much lovd, and that very much
lovd me, one that thought that the truest wisdom which
most conduced to our happynesse, and that it was not below
a man of sense to take satisfaction in the conversation of a
reasonable woman, one who did not think tendernesse a
disgrace to his understanding, who beleivd so well of me as
to fear I should not be easy in his absence (if that must ever
happen) rather than that I should make an ill of [*sic*] use of
it, one who would be as willing to be happy as I would be to
make him so. In short, quite the reverse of a race of people
who are obstinate in being wretched, nor is it in the power of
Fortune to make them otherwise. They never have a freind
that they do not suspect has a design to cheat 'em, or a mistresse that they do not beleive Jilts 'em. This humour deprives
them of all that is agreable in the trust of Freindship and
the most charming part of Love.

After this description of who I could like, I need not add
it is not you; you, who can suspect where you have the least
reason, that think so wrong of me as to beleive me every
thing I abhor. You need not say there is but a small chance
for my being easy with you. I see there is a certainty of my
being uneasy, not from my deprivation of pleasures that are
none to me, but from the living with one I could not please.

I wonder I was ever so mad to fancy I could. I desire you
to think no more of me. I had rather passe all my Life as I do,
than with one who thinks entirely ill of me and is resolvd
never to think otherwise. I am heartily glad I can have no
answer to this Letter, tho' if I could I should (now) have the
courrage to return it unopen'd.

You are unjust and I am unhappy—tis past—I will never
think of you more, never.

Text W MS i. 294–5   *Address* To Mr Edward Wortley Mountague   *End. by W* P. from the Country

To Wortley [*31 Oct. 1710*]

I am not surprizd that you find my Letters contradictory
one to Another, for I am not in the same mind 3 minutes
together. You have been prodigiously ill naturd in desiring
me to write and not takeing some way to have the Letter
as soon as possible. You have causd me so much trouble,
from uncertainty and difference of Imaginations, that I ought
not to suppose you have any regard for my quiet. I despair
of ever pleasing either you or my selfe. At this present I
can't tell whether I am glad or sorry or distracted.—

I am now gone about half way in your Letter and am
answering it allready.—I cannot go on. I foresee I shall meet
with something violently disobliging and can't answer for my
calmnesse of temper. I see very plain what you think of me.
—You think me every thing I am not.—What do you not
say, for tis impossible to speak plainer than you do!—I
beleive I am the most unfortunate thing living. I think you
so much in the right as to think I am intirely in the wrong.
I do heartily repent and am exceedingly sorry for these my
misdoings.[1] ⟨I⟩ can see no way of remedying it but forgett (as
I told you before) that all these things have been. How soon
I shall do that I can't tell, but I'm sure as soon as I can.

I beg you not to send me such another Letter. Tis full

---

[1] This sentence is adapted from the Communion Confession of the Anglican
Book of Common Prayer.

enough ⟨?⟩ conscience. I understand every word of it, and
am perfectly sensible that in writeing this, I prove my selfe
a most extreamly contemptible and ridiculous creature, but
there is no ⟨abso⟩lute necessity for your telling me so.

You desire me to write no ⟨more.⟩ I write.—I am certainly
very humble.—I have finishd your Letter. Why did you
send it? It would have been much better not to have writ,
and let me remain in uncertainty of the reason of your silence.
The pritty figure I make to Mr. St[eele]!

I suppose this is nonsense. You are mightily in the wrong
if you wonder at it.

Text W MS i. 188–9   *Address* To Mr Edward Wortley Mountague
[*in another hand*] Memb: of Parliamt at Wortley near Sheffeild Yorkshire Free¹ *Postmark* oc 31 mc *End. by W* From M. P. Oct. 31
Answ. to 24 Oct.

From Wortley 4 Nov. [1710]

[Passage omitted]

You dont say whether, if the treaty were to be renew'd, it must be
on the same foot with the former. I own I heartily wish that person
(whom I honour very much) woud think I deserv'd what you mention'd. Not that I shou'd take my selfe to be richer for such an addition
(unless for your figure) but I shoud be much more encourag'd to hope
for your Esteem. I beg you will this once try to avoid being witty
and write in a style of business, tho it shoud appear to you as flat as
mine. Dont fancy it is below you to be as open and plain with me on
such an occasion as you woud with an intimate friend. Let me know
what I might expect to hear on a second offer of my selfe. When such
treaties end in nothing they are commonly a disadvantage to both,
always to one.

I need not say I answerd your letter by the first post. Business
obligd me to be in the Country and I must stay a fortnight more, at
least ten days.

4 Nov'ber

Text W MS i. 33 (draft)   *End. by W* 4 Nov. Answ. to 31 Oct.

¹ As an M.P. (Huntingdon Borough), W was allowed by the post office to send
and receive letters without charge.

To Wortley [*14 Nov. 1710*]

I am going to comply with your request and write with all the plainesse I am capable of. I know what may be said upon such a proceeding, but sure you will not say it. Why should you allwaies put the worst construction upon my words? Beleive me what you will, but do not beleive I can be ungenerous or ungratefull. I wish I could tell you what answer you will receive from some people, or upon what terms. If my opinion could sway, nothing should displease you. No body ever was so disinterested as I am. I would not have to reproach my selfe (I don't suppose you would) that I had any way made you uneasy in your Circumstances. Let me beg you (which I do with the utmost Sincerity) only to consider your selfe in this Affair; and since I am so unfortunate to have nothing in my own disposal, do not think I have any hand in makeing Settlements. People in my way are sold like slaves, and I cannot tell what price my Master will put on me. If you do agree, I shall endeavor to contribute as much as lies ⟨in⟩ my power to your happynesse. I so heartily dispise a great Figure, I have no Notion of spending money so foolishly tho' one had a great deal to throw away. If this breaks off, I shall not complain of you; and as whatever happens I shall still preserve the opinion you have behavd your selfe well, let me entreat you, if I have committed any follys to forgive em, and be so Just to think I would not do an ill thing.

I say nothing of my Letters. I think them intirely safe in your hands.

I shall be uneasy till I know this is come to you. I have tryd to write plainly. I know not what one can say more upon Paper.

Text W MS i. 266–7   *Address* To Mr Edward Wortley Mountague [*in another hand*] Memb: of Parlt at Wortley near Sheffeild Yorkshire *Postmark* NO 14 MC *End. by* W Answ. to 2 of 4 Nov. M. P. 14 Novber.

From Wortley [*c. 17 Nov. 1710*]

I am far from being resolv'd to break off but I own I am not yet determin'd to close the bargain, nor do I know what woud close it. I think it coud not suddenly be done were both of us and all concern'd for us agreed. I was told before I went abroad your money was to be raisd by the Marriage of your brother; that may, for ought I know, be near, but I have not heard it is over. My affairs will, I believe, oblige me to engage my estate for a considerable sum. It may, indeed, be clear again in two months and I be the richer for doing this. But I did not know it woud be so when I treated, nor did I mention it. So that it seems as if neither side were ready to finish. Matters of this sort shoud not be long in Agitation, and till there is a prospect of ending speedily, it is better to be quiet, most certainly not to engage. If you think it will be well taken in me to enquire of the person I spoke with how the affairs of your family now are, I will go to him. Perhaps I may before I have your answer. My own opinion at present is to do so, tho I am sure no offer whatever has bin rejected or kept back on my account, for I never appeard satisfy'd with the demands that were made, and only said as every civil body shou'd do in such a case, that when I came to town I woud desire again to know what was expected.

Coud I see into your heart and find in it a partiality to me, I might break thrô all difficulties and run the hazard of losing it soon, which you must own woud be no small hazard. You cant wonder if so long an Absence, variety of other Acquaintance, and your Unkindness shoud make me less forward than I have bin. But I yet think it not unlikely for us to agree and that in less than two months. If it is not before the Spring, I take it for certain it will never be.

Text W MS i. 46–47   *Address* To Lady Mary   *End. by W* After travelling and seeing into her heart.

To Wortley [*c. 19 Nov. 1710*]

Indeed I do not at all wonder that absence and variety of new faces should make you forget me, but I am a little surpriz'd at your curiosity to know what passes in my Heart (a thing wholly insignificant to you) except you propose to your selfe a peice of ill naturd satisfaction in finding me very much disquieted. Pray, which way would you see into my Heart? You can frame no guesses about it from either my speaking or writeing, and supposeing I should attempt to shew it you, I know no other way.

I begin to be tird of my Humillity. I have carryd my Complaisances to you farther than I ought. You make new scruples, you have a great deal of Fancy, and your distrusts being all of your own makeing are more immovable than if there was some real ground for them. Our Aunts and Grandmothers allwaies tell us Men are a sort of Animals, that if ever they are constant 'tis only where they are ill us'd. Twas a kind of Paradox I could never beleive. Experience has taught me the truth of it. You are the first I ever had a Correspondance with, and I thank God I have done with it for all my Life. You needed not to have told me you are not what you have bin.—One must be stupid not to find a difference in your letters. You seem in one part of your last to excuse your selfe from having done me any injury in point of Fortune.—Do I accuse you of any?

I have not spirits to dispute any longer with you. You say you are not yet determin'd. Let me determine for you and save you the trouble of writeing again. Adeiu for ever. Make no answer. I wish amongst the variety of Acquaintance you may find some one to please you, and can't help the vanity of thinking, should you try them all, you won't find one that will be so sincere in their treatment, tho' a thousand more deserving, and every one happier. Tis a peice of vanity and injustice I never forgive in a Woman to delight to give pain. What must I think of a Man that takes pleasure in makeing me uneasy? After the folly of letting you know it is in your power, I ought in prudence to let this go no farther, except I thought you had good nature enough never to make use of that power. I have no reason to think so. However, I am willing, you see, to do you the highest obligation tis possible for me to do; that is, to give you a fair occassion of being rid of me.

Text W MS i. 264–5   *Address* To Mr Edward Wortley Mountague. *End. by* W Ans. to 4. P. Answ. to 4.

From Wortley *21 Nov.* [*1710*]

Tis now very late; I woud not willingly lose my Sleep after the
fatigue of a long journey on horseback, and therefore hope you will
excuse me if I endeavour to lay aside the thoughts of your letter and
to take a little time for answering it. Were I in circumstances that
I was sure woud make you live suitably to your Condition, I shoud
not take one minute to consider what to say. The case I fear is such
that were I a good deal richer I coud hardly think you had your due.
There are some things in yours I coud never acknowlege enough
were I sure you spoke your mind. I will not suppose the contrary
and rather be vain than displease you. But is it not wonderful you are
ignorant what the terms are on which you are to be disposd of? Was
you ever free in any other family where discourses of that kind did
not make up a great part of the Conversation? Those you have to do
with cannot set a low value on themselves and must set a very high
one upon you, and cannot have thought on this subject less than others.
I shoud hope you might find out some way to know what is intended.
I will, if I can, delay giving an answer till I hear from you again, and
desire you will lay no stress upon any thing I say at present.

London
21 Nov.

[Passage omitted]

Text W MS i. 12

To Wortley [*c. 22 Nov. 1710*]

I confesse women very seldom speak truth, but it is not
utterly impossible, and with all sincerity, I assure you, I
know no more of my own Affairs than a perfect stranger,
nor am capable of returning you any other answer than I
have allready done. I do not know that I ever told you a Lie
in my Life. If you will not beleive what I say, I ⟨can⟩'t help
it, nor shall not very much blame you, because I know it's
improbable that a Woman should be sincere. But tis a natural
defect that even Experience can't cure me of, tho' I am convinc'd tis against all prudence to speak what one thinks,
especially where people will not beleive one. If you ask me to

enquire, tis what I never did, nor ever will do, and perhaps would be unavailing if I did. I once more desire you not to act any thing against the most prudent consideration, and assure you I ⟨am⟩ so far from the usual vanity of ⟨my⟩ sex, as not to expect any su⟨ch jus⟩tice upon my account. I suppose this will pass for Affectation, but I know there may be a Woman uninterested and artlesse.

I thank you for considering my uneasynesse in regard of ⟨your⟩ Letters, and desire you to be so good natur'd to let me know as soon as your conveniency will permit, that mine comes safe. Tho' my fears are improbable and foolish, I can not forbear fearing the discovery of what will bear a Refflexion, and what I cannot justifye.

Text W MS i. 248–9   *Address* To Mr Edward Wortley Mountague
End. by W Ans. to that of 21 Nov. From P.

From Wortley [*c. 24 Nov. 1710*]

[*Passage omitted*]

.... I will suppose it possible you may speak the sincerity of your heart in affirming you know nothing of your money matters, and I will say what woud be great folly in me to say but upon that supposition, and this I do with no other view but to serve you. It may do me a great prejudice only to meddle in such an affair and perhaps your success in it may render it impossible for me to succeed.

If £60,000 shoud be added to the estate of your family (as I hear it will)[1] the giving £20,000 or £25,000 out of it for portions is a very trifle. I am sure it is advantageous to those that do it for money they don't want and this is very much for their honour. How can any one suppose less will be done where there is an estate already too big? Can it be thought a great estate suffers if £40,000 be added to it instead of £50,000? The taking from the land so much in present as you two[2] want, tho the greatest part of this fortune shoud not be receiv'd immediatly, can be no less even in the point of money. For what you now cost is certainly more than the interest of 2 very large portions. If your father and brother joyn in this it may easily be done and surely a brother cant take it ill to hear such a thing mention'd, or, if he shou'd,

---

[1] Through the imminent marriage of her brother to a great heiress (see above, p. 53).   [2] LM and her sister Frances.

how easy is it to get a friend to discourse the case with both of 'em and I am convinc'd it woud easily be granted.

[*Passage omitted*]

Text W MS i. 37–38 (draft)

To Wortley [*c. 27 Nov. 1710*]

If I had halfe the vanity of most people, I should think I ought no longer to be sincere with one that tells me he seldom relys on what is said unlesse by such as by long experience he has found uncapable of dissembling, nor even then, if their manner of acting contradicts their words. This is plainly meant to me, and yet might with more justice be meant to any other. I am sensible (in spight of my blindnesse) that what I say makes no impression on your mind, but I will once more talk truth to you, thô I expect you will tell me in return you don't beleive a word on't.

Interest is the last thing I shall think on. You'l think me Mad, but tis indifferent to me whither I have £10,000 or £50,000, and shall never quarrel with my family by pretending to direct in the Matter. However, I give you thanks for the service (you say) you intend me. I am willing to receive your Advice as comeing from a freind, but should eternally ruine my own repose should I offer to follow it. Tis no deceit to tell you I dare not venture the exasperateing those that have the disposal of me, by a Curiosity which I am sure would be unavailing, and which they would think impertinent. Tho' your thoughts of me are far from what pleases me, I think so well of you as to trust my ruine in your hands by telling you I am not entirely satisfyd with the proceedings of my Family, but—tis my Family, and I must endeavor to make my happynesse in my Mind, which if I can't do I am very much to be pityd, for I know no other remedy.

You wrong me (as you often do) in wresting my words about the time of your answering. I generally mean as I write, and meant no otherwise then but that you should not put your selfe to any trouble about me, being very far from thinking a Woman the most important busynesse of a Man's life. In recompence for so much trust and so much sincerity, be generous in your Turn, and since you resolve to break off, do it handsomely. Don't charge me with using you ill. Forget me, if you please, but don't remember me to my disadvantage. I should not have confidence to ask this if I thought you had reason for a different conduct, but I know no injury I have done you. I can accuse my selfe of nothing, nor if I look back can I find any ground of the difficulty you find in beleiving me.

I have more reason than ever to desire to know how this comes to your hands. Write, if it be but 2 lines. You seem in some concern about your Letter. If that be real, my answering so soon is not so impertinent as it used to be.

How ill naturd is yours! and how ridiculous am I in telling you so!

Text W MS i. 292–3   *Address* To Mr Edward Wortley Mountague
End. by W Ans. to 3. P.

To Anne Justice [*c. 3 Feb. 1711*]

I hope, Dear Nanny, you do not think I forget you, but I'll swear this town is such a place, and one is so hurryd about, tis with vast difficulty ⟨ ? ⟩ to get pen, ink, and paper, and perhaps when they are all in readynesse, whip, there comes some impertinent visiter or another and puts all into Confusion again. So that—you must forgive me—that's the short on't.

I am heartily sorry for the misfortunes of Oroonoko, and hope he'l find as much mercy in the Court of Heaven as in the Court Marshall.[1] As to Dresse, tis divided into Partys; all the High Church Ladies affect to wear Heads in the Imitation of Steeples, and on their Muffs roses exactly like those in the ⟨ ? ⟩ Hats. On the other Side, the low Party (of

[1] LM refers either to Aphra Behn's tale, 'Oroonoko: or, The Royal Slave' (1688) or to Thomas Southerne's dramatic adaptation (1696), which was popular on the London stage. It played at Drury Lane on 9 and 19 Dec. 1710 (*London Stage, 1660–1800*, Part 2, ed. E. L. Avery, 1960, p. 238).

which I declare my selfe)[1] wear little low Heads and long ribands to their Muffs. This [is] a full Account of that Important Busynesse, Dresse, which is at present much talk'd off against the Birth night where every body is endeav'ring to outshine the other.[2] The Town is very full and diversion more follow'd than ever I knew it. I am invited to a Ball to Night; I beleive I shall dance with some ⟨of the⟩ same companny I did at Mrs. Ba⟨nks⟩.[3] We talk of Mrs. Banks; pray d⟨id the⟩ Match go on? or is it only a ⟨false⟩ report?[4] The best way to make ⟨sure⟩ an old Lover is certainly to eng⟨age⟩ to a New one. I wish her ex⟨ceeding⟩ well, as I dare say you do ⟨too. I⟩ hope Next Summer we shall ⟨meet⟩ again. I long mightily to See dear Nottinghamshire and dear Nanny who has a most faithfull Freind of me.

Text MS in Pierpont Morgan Library   *Address* To Mrs Anne Justice at Mr Justice's upon the Pavement at York Yorkshire   *Postmark* ⟨?⟩

From Wortley [*9 Feb. 1711*][5]

Friday, 6 a clock.

Your resenting what I said is an Argument of its being pretty near the truth. Your expressing the resentment in such a manner shews how little you value me. I need not tell you that where there is any thing of Friendship, no words are thought a Crime, which are not spoke with design to give offence. You coud not but see I meant to be on better terms with you than ever, and certainly the passing over what I mention'd woud have bin the highest proofe of Esteem.

---

[1] LM was 'Whig to the teeth— Whigissima' (Lady Louisa Stuart [her granddaughter], *Letters to Louisa Clinton*, ed. J. A. Home, 1901, i. 86).

[2] Queen Anne's official birthday was 6 Feb. The nobility and gentry went 'in richer habits than has been known since 1660' (Luttrell, *Hist. Relation*, 1857, vi. 688).

[3] Words in angle brackets are torn from the MS but restored in pencil on the mounting sheet.

[4] At the end of Jan. 1711 Mary Banks, who had rejected an earlier suitor (see above, p. 42), definitely rejected Colonel Talbot's son, assuring her uncle (the negotiator): 'Whatever suspitions you and Mr. T——t might have of his being played against some other, as he hinted to you so often, yet I declare to you I don't believe anything of that nature was ever intended' (*Letters and Papers of the Banks Family*, 1952, p. 15).

[5] This letter is the aftermath of a meeting; both LM and W had been in London since the previous Nov., evidently without corresponding.

Tho your opinion of me is extremely low, I am sure you think me
uncapable of talking such things to one I did not suppose willing at
least to seem a friend. If such a supposition was my fault, you will own
it pardonable. If it was not, I am innocent.

But I shoud not wonder you say today you hate me, t'other night
I was silly. I cant imagine you took either of these Compliments to be
literally true, but you thought I deserv'd little less, or how coud you
have us'd 'em? Woud any other have given you a reply? You have
now reason to call me silly. I still value you too much to take you at
your word and shoud be pleas'd to hear you think better of me than
you pretend to do. But I own it will not grieve me much to know you
have quite laid aside the thoughts of me, for indifference is to me
Absence. Tis a Refusal and every thing that can relieve a Passion, and
this I suspected the moment you told me I must give over writing. At
the same time I own your Beauties to be such as are capable of charming me to the highest degree, otherwise I had taken one of those
opportunities, which you woud never have given to one you valu'd
much, of ending easily. I had never desir'd one halfe hour's discourse
for convincing you how much greater the misfortune woud be to your
selfe than me, shoud we disagree when it was too late, and how
difficult it was for two such tempers to agree. I am afraid it is not
possible to enter fully into these points by letter and hope you will
contrive to see me unless you are resolv'd to break off.

[*Passage omitted*]

Text W MS i. 73–74 (draft)   *End. by W* 9 Feb.

To Wortley [*10 Feb. 1711*]

If I refflect on what you said, on the pain you have given
me, the uneasynesse I have endur'd ever since, the disorder
which you caus'd me and which it was impossible wholly to
suppresse so as to make it unperceiv'd by the Companny I
was with, ought I ever to write to you again? But I will not
think it possible you could be in earnest. I freely own I
cannot be angry with you without pain. The softnesse of my
temper (which I confesse to be a very great deffect) makes me
uncapable of Anger, and the height of my resentment falls
into Sorrow, and a greife for being ill us'd is a more natural
consequence of my being wrong'd than Hatred or Revenge.

Let me beg you never more to give me that Greife. If you are weary of me, say that, but never say such a reason for it. I may want a thousand things necessary to please, but can accuse my selfe of no irregularitys but what I have done for you, and them ought to be excusable to you.

I should not be sorry to see you was it possible to discourse with you for half an hour. How to do that in a shop is very difficult, and I know no place where you visit. Lady Jekyl[1] has desir'd to be introduce'd to me. I think she is your Acquaintance. Consider if I can see you at her house. As to my forbiding you to write, I am necessitated to do it. A Letter intercepted would forfeit my eternal repose, especially with people that have entertaind a suspicion that I am partial to you.

I am going to speak very plain—it is very hard to alter a receiv'd Opinion; I have accustom'd my selfe to esteem you, and know not how to do otherwise. My Schemes of Happynesse are pritty near what I have sometimes heard you declare yours. I am not very old, but know enough of the Town to hate it, and allwaies hate it most when I am in it. I'm afraid you'l think this out of the bounds of what is probable, but tis truth, the way I now live in is intirely disagreable to me, from the same reasons most women would be pleas'd with it. I detest the croud I am oblig'd to live in, and wish it in my power to be retir'd. (You will think me too free, but I will proceed and tell you.) I like your conversation, I think you have no faults but what are grounded upon Mistakes, that I am sure will vanish when you are better acquainted with my Inclinations. I propose to my selfe a Happynesse in pleasing you and do not think it impossible.

And now—what shall I say to e⟨xcuse⟩ this declaration? You would like me better if I was more reserv'd, but why should dissimulation be meritorious? I have told all my Heart and must leave it to you, how you will like my Sincerity.—If you should think my behaviour too indiscreet and that I say more than ought to be said—I can't help it. How ever my Actions may appear, I am conscious to my selfe of

---

[1] Elizabeth (1655–1745), da. of John Somers, m. Sir Joseph Jekyll, M.P.

principles that would not suffer me to do any thing even for you that was not in some degree Justifiable.

An Answer cannot be directed to me. 2 penny post Letters would give Occassion for Enquiry. Direct to Lady Margaret Creichton at the Earl of Loudoun's in the Pall Mall, near St. James.[1]

Text W MS i. 207–8   *Address* To Mr Edward Wortley Mountague to be deliver'd with care and speed.   *End. by W* Feb. 10.

From Wortley [*13 Feb. 1711*]

Tuesday night, 6 a clock

Had you bin so well pleas'd with my conversation you woud have had it long since at forty different places. Who is there you do not visit, besides Mrs. Steele and Mrs. Hampden,[2] at whose houses I am at home? Your friend Lady Wharton[3] is continually with Mrs. Hampden. Lady Evelyn must know several Buckinghamshire women that are intimate with her.[4] She lives in Marlborough Street and visits all that neighbourhood. Mrs. Steele goes little abroad but Mrs. Bins that knows every body is often with her.[5] I not only visit Lady Jekyl but the Dutchesses of Grafton, Northumberland, Kent,[6] in all which

---

[1] Lady Margaret Crighton, da. of Charles Lord Crighton (d. 1690), son of 2nd Earl of Dumfries. Her cousin was married to Hugh Campbell (d. 1731), 3rd Earl of Loudoun, at whose house she died in 1721 (*London Journal*, 7 Jan. 1721).

[2] Mary Scurlock (1678–1718) m. (1707) Richard Steele (Steele, *Corr.*, ed. R. Blanchard, 1941, p. 189); probably Isabella (d. 1736), da. of Sir William Ellis, who m. (1701) Richard Hampden (G. Lipscomb, *Hist. and Antiquit. of Bucks.*, 1847, ii. 265, 267).

[3] Lucy Loftus (1670–1717), da. of 1st Viscount Lisburne, m. (1692) Thomas, Earl and later Marquess of Wharton, prominent Whig politician. In her journal, LM characterized Lady Wharton as an abandoned and unscrupulous woman who affected an air of prudery and even sanctity (Stuart, p. 70).

[4] LM's youngest sister lived with their aunt Lady Cheyne, whose husband owned several manors in Bucks. (Lipscomb, iii. 270, 332, 338). Mrs. Hampden's husband had sat in the Parliaments of 1705 and 1708 for constituencies in that county.

[5] Mrs. Binns (or Bins) was an intimate friend and companion of Mrs. Steele (Steele, *Corr.*, pp. 227, 247, 261).

[6] Isabella Bennet (1667–1732), da. of 1st Earl of Arlington, widow of 1st Duke of Grafton, m. (1698) Sir Thomas Hanmer; Catherine Wheatley (d. 1714), widow of Thomas Lucy, m. (1686) 1st Duke of Northumberland; Jemima Crew (d. 1728), da. of 2nd Baron Crew, m. (1695) Henry Grey, later Marquess, then Duke, of Kent.

places I have formerly met you; besides the Dutchess of Shrewsberry,[1] Lady Harvey, Lady Betty Germain, Mrs. Chetwind and Lady Clarges.[2] Is there any of these you dont know? But perhaps at most of 'em it is not possible to whisper any longer than for making a Peace when it is broke and renewing an old treaty, but not for finishing one that is but newly begun. In more than 3 [*sic*] years we have not bin able to settle preliminaries. In this time what have I seen? But my eyes were of no use for me. That I shoud at last beg your Pardon for being abus'd by you! Indeed it has had this good effect: the many pretty things it fetch'd from you destroy'd a Resolution of never troubling you more, which I took on Saturday upon your not sending an Answer. I believ'd I shoud keep it all Sunday and yesterday till I had yours. I now own I am so far gone as to think my selfe oblig'd to you for it, tho I am not able to draw this Consequence from it, that you have forborn one day to write more tenderly even where one line of any kind under your hand woud be sufficient; nay, tho I know that a whisper or but a look may be worth a thousand such Epistles. I am thankful for it thô what you talk of the softness of your Temper, of your committing no Irregularities, of the Nicety of your Principles, takes away that little Air of truth which might have appeard in the rest. I am sorry to tell you I intended last night to be as long before I answerd as you was, but a money matter of moment is on my hands and I find I cannot be at leisure to follow it without paying this Duty. I have not said a word of the most material points, for I dont know when I shoud give over if I enterd upon 'em. It is not unlikely I may write something of 'em in 2 or 3 days unless I see you, which I take to be the shortest way of ending. I saw you once (if you remember such a thing) at Colman's. Why not there again? But Corticelli's[3] early after dinner might be better. Mrs. Corticelli or I might introduce you to Signora Checa[4] who lodges there, and while she sings it will be no ill compliment to talk very softly. Dont go on an Opera day unless it be in the morning. I forgot to say that talking English is whispering

---

[1] Adelaide Paleotti (d. 1726), da. of Marquis Paleotti of Bologna, m. (1705) 1st Duke of Shrewsbury. Her assembly was one of the most prominent in London (*Wentworth Papers*, p. 208). She appointed W to be one of her executors, and left him £400 (*Brit. Journal*, 16 July 1726), which may explain why some of her papers are among the W MS (vi. 214–74).

[2] Elizabeth Felton (1676–1741), da. of Sir Thomas Felton, m. (1695) John 1st Baron Hervey, later 1st Earl of Bristol; Lady Elizabeth Berkeley (1680–1769), da. of 2nd Earl of Berkeley, m. (1706) Sir John Germain; Mary Berkeley (1671–1741), da. of 4th Viscount Fitzhardinge, m. (1703) Walter Chetwynd, M.P.; Barbara Berkeley, her sister, m. Sir Thomas Clarges.

[3] An Italian warehouse in Suffolk Street, much frequented by fashionable people for raffles, purchases, and assignations (H. B. Wheatley, *London Past and Present*, 1891, iii. 331).

[4] Not identified.

before her. The Dutchess of Montague and Lady Bridgewater visited
her without any introduction.[1] I coud give her notice of your desire
to see her but it seems better to do it by Mrs. Corticelli. Lady Bridgewater (now I think of her) is acquainted with Mrs. Hampden and
can carry you to her. On the days the Post comes in my letters are
calld for at Mr. G[oodwin]'s at noon. On a sudden occasion enclose
to Mr. Knapton, a Glass Shop against the Tavern, Q[ueen] Street.

Text W MS i. 76–77   *End. by W* Feb. 12.

To Wortley [*15 Feb. 1711*]

I have no Acquaintance with Mrs. Hampden, Mrs.
Steele, or Mrs. Bins. Lady Wharton, that you call my
Freind, I have not seen above thrice very near this 2 year.
The Dutchesses of Grafton, Northumberland, and Kent I
visit seldom, and if we should meet there, it would be
impossible to speak without observation. Tis harder for me
than you imagine to meet any body. Corticelli's I don't much
care to go to. I have not been there a vast while, and if I
should go, it would look odd to my Sister and to Corticelli
her selfe, who would not fail to guesse the Occassion of so
unusual a visit.

Lady Jekyl was presented to me last Monday. I like her
very well, and hope to contrive to see you at her house,
which I look upon to be the easiest and safest place.[2] I am
not acquainted with Lady Clarges, Mrs. Chetwynd, or
Lady Betty Germain. I seldom see Lady Harvey and the
Dutchesse of Shrewsbury and never at their assemblys. I very
well remember seeing you at Coleman's, but dare not venture
again. Tis allmost a certainty of its being discover'd to be
a design'd thing. You do not know the ill Consequences
such a matter would have.

I answer'd your Letter the moment I receiv'd it, but was
forc'd to stay to send it, till I could see that only Lady I dare
trust. The same reason will I fear delay this, but tis your

[1] Mary Churchill (1689–1751), da. of
Duke of Marlborough, m. (1705) 2nd
Duke of Montagu; and her sister
Elizabeth (1688–1714), m. (1703) 5th

Earl of Bridgewater.
[2] Lady Jekyll lived in Lincoln's Inn
Fields (Somers MS, Reigate Town
Hall).

way to blame me for every thing.—If you are sincere in what you say of mistrusting my Nicety of principles, and doing no irregularitys, I ought not to see you again, but I hope you do not, cannot speak your thoughts—that is, you cannot be so entirely mistaken, at least if your Judgment is as good as I fancy it is.

I shall go very soon to the drawing room.[1] If you please, twill be mighty easy to enter into discourse there with lesse suspicion than any where else. I cannot tell you what day it will be; perhaps I shan't know my selfe above halfe an hour before I go. Next Sunday I will be at St. James' Chappel in the a⟨fternoon⟩ in the Ladies' Closet.[2] You may lead me d⟨own⟩stairs, if you have any thing to say that can be said in so short a time. It may be, by then, I shall be able to tell you when we may meet at Lady Jekyl's.

This is nonsense I'm afraid, but I write both in haste and danger.

Text W MS i. 203–4   *Address* To Mr Edward Wortley Mountague
End. by W Friday 15. Answ. to that of 12.

From Wortley [*15 Feb. 1711*]

I wish your business had not bin too pressing to let you go for a minute to Lady Kent's.[3] She is my friend and I might at least have gone down stairs with you. You know before I say it I shall wait for you at the Chappel. Since you name no other place let me name one more, Mrs. Farmer's.[4] A friend of mine promis'd to carry me [there] just before I had yours forbidding me to write, but perhaps I may not suddenly find him now and this may not suit with your Affairs.

I did venture to tell Mr. St[eele] I long'd to say something to you and coud not find the means and therefore beg'd he woud get his wife

---

[1] The Drawing Room at St. James's Palace.

[2] The chapel in St James's Palace; in the section set aside for ladies, the pews had been raised and made into closets to prevent flirtations (Wheatley, *op. cit.*, ii. 276).

[3] A slip for the Duchess of Kent, whose husband had been raised to the Dukedom in April 1710.

[4] Probably Ellen Brown (d. 1741), widow since 1703 of Henry Fermor; one of her daughters was Arabella, heroine of *The Rape of the Lock* (Joseph Jackson Howard and H. F. Burke, *Genealogical Collections Illustrating the History of Roman Catholic Families of England*, Part i, 1887, p. 6). She had a house in St. James's parish.

to visit you. You wont, I'm sure, say this was a reflection upon you.
He told me my Lord was his good friend[1] and you had talk'd of visiting
her and therefore she might go without being introduc'd. I said I feard
L[ady] M[ary] woud suspect it was a Contrivance of mine. But sure
you that are in a higher rank may go without any ceremony. Don't
tell me again you dare not trust Sister F[rances]. I will for once grant
it to be true and advise you to pretend to her Mrs. St[eele] sent you
a message desiring leave to see you. She really has the nice principles
you talk of, is simple enough to be in love with a husband, and thinks
he is my friend. You can be no where so free from observation as with
her. If you must be introducd, get Lady Warwick to do it.[2] Dr. Garth,
who lives near you,[3] will tell you how you may go in an hour's time
to either of 'em. He himselfe may introduce you or may give Mrs.
St[eele] notice of your desire. She is visited by Mrs. Cottons;[4] I fancy
you know 'em. Before Mrs. St[eele] we may talk for hours if you like
it. Lady Je[kyll] has a niece,[5] and few young woman [*sic*] care to see
others whisper, nor am I sure Lady Je[kyll] woud not tell her Brother.[6]
I fear we coud not talk more before her than at the D[uches]s of Kent's.
At Mrs. Hampden's I coud call for cards and tally or whisper with
you and it woud pass for nothing. Perhaps your Aunt[7] will not like
your going thither, else you might easily get acquainted.

You may write to morrow and by answering a few questions save
some of our Debates. If you dont care to send your thoughts on such
high points, you may put a paper into my hands. You had better not
attempt to disprove what you never can, but—When a woman has bin
irregular as far as she coud with safety, which way can she prevent all
future suspicions or be pleas'd with the man that has entertaind any?
Can a woman us'd to Splendor submit with satisfaction to that way of
living which pleases the man tho never so low, and this when she is
not far from the Place in which she made a Figure?

It was said by one that treated he hop'd her father might give a
4th part more than he offer'd. It was not insisted upon. But if the
want of it shoud be thought inconvenient, might not that be obtain'd?
If the Lady agrees to it why may not a much higher sum be ask'd than

[1] Steele and Lord Dorchester were
fellow members of the Kit-Cat Club.
LM later told Joseph Spence that she
knew Steele through her father (*Anecdotes*, ed. J. M. Osborn, 1966, § LM 1).

[2] Charlotte (1679–1728), da. of Sir
Thomas Middleton, widow of 27th
Earl of Warwick. In 1716 she married
W's friend Addison.

[3] Dr. Samuel Garth's house was in
Covent Garden (*DNB*).

[4] Not identified.

[5] Margaret (d. 1761), da. of Charles
Cocks, m. John Lygon and then (1719)
Philip Yorke, later 1st Earl of Hard-
wicke. Her mother and Lady Jekyll were
sisters of Lord Somers.

[6] John (1651–1716), 1st Baron
Somers, the former Lord Chancellor,
was a political crony of LM's father.

[7] See below, p. 172.

will be taken? Is it reasonable to press a man to settle more than he is willing to settle? Where two live well together 'tis a thousand to one that her heirs will have the greatest of what he has. But why shoud a man be forc'd to it, let what will happen, which really makes the reversion of the estate hers and not his?

How can a man promise that even after 7 years he shall be easy to see a lady near the Company that has given him offence?

When you have satisfy'd me in these it will be your turn to raise Scruples, and you cant be too plain with me in telling 'em.

Thursday, 9 at night.

You dont care to put any date.

Text W MS i. 61–62 (draft)

To Wortley [*16 Feb. 1711*]

I would have gone to Lady Kent's if I had known you desir'd it, tho' it could have given us no oppertunity of speaking. Mrs. Farmer's is the most inconvenient place in the World. I do not go very often; the House is allwaies full of a mixture of Giddy and mallicious people. I am no where so much upon my guard, and should quite leave off them sort of Assemblys if I was so much my own Mistrisse as not to fear disobliging a companny of silly impertinent women.

I am ready to beleive the good Charecter you give Mrs. Steele and wish with all my Heart you could perswade her Husband to send her to see me. I dare not make the first visit, for I should certainly be examin'd why I did it, and tis what I never do. I have proceeded so far as to ask a Lady, who told me she was Intimate with her, to bring her to see me. Perhaps she never deliverd my Message, for twas one of those gay happy Ladies that mind nothing beside their own faces. I know no other that is acquainted with her. I would speak again to that Lady, but tis uncertain when I shall see her, for I don't much care to enter into an Intimacy with her. Tis Lady Ernley;[1] she visited me this summer in the country.

If you can oblige Mrs. Steele to come to see me, I shall be very glad, and after the first visit, there is no farther

[1] Frances (d. 1728), da. of Thomas Erle, m. Sir Edward Ernle (or Ernley), M.P.

difficulty. I will alow for her Modesty, and make the first
offers of Freindship, to entitle me to that freedom you
speak of.

I am now going to Answer without reserve to your
Questions. I beg you to put the mildest censure upon
my Sincerity. I am afraid you should think I say too much,
but I must write, for I'm sure I shall never be able to
speak it.

That irregularity you speak of is nothing more than a
native openesse of temper, and something of the gaity of
Youth, which is only ill construed for want of being known,
and there is nothing to be suspected where there is nothing
but what is visibly undesign'd. A Man that had once
show'd a Jealousie of Humour would be only disagreable to
one that propos'd all her future happynesse in the Enjoyment
of the foolish unsatisfactory Pleasures of the Town.

A Low manner of living has been my entire Inclination
ever since I can remember having an Inclination, and your
Likeing that is one of the best things I like in you.

As to the fortune, I cannot name positively what shall be
given. Some people Love to make those things secrets. You
may ask what you please, you cannot suppose I should not
be glad to have your fortune encreas'd. I should be glad if
it was nothing to me. Only let me give this caution: be not
any thing that may [be] thought unreasonable in your
demands, for if one Person is disoblig'd, He is irreconcilable.—You understand these things better than I.—Do what
you please, but I beg you, do not disoblige one that has the
disposal of me.—Sure, you will not.—As to settlements,
remember tis not I that am to make 'em, and my thinking
you in the right will not perswade others that you are so.

My Love is not divided into manny branches. Except 3
or 4 women or relations, for the generallity of my Acquaintance tis equal to me whether I dont see them in 7 year or as
long as I live.

I have now answer'd all your Questions; tis my turn to
raise objections. I have but one, and that is what I think
upon very often. You dont Love me.—If this is realy true,
I shall be very unhappy. Tis impossible to please any body
that has no Inclination to be pleasd with me. To live with

you and not to please you would be something very Miserable. I had rather stay as I am.—I am not willing to dwell upon this thought—you force me upon it.—Can any one have a degree of Kindnesse and raise so manny objections?

Friday night.

Sunday afternoon I will be at Chappell and Monday in the drawing room.

Text W MS i. 280–1

To Wortley [*17 Feb. 1711*]

I must write 3 words in great Haste. I shall stay at home all the Afternoon to morrow, by the command of people not to be disputed with. I am only sorry because I must disapoint you. Monday night at the drawing room I hope to have better fortune.

Text W MS i. 197–8   *Address* To Mr Edward Wortley Mountague *End. by W* Sunday [*sic*] 17 Feb.

To Wortley [*22 Feb. 1711*]

I was never more out of Countenance in my Life than to Night. I certainly made a very silly figure. Between Fear and Confusion it was Impossible to suffer more than I did. I fancy'd every body perceiv'd the reason of my comeing, and that fancy gave me a thousand Disorders. I had reason for more when I came into the coach. My Sister read me a long Lecture on your Account. I wish there had not been so much reason in what she said. I cannot Justifie my Actions in that point. Mrs. Steele and her Husband certainly think me as ridiculous as she does.—

What recompence have I for all this? Have I the pleasure of obliging a Man that I esteem? On the contrary, you think me more inexcusable than they do, and that I would

do the same for every Man in the world. After your Manner
of thinking, every fresh instance of kindnesse is a New
Crime.—How can you use me so? You call all things
Criminal; my Confusion (which I know not how to overcome
when I see you) is Peevishnesse, and my very sincerity is
design. Am I to think you love me? I must come over to the
Opinion of my Sister and own that (at least) I ought not to
think so.

But to your Question. I have nothing to say but that
(which is saying all in a few words) if you have the disposal
of me, and think it convenient either for your Pleasure or
Affairs to passe your Life in Yorkshire, I shall not be dis-
pleasd with it. A Town Life, in the public Station I now am,
is utterly disagreable to me. I am weary of it, and should quit
it with Pleasure. And now, consider with your Selfe the
degree of Inclination you ⟨have for⟩ me.

Do not think of marrying me except you think it will make
you happy. I had rather never see you than see you dislike
me.

After saying so much, permit me to say no more to you.
If you are determin'd to think ill of me, my Arguments
cannot convince you. If you think well—I need add no
farther.

I should be very glad if Mrs. Steele would return my
visit soon. I am asham'd to make manny advances. She will
think tis upon your Account, and (perhaps) she knows you
don't care for me.—I wish I could be convinc'd one way
or other. Do something to shew me your Partiallity or
Indifference; the first would give me pleasure, and the last
would free me from Pain.

Text W MS i. 178–9   *Address* To Mr Edward Wortley Mountague
End. by W P. 22d Feb. Friday

From Wortley [*24 Feb. 1711*]

Saturday [*Passage omitted*] I have resolv'd to bear any thing with
temper and in spight of you we shall one time or other be good friends.
I can excuse the pleasure you will take in an ill usage of me, for it is

to be ascrib'd to Vanity, which commonly attends a great deal of merit. Even at present I am generous enough to own that the new man[1] you have encourag'd and that attended you last night may be very proper for any of your purposes. If his father's estate shoud be less than £2,000 a year (one of his Country-men told me that is the value of it, but it may be a great deal more;[2] I shall know in a day or two) the part your lover may have of it may be very sufficient for the Country especially so far Northward, or if you like the town it is better living on a little there than not at all. For my part, I own it must be long experience of your sincerity that can make me bear the thoughts of being your Companion in town. If this is to be only a lover during his good behaviour, he is less inconvenient than several others, because it may be suppos'd your affair tends towards Matrimony. You see how just I am to You tho in favour of a Rival. In return end with me calmly, but if you will use the rough way, it is true I shall be more vex'd at present, but after a little time what I lose will appear the less. [*Passage omitted*] Saturday night.

Text W MS i. 50–51   *End. by W* 25 Feb.

To Wortley [*26 Feb. 1711*]

I intended to make no Answer to your Letter. It was something very ungratefull, and I resolv'd to give over all thoughts of you. I could easily have perform'd that resolve some time ago, but then you took pains to please me. Now you have brought me to Esteem you, You make use of that Esteem to give me uneasynesse, and I have the displeasure of seeing I esteem a Man that dislikes me. Farewell then, since you will have it so. I renounce all the Ideas I have so long flatterd my selfe with, and will Entertain my fancy no longer with the Imaginary Pleasure of pleasing you. How much wiser are all them women I have dispisd than my selfe! In placeing their Happynesse in triffles, they have plac'd it in what is attainable. I fondly thought Fine Cloaths and Gilt Coaches, Balls, Operas and public adoration rather

---

[1] Probably LM's suitor, Clotworthy Skeffington, son of 3rd Viscount Massereene (see below, p. 122, n. 1).

[2] In 1697 his father's estates were valued at £800 p.a. in England and £600 in Ireland (GEC *Peerage*).

the fatigues of Life, and that True Happynesse was justly
defin'd by Mr. Dryden (pardon the romantic Air of repeating verses) when he says

> Whom Heaven would bless it does from pomps remove,
> And makes their Wealth in Privacy and Love.[1]

These Notions had corrupted my Judgment as much as
Mrs. Biddy Tipkin's.[2] According to this Scheme, I propos'd
to passe my Life with you. I yet do you the Justice to beleive
if any Man could have been contented with this Manner of
Living, it would have been you. Your Indifference to me
does not hinder me from thinking you capable of tendernesse
and the Happynesses of Freindship. But I find tis not to me
you'l ever have them. You think me all that is detestable.
You accuse me of want of sincerity and Generosity. To
convince you of your Mistake, I'll shew you the last extremes
of both.

While I foolishly fancy'd you lov'd me (which I confess
I had never any great reason for, more than that I wish'd
it) there is no condition of Life I could not have been happy
in with you, so very much I lik'd you. I may say Lov'd,
since tis the last thing I'll ever say to you. This is telling
you sincerely my greatest weaknesse, and now I will oblige
you with a new proofe of Generosity—I'll never see you
more.—I shall avoid all public places, and this is the last
letter I shall send. If you write, be not displeas'd if I send
it back unopen'd. I shall force my Inclinations to oblige
yours, and remember that you have told me I could not
oblige you more than by refuseing you. Had I intended ever
to see you again, I durst not have sent this Letter. Adeiu.

Text W MS i. 268–9   *Address* To Mr Edward Wortley Mountague
End. by W Feb. 26.

[1] The closing lines (slightly altered)
of *Aureng-zebe* (1676), Act III.

[2] The heroine of Steele's *The Tender
Husband* (1703). As described by another character in the play: 'She has
spent all her Solitude in reading
Romances, her Head is full of Shep-
herds, Knights, Flowery Meads, Groves
and Streams, so that if you talk like a
Man of this World to her, you do
nothing' (ed. 1734, p. 19).

From Wortley [*26 Feb. 1711*]

Monday night.

What woud I not give to prove I writ the other sheet on Saturday night! I hope the Colour of the Ink and the folly of what I say about a Rival will convince you. How true a Prophet have I bin! Had you ended with me in a better manner I shoud have bin extremely surpriz'd. Since this has not fall'n upon me unexpected, I am the more able to bear it. After this you must never pretend to be either sincere or generous. Can it possibly be true that you are angry at a letter which shew'd I endeavourd to conceal a Passion but coud not? Has it not appeard in almost every one of those unmannerly lines I have at any time sent you as plainly as the want of one is seen in all your civil expressions, nay, I will add, in your Angry ones? How coud any woman break off so suddenly with one she had lately valu'd? That you are not sincere is plain. Then for your Generosity: Coud one that had any Humanity give a reason so mortifying as this must have bin had I intirely believ'd it? But never imagine that from your former carriage I fancy you ever lov'd me or that I can take this letter for any thing but a proofe you never did, and conclude I shall be free from Pain sooner than you intend I shou'd. I will, however, gratify you in this. I own I am griev'd at present when I ought to be no more than angry. Since I perceive you tell me very truly, tho you conceal the true reason, that you have laid aside the thoughts of me, All I have left to do is, as soon as I am able, to separate my Love from Esteem. I had bin very long about it coud I have charg'd upon my selfe the loss even of that small appearance of your Partiality. I send you Mr. Steele's letter to prove how diligent I have bin in going and writing often about the return of your visit. I wish you coud shew me as clearly that my complaints, or but the last, was as groundless, and then all might be right again. I mean we might be as well together as we were before I writ the last letter. I own I coud never forbear urging you to consider your danger till all was agreed. I once more beg of you what I did before, to give me for the reason of your refusal your not liking me. When you tell me this calmly, I shall be convinc'd I am dismiss'd in good earnest and we may both bid Adieu together. Your saying you resolve not to see me is too great a Compliment. It is beneath you to admit I am able to raise in you so much anger. If Mrs. St[eele]'s is not convenient let me know at what hour you think of visiting some other. I coud name a place without exception but it is now too late for me to appoint. [*Passage omitted*]

Monday night, 7 a clock.

Text W MS i. 69–70 *End. by* W 28 Feb.

To Wortley [*27 Feb. 1711*]

I am yet weak enough to write to you, and so asham'd of it I know not what to say to you.—This will be a very good jest between you and Mr. Steele.—

I am sorry she did not return my visit sooner.—I can not see you without a vast Confusion and yet I would.—What shall I do? You will dispise me for this. I own tis Impudence to think of seeing you. After so much Indiscretion I cannot blame you if you think me capable of every thing.

I will come to Mrs. Steele early on friday. I am afraid of finding companny there. I hope it is not Mr. St[eele]'s custom to carry his Acquaintance up stairs. Men are more Censorious than Women. I know I deserve it, but I could not bear to be shew'd as a sight to his Freinds. I hope I shall see none of them.—

Perhaps I shall be at the play Thursday. If I ⟨am⟩ not, I will be at Mrs. Steele's. This is nonsense. I tremble at the ⟨thing I⟩ am doing. I deserve your contempt and expect to find it. My time not being [my] own, I can very seldom tell long before what I am to do. I will be positively at Mrs. Steele's Thursday or at the play, but I cannot tell which. Think as favourably of me as you can. I am very silly. What is become of my anger?   Tuesday Night 11

Text W MS i. 213–14   *Address* To Mr Wortley at his Lodgings over against the Tavern in Great Queen Street a Looking-Glasse shop   *End. by* W From P. 1 Mar.

From Wortley [*3 March 1711*]

Saturday Morning.

Every time you see me you give me a fresh proofe of your not caring for me. Yet I beg you will meet me once more. How cou'd you pay me that great Compliment of your loving the Country for Life, when you woud not stay with me a few minutes longer? Who is the happy man you went to? I agree with you I am often so dull I cannot explain my meaning but will not own the expression was so very obscure,

when I said If I had you I shoud act against my Opinion. What need
I add? I see what is best for me, I condemn what I do, and yet I fear
I must do it. If you cant find it out that you are going to be unhappy,
ask your sister, who agrees with you in every thing else, and she will
convince you of your rashness in this. She knows you dont care for me
and that you will like me less and less every year, perhaps every day,
of your life. [*Passage omitted*]

Now you have bin so free before Mrs. St[eele] you may call upon
her or send for her to morrow or next day. Let her dine with you or go
to visits, Shops, Hide Park, or other diversions. You may bring her
home. I can be in the house reading, as I often am, tho the master is
abroad. If you will have her visit you first, I will get her to go to
morrow. I think a man or a woman is under no engagement till the
writings are seal'd, but it looks like indiscretion even to begin a treaty
without a probability of concluding it. When you hear all my objections to you and to my selfe, you will resolve against me. Last night
you was much upon the reserve. I see you can never ⟨be⟩ thoroughly
intimate with me; 'tis because you ⟨can⟩ have no pleasure in it. You
can be easy and complaisant, as you have sometimes told me, but never
think that enough to make me easy unless you refuse me.

Write a line this evening or early to morrow. If I dont speak plain,
do you understand that I write? Tell me how to mend the stile if
the fault is in that. If the Characters are not plain I can easily mend
them. I always comprehend your expressions, but woud give a great
deal to know what passes in your heart.

In you I might possess Youth, Beauty, and all things that charm.
It is possible they may strike me less after a time, but I may then consider I have once enjoyd 'em in perfection, that they woud have decay'd
as soon in any other. You see this is not your case. You will think you
might have bin happier. Never engage with a man unless you propose
to your selfe the highest satisfaction from him or none other.

Text W MS i. 96–97   *Address* To Lady Mary Pierpont with Care
and Speed.

To Wortley [*7 March 1711*]

I know not what thoughts you left me with, last night,
but mine are all in your Favour. Tho' your Letter had several
things in it that had an Air of Indifference, you reconcil'd
your selfe by your behaviour, and I fancy that you do think
tolerably of me. I can write what I cannot say. I will certainly

see you on Satterday, and will endeavor to speak, but I am so conscious to my selfe of doing wrong while I do it, ⟨that I⟩ cannot without great difficulty.

My sister perswades me you deceive me. I do not easily admit of such a suspicion and cannot think ill of you till you force me upon it. The sincerity and openesse of my temper ought to make you treat me with more Confidence than you do. I am incapable of deceiving you, and say nothing but what I think Truth. Tis easy for you (with the good opinion I have of you) to impose upon me. But sure you cannot do it. —My Father has allready entertaind a suspicion of my favouring you. To give him any knowledge of a Private Correspondance with you would ruine me. Tis hardly possible for me to do any thing without his finding it out. I am sure he will if I repeat it often. This will convince you of the Nec⟨essity⟩ of Satterday being the last time of our Meeting. I cannot promise from my foolish temper that I shall then be able to talk of any thing Important. I am confus'd, I tremble and know not what I say. Tis therefore absolutely necessary for me to write what I ought to speak, however it may seem.

I could be content to passe my Life in the Country. A private manner of Living suits my Inclination; and I am very well assur'd the more you know, the lesse you will suspect me.

This is saying all in a few words. As to the demand you make me, tis willingly granted, and nothing of that Kind can be difficult to me. Writeing is much more so at this time, for my sight is so weak I am oblig'd ⟨to⟩ leave off.

Adeiu. Use me ⟨we⟩ll. I deserve more Esteem than you give me. Tis not manny Women that could renounce all the world for any one. I could do that was I sure of pleasing that One.

Text W MS i. 174–5 *Address* To Mr Wortley at his Lodgings over against the Tavern in Great Queen Street ⟨a⟩ Looking Glasse ⟨shop⟩ *End. by W* P. 7 Mar.

From Wortley [*10 March 1711*]

I was extremely concern'd to see your Coach go away from Mrs.
St[eele]'s. Her Husband was hinderd all night from sleeping by the
Gout and she coud not sleep while he was in pain. She was ill and in
bed when you came. This unlucky accident troubles me the more
because it brings this Reflection into my mind. Is there any of your
Acquaintance but myselfe whom you do not meet at more places than
one? When you delay'd me so long did you not expect many things
might prevent our meeting? Dont imagine I am concern'd for missing
this Conference, because I hop'd to be made happy by it. I am not
vain enough to conclude I shall please you after you [have] given me so
many proofs that I cannot, but I am sorry your trouble about me, if
you have had any, is not yet over. [*Passage omitted*]
Saturday 6 a clock.

Text W MS i. 54–55   *Address* To Lady Mary Pierpoint.

To Wortley [*12 March 1711*]

I have been sick ever since I was at the Opera, and had
so great Weaknesse in my sight, I have not been able to read
nor write. It was with difficulty that I read your Letter, which
I receiv'd on friday night. I design'd to answer it by word
of Mouth and went Satterday in a scarfe to Mrs. Steele.
I found [her] not at home, which very much surpriz'd me.
It is not often my time is at my own disposal, and my sister
not of a Humour to suffer me to engage my selfe where she
don't like.—

I ⟨am⟩ at present very much out of Humour, and doubly
indispos'd from a very great Cold and some Expressions in
your Letter. I write in pain, for my Eyes are not yet perfectly recover'd.

You continue to be unjust and to suspect my sincerity.
I suffer every way. My sister reproaches me with fondnesse
for a Man that does not care for me. The Plague of Companny
is added to my Misfortunes. I must leave off.—

I will come to morrow to Mrs. Steele's early but cannot stay. I am engagd against my will to Lady K. Sidney.[1]

Text W MS i. 215–16   *Address* To Mr Wortley at his Lodgings over against the Tavern in Great Queen street a Looking Glass shop *End. by W* P. 12 Mar.

To Wortley [*13 March 1711*]

I have this minute receiv'd your 2 Letters.

You very much mistake me. I am not so ridiculously vain to take a Pleasure in giving uneasynesse was it in my Power. If I could make you happy, you should be allwaies so, and the cheif of my wishes is to please you. I hazard a great deal to meet you, and every letter is a proof of my desire to please at any Expence.

I tell you with all that freedom you require: If you can like me for a Compannion I shall think my selfe happier in such a retirement than any of those that place their happynesse in the Gayeties of a Court, and shall not only be contented but pleasd in returning no more to this Hurry.

I tell you this with the utmost sincerity. Consult your own Heart and do what you please. If you have a mind to see me once more, I will venture it to oblige you. Tis better to make a ridiculous figure to few than to a manny, and having allready been laugh'd at at Mrs. Steele's, I had rather be so there again than in new Companny.

Give your selfe no trouble to day. I am not one of those foolish vain Women [who] think nothing so Impor⟨tant⟩ as themselves.

Write me word what day would be most convenient, and if possible it shall be then. It cannot be Thursday. Dr. Garth's Ball is that day, I fancy, and I must feign a sicknesse or I shall entirely disoblige my sister that has a mind to go. Neither will it be in my power to refuse, for my Father has promis'd I shall be there.—I don't speak this by way of

[1] Lady Catherine Sydney (d. 1722), da. of 4th Earl of Leicester, m. William Barker.

Excuse, for if you please I'll say I am ill and keep my Chamber 2 or 3 days. Let me know what you'd have me do.

Text W MS i. 251–2   *Address* To Mr Wortley at his Lodgings over against the Tavern in Great Queen street a Looking Glass shop *End. by W* From P. 13 Mar.

To Wortley [*13 March 1711*]

Tuesday 10 a Clock

I am in Pain about the Letter I sent you this Morning. I fear you should think after what I have said, you cannot in point of Honnour break off with me. Be not scrupulous on that Article, nor affect to make me break first to excuse your doing it. I would owe nothing but to Inclination. If you do not love me, I may have the lesse Esteem of my selfe, but not of you. I am not of the Number of those Women that have the Opinion of their persons Mr. Bayes had of his Play, that tis the touchstone of sense, and they are to frame their Judgment of people's understandings according to what they think of them.[1]

You may have Wit, good Humour, and good Nature, and not like me. I alow a great deal for the Inconstancy of Mankind in general and my own want of Merit in perticular. But tis a breach at least of the 2 last to Deceive me. I am sincere, I shall be sorry if I am not now what pleases, but if I (as I could with Joy) abandonn all things to the Care of pleasing you, I am then undone if I do not succeed.—Be Generous.

Text W MS i. 270–1   *Address* To Mr Wortley at his Lodgings over against the Tavern in Great Queen Street a Looking Glasse shop *End. by W* from P. 13 March

[1] 'I know you have wit by the judgement you make of this Play; for that's the measure I go by: my Play is my Touch-stone' (Duke of Buckingham, *The Rehearsal*, 1671, Act III, Sc. i).

From Wortley [*14 March 1711*]

Coud I believe all you say, there woud be no need of a further Conference between us on this subject, but you know how little reason I have to be convincd by what you say. I shoud set you right in one mistake. I have determin'd to pass my life out of London, not out of a particular humour which may alter, but no man living is so much oblig'd to avoid the town as I am. I have seldom had a perfect settled health in it, thô I have not often wanted it in the Country. One halfe hour's sleep or a keener appetite every day is what I woud not quit for the Duke of M[arlborough]'s Fame or Riches. This is a fixt Resolution which nothing but Love can overcome, and if I must Love, it shall be an object that is not to be found here. Tis plainly my interest to take leave of the town and all business whatever, and I have bin vext this 2 or 3 years at my being detaind by a money affair of moment which is now almost settled. The man I am best pleas'd with presses me to do this for our pleasure, and unless I promise him shortly he will seek another companion.[1] If you and I agree, I shall not bear to have him or any other near me that I like very well, and whether I shall be so well satisfy'd with your carriage to me that I shall want no other, you best tell. I must forbear going into a delightfull Climate for your sake if I love you. If I do not, I must endeavour to be happy at a distance from you, and my present circumstances are such that I cannot content my selfe with much less money than I have now I am single. [*Passage omitted*]

Wednesday 9 a clock in the Morning.

Text W MS i. 6–7 (draft) *End. by W* 14 Mar.

From Wortley [*c. 20 March 1711*]

Tho your putting me off till Saturday seems in favour of another, thô an Air of Truth is wanting in almost every line you write, there are some things you say that oblige me more than I can express. Now is the time to dismiss me, change the Lover for a friend. I am both able and ambitious to serve you, and shall think my selfe bound in Gratitude to endeavour it as long as I live. But if you take me, see what your

---

[1] On at least two occasions Addison proposed sharing a house with W: in July and in Oct. 1711 (Addison, *Letters*, ed. W. Graham, 1941, pp. 264, 265).

hazard is. It will not be long 'ere you will seem pleas'd with another or negligent of me. I shall presently conclude you have given over Acting and look upon you as one that has cheated me of a good part of my fortune and sunk my Credit. The very engaging with one that is acquainted with every man of fashion in town and with several of 'em too much will pass for a great piece of Folly, but when it proves as every one expected, I shall be brought under the utmost Contempt. These are the least of the disadvantages I shall suffer from being deceiv'd or (if you please I'll say) from a change of your humour. I need not shew you that your condition will be alterd for the worse as much as mine. One that has so bright an Imagination must discern what will be the consequences of a breach between us and how likely it is to happen. The Clearness of your Understanding is the only argument for my thinking of you, for unless you can be sure to please me, you will at last reject me and not commit the greatest of Follies after so long a deliberation.

You was yesterday much in the right when you made a doubt of being able to please me. Your offers, tho very large, are not enough. If woman shoud seem more desirous than your selfe to please a man, more fearful of displeasing him, or of losing his kindness, or less fond of pleasing others, I shou'd fancy my selfe ill treated. My Demand proves at last to be very high, but I can abate nothing of it. I believe you may before Saturday come to a very right Determination. Think seriously on the most weighty point you will ever have to decide.

Text W MS i. 65–66   *Address* To Lady Mary Pierpont.

To Wortley [*21 March 1711*]

Wednesday morn.

I obey'd your Commands and staid at home Yesterday. If I pleas'd you, it is giving my selfe more pleasure than the opera could have done.[1]

This is to desire you to direct your next enclos'd to Mrs. Dupont at this house.[2] I shall have it sooner, which I would fain have, for somebody goes out of Town next Week and

---

[1] On Tuesday, 20 March, the opera at the Queen's Theatre in the Haymarket was Handel's *Rinaldo* (*London Stage 1660–1800*, Part 2, ed. E. L. Avery, 1960, p. 245).

[2] For Mrs. Dupont see above, p. 41, n. 1.

perhaps we do the latter end of this. Monday or Tuesday
we shall at farthest.

[*Postscript*] You know the name of this Street near St ——.

Text W MS i. 201–2   *Address* To Mr Wortley at his Lodgings in
great Queen Street over against the Tavern a Looking Glasse Shop
End. by W from P. 21 Mar.

From Wortley [*22 March 1711*]

I cannot believe I am less unacceptable to you than I was a few
days ago, but your writing proves you to be something less ill-natur'd
and by shewing me you have not broke with me for ever it has destroy'd the Resolution I had taken of giving you no more trouble.
Why will you oblige me to write again? Is it possible for you to remove
the strong suspicions which you know I have entertaind with so much
reason? Can you convince me I shall have no more of 'em? It is
pretty clear to me you cannot. However, if you fancy otherwise, it is
not for me to desire you will forbear endeavouring to satisfy me as
you told me you woud when I had writ. But I am bound in justice
to own I think it is now too late for you to say any thing, and you had
better give me no answer.

If you shoud write as fully as you promis'd and I continue in my
present opinion (as I believe I shall) you may be assur'd I will return
your letter by the Post, or, if you please, by a faithfull messenger that
does not know you. I may deliver it inclos'd to Lady Margaret
C[righto]n[1] or any other.

Thursday night.

Text W MS i. 39 (?draft)   *End. by W* 22d Mar.

To Wortley [*24 March 1711*]

Tho' your Letter is far from what I expected, haveing
once promis'd to answer it with the sincere account of my
inmost thoughts, I am resolv'd you shall not find me worse
than my word, which is (what ever you may think) inviolable.
Tis no Affectation to say, I dispise the Pleasure of pleasing

---

[1] At the Earl of Loudoun's house (see above, p. 74).

people that I dispise. All the fine Equipages that shine in the Ring never gave me another thought than either Pity or Contempt for the Owners, that could place Happynesse in attracting the Eyes of strangers. Nothing touches me with Satisfaction but what touches my Heart, and I should find more Pleasure in the secret Joy I should feel at a kind Expression from a freind I esteem'd, than at the Admiration of a whole Play house, or the Envy of those of my own Sex who could not attain to the same Number of Jewells, fine Cloths etc., supposing I was at the very top of this sort of Happynesse.

You may be this freind, if you please. Did you realy esteem me, had you any tender regard for me, I could, I think, passe my Life in any station, happyer with you than in all the Grandeur of the World with any other. You have some Humours that would be disagreable to any Woman that marryd with an Intention of finding her Happynesse abroad. That is not my Resolution. If I marry, I propose to my selfe a Retirement. There is few of my Acquaintance I should ever wish to see again, and the pleasing One, and only One, is the way I design to please my selfe.

Happynesse is the natural design of all the World, and every thing we see done, is meant in order to attain it. My Imagination places it in Freindship. By Freindship I mean an intire Communication of thoughts, Wishes, Interests, and Pleasures being undivided, a mutual Esteem, which naturally carrys with it a pleasing sweetnesse of conversation, and terminates in the desire of makeing one or Another happy, without being forc'd to run into Visits, Noise, and Hurry, which serve rather to trouble than compose the thoughts of any reasonable Creature. There are few capable of a Freindship such as I have describ'd, and tis necessary for the generallity of the World to be taken up with Triffles. Carry a fine Lady or a fine Gentleman out of Town and they know no more what to say. To take from them Plays, Operas, and fashions is takeing away all their topics of discourse, and they know not how to form their thoughts on any other Subjects. They know very well what it is to be admir'd, but are perfectly ignorant of what it is to be lov'd.

I take you to have Sense enough not to think this Scheme

Romantic. I rather chuse to use the word Freindship than
Love because in the general Sense that word is spoke, it
signifies a Passion rather founded on Fancy than Reason,
and when I say Freindship I mean a mixture of Tendernesse
and Esteem, and which a long acquaintance encreases not
decays. How far I deserve such a freindship, I can be no
Judge of my selfe. I may want the good sense that is necessary to be agreable to a Man of Merit, but I know I want
the vanity to beleive I have, and can promise you shall never
like me lesse upon knowing me better, and that I shall never
forget you have a better understanding than my selfe.

And now let me intreat you to think (if possible) tolerably
of my Modesty after so bold a declaration. I am resolv'd to
throw off reserve; and use me ill if you please. I am sensible
to own an Inclination for a Man is puting one's selfe wholly
in his Power, but sure you have generosity enough not to
abuse it. After all I have said, I pretend no tye but on your
Heart. If you do not love me, I shall not be happy with you;
if you do, I need add no farther. I am not Mercenary and
would not receive an obligation that comes not from one that
Loves me.

I do not desire my Letter back again. You have honnour
and I dare trust you. I am going to the same place [Acton]
I went last Spring. I shall think of you there; it depends
upon you, in what Manner.

Text W MS i. 257–8   *End. by W* from P. 24 Mar.

From Wortley [*29 March 1711*]

You judge very right that the secret of your esteeming me so much
will be safe. Were I vain enough to believe it my selfe, I shoud never
hope to convince any other or expose my selfe to ridicule in attempting
it. Coud I have imagin'd your respect for me halfe what you say it is,
I had long since endeavourd to be much more or less happy than I am
at present. After all the unkindness you have express'd, my Passion is
yet at such a height that I woud part with Life it selfe to be convinc'd
your esteem is as you represent it. At last I own this weakness to you
with a great deal of shame. I cannot help owning it now you have

put it out of your power to take advantage of the Confession. After —
(I am still griev'd at the thoughts of it and will not say what it is) no
one can be persuaded he is esteemd. I shoud have taken my selfe to be
the most fortunate man alive, whatever price I had paid for you, coud
I but have believ'd you as indifferent to all others as to me. To see you
too well pleas'd with another is the only hard Condition to which
I cou'd not have submitted. That I did not yield to this is your good
Fortune as well as mine, thô I am worth a great deal more than I
pretended to be, for you will certainly have many offers of those that
are above me in wealth, in wit, in every thing that pleases you, thô
you will never hear of one that loves you more. I shall, as soon as I
am able, cease to be such a Lover, but you will never find me other
than your servant.

[Passage omitted]

I am so foolish in all that relates to you, I cannot forbear thanking
you for this letter, tho it plainly appears in it that all these obliging
expressions are us'd to one that is valu'd very little. Did you ever see
a line from me that did not prove a Passion? ⟨?⟩ will pardon the
impertinence I have now bin guilty of in confirming the past. I coud
not forbear doing it in answer to a letter which seems to be your last.

Text W MS i. 13–15   *Address* To the Right Honble Lady Mary
Pierrepont.   *End. by W* 29 Mar.

To Wortley [2 April 1711]

To receive such a Letter after all I have said, after all
I have done to find so much ill usage, is something surprizing. Had you told me sincerely you thought my fortune too
little, I should have thought You like the rest of the world
and not have wonder'd at your proceeding. Had you told
me I had behavd my selfe too indiscreetly in regard of you,
that I have shewn a fondnesse of you that entirely disgusted
you, however hard, this would have been speaking to be
beleiv'd. But this—this Dissimulation! I thank God, foolish
as I am, I am not yet weak enough to fancy any Man a Lover
that has it in his own power to have a Woman that he has
reason to think does not hate him allwaies with him, and
would not. Let the pretence be what he will, want of Inclination is the true Cause.

And now, since you have no thoughts of makeing me happy, for God's sake do not render me wretched. I know you have no Faith in what I say, but by all that's Sacred I am sincere. Tis with the utmost hazard I send this to you. Should my Father find it out, he is of a humour never to forgive it. Your Letter might have falln into his Hands and then I am ruind. And indeed, why would you write? Why will [you] persecute one that cannot yet perswade her selfe to wish you ill? Suffer me, if possible, to forget a Man that has given me all the uneasy moments of my Life. Do not fancy any thing can perswade me you love me, nor is it of Importance I should beleive it, except tis necessary to your repose I should be wretched. I am now of the Opinion of those I once would not hear, that Had you had any real Affection for me, you would have long ago apply'd your selfe to him from whose hand only you can receive me.

The silly proofes of my Esteem I have given you have been without a thought of your Estate. Could I bring my selfe to value a Man with no other Merit, I might be happier than I am.

I am here alone in a place that I like and where every thing inspires peace and tranquillity. What Injury have I done you to make you poison all the pleasure I should otherwise take in being alone and at quiet?

Do not imagine I shall take it for a Complement to say I have refus'd. I appeal to your selfe, however partial against me, if I have ever us'd you like a property to my Vanity. I have so little, I shall not be mortify'd if you tell people you have refus'd me. Nothing can mortify me after knowing it is so.

[*Postscript*] How hard is it to destroy an Idea that is once fixd! How happy had I been in any part of the world with ⟨?⟩[1]. You have thrown away a Heart you knew not how to value.

Text W MS i. 286–7   *Address* To Mr Wortley at his Lodgings over against the Tavern in Great Queen Street a Looking Glasse Shop   *Postmark* PENY POST PAYD   *End. by W* From P. 2 April.

---

[1] A line here is not visible.

To Wortley [9 *April 1711*]

I thought to return no answer to your Letter, but I find I am not so wise as I thought my selfe. I cannot forbear fixing my Mind a little on that Expression, tho' perhaps the only insincere one in your whole Letter.—I would die to be secure of your Heart tho' but for a moment.—Were this but true, what is there I would not do to secure you?

I will state the case to you as plainly as I can, and then ask your selfe if you use me well. I have shew'd in every Action of my Life an Esteem for you that at least challenges a gratefull regard. I have trusted my reputation in your hands. I have made no scrupale of giving you under my own hand an Assurance of my Freindship. After all this I exact nothing from you. If you find it inconvenient for your Affairs to take so small a fortune, I desire you to sacrifice nothing to me. I pretend no tye upon your Honnour; but in recompence for so clear and so disinterested a proceeding, must I ever receive Injurys and ill usage?

I have not the usual Pride of my Sex. I can bear being told I am in the wrong, but tell it me gently. Perhaps I have been indiscreet; I came young into the Hurry of the World. A great innocence and an undesigning Gaity may possibly have been constru'd Coquettry and a desire of being follow'd, tho' never meant ⟨by⟩ me. I cannot answer for the ⟨?⟩ that may be made on me—all ⟨the⟩ Mallicious attack the carelesse and defencelesse. I own my selfe to be both. I know not any thing I can say more to shew my perfect desire of pleasing you and makeing you easy, than to proffer to be confin'd with you in what manner you pleas'd. Would any woman but me renounce all the world for One, or would any Man but you be insensible of such a proofe of Sincerity?

Text W MS i. 259–60   *Address* To Mr Wortley at his Lodgings over against the Tavern in Great Queen street a Looking Glasse shop   *Postmark* ⟨PENY⟩ POST PAYD   *End. by W* From P. 9 April.

From Wortley [*c. 16 April 1711*]

At last I am ready to confess my Errors, to retract all I have said of you and ask your forgiveness. I own I was very uneasy at the beginning of the last winter when I saw you and Mr. K.[1] pressing so close upon each other in the drawing-room and found that you coud not let me speak to you without being overheard by him. What pass'd between you two at the Trial confirmd my suspicion.[2] T'wou'd be ⟨e⟩ndless to reckon up all the Passages that gave me pain. The second time I saw you at the Play this year I was inform'd of your Passion for him by one that I knew woud not conceal it from others. At the Birthnight you remember the many proofs of your Affection for him and cannot have forgot what pass'd in his favour at the ⟨? Dr.⟩'s Ball. My observing you have since bin present at the Park, Operas, Assemblys together, and absent together, and, to finish all, your contriving to have him for one of that select number that serenaded you at Acton ⟨and⟩ afterwards dancd at the Dutchess's: all this had gone a great way in settling my opinion that he, and none but he, possess'd your heart. But I will now, if you please, acknowlege that all my uneasiness was owing to an excess of Passion and that none but my selfe woud have drawn the same Consequences. So that this Dispute is now over. I confess the fault to have bin in my temper. But at the same time I must have some regard to what was told me by others within these 3 days, by two persons that neither love nor hate nor envy you. They have met you several times in private Companys with that happy Gentleman and both of em plainly discoverd you was in Love with him before they had mention'd it to each other or heard any thing of the story. They tell me it has bin publick for some time and cou'd not have escap'd me had I not bin taken for a Rival. They also confirmd me in an opinion I had form'd from seeing Mr. D. often where you were not, that your familiarities with him were only to hide your fondness of the other. The report, which they say some of your Acquaintance have put about of my being in love with you, may have bin of some use too in this Affair, which cannot be approv'd by your family. Your sending the first letters in such a manner I dont wonder at, since you was quite free from the scandal of being pleas'd with me, and it was not in your power to bring it upon you.

[Passage omitted]

[1] Perhaps Clotworthy Skeffington, LM's most successful suitor (see below, p. 122, n. 1).

[2] The trial may have been that of George Mordaunt, Lord Peterborough's brother, charged with bigamy; on 14 Feb. 1711 he was acquitted (Luttrell, *Hist. Relation*, 1857, vi. 691).

Your father will think I have abus'd him in not applying to him as
I desird leave to do. Telling him the truth wou'd reconcile him to me,
but I will rather do wrong to my selfe than any thing that may hurt
or displease you. When you are married, he shall know it. In the mean
time, tell me, shall I go to him? And what excuse shall I make? Shall
I say in general I have taken exception to your Conduct which others
might not have taken? Whatever you please I will say. I will even
tell him, if you desire it, I cannot engage because I am in straits for
money, tho I woud really pay a great deal more for you than he will
give with you, were it possible to hope I shoud be as well us'd as many
men are. Not going near him is the most uncivil thing I can do; however, without your directions I will do nothing.

I was to blame for saying in my last you had us'd me ill. You never
did, for Love is an Excuse for a Breach of Friendship. I am so far from
being Angry, tho I am griev'd, that I sincerely wish you may ever
enjoy your present happiness of being pursu'd by the man you are in
Love with.

Text W MS i. 30–31

To Wortley [*17 April 1711*]

I have done disputeing with you. ⟨I⟩ am very sorry that
ever I ⟨at⟩tempted it. Had I realy the Inclination you charge
me with, I should not deny it, but I cannot confesse what
I was never guilty of, to make your Accusation appear just.
I know not how to prove it to you otherwise than by my
own words, and I am now very well convinc'd they are of no
force with you. However, I will do my selfe the Satisfaction
of solemnly protesting to you (since tis the last time I shall
say any thing to you) That Gentleman has no interest in my
Heart, nor ever endeavor'd haveing any. I have often seen
him makeing Love to Another, which I suppose he would
not have done before my face, had he had any design upon
me. His comeing to A[cton] was who⟨lly⟩ to[o] without my
knowledge; neither was it to wait upon me, but those that
came with him.—

Here's enough of this Matter. I shall make none of the
complaints another Woman would do. I thank God I can
now refflect on your proceeding without being angry at you.

I have nothing farther to desire but that for your own sake you would do nothing that you must one Day repent of, for I am perswaded no Man of Honnour (which I still beleive you to be) can wrong any one, without sometime feeling a Sorrow for having done it. Except in writeing to you, I know nothing I have done against the knowledge of my Father. I confesse I ought to be punishd for that Indiscretion. I am punish'd, but would it be right in you to complain of a Conduct, which has been only faulty upon your Account? Neither do I think he would take such an Excuse for a Complement. He has now a very good Opinion of you, and I wish he may allwaies retain it. If you Judge it absolutely Necessary to say something, let m⟨e⟩ beg you to find out some other pretence than one that must render my Life uneasy to me. As to what you say of my Acquaintance reporting you a Lover of mine, tis a falsity I never told to any one in the world. I have nothing more to say, but that I wish you all possible Happynesse and my selfe the Quiet of never hearing from you more.

[*Postscript*] I am to thank you for not meeting me at Mrs. St[eele's] as I desird. It would possibly have done me some harm and could do me no good.

Text W MS i. 164–5   *Address* To Mr Edward Wortley Mountague
End. by W 17 Apr.

From Wortley *23 April* [*1711*]

Yorkshire, 23 Apr.

Had I doubted of your Passion, this letter wou'd have convinc'd me. One halfe of it is fill'd with his Praises, the other with your fears of losing him. To make you easy without more delay, I give you my word I will not find fault with your Conduct. I told you in my last very clearly I wou'd do nothing but by your order. As meanly as you think of me, how coud you be persuaded I was capable of changing my resolution so soon? You knew too I coud not disobey you. What need was there of your shewing so much concern about him? You judge right that I envy him extremely, but I am not malicious enough to hurt him when it vexes you. Coud I propose to succeed him, I might do any thing, but you have made it impossible for me to hope it. You know it is not true when you tell me your father woud not be better with me did I give him the true reason of my ceasing to pursue you. You know he woud esteem me for it. But I woud fall out with him and all that are even as considerable as himselfe rather than disobey you in the least of your Commands.

You tell me you shou'd own an Inclination for him if you had it. You are happy in having the man you think worthy of you. You say he is a lover of that Lady's. Your jealousy is not quite so great; you cannot persuade your selfe what no one else does or can believe. Tho you fancy those you despise are neglected by all the world, you can never imagine those you love are welcome to every other. Coud I credit what you solemnly protest of his never having aim'd at you, I shoud be the weakest of all that know him or you. His passing most of his time among the women, his attempting to recommend himselfe to so many, is as well known as your desiring to be follow'd. We happen'd to talk of him; had we been upon Mr. D. you woud have deny'd his making Love to you as solemnly, tho by Accident I have heard of the very words he has us'd, not to mention the whispers, looks, etc., which I have seen and pass for strong assurances from other women. But enough of this happy man; I beg you will say no more of him. Why woud you say nothing but of him?

What you tell me of my not meeting you at Mrs. St[eele]'s was a Continuation of the Subject. You know you was going to dance with him when you call'd there and you gave me no notice of your design to be there, thô you spoke to me but the night before. I might have press'd you to stay too late. I beg I may hear no more of Rivals; if you have no other Subject, say nothing. I cannot desire you to write at all unless to tell me by your selfe, or your servant, you have had this. I woud know I have put you out of Pain. If you add anything to that, I must answer. Converse with me or not according as you fancy. If you give over, I own I may be more uneasy for the present, but in all appearance, shall be sooner free from the disease.

Your letter was unanswerd one post, but I cannot leave off first, tho nothing can now restore my Vanity.

Text W MS i. 16–17 (draft)

From Wortley 25 *April* [1711]

Yorkshire, 25 April.

I cannot avoid thanking you for the 3 lines you sent me the day I left the town, the moment I receive 'em. Had I seen 'em before I

went they had stopt me. I do not presume to hope for an answer to
this. That I writ last Post assurd you of my obedience to your Command. I think you shou'd either by your own hand, or another's, give
your selfe the trouble of owning you had it. If you say more, I must
reply. What I may have writ too freely you ought to pardon, since it
comes from one that has sufferd so much and coud not have come from
one that did not still suffer a great deal.

Text W MS i. 75

To Wortley [*28 April 1711*]

I cannot write and only say I have receiv'd yours; I have
allwaies ten thousand things to say to you, and yet I solemnly
and sincerely desire you to desist writeing. I could wish it
was possible to keep a Correspondance with you without
scandal or discovery, but as that cannot be, in Generosity do
not make me uneasy. There is nothing I would not do to
make you easy. That Gentleman has no interest in my heart,
and yet I think he has as much as he deserves. I have the
vanity to beleive a Man that could engage me must have a
greater share of understanding. Had he desir'd it, it could
never have been, but tis no Lie to assure you, he never
attempted it. Mr. D. is one of those fine people [that] have
the same way of talking to all the Women they see, that
every body suffers and no body esteems. I cannot deny he
has often entertaind me in that manner he does a thousand
others, which I never took to be in earnest because I knew he
never meant it so. I beleive he may have been well with some
women, but I hope they have been women of a charecter
very different to mine. All I know is that there was never
any thing between us but a little raillery. I suppose it will
[be] no hard matter for you to beleive this. I wish I could as
easily clear my selfe from the other. My word is not sufficient
for that, in your Opinion. Time and observation would soon
do it, but then you may imagine me forsaken, or that we
are broke off from some other cause, but it will be impossible
to convince you of the truth.

I have seen enough of the world not to be very fond of it.

I have seen so manny Acquaintance unhappy, and heard so manny secret complaints of Husbands, I have often resolvd never to marry, and allwaies not to Sacrifice my selfe to an Estate. Having done with your Heart, I have no pretensions to yours. As I am, I enjoy every satisfaction but your Conversation. Marrying you is ⟨to⟩ part with every other for that; ⟨that⟩ I once resolvd to do it shews ⟨I⟩ set no common value on it. While I thought you lovd me, I could have liv'd with you in any place or Circumstances. I have but this satisfaction, that one time or other, I am assur'd, you will think of me and regret you have wrong'd me. Adeiu. I desire you not to answer.

Text W MS i. 288–9   *Address* To Mr Edward Wortley Mountague [*in another hand*] at Wortly near Sheffeild Yorkshire Free   *Postmark* AP ⟨?⟩   *End. by W* 28 Apr. Ans. to 25.

From Wortley [*2 May 1711*]

To tell me one of those never endeavour'd to engage you and the other had indeed said fine things but was never in earnest, shews how much you despise me, whether you fancy I shall believe you or not. To think I shall believe you is concluding me a fool. To write it when you fancy I shall not, proves you take me to be unworthy of the lowest degree of your friendship. When you say one of 'em has not understanding enough to charm you, besides the fondness of him you have express'd before me, you forget how you extolld his Cunning to me, which I know you take to be the best sign of a great Genius by the high praises I have heard you bestow on one that is thought to excel in that Faculty. That the other has ever charmd the women you mean, I cannot admit; I am credibly inform'd he has not. He may have bin well with them, as you term it, but not so well as he has bin with you. Why woud you use me thus at parting? Did I not beg you woud not mention em? There are some expressions that relate to one of 'em which you woud agree (were it of any use to dispute with you) to be us'd out of kindness to him, but what have I to do with your concerns? You will say, why then do I answer your letter. I will tell you. It is not to convince you I know how [you] treat me and therefore don't deserve to be so despis'd. I have told you so often and yet I find you ever will despise me and I shall never fancy you do not. Nor is this to express to you the Violence of my Passion; I know it is as impossible

for me to make it appear less as for you to prove that you value me.
I fairly own I have no reason to write but I cannot help it. Every word
of yours that shews you woud be contented with me were it in your
power is an obligation and there is something of that in your letter.
You express very naturally a caution against suffering in your Reputa-
tion upon my account. It requires your utmost skill to do that. However,
I cannot be so unjust as to persuade you to give your selfe any trouble
where you can have no pleasure to pay you. Adieu, Dearest L[ady
M[ary]. This once be assurd you will not deceive me. I expect no
Answer.[1]

Text W MS i. 8–9   *Address* To Lady Mary Pierrepont.   *End. by W*
2 May To P.

To Philippa Mundy[2] [*c. 4 May 1711*]

I begin to discover that I am cursed proud, which amongst
my other innumerable faults, I never found out before.
Nothing else Dear Phil: could hinder me from answering
your Letters the Minute I receive them, but I find I must
have manny Ejaculations for the Grace of Humillity, before
I can bring down my proud stomach to convince you, in
reality, I am very dull and stupid, which I am now forc'd
to do, if I write at all. At length I am content to shew my
Infirmitys, especially being brib'd by the agreablenesse of
your Letter. The Hopes of such another shall prevail, tho'
at the same time, tis mortifying enough to see you so capable
of diverting me, while the greatest power I can have over
you, is to lull you to sleep. Such is my Indolent state, I am
hardly to be wak'd by animateing Hopes and fears, the
Ideas of things past grow faint and Languid, and my
Imagination grows so dull, I cannot form to my selfe one
pleasing castle, my reason not being able to furnish me with
one probable foundation. Thus are all my Facultys so stupify'd that I don't think it at all proper, in speaking of my

[1] W received none, so far as we know, until he wrote again in June 1712.
[2] Philippa (1689–1762), eldest da. of Francis Mundy of Markeaton, Derby-
shire (W. O. Massingberd, *Hist. of the Parish of Ormsby-cum-Ketsby*, [1893], p. 327). Here begins a hitherto unpub-lished correspondence.

selfe, to say Me, but that which ⟨once⟩ was Me, being dead to all most all intents and purposes.

My Dear Phil: if your star carrys you to London, the first step to Paradise,[1] remember your freinds in Distresse, and once Sisters in Affliction, and write often to me, in spight of interruptions and temptations to the contrary. Where ever you are, continue to me your Remembrance and Correspondance, as I shall ever my Freindship, and desire (if I am deny'd othe⟨r⟩ ways) to serve you. So may ⟨?⟩ an Image of the first design of our Creation (as the Parsons say) and live in Paradice till you remove to Heaven.

Text MS M/M 11/5/4   *Address* To Mrs Phillippa Mundy at Osbaston near Leicester Leicestershire by way of London[2] *Postmark* TUXFORD MA 9

To Anne Justice [*c. 4 Aug. 1711*]

I am very glad you divert your Selfe so well. I endeavour to make my Solitude as agreable as I can. Most things of that kind are in the power of the mind; we may make our selves easy if we cannot perfectly happy. The News you tell me very much surprizes me. I wish Mrs B[anks] extreamly well,[3] and hope she designs better for her selfe than a stolen wedding with a Man who (you know) we have reason to beleive not the most Sincere Lover upon Earth; and since his Estate [is] in such very bad order, I am clearly of your Opinion his best course would be to the Army, for I suppose 6 or 7 thousand pound (if he should get that with his Mistrisse) would not set him up again, and there he might possibly establish his Fortune, at least better it, and at worst be rid of all his Cares. I wonder all the young Men in England

[1] In the private language used by the two young ladies, Paradise meant being married to a man one loved, Hell to a man one detested, and Limbo or Purgatory to a man one merely tolerated.

[2] Osbaston Hall, ten miles west of Leicester, had come to Mundy through his wife Philippa Wrightson (John Nichols, *Hist. and Antiquit. of the Co. of Leicester*, 1811, IV, ii. 525). When LM was at Thoresby—the Tuxford postmark shows she was at this time—she had to send her letters by way of London since there was no by-post from Nottingham to Leicester.

[3] Mary Banks (see above, p. 42).

dont take that method, certainly the most profitable as well the noblest. I confesse I cannot beleive Mrs B[anks] so imprudent to keep on any private Correspondance with him. I much doubt her perfect happynesse, if she runs away with him; I fear she will have more reason than ever to say there is no such thing.

I have Just now receiv'd the numbers of the Great Lottery which is drawing.[1] I find my selfe (as yet) among the unlucky, but Thank God the great prize is not come out and there's room for hopes still. Prithee Dear Child, pray heartily for me. If I win, I don't question (in spite of all our Disputes) to find my selfe perfectly happy. My heart goes very much pit a pat about it, but I've a horrid ill bodeing Mind that tells me I shan't win a farthing; I should be very very glad to be mistaken in that case.

I hear Mrs. B[anks] has been at the Spaw; I wonder you dont mention it,—Adeiu my dear, pray make no more excuses about long letters and beleive yours never seem so to me.

Text MS owned by the Duke of Newcastle   *Address* To Mrs Anne Justice at Mr Justices on the pavement at York Yorkshire by way of London   *Postmark* AV 7

To Philippa Mundy [*c. 6 Sept. 1711*]

Your Excuses, dear Phil, are very needlesse, and carry a complimental Air I would have unknown between you and Me. Let us retrench the superfluous ⟨words⟩ of Madam and Ladyship, to give place to the Agreable Freedom of our usual Conversations. I shall never forget the pleasure those conversations gave me, and the eternal Impression made by your good Nature and good Sense, which perswades me 'tis impossible you can ever Die, since all them that have once lov'd you can never do other wise. Beleive your Glasse and your Freinds, and let no Omens or Symptoms discourage

---

[1] In the 'Two Million Lottery' many of the aristocracy subscribed. The draw for prizes was held in London from 1 to 15 Aug. (C. L'E. Ewen, *Lotteries and* *Sweepstakes*, 1932, pp. 136–8; Swift, *Corr.*, ed. H. Williams, 1963–5, i. 257, n. 1).

you. I am Glad to hear of your Ball. Think not of the Grave, the Meditation of declineing Beauties, but look Forward upon the Paradise you may reasonably promise your selfe, and depend upon it, that you have a freind entirely devoted to your Service in

M. P.

Write with entire freedom, and be assur'd I will never shew your Letters to any mortal living.

Text MS M/M 11/5/17   *Address* To Mrs Philippa Mundy at Osbaston near Leicester Leicestershire by way of London *Postmark* TUXFORD SE 10

To Philippa Mundy *25 Sept.* [*1711*]

Realy, my dear Philippa, tho' nobody can have more exalted Notions of Paradise than my selfe, yet if Hell is very tempting, I cannot advise you to resist it, since Virtue, in this wicked World, is seldom any thing but its own reward. I guesse Mr. Chester to be the Man; in point of prudence (contrary to point of Pleasure) you ought Not refuse him.[1] I give you better Counsell than I can take my selfe, for I have that Aversion to Hell, I shall resist it all my Life, tho' without Hope of Paradise, and I am very well convince'd I shall never go to Hell, except 'tis to lead Apes there.[2]

I pray for the Successe of your Endeavors to come to London, where I hope we shall meet, and I be happy in discourseing with you with that Freedom I would discourse with nobody else. You need not doubt my fidelity; I never take notice to any body when I receive a Letter from you, to avoid Enquirys.

Dear Phil, write me longer Letters and be assur'd to my

[1] William Chester (1687–1726) was an intimate friend of Burrell Massing-berd. of South Ormsby, Lincs, who had begun to court Miss Mundy in the autumn of 1710, and who asked Chester to use his good offices with her father (R. E. C. Waters, *Geneal. Memoirs of the Extinct Family of Chester*

of Chicheley, 1878, ii. 604). Either LM misunderstood Chester's role as go-between, or perhaps he was himself a declared suitor.

[2] A proverbial consequence of dying an old maid; used by Shakespeare in *The Taming of the Shrew*, 11. i. 34.

little Power, I will faithfully serve you. My Freindship is more sincere than the Generallity of our Sexe's, and I would do any thing that you could Imagine, of service to you.

I've had a general Hunting Day last Tuesday, where we had 20 Ladys well dressd and mounted, and more Men. The Day was concluded with a Ball. I rid and danc'd with a veiw of Excercise, and that is all—how dull that is!

Dear Phil, adeiu. I'm oblig'd by your Confidence, and you shall never repent it.

Sept. 25.

Text MS M/M 11/5/15   *Address* To Mrs Phillippa Mundy at Osbaston near Leicester Leicestershire by way of London *Postmark* TUXFORD OC 1

To Philippa Mundy [*c. 2 Nov. 1711*]

I am glad, dear Phil: that you begin to find Peace in this world. I dispair of ⟨it⟩, God knows; the Devil ⟨to⟩ pull, and a father to drive, and yet—I don't beleive I shall go to Hell for all that, tho' I have no more hope of Paradice than if I was dead and bury'd a 1,000 Fathom. To say truth, I have been this 10 days in debate whether I should hang or marry, in which time I have cry'd some 2 hours every day, and knock'd my head against the Wall some 15 times; 'tis yet doubtfull which way my resolution will finally carry me.[1]—

So much for my own Affairs; as to my advice concerning yours, you know it allready. Scrupules and demurs are as fatal to some young Women as the Flesh and Devil to others, and there are some proverbs written for our Edification, as Faint heart, etc., nothing venture nothing have, and

[1] Suitors other than W applied to LM's father for her hand. To one of them, an unidentified peer, Lord Dorchester wrote: '. . . haveing had lately occasion to talk seriously to my daughter of marrage, I find she is in very good earnest when she declaires against it, which I am very sory for. What more I can assure Your Lordship from her owne mouth is, that she has not forgott the zeale You exprest for her deliverance onse upon a time [April 1710?] so that she heartely wisshes You a long and perfect happynes, and hopes You'l meet it in somebody [who] deserves and can return Your affection. . . .' (MS in Osborn Collection, Yale University).

Letter of Lady Mary Pierrepont to

From the

PLATE 2

I am glad dear Phil: that
you begin to fine Peace in
this world, I dispair of
God knows, the Devil
wll, & a father to drive
& yet — I don't beleive I
shall go to Hell for all
that, tho' I have no more
hope of Paradice than if
I was dead & bury'd a 1000
Fathom. to say truth, I have
been this 10 days in debate
whether I should hang or
marry. in wch time I have

more of the same Nature. You know where you may have a faithful Messenger—I say no more, you understand me.

Dear Phil, infuse into me notions of Moderate happy-nesse. I am yet so miserable to be incapable of Limbo, and such an Infidel I cannot perswade my selfe there is any such place in the Creation. I rave of nothing but Fire and brim-stone, God help me. For you, if y⟨ou⟩ do abandonn hopes of the pritty Paradice you once plac'd your Heaven in, however may you find another flowing with Milk and Honey, as charming, as Enchanting, and every way worthy of such a Lovely Eve.

Text MS M/M 11/5/11 *Address* To Mrs Phillippa Mundy at Osbaston near Leicester Leicestershire by way of London *Postmark* TUXFORD NO 6

To Philippa Mundy *23 Nov.* [*1711*]

Your obliging interesting Letters, Dear Phil, are some Consolation to a poor distracted Wretch of wretches. My head and my Heart are both very full at this instant. I shall stay in the Country all Winter. I have only such Dark and Dismal prospects of Futurity, I cannot raise my spirits to build one dear castle. My Will is still good to serve you, but Fortune never fails to put it out of my Power to do any thing I propose a pleasure in doing.

'Tis yet dubious whether I go to Hell or no, but while I delay between doubting and choosing, here I stay spending the irretreivable days of youth, in looking upon wither'd Trees and stone walls. I have generosity enough, dear Phil, to wish you in London, tho' I have no hopes of meeting you there; but when you are in the Playhouse, I don't question one powerfull Glance can recall any heart
—if it can be
That any Lover can be false to thee—
And fix it ever yours.

If Predestination carrys me to Hell (Nothing else can), it will [be] a sort of comfort even there to look up and see you in

Heaven, and I shall taste of happynesse by Refflection. The
Consideration you mention goes a great way in tempting me
to prefer Common Hell to the uncommon joyn'd to my
Dispair of Paradice. I'm afraid I jog on to the devil.—Mercy
on me!

Dear Phil: ⟨if⟩ your good Fortune brings you ⟨to⟩ happy
London Town, don't forget your Quondam Sister in Affliction. Write often, long and comforting Letters, to your poor
distressed yet ever Faithfull Freind,

M. P.

Nov. 23.

Text MS M/M 11/5/16   *Address* To Mrs Phillippa Mundy at
Osbaston near Leicester Leicestershire by way of London.
Postmark TUXFORD NO 26

To Philippa Mundy *12 Dec.* [*1711*]

I am glad Dear Phil: you still retain Hopes of seeing
London. I begin to think of it, as I have done of Salisbury
Steeple, when I took the air upon the Downs at 4 year old,
that it runs away from me.

You penetrate to the very bottom of My Heart, my Dear;
I have a Mortal Aversion to be an old Maid, and a decaid
Oak before my Window, leavelesse, half rotten, and shaking
its wither'd Top, puts me in Mind every morning of an
Antiquated Virgin, Bald, with Rotten Teeth, and shaking of
the Palsie. Since therefore Hell must be, why not now?
These cruel Refflections have nothing to do with your for-
tune. Paradise is in your veiw, fresh, young and blooming.
Write but to him with halfe the spirit, Life and agreable-
nesse you do to me, and tis impossible but you must attain
it, at least if he has the good taste I don't doubt him
Master of.

Neither have you any reason to repeat that dismal Poesy
you do—rather remember:

> Ill grounded Passions quickly wear away,
> What's built upon Esteem can ne'er decay.

I prophesy nothing but happynesse if he either sees or hears

from you; he can neither resist your Eyes or Pen, but
Absence and silence are capable of wearing out the strongest
Impressions. My Dear, I heartily thank you for your good
wishes to serve me; a little rats' bane is all the remedy can
be given me. For want of that I go to Hell—Fire, brimstone,
Frosts and burnings, Favours, a Parson and wedding
Cloaths.—Adieu, my Head turns with these Mixtures, but
allwaies fix'd in being Faithfully Yours.

Dec. 12.

Text MS M/M 11/5/8   *Address* To Mrs Phillippa Mundy at
Osbaston near Leicester Leicestershire by way of London.   *Postmark* TUXFORD DE 17

To Mrs. Frances Hewet [*Jan. 1712*]

I have a thousand thanks to give dear Mrs. Hewet for
her news, and, above all, the letter, and I would not have
delaid them but the messenger was in haste, and I was resolv'd
to write you a long scribble.

My advices of Satterday say a Peace will be possitively
concluded;[1] this came from the same hand that writ so contrary Thursday, and I depend very much on the Intelligence. I am charm'd with your Correspondante; I hope tis
a woman and, if it is, I reckon her an Honnor to the sex.
I am in no fear of the Refflection you mention, and being
perfectly innocent, God knows, am far from thinking I can
be suspected—perhaps this is a wrong manner of reasoning, but it has ever been mine. Your news and no news,
I know not what to make of. At present my domestic affairs
are so ill, I want spirits to look abroad. I have got a cold that
disables my eyes and disorders me every other way. Mr.
Mason has ordered me blooding,[2] which I have submitted

[1] Soon after coming into power in
1710 the Tory ministry began to negotiate a treaty to end the War of the
Spanish Succession. 'Sure it will be
worth your while to hear the peace
Treated in the House of Commons . . . .
we talk of nothing but a peace,' Addison
wrote to W on 13 Oct. 1711 (*Letters,*
ed. W. Graham, 1941, pp. 265–6). A
treaty was not signed until 1713 at
Utrecht.

[2] Probably George Mason of Worksop, an apothecary. In 1744 he attended
the Countess of Oxford at nearby
Welbeck Abbey (Lady Oxford to LM,
5 Dec./24 Nov., Harley MS, BM).

to after long contestation. For how stupid I am; I entertain you with discourses of Physic, But I have the oddest Jumble of disagreable things in my head that ever plagu'd poor mortals: a great cold, a bad peace, people I love in disgrace,[1] sore eyes, the horrid prospect of a civil war, and the filthy thought of a potion to take—I beleive no body ever had such a melange before.

Our coachman, dear man, arriv'd safe last night, but when we remove,[2] God only knows. If possible I will wait on you at Clipston,[3] but this Physic may prevent all my good intentions.

My companions[4] are your Servants. I had forgot the Spectators; one is not worth mentioning, the other so plain and so good sense, I wonder any body above 5 year old does not find out he's in the right.

Text Wh MS 439 (transcript)[5]   *End. by Lord Wharncliffe* Copy of W[illiam] Upcott's letter of Ly Mary

To Philippa Mundy [*Jan. 1712*]

I am heartily sorry for the ill Situation of your Affairs, Dear Phil, but am glad tis in my power to give you such full Information about what you desire ⟨to⟩ know. No body knows Harriot ⟨be⟩tter than I do; we are of the same age and us'd to be play fellows in the happy days of ignorance.[6] She is no beauty, but is generally thought very pritty,[7] but

[1] Perhaps the Whig leaders; Marlborough and Walpole were dismissed in Jan. 1712.

[2] On 19 Jan. [1712] Lady Frances Pierrepont wrote to Miss Mundy: 'I thought long before this . . . to have been at London' (M/M 11/5/31).

[3] Clipstone, a village about three miles from Thoresby.

[4] Lady Frances and probably Sarah Chiswell (d. 1726), a childhood friend from Nottingham, who—Lady Frances wrote to Miss Mundy on 19 Nov. [1711]—was staying with them (M/M 11/5/25).

[5] Probably in the hand of John Martin (1791–1855), bibliographer, who assisted Lord Wharncliffe in preparing the 1837 ed. of LM's letters.

[6] Lady Henrietta Cavendish Holles (1694–1755), only da. of 1st Duke of Newcastle, later Countess of Oxford. She lived at Welbeck, near Thoresby, and was a distant relation of LM through their common ancestor the Hon. William Pierrepont (1608–78).

[7] '. . . they say the girl is handsome, and has good sense, but red hair' (Swift, *Journal to Stella*, ed. H. Williams, 1948, p. 407).

crooked to Deformity twice as much as Mrs. Dickey,[1] peevish and ill temper'd, and so stupid, that to a Man of his Wit and Fire she must be Hell to the very centre, beyond the comfort of £22,000 to turn her into Purgatory.[2] I cannot beleive that any mortal capable of being charm'd by a pritty blackey'd Lady of my Acquaintance, can ever descend to the most insipid thing breathing. Tis a meer flying report, as I take it. She may be fatal, but she's no charmer, upon my Word.

The Lottery is drawn, and neither you nor I so happy to gain a Wooden Conveniency. Mis Chiswell won a table, of 6 shillings; you may Judge the beauty of it.[3] I am so unlucky in all sort of busynesses, I have some thoughts of hanging my selfe, none of going to Hell, being resolv'd to endure all extremitys first, tho' I know all my hopes are sly deceivers. My own dispair does not make me Envious, and to see my Dear Phil in Paradice is the sincerest wish of
Your Faithfull Freind.

Text MS M/M 11/5/12   *Address* To Mrs Philippa Mundy at Osbaston near Leicester Leicestershire by way of London.   *Postmark* TUXFORD

To Philippa Mundy [*6 Feb. 1712*]

To day, my Dear Phil:, Feb. 6, am I fancying I see all the Beaux and Belles dressing in a Hurry to make their Bows, and Cursies [*sic*] to the Queen;[4] Your Paradise, and several other paradises, in Fring'd Gloves, embrodier'd Coats, and powder'd wigs in irresistable Curl; Lady Atkyns[5] and her fair Sister tiffing before the Glasse, and wishing for double Charms; while we, my Dear, in our several little Cells are

---

[1] Probably a daughter of Sir Wolstan Dixie, of Market Bosworth, Leics.

[2] By her father's will Lady Henrietta had been left a dowry of £20,000 and lands worth £5,000 a year (S. H. Nulle, *Newcastle: His Early Political Career*, 1931, p. 12).

[3] Besides state lotteries for money, lotteries were held for goods from shops

(*Wentworth Papers*, p. 126; John Ashton, *Social Life in the Reign of Queen Anne*, 1897, pp. 86–87).

[4] The Queen's birthday was officially celebrated on 6 Feb.

[5] Rebecca Maria Dixie (d. 1731), another da. of Sir Wolstan Dixie, m. (1707) Sir Henry Atkins.

perhaps more happy than they, at least more easy. If nothing pleases, in our solitary walks, at least nothing offends, while a favourite, ill pinn'd up, goes to the very heart of them, and an ill natur'd blast of Wind as they enter the drawing room, enough to discompose their Looks and humours for all Day.

Notwithstanding all the Charms of Quiet, I hope in a Little while you will exchange them for Pleasures more touching, and that I may soon see you in Town, happy in your present Paradice, or some other, every way as pleasing. For me, I begin my Journey next Tuesday, and am fretting at the Thought of not passing by Leicester.

> I know the Fate of those by Interest wed,
> Doom'd to the Curse of a vexatious Bed,
> Days without Peace, and Nights without Desire,
> To mourn, and throw away my Youth for hire.
> Of Noble Maids, how wretched is the Fate!
> Ruin'd with Jointures, curs'd by an Estate,
> Destin'd to Greifs, and born to be undone,
> I see the Errors which I cannot shun.
> Pity my Fate, disclos'd to you alone,
> And weep those Sorrows which may be your own.

[*Postscript*] Direct to Arlington street, near St. James, London. Write soon and burn this.

Text MS M/M 11/5/9   *Address* To Mrs Philippa Mundy at Osbaston near Leicester Leicestershire by way of London   *Postmark* TUXFORD FE 13

To Philippa Mundy [*c. 11 Feb. 1712*]

Having all along design'd for Stamford Road, this morning the Coachman learn't by a Brother the way was better to Leicester, contrary to what he had before told me. My Dear Phil: cannot imagine how much I am vex'd to be here without hope of seeing her. I fear 'twill be too late for you to set out now, and to Morrow we persue our Journey by Day break. This is what writeing tackle the Inn affords, and my head and hand are both disorder'd with Fateigue, both of mind and body.

Text MS M/M 11/5/10   *Address* To Mrs Phil: Mundy at Osbaston. wth Care.

To Philippa Mundy *27 Feb.* [*1712*]

If I could have given Dear Phil: any Account of her Affairs or my own, I should not be so tedious in my Intelligence, but I am so melancholy, and see so few people, I know nothing of what passes in the World. I have been at Neither Opera nor Playhouse, nor don't intend it, and have but once (as Necessity requir'd) appear'd at the Drawing room. I look'd for your Paradice, but he was absent, and I had neither Pleasure nor Interest to move me to a Look upon the Croud. I make no enquiry for after News, and the little that is told me, I regard so little, I forget it the Minute after I have heard it.

Dear Philippa, I hope your Fortune will be kinder than your Fears, and that I shall see [you] in London, and we may passe some hours together, which however Melancholy will have something in them pleasing, since pass'd with you. Pray write, and depend upon't, reading your Letters will please me better than any thing I see here. My Dear, Adeiu. Feb. 27.

Text MS M/M 11/5/13   *Address* To Mrs Phillippa Mundy at Osbaston near Leicester Leicestershire   *Postmark* ⟨?⟩

To Mrs. Frances Hewet [*c. 8 March 1712*]

Arlington-street.

I do not doubt, but that before this time, my dear Mrs. Hewet has a thousand times called me ungrateful, and as often repented of the many kindnesses she has done me in the country. *Les apparences sont trompeuses*—I am as much your servant as ever, and think of you with the friendship and acknowledgment I owe you. A train of disagreeable events have hindered my having one leisure moment, and at this very time my poor head is distracted with such a variety of *gallimatias*, that I cannot tell you one bit of news. The fire I suppose you have had a long and true account of, though not perhaps that we were raised at three o'clock, and kept waking 'till five, by the most dreadful sight I ever saw in my life. It was near enough to fright all our servants half out of their senses; however, we escaped better than some of our neighbours.[1] Mrs. Braithwayte, a Yorkshire beauty, who had been but two days married to a Mr. Coleman,[2] ran out of bed *en chemise*, and her husband followed her in his, in which pleasant dress they ran as far as St. James's street, where they met with a chair, and prudently crammed themselves both into it, observing the rule of dividing the good and bad fortune of this life, resolved to run all hazards together, and ordered the chairmen to carry them both away, perfectly representing both in love and nakedness, and want of eyes to see that they were naked, our first happy parents. Sunday last I had the pleasure of hearing the whole history from the lady's own mouth.

The next most extraordinary adventure is the famous quarrel between her grace of Hamilton with captain Hero; but I suppose you cannot be ignorant of so surprising an event.[3]

Deaths nor marriages I know of none, but sir Stephen Evans, that hanged himself,[4] and my sister Evelyn, who will

---

[1] On 2 March 1712 the house of Sir William Wyndham (1687–1740), Tory politician, in Albemarle Street burned down; and two maids who jumped from a window were killed (Swift, *Journal to Stella*, ed. H. Williams, 1948, pp. 502–3; *Wentworth Papers*, pp. 274–5, 276).

[2] Neither is identified.

[3] Elizabeth Gerard (1682–1744), da. of 5th Baron Gerard, m. (1698) 4th Duke of Hamilton (who was killed in Nov. 1712 in his notorious duel with Lord Mohun); and James O'Hara (1682–1773), later 2nd Baron Tyrawley.

The quarrel took place 'at the play house . . . soe loud, that every body heard it, with such language as is seldom used but at Billingsgate, and he taking it in the best manner that could be, laughing extreamly at her' (*Wentworth Papers*, p. 276).

[4] Sir Stephen Evance, goldsmith and jeweller since 1684, and in 1710 listed as Jeweller to the Queen, went bankrupt at the beginning of 1712 (A. Heal, *London Goldsmiths 1200–1800*, 1935, p. 148; J. Chamberlayne, *Magnae Britanniae Notitia*, 1710, p. 544; Swift, *Journal to Stella*, p. 462). According to

be married next week.[1] The post bell rings; my next shall
be longer, with some account of your fair family.

Text 1805, v. 235–7[2]

To Philippa Mundy [*c. 20 March 1712*]

I have been so taken up with wishing Joy, and assisting
at the ceremonys that put 2 people in Limbo,[3] I have hardly
had time to look about me. I had however one Glance of
your Paradice who look'd as handsome as an Angel. I cannot
help thinking you are predestin'd to meet at last. For me,
'Hopes I have none, for I am all Dispair'. I have no choice
but Hell, or Leading Apes,[4] nor is that hardly a Choice, since
the first seems determin'd.

> Love, what a poor Omnipotence hast thou,
> When Gold and Titles buy thee!

My own Dispair does not damp my Zeal to serve you, and
if ever (which I'll endeavor) Fortune leads me in Companny
with your Paradice, I will refresh the charming Idea of you
in such a Manner, as shall easily betray his heart through
his Eyes, and yet not permit him to guesse my knowledge
of any thing.

I tell you nothing of the News of the Town, which I suppose, Dear Phil:, is as indifferent to you as it is to me.

My Dear, I wish you all kind of Happynesse, I'm sure
you deserve a great deal. I confesse that is a bad Omen,
But I hope Fortune in your Favour will change her Course
and once reward the Meritorious.

Text MS M/M 11/5/5   *Address* To Mrs Phillippa Mundy at
Osbaston near Leicester Leicestershire.   *Postmark* MR 2⟨?⟩

Peter Le Neve, he shot himself in the
temple (*Pedigree of Knights*, ed. G. W.
Marshall, Harleian Soc., viii, 1873,
p. 435).
    [1] On 13 March 1712 she was married
in London to John Leveson-Gower
(1694–1754), Baron, later 1st Earl,
Gower.

[2] MS sold at Sotheby's on 26 June
1829, lot 196.
    [3] Her sister Evelyn's marriage to Lord
Gower.
    [4] 'Leading Apes': remaining a spin-
ster, as LM had remarked six months
earlier.

To Philippa Mundy [*c. 25 March 1712*]

My Dear Phil: will wonder at seeing my hand again so soon, when she knows the Hurry I am in, in this damn'd Town, but I was resolv'd nothing should hinder me giving you an Account of a shock I receiv'd last Sunday in Hide Park. I saw your Paradise in Hell, I beleive, for he had the Devil of a Bride in a fine chariot. He has been wedded and bedded some time, and was so last time I saw him but I did not know it. The real concern I have for every thing touches you, made me fall into a deep Melancholy at a sight that I knew must give you some. At the same time, I made Refflections on the Folly and contemptible Falsehood of that designing Sex, and concluded they are certainly our Inferiors in good Sense, as well as most other Merit, since tis plain we have a truer taste of Happynesse.

> Vows, Oaths, and Contracts they devise,
> And Tell us they are sacred Tyes,
> And so they are, in our Esteem,
> But empty Names dispis'd by them.[1]

All that pleases me is that their Punishment is annex'd to their Crime; they are wretched from the Minute they are guilty, and those that barter a Heaven of Mutual Love and retir'd Happynesse (the Paradice we have so often talk'd over) for the silly shine of Equipage, and haveing it in their power to be formost in a croud, commit an Error against Judgment, as well as Honesty.

My Dear Phillippa, receive this Letter (which it vexes my Soul to send you) without much trouble, look upon his Falsehood as a vice inherent to his Sex, and depend upon it:

> That Man is Man, and all the Sex is One,
> Nor in Love's Ritual can we ever find
> Vows made to Last, or promises to bind.

I own this Accident will make me support Hell with more patience. Since it was possible to be unjust to so much Youth, Beauty, Wit, and tendernesse as you have, no body else has

---

[1] Edmund Waller, *The Maid's Tragedy Altered*, 1690, p. 31.

any thing to expect, and after sacrificeing an Age of Bloom and Innocence, I should expect to be forsaken and forgotten. Poets are seldom guilty of much truth, and yet I beleive he discover'd the very inside of his Sex that said:

> The Fire we boast, with force uncertain burns,
> And breaks but out as Appetite returns.

There is their true Charecter, strangers to our softnesse, truth, and fondnesse:

> By Nature prompted, and for Empire Made,
> Alike by Strength and Cunning they invade;
> Their Falsehood and their Arms have equal use,
> As they their Conquest or delight produce.

This Example, and halfe a dozen more, have determin'd me to submit to Hell, tho' with all due Horror.

My Dear, write to me.

Text MS M/M 11/5/2

To Philippa Mundy [*April 1712*]

If your Paradice (Dear Phil:) could see your last letter, so much softnesse and good sense would certainly shew him the Folly he has committed, so plainly as to make him hang himselfe.

My Refflections on the genneral Inconstancy and Ingratitude of Men proceed from no Experience in my own Affairs. I should be happyer than I am if I had not too much reason to think too well of one of them. I see no probable prospect of my ever entering Charming Paradice, but since I cannot convince him of the Necessity of what I do, I rack my selfe in giving him pain. This is the real state of my Heart, which is now so much perplex'd and divided, I change Resolves every 3 minutes. The apparent impossibillity of dear Paradice often makes me resolve to plunge to Hell and lose the Thought for ever. Sometimes I am on the point of determining to lead Apes, tho' I have much reason to fear the Consequence of that will be a settlement in the Country, and then perhaps after that mighty Sacrifice, I may find my selfe at one time wither'd and forgotten. These alternate Thoughts fight battles in my Breast; mean time I see daily preparations for my journey to Hell.[1] Something I must resolve on suddenly.—My head is so perplex'd I forgot to tell you, I have made enquirys concerning your Murdresse. No body says she is an agreable Woman; I suppose you know she was a great Fortune, and marry'd him for Love.

Text MS M/M 11/5/1   *Address* To Mrs Phillippa Mundy at Osbaston near Leicester Leicestershire.   *Postmark* AP ⟨?⟩

To Wortley [? *c. 7 June 1712*]

I was never more surpriz'd in my Life than at seeing a Letter from you.[2] I am willing to beleive only Curiosity made me weak enough to receive it.

In the whole course of your commerce with me I do not think you have allways done right to me, but I do not think you have ever deceiv'd me. Whatever you have to ask me, I shall answer you with the greatest sincerity. Nothing can be more hazardous than meeting you, but I am willing to remove some mistakes of your Letter. Indian Houses[3] are too public, nor at all proper for a long conversation. I will go Tuesday between 6 and 7 to Sir Godfrey Kneller's.[4] I set a real value on your freindship, and hope I shall never lose it.

Text W MS i. 242–3   *Address* To Mr Edward Wortley Mountagu with care and speed

[1] Her father had engaged her to Clotworthy Skeffington (*c.* 1681–1739), son and heir of 3rd Viscount Massereene, an Irish peer (James Brydges to Anthony Hammond, 29 Aug. 1712, *Times Lit. Suppl.*, 4 Sept. 1937). Skeffington was M.P. for Co. Antrim 1703–14.

[2] Apparently the first letter since that of [2 May 1711].

[3] Shops where Indian goods were sold.

[4] Kneller (1646–1723), the most fashionable portrait painter at the time, had lived in Great Queen Street since about 1704 (George Vertue, *Note Books*, Walpole Soc., xviii, 1930, p. 28).

To Wortley [*11 June 1712*]

I was at Sir G[odfrey] K[neller]'s yesterday a quarter after 7. It was so long after the time I had name'd I went allmost without expecting you, but I was unavoidably hinder'd comeing sooner. I cannot go there again soon, without giving suspicion to my Compannion. If I should meet you in a private house, I must trust the mistresse of it, and I know no body I dare trust. A formal visit will not permit us to talk. I cannot speak to you but before Wittnesses, and I chuse rather to tell you in this way that your Letter seems founded on a Mistake. I did not ask you to write, nor desire to see you. As my Circumstances are, I know no use it can be to me. I am very far from a thought of what you seem to hint at the end of your Letter. My Family is resolv'd to dispose of me where I hate. I have made all the Opposition in my power; perhaps I have carry'd that opposition too far. However it is, things were carry'd to that height, I have been assur'd of never haveing a shilling, except I comply. Since the Time of Mandana's we have heard of no Ladys ran away with, without fortunes.[1] That Threat would not have oblig'd me to consent, if it had not been joyn'd with an Assurance of makeing my Maiden Life as miserable as lay in their power, that is so much in their power I am compell'd to submit.—I was b⟨orn to⟩ be unhappy, and I must fullfill the course of my Destiny—

You see, Sir, the Esteem I have for you. I have ventur'd to tell you the whole secret of my Heart. Tis for the last time I indulge my selfe in complaints, that in a little while will become indecent. By this real and sincere Account of my Affairs you may ⟨see I⟩ have no design of any Engagement beyond freind⟨ship⟩ with you, since should we agree, tis now impossible, my fortune only following my obedience.

---

[1] Mandane, the heroine of Madeleine de Scudéry's *Artamène ou le Grand Cyrus* (1649–53), who in the course of the long romance is abducted several times before being won by Cyrus. LM's library in 1739 contained the *Grand Cyrus* in 10 vols. (Wh MS 135); and she had read it as early as 1705, when she listed its characters in a notebook (H MS 250).

Tis utterly inconvenient for you to write to me; I know no safe way of conveying a Letter to me. After this long Account, I don't suppose you have any farther enquirys to make, nor in my wretched circumstances is there room for Advice. If you have any thing to say (tho ⟨I cannot⟩ imagine what it should be) I will be at Coleman's friday between 4 and 5. I cannot be more exact; it may be very soon after 4, or very near 5. If you have nothing to say, or that now you know the true state of my Affairs you find Advice can be of no importance, do not come. I shall ever think you my Freind, and never give you Occassion to be otherwise. My busynesse is now to behave my selfe with my fortune, in a manner to shew I do not deserve it.—

Text W MS i. 176–7   *Address* To Mr Edward Wortley Mountague.

To Wortley [*c. 15 June 1712*]

I was told last night you desir'd to speak to me. It may possibly not be so, but however I will answer ⟨you⟩ as if I thought it was.—

⟨Witho⟩ut makeing a confidance with the people of the house, tis impossible to talk long either at Indian houses or painters'. Assemblys are no more, and should I meet you at a visit, the sense of the silly figure I should make would render that very indiscretion to no purpose, and I should not be able to speak to you. Neither can I guesse what it is you have to say to me. My circumstances are directly what I told you. I know of no advice can be given me. You said you had a great deal to say to me. If ⟨?⟩ to hear it, I know not how to ⟨find an⟩ Opertunity.

I have thought of a way to receive a Letter from you, but tis too dangerous to be us'd above once. I am very much watch'd, and particularly on your Account, some part of my family being perswaded you are the secret cause of my resisting their commands. I won't make you that complement. If you had never been born, I should have acted on that point exactly as I have done. I am perswaded the Man they force me to is of a humour to suffer me to do what I please, but what is Liberty to one that carrys her goaler in her breast? My Duty is more a chain to me than all others that could be impos'd on me.

Direct to Mr. Cassotti, at Mr. Roberts at the Queen's head in Litchfeild street, Soho. He is my Italian master.[1] I have made a kind of plausible pretence to him for one Letter to come that way, but I dare not trust him.

Text W MS i. 186–7   *Address* To Mr Edward Wortley Mountagu

From Wortley [*16 June 1712*]

I have bin for some time grievd to hear you was to be confind to one you did not like and in another country, but if the case is as you tell it, that you are to do what you please, I fancy the goaler you speak of will hurt you very little. I am not clear in it that you shoud not comply and cannot advise you against it. But if you say this as you have done many other things, because it is well said, and the real truth is that you are to be confind by such a one, follow the advice of one that knows something of mankind and has a real concern for you: think no more of this match. There is scarce any instance of a woman so fetterd that has not thought herselfe very miserable. Your relations, I am sure, whatever they threaten, will never treat you barbarously. They will, for their own sakes if not for yours, take as good care of you as they do now and if they coud be cruel they woud, however, give something to dispose of you, but they cannot offer to punish you for what the world will praise you. [*Passage omitted*]... for my part, I woud not marry a Queen [if] I did not love her as well as any one living, were I to be debard from choosing my company. But least you shoud differ with me in this notion and fancy me no ill match, tho you know it can be on no other terms than of being chang'd from a fine Court Lady into a plain Country Wife, and because I am satisfy'd this affair is not so very much determind as you make it, after having said so much about you (which perhaps was needless because your opinion is the same with mine) I will say a little of my selfe and that with the greatest truth and plainness.

If I marry I must have more liberty over my estate than your father seem'd willing I shoud, tho I was ready to go higher than men have done unless in the case of a Duke or perhaps a Lord or two. But

[1] Since 1710 (see above, p. 21).

those instances are of no weight with me. I shoud be more desirous of being allied your father were he a Squire than as he is. Don't take it ill that I shoud be for a reasonable settlement when you know, considering how you have carri'd yourselfe, the hazard I run of seeing you dislike me is visibly great. I woud not be uneasy in my fortune as well as my companion if I shoud not be well us'd. But if they wou'd make me easy in this I cannot say I am yet ready to close. I have a private affair of moment on my hands which may not be ended in less than two months and may oblige me to be abroad a part of the time. I woud willingly see this over and be satisfy'd the Publick will not be in Confusion before I take the care of a family upon me. And if all these objections were over, how can I promise you will convince me you are to be rely'd on after I have so often found you made a fool of me? So that upon the whole you ought not to alter your opinion about this match with any view towards me. I have said what seem'd most necessary (in as few words as I cou'd) because you tell me I must send but one letter. When I say this I know how simple it woud be to write all this and in such a homely blunt manner to any but one that knows I admire her more than I do any one living, and that I am capable of Loving her to excess. After thus much I want to say more but will tire you no longer.

This I writ yesterday when your letter came. I fancy I judg'd right, thô I did not dare to send it. After having slept upon it I find I dont yet know my own mind. Tell me as much of yours as you can; perhaps that may govern me. Sure you will be very plain if I am to write no more.

Tuesday Morn.

Whatever becomes of me I coud not lose the pleasure of seeing you at the park, but my friend is out of town, my own equipage is out of repair because I dont know when I shall live in town again, and for 3 or 4 days it woud look odd to fit it up.

Text W MS i. 44–45 (draft)

To Philippa Mundy [*21 June 1712*]

Dear Phil:

I beleive you wonder you have not heard from me so long; for my part, I wonder you hear from me now. I am in so manny distractions, I am by turns raveing and stupify'd, both improper times to write in. Judge how

incapable I am of adviseing. At the same time I am ready
to hang as the only way to avoid Hell, it would sound very
strange to advise another thither, but your case and mine
are widely distant. You are dead and bury'd, and tho' I am
as much barr'd the Entrance of Paradise as if I was dead,
yet I cannot make any Advances to Hell, without allmost
killing Paradise. All these things put together, I beleive you'l
agree with me, that I run mad with a great deal of reason.
In your Circumstance, I should call pride to my Aid, dresse,
look handsomer than ever and go to Hell with a very good
Air. I think this is the best advice I can give. For me, I pine
and pine, and am (I fear) every day nearer Hell than I was
the Day before.

Dear Phil: I long to see you, with a great deal of Impatience. My good wishes ever attend you.

Let me hear soon how your destiny is to be determin'd.

Text MS M/M 11/5/14   *Address* To Mrs Phillippa Mundy at
Osbaston near Leicester Leicestershire   *Postmark* IV 21

To Wortley [*c. 7 July 1712*]

If there was any thing in my last that you have a mind to
answer, tis impossible it can be by the same Direction. I shall
be Thursday at Lady Jekyl's. You visit her. If you come
there, you may find a way to give me a Letter. Let there be
nothing in it to require an Answer. Tis so very dangerous for
me to write to you, I tremble every time I do it. If you come
your visit must appear by chance, and we must not speak
in particular. That Lady is my Freind, but in my Circumstances, without it were possible to look into my heart,
I should not blame her if she thought very ill of such an
Appointment.

Text W MS i. 205–6   *Address* To Mr Edward Wortley Mountagu.

To Wortley [*10 July 1712*]

Thursday

I am more unlucky than any other body, and therefore I ought not to be surpriz'd at my Lady J[ekyll] sending me an excuse this Morning. You have so ill an Opinion of me, you may imagine I am to blame. It is usual in you to ascribe to me the faults of my ill fortune. She desires me to come to her next Satterday. I will go, but if you have been this Afternoon and should go again Satterday she might guesse the truth. I will make a 2nd Appointment when I am there what day you please, and you may come. You must answer this to let me know. I have no other direction, but the same must be venture'd again, tho' I tremble while I suffer you to do it.

In your last you seem to think I affect to place things in a nearer light than they are. I wish you may not be convinc'd of my truth fattally for my repose.

Text W MS i. 236–7   *Address* To Mr Edward Wortley Mountagu
End. by W From P. 14 July 1712

To Philippa Mundy [*15 July 1712*]

You are, however, tolerably happy, my Dear Phil, since Limbo is like to be your Fate, and Paradise not obstructing your Passage, since he has render'd himselfe unworthy of that Name.

> But I th'unhappiest of Womankind
> No help can hope, no Remedy can find,
> But doom'd to drag a restlesse Life in Care,
> And all my pleasures poison'd with Dispair.

This Quotation suits me too justly. I confesse to you the Suplications of Paradice, and the Pain I saw him in, at length rais'd my Spirit to oppose vigorously my progresse to Hell, but all my Opposition was vain, and all the Difference I could obtain was making it yet worse. Instead of going I

shall be drag'd to the lowest of Hells,[1] without the pleasure
of satisfying Paradise, who would perswade me to continue
Resisting. Tis certain the worst could befall me would be
Eternal Confinement. But you that have some degree of
knowledge of that kind of Life can Judge what a terrible
thing it must be for ever, since I can see no kind of probabillity of my entering Paradise except Miracles happen;
but if Miracles should happen, Distraction and Dispair,
I shall curse my selfe for not prefering every suffering, to
what I am now going to do.

This is a long Account of my Affairs; I hope you will be
as free in communicateing Yours. Be assur'd, my Dear Phil,
you cannot do it to a freind more entirely Yours than
                                                        M. P.

Text MS M/M 11/5/18   *Address* To Mrs Phillippa Mundy at
Osbaston near Leicester Leicestershire.   *Postmark* IY 15

To Wortley [*17 July 1712*]

Thursday

I have but just this minute receiv'd your letter. I see it
was writ Tuesday, but there is a g⟨reat⟩ deal of uncertainty
in my receiving letters this way. I am to be the whole
Afternoon with Lady J[ekyll] next Satterday.

You have not that confidence in me that you ought to
have. I tell you exactly Truth. Nothing is more in my power
than I say. Was I to chuse my Destiny (tho' I am sincere
enough to acknowledge, there are parts of your Humour I
could wish otherwise) I had rather be confine'd to a desart
with you than enjoy the highes⟨t of⟩ Rank and fortune in a
cou⟨rt with⟩ him I am condemn'd to. This is trusting you
with a very plain confession, but no great complement. I
have no notion of happynesse with a disagreable companion.

If you come to Lady J—— you may find a way to give
me a Letter.

[1] On 19 July her friend Mrs. Hewet
gossiped: 'Lady M. Perpoint is not yet
maryed but is to be very soon, before
Lord Do[rchester] coms to Nottinghamshire' (to the Duchess of Newcastle,
Portland MS at Longleat, xiv. 8).

[*Postscript*] I am sorry to open my Letter to tell you Lady J—
has sent this minute to me to say she is obligd to go into
Hartfordshire[1] on Satterday, and desires me to put off the
appointment till some day next week. I begin to be perswaded there is a destiny that hinders our meeting, like every
other pleasure to one so unfortunate as I am. I must once
more venture to hear from you this way.

Text W MS i. 219–20   *Address* To Mr Edward Wortley Mountagu.

To Wortley [*22 July 1712*]

Tuesday

I am very sorry that you have been ill, but as I suppose it
was nothing more than this Fever, I hope tis allready over.
You do me wrong in fancying ill health capable of lessening
my Freindship for any one. There is something of a softnesse in my temper that rather inclines me to think more
favourably of them when they are in a condition to move
compassion.

The Dutchesse entertain'd me from the Garden to London
with your praises. As no body knows better how to make
their court, I suspected she guess'd she was makeing her
selfe agreable to me. However, I had rather trust her than
Mrs. St[eele], for manny reasons. I intend to go there to
morrow in the Afternoon. If you come there, the best way
of speaking to me will be to excuse it to her with some compliment, and then ask me aloud to hear what you have to say
for the last time. I will answer you that you need not be
very solicitous about it, since with my Lady D[uchess]'s
leave, as odd as it might look, I had something to say to you.
We may go into the next room, for I beleive the conversation
may be very long.

I don't beleive she'll speak of me, or if she should, if we
agree, I'm sure it signifies nothing. If we do not, I shall be
so soon dispos'd of, it can do me no harm. Going in to the

---

[1] Sir Joseph Jekyll's seat was Brookmans, North Mimms, Herts (*DNB*).

next room will be more convenient for us than whispering, and I think civiller to the companny.

All your Letters came to me together. Adeiu. I hope you are well.

Text W MS i. 238–9   *Address* To Mr Edward Wortley Mountagu

From Wortley [?22 *July 1712*]

I am so far from disputing whether you have an esteem for me that I will own it is not easy for any one to persuade me you have not. There is always something of it (tho often to no great degree) when a man has lov'd as I have done, when althô ill usage or absence has made the passion easier it has always got strength again upon a prospect of better treatment. While you mention your Esteem you do not assure me you can comply with all the terms I have demanded, which are absolutely necessary for my quiet. You are in the right in not consenting to 'em. They seem hard for you to perform, and unless you are sure you can perform you will be much in the right to take the other rather than me, tho you have an aversion to him. Thô you seem not willing to comply with me in 'em I will not resolve against engaging with you till I hear from you again.

You have done right to satisfy me in one point, that what we do must be without your relations; and I affirm to you in answer I shall like that way full as well as the other, perhaps a great deal better. But whether any assurances you can give me will prevail with me to engage, I cannot tell. [*Passage omitted*] Tell your mind as plainly as I do. If you think you must speedily quit one of us, there can be no great hazard in trusting some woman with seeing us talk together on Tuesday or Wedensday. If you can't, get Mrs. Steele to be at home or to meet you, who has now a house in Bloomsberry Square, the 5th door on the right hand as you look towards Southampton-house.[1] The Dutchess you was with is goodnatur'd and I fancy woud never talk of such a thing. If my terms are too hard, spare your selfe the trouble of meeting me; it will give me pain and can do you no good. Your letter seems writ on Friday, but came not till to day. If Mr. Cassotti puts your letters into the post, why may he not leave 'em here?

Text W MS i. 22–23   *Address* To the Rt Honble the Lady Mary Pierrepont   Great care and speed.

[1] The Steeles had moved from Bury Street. On 15 July Steele mentioned their new house, and by 8 Aug. was living there (*Corr.*, pp. 277–8). Southampton House occupied the north side of Bloomsbury Square.

From Wortley [*23 July 1712*]

[*Passage omitted*] The Marriage of my kinsman has, I hope, furnish'd an example that will put an end to the disputes about our settlement. What his is I cant yet learn, but I shall never desire to be easier than one whose condition is so like my own, and your family must own themselves to be unreasonable if their demands are higher than those of the Lady's relations, who are very prudent people and skilful in managing their affairs. Whatever terms might be insisted on I coud not for a moment delay to close with them were I convinc'd of your Esteem, but unless I am better assur'd of that, I may perhaps be able to wait till I hear your family will not be too rigorous with me. [*Passage omitted*]

Is not Mrs. Hampden's a better place than Lady J[ekyll]'s? I have seen other meetings of the same nature at Mrs. H.'s and she is not censorious nor in the least given to tell what she observes. She is, too, very much my friend.

Wednesday Morn. 9 a clock.

Text W MS i. 59–60   *Address* To the Rt Honble the Lady Mary Pierrepont.

To Wortley [*c. 24 July 1712*]

You certainly beleive me very little. I don't suppose my familly would insist on better terms than your kinsman's, but I have allready told you, tis now to no purpose to talk of terms. I am too well convince'd they will not hear of any. If you persist in disbeleiving me, I know no way to be convince'd but trying. I am unhappily assur'd of the Answer you will meet, that you speak too late. Tis never too late for me to save my selfe from Ruine, but that is not what they think of.—

I do not understand what you call an Air of Sincerity. I speak, I am sure, with truth, I think with plainesse. To what end should I deceive you? I am not perswadeing you to make proposalls to my Familly; I know (and I freely confesse) it is too late for any hopes that way. I have neither folly nor vanity enough to suppose you would think of running away with me, and, in my Situation, perhaps it would be more prudent to tell you what is doing is with my own consent, and affect to be pleas'd with it. I have done with my pretensions to Happynesse. The Esteem I have for you makes me own it to you. As a Freind I shall ever be glad to see you, however melancholy my circumstances are.

I am very sorry I don't visit Mrs. Hampden.[1] She made me some advances last winter, but these affairs put me so much out of humour I was not gay enough to think of makeing new acquaintance. I shall go to Kensington Gardens,[2] but I cannot name exactly the day. If you have any inclination to see me, you may go every Evening, Satterday, Monday, and Tuesday. One of those days we may possibly meet. To a place like that, I cannot go alone. You may make by your manner our meeting appear accidentall to those with me. I go this Evening to Lady J[ekyll]. I am afraid you won't have this letter time enough to come. I receiv'd yours this minute.

Text W MS i. 180–1

To Wortley [*c. 26 July 1712*]

I am going to write you a plain long letter. What I have allready told you is nothing but the truth. I have no reason to beleive I am going to be otherwaies confine'd than by my Duty, but I, that know my own Mind, know that is enough to make me miserable. I see all the Misfortune of marrying where it is impossible to Love. I am going to confesse a weaknesse [that] may perhaps add to your contempt of me. I wanted courrage to resist at first the Will of my Relations, but as every day added to my fears, Those at last grew strong enough to make me venture the disobliging them. A harsh word damps my Spirits to a degree of Silenceing all I have to say. I knew the folly of my own temper, and took the Method of writeing to the disposer of me. I said every thing

---

[1] See above, pp. 74, 76.   Kensington Square (see below, p. 148,
[2] W probably lived at this time in   n. 2).

in this Letter I thought proper to move him, and proffer'd
in attonement for not marrying whom he would, never to
marry at all. He did not think fit to answer this letter, but sent
for me to him. He told me he was very much surpriz'd that
I did not depend on his Judgment for my future happynesse,
that he knew nothing I had to complain of etc., that he did
not doubt I had some other fancy in my head which encour-
rag'd me to this disobedience, but he assur'd me if I refus'd
a settlement he has provided for me, he gave me his word,
whatever proposalls were made him, he would never so
much as enter into a Treaty with any other; that if I founded
any hopes upon his death, I should find my selfe mistaken—
he never intended to leave me any thing but an Annuity of
£400;[1] that tho' another would proceed in this manner, after
I had given so just a pretence for it, yet he had goodnesse
to leave my destiny yet in my own choice;—and at the same
time commanded me to communicate my design to my
Relations and ask their Advice.—

As hard as this may sound, it did not shock my resolution.
I was pleas'd to think at any price I had it in my power to be
free from a Man I hated. I told my Intention to all my
nearest Relations; I was surpriz'd at their blameing it to the
greatest degree. I was told they were sorry I would ruin my
selfe, but if I was so unreasonable they could not blame my
F[ather] whatever he inflicted on me. I objected I did not
love him. They made answer they found no Necessity of
Loveing; if I liv'd well with him, that was all was requir'd
of me, and that if I consider'd this Town I should find very
few women in love with their Husbands and yet a manny
happy. It was in vain to dispute with such prudent people;
they look'd upon me as a little Romantic, and I found it
impossible to perswade them that liveing in London at
Liberty was not the height of happynesse. However, they
could not change my thoughts, tho' I found I was to expect
no protection from them. When I was to give my final answer
to [my Father] I told him that I prefer'd a single life to
any other, and if he pleas'd to permit me, I would take that
Resolution. He reply'd, he could not hinder my resolutions,

[1] As a girl living at home, she received from her father an allowance of
£200 a year (Manvers MS 4265, Univ.
of Nottingham).

but I should not pretend after that to please him, since pleaseing him was only to be done by Obedience; that if I would disobey, I knew the consequences—he would not fail to confine me where I might repent at Leisure; that he had also consulted my Relations and found them all agreeing in his Sentiments.

He spoke this in a manner hinder'd my answering. I retir'd to my chamber, where I writ a letter to let him know my Aversion to the Man propos'd was too great to be overcome, that I should be miserable beyond all things could be imagin'd, but I was in his hands, and he might dispose of me as he thought fit.—He was perfectly satisfy'd with this Answer, and proceeded as if I had given a willing consent. —I forgot to tell you he name'd you, and said if I thought that way, I was very much mistaken, that if he had no other Engagements, yet he would never have agreed to your proposalls, haveing no Inclination to see his Grandchildren beggars.

I do not speak this to endeavor to alter your opinion, but to shew the improbabillity of his agreeing to it. I confesse I am entirely of your Mind. I reckon it among the absurditys of custom that a Man must be oblig'd to settle his whole Estate on an eldest Son, beyond his power to recall, whatever he proves to be, and make himselfe unable to make happy a younger Child that may deserve to be so. If I had an Estate my selfe, I should not make such ridiculous settlements, and I cannot blame you for being in the right.

I have told you all my Affairs with a plain sincerity. I have avoided to move your compassion, and I have said nothing of what I suffer; and I have not perswaded you to a Treaty which I am sure my familly will never agree to. I can have no fortune without an entire Obedience.

Whatever your busynesse is, may it end to your Satisfaction. I think of the public as you do. As little as that is a Woman's care, it may be permitted into the Number of a Woman's fears. But wretched as I am, I have no more to fear for my selfe. I have still a concern for my freinds, and I am in pain for your danger. I am far from takeing ill what you say. ⟨I⟩ never valu'd my selfe as the daughter of ———, and ever dispis'd those that esteem'd me on that Account.

With pleasure I could barter all that, and change to be any Country Gentleman's daughter that would have reason enough to make happynesse in privacy.

My Letter is too long. I beg your pardon. You may see by the situation of my affairs tis without design.

Text W MS ii. 372–5   *Address* To Mr Edward Wortley Mountagu

From Wortley [*28 July 1712*]

I burnt a long letter which I writ yesterday relating to your circumstances as you describe 'em. I now fancy it is as well to say in few words, that you are best able to judge whether you are likely to have a pleasant life with the person design'd you. If you think you can not, you are in the wrong to put yourselfe into a condition from which there is no retreat.

Tho it may be useless to say more of you, I ought to add something about my selfe, because I find your match will be concluded soon unless I break it off by complying with what was demanded of me. Whatever you take this match to be, another who knows a great deal of your selfe and your Lover believes he is more proper for you than I am; otherwise he woud not again have insisted on his first demands. He knows that seldom any man can be so hard hearted and unjust as not to make the person his heir that by the law and custom of his Country has reason to expect it, and that in all appearance I shall, if I am able, leave him twice as much as what he woud force me to do. He knows too there is little reason to doubt of my being able. I am so far from being a Squanderer that I have by my own management made a large addition to my fortune. But I woud have my heir thank me and not another that he is so. This woud be my Notion were I sure I coud never be in danger of losing my Life or Liberty or be any way unhappy for want of a power over an estate.

I am now reasoning as if I had bin against complying with what is usual. So far from it that I was willing to part with double to what is customary, and he woud surely accept of it if he did not prefer the other. If ever I make an offer near so advantageous in point of Fortune to any other, condemn me for a fool that did not know your worth. It is not unlikely I may in a little time accuse my selfe as such for not having yielded to every thing. For at the same time I write this, there is no one upon earth admires you more than I do.

If your [Father] sets him above me for no other reason but that his proposals are better, he shoud have twice as much of him as he ask'd of me. Scarce any man woud give an estate here for one twice as big there, if he must change his Country and often live there. Th⟨e⟩ same rents will sell for near twice as much here a⟨s⟩ they will there. But I beg your pardon for entering into this, when for ought I know the bargain is quite concluded and fixt. It is with difficulty that I forbear burning this too. I dont know what to write. I woud have avoided saying any thing till I coud agree with him or differ without so much Pain. But your Affairs require a speedy answer.

Monday night.

Text W MS i. 80–81

From Wortley [*30 July 1712*]

When you desir'd I shoud write, I concluded what I heard from many others was true, that your match was off. I cannot yet be convinc'd it is not. Were it broke without any regard to me, I own I shoud be glad for your sake. My health will not suffer me to make any great progress in a bargain now, but if you shoud be free when I return, my opinion is I shall be desirous to engage, tho perhaps not upon unreasonable terms. But my return is not to be depended on, and therefore I cannot agree you shoud dismiss the other affair on my Account. If your circumstances shoud be such as not to allow me more than 3 or 4 days to determine, I shall be in so much pain that you must not wonder if I run away on a sudden in hopes of being easy. Wedensday Morn. 6 a clock.

Text W MS i. 18

To Wortley [*30 July 1712*]

Wednesday

I write from my bed, so ill I can hardly hold a pen. I was taken ill yesterday of a Fever which is worse to day. I should be sorry to hear you was gone out of Town while

I am not in a condition to answer, tho' as sensible as I ought to be of the Generosity of your first Letter.—

My head is giddy. Mr. White is dead.[1]

Text W MS i. 244–5   *Address* To Mr Edward Wortley Mountagu *End. by W* From P. 1 Augst.

From Wortley [*1 Aug. 1712*]

Friday afternoon.

By what you write I shoud ghess there is no way of engaging but without troubling your family. 'Tis what I shoud like best but cannot say my circumstances ⟨do⟩ not seem to you impaird by such a Match. You are unwilling to tell me plainly your thoughts, as I press'd you to do, but I will avoid saying much till you are better.

The letter came just now. It had no date. I hope you will always put one, especially when you are ill.

Text W MS i. 10–11   *Address* To the Rt Honble the Lady Mary Pierrepont.

To Wortley [*1 Aug. 1712*]

I know not what to say. I am sure I cannot say enough to thank you for the Generosity of your proposal. However I should shew very little to make use of it to your disadvantage. I do not very well understand how your Circumstances are, or how far they may be impair'd by marrying a Woman without a Fortune. Mr. White dy'd last week.

My Fever is much abated, and I have ventur'd to rise to write to you, but my head continues so much disorder'd, I fear you cannot read or understand what I write.[2]

You may let me hear from you.

Text W MS i. 240–1   *Address* To Mr Edward Wortley Mountagu *End. by W* 2 Augst.

[1] He was evidently an agent of LM's father who had been concerned with the financial negotiations of W's hesitant courtship (W to LM, W MS i. 24).

[2] Perhaps because she was making a special effort, the handwriting is unusually clear.

To Wortley [*c. 2 Aug. 1712*]

It has troubled me more than my illnesse, the Incapacity of reading your Letters as I should do. This Morning I am so much better, I hope to be able to answer you. I am very sorry if this unlucky sicknesse of mine has hinder'd your Journey to day, if that was necessary for your satisfaction. I should never forgive my selfe if I contributed any way to make you uneasy, tho you are unjust to me in manny things. You beleive every idle report concerning my Affairs sooner than what you hear from my selfe. My Marriage is so far from being broke, I beleive I shall be press'd to sign the writeings within this 2 days. Judge if it is now in my power to stop by any Aplications to my Family. Reading over both your Letters calmly I find my selfe mistaken in some parts of them. You think me much more designing and interested than I have any Notion of being.—

However, think what you please. Your mistakeing me does not hinder me from retaining the Opinion of you that I have ever had. I have a sincere Esteem for you. I wish, if ever you have Occassion for any one's service, they may offer it with as much ready Jo⟨y⟩ as I should do. You talk ⟨of⟩ next Winter. All the preparatio⟨ns⟩ for the finishing this hard Affair are allready concluded.

If you have any thing to say, write by the same direction. It must be soon. When I go into the Country, tis in order to ——

Text W MS i. 221–2   *Address* To Mr Edward Wortley Mountagu

To Wortley [*c. 4 Aug. 1712*]

I write this letter in a great deal of perplexity. I have not heard from you since my first Illnesse. My Master has not been here this morning.[1] I sometimes think my Letters have

[1] Casotti, her Italian master, was an intermediary in her correspondence with W (see above, p. 125).

miscarry'd, sometimes that yours have, and I sometimes imagine that you are sick. I hope I am mistaken. I am now very well. We may meet at the Dutchesse of Grafton's. I do not know, after often reading over your Letters, whither I understand them right. Explain them in one more, and do it very soon. I am afraid mine are very obscure, but I'm allmost distracted. I can delay no longer than the latter end ⟨of⟩ this week.

Text W MS i. 199–200   *Address* To Mr Edward Wortley Mountagu

To Wortley [*6 Aug. 1712*]

You do me wrong in several parts of your Letter. You seem not very well to know your own mind. You are unwilling to go back from your word, and yet you do the same thing as telling me you should think your selfe more oblig'd to me for a refusal than a consent. Another woman would complain of this unsteadinesse of resolution. I think in an Affair of this nature, tis very natural to think one minute one thing, and the next another, and I cannot blame you. I remember an expression in one of your letters to me which is certainly just. Should we not repent, we should both be happy beyond example; if we should, we should, I fear, be both wretched in as high a degree. I should not hesitate one moment, was I not resolv'd to sacrifice every thing to you. If I do it, I am determin'd to think as little of the rest of the World—Men, Women, Acquaintance and relations —as if a deluge had swallow'd them. I abandonn all things that bear the name of pleasure but what is to be found in your companny. I give up all my Wishes, to be regulated by yours, and I resolve to have no other study but that of pleasing you.

These Resolutions are absolutely necessary if we are to meet; and you need have no doubt but I will perform them. I know you too well to propose to my selfe any satisfaction in marrying you that must not be center'd in your selfe. A Man that marrys a Woman without any advantages of

Fortune or Alliance (as it will be the case) has a very good title to her future Obedience. He has a right to be made easy every other way, and I will not impose on your Generosity, which claims the sincerest proceeding on my side. I am as sensible as you your selfe can be of the generosity of your proposal. Perhaps there is no other man that would take a woman under these disadvantages, and I am gratefull to you with all the warmth gratitude can inspire. On the other side, consider a little whither there are manny other Women that would think as I do. The Man my familly would marry me to, is resolv'd to live in London. Tis my own fault if I do not (of the humour he is) make him allways think whatever I please. If he dies, I shall have £1,200 per Annum rent charge; if he lives I shall enjoy every pleasure of Life, those of Love excepted. With you, I quit all things but your selfe, as much as if we were to be plac'd alone together in an inaccessible Island, and I hazard a possibillity of being reduce'd to suffer all the Evils of poverty. Tis true I had rather give my hand to the Flames than to him, and cannot think of suffering him with common patience. To you—I could give it, without reluctance (it is to say more than I ought) but perhaps with pleasure.

This last consideration determines me.—I will venture all things for you. For our mutual good, tis necessary for us to consider the method the most likely to hinder either of us from repenting; on that point our whole repose seems to depend. If we retire into the country, both your fortune and Inclination require a degree of privacy. The greatest part of my Familly (as the greatest part of all famillys) are fools; they know no happynesse but Equipage and furniture, and they Judge of every body's by the proportion they enjoy of it. They will talk of me as one that has ruin'd her selfe, and there will be perpetual enquirys made of my manner of living. I do not speak this in regard of my selfe; I have all-ways had a hearty contempt of those things, but on these and some other considerations I don't see why you should not persue the plan that you say you begun with your Freind. I don't mean take him with you, but why may not I supply his place? At Naples we may live after our own fashion. For my part, as I design utterly to forget there is such a place as London, I shall leave no directions with nobody to write after me. People that enter upon a solitude are in the wrong if they do not make it as agreable as they can. A fine Country and beautifull prospects to people that are capable of tasting them are (at least) steps to promoteing happynesse. If I liv'd with you, I should be sorry not to see you perfectly happy. I foresee the Objection you will raise against this, but it is none. I have no Acquaintance, nor I will make none, and tis your own fault if I ever see any creature but your selfe. Your commands shall regulate that. If you please, I can take with me a Lady you have heard me speak of, whom I am sure will follow me over all the world if I please, and I don't care if I never see any body else but her and you. If you agree to this, there is but one point farther to be consider'd, whether you can make me any Assurance of a provision if I should be so unhappy to lose you. You may think this an odd thing for me to name, when I bring you no fortune.[1] My Brother would keep me, but there is something very severe to submit to a dependance of that Nature, not to mention a possibillity of his Death, and then, what am I to expect from the guardians of his son?[2] I am sure I have nothing to expect from my F[ather]. By Assurance I only mean your word, which I dare entirely depend on.

I know no faults that you are ignorant of; on the contrary, I beleive you forgive more than you have occassion to forgive. I do not however look upon you as so far engag'd that you cannot retreat. You are at Liberty to raise what objections you please. I will answer them, or freely confesse any that are unanswerable. I make no reply to the accusation of haveing no value for you; I think it needs none when I proffer to leave the whole World for you. I say nothing of pin money etc. I don't understand the meaning of any divided interest from a Man I willingly give my selfe to. You speak of my F[ather] as if 'twere in my power to marry you with his

[1] In the *Tatler* No. 223 of 12 Sept. 1710, based on W's notes (see above, p. 51, n. 2), is the sentence: 'I ordain, That no Woman ever demand one Shilling to be paid after her Husband's Death, more than the very Sum she brings him, or an Equivalent for it in Land.'

[2] Lord Kingston's son, Evelyn Pierrepont, was born 3 April 1712 (Lady Frances Pierrepont to Philippa Mundy, 4 April 1712, M/M 11/5/27) He later became 2nd Duke of Kingston (d. 1773), succeeding his grandfather.

consent. I know it is not. All is concluded with this other,
and he will not put it off. If you are not of my Opinion
(which however I am sure is right) you may do what you
please in it, without nameing me, which will only serve to
expose me to a great deal of ill usage, and force me to what
he will.

Adeiu. I say nothing of time and place because I know
not whither you will agree to what I speak of. We have now
time enough, and I think we are in the wrong if we do not
settle every thing before we meet. I will not [*last page
missing*]

Text W MS i. 209–12

To Wortley [*6 Aug. 1712*]

Wednesday Night

I sent my last letter but this morning, and I begin (allmost) to repent it allready. I foresaw when I writ it, I should
be ready to unsay part of it before it could get to your hands.
Should I examine my own heart, it would now tell me I am
in the wrong to scruple what kind of Life pleases you most,
and that if I am to be happy but a few weeks, it is yet better
than never being so. I resolve my heart shall not overcome
my reason. I will not—to please my selfe—venture seeing you
unhappy; and sure, I have now some title to your Esteem.
There are not manny Women that would so far mistrust their
own power of pleasing. Tis not very easy to renounce what
one likes, and accept what one hates.—I will not persue
that hard Refflection.—

I now set you free from all your Fears, which your late
letters have evidently shewn you have been under, that I
should accept of your Offer. I will not accept it without a
probabillity of makeing you happy; however I thank you for
the generosity of the proposal. I hope this shews you I had
no design upon your Fortune, which you seem to imagine
in your last. Perhaps my future conduct may shew you that

your Freinds, who may know Womankind perfectly, know nothing of me.

I go next Monday; probably I shall see you no more. Your pity, even your Esteem will then be unavailable to me, yet I shall take some pleasure in it. I think you cannot without some degree of Esteem remember a Woman who would have left all the World for you, and who would rather be certainly miserable her selfe than hazard the seeing you so. I can refflect with an honest satisfaction, I have deceiv'd you in Nothing. I have told you the most disadvantageous truths in regard of my Fortune, and the Letter you accuse me of a trick in, came, it may be too sincerely, from my heart; yet with the same sincerity I own to you, was I in circumstances to choose my condition, I would be allways single, except it were possible (which I don't think it is) to change some parts of your temper. I do not blame you for n⟨ot⟩ agreeing with what I propose; and without Affectation I wish whoever you chuse may make you too happy to think of me.

Sometime or other I shall desire you to return my letters. They can be of no Value to you.

Text W MS i. 253–4   *Address* To Mr Edward Wortley Mountagu

From Wortley [7 *Aug. 1712*]

I had no sooner sent away an answer to your long letter but I accus'd my selfe of too much dissimulation in not having told you what effect it had upon me.

I can now no longer forbear laying my heart quite open and telling you the Joy I am in for being so near the greatest happiness I am capable of enjoying. Your letter of 3 sheets, which woud have pleasd me more than the rest for being the longest had it only bin of the same kind with them, has transported me by removing those doubts which I resolve shall never rise up again. I now, with the utmost pleasure, own you have convinc'd me of an esteem. The firm resolutions you have taken of putting yourselfe in my power and being pleas'd with any re-tirement in my company, I acknowledge to be such proofs of kindness as not many women of your condition woud have given . . . without some degree of Passion. These assurances, which might have bin acceptable

from any woman of merit, are given me by her I have, ever since I
knew her, believ'd to possess more charms than any other upon earth.
[*Passage omitted*]
You tell me of your Gratitude. Be assur'd I will always express
mine in the best manner I am able. The greatest part of my life shall
be dedicated to you. From every thing that can lessen my Passion I
will fly with as much speed as I shoud from the Plague. I shall sooner
choose to see my heart torn from my breast than divided from you.
You have often spoke as if I were about to save you from ruin.
I am now to ask relief of you. Since you have given me these assurances
of kindness it is with impatience I want to know when we must begin
to live together. I beg you will not recant any part of what you writ.
It will now fall heavy upon me to be dismiss'd and I can hope for no
ease but from You.

But I am indispos'd or I had said much more. The perplexity I was
in for want of knowing what to do has made for some nights past
my slumbers very short and [a] good part of last night, which I was
under apprehensions of being so long without you. I now declare to
you that I am already, if you please, marri'd to You. If you will
condescend to say something like it, such a declaration on both sides
I believe is as good a marriage as if it were by a minister, and I shall
have this advantage if you make it, that you will go before one very
soon and with a great deal of ease when you think you are doing but
what you have already done, and is of no use but to satisfy others.
I have more than once before bin indispos'd in the same manner and
therefore am in no fear of not being well in a few months especially
if I have your kindness, which I believe will be the best cordial to me.
If this or any other illness carries me off I will, if I am able, take care
you shall not fancy your fortune has bin diminish'd for my sake.

The gaining you in such a manner seems now to be the greatest
good Fortune. Each of us has now reason to believe the other is
sincere in promising an inviolable friendship and a lasting Affection.
You will say perhaps these professions are not always made good,
but when they are not, it is owing to the folly of one, if not both, of
the parties that engage.

As you have more spirit I believe you are more generous than other
women, otherwise I shoud not have trusted you with all this, for I
know a warm letter is generally rewarded with a cool answer. Unless
you think you can oblige me yet more than you did in that long letter,
which I coud not help kissing very often, say nothing for fear I shoud
not think you say enough. Name the hour and the place; Friday or
Saturday if you please.

Text W MS i. 102–3 (rough draft)

To Wortley [7 *Aug. 1712*]

Thursday

There is something of ill Fortune that mixes in all my
Affairs. My F[ather] has taken a fancy to go dine with my
B[rother], which will consequently prevent his comeing to
Town. To morrow I go to Acton. I am willing to talk with
him before I absolutely determine a thing of this consequence.
If you please to permit me one Day longer, since I cannot
see him before, on Satterday Morning I will write to you
from Acton. I hope a day's delay of my Answer can be no
considerable injury to you any way.

I tremble when I think what I am about. When I see you,
I am of Opinion tis a clear case, and had there been a parson
in the room with us, I had certainly marry'd you last night,
in defiance of consequences. When I come to consider,
I should be glad if I could have my Bro[ther's] promise of
protection in case of Accidents. I know my selfe better since
yesterday than I did before. I find my Inclinations are more
of your side than I imagin'd, but——

I will write Satterday morning without fail. If I resolve
to be so at all, Sunday night I beleive I must be yours.

Forgive the irresolution of this Letter. I know not what
I shall do. I know I wish you perfectly well.

Text W MS i. 217–18   *Address* To Mr Edward Wortley Mountagu

To Wortley [7 *Aug. 1712*]

Thursday Night

If I am allways to be as well pleas'd as I am with this
Letter, I enter upon a state of perfect happynesse in com-
plying with you. I am sorry I cannot do it entirely as to
Friday or Satterday. I will tell you the true reason of it.
I have a relation that has ever shew'd an uncommon par-
tiality for me. I have gennerally trusted him with all my

thoughts, and I have allways found him sincerely my freind. On the Occassion of this marriage, he receiv'd my complaints with the greatest degree of tendernesse. He proffer'd me to disoblige my F[ather] by representing to him the hardship he was doing, if I thought it would be of any service to me, and when he heard me in some passion of greife assure him it could do me no good, he went yet farther, and tenderly ask'd me if there was any other ⟨ma⟩n tho' of a smaller fortune I could be happy with, and how much so ever it should be against the will of my other relations, assur'd me he would assist me in makeing me happy after my own way. This is an obligation I can never forget, and I think I should have cause to reproach my selfe if I did this without letting him know it. He knows you and I beleive will approve of it.—You guesse whom I mean.—

The generosity and the goodnesse of this Letter wholly determines my softest inclinations on your side. You are in the wrong to suspect me of artifice. Plainly shewing me the kindnesse of your heart (if you have any there for me) is the surest way to touch mine, and I am at this minute more encl⟨in'd⟩ to speak tenderly to you than ever I was in my Life—so much enclin'd, I will say nothing. I could wish you would leave England, but I know not how to object against any thing that pleases you. In this minute I have no will that does not agree with yours. Sunday I shall see you, if you do not hear from me Satterday.

Text W MS ii. 376–7   *Address* To Mr Edward Wortley Mountague

From Wortley [*c. 8 Aug. 1712*]

If you are yet in any doubt what to do I am very certain you ought to resolve against me. To marry one of my humour unless you can place all your pleasure in his Company, is to depart this life. It was a great piece of folly in me to persist in leaving it to you to decide after you had assur'd me you did not value me much. You know I have formerly broke with you upon that point. All your letters of late have implied the contrary of what you said or I cou'd not have determin'd as at last I did. [*Passage omitted*]

You do extremely well in asking your brother's consent. I wish too you coud try with your f[ather] to break of[f] the new affair; but perhaps you may think, and with some reason, that while he is treating with me, you shall break with me too, as you have done with better. [*Passage omitted*] You may appoint the time and place, and I will provide a Coach, a Licence, Parson, etc. A Coach and six looks much better than a pair for such a service, but will it not be more likely to have company about it while it stands near your house?

If we shoud once be in a coach let us not say one word till we come before the parson, least we should engage in fresh disputes; but why shoud we meet at all, if we are so likely to have 'em? It is plain we shou'd not. [*Passage omitted*]

Text W MS i. 98–99 (rough draft)

To Wortley [*c. 8 Aug. 1712*]

I am just come to Acton. I found my B[rother] in bed, just taken very ill of this fever. Something has been mistaken in the writeings, that they must go back into Ireland[1] to be sign'd over again. This is at least a repreive of 3 weeks, and if you please, allows us more time for consideration, and I hope, for the Establishment of your health. However if you find it necessary you should go to the Spaw soon, I will positively determine in my next letter.—

I wish I could see you. Letters are an imperfect intelligence compar'd to Conversation, and I have a great deal to say, but I know not how to contrive a meeting. I would not have you injure your health by staying in London, but you may be with your Freind at Kensington, and enjoy the benefit of the Air and the Gardens.[2] I should be sorry (except all things were ended between us) that you was farther from me, daily unforeseen chances happening in my Affairs. I talk of 3 weeks. Possibly these writeings may be

[1] Lord Massereene's seat was in Co. Antrim.

[2] The previous autumn Addison had invited W to lodge with him in a house he proposed taking in Kensington Square, where (he promised) the air would be as good as in Yorkshire (*Letters*, ed. W. Graham, 1941, pp. 265–6). Addison was living there in July 1712 (Swift, *Journal to Stella*, ed. H. Williams, 1948, p. 550).

return'd in a fortnight, and when ever they are, I may be press'd to marry at 2 days', or a day's warning.

Sick as my Brother is, I have spoke to him concerning my Affair. He agrees with me there is nothing to be treated with my F[ather], who is resolv'd. Upon the least Suspicion he will send me farther into the country, and put it out of our power ever to meet.

Take care of your Health, in the first place. Let me hear how you do, and if it is necessary for me to say what I intend to do possitively in my next Letter, and I will do it, tho' since we have time, I should be glad to delay engageing for some little time. I own I tremble at the thought of irrevocably promiseing, and yet I tremble too at the thought of parting for ever. If it suits with your conveniency to be at Kensington, we may write often, and you may alow m⟨e tim⟩e.—

Do what is most convenient for you. Write soon. You may direct without any enclosure to me, at my Father's, here. No body will examine who I receive Letters from. But you must take care who you trust with a Letter to the pp [penny post] if my Name is on the outside.

Text W MS i. 184–5   *Address* To Mr Edward Wortley Mountagu.

To Philippa Mundy [*Aug. 1712*]

My dear Phill,

I am very sorry that your Affairs are not in a posture to expect Paradise, but I think you much in the right to accept of Limbo; there is nothing that is not preferable to the state you are now in,

> For when the Mind so cool is grown
> As neither Love, nor Hate to own,
> Then Life but dully lingers on.

For my part, I know not what I shall do; perhaps at last I shall do something to surprize every body. Where ever I am, and what ever becomes of me, I am ever yours. Limbo is better than Hell. My Adventures are very odd; I may go into Limbo if I please, but tis accompanny'd with such circumstances, my courrage will hardly come up to it, yet perhaps it may. In short I know not what will become of me. You'l think me mad, but I know nothing certain but that I shall not dye an Old Maid, that's positive.[1]

Dear Phil: let me know if you go to Nottingham Race, and what new conquests you make there. I wish you all the happynesse you are capable of tasting, which is all that is most exquisite and delicate.

Text MS M/M 11/5/6 *Address* To Mrs Phillippa Mundy at Osbaston near Leicester Leicestershire. London and forward. *Postmark* PENY POST PAID. AV ⟨?⟩

To Wortley [*11 Aug. 1712*]

Monday

My F[ather] has been here to day. He bid me prepare to go to Dean this day sennight. I am not to come from thence but to give my selfe to all that I hate. I shall never see you more. These considerations fright me to Death. Tell me what you intend to do. If you can think of me for your compannion at Naples, come next Sunday under this Garden wall, on the road, some little distance from the summer house, at 10 a clock. It will be dark, and it is necessary it should be so. I could wish you would begin our Journey immediately; I have no fancy to stay in London or near it. I will not pretend to Justifye my proceeding. Every body will object to me, why I did not do this sooner, before I put a man to the charges of Equipage etc.? I shall not care to tell them, you did not ask me sooner. In short, as things have

---

[1] In 1741 LM told Joseph Spence that 'she had a vast number of offers . . . and the thing that kept her awake was, who to fix upon. Most part of the Month she was determind but as to two points, which were: to be married to some body, and not to be married to the man her Father . . . advisd her to' (Eg MS 2234, f. 247). In the opinion of her granddaughter Lady Louisa Stuart this account 'appears to have been mere rattle; yet it is likely enough that she more than once wavered between Mr. Wortley and others though unwilling ever to lose her hold of him intirely. It is pretty plain that he suspected this' (to Stuart Corbett, 7 Sept. 1834, Wh MS 439).

been mannag'd I shall never care to hear any more on't. Tis an odd step, but something must be venture'd when the happynesse of a whole Life is depending. I pretend to be happy with you, and I am sure tis impossible with him.

If on the account of your health, or for any other reason, you had rather delay this till I return from Dean, tis certain I shall come hither, from thence, and twill be then in our power to do the same thing. But as the time of my return is uncertain, you must not be far off if you intend to do it, for I own I cannot, nor dare not, resist my Father, and I know he has power over me to make me do whatever he pleases.

I shall not be surpriz'd if you have chang'd your mind, or even if you should change your mind after you have consented to this. I would have no tye upon you but Inclination; I have nothing to do with your word or your honnour etc.

The Scheme I propose to my selfe is living in an agreable Country, with a Man that I like, that likes me, and forgetting the rest of the world as much as if there was no other people in the world, and that Naples were the Garden of Eden. If there is any part of this Scheme that does not agree either with your Affairs or Inclinations, do not do it. I own I know not how to disoblige all my relations and live in the midst of them. If you will leave England immediately I am ready to wait on you, either next Sunday at 10, or I'll wait till I come back, and leave you all the time of my stay at Dean to consider. I shall be sorry if you resolve against me, but I should be doubly sorry to have you take me without your own Inclination being intirely for it.

If you come Sunday, 'tis indifferent to me whether tis with a coach and six or a pair. For my part I could wish to make our first stage that night. Do what you please for that matter.——

I say nothing of Jointure. I begin to think my selfe in the wrong to imagine a Man so generous to take me without a fortune would not be also generous enough to make me easy every other way. Consult your own heart, and let that determine you. Make no scruple of going back from your word, if you cannot resolve upon it. Should I go to the Garden door and not find you there, the disapointment would

not be so hard as seeing you uneasy afterwards. On my side,
if I find I cannot live with you at Naples without another
wish, if I cannot answer for my own renouncing the pomps
and vanitys of this world,[1] you shall not be troubled with
me, and Satterday receive a Letter that I cannot bring my
selfe to it. In the Opinion I am in this Minute I think I can
abandonn the whole World for you.

Do not be apprehensive I shall take it for a mark of
Indifference if you delay till my return. Perhaps your health
may require it, or the situation of your Affairs, which may
not be in order to travell before. I will think of it what you
please, and will not reproach you if you do not do it then.
Let us both be at Liberty till the Parson puts an end to it.

Text W MS i. 282–5   *Address* To Mr Edward Wortley Mountagu

From Wortley [*11 Aug. 1712*]

This kind letter brings me yet more pleasure than the other because
it fixes the day. I shall go to meet you with more joy than I shoud to
take possession of Riches, Honour or Power; nay, then I shoud to
meet you if you brought 'em along with you because I coud not so
well convince you how much I value you. I never thought them
necessary to make life happy. You will prove that I was in the right
by making me without their assistance believe that I am the most fortunate man upon Earth. There are no difficulties that I shoud not
undergo to preserve this kind usage. [*Passage omitted*]

Text W MS i. 160

To Wortley [*12 Aug. 1712*]

Tuesday night

I receiv'd both your Monday Letters since I writ the
Enclos'd, which however I send you. The kind Letter was
writ and sent Friday morning, and I did not receive yours till
the Satterday noon, or (to speak truth) you would never have

---

[1] LM's renunciation repeats a phrase of the Anglican Catechism.

had it, there were so manny things in yours to put me out of Humour. Thus you see it was on no design to repair any thing that offended you. You only shew me how industrious you are to find imaginary Faults in me. Why will you not suffer me to be pleas'd with you?

I would see you if I could (tho' perhaps it may be wrong), but in the way I am here, tis impossible. I can't come to Town but in companny with my sister in law.[1] I can carry her no where but where she pleases, or if I could I would trust her with nothing. I could not walk out alone without giving Suspicion to the whole Family. Should I be watch'd and seen to meet a Man—judge of the Consequence.

You speak of treating with my Father, as if you beleiv'd he would come to Terms afterwards. I will not suffer you to remain in that thought, however advantageous it might be to me; I will deceive you in nothing. I am fully perswaded he will never hear of terms afterwards. You may say, tis talking oddly of him. I can't answer to that, but tis my real Opinion, and I think I know him. You talk to me of Estates as if I was the most interested Woman in the World. Whatever faults I may have shewn in my Life, I know not one Action of it that ever prov'd me Mercenary. I think there cannot be a greater proof of the contrary than treating with you, where I am to depend entirely on your generosity, at the same time that I have settle'd on me £300 per Annum pin money and a considerable jointure in another place, not to reckon that I may have by his temper what command of his Estate I please; and with you I have nothing to pretend to. I do not however make a Merit of this to you. Money is very little to me because all beyond necessarys I do not value that is to [be] purchas'd by it. If the man propos'd to me had £10,000 per Annum and I was sure to dispose of it all, I should act just as I do. I have in my Life known a good deal of shew, and never found my selfe the happier for it.

In proposeing to you to follow the scheme begun with your Freind, I think tis absolutely necessary for both our Sakes. I would have you want no pleasure which a single Life would afford you; you own that you think nothing so agreable.

---

[1] Lady Kingston, whom LM elsewhere characterized as silly and childish (Stuart, p. 68).

A Woman that adds nothing to a Man's fortune ought not to take from his happynesse. If possible I would add to it, but I will not take from you any satisfaction you could enjoy without me. On my own side, I endeavor to form as right a judgment of the Temper of Humane Nature, and of my own in particular, as I am capable of. I would throw off all partiallity and passion, and be calm in my Opinion. Allmost all people are apt to run into a mistake, that when they once feel or give a passion, there needs nothing to entertain it. This Mistake makes, in the Number of Women that inspire (even) violent passions, hardly one preserve one after possession. If we marry, our happynesse must consist in loveing one Another. Tis principally my concern to think of the most probable method of makeing that Love Eternal.

You object against living in London. I am not fond of it my selfe, and readily give it up to you, tho' I am Assur'd there needs more art to keep a fondnesse alive in Solitude, where it gennerally preys upon it selfe. There is one Article absolutely necessary: to be ever belov'd, one must be ever agreable. There is no such thing as being agreable without a thorrough good humour, a natural sweetnesse of temper, enliven'd by Cheerfullnesse.—Whatever natural Fund of gaity one is born with, to keep that up tis necessary to be entertain'd with agreable Objects. Any body capable of tasting pleasure, when they confine them selves to one place should take care tis the place in the World the most pleasing. Whatever you may now think (now perhaps you have some fondnesse for me), tho' your Love should continue in its full force, there are Hours when the most beloved Mistrisse would be troublesome. People are not ever (nor is it in Humane Nature they should be) dispos'd to be fond. You would be glad to find in me the Freind and the Compannion. To be agreably this last, it is necessary to be gay and Entertaining. A Perpetual Solitude in a place where you see nothing to raise your spirits at length wears them out, and Conversation insensibly falls into Dull and insipid.—When I have no more to say to you, You will like me no longer. How dreadfull is that veiw! You will refflect, for my sake you have abandonn'd the conversation of a Freind that you like'd and your Situation in a Country where all things would have contributed to make your Life passe in (the true volupté) a smooth Tranquillity. I shall lose the vivacity that should entertain you, and you will have nothing to recompense you for what you have lost. Very few people that have settled entirely in the Country but have grown at length weary of one another. The Lady's conversation gennerally falls into a thousand impertinent Effects of Idlenesse, and the Gentleman falls in Love with his dogs and horses, and out of Love with every thing else. I am not now arguing in favour of the Town; you have answer'd me as to that point. In respect of your health, tis the first thing to be consider'd, and I shall never ask you to do any thing injurious to that. But tis my Opinion tis necessary to being happy that we neither of us think any place more agreable than that where we are. I have nothing to do in London, and tis indifferent to me if I never see it more. I know not how to answer your mentioning Gallantry, nor in what sense to understand you; I am sure in one: whoever I marry, when I am marry'd, I renounce all things of that kind.[1] I am willing to abandonn all conversation but yours; if you please I will never see another Man; in short, I will part with any thing for you, But you. I will not have you a month, to lose you for the rest of my Life. If you can persue the plan of happynesse begun with your Freind and take me for that Freind, I am ever yours.

I have examin'd my own heart whither I can leave every thing for you. I think I can. If I change my Mind, you shall know before Sunday. After that I will not change my Mind. If tis necessary for your Affairs to stay in England to assist your father in his busynesse, as I suppose the time will be short, I would be as little injurious to your fortune as I can, and I will do it. But I am still of Opinion, nothing is so likely to make ⟨us⟩ both happy as what I propose. I foresee I may break with you on this point, and I shall certainly be displeas'd with my selfe for it, and wish a thousand times that I had done whatever you pleas'd, but however, I hope I shall allways remember how much more miserable than any thing else could make me, should I be to live with you and please

---

[1] A reference to W's sentiment about 'Cuckoldom', as repeated in his letter three days later (p. 158).

you no longer. You can be pleas'd with nothing when you are not pleas'd with your selfe. One of the Spectators is very Just, that says a Man ought allways to be on his guard against Spleen and too severe a Philosophy, a Woman against Levity and Coquettry.[1] If we go to Naples, I will make no Acquaintance there of any kind, and you will be in a place where a variety of agreable Objects will dispose you to be ever pleas'd. If such a thing is possible, this will secure our everlasting Happynesse, and I am ready to wait on you without leaving a thought behind me.—

Text W MS ii. 361–4   *Address* To Mr Edward Wortley Mountagu

From Wortley [*13 Aug. 1712*]

Before you are to leave Acton, the Post will go out but thrice, and I cannot omit using it every time. I have now done disputing with you. Say what you please to the contrary, I will go to Acton at the hour you nam'd and stand near the summer house which looks upon the great road that goes into the town. Whatever you may tell me in the mean time I cannot be assurd how you will stand affected then. You must judge for both of us. A mistake may be fatal. I am Yours till you turn me away.

Text W MS i. 58

To Wortley [*15 Aug. 1712*]

Friday, 7 a clock

If I think till to morrow after the same manner I have thought ever since I saw you, the wisest thing I can do is to do whatever you please. Tis an odd thing to confesse, but I fear nothing so much as a change in my mind when there can be none in my condition. My thoughts of you are capable of improvement both ways. I am more susceptible of gratitude than any body living. You may mannage in a manner to make me passionately fond of you. Should you

[1] *Spectator* No. 128 (27 July 1711) by Addison.

PLATE 3

Letter of Lady Mary Pierrepont to Edward Wortley Montagu,
[15 Aug. 1712]
Wortley MSS i. 170

use me ill, can I answer that I should be able to hinder my selfe from refflecting back on the sacrifice I had made? An engagement for my whole Life is no triffle, and should we both be so happy as to find we like'd one another, yet even Years of Exquisite happynesse, when they are past, could not pay me for a whole Life of misery to come. I think perhaps farther than I have Occassion to think, but in an affair like this, all possible as well as all probable Events are to be foreseen, since a mistake is not to be retreiv'd. In my present Opinion, I think that if I was yours and you us'd me well, nothing could be added to my misfortune should I lose you. But when I suffer my reason to speak, it tells me that in any circumstance of Life (wretched or happy) there is a certain proportion of Money, as the world is made, absolutely necessary to the liveing in it. I have never yet found my selfe in any straits of Fortune, and am hardly able to imagine the misery ariseing from it. Should I find my selfe 20 year hence your Widow, without a competency to maintain me in a manner suitable in some degree to my Education, I shall not then be so old I may not possibly live 20 year longer, without what is requisite to make Life easy. Happynesse is what I should not think of.

After all these prudent considerations, the Bias of my heart is in your Favour. I hate the Man they propose to me. If I did not hate him, my reason would tell me he is not capable of either being my Freind or my Compannion. I have an Esteem for you, with a mixture of more kindnesse than I imagin'd. That kindnesse would perswade me to abandonn all things for you, my Fame, my Family, the Settlement they have provided for me, and rather embark with you through all the hazards of perhaps finding my selfe reduce'd to the last extremes of Want (which would be heavier on me than any other body) than enjoy the certainty of a plentifull Fortune with another. I can think with pleasure of giveing you with my first declaration of love the sincerest proof of it. I read over some of your first Letters, and I form romantic Scenes to my selfe of Love and Solitude. I did not beleive I was capable of thinking this way, but I find tis in your power to make me think what you please.

One would think this Letter were determin'd; yet I know

not what I shall do.—I know if I do not venture all things
to have you, I shall repent it.

Text W MS i. 168–71   *Address* To Mr Edward Wortley Mountagu

From Wortley [?c. *15 Aug. 1712*]

[*Passage omitted*] I had rather live in any part of Italy than in England
and shall never wish to be here unless my affairs suffer too much by
my absence. We can never differ I think upon this point. I have now
complied with all your demands. Have you any thing more to ask?

Too much of this short time has bin spent in useless disputes. Out
of tenderness to you I have forborn to state your case in the plainest
light which is thus. If you have no thoughts of Cuckoldom, you are
mad if you marry him. If you are likely to think of Cuckoldom, you
are mad if you marry me. Surely in one minute you may tell which of
us ought to be your choice. Lady Harpur[1] has £400 a year pin-money,
is brought to town for some months every year, as the husband promis'd when he marri'd her against her inclination by her mother's[2]
persuasion, and yet she declares to her friends (she has done it to me
among the rest) that one had better be buried alive than married to
one that gives disgust. Pin-money is worse than nothing unless the
husband is extravagant or you cuckold him. My present income is
better than his and I have a power to make settlements of every part of
it. My reversions, I believe, are much more than his too. But perhaps
the difference of our circumstances may be small; I am sure not enough
to have any weight in your decision of this great affair. If both of us
are likely to be little better than goalers in your eye, hazard all rather
than think of either. And now I think I shoud give over arguing.

Are you sure you shall come back from Dean before you are marri'd?
You have no reason to trust to that. Some say you are to live in
Ireland when you are married, but I suppose you know how that is
to be. All I can say is that for two days more you are mistress of your
selfe and me.

Your letter writ on Wednesday night seems unkind. However,
I will come to Acton on Sunday night, 10 a clock. If you do not come
yourselfe to take leave of me or go with me, you may send your maid
with a compliment.

[1] Probably Catherine (1682–1745),
da. of 2nd Baron Crew, m. (*c.* 1709) Sir
John Harpur or Harper (1679–1741).
[2] Anne (d. 1719), da. of Sir William

Armine, m. (1674, as 2nd husband)
Thomas 2nd Baron Crew, and (1704,
as 3rd) 3rd Earl of Torrington.

Till Sunday night I will leave word where I may be found every minute in the day. I have a faithful servant that is too good to wait behind me. He may meet your maid at Kensington, Acton or where you please, if it be of any use, and letters may pass very speedily.

Perhaps it gave you some disgust when I told you for the sake of my health I had better not be in the same bed for a time. I had no sooner left you but I thought I had better suffer any thing than give you a suspicion which must be very natural in such a case. I have since bin very uneasy and I am sure the quiet of mind I shall gain by being near you will effectually prevent my receiving any harm and do me more good than any other remedy.

Text W MS i. 40–43 (?draft)

To Wortley [*15 Aug. 1712*]

Friday Night

I tremble for what we are doing. Are you sure you will love me for ever? Shall we never repent? I fear, and I hope. I foresee all that will happen on this Occassion. I shall incense my Familly ⟨to⟩ the highest degree. The gennerallity of the World will blame my conduct, and the Relations and freinds of —— will invent a thousand storys of me, yet—tis possible you may recompence every thing to me. In this Letter (which I am fond of) you promise me all that I wish. —Since I writ so far, I receiv'd your friday Letter. I will be only yours, and I will do what you please.
[*Postscript*] You shall hear from me again to morrow, not to contradict but to give Some directions. My resolution is taken—Love me and use me well.

Text W MS ii. 378–9   *Address* To Mr Edward Wortley Mountagu. *End. by LM* ⟨?⟩ did not. [*struck out*]

To Wortley [*16 Aug. 1712*]

Satterday Morning

I writ you a Letter last night in some passion. I begin to fear again; I own my selfe a coward.——

You made no reply to one part of my Letter concerning
my Fortune. I am afraid you flatter your selfe that my
F[ather] may be at length reconcile'd and brought to
reasonable terms. I am convince'd by what I have often
heard him say, speaking of other cases like this, he never
will. The fortune he has engag'd to give with me was settle'd,
on my B[rother's] marriage, on my sister and my selfe, but
in such a manner that it was left in his power to give it all to
either of us, or divide it as he thought fit.[1] He has given it
all to me. Nothing remains for my sister but the free bounty
of my F[ather] from what he can save, which notwithstanding the greatnesse of his Estate may be very little. Possibly
after I have disoblig'd him so much, he may be glad to have
her so easily provided for, with Money allready rais'd,
especially if he has a design to marry him selfe, as I hear.[2]

I do not speak this that you should not endeavor to come
to terms with him, if you please, but I am fully perswaded
it will be to no purpose. He will have a very good Answer
to make, that I suffer'd this Match to proceed, that I made
him make a very silly figure in it, that I have let him spend
£400 in wedding cloaths, all which I saw without saying
any thing. When I first pretended to oppose this Match,
he told me he was sure I had some other design in my head.
I deny'd it with truth, but you see how little appearance
there is of that Truth. He proceeded with telling me that
he never would enter into treaty with another Man, etc., and
that I should be sent immediately into the North, to stay there,
and when he dy'd he would only leave me an Annuity of
£400.

I had not courrage to stand this Vein, and I submitted to
what he pleas'd. He will now object against me, why, since
I intended to marry in this Manner, I did not persist in my
first resolution? that it would have been as easy for me to
run away from T[horesby] as from hence, and to what
purpose did I put him and the Gentleman I was to marry
to Expence etc.? He will have a thousand plausible reasons
for being irreconcilable, and tis very probable the World
will be of his Side.—Refflect now for the last time in what
manner you must take me. I shall come to you with only

---

[1] See above, p. 53.   [2] He married two years later.

a Nightgown[1] and petticoat, and that is all you will get with
me.

I have told a Lady of my Freinds what I intend to do.
You will think her a very good Freind when I tell you she
has proffer'd to lend us her house, if we would come there
the first Night. I did not accept of this, till I had let you
know it. If you think it more convenient to carry me to
your Lodging, make no scrupule of it. Let it be what it will;
if I am your Wife, I shall think no place unfit for me where
you are. I beg we may leave London next morning, where
ever you intend to go. I should wish to go out of England if
it suits with your Affairs. You are the best Judge of your
father's temper. If you think it would be obliging to him,
or necessary for you, I will go with you immediately to ask
his pardon and his blessing. If that is not proper at first,
⟨I⟩ think the best Scheme is going to the Spaw. When you
come back you may endeavor to Make your Father admit of
seeing me, and treat with mine (tho' I persist in thinking
it will be to no purpose). But I cannot think of living in the
midst of my Relations and Acquaintance after so unjustifiable a step—unjustifiable to the World.—But I think I can
justify my selfe to my selfe.—

I again beg you to hire a Coach to be at the door early
Monday morning to carry us some part of our way, wherever
you resolve our Journey shall be. If you determine to go to
that Lady's house, you had better come with a coach and
6 at 7 a clock to morrow. She and I will be in the balconey
that looks on the road; you have nothing to do but to stop
under it, and we will come down to you. Do in this what you
like best. After all, think very seriously. Your ⟨letter⟩, which
will be waited for, is to determine every thing. I forgive
you a coarse Expression[2] in your last, which however I wish
had not been there. You might have said something like it
without expressing it in that Manner, but there was so much
complaisance in the rest of it, I ought to be satisfy'd. You
can shew me no goodnesse I shall not be sensible of. However, think again, and resolve never to think of me if you
have the least doubt, or that it is likely to make you uneasy
in your Fortune. I beleive to travell is the most likely way

---

[1] Formal evening dress.   [2] 'Cuckoldom'.

to make a Solitude agreable, and not tiresome. Remember you have promis'd it.

Tis something Odd for a Woman that brings nothing to expect any thing, but after the way of my Education I dare not pretend to live but in some degree suitable to [it]. I had rather die than return to a dependancy upon Relations I have disoblig'd. Save me from that fear if you Love me. If you cannot, or think I ought not to expect it, be sincere and tell me so. Tis better I should not be yours at all, than for a short happynesse involve my selfe in Ages of Misery. I hope there will never be Occassion for this precaution but however tis necessary to make it. I depend entirely on your honnour, and I cannot suspect you of any way doing wrong. Do not imagine I shall be angry at any thing you can tell me. Let it be sincere. Do not impose on a Woman that leaves all things for you.

Text W MS ii. 384–7   *Address* To Mr Edward Wortley Mountagu

To Wortley [*16 Aug. 1712*]

Satterday

Since I writ the Enclos'd, I hear my F[ather] intends us a visit to morrow. You cannot come at 7 a clock. I have had a Letter from that Relation I said I would speak to; he is prevented comeing to me. I would (if possible) consult him ⟨befo⟩re I do an Action of this consequence. Upon second thoughts it will not be so convenient to go to the Lady I spoke of, for several reasons both in regard to her and my selfe.

I am in so much disorder, I can hardly form a Letter. Tis very plain as you state the case, but a Woman that disobliges her Familly and engages the world against her, risques a great deal.

I will write to my relation and send away the Letter to night, and write to you to morrow.—I have just receiv'd your friday Letter.—A mistake may be fatal—It may indeed. —How hard is it to decide a Question where my whole

Happynesse is depending! I must be perfectly happy, or I must be lost and ruin'd. I am fainting with Fear.—Forgive my Instabillity.—If I do it, Love me; if I dare not, do not hate me.—

You shall hear from me again to morrow Morning. If I find I cannot do it, why should you come? You must not be expos'd to that trouble.

Text W MS i. 223–4   *Address* To Mr Edward Wortley Mountagu

To Wortley [*17 Aug. 1712*]

Sunday

Your Letter, which I receiv'd this morning in bed, distracts me. If my F[ather] knows of it,[1] tis past; I shall be sent to Dean early to morrow morning, and hinder'd to Night. He comes to day. I am coward enough to aprehend his rage to a degree of being ready to swoon. I know he may make me do what he will.—

I can write no longer. If you dont hear from me again to day, do not come, for we are certainly prevented. By several little things, I fear'd he suspected it before. I tremble so I can't write.

Text W MS i. 162–3   *Address* To Mr Edward Wortley Mountagu Speed

To Wortley [*17 Aug. 1712*]

Every thing I apprehended is come t⟨o p⟩asse. 'Tis with the utmost difficulty ⟨and da⟩nger I write this. My father is in the house. After a long conference with him I am sent up to my chamber, from whence I shall not move till early to morrow morning to go into the coach, to begin my Journey.—

I am frighted to death and know not what I say.

---

[1] W's marriage licence, as she makes clear in her second letter of the next day.

I had the precaution of desiring Mrs. —— to send her servant to wait here for a Letter, yet I am in apprehension of this being stopp'd. If tis, I have yet more to suffer, for I have been forc'd to promise to write no more to you.

Text W MS i. 182–3

To Wortley [*18 Aug. 1712*]

I cannot easily submit to my fortune; I must have one more tryal of it. I send you this Letter at 5 a Clock, while the whole familly is asleep. I am stole from my Sister to tell you we shall not go till 7, or a little before. If you can come to the same place any time before that, I may slip out, because they have no suspicion of the morning before a Journey. Tis possible some of the servants will be about the house and see me go off, but when I am once with you, tis no matter.——

If this is impracticable, Adeiu, I fear for ever.

Text W MS i. 250

To Wortley [*18 Aug. 1712*]

I would not give my selfe the pain of thinking you have suffer'd as much by this misfortune as I have done. The pain of my mind has very much affected my body. I have been sick ever since, yet tho' overcome by fateigue and misfortune I write to you from the first Inn.

I blame my selfe for my cowardice and folly. I know not how my [Father] receiv'd his Intelligence but out of my fright. When I refflect, I don't beleive he knew of the takeing out the License,[1] since he did not name it particularly,

---

[1] To avoid publishing banns, W had applied for a special marriage licence on 16 Aug. He applied twice on that day— the first time to be married in the Church of St. Dunstan in the West, the second to be married 'at any convenient time and place' (Marriage Allegations, Vicar General's Office, Westminster). The actual licence (H MS) is dated 17 Aug. 1712.

but in genneral terms spoke of my keeping a correspondance, etc. I was so frighted and look'd so guilty, I beleive it was the worse for me. I had perhaps better have deny'd it, but instead of that I foolishly made what promises he would.—

I lament my folly, but would remedy it if possible, tho' I cannot blame you if after so much trouble about it you resolve never to think more of so unlucky a creature as I am. But if like me you are still determin'd, if possible I will write to you every post, and what I can do I will.

I suppose I shall not be remov'd from hence till the night before my intended ——. If that should happen sooner than is convenient for you, perhaps sicknesse may serve for a pretence to delay it 2 or 3 days. I am afraid your Affairs may suffer if you stay from your [Father]. If so, do what is right for your selfe in the first place. Neglect nothing upon my Account. Go to him, if you can be back in 10 days, to be sure I shall not be persecuted sooner. But do no harm to your health by fateigue or vexation; rather forget what becomes of me t⟨han⟩ any way injure your selfe. I am ⟨?⟩ distracted when I think how much t⟨rouble⟩ I have allready given to the Man ⟨on⟩ Earth I have most reason to esteem, and for whose happynesse I would do every thing. If on my Account your health or your fortune should ever be impair'd I should wish I had never been born.

Write to me soon, to West Dean, near Salisbury, Wiltshire, by my own name. Did you write Sunday? I had no letter.

[*Postscript*] I made shift to get into the Balconey at 6 and sta'ed till 7 this morning. But heaven was not so kind to bring you. You once call'd my kindnesse a cordial to you. I wish it was so, for it runs in my head you are ill. Whatever is ordain'd for me, if my wishes were heard, you should never feel any.

Adeiu. I could say a great deal more.

Text W MS i. 172–3   *Address* To Mr Edward Wortley Mountague. if not in Town, to be sent after him wth speed.[1]

> [1] Delivered the next day, while both lodged at the same inn.

To Wortley [*19 Aug. 1712*]

I have no servant with me I dare trust. I was oblig'd to leave my own behind. I beleive You have no conveniency of carrying me off now, nor is it very decent for me to go without a servant. I dare not come to you, and hope not to have if known, except we meet not to part.—Tell me how you intended that.—

Here is enclos'd a Letter I writ last night, with an Intention to send by the post.

Text W MS i. 225

To Wortley [*19 Aug. 1712*]

If you have provided conveniency to carry me away decently I will come, if not I dare not. Your way would be exposing my B[rother] to use me ill if I return, or disoblige my fath[er] for ever. I would not see a relation after tis over.

Text W MS i. 300–1[1]

To Wortley [*19 Aug. 1712*]

Why did not you bring a coach etc. to be set up at another Inn? I would fain come but fear being stopp'd. If you could carry me with you, I would not care who saw me. Or if you had been lodg'd on the same floor with me, I might have been marry'd perhaps, and return'd unsuspected.

Text W MS i. [301*a*]–2[1]

To Wortley [*c. 20 Aug. 1712*]

We have more ill Luck than any other people. Had you writ in your first Letter where you intended to be etc. I could have ris up by my selfe at 4 a clock and come to your

[1] This coarse note-paper is badly blotted.

chamber, perhaps undiscover'd. At worst you could but have done what you resolv'd on at first if it had been known, which could not have been till after it was over, all our people being in bed. After my woman was up, she watch'd me so much it was impossible; she apprehended you was in the house, but I beleive has now lost that thought. Had I not been sick and gone to bed sooner than usual, I should have seen your Gentleman, and then he would have told me where you was.—All things conspire against the unfortunate, but if you are still determin'd, I still hope it may be possible one way or other. Write to me allways what contrivance you think on; I know best what is practicable for me. I have since ask'd my B[rother] what he could have done if I had been marry'd in that way. He made answer, he durst not have taken me with him; we must have staid in the Inn, and how odd that would have been!

If there had been any Robbery lately committed, you had been taken up. They suspected you in the House for Highway men. I hope some time of our Lives we may laugh together at this Adventure, tho' at this minute tis vexatious enough.

Do what is most convenient for your own Affairs, but if you intend to go the Spaw, we are very near a sea port here, tho' if possible I would delay my flight till the Night I come to Acton, or I must come quite alone. I should not much care to have this said, but if you judge it most convenient I will drop that scruple, and in every thing prefer you to the world. I am ⟨?⟩ of what you do for me, and my thoughts ⟨?⟩ it are all you would have them.

Pray write. If possible I would do what you desire, and say No, tho' they brought a parson, but I hope we shall not be put to that hard Necessity, for I fear my own woman's weaknesse.

Adeiu. I am entirely yours if you please.[1]

Text W MS i. 298–9 *Address* To Mr Edward Wortley Mountagu.
End. by W M. P. from Dean

[1] The most authoritative account of LM's elopement is that in a letter from Lady Frances Pierrepont to Philippa Mundy on 15 Oct. [1712]: 'As for my Sister I don't know what account you may have heard of her flight, which to be sure has been told with many additionall Circumstances and is but

To Wortley *22 Oct.* [*1712*]

Walling Wells,[1] Oct. 22, which is the first post I could write, Monday Night being so fateigu'd and sick I went strait to Bed from the Coach.

I don't know very well how to begin; I am perfectly unacquainted with a proper matrimonial stile. After all, I think tis best to write as if we were not marry'd at all. I Lament your Absence as if you was still my Lover, and I am impatient to hear you are got safe to Durham[2] and that you have fix'd a time for your return.

I have not been very long in this Familly, and I fancy my selfe in that describ'd in the Spectator.[3] The good people here look upon their children with a fondnesse that more than recompences their care of them. I don't perceive much distinction in regard to their merits, and when they speak sense or nonsense it affects the parents with allmost the same pleasure. My freindship for the Mother and kindnesse for Mis Biddy makes me endure the Squalling of Mis Nanny and Mis Mary with abundance of patience, and my fore-telling the future conquests of the Eldest Daughter makes me very well with the Familly.—[4]

I don't know whether you will presently find out that this seeming Impertinent Account is the tenderest expressions of my Love to you, but it furnishes my Imagination with agreable pictures of our future Life, and I flatter my selfe with the hope of one day enjoying with you the same satis-factions, and that after as many Years together I may see

too liable to ill natur'd remarks. The matter of fact is this: that a week after her arrival to this place [Dean, *c.* 27 Aug.] she went off with Mr. Wortley Mountagu and was marry'd at Salisbury. My Father is not yet reconcil'd to her. She wri⟨tes⟩ ev'ry body word she's perfectly happy, and it seems has found paradise (as she terms it her selfe) when she expected but limbo. . . .' (M/M 11/5/28).

[1] In Notts., near Worksop.

[2] Where his uncle was Dean (see above, p. 31).

[3] No. 500 (3 Oct. 1712), by Addison, is a letter from Philogamus about the pleasures of a large family.

[4] Thomas White (1667–1732), M.P. for Retford 1708–10, and related to LM through his Pierrepont great-grandmother, m. (1698) Bridget Taylor (d. 1761). Besides two sons, they had the three daughters mentioned here: Bridget (b. 1703), Anne (1709–44), and Mary (b. 1710) (*Memoirs of the House of White of Wallingwells*, 1886, p. 22).

you retain the same fondnesse for me as I shall certainly mine for you; and the noise of a Nursery may have more charms for us than the Music of an Opera. ⟨?⟩ as these are the sure Effect of my Sincere Love, since tis the Nature of that passion to entertain the Mind with pleasures in prospect, and I check my selfe when I greive for your Absence by remembering how much reason I have to rejoyce in the hope of passing my whole Life with you, a good fortune not to be valu'd.—I am afraid of telling you that I return thanks for it to Heaven, because you will charge me with Hipocricy, but you are mistaken. I assist every day at public prayers in this familly, and never forget in my private Ejaculations how much I owe to Heaven for makeing me Yours.

Tis candle light, or I should not conclude so soon.

Pray, my dear, begin at the top and read till you come to the bottom.[1]

Text W MS ii. 388–9   *End. by W* L. M. to Durham

To Philippa Mundy [*Oct. 1712*]

Dear Phil:

With much Justice you may accuse me of ingratitude or Stupidity, and I am afraid have by this time entirely banish'd me your thoughts, as unworthy of a place there, but upon my word you have allways the same share in mine, tho' the various hurrys of my Life these many weeks past have been such as not to afford me Leisure to expresse my thoughts, which have been full of You.

At this minute I am in Yorkshire, but shall be in a few days not many Mile from Newark.[2] I think you are some-times with a Relation there. If there was any possibillity of having you with me for a week or longer, I would send my Coach with pleasure.

---

[1] A wide space separates the first two paragraphs of the letter.

[2] LM must have been visiting her husband's family at Wortley, about ten miles north of Sheffield. This letter may precede the one from Wallingwells on 22 Oct.; if so, it would have been written while LM and W were still together.

Knowing me for such a coward as you do, I don't doubt but you were very much surpriz'd to hear I had pluck'd up a spirit, and enter'd upon Rebellion with so much courage. It was certainly my good Genius that inspir'd me, and I am more than ever perswaded:

> An unseen hand makes all our Moves,
> And some are great, and some are small [. . . .]
> Figures alas! of speech, for Destiny plays us all.[1]

I have no longer reason to complain of mine; I hope to hear you say the same of yours.

My Dear Phil, let me have a quick answer; I am ever and entirely Yours,

M.W.M.

Direct your answer to Scoffton, near Worksop, Nottinghamshire, by way of London.

Text MS M/M 11/5/19   *Address* To Mrs Phillippa Mundy at Osbaston near Leicester Leicestershire by way of London   *Postmark* OC 27

To Wortley [*Oct. 1712*]

I am at present in so much uneasynesse, my Letter is not likely to be intelligible if it all resembles the confusion in my head. I sometimes imagine you not well, and sometimes that you think it of small importance to write, or that greater matters have taken up your thoughts.—This last imagination is too cruel for me; I will rather fancy your Letter has miscarry'd, tho' I find little probabillity to think so. I know not what to think, and am very near being distracted amongst my variety of dismal Apprehensions. I am very ill companny to the good people of the house, who all bid me make you their compliments. Mr. White begins your health twice every day. You don't deserve all this if you can be so entirely forgettfull of all this part of the World. I am peevish with you by fits, and divide my time between anger and sorrow,

---

[1] Quoted from Cowley's *Pindarique Odes*, 1668 (*Poems*, ed. A. R. Waller, 1905, p. 193).

which are equally troublesome to me. Tis the most cruel thing in the world to think one has reason to complain of what one loves. How can you be so carelesse? Is it because you don't love writeing? You should remember I want to know you are safe at Durham. I shall imagine you have had some fall from your horse, or ill accident by the way, without regard to probabillitys; there is nothing too extravagant for a Woman's and a Lover's fears. Did you receive my last letter?—If you did not, the Direction is wrong; you won't receive this and my question is in vain. I find I begin to talk nonsense, and tis time to leave off. Pray, my dear, write, ⟨or⟩ I shall be very mad.

Text W MS ii. 394–5   *Address* To Mr Edward Wortley Mountagu at the Deanary of Durham by Durham bag.   *End. by W* L. M. to Durham.

To Wortley [*c. 4 Dec. 1712*]

I don't beleive you expect to hear from me so soon. If I remember, you did not so much as desire it, but I will not be so nice to quarrel with you on that point. Perhaps you would laugh at that delicacy which is however an Attendant of a tender Freindship.

I open'd the closet where I expected to find so many books. To my great Disapointment there were only some few peices of the Law and folios of mathematics, my Lord Hinchingbrook and Mr. Twiman[1] having dispos'd of the rest, but as there is no Affliction no more than no happynesse without Allay, I discover'd an old Trunk of papers, which to my great diversion I found to be the letters of the first Earl of Sandwich, and am in hopes that those from his Lady will tend much to my Edification, being the most extrodinary Lessons of Oeconomy that ever I read in my Life.[2] To the

[1] Edward Richard Montagu (1692–1722), Viscount Hinchingbrooke, son and heir of 3rd Earl of Sandwich; Anthony Twyman (1677–1722), his tutor (J. Venn, *Alumni Cantab. to 1751*, iv. 282). For Hinchingbrooke, the house where LM is staying, see above, p. 7.

[2] Edward Montagu (1625–72), 1st Earl of Sandwich, m. (1642) Jemima Crew (1625–74), da. of 1st Baron Crew. These personal letters are described

Glory of your father, I find that his look'd upon him as destin'd to be the honnour of the Family.

I walk'd yesterday 2 hours on the Terrace. These are the most considerable Events that have happen'd in your absence, excepting that a good Natur'd Robin red breast kept me companny allmost all the afternoon, with so much good humour and Humanity as gives me faith for the peice of charity ascrib'd to them little Creatures in the Children in the Wood, which I have hitherto thought only a poetical Ornament to that history.

I expect a Letter next post to tell me you are well in London, and that your busynesse will not detain you long from her that cannot be happy without you.

Text W MS ii. 382–3   *Address* To Mr Edward Wortley Mountagu to be left at Mr Tonsons Bookseller at Shakespears head overagainst Catharine Stre⟨et⟩ in the Strand[1] London free   *Postmark* ⟨HUNTI⟩NTON *End. by W* L. M. from H[inchingbrooke] 6 Dec.

To Wortley [*c. 6 Dec. 1712*]

I am not at all surprizd at my Aunt Cheyne's Conduct.[2] People are seldom very much greiv'd (and never ought to be) at Misfortunes they expect. When I gave my selfe to you, I gave up the very desire of pleasing the rest of the World, and am pretty Indifferent about it.

I think you are very much in the right for designing to visit Lord Pierrepont.[3] As much as you say I Love the Town, if you think it necessary for your Interest to stay some time here, I would not advise you to neglect a certainty for an uncertainty. But I beleive if you passe the Christmas here, great matters will be expected from your Hospitality; however, you are a better Judge than I am.

in F. R. Harris, *Life of Edward Montagu, First Earl of Sandwich*, 1912, i. 227–32 *passim*. Pepys considered Lady Sandwich most excellent, good, and discreet (9 Oct. 1667).

[1] Jacob Tonson (1656?–1736), leading publisher, had been at this address since 1710.

[2] Gertrude Pierrepont (1663–1732),

m. (1680) William Cheyne, 2nd Viscount Newhaven and 2nd Lord Cheyne.

[3] Gervase Pierrepont (*c.* 1656–1715), 1st Baron, uncle to LM's father, was wealthy and childless. Besides, his wife was aunt to Lord Pelham, later Duke of Newcastle, who was about to enter his majority as a powerful Whig magnate.

I continue indifferently well, and endeavor as much as I can to preserve my selfe from Spleen and Melancholy, not for my own sake—I think that of little importance—but in the condition I am,[1] I beleive it may be of very ill consequence; yet passing whole days alone, as I do, I do not allways find it possible, and my constitution will sometimes get the better of my Reason. Humane Nature it selfe, without any Additional misfortunes, furnishes disagreable meditations enough. Life it selfe, to make it supportable, should not be consider'd too near. My reason represents to me in vain the inutillity of Serious Refflections. The idle Mind will sometimes fall into Contemplations that serve for nothing but to ruine the Health, destroy good Humour, hasten old Age and wrinkles, and bring on an Habitual Melancholy. Tis a Maxim with me to be young as long as one can. There is nothing can pay one for that invaluable ignorance which is the compannion of youth, those sanguine groundlesse Hopes, and that lively vanity which makes all the Happynesse of Life. To my extreme Mortification I grow wiser every day than other. I don't beleive Solomon was more convinc'd of the vanity of temporal Affairs than I am. I lose all taste of this World, and I suffer my selfe to be bewitch'd by the Charms of the Spleen, tho' I know and foresee all the irremediable mischeifs ariseing from it.—

I am insensibly falln into the writeing you a Melancholy Letter, after all my resolutions to the Contrary, but I do not enjoyn you to read it. Make no scruple of flinging it into the Fire at the first dull Line. Forgive the ill Effects of my Solitude, and think me (as I am) ever Yours.

Text W MS ii. 390–1   *End. by W* L. M. 9 Decr.

To Wortley [*8 Dec. 1712*]

Your short Letter came to me this Morning, but I won't quarrel with it since it brought the good News of your health. I wait with Impatience for that of your return. The Bishop of Salisbury writes me word[2] that he hears my Lord

---

[1] Her son was born the following spring.

[2] All that survives of LM's correspondence with Gilbert Burnet is her letter of 20 July 1710.

Pierrepont declares very much for us. As the Bishop is no Infaillible Prelate I should not depend much on that Inttelligence, but my sister Francesse tells me the same thing. Since it is so, I beleive you'l think it very proper to pay him a visit, if he is in Town, and give him thanks for the good offices you hear he has endeavor'd to do me unask'd. If his kindnesse is sincere, tis too valuable to be neglected; however, the very Appearance of it must be of use to us. If I know him, his desire of makeing my F[ather] appear in the wrong will make him zealous for us. I think I ought to write him a Letter of Acknowledgment for what I hear he has allready done. The Bishop tells me he has seen Lord Halifax,[1] who says besides his great Esteem for you he has particular respects for me and will take pains to reconcile my F[ather] etc.

I think this is near the Words of my Letter, which contains all the News I know, except that of this place, which is, that an unfortunate Burgesse of the Town of Huntingdon was Justly disgrac'd yesterday in the face of the Congregation for being false to his first Love, who with an audible voice forbid the banns publish'd between him and a greater fortune. This Accident causes as many disputes here as the Duel could do where you are.[2] Public Actions, you know, allways make 2 partys. The great Prudes say the young Woman should have suffer'd in silence, and the pretenders to Spirit and Fire would have all false Men so serv'd, and hope it will be an Example for the terror of Infidelity through out the whole County. For my part, I never rejoyc'd at any thing more in my Life. You'l wonder what private Interest I could have in this Affair. You must know, it furnish'd discourse all this afternoon, which was no little service when I was visited by the young Ladys of Huntingdon.

This long Letter I know must be particularly impertinent to a Man of busynesse, but Idlenesse is the root of all evil.

[1] Charles Montagu (1661–1715), 1st Baron Halifax, had held important posts in Whig administrations. Although LM calls him W's 'near relation' ('Account of the Court of George the First', 1861, i. 123) he was only distantly related, their common ancestor having been Sir Edward Montagu of Boughton (1532–1602).

[2] The famous duel between the Duke of Hamilton and Lord Mohun in Hyde Park on 15 Nov. 1712 (Swift, *Journal to Stella*, ed. H. Williams, 1948, pp. 570–1).

I write and read till I can't see,[1] and then I[2] walk; sleep succeeds; and thus my whole time is divided. If I was as well qualified all other ways as I am by idleness, I would publish a daily paper called the *Meditator*. The terrace is my place consecrated to meditation, which I observe to be gay or grave, as the sun shews or hides his face. Till to-day I have had no occasion of opening my mouth to speak, since I wished you a good journey. I see nothing, but I think of every thing, and indulge my imagination, which is chiefly employed on you.

Text W MS i. 255–6

From Wortley [*11 Dec. 1712*]

Tho I had no letter of yours by the last and I have writ every post day since I have bin here, I cannot avoid doing it again. I cannot believe you have been too ill to write without letting me know it by another hand, and can think of no other reason for your silence but your having better company than the Robin, who woud not have hindred you in writing. Whoever was with you, sure your absence might have bin excus'd for a minute to tell me of your health. Wherever I am, you see I can always be alone to write to you. But till I see you or hear from you again, I will not enter into the particulars of that concerns you but only tell you in general what I am sure will not displease you much. Your unkle Lord P[ierrepont] has already said something in favour of you to your f[ather]. I am told Lord P. seems willing to mention a reconciliation as a thing proper for your father to agree to, but not as a favour he woud ask. How far this is likely to weigh, you can best tell. By the next post I may write what day I may hope to see you. Till I can have that pleasure why will you deprive me of the next to it, that of hearing from you?

Thursday.

Text W MS i. 154–5 *Address* To the Rt Honble Lady Mary Wortley at Hinchingbrook near Huntington Frank Edw. Wortley. *Postmark* ⟨?⟩

[1] At about this time she read a manuscript draft of Addison's *Cato*, and composed a lengthy critique which she later endorsed 'Wrote at the Desire of Mr. Wortley; suppress'd at the desire of Mr. Adison' (W MS vii. 388–98). When the play was staged in April of the following year, it embodied several of the improvements she had suggested (Halsband, *LM*, pp. 32–33; Peter Smithers, *Life of Addison*, 1954, pp. 250–6). She also wrote an epilogue to the play (1861, ii. 453), but Dr. Garth's was spoken during the play's run.

[2] The rest of the letter (including the *End*. '9 or 11 Dec.') is missing in MS· the text is from 1861, i. 203.

To Wortley [*c. 13 Dec. 1712*]

I am alone without any Amusements to take up my thoughts, I am in Circumstances in which melancholy is apt to prevail even over all Amusements, dispirited and alone, and you write me quarrelling Letters!

I hate complaining. Tis no sign I am easy, that I do not trouble you with my Headachs and my spleen. To be reasonable one should never complain but when one hopes redresse. A Physician should be the only Confidante of Bodily Pains, and for those of the Mind, they should never be spoke of but to them that can and will releive them. Should I tell you that I am uneasy, that I am out of Humour and out of patience, should I see you halfe an hour the sooner? I beleive you have kindnesse enough for me to be very sorry, and so you would tell me, and things remain in their primitive state. I chuse to spare you that pain; I would allways give you pleasure. I know you are ready to tell me that I do not ever keep to these good Maxims. I confesse I often speak impertinently, but I allways repent of it. My last stupid Letter was not come to you before I would have had it back again, had it been in my power. Such as it was, I beg your pardon for it.

I did not expect that my Lord P[ierrepont] would speak at all in our favour, much lesse shew zeal upon that Occassion that never yet shew'd any in his Life. I have writ every post, and you accuse me without reason. I can't imagine how they should miscarry; perhaps you have by this time receiv'd 2 together.

Adeiu, je suis à vous de tout mon cœur.

Text W MS ii. 400–1   *Address* To Mr Edward Wortley Mountagu to be left at Mr Tonsons bookseller, at Shakespears head, overagainst Catharine Street in the Strand London   *Postmark* ⟨HUNTI⟩NTON *End. by W* L. M. Decr.

To Philippa Mundy [*10 Jan. 1713*]

You will be convince'd, my Dear Phil: that Absence and Distance can make no Alteration in my heart, or dimunition of your power there, by my sudden Answer to your obliging Letter, notwithstanding the Impediments to writeing, ariseing from Companny, or my own Indisposition which renders it allmost allways uneasy to me.

You ask my Advice in a Matter too difficult, but since you ask it, my freindship obliges me to give it to the best of my Understanding. You have not made your case very clear, but I think you ask whether it would conduce most to your happynesse to comply with your Relations, in takeing a Man whose Person you dislike, or to dispose of your selfe according to your Inclination. By that Expression of a thorrough Contempt of the Pomps and vanitys of this wicked World,[1] I suppose your Inclination is in favour of one unequal in point of Fortune to him proposd by your father. I know there is nothing more Natural than for a Heart in Love to imagine nothing more easy than to reduce all Expenses to a very narrow compasse. If you like a Man of a £500 per Annum, I am sure you imagine you can live without one thought of Equipage, or that proportion of Attendance, New Cloaths, etc., that you have been us'd to. But, my Dear, can you be very sure of this? The Cares, the Selfe Denial, and the Novelty that you will find in that manner of Living, will it never be uneasy to you? Accidental Losses, thousands of unforseen Chances, may make you repent a hasty Action, never to be undone. When time and Cares have chang'd you to a downright housekeeper, will you not try,

> Tho then, alas, that Tryal be too late,
> To find your Father's Hospitable Gate,
> And seats where Ease and Plenty brooding sate,
> Those seats which long excluded you may Mourn,
> That Gate for ever barr'd to your Return?

My Dear Phil, my kindnesse for you makes me carry it very far, and beg you to look a little on the other side. If the

---

[1] LM had also used this phrase of the Catechism (above, p. 152).

Gentleman propos'd to you has realy no other fault but a disagreable Person, if his Conversation is to be lik'd, his principles to be Esteem'd, and there is nothing Loathsome in his Form, nor no disproportion in your Ages, if all your Dislike is founded on a displeasing Mixture of Features, it cannot last long. There is no figure that after the Eyes have been accustom'd to, does not become pleasing, or at least not otherwise. I fancy it is him that I dance'd with at N.; if so, I cannot commend his Person; but if his understanding is to be valu'd, the progresse from Esteem to Love is shorter and easyer than it is gennerally imagin'd.

However, after all I have said, if the Difference between your choice and your Father's is only between a great Estate and a Competency, tis better to be privately happy than Splendidly Miserable. The reputation of having acted prudently will be no Comfort. Follow your Inclination, but in the first Place remember, tho' tis easy to be without superfluitys, 'tis impossible to be without Necessarys, and as the World is made (and I see no prospect of its being reform'd) there are some superfluitys become Necessarys. You can be without 6 horses, you can't be without a Coach; you can be without lac'd Liverys, you can't be without foot-men.[1] Consider over these things calmly, but if you have a belov'd Lover with an easy fortune, consider also 'tis possible to be very happy without the Rank and Show of Mr. Ch[ester]'s[2] Wife, and (as an experienc'd person) I advise you to consult cheiffly and firstly if you can be pleas'd and 2ndly the World. But if both is impossible, please your Selfe, and beleive from my Experience there is no State so happy as with a Man you like.—I should not be so free in giving my Opinion, dear Phil: but through an entire zeal for your happynesse, which I heartily wish for, and conclude my Letter with a seasonable remembrance,

> Now is your hour, or to comply or shun,
> Better not do the deed, than weep it done.

If you would avoid Mr. C. only because he is not well

---

[1] Many years later LM boasted that she and W had lived on less than £800 during the first year of their marriage (letter sent to her errant, extravagant son on 3 March [1761]).

[2] See above, p. 109.

made, don't avoid him; if you would marry another only
because you like him, don't marry him.

One word of your little Freind, and I have done. If you
was to meet, she would be as fond as ever. There are some
people no more made for freinds than Politicians.

Text MS M/M 11/5/23   *Address* To Mrs Phillippa Mundy at
Osbaston near Leicester Leicestershire.   *Postmark* IA 10

To Philippa Mundy [*27 Feb. 1713*]

To own the Truth, my Dear Phil, I am realy sorry that you
have utterly refus'd your disagreable Lover; 'tis against my
Advice, if that disagreablenesse reaches no farther than his
Person. You say he has good Sense with all the Improvement
that is capable of. If Good Nature is added to that, I am sure,
my Dear, by numerous Examples, you will forget and overlook all that displeases you in his Person. You speak of him
with Esteem; beleive me there is no such thing as a lasting
Aversion that is not founded on Contempt. The first Qualification to be consider'd in a Compannion for Life, and the
greatest charm they can have, is a sweetnesse and complaisance of temper. Examine nicely into that; if your Lover's
joyns that to a good Understanding and Polite behaviour,
endeavor to recall the rash Denial you have given him.
A Man that Loves you enough to have waited Years for your
Answer will not be easily disgusted, and I am yet of Opinion
tis in your power to marry him, which I wish you would do,
if you are sincere in assuring me you have no other Inclination. I can figure to my selfe Mrs. Ashburnham.[1] In a Man
there is nothing Loathsome in Forms, and if he has no other
Deffect but a very lo⟨w⟩ size, a face not Beautiful, you will
be soon reconciled to his figure by a continu'd good humour
and agreable Conversation, especially when your Gratitude
obliges you to it.

> Weak the Bare Tye of Man and Wife we find,
> But freind and Benefactor allways bind.

[1] This allusion is puzzling.

My Paper makes me conclude. Adeiu my Dear, ever faithfully yours.

Text MS M/M 11/5/7   *Address* To Mrs Phillippa Mundy at
Osbaston near Leicester Leicestershire   *Postmark* FE 27

To Philippa Mundy [*April 1713*]

Dear Phil:

I beleive you think me much slower in my answers than
formerly, but one thing or other, I have been intterupted
fifty times, after I had set out pen, Ink and paper with an
Intention of thanking you for your last. I wish you was in
Town from the very bottom of my Soul, a wish much for my
own Advantage; the Scarcity of agreable people is incredible,
as indeed of all agreable things, in this dismal Damn'd London, in which the Spirit of Discord is gone forth, as Satan
did once on the face of the Earth.[1] I am easy while it keeps
out of my small Family; I move in my little sphere in the
height of noise and contention, with the same tranquillity
as if I was in one of the little planetary worlds in Monsieur
Fontenelle's Theory:—[2]

> 'From whence I can with scorn look down
> 'Upon a Worthlesse, witlesse, tastlesse Town.'

I cannot beleive, my Dear Phil: your Merit and Beauty
was made to moulder in old Maiden Lane, notwithstanding
all your Melancholy Imagination. I hope to see a happy end
of them; preserve your Health with care, and there is nothing
you may not hope for this Dozen Year.

Direct to Mr. Tonson's etc.

Text MS M/M 11/5/3   *Address* To Mrs Phillippa Mundy at
Osbaston near Leicester Leicestershire   *Postmark* ⟨?⟩

[1] Referring to Job i. 7, 12.
[2] *Entretiens sur la pluralité des mondes* (1686, transl. 1688), Bernard de

Fontenelle's popular exposition of Newton's astronomy.

To Wortley [*22 June 1713*]

You have not been gone 3 hours, I have call'd at 2 people's doors, and without knowing it my selfe, I find I am come home only to write to you. The late Rain has drawn every body to the Park. I shall passe the whole Evening in my chamber, alone, without any busynesse but thinking of you, in a Manner you would call Affectation, if I should repeat to you. That Refflection brings me back to remember I should not write my thoughts to you. You will accuse me of Deceit when I am opening my Heart to you, and the Plainesse of expressing it will appear Artificial. I am sorry to remember this, and check the Inclination that I have to give a loose to my tendernesse, and tell you how melancholy all things seem to me in your absence, how impatient I am for the End of this Week, and how little possible I find it would be for me to live without you.—My Eyes are so weak I can go no farther. Tis allmost dusk. I dare not write by Candle light; I will finish my letter to Morrow.

Tuesday. My first News this Morning is what I am very Sorry to hear. My Brother has the Small pox. I hope he will do well; I am sure we lose a Freind, if he does not.

I expect to Morrow impatiently. If you break your Word with me, and I have no letter, you do a very cruel thing and will make me more unhappy than you imagine.—The length of this letter will tire you.—Adeiu. May every thing go as you would have it. Your little Boy is very well, and would present his Duty to you, if he could speak.[1]

Text W MS ii. 305–6   *Address* To Mr Edward Wortley Montagu at Hinchingbrook by Huntington bag Huntingdonshire   *Postmark* IV 23   *End. by W* L. Mary

To Wortley [*25 June 1713*]

I am ready to chide you for takeing more care of your promises to your Freind than to me. You write to him first

[1] Edward Wortley Montagu, Jun., *Edward Wortley Montagu 1713–1776*, was born 16 May 1713 (J. Curling, 1954, p. 14).

and then you have no time left.——However I keep all mine to you. I took care to send your Letter, and it was deliver'd into his own hand. I hope your next will make me some Amends. If loving you beyond all things and being insensible of any pleasure but what regards you is any Merit, I have some to you.

My Brother, they send me word, is as well as can be expected. But Dr. Garth says 'tis the worst sort, and he fears he will be too full, which I should think very forebodeing if I did not know all Doctors (and particularly Garth) love to have their Patients thought in Danger.[1]

Your Son is at present in better Health and much happier than his Mother. I am apprehensive of a little return of my sore throat, and am very impatient of your absence. The weaknesse of my Eyes is most troublesome to me since it hinders my writeing you long letters.

I hope you presented my Duty to your Father, thô I forgot it in my last. Pray do now.

I expect a letter to morrow, and to see you Satterday.

Text W MS i. 226–7   *Address* To Mr Edward Wortley Montagu at Hinchingbrook by Huntington bag Huntingtonshire.   *Postmark* IV 25   *End. by W* L. M. 26 June.

To Wortley [*3 July 1713*]

Friday

I sent for Mr. Banks[2] according to your order, and find by him the House he mention'd at Sheffeild is entirely unfurnish'd, and he says he told you so; so that I cannot go

---

[1] In her town eclogue 'Saturday, or The Small-Pox' LM describes Dr. Garth during her own illness (in Dec. 1715), when he attended her:

> MACHAON too, the great MACHAON, known
> By his red cloak and his superior frown;
> And why, he cry'd, this grief and this despair?

You shall again be well, again be fair;
Believe my oath; (with that an oath he swore)
False was his oath; my beauty is no more!

(*Six Town Eclogues*, 1747, p. 36; identification from Horace Walpole's annotated copy, owned by Mr. W. S. Lewis).

[2] Joseph Banks, land agent (see above, p. 42, n. 2).

there. He says there is a house 5 mile from York, extremely
well furnishd and every way proper for us, but the Gentleman
who owns it is gone to France,[1] and nothing can be done till
an answer can be had from thence. I have yet no Letter from
Mrs. Westby[2] concerning Mr. Spencer's.[3] And he says 'tis
very doubtfull whither we can have Mr. Gill's;[4] that we
should be welcom to stay at Scoffton till better provided,
but tis halfe down, and all the Furniture taken down and
lock'd up; that if we will dispence with the Inconveniency
of being in a Town, we may be easily fitted in York, and
not obligd to stay but by the week, that we may be at
Liberty to remove when we can please our selves better.
I am in a great perplexity what to do. If I go to Pule Hill[5]
without giving them warning I may find the house full of
people, and no room to be made for us. If I determine to go
to York, besides the Inconvenience and disagreablenesse of
a Country Town, it may be perhaps out of your way. I know
not what to do, but I know I shall be unhappy till I see you
again, and I would by no means stay where I am. Your
absence encreases my Melancholy so much I fright my selfe
with Imaginary terrors, and shall allways be fancying
Dangers for you while you ⟨are out⟩ of my sight. I am afraid
of Lord H. I am afraid of every thing. There wants but little
of my being affraid of the Small pox for you, so unreasonable
are my fears, which, however, proceed from an unlimited
Love. If I lose you—I cannot bear that If, which I blesse
God is without probabillity, but since the losse of my poor
unhappy Brother, I dread every Evil.[6]

Satterday.   I have been to day at Acton to see my poor
Brother's melancholy Family.[7] I cannot describe how much

[1] See below, p. 186 and n. 1.

[2] Anne, sister of Thomas White of
Wallingwells, m. (after 1699) Thomas
Westby, M.P. (J. Foster, *Pedigrees of
the Co. Families of Yorks.*, 1874, vol. ii,
part i).

[3] William Spencer (d. 1737), Mr.
Westby's relation, owned Attercliffe
Hall and Bramley Grange, both near
Wortley (Burke, *Landed Gentry*, 1852–
3, ii. 1271; Jos. Hunter, *Familiae
Minorum Gentium*, Harl. Soc., xxxviii,

1895, pp. 528–9).

[4] Probably Westby Gill (1679–1746),
of Carhouse, Yorks. (J. Venn, *Alumni
Cantab. to 1751*, ii. 217).

[5] Near Wortley, and owned by Mr.
Phipps (see below, p. 187).

[6] Lord Kingston d. 1 July 1713; he
was buried at Holme Pierrepont, near
Nottingham, on the 9th.

[7] Besides his wife he left his son
Evelyn, and a daughter Frances Pierrepont, b. 22 April 1713 (Eg MS 3531).

it has sunk my Spirits.—My Eyes are too sore to admit of a long Letter.

Text W MS ii. 396–7

To Wortley [*12 July 1713*]

I thank God my Child and my selfe are arriv'd safe at the Lodge,[1] but I am much concern'd to hear by M. N.[2] you had not a long letter that Mr. Chevaleir[3] enclos'd to you from me directed to Burrowbridge, by order of Mr. Jessop.[4] I writ again the day before I set out but suppose you had not that neither. I lay at Worsop. Mrs. White came to see me in the morning there, and would fain have perswaded me to her house.[5] My Impatience to see or hear from you, which I thought I should do here, made me refuse her, thô she press'd it extremely. But if your Affairs do not permit me to see you soon, after I have seen how the Child is in this Air, and that I am a little recover'd the Journey, which has much fatigu'd me, I will go there and stay till you return from B[oroughbridge], if you like of it. I find my selfe weaker than I imagin'd, and tis necessary to recover my strength. I should not be too much alone, which leads me into a Melancholy I can't help, thô I know tis very

[1] Wharncliffe Lodge, occupied by W's father, had been built in 1510 by Sir Thomas Wortley 'on this crag in the midst of Wharncliffe for his pleasure to hear the hart's bell' (stone inscription at Lodge). In Horace Walpole's jaundiced view (in 1756), it was 'a wretched hovel' (*Letters*, ed. Mrs. P. Toynbee, 1903, iii. 444).

[2] Matthew Northall was a trusted servant, also steward, of the Wortley household at the Lodge.

[3] Probably Charles Chevallier, who was later a clerk in the Treasury (*Cal. of Treasury Books*, ed. W. A. Shaw, xxix, 1957, *sub* 17 Oct. 1715 *et seqq.*).

[4] William Jessop (d. 1734) legal adviser to Lord Pelham, had been M.P. for Aldborough, Yorks., 1702–10.

Aldborough, like the adjoining Boroughbridge, was a pocket borough controlled by John Holles, Duke of Newcastle. After the Duke's death in 1711 his widow and his nephew Lord Pelham disputed the terms of his will, and set up rival candidates for both boroughs. Along with Jessop, W had been chosen (on 1 July 1713) as Pelham's candidate for Aldborough. One of W's qualifications, Jessop wrote, was that LM was a relation of Pelham (T. S. Lawson-Tancred, *Records of a Yorkshire Manor*, 1937, pp. 228–9, 257). Besides being cousins through marriage (see above, p. 172, n. 3) they had a common ancestor in the Hon. William Pierrepont.

[5] Wallingwells.

prejudicial to my Health. Not that I do not think my selfe happy in you, and I am sure, to me you can recompence every Losse. While you are well and Love me, I am insensible of any Misfortune, but 'tis impossible for me to hinder makeing some Melancholy Re⟨flections⟩ on the untimely Death of my ⟨Brother⟩ and the Manner of it.

I have done nothing concerning Mr. Gill's house, for fear of doing something you should disapprove. I don't think you will like his proposals. The Enclos'd came from Mr. Aisleby[1] the Night before I set out from London. That House of Mr. Thompson's[2] I fancy you will like better. I am, with the greatest Tendernesse, faithfully yours.

I thank you for the Ven'son.

Text W MS ii. 329–30   *Address* To Mr Edward Wortley Montagu
End. by W L. M. 12 July

To Wortley [*15 July 1713*]

I am allways overjoy'd when I hear from you that you are well, and I cannot forbear beginning my Letter with telling you so. We are both, the child and me, in health. About 3 hours ago Mrs. White sent me the Enclos'd which she desir'd me to send you by the first oppertunity and let you know that Mr. White depended upon having what you desird done. She press'd me again to come to her, and I writ her word that I would come in 2 days if nothing happen'd to hinder me, as I was in hopes your coming would. I am afraid you won't like Mr. Gill's proposals. If you would come to Mr. White's for a day or two, you would be very welcome. I went to Acton before I left London, and my sister F[rances] told me she thought my father did not intend to come into this Country this Summer, but could not be possitive in any thing relateing to him, for he had not seen her nor nobody, nor spoke of any kind of Busynesse.

---

[1] John Aislabie (1670–1742), M.P. for Ripon (Yorks.), statesman and politician.
[2] A member of the large and prominent Yorkshire family (Jos. Hunter, *Familiae Minorum Gentium*, Harl. Soc., xxxviii, 1895, pp. 532–35).

Mr. Banks spoke to me about a house of Mr. Barlow's near where you are, which I have often heard of for a pritty place well furnish'd, and he said will be let cheap, for Mr. Barlow is gone to France.[1] I desir'd him to write to him about it, and he promis'd to do it. Mrs. Spencer[2] will not let her House for longer than till Michaelmass, and I suppose you won't think of leaving the country so soon. I don't know whether I should send the Messenger back, but I have no mind to delay answering your Letter. When I am at Mrs. White's I can write constantly easily by Retford, but the Northern posts are very uncertain. However I'll try my Luck.

My dear Life, write to me, take care of your Health, and let me see you as soon as you can. Your little boy deliver'd me your Letter. The Nurse thought it would be an Acceptable present, and put it into his hands. You will laugh at this Circumstance, which you will think very ridiculous, but it pleas'd me mightily.

Wednesday. Candle light .

I open my Letter to tell you Lord S[andwich][3] is come to Wortley and they are allready inquisitive about my staying. I go to Morrow.

Text W MS ii. 264–5   *End. by W* from L. M. 13 July

To Wortley [*16 July 1713*]

I am sorry I forgot to ask you upon what terms you would have me leave my small family here. I beleive tis best to put John to Board wages, and give Mrs. Northall so much a week for the Nurse.[4] While I am here we live in an irregular way, and I know not how to help it. Some Tennant or other is allways coming in; besides, Mrs. Northall and her Maids eat with us.

---

[1] Probably Thomas Barlow, who died in France in 1713 (J. W. Walker, *Yorks. Pedigrees*, Harl. Soc., xciv, 1942, pp. 38–39).

[2] Not identified.

[3] W's cousin (see above, p. 7).

[4] Before leaving Wharncliffe Lodge, where she has been staying, LM discusses the domestic arrangements of John, her coachman, and of other servants.

For want of something else to do, I went to see Mr. Gill's house and Gardens, and am more than ever of opinion that his Terms are extravagantly unreasonable. I fancy Mr. Barlow's will do our busynesse much better.—I just now receivd Your Letter, and hope by it that your busynesse goes to your Mind, and that I shall see you soon. Mr. Phipps[1] will fancy Lending Pulehill an obligation, and I had as leive be here, so that I can see no reason for borrowing it at any time. Mrs. White said something to me about a House of Mr. Wigfeild.[1] I will make farther enquiry concerning it, but I am of opinion Mr. Barlow's will be most convenient in every respect. I am just removing, in some little hurry and afraid I write nonse⟨nse.⟩ Your little Son is in good Health. I am, with all my Heart, Yours.

They whisper here that Lord S[andwich] does not intend to stay, but will go to London.

Pray send me the direction to write to you, which I'm afraid I don't know exactly.

I writ by a Messenger yesterday.

Text W MS ii. 331–2   *Address* To Mr Edward Wortley Montagu *End. by W* From L. M. 17 July

To Wortley [*23 July 1713*]

I have just now receiv'd a letter from you which has been at London. I could be allmost angry with you for seeming to imagine in it that I could be a post without thinking of you. —I think of you too much, and I hope I am often uneasy without cause. But I cannot forbear cautioning you to take care of your Health. If you love me, you will study to preserve it, as the Thing upon Earth dearest to me. I am Affraid the busynesse you are upon is very disagreable and fatiguing. I wish a happy end to it, as what would be pleasing to you. For my part I can make my selfe easy (I think) with any thing but loseing you. I am now at Walling Wells. Mr. Chevaleir let me know by Mr. Banks' desire, that Mr. Gill insists upon what he mention'd when I was in Town,

[1] Not identified.

reserving an Apartment for himselfe, which on many Accounts I think entirely Inconvenient. The north post brought me no letter, but I suppose (thô I wonder at it) you have not had my last. I have never, nor never can, miss any Opertunity of writeing. Mr. White has entertain'd me much with your glorious speeche and Victory over A[rthur] M[oore] this session.¹ You know I must allways find a sort of pleasure in hearing people joyn with my own thoughts in your praise.

Text W MS ii. 270–1   *Address* To Mr. Edward Wortley Montagu at Mr Mans² at Burrowbridge.   *End. by W* L. M. 23

To Wortley [*25 July 1713*]

I am at this Minute told I have an opertunity of writeing a short Letter to you, which will be all reproaches. You know where I am, and I have not once heard from you. I am tir'd of this place³ because I do not, and if you persist in your silence I will return to Wharncliffe. I had rather be quite alone and hear sometimes from you than in any Companny and not have that Satisfaction. Your Silence makes me more Melancholy than any Solitude, and I can think on nothing so dismal as that you forget me. I heard from your little Boy yesterday, who is in good Health. I will return and keep him companny.

The good people of this family present you their services and good wishes, never failing to drink your Health twice a day. I am importun'd to make haste, but I have much more

---

¹ On 14 May 1713 Arthur Moore, a Commissioner of Trade, had defended the Treaty of Commerce with France. W, among others, had spoken against it. On 18 June, when Moore and W again spoke for and against the Bill, it was put to a vote and defeated by a majority of nine (Rich. Chandler, *Hist. and Proc. of the H. of C.*, 1742–4, v. 11, 40–41; *Wentworth Papers*, pp. 334, 338). W's speeches may have helped win his nomination to the Aldborough seat, for in listing his qualifications Jessop,

his fellow candidate, wrote that he was instrumental in throwing out the Bill which would have destroyed the woollen industry (T. S. Lawson-Tancred, *Records of a Yorkshire Manor*, 1937, p. 257).

² William Mann, postmaster of Boroughbridge (T. H. Oldfield, *Rep. Hist. of Great Britain and Ireland*, 1816, v. 331).

³ Wallingwells, where LM was staying with Thomas White's family.

to say, which may be however all comprehended in these words: I am Yours.

Say something of our Meeting.

Text W MS ii. 402–3   *Address* To Mr Edward Wortley Montagu at Mr Mans at Burrowbridge Yorkshire. *End. by* *W* L. M. 25 July.

To Mrs. Frances Hewet [*? July 1713*]

I would willingly return dear Mrs. Hewet something more for diverting me so well than dry thanks impertinently express'd, but I know [by] this post but that tis reported Lady Charlot Finch is to marry Lord Conaway, and Lady Marg[are]t Tufton Lord Brookes;[1] besides the dismal Changes of state,[2] this all I know. I fear I write Nonsense, but it happens miraculously to be in a room full of Companny, and if I omit this Opertunity, I know not when I may have another of sending. Mr. Sterne, the titular Bishop, was last week marry'd to a very pritty Woman, Mrs. Bateman,[3] whom he fell in Love with for falling backward from her Horse, Leaping a ditch, where she display'd all her Charms, which he found irresistable.[4] Mrs. White, Mrs. Sutton, and Mrs. More are all with me,[5] and I am so embarrass'd with my Civillitys tour à tour, I have hardly calmnesse of Spirit enough to tell you in a compos'd way, I am your thankfull humble servant.

Text MS in Brooke Collection, Soc. of Antiquaries, Newcastle upon Tyne   *Address* To Mrs Hewet to be left at Mr Masons[6] at Worksop

[1] None of this gossip was true: Lady Charlotte Finch (1693–1773), da. of the Earl of Winchilsea and of Nottingham, m. (1726) 6th Duke of Somerset; Francis Seymour Conway (1679–1732), 1st Baron, was at this time married to his second wife (d. 1716); Lady Margaret Tufton (1700–75), da. of 6th Earl of Thanet, m. (1718) Thomas Coke, later 1st Earl of Leicester; and William Greville (*c.* 1694–1727), Baron Brooke, m. (1716) Mary Thynne.

[2] Parliament having been dissolved, the Tories were expected to win again in the forthcoming elections.

[3] Not identified.

[4] John Sterne or Stearne (1660–1745), consecrated Bishop of Dromore 10 May 1713, never married. He was considered a man of learning and piety (Swift, *Corr.*, ed. H. Williams, 1963–5, i. 62, n. 1).

[5] Mrs. White of Wallingwells, with whom LM was staying; Mrs. Sutton, probably Eleanora Margaretta (d. 1715), elder da. of 2nd Baron Lexington; and Mrs. More, unidentified.

[6] An apothecary (see above, p. 113).

To Wortley *3 Aug.* [*1713*]

I have been to day as you order'd me at Bank Top,[1] and have seen a very pritty house, in a pritty place, much superior to Mrs. Spencer's, But not one bit of Furniture, nor halfe the rooms finish'd. I enquir'd when they propos'd to have them done. They answer'd about 2 months hence, and they had some old furniture of their own spinning to put up. If I had not made this Journey, I could never have beleiv'd there had been people capable of building such a House, and not haveing any thing to put into it. The master and Mistress[2] lie at present in a kind of Larder behind the Kitchin. I made no farther enquiry concerning price etc., being I see there's time enough to think on't.

You see I write the very first post, but I propose to follow your example and say nothing of the pain I felt in parting with you, the desire I have to see you, and the uneasynesse it is to me to be from you. Your little Boy presents his duty to you. Pray let me hear from you, but no more ungracious letters.

There came an Aldborrough Man to seek for you at 11 this morning.

Aug't 3.

I forgot part of my Adventure. I was overturn'd going.

Text W MS ii. 341–2   *Address* To Mr Edward Wortley Montagu at Mr Mans at Burroughbri⟨dge⟩ Yorkshire   *End. by W* L. M. 3 Aug.

To Wortley [*4 Aug. 1713*]

Tho' I writ to you but the last post, and have had as yet no news from you, I cannot forbear writeing again, thô

[1] William Adams (1667–1714), an attorney, lived at Bank Top, in Worsborough (Jos. Hunter, *Familiae Minorum Gentium*, Harl. Soc., xxxix, 1895,

p. 902).

[2] Martha (1670–1717), da. of John Barber of Gawberhall.

(perhaps) I am more importunate than obliging. I have hitherto heard nothing from Mrs. White. I intend to send friday, if I have no letter to morrow, and am determin'd, however it falls out, to leave this place on Satterday, not being able any longer to govern the Impatience I have to see you. I hardly think it possible we can misse the House, but after enquiring the Name of Mr. White's Homme d'affairs,[1] rather than stay here 10 days longer for an Answer, I may go to York and treat with him my selfe. But I hope there'll be no occassion for this Expedient, but that on Thursday or friday I may receive an Answer, and I will send you immediate word of it.

I am assur'd by the People here that Mr. Brook's house at Dodworth is quite empty,[2] and sometime since the goods sold by Auction, for which reason I have not been to see it.

Your little Boy is well, and presents his Duty. I am faithfully Yours.

Text W MS ii. 337–8　　*Address* To Mr Edward Wortley Montagu
End. by W L. M. 4 Aug.

From Wortley [*Aug. 1713*][3]

I was surpriz'd very much at the sight of your letter but not so agreably as you imagine. Within an hour or two after you left me my care about a house was ended, and I was contriving which way I might make Mr. Barlow's most pleasant to us. It was no small advantage to it that I coud propose to be with you on Tuesday night after our Election.[4] The distance of the place you are gone to will make me like it worse than this till I see you. If you shoud not have Mr. Adams's or not like it, perhaps it may be no prejudice to us if we are not thought upon ill terms with my sister[5] and I think it cannot be expected we shoud have her much with us. In other respects I think it must be near as good as Mr. Adams's. You must not say a word of Dodworth till Matthew's father in law has made a bargain for fear of spoiling it.[6] If Mr. Barlow's will, in your opinion, do better than any of them for

---

[1] Alexander Harrison.
[2] Thomas Brooke (1669–1739) of Field Head and Dodworth, rector of Richmond (Yorks.) (Jos. Hunter, *Familiae Minorum Gentium*, Harl. Soc., xxxviii, 1895, p. 766).

[3] Perhaps in answer to LM's first letter of 26 Aug.
[4] At Aldborough on 31 Aug.
[5] Catherine (see above, p. 7).
[6] W suggests using Mrs. Northall's father as intermediary in renting.

the present and it is still to be had, believe me I shall be contented with it if you are. It is also very certain I shall not be easy where you are not pleas'd. Whether your suddain change to day was a compliment to the child or me I hope you will not repent it, but enjoy all that can make you happy in every place. I liked Mr. Barlow's[1] very well before I had your letter and whatever other habitation is your choice will please me as well as if it were mine. I therefore beg you will settle to your own mind as soon as is convenient ⟨to⟩ you.

Aldborough, Wedensday night.

If it be of use for you to ask any questions about Dodworth, Mrs. Northal can send for her father, but he must be charg'd not to say you ask'd about it because he has hopes of getting so good a bargain that we may let it for more than we give.

Text W MS i. 156–7   *Address* To Lady Mary Wortley.

To Wortley [7 *Aug. 1713*]

I am of your opinion that the Objections to Mr. Barlow's house are not very material. As to the want of Iron bars, it will give me no apprehensions in a House where I know there is nothing to be stole but chairs and stools. The small distance from York is much more convenient than was it 5 or 6 mile. I have no acquaintance there, and whoever would have a mind to make me a visit would come to Dinner, which we should have found very troublesome. As it is, no body will pretend farther than an Afternoon visit, which cannot be very importunate if not repeated too often, which without an Intimacy is not probable, especially in a place where we have no Interest to mannage. The worst part of the story is the want of Kitchin furniture, which is a very considerable want, and should be allow'd for in the rent.

Whatever Mrs. Spencer's Terms are, I am sure her house must be preferable to Mr. Gill's. I will make immediate Enquiry, but I beleive we shall be much in the wrong if we misse Mr. Barlow's, but great Allowances should be made for the deffect of furniture and people's living in the House.

I am allmost ready to beleive 'tis some mistake that Lord

---

[1] Middlethorpe Hall, one and a half miles south of York, built by Thomas Barlow (see above, p. 186)

Gower is at York, but if he is, I am fully assur'd he will leave it as soon as possible. However I would not put meeting him to the hazard, for it would be an Adventure extremely disagreable to me,[1] for which reason I will go to Knarsburgh, where I hope you will meet me, and go with me to York, if he is gone by that time. The season of drinking the Waters being over, I think I am in no danger of meeting Companny, and I suppose tis a place of tolerable Accomodation. If you do not come hither before that time, on Monday next I will begin my Journey. I can delay no longer the pleasure of seeing you. If you lov'd me as well as I do you, it would be as uneasy to you, but I am afraid you are far from being equally disatisfy'd, and (perhaps) have more reason to be comforted.

Text W MS ii. 353–4   *Address* To Mr Edward Wortley Montagu
End. by W L. M. 7 Augst

To Wortley [*c. 10 Aug. 1713*]

I have just now receiv'd the Mortifying News that Mrs. Spencer has Occassion to live in her house her selfe, and will not let it till the next spring, and then not under a term of Years. At the same time Mr. White has sent me a letter from Mr. Alex[ander] Harrison his agent, in which there is a list of Mr. Barlow's goods, and he proffers to take care at your desire to lay in what Quantity of Beer, Coals etc. you would have, and take care of the rooms being air'd, and see to get Pewter and Brass as much as you will have occassion for. He has sent a copy of the Agreement, by which the Bargain is to be void except confirm'd by you before the 16th.

If we misse of it, I can't tell what we shall do. I know of no house here but Mr. Adams', and he told me that he could have it ready in 2 months, but did not seem willing to make it so without being sure of a Bargain for it afterwards. I beleive he repents of the Expence, and does not intend to lay out money to finish it. He ⟨and⟩ his Wife lie in a dirty room

---

[1] LM was still estranged from her family, perhaps including her brother-in-law.

next the Kitchin. He said they were removing to another House. Above Stairs, the rooms are halfe wainscotted, what wainscot is put up halfe painted, the stairs not finish'd, and the sorry furniture all pull'd down and lying on the floors. 'Tis a very pritty place, and surprizing those people should think of building it and have nothing to put in it. While I am here,[1] we live at a great Expence to no purpose. The Butchers (besides cheating in the weight) make us pay $2\frac{1}{2}$d. per pound for all meat. I lost all patience with his Bill yesterday, and sent to day to Sheffeild where in the public Market they ask'd but 2d. for better meat than any we have had yet. I am afraid we shall find our selves proportionably cheated in all other things.

I have taken care to break my little Horse of his kicking, and beleive I shall like him mightily. I shall be easy in any place where your Affairs or your Pleasure makes it necessary for me to be, and upon no Occassion will ever shew an Inclination contrary to yours. You need be in no pain about me, farther than consulting your own Mind what will please you best, and you may securely depend on its pleasing me.

Text W MS ii. 355–6

To Wortley *22 Aug.* [*1713*]

York, Aug'st 22

I have once more veiw'd the House, but not taken it, and am determin'd I will not till I hear from you, and beg you to consider in your own Mind what you would have me do. There is Vessells in the house, but Mr H[arrison] tells me no Vessells can be good out of constant use, and that it will be cheaper (he engages) to have Beer from him than of our own brewing, and he take care to have it to your taste and in what Quantity you please. Perhaps he may speak this with an Eye to his own Interest. He would perswade me, tis better to buy what is wanting in the Kitchin and sell again than hire, and I may do it with lesse losse. There will be none

<hr>

[1] At Wharncliffe Lodge.

or very little trouble of this kind at Mr. Gill's, and tis for you to Judge of other Inconveniencies.

I beg you would write by a special messenger to morrow Morning, and your Letter shall put an end to all future care about it. I will either send the Coach and take the House, or go my selfe to Wh[arncliffe] and proceed with the Ch[ild] to Mr. Gill's. If you take the House for 4 months, I have perswaded Mr. H[arrison] that the people shall remove and we not be troubled with any body in the house but our own Servants, which I think a considerable point. —The country round is disagreable, and you may have sports about Rotherham[1] you can not have here, beside the advantage of the Gárden, but I fear Mr. G[ill] will expect we shall keep the Gard'ner, and at that rate I'm sure that Garden will be no advantage at all. Perhaps also we shall find the price of meat much higher there than here; I think I have heard Mrs. White say so. Pray let me have your last thoughts, and don't leave it again to me, for upon farther thoughts, without affectation, they are equal to me, and I have no sort of partiality to this, Thô I am gratefull, as I ought to be, for your goodnesse in leaving me my choice, which I shall allways remember with an unfeign'd sense of it.

Since I writ this, Mr. H[arrison] is come to tell me I may hire pewter plates at 2s. 6d. a dozen for 4 months. I beleive one or 2 doz. is all I shall want and then you have plates hir'd for 5s., and other Pewter at the rate of one d. per pound. But we are like to have a good deal of trouble to get Brazerie.—In Sumn, say which way you would have me take. You know all that is to be said on both sides. I beg you not to think of any thing but what will be most convenient for you, and upon my word that will be most pleasing to me.

Text W MS ii. 313–16   *Address* To Mr Edward Wortley Montagu at Burrough Bridge with care.   *End. by W* L. M. 22 August

[1] Carhouse, where Mr. Gill had his property, was one half mile from Rotherham (Thomas Langdale, *A Topographical Dictionary of Yorkshire*, 1822). W enjoyed shooting (W to Addison, 8 Oct. 1711, *Cat. of Alfred Morrison Coll.*, 1883–92, iv. 285).

From Wortley *23 Aug.* [*1713*]

23 Aug'st.

Having not bin able to see Mr. Gill's it is impossible for me to tell how weighty the objection to it is; and shoud we wait till the Election is over, it may not be in our power to have either, so that you must decide, if one of us must. But I think it is better not to be oblig'd for above 3 months, unless you think the removing the people worth the price of a month.

I have been at Mr. Aisbalie's[1] this afternoon and came home late to night. Shoud I sit up to think of this affair I shoud scarce be able to say any thing more to your satisfaction. M[atthew] Northal will be here to morrow morning and ⟨I will⟩ know what Mr. Gill's brother says.[2] If I think it of any use to let you know it, I will send a messenger. If you woud resolve on Mr. Barlow's, perhaps it may be as well not to engage absolutely till night, but that need not hinder preparing beds etc.

It has struck Eleven a clock.

Text W MS i. 152–3   *Address* To Lady Mary Wortley

To Wortley [*24 Aug. 1713*]

I could chide you (if I could chide you at all) for not saying something positive. Upon my word this place is entirely indifferent to me. Here is not a creature I ever saw, and I have not one reason for wishing to stay, and would fain guesse what would please you best. You seem to answer some objections, for which reason I will take this if you do not send me a Messenger to the contrary to morrow morning to be with me about 9.

Pray speak of it, and depend upon it that the other is equal to me.

Your Messenger was so long coming I thought you would not send at all, for which reason I have sent to Burrough Bridge. The Man will be back here to morrow Early, and

---

[1] John Aislabie (see above, p. 185).   *Minorum Gentium*, Harl. Soc., xxxix,
[2] Probably John, Westby Gill's   1895, p. 1142).
younger brother (Jos. Hunter, *Familiae*

if you do not say any thing to the contrary, I will go into the House, but I wish you would decide it.

Text W MS ii. 347–8   *Address* To Mr Edward Wortley Montagu
End. by W L. M. 23 Aug.

To Wortley [*25 Aug. 1713*]

I have pass'd this morn in tedious waiting for a Letter from you, and begin to think that mine by the post miscarry'd. It was very Long, but the Sumn of it: I will not take the house without your final determination. If we agree for 4 months, the people will quite remove. The Hire of Necessarys will come to about 20s., but I have no kind of partiality to the House. You know all that is to be said on both sides. I beg you to determine, and according to your determination I will either go my selfe, or send the Coach to W[harn]c[li]ffe immediately. There is not here one single Soul I ever saw or heard of. Mr. H[arrison] presses my final Answer. Pray send it early to morrow morning, that I may prepare for my Journey, being impatient to be somewhere and Indifferent where, provided you like it.

Text W MS ii. 335–6   *Address* To Mr Edward Wortley Montagu At Mr. Wilkinsons¹ at Aldborrough   *End. by W* L. M. 25 Aug.²

To Wortley [*26 Aug. 1713*]

I fancy'd you look'd after me as if you repented your orders, or at least that complaisance had some share in them, which determine'd me to take the road to Ferrybridge. At worst I can but stay at Pulehill while B[ank] Top is fitting up, and I have much ado to beleive Mr. Adams would proffer his House and then go back from his word. There is no

¹ Charles Wilkinson (1672–*c.* 1729) was Lord Pelham's agent in Boroughbridge, and hence concerned with the imminent election (T. S. Lawson-

Tancred, *Records of a Yorkshire Manor*, 1937, pp. 191, 267).
² End. altered by W to 27 Aug.

Inconvenience so great as the possibillity of your being uneasy, and there is nothing upon Earth so dear to me as your Quiet; and if I can any way convince you of my Love, I am happy.

[*Postcript*] Don't forget to send to Mr. Harrison.

Text W MS ii. 321–2   *Address* To Mr Edwd Wortley

To Wortley [*26 Aug. 1713*]

Ferrybrige

I hope you do not think I have committed an Indiscretion in coming hither. I should not easily forgive my selfe if I omitted any endeavors of settling in the place you think properest; and supposing Mr. Adams does change his mind, the charge of my coming with the Coach is little more than it would have been by it selfe, and I fancy that other Gentleman being about Middle[thorpe] was a Lye, and if so I may come back if there be an Necessity (without it I won't); and I shall have the satisfaction of takeing care of the Child in its Journey.

Text W MS ii. 278–9   *Address* To Mr Wortley at Burrough Brige
End. by W L. M. 26 Aug.

To Wortley [*28 Aug. 1713*]

Between fatigue and vexation I am halfe dead.—I call'd at Bank T[op], in my way hither. Tis late and My Eyes wont suffer me to tell a long story, but in short they are resolv'd neither to let nor lend. He says he never thought of doing it till after Candlemas etc. I have given my selfe trouble to no purpose. I think there is nothing to be done but to send an immediate Note to Mr. H[arrison] to let him know I will be at M[iddlethorpe] with my family Tuesday next. You will do this. I hope you won't find it let, for I am of opinion if we are obligd to go to Mr. G[ill's] we

shall very much repent it. I am comforted, thô sick, with
seeing your Little Boy very well and mightily grown.

I will conclude you have taken M[iddlethorpe] and set
out Monday if you don't say any thing to the Contrary
between this and then.

Text W MS ii. 357–8   *Address* To Mr Wortley at Aldborrough
End. by W L. M. 28 Aug.

To Wortley [*30 Aug. 1713*]

You could send a Letter to Mr. Adams, and know the
same Messenger would come to me, and yet neglect writeing. How have I deserv'd this unkindnesse?—Do what you
please. I had rather you should not write, than write when
you could as willingly let it alone.—

He brought hither this Answer from Mr. A[dams].
I open'd it because I thought he might have chang'd his
mind and resolv'd to let or lend his house, and then there
would have been a necessity of sending it to you immediately,
and John said his orders were not to return till Sunday. But
I find he has no such intention, thô I beleive he would willingly do it, but his Wife won't let him, who I perceive is
very arbitrary in her government. I told her I understood
that she had another House she design'd to go to. She made
answer, she had a house, but there needed a great deal of
Preparation to go into it, at least a Quarter's warning. I said
that Mr. Ad[am]s had proffer'd to lend it. She said she knew
nothing of that, and was much surpriz'd to hear it, but she
would call him. When he came, he said there was some
Mistake, but he hop'd that you would not take it ill, that
he would do more to oblige you than any Gentleman in the
World, and many things to that purpose, which ended in
nothing. I saw he did not care to confesse any such proffer,
and talk'd of our buying the Goods, which I am sure is not
our busynesse. He said it would be 4 or £500 losse to him
to remove presently. I mentiond a fortnight or 3 weeks, and
he answer'd, after Candlemasse at soonest. This is the
Historiette of my treaty with Mr. A.

My letter concluded in this manner, for I was angry at your neglect of me, and would not trouble you with kindnesse I begun to think you weary of. But a Messenger has brought me 2 letters, and given me the pleasure of finding you think of me. Whenever you forget me, you forget one that sumns all her thoughts and wishes in you, and the design of pleasing you is the real motive of all I do. I Love the Child, but after you, and because it is yours. I set out Monday. I wish you successe.[1]

I open my Letter to tell you, we may have the House, and I set forward monday.[2]

Text W MS ii. 351–2   *Address* To Mr Edward Wortley Montagu
End. by W L. M. 30 Aug.

To Wortley [*29 Oct. 1713*]

'Tis now candlelight, and I have but Just receiv'd your Letter, but I need no Excuse but your Example for makeing it a short one.

I have not writ because I expected you every day. I return thanks for your Woodcocks. Your little Boy is very well.

The Man is obstinate in having the Letter this Night. Here are others of more Importance which I will not delay sending to you for fear there should be busynesse.

Text W MS ii. 368–9   *Address* To Mr Edward Wortley Montagu
End. by W L. M. 29 Oct.

To ——[3] [*Nov. 1713*]

I return you a thousand thanks, my dear, for so agreable an Entertainment as your Letter.

In this Cold Climate where the Sun appears unwillingly

---

[1] In the election, on 31 Aug., W and Jessop were defeated by the Duchess of Newcastle's nominees; and although they later appealed to the House of Commons to void the election, charging that their opponents had used bribery, their petition was lost in committee (T. S. Lawson-Tancred, *Records of a Yorkshire Manor*, 1937, pp. 263–5).

[2] Apparently at this time they rented the house at Middlethorpe. Later that year W addressed a letter to LM there (W MS i. 148–9).

[3] Thomas's conjecture (1861, i. 206) that LM's correspondent was W's sister Catherine is unlikely.

—Wit is as wonderfully pleasing as a Sunshiny day, and, to speak poetically, Phœbus very sparing of all his favours. I fancy'd your Letter an Emblem of your selfe. In some parts I found there the Softness of your voice, and in others the vivacity of your Eyes. You are to expect in return but humble and hearty thanks,[1] yet I cant forbear entertaining you with our York Lovers (strange Monsters, you'l think, Love being as much forc'd up here as Melons). In the 1st form of these Creatures is even Mr. Vanbrug.[2] Heaven no doubt compassionateing our Dullness has inspir'd him with a Passion that makes us all ready to die with laughing. Tis credibly reported that he is endeavouring at the Honourable state of matrimony and vows to lead a sinfull life no more.

Whether pure Holiness inspires his mind or Dot⟨age⟩ turns his Brain is hard to find. Tis certain he keeps mondays' and Thursdays' market (assembly days) constant; and for those that dont regard Worldly Muck there's extrodinary good Choice indeed. I beleive last Monday there were 200 peices of Woman's flesh (fat and lean), but you know Van's taste was allways odd. His Inclination to Ruins has given him a fancy for Mrs. Yarborrough.[3] He sighs and ogles, that it would do your heart good to see him; and she is not a little pleas'd, in so small a proportion of men amongst such a Number of Women, a whole man should fall to her share.—

My dear, Adeiu. My service to Mr. Congreve.[4]

Text W MS v. 9–10   *End. by W* L. M.'s letter on Mr Vanbrugh

[1] This phrase is from the General Thanksgiving in the *Book of Common Prayer*.

[2] John Vanbrugh (1664–1726), playwright and architect—knighted the following year—was visiting Castle Howard, near York, at the end of Oct. 1713 (B. Dobrée, *Essays in Biography*, 1925, p. 139). Castle Howard was one of his famous creations.

[3] Henrietta Maria Yarburgh (d. 1776), m. (1719) Vanbrugh. Authorities differ as to her age: nineteen (*DNB*, sub Vanbrugh), twenty-two (Burke, *Landed Gentry*, 1852–3, ii. 1666), or twenty-seven (*Annual Register*, 1776, p. 224). LM here alludes to Vanbrugh's taste for architectural ruins; and she is perhaps ironic about his courtship—he was forty-nine—of a very young woman. Dobrée (p. 350) suggests that her mother, wife of Col. James Yarburgh (who d. 1728), is meant, but LM points to Vanbrugh's matrimonial intentions.

[4] As a girl, LM knew William Congreve, the dramatist. In 1741 she told Spence that Congreve had helped her study Latin (Eg MS 2234, f. 247). She also recalled, once, that he had advised her to hide her temper (MS Commonplace Book, f. 22, Fisher Library, University of Sydney).

To Mrs. Frances Hewet [*c. 29 Nov. 1713*]

'Tis neither owing to insensibillity or ingratitude that I have not yet return'd my thanks to dear Mrs. Hewet for her obliging letter, but the weaknesse of my sight will not permit my pen to expresse the dictates of my heart, and I am forc'd to sit by the fireside and think you a thousand thanks when I would be putting them upon paper.

I rejoyce that Lady Harriot has shew'd some sensibillity, as unworthy an object as she has chosen, yet I think tis better than (as I fear'd she had) dutifully makeing over all her senses along with her fortune for the use of her Grace.[1] I thought her other facultys as imperfect as her sense of hearing. You know smelling a stink is a certain proofe people have some Smell thô disagreably employ'd, and I am glad she is not such a stock as I took her to be.

I beg your pardon that I must write a Letter without news, but I don't know one bit, if it was to stand me instead of my neck verse.[2] I am here waiting the meeting of the Parliament,[3] and am perswaded you will be in London before me; if not, I will endeavor to see you. You talk of the Duke of Leeds;[4] I hear he has plac'd his heroic Love on the bright charms of a Pewterer's wife, and, after a long Amour and many perilous adventures, has stoln the fair Lady, which, in spite of his wrinkles and grandchild,[5] perswades people of his Youth and Gallantry—you see what stuff I am forc'd to

---

[1] Margaret Cavendish (1661–1716), da. of 2nd Duke of Newcastle, m. (1690) Earl of Clare, later (1694) Duke of Newcastle. Among suitors for Lady Henrietta (see above, p. 114) her mother had put forward the Earl of Hertford, and her cousin Lord Pelham had put himself forward; but she was finally won by Edward Lord Harley (1689–1741), later 2nd Earl of Oxford, whom she married 31 Aug. 1713. Just before the wedding the Duchess had become estranged from the Harleys and her daughter (S. H. Nulle, *Newcastle: His Early Political Career*, 1931, pp. 14–15). The disagreement between mother

and daughter made 'a great noise' (*Wentworth Papers*, p. 350).

[2] 'A Latin verse printed in black-letter (usually the beginning of the 51st Psalm) formerly set before one claiming benefit of clergy, by reading which he might save his neck' (*OED*).

[3] The new Parliament, in which W did not have a seat, met on 16 Feb. 1714.

[4] Peregrine Osborne (1659–1729), 2nd Duke of Leeds. By reputation he was 'wild and . . . loose in his life and conduct' (HMC *Stuart Papers*, ii, 1904, p. 420).

[5] Thomas Osborne (6 Nov. 1713–1789), later 4th Duke.

write, but to such I am compell'd except I should entertain
you with York Loves and piques, which would be as dull
to you as what pass'd at the last wake; 'tis impossible to
laugh at what they do, without having first laugh'd at what
they are. I am, Madam, Yours,

M.W.M.

This is aprubt [*sic*], but the post will stay for no man.

Text MS at Yale University   *Address* To Mrs. Hewet at Shireoaks to
be left at Worksop Nottinghamshire   *End.* 29 November 1713 Then
send thro' the Tuxford Bye post. W:G:[1]

To Wortley [*Jan. 1714*]

I am equally surpriz'd and afflicted at your Long stay. For
your sake I should be sorry that absence was as uneasy to
you as to me; I am in hopes by your delays that it is not.

According to your orders I have sent all our goods that
are to go by Water. I hear from Mrs. Smith that she has
taken a House for us.[2] I wish it may be such as you may like,
but for a few months, whatever it is, I think tis of no great
Importance. I know not what to do with the things in your
Closet of which you have the Key, and I dare not break it
open. I hope'd before this to have seen you and have staid
at home expecting every noise made by the Wind was you
coming in. At length I am oblig'd to send this messenger,
not knowing whether you have not chang'd your mind concerning your Journey, which would now be inconveniently
delay'd because of our things being sent away. Mrs. Smith,
without my desire, has officiously laid in provision of Coals
and Beer, I hope not in too large a Quantity. If you are
determind not to come, if you please to send back this
Messenger to morrow with the Key of your Closet, I will
faithfully put up your papers in the best manner I am able,
and upon my word without looking in one of them. The
Carriers go out on Tuesday, and we may set out on that day

---

[1] Perhaps the initials of the postmaster at Worksop.

[2] Perhaps Jane Smith (see below,
p. 250, n. 2); a house in London.

and meet you at Doncaster.[1] If you have alter'd your Resolution of going, pray let me know it. Whatever you please, I am too much yours not to be pleas'd with. Your child, I thank God, is very well, which I can't omit speaking of, thô you never ask after him.

Mrs. Smith says the Q[ueen] is ill.[2]

Text W MS ii. 349–50   *Address* To Mr Edward Wortley Montagu
End. by W L. M. at Middlethorp

To Wortley [*Jan. 1714*]

Your Father has just sent a Complement with your Letter and inttelligence that a Messenger goes to Wharncliffe to morrow. I hope you will be set out, but however if my Letter meets you on the road 'tis no matter. I had writ you a long one to send by a Messenger on purpose. When we meet, wee'l talk what is best as to our Journey. Most of our Goods are gone.

Tis candle light and I can not read what I write. My Eyes are much impair'd by this long Absence and sitting at home in vain expecting you.

You have forgot, I suppose, that you have a little Boy.

Text W MS ii. 309–10   *Address* To Mr Edward Wortley Montagu at Wharncliffe   *End. by* W L. M.

To Philippa Mundy [*4 March 1714*]

Dear Phil,

Not knowing where you were till I met your Brother at Leicester, hinder'd my renewing my Pleasing Correspondance with you. I am now to wish you Joy of his Marriage[3]

[1] Doncaster, on the Great North Road, would be a convenient place for LM (coming from Middlethorpe) and W (from Wharncliffe) to meet on their way to London.

[2] Queen Anne was taken violently ill on Christmas Eve 1713, and did not recover until the beginning of Feb. 1714 (*DNB*).

[3] Francis Mundy (1691–1720) m. Anne, da. of Sir John Noel (John Nichols, *Hist. and Antiquit. of the Co. of Leicester*, 1811, IV. ii. 523, *526; J. Venn, *Alumni Cantab. to 1751*, iii. 227).

and the near Approaches of your own.[1] I heartily wish your
change of condition may render you yet happyer than you
are. I know your own Prudence so well, I am sure you will
contribute as much as is possible to your own Happynesse,
which is one of the most Important Cares to every body. Had
I known you were at Osbaston, I had not fail'd to appoint
you a meeting upon the road; I hope to have better luck
another time. Oblige me with your usual freedom with an
account of your Intended Marriage, which very much surpriz'd me when I first heard of it.

My Dear Phil, I am with my accustom'd Sincerity and
tender Affection faithfully Yours,

M.W.M.

Direct as Last year to be kept at Jacob Tonson's.

Text MS M/M 11/5/21   *Address* To Mrs Phillippa Mundy at
Osbaston near Leicester Leicestershire.   *Postmark* 4 MR

To Philippa Mundy [*17 April 1714*]

Such agreable freinds as you (Dear Phil:) are so seldom
met with, that tis impossible to forget them, or not to
endeavor to preserve so great a treasure. Without Affectation, I feel a concern for you that I am not often sensible of,
and I cannot hear of your entering on so important an
Action as a Settlement for Life, without a degree of Doubt
and fear inseparable from a real Concern. I wish I had been
so fortunate to have met with Mr. M[assingberd], and convers'd with him, but whatever he is, if he has a good understanding, so much Virtu and so many Charms as you have
must engage ⟨him⟩ to be whatever you wish him.

I saw the other Gentleman's Bride some time ago, the most
disagreable old Woman I ever saw, but Money can guild
every thing, and perhaps that way of thinking is not quite
ridiculous, except the World could be alter'd from what it is.

When I come down, which I hope will be very soon, I will
let you know it, and expect the pleasure of seeing you at
Leicester. 'Tis so common a thing to see our sex unhappy

[1] See below, p. 207.

that chuse Husbands without any Guide but Fancy, which is every hour changeable; I form better Veiws for you that are so reasonable, and lay your Happynesse on a more lasting foundation.

Dear Phil: I wish Mr. M. may be sensible how happy he is in that uncommon thing (so rare that like the Phœnix its very existence is disputed), a Woman of Youth and Beauty without Coquetry. In this vile Town, the ⟨?⟩ Universal follys of the fair, the ugly, in short, the whole sex that way ought to make all Husbands revere those Wives that have sense enough not to be led by the Croud, and Virtuous Courrage enough to stand the Laugh that will infailibly insult them with the name of Prudes.[1]

Dear Phil, I am with an unalterable freindship, and a tender Affection, Yours,

M.W.M.

Text MS M/M 11/5/22   *Address* To Mrs Phillippa Mundy at Osbaston to be left at the Posthouse at Leicester Leicestershire. *Postmark* 17 ⟨AP⟩

To Mrs. Philippa Massingberd[2] [*10 July 1714*]

I have not yet express'd my sorrow for your Indisposition and Joy for your recovery, every post expecting I might let you know when there was a possibillity of seeing you at Leicester. I now think I am sure of setting out from hence on next Tuesday. Thursday night I hope to be at Leicester where, if I am so happy to meet my dear Phil: I shall think the fatigue of my Journey more than recompenced. Forgive the disagreable Hurry of Tradespeople etc. at leaving the Town, which forces me to shorten my Letter. You may beleive me in these few plain words, I am Ever Yours,

M.W.M.

Text MS M/M 11/5/20   *Address* To Mrs Phillippa Mundy at Osbaston near Leicester Leicestershire.   *Postmark* 10 IY

[1] LM's thoughts on marriage in this letter may be related to the anonymous essay she contributed to *Spectator* No. 573, published on 28 July 1714. In it she regards with cynical humour the shortcomings of husbands (Halsband, *LM*, p. 37).

[2] LM did not yet know that her friend had been married on 8 July (see next letter).

To Mrs. Philippa Massingberd[1] [*c. 18 July 1714*]

My Dear Phil: (for so I will still call you),

Tis impossible to have heard any News with more satisfaction than I did that of your happynesse, and the obliging Complement you make me of having contributed to it. I do not doubt the continuation of it, as I know you have every Quality to make a good Husband as well as a passionate Lover. I confesse, contrary to the Generallity of my Sex, I am of Opinion that both good and ill Husbands are their Wives' makeing, for as Folly is the root of all matrimonial Quarrells, that distemper commonly runs highest of the Woman's side. I have nothing to fear of that Nature from you; your good humour and good Sense will raise the Esteem of Mr. Massinberd every day, and as your Beauty grows Familiar to his Eyes, your conduct and Conversation will fix his Love on a Foundation that lasts for ever.

Whatever Romances and heat of youth impose on the minds of young people, Passion is soon sated, and a real freindship and mutual Value the only tye that makes Life pass easily on, when 2 Freinds agree to lessen each other's care, and joyn in promoteing one and the same Interest.

I am extreamly glad, my dear Phil, you are happy in a Husband capable of this freind⟨ship⟩. I do not doubt Mr. Massingberd ⟨?⟩ sensible of the Advantage he has above the rest of Man kind, for tis a thing more uncommon, and a greater Blessing, to marry a reasonable Woman than a fortune of £40,000.[2]

I am, my dear Mrs. Massinberd, with a sincere pleasure in your happynesse, faithfully Yours,

M.W.M.

Text MS M/M 11/5/24[3]   *Address* To Mrs Massingberd at South Ormesby near Horn Castle Lincolnshire

[1] On 8 July 1714 Philippa Mundy was married at Cadeby, near Market Bosworth, to Burrell Massingberd (1683–1728) of South Ormsby, Lincs. (MS Bishop's Transcript, Cadeby Church Register; J. Venn, *Alumni Cantab. to 1751*, iii. 159). He had been her suitor for more than three years.

[2] Their marriage settlement, dated 7 July 1714, shows her dowry to have been £3,000 (W. O. Massingberd, *Hist. of Ormsby-cum-Ketsby*, [1893], pp. 177–8).

[3] Extract in *ibid.*, pp. 176–7.

To Wortley *20 July* [*1714*]

I went to Hanslip from Newport Pagnel, hearing Lord Pierrepont was there.[1] They kept me that night and Sunday with a great deal of kindnesse, and seem'd mightily oblig'd by my visit, particularly my Lord. He made me engage that you would take it in your road down, and was extremely desirous of your Company, and pleas'd with mine. I think tis worth your while to hire some footman to go with you so far, and stay with you there. I look upon't as an easy thing for you to be more in his favour than you Imagine. If you have a mind to travel you may easily make it agreable to him, and he will take it kindly to be spoke to of what you intend to do. He loves travelling himselfe to this day so much that my Lady[2] told me he would now go to the Spaw if her Health would permit her to go with him. Therefore he won't dislike your doing it.

I am impatient to see you and ever yours. To Morrow I'll give your service to your Boy.

Nottingham, July 20

Text W MS ii. 286–7   *Address* To Mr Edward Wortley Montagu to be left at Mr Jacob Tonsons Bookseller at the Shakespears Head overagainst Catharine Street in the Strand London   *Postmark* 23 IY *End. by W* L. M. 20 July.

To Wortley [*26 July 1714*]

I should have writ to you the last post, but I slept till it was too late to send my Letter. I found our poor Boy not so well as I expected. He is very lively, but so weak that my heart achs about him very often. I hope you are well; I should be glad to hear so, and what successe you have had in your busynesse. I suppose my sister is marry'd by this

---

[1] Lord Pierrepont (see above, p. 172) lived at Hanslope, Bucks.
[2] Lucy Pelham (*c.* 1663–1721), da.

of Sir John Pelham, m. (1680) Gervase, later Lord Pierrepont.

time.[1] I hope you intend to stay some days at Lord Pierrepont's. I 'm sure he 'l be very much pleas'd with it. The house is in great disorder, and I want Maids so much that I know not what to do till I have some. I have not one bit of paper in the House but this little sheet or you would have been troubled with a longer scribble. I have not yet had any Visiters. Mrs. Elcock[2] has writ me word she has not found any cook. My first Enquirys shall be after a country house, never forgetting any of my promises to you. I am conce⟨rned⟩ that I have not heard from ⟨you⟩. You might have writ while ⟨you⟩ was on the road, and the Letter would have met me here.

I am in abundance of pain about our dear child. Thô I am convinc'd in my reason tis both silly and wicked to set one's heart too fondly on any thing in this world, yet I cannot overcome my selfe so far as to think of parting with him with the resignation that I ought to do. I hope, and I beg of God he may live to be a comfort to us both. They tell me there is nothing extrodinary in want of teeth at his age, but his weaknesse makes me very app⟨rehensive⟩. He is allmost never out of my sig⟨ht⟩. Mrs. Behn says that the cold Bath is the best medicine for weak children,[3] but I am very fearfull and unwilling to try any hazardous Remedys. He is very cheerfull and full of play.

Adeiu my love, my paper is out.

Text W MS i. 272–3   *Address* To Mr Edward Wortley Montagu to be left at Mr Jacob Tonsons Bookseller at the Shakespears head over against Katharine Street in the Strand London   *Postmark* 2⟨?⟩ IY   *End. by* W L. M. 26 July 1714

by her aunt Lady Cheyne (see below, p. 216).

[2] Not identified.

[3] LM's son suffered from rickets, for which cold baths had recently been advocated by Sir John Floyer, a leading physician of the day. Mrs. Behn is unidentified, evidently not the writer.

To Wortley 27 *July* [*1714*]

I fear that I frighted you in my last concerning the Child. thank God he grows Stronger every day and I hope will overcome his illnesse.

I think tis absolutely necessary to call at Lord Pierre-pont's, for I promis'd you should do it, and he seem'd very earnestly to desire it, repeating it several times. If you think it necessary for your Interest you may go cross from North-ampton to Huntington. I am glad you have got some News to please me; I am sure none can do it more than to hear you are well. I have set my heart upon You and my Boy.

I don't understand what you mean b⟨y⟩ desiring me to send you ⟨?⟩ horses. I suppose you don't mean Coach horses, and here is but one Saddle horse. Pray explain next post.

I think any other will do better than Jos[eph] since he was with me.[1] My opinion is that you will be very much press'd to stay. I look upon it as very easy to be very much in his favour, but he is likely to live a long time.[2] I have no thought of any kind but for your sake.—I cannot forbear filling my paper tho I see you don't love long letters.

July 27.

Text W MS ii. 323–4   *Address* To Mr Edward Wortley Montagu to be left at Mr Tonsons Bookseller at the Shakespears head over-against Katharine Street in the Strand ⟨London⟩   *Postmark* 30 IY

To Wortley [*c. 30 July 1714*]

I have no great Inclination to answer this last Letter. It might have been directed to any body else, and I had rather it had been writ to Grace, or to Mathew Northall; and you mention your little Boy with so slight a regard, I have no

[1] Evidently LM had been accompanied on her visit by a footman named Joseph; she instructs W to take a different one.

[2] W thought that Lord Pierrepont's fondness for LM would eventually bring her a large legacy (see below, p. 230, n. 1). But at his death the next year, his will—drawn up in 1682 (P. C. C. Fagg, f. 120)—did not mention her.

mind to inform you how he does. I have had a doctor to him, and he has advis'd me to a cold well 3 mile off. Thither I carry'd him with a beating heart tother day. I thank God he appears to gather strength since. To day Grace is gone with him again. He must go 9 times.

The Races at York have been this 3 days.[1] I never went but once. Lady Betty Howard and her sisters came here to desire my company with them.[2] There was very little compan⟨y⟩; I saw nobody I knew but Mrs. Margaret Boswell in a mourning Coach.[3] Lady Betty told me Lord Wharton was at their house, and that he presented his service to me, and said he was oblig'd to go from hence to Nott[ingham] Race and much straiten'd in time, or he would have waited on me.[4]

Lord Pierrepont's house is near Newport Pagnel. I beleive in the course of your Journey you must come there to dinner. I beleive you need not doubt being press'd to stay. Giveing moderately to the servants, I dare say, will please him best. I told him that you would come sooner than your busyness has permitted you. You may enquire at Newport if he is still at Hanslip. I hope you leave no part of your busynesse of any kind ⟨in⟩ London unfinish'd, that we may have no more expensive Journeys. I can't help wishing to see you, thô you don't write as if you did.

The horses shall set [out], according to order.

Text W MS ii. 280–1   *Address* To Mr Edward Wortley Montagu to be left at Mr Tonsons bookseller at the Shakespears head over-against Katharine Street in the Strand London   *Postmark* 2 AV

[1] The races, at Hambledon Down near the city, were a great social event for the gentry, especially the ladies (Daniel Defoe, *A Tour thro' Great Britain*, 1726, ed. 1927, ii. 642–3).

[2] The daughters of Charles Howard (1669–1738), 3rd Earl of Carlisle: Lady Elizabeth (d. 1739) m. Nicholas Lechmere, and (1728) Sir Thomas Robinson; Lady Anne (before 1696–1764) m. (1717) 5th Viscount Irwin or Irvine, and m. (1737) Col. William Douglas; and Lady Mary (d. 1786). They lived at Castle Howard, about 14 miles north of York.

[3] Margaret Bosville, da. of William and Mary Bosville of Gunthwaite, was in mourning for her brother Godfrey, who died 18 June 1714 (Alice Macdonald, *Fortunes of a Family*, 2nd ed., 1928, p. 233).

[4] Thomas Wharton (1648–1715), Earl, later Marquess, of Wharton, may have been tactful in not calling on LM because he was a friend and political colleague of her father. By mid-Aug. he had returned to London from Yorks. (Addison, *Letters*, ed. W. Graham, 1941, p. 291).

To Wortley [*c. 1 Aug. 1714*]

I am very much surpriz'd that you do not tell me in this last Letter that you have spoke to my F[ather]. I hope after staying ⟨so⟩ long in the Town on purpose ⟨you⟩ do not intend to omit it. I beg you would not leave any sort of busynesse unfinish'd, remembering them 2 necessary Maxims: whatever you intend to do as long as you live, to do as soon as you can; and to leave nothing to be done by another that tis possible for you to do your selfe.

I have not yet sent the horses. I intend'd to do it yesterday, but John is very Arbitrary, and will not be perswaded to hire a horse from York to carry the Child to Fuforth.[1] He says there is ⟨?⟩ that can go, and they will ⟨?⟩ ours, and a great many other things that may be all Excuses, but I know not what Answer to make him, and tis absolutely Necessary now the Child has begun his Bathing he should continue it. Therefore I'll send the Saddle horse to morrow According to your Order to Mathew Northall, and he may hire Another to send with it to you.

I thank God this cold well agrees very much with the Child, and he seems stronger and better every day, but I should be very glad if you saw Dr. Garth if you ask'd ⟨his⟩ Opinion concerning the use of cold Baths for young children. I hope you love the Child as well as I do, but if you Love me at all, you'l desire the preservation of his health, for I should certainly break my heart for him.

I writ in my last all I thought necessary concerning Lord Pierrepont.

Text W MS ii. 398–9   *Address* To Mr Edward Wortley Montagu to be left at Mr Tonsons Bookseller at the Shakespears head overagainst Katharine Street in the Strand London   *Postmark* 4 AV

---

[1] Probably Water Fulford, about 2½ miles south of York.

To Wortley [*c. 3 Aug. 1714*]

I cannot forbear takeing it something unkindly that you do not write to me when you may be assur'd I am in a great Fright, and know not certainly what to expect upon this sudden change.[1] The Arch Bishop has been come to Bishopthorp but 3 days.[2] I went with my Cousin to day to see the K[ing] proclaim'd, which was done, the Archbishop walking next the Lord Mayor,[3] all the Country Gentry following, with greater Crouds of people than I beleiv'd to be in York, vast Acclamations and the appearance of a genneral satisfaction, the Pretender afterwards dragg'd about the streets and burnt, ringing of Bells, bonfires and illuminations, the mob crying liberty and property and long live K[ing] George.

This morning all the principal men of any figure took post for London, and we are alarm'd with the fear of attempts from Scotland, tho all Protestants here seem unaminous [*sic*] for the Hannover Succession. The poor young Ladys at Castle Howard are as much afraid as I am, being left all alone, without any hopes of seeing their father again (thô things should prove well) this 8 or 9 months.[4] They have sent to desire me very earnestly to come to them and bring my Boy. Tis the same thing as pensioning in a Nunnery,[5] for no mortal man ever enters the doors in the absence of their father, who is gone post. During this uncertainty I think it will be a safe retreat, for Middlethorp stands expos'd to Plunderers. If there be any at all, I dare say after the Zeal the A[rch] B[ishop] has shew'd, they'll visit his house (and consequently this) in the first place. The A.B. made me many complements on our near Neighbourhood and said he should be overjoy'd at the happynesse of improving his Acquaintance with you.

[1] The death of Queen Anne on 1 Aug.

[2] Sir William Dawes (1671–1724), translated to York at the beginning of 1714, was 'a fine young bishop. . . . All the ladies of the town resolve to endeavour to charm him' (Isabel, Dowager Lady Irwin, HMC *MSS in Var. Coll.*, 1913, viii. 90).

[3] William Redman, hosier (*Reg. of Freemen of the City of York*, Surtees Soc., cii, 1900, p. 203).

[4] Lord Carlisle was one of the twenty-five Lords Justices of the Realm who ruled from the Queen's death until George I's arrival in England on 18 Sept.

[5] Many years later LM recollected

I suppose you may now come in at Alburgh, and I
heartily wish you was in Parliament.[1] I saw the A.B.'s list of
the Lords Regents appointed and perceive Lord W[harto]n
is not one of them, by which I guesse the new scheme is not
to make use of any Man grossely infamous in either party;[2]
consequently those that have been honest in regard to Both
will stand fairest for preferment.

You understand these things much better than me, but
I hope you will be perswaded by me and your other freinds
(who I don't doubt will be of my Opinion) that tis necessary
for the common good, for an honest man to endeavour to be
powerfull, when he can be the one without loseing the first
more valuable title; and remember that Money is the source
of power.

I hear the Parliament sits but 6 Months.[3] You know best
whether tis worth any Expence or Bustle to be in for so short
a time.

Text W MS ii. 290–2   *Address* To Mr Edward Wortley Montagu
to be left at Mr Tonsons Bookseller at the Shakespears head over-
against Katharine street in the Strand London   *Postmark* 6 AV

To Wortley [6 *Aug. 1714*]

You made me cry 2 hours last night. I cannot imagine
why you use me so ill, or for what reason you continu silent
when you know at any time that your Silence cannot fail of

that at this time W had 'that sort of
passion for me, that would have made
me invisible to all but himself, had it
been in his power' ('Account of
George I', 1861, i. 123).

[1] By law, at the death of the Sovereign, Parliament was to continue to sit
for no longer than six months while new
elections were arranged (Wolfgang
Michael, *Engl. under George I*, transl.
1936–9, i. 4–5, 113). Hence LM suggests
that W stand again.

[2] The Archbishop of York was one
of the Lords Justices—called Lords
Regents by LM. The omission of

Wharton's name from the list came as
a great surprise to those closer to the
political scene (*Wentworth Papers*,
p. 409). In W's opinion, Wharton was
'very wisely left out, having been too
violent and too odious to a great part
of the nation' ('On the State of Affairs
when the King Entered', LM 1861, i.
135). But Wharton's reward came six
weeks later, after the King's arrival,
when he was appointed Lord Privy Seal.

[3] LM is probably repeating an un-
founded rumour about the new Parliament to be elected.

giving me a great deal of pain, and now to a higher degree because of ⟨the⟩ perplexity that I am in, without knowing where you are, what you are doing, or what to do with my selfe and my dear little Boy. However, being perswaded there can be no objection to it, I intend to go to morrow to Castle Howard and remain there lock'd up with the young Ladys till I know when I shall see you or what you would command.

The Arch Bishop and every body else are gone to London. We are alarm'd with a story of a fleet being seen from the Coasts of Scotland. An Expresse went from thence through York to the Earl of Mar.[1]

I beg you would write to me. Till you do, I shall not have any easy minute. I am sure I do not deserve from you that you should make me uneasy.—I find I am scolding. Tis better for me not to trouble you with it, but I cannot help takeing your silence very unkindly.

Text W MS ii. 319–20   *Address* To Mr Edward Wortley Montagu to be left at Mr Tonsons Bookseller at the Shakespears head over-against Katharine street in the Strand London. *Postmark* 9 AV *End. by W* L. M. 7 Augst   goes the 7th to Castle howard.

To Wortley [*c. 9 Aug. 1714*]

I am very glad to hear from you when I do, tho' you make me wait for that happynesse. I am very much trouble'd (tho not at all upon my own Account) at my F[ather]'s pro-digious proceedings.[2] I think you should let Lord P[ierre-pon]t know that he made you an offer of treating after my S[ister]'s marriage and then flew off.

I suppose twill be near 3 weeks before I see you, and since you say nothing against it, I am retir'd to Castle Howard, which is the same thing as pensioning in a convent. The

---

[1] LM's brother-in-law (p. 209, n. 1).

[2] On 2 Aug., after being a widower for twenty-two years, Lord Dorchester m. Lady Isabella Bentinck (1688–1728), da. of 1st Earl of Portland; she was only a year older than LM. He had pursued her a long time (see above, p. 160; Walpole, *Corr.*, ed. W. S. Lewis *et al.*, xiv, 1948, p. 243; Stuart, p. 78).

Ladys have no Coach, and I have sent my horses to Wortley, that they may be kept with the least Expence. My Boy I hope grows better, which is a very considerable pleasure to me. Pray write oft to me. I cant help flattering my selfe, if you knew how uneasy your silence makes me, you would not punnish me with it.

I am in no pain concerning my Sister M[ar] living in greater figure than my selfe,[1] but I hope there's no sin in being a little pleas'd if it should prove to the Town that matches of my Aunt Cheyne's makeing are not allways extreme prudent.[2]

Text W MS ii. 370–1   *Address* To Mr Edward Wortley Montagu to be left at Mr Jacob Tonsons Bookseller at the Shakespears head overagainst Catharine Street in the Strand London   *Postmark* 11 AV

To Wortley [*c. 11 Aug. 1714*]

I hope the Child is better than he was, but I wish you would let Dr. Garth know he has a bignesse in his joynts, but not much. His Ankles seem cheifly to have a weaknesse. I should be very glad of his Advice upon it, and whither he approves rubbing them with Spirits, which I am told is good for him.

I hope you are convinc'd I was not mistaken in my Judgment of Lord Pelham; he is very silly but very good natur'd.[3] I don't see how it can be improper for you to get it represented to him that he is oblig'd in Honnour to have you chose at Alburgh, and may more easily get Mr. Jessop chose

[1] Although the Tory leaders, Bolingbroke and Oxford, were dismissed by the Queen shortly before her death, Lord Mar had retained his posts; and Lady Mar optimistically presumed that he would continue to prosper under the new monarch.

[2] The marriage stung one Whig to remark: 'My Lord Marr is marryd to my Lady Frances Pierpoint so that there is a good Whig *marr'd* by taking a Scotch Jacobite for her Husband' (*Letters of Thomas Burnet to George*

Duckett 1712–1722, ed. D. N. Smith, 1914, p. 69).

[3] This is the first surviving contemporary estimate of Thomas Pelham-Holles (1693–1768), 2nd Baron Pelham, future Duke of Newcastle. Now in the infancy of his career as election manager of the Whig party, he controlled approximately twenty parliamentary seats in three counties (S. H. Nulle, *Newcastle: His Early Political Career*, 1931, pp. 22, 53).

at Another place.[1] I can't beleive but you may manage it in such a Manner, Mr. Jessop himselfe would not be against it, nor would he have so much reason to take it ill (if he should not be chose) as you have, after so much money fruitlessly spent. I dare say you may order it so that it may be so, if you talk to Lord Townshend[2] about it etc. I mention this because I cannot think you can stand at York or any where else without a great Expence.[3] Lord Morpeth is just now of Age, but I know not whither he'l think it worth while to return from Travel upon that Occassion. Lord Carlisle is in Town. You may, if you think fit, make him a visit, and enquire concerning it.[4] After all, I look upon Alburgh to be the surest thing. Lord Pelham is easily perswaded to any thing, and I am sure he may be told by Lord Townshend that he has us'd you ill, and I know he'l be desirous to do all things in his power to make it up.

In my opinion, if you resolve upon an Extrodinary Expence to be in Parliament, you should resolve to have it turn to some Account. Your father is very surprizing if he persists in standing at Huntingdon,[5] but there is nothing surprizing in such a world as this is.

Text W MS ii. 380–1

[1] Pelham was obliged to nominate W for Aldborough, LM thought, because W had been defeated as his candidate in Aug. 1713. On 17 Aug. 1714, however, Pelham named Jessop and General James Stanhope for the Aldborough seats (T. S. Lawson-Tancred, *Records of a Yorkshire Manor*, 1937, p. 265).

[2] Charles Townshend (1675–1738), 2nd Viscount, powerful Whig leader who won great favour with George I. His first wife (d. 1711) was Pelham's half-sister.

[3] In the constituency of York the franchise was vested not in the corporation alone but in all the freemen (Robert Walcott, *Eng. Politics in the Early Eighteenth Century*, 1956, p. 18). Hence an election campaign there would be very expensive.

[4] Carlisle's son and heir—Henry Howard (d. 1758), later 4th Earl—was styled Viscount Morpeth. Baptized 14 April 1693 (R. A. Austen-Leigh, *Eton College Reg. 1698–1752*, 1927, p. 242), he had been of age four months. Besides one seat for Carlisle, Lord Carlisle controlled both seats for Morpeth (Walcott, p. 50); and in the 1715 election Lord Morpeth was returned for one of them.

[5] Although W had sat for Huntingdon in the 1710 Parliament, his father, who controlled the borough, had nominated himself and Lord Hinchingbrooke in 1713 (when W lost at Aldborough) and did so again for the 1715 Parliament.

To Wortley [*c. 18 Aug. 1714*]

I mean't you should tell Lord P[ierrepon]t when you see him,[1] but if he has left Hanslip, which is very probable, when we meet 'tis time enough to form a letter between us. I am very Impatient for that time, tho I would [not] have you leave London without seeing the K[ing]. I had a letter this post from my sister M[ar] that seems very much confirm'd in her beleife of Lord Mar's keeping his place or getting an Equivalent pension,[2] for she talks of nothing but living in London, fine preparations for the Coronation, etc.[3]

I wish you was sure of ⟨?⟩ place of being chose without Expence. You made me no Answer concerning what I said about Lord Pelham. I still think it very possible you may mannage so with him to come in easily at Alburgh or else-where, when his Interest is undisputed.

You don't speak one word of your Boy in this letter nor what Dr. Garth says concerning the use of Spirits to his Joynts, which are something big. Pray don't forg⟨et⟩ to write. I have your Letters constantly.

Text W MS i. 228–9   *Address* To Mr Edward Wortley Montagu to be left at Mr Tonsons Bookseller at the Shakespears head over against Catharine street in the Strand London   *Postmark* 20 AV

To Wortley [*c. 20 Aug. 1714*]

I have at this instant so terrible a tooth Ach, if it was not to write to you I should not be able to hold a pen, and even

---

[1] That her father had gone back on his promise to negotiate with W.

[2] The 'Equivalent' was a sum of money (almost £400,000) which by the 1707 Act of Union was to be paid to Scotland (Daniel Defoe, *Hist. of the Union*, 1786, pp. 201–3). Apparently Lady Mar believed that if her husband lost his post as Secretary of State for Scotland, he would be compensated by a pension from this fund.

[3] In spite of Lady Mar's boasting, her husband was more realistic; he wrote to his brother on 7 Aug. that he did not expect to retain his post. 'And then,' he added, 'I must do the best I can for myself' (HMC *Mar and Kellie MSS*, 1904, p. 505). He offered his loyal services to the King, but was dismissed from office at the end of Sept.; a year later he joined the Jacobite rebellion and helped lead it to disaster.

that consideration won't, I fear, enable me to do it long.
I would not have you miss seeing the K[ing] after waiting so
long.[1] Lord P[ierrepont] I don't doubt is remov'd to Tong
Castle[2] before this time. He intended to do it in a fortnight
when I was with him. I will go back to Midlethorp in a few
days on purpose to make what enquirys I can from the
Tomsons[3] etc. Here we live directly as in a convent, and
know no more the affairs of York than those of Constantinople. If you are yet undetermin'd where to stand, I fancy
you may meet as little opposition there as any where. If Lord
Carlisle is unengag'd I suppose he'l make no scruple of
promising you his Interest, which is very great; but it would
be convenient to ask it as soon as you can, and Sir William
Robinson will, I dare say, be very willing to joyn with you.[4]
If he is [in] Town you may speak to him about it; if at York,
if you please, I may hint it to my Lady[5] and probably be able
to give you an Account what difficultys will arise in the
undertaking. I think tis prodigious your father persists in
standing at Huntingdon.

The child is very lively but not so strong as I could wish
him. My insupportable teeth forces me to conclude.

I won't mention any thing till farther orders from you.

Text W MS ii. 262–3   *Address* To Mr Edward Wortley Montagu
to be left at Mr Tonsons Bookseller at the Shakespears head over-
against Catharine Street in the Strand London   *Postmark* ⟨?23⟩ AV
End. by W 23 Aug.

To Wortley [*c. 1 Sept. 1714*]

I came to day from Castle Howard. Tis candle light and
I must not pretend to a long letter. I hope you are secure of
some other place, for I beleive tis impossible to carry it at

[1] George I did not hasten to his new
throne; he left Hanover on 31 Aug.

[2] In Shropshire; it had come to him
through his mother, Elizabeth, da. of
Sir Thomas Harris.

[3] For this family, see above, p. 185,
n. 2.

[4] Sir William Robinson (*c.* 1656–
1736) sat for York without interruption
from 1698 to 1722.

[5] Lady Anne Capell (1675–1752), da.
of 1st Earl of Essex, m. (1688) 3rd Earl
of Carlisle.

York. Allmost the whole Town are engag'd for Mr. Fairfax.[1]
Sir W[illia]m Robinson is at London and perhaps may give
you farther Information, but I am of Opinion it would be
a great Expence to no purpose. Adeiu. If the K[ing] is at
Hague,[2] I hope your respects will be soon paid and I shall
see you here.

Text W MS ii. 343–4   *Address* To Mr Edward Wortley Montagu
to be left at Jacob Tonsons Bookseller at the Shakespears head over-
against Katharine Street in the Strand London   *Postmark* 3 SE
End. by W L. M. Sept.

To Wortley *3 Sept.* [*1714*]

Midlethorp, Sept. 3.

I see here is nothing to be done at York, where every body
is engag'd for Mr. Fairfax or Mr. Jenkins.[3] I hope you are
sure of some place, for all the country is full of people
makeing Interest at every Burrough. There is allmost no
body left at York, all gone to London. I beleive you'l be
sorry to hear Mr. Topham[4] is given over by his Physicians,
but I am much more so at a report that Lord Irwin is kill'd
in Scotland. I realy compassionate poor Lady Irwin with a
sense of a Mother's sorrow upon so dismal an Occassion.
They say he was much a prittyer sort of Gentleman than the
Elder Brother.[5]

I am at present lock'd up. The day after I came from
Castle Howard I thought it more convenient and cheaper
to send 2 horses to Grass at Wharncliffe than keep them

[1] Robert Fairfax, a retired admiral,
had been elected for York in a 1713
by-election but was defeated in 1715
(C. R. Markham, *Life of Robert Fairfax
of Steeton 1666–1725*, 1885; W. W.
Bean, *Parl. Rep. of Six Northern Cos.
1603 to 1886*, 1890, pp. 1112, 1125).

[2] The King did not arrive at the
Hague until 5 Sept., and his departure
for England was further delayed eleven
days by unfavourable winds (Wolfgang
Michael, *Engl. under George I*, 1936–9,
i. 73).

[3] Tobias Jenkins, who had sat for
York in previous Parliaments, was defeated in 1713 but stood successfully in
1715 (Bean, *op. cit.*, p. 1128).

[4] An unidentified member of the
well-known Yorkshire family.

[5] The Dowager Lady Irwin or
Irvine was Isabella Machell (1670–1764),
widow of the 3rd Viscount. Her eldest
son, Edward (b. 1686), had died in May
1714; and his next brother, Richard
Ingram (1688–1721), 5th Viscount, is
the Lord Irwin falsely reported killed.

here, especially haveing no probable Occassion of going
often out this winter and having no body in the house but
George to lay the cloth etc. I sent to John to carry the horses
to Mathew.¹ He sent me word he would not, and that he
desir'd to be discharg'd. I took no notice of what he said
that night, but put my selfe to the Inconvenience of sending
George in his Stead, and next morning (having no mind to
part with him at this time) I bid Grace tell him if he would
beg pardon he might stay. But he sent me up his Bill and
desir'd to be discharg'd, which I was forc'd to do, very
unwillingly because tis hardly possible in the Country to
get any that is tolerable safe, thô he has been very troublesome and grumbling ever since we left London. He told
Grace sometime ago that he heard we intended to live in the
Country and he resolv'd not to stay. I wish you would enquire for one that can drive 4 horses well and is sober, and
bring him down with you, for tis impossible to get one here
that I durst trust to drive me. I am very Impatient to see
you. Adeiu.

Mrs. Listers are just come² and say Topham is dead.
I have made what enquiry I can concerning a House, but
can hear of none ready furnish'd. There will be a great deal
of trouble in removing.

Since I writ the Enclos'd, I have a very quiet sober
Country Coachman recommended to me, whose honesty is
answer'd for, but I fear that his skill is not sufficient to drive
a Journey, especially with 4 horses. However, I may take
him for some time, that we need not be press'd to take one
without much Enquiry.

Text W MS ii. 365–7   *Address* To Mr Edward Wortley Montagu
to be left at Mr Tonson's Bookseller at the Shakespears head over-
against Catharine Street In the Strand London   *Postmark* 6 SE
End. by W L. M. Sept.

¹ Matthew Northall was the steward   *Pedigrees of the Co. Families of Yorks.*,
at Wharncliffe Lodge.   1874, vol. i, part ii.
² For the Lister family, see J. Foster,

To Wortley [*c. 6 Sept. 1714*]

I am very much surpriz'd that you complain of my silence. I have not omitted writeing and am very sorry that my Letters have miscarry'd. You say nothing of your Election. I hope you are sure of comeing in somewhere. I beleive most people have made Interest where they intend to stand, and Delay in those Cases (as you have found it with Lord Pelham) is a certain way of being disapointed. I suppose you are now with Sir Peter King,[1] and therefore will not intterupt your Conversation with an insignificant long Letter. I am ex⟨tream⟩ly glad you are comeing down, ⟨for⟩ I live the most melancholy Life in the World.

The Boy is very well but not so strong as to make me entirely easy upon his Account.

Text W MS ii. 268–9   *Address* To Mr Edward Wortley Montagu to be left at Mr Tonsons Bookseller at the Shakespears head over-against Katharine Street in the Strand London   *Postmark* 8 SE *End. by W* L. M. 8 Sept.

To Wortley [*c. 10 Sept. 1714*]

I am surpriz'd I don't hear from You. I never fail writeing every post, and I beleive you do not receive my Letters, a misfortune I lament, without knowing how to remedy it. In my last (if you receiv'd it) I gave you a peice of false news, that my Lord Irwin was shot. I hear since he is gone to London. I am very sorry that you did not [in] time enough declare you would stand at York, where you had undoubtedly been chosen. All the Interest Mr. Jenkins has would have been yours. The Thompsons were here yesterday, and without my saying any thing begun to t⟨ell m⟩e that they were very much ⟨conce⟩rn'd you did not stand here, and the Interest of all their family[2] would sooner have been yours

---

[1] Peter King (1669–1734), a prominent Whig and close friend of W's. Knighted in 1708, he became a baron and Lord Chancellor in 1725.

[2] Various members of the Thompson family sat for York in Parliaments before and after this time.

than any man in England; and tis they that chuse Mr.
Jenkins if he is chose, as I beleive now he will. I hope you
stand some where, for I think tis as reasonable to stand now
as it was unreasonable last year, for I suppose one sort of
petitions will be as favourably receiv'd now, as the other
were before.

The Boy has been pritty well, but is to day out of order.
We hope tis only teeth. I wish ⟨to⟩ God you was as impatient
to see me as I am to see you.

John is gone to London. I would not bear his charges
because he went away so impertinently. May be he'l come
to you about it, but I beleive you'l think me in the right.

Text W MS ii. 272–3   *Address* To Mr Edward Wortley Montagu
to be left at Mr Tonsons bookseller at the Shakespears Head over-
against Katharine Street in the Strand London   *Postmark* 13 SE
End. by W L. M. Sept.

To Wortley [*c. 15 Sept. 1714*]

I cannot be very sorry for your declineing at Newark,
being very uncertain of your Successe,[1] but I am surpriz'd
you do not mention where you intend to stand. Dispatch
in things of this nature, if not a security, at least delay is
a sure way to lose, as you have done being easily chose
at York for not resolving in time, and Alburgh for not
applying soon enough to Lord Pelham. Here are people
here had rather chuse Fairfax than Jenkins, and others that
prefer Jenkins to Fairfax, but both partys separately have
wish'd to me you would have stood, with assurances of having
prefer'd you to either of them.[2] At Newark Lord Lexington[3]
has a very considerable Interest. If you have any thoughts of
standing you must endeavor to know how he stands affected,

[1] Newark-on-Trent was a borough
with a fairly democratic franchise, all its
tax-paying inhabitants having the right
to vote (Robert Walcott, *Eng. Politics
in the Early Eighteenth Century*, 1956,
p. 12).

[2] In this 1715 election Robinson in-

structed some of his voters to support
Jenkins; consequently they were both
elected, and Fairfax was defeated (C. R.
Markham, *Life of Robert Fairfax of
Steeton 1666–1725*, 1885, p. 258).

[3] Robert Sutton (1662–1723), 2nd
Baron Lexington.

thô I am afraid he will assist Brigadeir Sutton[1] or some other Tory. Sir Mathew Jenison has the best Interest of any Whig, but he stood last year himselfe, and will perhaps do so again.[2] Newdigate will certainly be chose there for one;[3] upon the whole tis the most Expensive and uncertain place you can stand at.

Tis surprizing to me that you are all this while in the midst of your freinds without being sure of a place when so many insignif⟨icant⟩ creatures come in without any opposition. T⟨hey⟩ say Mr. Strickland is sure at Carlisle, where he never stood before.[4] I beleive most places are engag'd by this time. I am very sorry for your sake that you spent so much money in vain last year, and will not come in this, when you might make a more considerable figure than you could have done then. I wish Lord Pelham would compliment Mr. Jessop with his Newark Interest,[5] and let you come in at Alburgh.[6]

Text W MS ii. 297–8   *Address* To Mr Edward Wortley Montagu to be left at Mr Tonsons Bookseller at the Shakespears head over-against Katharine Street in the Strand London   *Postmark* 17 SE *End. by W* L. M. Sept.

To Wortley [*c. 17 Sept. 1714*]

I am very sorry you have not yet a more sure place than Newark. The Tory Interest there is very strong. The Duke

[1] Richard Sutton (1674–1738), a relation of Lord Lexington, and Brigadier-General under Marlborough (Charles Dalton, *George the First's Army 1714–1727*, 1910–12, i. 55–58). He had sat for Newark in the Parliament of 1708, and again since 1712 (as a replacement for the Member who had been called to the House of Lords). He was successful in the current election of 1715.

[2] Sir Matthew Jenison (1653–1734) had sat for Newark only in 1701 and 1702.

[3] Richard Newdigate (1679–1745) was returned for Newark; he had also

been successful in 1713 (J. Foster, *Alumni Oxon. 1500–1714*, iii. 1060).

[4] William Strickland (*c.* 1686–1735) succ. his father as 4th baronet in 1724; he sat for Malton 1708–14, and was brought in for Carlisle in 1715.

[5] The borough of Newark-on-Trent was the property of Lord Pelham, who nominated its candidates (S. H. Nulle, *Newcastle: His Early Political Career*, 1931, p. 52).

[6] Pelham had already chosen his nominees for Aldborough (see above, p. 217, n. 1). Perhaps LM hoped he would reconsider.

of Newcastle (who you know had more than double the power of Lord Pelham there) set up Brigadeir Sutton there a few years ago, and he lost it, after an Expence of £1,200 as I heard him say; but if he did not spend that, tis certain he spent a great deal to no purpose.[1] All the Interest the D[uche]sse of Newcastle now has is thereabouts, and out of spite to Lord Pelham she will employ it all against you.[2] My Opinion is, if he does not appear here himselfe, his name will signify nothing, and if he does, 'tis still uncertain. It has allways been famous for opposition, and I beleive more Money spent there lately than in most of the Towns in England. I am very much concernd you did not think of York in good time, being fully convince'd you would have carry'd it with very little trouble. I should be very glad to hear you have a sure place; and in the mean time would not have you refuse Newark, thô tis the very worst to be depended on. I am afraid most of the Burroughs are engag'd. I am sure they are hereabouts, for I hear of treating every day.

If Lord Pierrepont is comeing to Town, and it is consistent with your other Affairs, I think tis very right to stay to wait on ⟨him⟩ for fear of missing him on the ⟨road⟩ in the Journey, and I should be g⟨lad⟩ you gave him a clear account of my F[ather] breaking his word with you; and after that, tell him you will give him no farther trouble about it. I think tis very probable Lord Pierrepont should invite you to his house in the country. If he does, I suppose you'l take the first oppertunity of going to it. Pray return him thanks for having done it; and let him know that you did not intend to go near his house without waiting on him.

I am very melancholy and want to see you extreamly. Every body is at London, that keeps a Coach. I read all Day.

Text W MS ii. 260–1   *Address* To Mr Edward Wortley Montagu

[1] Sutton had been defeated in the 1710 election, which he then contested on the grounds that his opponent had used bribery and violence to deter voters from electing him (*Journ. of H. of C.*, xvi. 418).

[2] John Holles (1662–1711), 1st Duke of Newcastle, had made his nephew Lord Pelham his heir, even bequeathing to him the Cavendish estates inherited by the Duchess from her father (A. S. Turberville, *Hist. of Welbeck Abbey and Its Owners*, 1938–9, i. 302–3). The Duchess's protracted litigation with Pelham about his inheritance had been settled in July 1714 in her favour.

to be left at Mr Tonsons Bookseller at the Shakespears head over-against Catharine Street in the Strand London *Postmark* 19 SĒ *End. by W* L. M. Sept.

To Wortley [*c. 24 Sept. 1714*]

Thô I am very impatient to see you, I would not have you by hastening to come down lose any part of your Interest. I am surpriz'd you say nothing of where you stand. I had a letter from Mrs. Hewet last post who said she heard you stood at Newark and would be chose without opposition, but I fear her Inttelligence is not at all to be depended on. I am glad you think of serving your freinds; I hope it will put you in mind of serving your selfe.

I need not enlarge upon the Advantages of Money. Every thing we see and every thing we hear puts us in remembrance of it. If it was possible to restore Liberty to your Country or limit the Encroachments of the Pre[rogati]ve by reduceing your selfe to a Garret, I should be pleas'd to share so glorious a poverty with you, but as the World is and will be, tis a sort of Duty to be rich, that it may be in one's power to do good, Riches being another word for Power, towards the obtaining of which the first necessary qualification is Impudence, and (as Demosthenes said of Pronunciation in Oratory) the 2nd is Impudence, and the 3rd, still, Impudence.[1] No modest Man ever did or ever will make his Fortune. Your freind Lord H[alifa]x, R[obert] W[alpo]le[2] and all other remarkable instances of quick Advancement have been remarkably Impudent. The Ministry is like a play at Court. There's a little door to get in, and a great Croud without, shoveing and thrusting who shall be foremost; people that knock others with their Elbows, disregard a little kick of the shinns, and still thrust

[1] LM may be citing Francis Bacon's essay 'Of Boldness', where he quotes Demosthenes as saying that Action, Action, and Action are the three chief requisites in oratory; Bacon then says that Boldness, Boldness, and Boldness are the chief ones in civil business. LM's library in 1739 contained a copy of Bacon's *Remains* (Wh MS 135).

[2] By this time the future Prime Minister had been lord high admiral, secretary at war, treasurer of the navy, and had been expelled from the House of Commons on charges of bribery.

heartily forwards are sure of a good place. Your modest man stands behind in the Croud, is shov'd about by every body, his Cloaths tore, allmost squeez'd to death, and sees a 1,000 get in before him that don't make so good a figure as him selfe. I don't say tis impossible for an Impudent Man not to rise in the World, but a Moderate Merit with a large share of Impudence is more probable to be advance'd than the greatest Qualifications without it.

If this Letter is impertinent it is founded upon an opinion of your merit, which if tis a mistake I would not be undeceiv'd in. Tis my Interest to beleive (as I do) that you deserve every thing, and are capable of every thing, but no body else will beleive it if they see you get nothing.

Text W MS ii. 303–4   *End. by W* L. M. 24 Sept.

To Wortley [*26 Sept. 1714*]

I am sorry you resolve upon Newark, being perfectly convince'd you will not be chose there, and tis one of the most expensive places in England. I beleive Lord Lexington's Interest in that Town superior to Lord Pelham's, and you don't say that you are sure he will be Idle, which I beleive is the most you must expect from him, and tis certain he will not be that if Brigadeir Sutton stands. You say you hope you shall be sure else where, but you don't seem to know where, and I am afraid it will be finally no where.

Undoubtedly you should have told the story of my F[ather] to Lord P[ierrepont] the first time you saw him, which would have look'd much more natural and undesign'd, but however tis necessary to tell it in these words: I beleive I told your Lordship, Lord D[orchester] bid me apply to him again when Lady F[rances] was marry'd, but he would not put it out of his power to dispose of her. If he makes answer: no, you did not tell me so, you may reply: I thought I had, but perhaps it was after you had left the Town, but he did tell me so; accordingly I apply'd to him, etc.

I hope you visit Lady Dowager Denbeigh.[1] She will have reason to take it unkindly if you do not, and I promis'd her you should. Pray do before you leave the Town.

Text W MS ii. 274–5   *Address* To Mr Edward Wortley Montagu to be left at Mr Tonsons Bookseller at the Shakespears head over-against Catharine Street in the Strand London   *Postmark* 29 SE *End. by W* L. M. 26 Sept.

To Wortley [*1 Oct. 1714*]

I am very glad to hear from you, thô by so short a letter, but am willing to beleive your Affairs hinder'd its being longer. I hope you will not fail this 2nd Appointment, and that Mr. Wil:[2] will send for his daughter in due time. She is not in the Least silly and not in the Least entertaining. Adeiu.

Candle light.

My duty to Papa.[3] I will tell you the child is well thô you don't ask after it.

Text W MS ii. 288–9   *Address* To Mr Edward Wortley Montagu *End. by W* L. M. 1 Oct.

To Wortley [*5 Oct. 1714*]

I cannot imagine why you should desire that I should not be glad, thô from a Mistake, since at least tis an Agreable one. I confesse I shall ever be of Opinion, if you are in the Treasury[4] it will be an Addition to your figure and facilitate your Election, thô tis no otherwise Advantageous; and that if you have nothing when all your Acquaintance are pre-ferr'd, the World gennerally will not be perswaded that you neglect your fortune, but that you are neglected.

[1] Mary Cary (*c.* 1623–1719), da. of 2nd Earl of Monmouth, was second wife of William Feilding, 3rd Earl of Den-bigh. LM's mother had been his daughter by his first wife; hence the Dowager was LM's step-grandmother.

[2] Not identified.

[3] The first sign that LM's father had become reconciled to her.

[4] To which he was shortly appointed.

Text W MS ii. 299–300   *Address* To Mr Edward Wortley Montagu
to be left at Mr Tonsons Bookseller at the Shakespears head over-
against Catharine Street in the Strand London.   *Postmark* 6 OC
End. by W L. M. 5 Oct.

To Wortley [*9 Oct. 1714*]

You do me wrong in Imagining (as I perceive you do)
that my reasons for being solicitous for your having this
place was in veiw of spending mere [*sic*] money than we do.
You have no cause of fancying me capable of such a thought.
I don't doubt but Lord H[alifa]x will very soon have the
staff,[1] and tis my beleife you will not be at all the richer.
But I think it looks well and may facilitate your Election,
and that is all the advantage I hope from it. When all your
Intimate Acquaintance are preferr'd, I think you would have
an ill Air in having nothing. Upon that Account only I am
sorry so many considerable places are dispos'd on. I suppose
now you will certainly be chose some where or other, and I
cannot see why you should not pretend to be Speaker.[2]
I beleive all the Whigs would be for you, and I fancy you
have a considerable Interest amongst the Torys, and for that
reason would be very likely to carry it. Tis impossible for
me to Judge of this so well ⟨as⟩ you can do, but the reputation
of being thoroughly of no party is (I think) of use in this
affair, and I beleive people gennerally esteem you Impartial;
and being chose by your Country is more Honnourable
than holding any place from any King.

Text W MS ii. 295–6   *Address* To Mr. Edward Wortley Montagu
to be left at Mr. Tonsons Bookseller at the Shakespears head over-
against Catharine Street in the Strand London   *Postmark* 11 OC
End. by W L. M. 9 Oct.

[1] Although the Whig leaders had promised Halifax the staff as Lord High Treasurer, the King insisted that the Treasury be put into commission (William Lord Cowper, *Private Diary*, ed. E. C. Hawtrey, 1833, p. 58). On 1 Oct. it was settled that Halifax would be First Lord (*Wentworth Papers*, p. 425).

[2] In the House of Commons (after his election).

To Wortley [*c. 12 Oct. 1714*]

Your Letter very much vex'd me. I cannot imagine why you should doubt being the better for a place of that consideration,[1] which 'tis in your power to lay down whenever you dislike the measures that are taken. Supposing the Commission lasts but a short time, I beleive those that have acted in it will have the offer of some other considerable thing.[2] I am perhaps the only Woman in the world that would disuade her Husband (if he was inclin'd to't) from accepting the greatest place in England upon the condition of giving one Vote disagreeing with his principle and the true Interest of My Country; but when tis possible to be of Service to that Country by going along with the ministry, I know not any reason for declining an honnourable post. The World never beleives it possible for people to act out of the common tract, and who ever is not employ'd by the Public may talk what they please of having refus'd or slighted great offers, but they are allways look'd upon either as neglected or discontented because their pretensions have fail'd, and whatever efforts they make against the Court are thought the Effect of Spleen and disapointment, or Endeavors to get something they have set their Heart on—as now Sir T[homas] H[anme]r is represented (and I beleive truly) as aiming at being Secretary.[3] No man can make a better figure than when he enjoys a considerable place, being

---

[1] W was appointed by Halifax one of the four junior Commissioners of the Treasury at an annual salary of £1,600 (commission 13 Oct. 1714, *Cal. of Treasury Books*, ed. W. A. Shaw, xxix, 1957, pp. 16, 323). LM later wrote that W, thinking any offer below that of Secretary of State unworthy, was persuaded to accept the Treasury appointment 'by a rich old uncle of mine, Lord Pierrepont, whose fondness for me gave him expectations of a large legacy' ('Account of George I', 1861, i. 123).

[2] In May 1715 Halifax died, and when the Treasury Board was reconstituted under Robert Walpole in Oct.,

W was dismissed. He was then rewarded with the reversion of Auditorship of the Imprest (11 Oct. 1715, news-letter from Jean de Robethon, Staatsarchiv Hannover, 24/123). He surrendered the reversion in 1720 (*Cal. of Treasury Books and Papers 1735–1738*, ed. W. A. Shaw, 1900, p. 394).

[3] Sir Thomas Hanmer (1677–1746), who had been Speaker in the House of Commons, was offered the post of Chancellor of the Exchequer, but like most other prominent Tories refused, wishing to be free to serve his party (*Wentworth Papers*, p. 423; Wolfgang Michael, *Engl. under George I*, 1936–9, i. 101).

for the place Bill;[1] and if he finds the ministry in the wrong, withdrawing from them when tis visible that he might still keep his places, if he did not chuse to keep his Integrity.

I have sent you my thoughts of places in genneral, I solemnly protest without any thought of any particular advantage to my selfe; and if I was your freind and not your Wife, I should speak in the same Manner, which I realy do without any consideration but that of your figure and Reputation, which is a thousand times dearer to me than Splendor, Money etc.

I suppose this long Letter might have been spar'd, for your Resolution I dont doubt is allready taken.

Text W MS ii. 301–2

To Wortley [*20 Oct. 1714*]

I hear the Parliament will be certainly dissolv'd soon after the Coronation.[2] I wish it be not then too late to begin to make an Interest at any place, and I wonder to hear no Account of your being sure somewhere. I hope you do not forget that now is the time to make sure of the Colleirys and put an end to your trouble about 'em, which perhaps may not be so easily done if delay'd.[3] I am surpriz'd you do not mention them in your Letters. Lord Gower has got a decree in his favour against Lord Lansdowne.[4] Lady Hinchingbrook is with Child.[5]

[1] In 1710, when he saw no possibility of a government appointment (the Tories being in power), W had introduced a place Bill, forbidding Members of Parliament from serving in the government; but it was defeated. Such a Bill was introduced (and defeated) in March 1714 (Luttrell, *Hist. Relation*, 1857, vi. 662, 725–6). LM is now trying to persuade him that he will not violate his conscience by accepting the Treasury post and at the same time winning election.

[2] On 21 Oct., the day after the Coronation, Parliament was prorogued until Jan. 1715, when it was dissolved.

[3] W and his father, owners of exten-

sive coal-mining interests in the North Country, were members of a 'Regulation' or monopoly of owners and lessors; and a break-up of this Regulation was impending (Edward Hughes, *North Country Life in the 18th Century*, 1952, pp. 193–4).

[4] This must have some connexion with the pension inherited by Lord Gower through his grandmother, who was a daughter and co-heir of John Granville, 1st Earl of Bath (*Cal. of Treasury Books*, ed. W. A. Shaw, xxix, 1957, pp. 109, 197). George Granville (1667–1735), Baron Lansdown, was a nephew of the Earl.

[5] Elizabeth Popham (d. 1761) m.

I have not heard from you this long time, but I confesse from writeing such Letters as you ⟨do⟩, tis a very natural Transition no⟨t⟩ to write at all.

Text W MS ii. 276–7   *Address* To Mr Edward Wortley Montagu to be left at Mr Tonsons Bookseller at the Shakespears head over-against Catharine Street in the Strand London   *Postmark* 22 oc *End. by W.* L. M. 20 Oct.

To Wortley [*c. 23 Oct. 1714*]

You seem not to have receiv'd my Letters, or not to have understood them. You had been chose undoubtedly at York if you had declar'd in time, but there is not any Gentleman or tradesman unengag'd at this time. They are treating every night. Lord Carlisle and the Thompsons have given their Interest to Mr. Jenkins. I agree with you of the necessity of your standing this Parliament, which perhaps may be more considerable than any that are to follow it, but as you proceed 'tis my opinion you will spend your Money and not to be chose. I beleive there is hardly a burrough unengag'd. I expect every letter should tell me you are sure of some place, and as far I can perceive you are sure of none. As it has been mannag'd, perhaps it will be the best way to deposite a certain Sumn in some freind's hands, and buy some little Cornish Burrough.[1] It would undoubtedly look better to be chose for a considerable Town but I take it to be now too late.

If you have any thoughts of Newark, it will be absolutely necessary for you to enquire after Lord Lexington's Interest, and your best way to apply your selfe to Lord Holdernesse, who is both a Whig and an honest man.[2] He is now in Town, and you may enquire of him if Brigadeir Sutton

(1707) Lord Hinchingbrooke. Her child did not live, and this may have been the occasion for LM to write in her diary (which no longer exists): 'Lady Hinchinbroke has a dead daughter—it were unchristian not to be sorry for my cousin's misfortune; but if she has no live son, Mr. Wortley is heir—so there's comfort for a Christian' (Stuart, p. 65).

[1] Pocket boroughs in Cornwall were relatively cheap constituencies to 'buy'; in 1698 one went for only £400 (Edward Porritt, *The Unreformed House of Commons*, 1909, i. 356–7).

[2] Lord Lexington was Lord Holdernesse's uncle.

stands there, and if not, try to engage him for you. Lord Lexington is so ill at the Bath that it is a doubt if he will live to the Election; and if he dyes, one of his heiresses and the whole Interest of his Estate will probably fall on Lord Holdernesse.[1]

Tis a surprize to me that you cannot make sure of some burrough, when so many of your freinds bring in several parliament men without trouble or expence. Tis too late to mention it now, but you might have apply'd to Lady Winchester, as Sir Joseph Jekyl did last year, and by her Interest the D[uke] of Bolton brought him in for nothing.[2] I am sure she would be more zealous to serve me than Lady Jekyl.[3] You should understand these things better than me.

I heard by a letter last post that Lady M. Montagu and Lady Hinchingbrook are to be Bedchamber Ladys to the Princesse, and Lady Townshend Groom of the Stole.[4] She must be a strange princesse if she can pick a favourite out of them, and as she will be one day Queen, and they say has an influence over her Husband,[5] I wonder they don't think fit to place Women about her with a little common sense.

Text W MS ii. 307–8

[1] None of these predictions came to pass: Lord Lexington lived until 1723; his elder daughter, Eleanora Margaretta, d. (1715) unmarried; and Bridget (1699–1734) m. (1717) the Marquess of Granby, later 3rd Duke of Rutland.

[2] Lady Anne Vaughan (*c.* 1689–1751), da. of 3rd Earl of Carbery, m. (1713) Charles Paulet or Powlett (1685–1754), Marquess of Winchester, son and heir of Charles (1661–1722), 2nd Duke of Bolton. The Duke controlled one of the seats for Lymington, Hants (Robert Walcott, *Eng. Politics in the Early Eighteenth Century*, 1956, p. 17), for which Jekyll (1663–1738) was returned in 1715.

[3] Lady Winchester had been LM's intimate girlhood friend (Stuart, p. 57). They were also related by marriage, through the 1st Marquess of Halifax,

whose second wife was a Pierrepont.

[4] Caroline of Anspach (1683–1737), Princess of Wales, had arrived in England on 15 Oct. 1714, and she settled her Court between the Coronation, on 20 Oct., and the public announcement on 28 Oct. (Mary, Countess Cowper, *Diary*, ed. S. Cowper, 2nd ed., 1865, pp. 6–10). The ladies named here, none of them appointed, were: Lady Mary Lumley (1690–1726), da. of 1st Earl of Scarborough and 2nd wife of George Montagu; Lady Hinchingbrooke (see previous letter); and Dorothy Walpole (1686–1726), who m. (1713) Lord Townshend.

[5] After having been at Court herself, LM analysed Princess Caroline's influence over the future George II in her brilliant 'Account of George I', 1861, i. 133–4.

To Wortley [*c. 25 Oct. 1714*]

I am told that you are very secure at Newark. If you are so in the West, I cannot see why you should set up in 3 different places except it be to trebble the Expence.[1]

I am sorry you had not oppertunity of paying Lord P[ierrepon]t that complement, tho' I hope that it will not weigh much with him in favour of another. I wish you would remember the common usefull Maxim, what ever is to be done at all ought to be done as soon as possible. I consider only your own Interest when I speak, and I cannot help speaking warmly on that Subject. I hope you will think of what I hinted in my last Letters; and if you think of it at all, you cannot think of it too soon.

Adeiu. I wish you would learn of Mr. Steele to write to your Wife.[2] Pray order me some Money, for I'm in great want and must run in Debt if you don't do it soon.

Text W MS ii. 293–4   *Address* To Mr Edward Wortley Montagu to be left at Mr Tonsons at the Shakespears head overagainst Katharine Street in the Strand London   *Postmark* 27 oc   *End. by W* L. M. 27 Oct.

To Wortley [*29 Oct. 1714*]

I am very much oblig'd to My Lady Denbeigh and the Bishop of Salisbury ⟨for⟩ their kind enquirys after the Child, and the more because 'tis certainly neither of theirs. You may tell them that he is very well, and has got some teeth, thô he is not so strong as I could wish he were. He is all the comfort of my Life.

You say nothing of a Coachman. I hope you won't forget to bring down one with you. He that I have got overturn'd

---

[1] W finally stood for Westminster, a seat controlled by the Court (Robert Walcott, *Eng. Politics in the Early Eighteenth Century*, 1956, p. 13), and was returned on 24 Jan. 1715.

[2] Steele's missives to his 'Dear Prue' were frequent even when they were living in the same place. During her courtship LM had been a visitor at their house, where she could have observed his solicitude in informing his wife of his activities.

me about a week ago at the side of the Ditch, that twas the particular providence of God or I had undoubtedly been kill'd. Since that time I have not stir'd out, nor know not when I shall have courrage to venture. No body comes hither and tis not possible to live in a more melancholy Solitude than I do.

Text W MS ii. 284–5   *Address* To Mr Edward Wortley Montagu to be left at Mr Tonsons Bookseller at the Shakespears head over-against Catharine Street in the Strand London   *Postmark* 1 no *End. by W* L.M. 29 Oct.

To Wortley [*c. 10 Nov. 1714*]

I was not well when I writ to you last; possibly the dis-order in my health might encrease the uneasyness of my Mind. I am sure the uneasyness of my Mind encreas'd the disorder of my health, for I pass'd the Night without sleep-ing, and found my selfe next morning in a fever. I have not since left my chamber. I have been very ill and kept my Bed 4 days, which was the reason of my Silence, which I am afraid you have attributed to being out of humour, but was so far from being in a condition of writeing I could hardly speak, my face being prodigiously swell'd, that I was forc'd to have it lance'd to prevent its breaking, which they said would have been of worse Consequence. I would not order Grace to write to you for fear you should think me worse than I was, thô I don't beleive the fright would have been con-siderable Enough to have done you much harm. I am now much better and intend to take the air in the Coach to day, for keeping to my chair so much as I do, will hardly recover my Strength.

I wish you would write again to Mr. Phipps,[1] for I don't hear of any money and am in the utmost Necessity for it.

Text W MS ii. 404–5   *Address* To Mr Edward Wortley Montagu to be left at Mr Tonsons Bookseller at the Shakespears head over-against Catharine Street in the Strand London   *Postmark* 12 no *End. by W* L. M. 14 Nov.

[1] Perhaps the Mr. Phipps from whom LM considered borrowing a house near York (see above, p. 187).

To Wortley [*c. 24 Nov. 1714*]

I have taken up and laid down my pen several times, very much unresolv'd in what style I ought to write to you. For once I suffer my Inclination to get the better of my reason. I have not oft opertunitys of indulging my selfe and I will do it in this one letter. I know very well that no body was ever teiz'd into a Likeing, and 'tis perhaps harder to revive a past one than to overcome an Aversion, but I cannot forbear any longer telling you I think you use me very unkindly. I don't say so much of your absence as I should do if you was in the Country and I in London, because I would not have you beleive I am impatient to be in town when I say I am impatient to be with you. But I am very sensible I parted with you in July, and tis now the middle of November. As if this was not hardship enough you do not tell me you are sorry for it. You write seldom and with so much indifference as shows you hardly think of me at all. I complain of ill health and you only say, you hope tis not so bad as I make it. You never enquire after your Child.—

I would fain flatter my selfe you have more kindnesse for me and him than you express, but I reflect with greife, a Man that is asham'd of passions that are natural and reasonable is gennerally proud of those that [are] shamefull and silly.

You should consider solitude and spleen (the consequence of Solitude) is apt to give the most melancholy Ideas, and there needs at least tender Letters and kind expressions to hinder uneasynesses allmost inseparable from absence. I am very sensible how far I ought to be contented when your affairs oblige you to be without me. I would not have you do them any prejudice, but a little kindnesse will cost you nothing. I do not bid you lose any thing by hasting to see me, but I would have you think it a misfortune when we are asunder. Instead of that, you seem perfectly pleas'd with our separation, and indifferent how long it continues. When I refflect on all your behaviour I am asham'd of my own. I think I am playing the part of my Lady Winchester. At least be as gennerous as my Lord; and as he made her an early confession of his aversion, own to me your Inconstancy, and upon my word I will give you no more trouble about it.[1] I have conceal'd as long as I can the uneasyness the nothing-ness of your Letters have given me, under an affected Indif-ference, but Dissimulation allways sits aukardly upon me. I am weary of it, and must beg you to write to me no more if you cannot bring your selfe to write otherways. Multi-plicity of busynesse or Diversions may have engag'd you, but all people find time to do what they've a mind to. If your Inclination is gone, I had rather never receive a Letter from you, than one which in leiu of comfort for your absence gives me a pain even beyond it. For my part, as tis my first, this is my last complaint, and your next of that kind shall go back enclos'd to you in blank paper.

[*Postscript*] I have receiv'd your money.

Text W MS i. 303-4   *End. by W* L. M. 24 Nov.

To Wortley [*27 Nov. 1714*]

I am very sorry my letters have been open'd (if they have been so) and wish you had let me know it sooner. I am sorry you have taken a house in Duke street, both from the Damp-ness of the situation and that I beleive there is hardly one sound house that looks into the Park in that street.[2] I know my Lord Loudoun liv'd in one, which he staid in but a single week, being every moment in apprehension of having it fall upon their heads. Mr. G[eorge] Montagu left another for the same reason, which has stood empty ever since.

[1] Lord and Lady Winchester (see above, p. 233, n. 2) separated soon after their marriage in July 1713. She was considered (in 1706) 'exstreemly good, and very handsom, and very modist and vertuously brought up' (*Wentworth Papers*, p. 51). Horace Walpole called her an ugly monster, and said that Winchester's father had forced him to marry her for the sake of her money (*Corr.*, ed. W. S. Lewis *et al.*, ii, 1937,

p. 329). Her marital ill fortune was ascribed by LM to an excess of virtue and lack of passion (8 Dec. [1754]).

[2] Duke Street, Westminster, on the east side of St. James's Park, no longer exists, swallowed up by government buildings in Whitehall. W and LM remained in the same street when, a year later, they took the house of Sir Charles Wager (Rate Books for St. Margaret's, Westminster Public Library).

I am very much afraid you have taken one of these houses. Pray tell me if you have; I hope not Mr. George Montagu's.[1]

You seem to have forgot I have no Coachman. Here are none to be got, either acquainted with the roads or that know how to drive in the streets at London, for which reason it may be as well to send one down with a postillion and a pair of horses from London. I don't beleive there is a pair of horses to be hir'd at York able to draw to London.—But tis time enough to consider this. I'll make what Enquiry I can.—The consideration whither I should bring the Child with me is of much more Importance. I would fain do what is best for him without any regard to my selfe and my unwillingness to part with him. I would speak of some other things, but I remember my Letter will [be] open'd.

Text W MS ii. 325–6   *Address* To Mr Edward Wortley Montagu to be left at Mr Tonsons Bookseller at the Shakespears head over-against Catharine Street in the Strand London   *Postmark* 1 DE *End. by W* L.M. 27 Novr.

To Wortley [*c. 6 Dec. 1714*]

Pray let me know what house you have taken, for I am very much afraid it should be that where Mr. George Montagu liv'd and out of which Mrs. Montagu and her Child both dy'd of the Small pox, and nobody has liv'd in it since.[2] I know tis 2 or 3 year ago, but tis gennerally said, that Infection may lodge in Blankets etc. longer than that. At least I should be very much afraid of coming into a house from whence any body dy'd of that Distemper, especially if I bring up your Son, which I beleive I must, thô I am in a great deal of concern about him. One Saddle horse is enough, that you need not send down any more. George is very honest, I beleive, and has behav'd himselfe very well to his power, but he and all like him are too Aukard to serve in London, for visiting or any thing of that Nature, but I had much rather carry him up than any other of his Country-Men, that would add to their Aukardness want of use.

[1] George Montagu (d. 1739), nephew of Lord Halifax, and himself cr. (1715) Earl of Halifax.

[2] Montagu's first wife, Ricarda Posthuma Saltonstall (b. 1689), had died shortly before 5 April 1711.

I have sent your Nightgown and the rest of your things to day, directed to Jacob Tonson's. The hire of 2 Coach horses and a postillion from hence to London is £6 if they bear their own charges, and 5 if I do. You can Judge which is cheaper, to hire them here or from London. I have taken a Coachman for present use, but I have had him but 3 days, so can make no Judgment what he will prove. If you have one to send down, to be sure (I think) twill be as cheap to send him upon a Coach horse and a postillion upon another. He that I have taken says he has been us'd to the roads, but there is no great trust to be given to their words. I can neither be sure how he'l drive in London, but he says he has been a Coachman there. Let me know if you would have me keep him, or whither you have hir'd another.

I have receiv'd your 2nd Letter, and hope by your mentioning another house of Mr. G. Montagu's that you have not taken that which Mrs. Montagu dy'd in. I know of but one he liv'd in, in that street.

I don't desire to be trouble'd with John any more after his impertinence to me, but I can not move till the 1st day of Jan. The Nurse the Child now has won't go to London, and I am enquiring for another, which I would willingly have some tryal of before I take her.

Text W MS ii. 327–8   *Address* To Mr Edward Wortley Montagu to be left at Mr Tonsons Bookseller at the Shakespears head over-against Catharine Street in the Strand London   *Postmark* ⟨?⟩ *End. by W* L. M. 6 Dec.

From Wortley 9 *Dec.* [*1714*]

You speak of beginning your journey on the first of January. It falls upon a Saturday. If you mean the Monday after Christmas Day, as I believe you do, it is four or 5 days sooner. I believe the Coach horses from York will be altogether as cheap as from London. If they are as good it is better to have them because you will be sure of them on the day you will want them. Those that furnish the horses will find a Coachman and Postillion, which may return with them. I had rather we did not take a Coachman but for the journey because I think it will be best to hire Coachman and horses in town. I have too much business to look after them and if I were idle it is as cheap or cheaper to do so. My own horses I woud sell, and buy again when there is occasion. I have another Country servant who is the best footman I ever had. But for George, do as you like best. As to the Child, if you do wrong about him, you will have no reason to blame me, for I desire it may be as you like best. You shall know by next post which of Mr. Montague's two houses we have taken. It is certainly not that which was thought in danger of falling. If you take horses etc. from the Country, the sooner you secure them the better. But for the time of going, it is better to be at liberty with them.

9 Dec'r.

Text W MS i. 150–1   *Address* To Lady Mary Wortley at Middle-thorp near York   *Postmark* ⟨9⟩ DE

To Wortley [*11 Dec. 1714*]

I am still in great trouble and irresolution whither to leave the Boy behind me or carry him this long Journey. I am very fearfull and unwilling to part with him, and 'tis pity you should not be Acquainted with him, but I fear his catching cold on the road or any Overturn. I hope if you would not have me make use of the Coachman I have and hire horses here, that you will send down a Coachman, postillion, and pair of horses to be ready to set out from hence the first day of January. I am entirely of your opinion concerning the figure, but I beleive the roads will now be very bad, and it will be allmost impossible to travel with 4. Besides that, it is hazardous with a Coachman that I am not very well assur'd of.

My Lord Duplin[1] came to see to [*sic*] me 2 days ago, or more properly to see the house, for I found that was his busyness. I did not suppose that it was for him you would have taken it, and so told him that I thought you had spoke for it for another year, but I beleive Mr. Barlow thinks of living in it himselfe.[2] I have sent to enquire of his Steward.

Text W MS ii. 317–18   *Address* To Mr Edward Wortley Montagu

[1] George Hay (d. 1758), Viscount Dupplin, later 8th Earl of Kinnoull.
[2] Since Thomas Barlow had died in France in 1713 (see above, p. 186, n. 1), this must have been his son and heir, Francis (1690–1771).

PLATE 4

Lady Mary Wortley Montagu
From a painting by Godfrey Kneller, [1715]

to be left at Mr Tonsons Bookseller at the Shakespears head over-
against Catharine Street in the Strand London. *Postmark* 13 DE
End. by W L. M. 11 Decr.

To Wortley [*12 Dec. 1714*]

I am still in great concern about the child. He has now a
Nurse about him that I very much confide in, but She won't
go to London but would fain take him home to her house.
I know no objection to it but my own fears and the uneasyness I shall be in for want of him, who is now company for
me at all times. Mrs. Cromwell[1] I beleive would not care
to take him again, and if she would, after so severe an illness
there I should not care to leave him. When I took him he
was so extreme weak that I durst hardly hope for his Life,
and he is now (as every body thinks as well as me) as fine a
Child as ever was seen, and allways merry and at play from
morning till Night, for which reason I don't desire to change
the Nurse that is about him, which I must do if I carry him
from hence. I can leave him in charge with Mrs. Thompson[2]
and some other good Wives of York that will see him every
day, the same thing as if I left him in their houses. But I
wish I could tell if you have any thoughts of coming here
again, for my determination would depend a good deal on
that, thô I dread this long Winter Journey and change of
Air for him.

I hope you'l take care to have the house all over very well
Air'd, which I am sure is particularly damp in that Situation.
There should be fires made in all the rooms, and if it be the
house Mrs. Montagu dy'd in (which I hope it is not) that
all the bedding (at least) be chang'd. Lady Mary Montagu[3]
got the Small pox last year by lying in blankets taken from
a bed that had been laid in by one ill of that Distemper some
months before.

[*Postscript*] Your Sister has been here. Having occassion to
say something of her, and some other Affairs de famille which

---

[1] Not identified.
[2] Possibly LM's former correspondent, Anne Justice (see above, p. 42).
[3] George Montagu's second wife.

I had no mind should be seen, I sent a box by the stage Coach and put a letter in the Sleeve of my Calico Manto.

Text W MS ii. 282–3   *Address* To Mr Edward Wortley Montagu to be left at Mr Tonsons bookseller at the Shakespears head over-against Catharine Street in the Strand London   *Postmark* 15 DE   *End. by W* L. M. 12 Decr.

To Wortley [*15 Dec. 1714*]

I intend to set out the monday following, if the 1st of Jan. falls on a Satterday, thô that is not very important, for I don't beleive it possible to avoid being a Sunday on the road, which these late Snows have made as bad as they can be. If it is not cheaper to hire horses here I had rather you sent a pair with a postillion and coachman from London because I beleive the postillion is more likely to be a good one from thence. Pray answer this the very first post because if I hire horses etc. here, I must bespeak them a week beforehand. I have a great mind to bring your boy, for I'm sure you'd be very fond of him, but his health ought to be the first consideration.

Text W MS ii. 311–12   *Address* To Mr Edward Wortley Montagu to be left at Mr Tonsons Bookseller at the Shakespears head over-against Catharine Street in the Strand London   *Postmark* 17 DE   *End. by W* L. M. 15 Decr

To Wortley [*c. 18 Dec. 1714*]

I forgot in my last letter to ask you if you can hire Linnen to serve us, while that we have here can come up by Water, Land Carriage being so excessive dear, and I cannot hire any here. I wish you would tell me if in the house you have taken there is a convenient Nursery. I have a great mind to bring my Boy, but if any harm should come to him, I should never be comforted, and I'm sure I can safely trust him with the Woman that has now the care of him.

I hope you take care to send for the 2 Boxes I have sent
directed to J[acob] Tonson's, one by the Coach and one by
the Carryer. I will make what Enquiry I can about selling
your horses, but being entirely without assistance from any
body, and ignorant in things of that nature, I fear it is not
possible. Here is no body in the Town that wants horses.
Since tis saving £3 I beleive it may do as well to hire here.

Text W MS ii. 339–40   *Address* To Mr Edward Wortley Montagu
to be left at Mr Tonsons Bookseller at the Shakespears head over-
against Catharine Street in the Strand Lôndon   *Postmark* 20 DE
End. by W L. M. 20 Decr

To Wortley [*20 Dec. 1714*]

I am very well satisfy'd about the house, and I think to
hire horses here, but you say nothing to my Question
whither you have thoughts of returning soon, till which I
know not what to resolve upon in relation to the Boy, thô
I have a great Inclination to bring him with me. I chuse to
stay till Monday after new year's day for the sake of the
Moon, which is absolutely necessary in so long a Journey.
I love travelling, and if I did not, I should not think any
thing uneasy to come to you. I am only in care about your
little child, who is now, I thank God, in perfect health.

Text W MS ii. 345–6   *Address* To Mr Edward Wortley Montagu
to be left at Mr Tonsons Bookseller at the Shakespears head over-
against Catharine Street in the Strand London   *Postmark* 22 DE
End. by W L. M. 20 Dec.

To Wortley [*20 Dec. 1714*]

Tis very surprizing to me that you should take a house to
be ready on Christmas Day, and my Lord Seafeild be in it
yet. I don't doubt he intends to stay till the Parliament is

dissolv'd, and I hear that is not expected till Feb.[1] I have sent for the horses from Wharncliffe, and they came hither last night. I have given Earnest for the hire of 2 horses etc. I have prepar'd all things for my Journey, and it will now be a considerable Expence to stay. I must lay in more Coals etc., which cannot be bought in a small Quantity. If you have realy taken the house, as you told me you had, my Lord Seafeild has no right to stay in it but till you please to come in it; and tis your busynesse to tell the LandLady or whoever lets it to give him warning, unless you have some particular tyes to be over and above civil to my Lord Seafeild.

What you are told about Linnen is no Sign there will be any when I come. I wish you would enquire at what rate they are to be let, and perhaps it will be as cheap to send up by the carryer what I have. At least I desire I may be su⟨re⟩ of some the first night I come, sheets and table cloaths not being for show but being absolutely necessary.

I shan't bring the Boy, for I suppose there won't be a place to put him in, and tis easier for me to endure any hardship than see him do it.

Pray answer this by the first post. I can't beleive but my Lord Seafeild will agree to take another lodging, or that I may not come to yours, except you want an Excuse to be without me.

Text W MS ii. 333–4   *Address* To Mr Edward Wortley Montagu to be left at Mr Tonsons Bookseller at the Shakespears head over-against Catharine Street in the Strand London   *Postmark* ⟨?⟩ DE *End. by W* L. M. 20 Decr

To Wortley [5 *Jan. 1715*]

I set out to Day from Middlethorp. I intend to stay one Day at Mrs. White's,[2] and hope to see you in London on Sunday or Monday next. I leave [by] the advice of all people my dear little one, who (they say) would hazard his Life in travelling at this time of year. Now he is about ⟨to

[1] James Ogilvy (1663–1730), 1st Earl of Seafield, was a Scottish Representative Peer, and for that reason stayed in London while Parliament was in session. It was dissolved on 5 Jan. 1715.   [2] At Wallingwells (see above, p. 168).

tee⟩th, I would take the more care of him because if you have 20 children you may never [have] one like him, for he is very pritty, and has more apprehension than is usual at his Age.

Text W MS i. 305–6   *Address* To Mr Edward Wortley Montagu to be left at Mr Tonsons at the Shakespear head overagainst Catharine Street in the Strand London   *Postmark* 7 IA

From Baroness von der Schulenburg[1] [*1715*]

Je crains de n'avoir pas des termes assez forte pour vous exprimer la joye que j'ay conçu en ⟨?⟩ ⟨?⟩ que vous ⟨m'avez fait⟩ l'honneur de m'écrire, vous assurant qu'on ne sçauroit estre plus reconnoisante que je suis des bontez que vous me temoigner, et vous me ferez bien du plaisir et d'honneur de venir icy[2] quand il vous plaira. Vous pouvez bien estre persuade que le plutos me sera le plus agreable; ainsy je me flatte d'avoir bientost l'honneur de vous pouvoir dire de bousche combien je vous aime et combien je suis, ma chere madame, Votre tres humble et tres obeysante Servante,

M. de Schoulenbourg.

C'est a moy de faire bien des excuse d'un tell griffonage[3] mais come je suis fort pressé ainsy j'espere que vous ne regarderay pas de si pres.

Text W MS iv. 240–1   *End. by W* Madlle Scholenbourg

To Lady —— *13 Jan. 1716*

[*A spurious letter, printed 1767, pp. 3–13; 1861, ii. 6–9*]

[1] Ermengarde Melusina, Baroness von der Schulenburg (1667–1743), later Duchess of Munster and Duchess of Kendal, was the more influential of the two mistresses in the King's German entourage. She must have met LM early in 1715 when (as Lady Loudoun reported on 5 March) LM was learning German in order 'to make her court to the King' (Huntington Library MS Lo 11254). In her 'Account' of the Court, written many years later, LM described the Baroness as so much of

the King's own temper 'that I do not wonder at the engagement between them. She was duller than himself, and consequently did not find out that he was so. . . .' (1861, i. 127).
    The letter is translated on p. 454 below.

[2] The Baroness occupied a lavishly furnished apartment in St. James's Palace (*Cal. of Treasury Books*, ed. W. A. Shaw, xxix, 1957, *passim*).

[3] The Baroness's writing is indeed a scribble.

To Wortley [*19 April 1716*]

at Lady Jekyl's[1]
Ap. 18 [*sic*]

The bill has been read to day, with little opposition.
There was however a divission, in which the Court had 276
to 156. Sir J[oseph] J[ekyl] voted with the Majority, and
will continu to do so.[2] I hear no mention of the place bill.[3]
I hope you have had a good Journey. Your Son presents his
Duty to you.

Text W MS ii. 266–7   *Address* To Mr Edward Wortley Montagu
Wharncliffe Lodge by Sheffield bag Yorkshire   *Postmark* 19 AP
End. by W L. M. 18 Apr.

To Wortley [*20 April 1716*]

By your last I should hope to see you in Town before this
can get into Yorkshire, but however I will not forbear writeing. The Bill was carry'd yesterday by more than 100. Sir
J. Jekyl spoke for it, with great earnestness, and I hear
extremely well. I have done nothing concerning Liverys,
having not your particular directions about 'em.[4]

I hope M[atthew] Northall's sister will come up soon, or
refuse it, for tis necessary the child should be some time
accustom'd to his maid before he goes a Journey under her
Care. I have been sick all day with a Cold, which is a genneral
Distemper. I hope you have escap'd very bad Weather.

[1] LM had known Lady Jekyll since
1711 (see above, p. 76).

[2] On 19 April, a Bill to repeal the
Triennial Act came before the House
of Commons, and a motion was carried
that it be read a second time the following week. The voting was exactly as
given by LM (*Journ. of the H. of C.*
xviii. 425; Rich. Chandler, *Hist. and
Proc. of the H. of C.*, 1742–4, vi. 68).
Jekyll usually voted with the Whigs, as
he did now, but he was a man of prin-

ciple capable of independent judgement.
[3] See next page.

[4] In April 1716 W was nominated by
the King to be Ambassador to Turkey
(*Evening Post*, 5–7 April 1716), and
his appointment was confirmed by the
Levant Company on 10 May 1716
(Alfred C. Wood, *History of the Levant
Company*, 1935, p. 251). While he is in
Yorkshire, LM is looking after such
preparations for the Embassy as choos-
ing liveries for the servants.

I hear some people Question your right of sitting in Parliament, and suspect there is somebody ready to supply your place.[1] You know your own affairs better than I do, and shall therefore say nothing. If you would have me bespeak Liverys, say whether You would have them plain or Lace'd. Any sort of Lace will very considerably encrease the Expence but perhaps it may be necessary.

Mr. Cook was to see me,[2] to little purpose, for he said he knew nothing of what was fit for me to do. I long to see you for variety of reasons. Your boy presents his Duty.

Text W MS ii. 359–60   *Address* To Mr Edward Wortley Montagu
End. by W L. M. April

To Wortley [*c. 30 April 1716*]

I am extremely concern'd at your illness. I have expected you all this day, and suppose'd you would be here by this time if you had set out Satterday afternoon as you say you intended. I hope you have left Wharncliffe, but how-ever will continu to write till you let me know you have done so. Dr. Clarke has been spoke to, and excus'd himselfe from recommending a chaplain, as not being acquainted with many Orthodox Divines.[3] I dont doubt you know the Death of Lord Sommers, which will for some time interupt my commerce with Lady Jekyl.[4] I have heard he is dead without a Will, and I have heard he has made young Mr. Cox his Heir; I cannot tell which Account is the truest.[5]

[1] By the 1701 Act of Settlement, any Member who accepted an office from the Government was required to stand immediately for re-election (Robert Walcott, *Eng. Politics in the Early Eighteenth Century*, 1956, pp. 89, 117). W, however, did not do so.

[2] Perhaps James Cook (d. 1746), a Turkey merchant, or Thomas Cook (1672–1752), a Director of the Bank of England and a Turkey merchant (*London Mag.*, 1746, p. 591; 1752, p. 384).

[3] Samuel Clarke (1675–1729), rector of St. James's, Piccadilly, was an out-

standing liberal churchman, condemned by orthodox divines for preaching a disguised deism. Eventually William Crosse (b. 1684), chaplain to the English factory at Constantinople in 1712, was reappointed (J. Foster, *Alumni Oxon. 1500–1714*, i. 357).

[4] Lord Somers (see above, p. 78, n. 6) died on 26 April. He was survived by two sisters, Lady Jekyll and Mary, wife of Charles Cocks, M.P.

[5] The former rumour was the correct one; letters of administration were granted to his sisters (P.C.C. Acts of

I beg of you with the greatest Earnestness that you would take the first care of your Health; there can be nothing worth the least loss of that. I shall be sincerely very uneasy till I hear from you again, but I am not without hopes of seeing you to morrow. Your Son presents his duty to you, and improves ev'ry day in his Conversation, which begins to be very entertaining to me. I directed a Letter for you last post to Mr. B.[1]

I cannot conclude without once recommending to you if you have any sort of value for me to take care of your selfe. If there be any thing you would have me do, pray be particular in your Directions. You say nothing possitive about the Liverys. Lord B[ingley's] lace is silk with very little silver in it, but for 20 liverys comes to £1 10.[2]

Adeiu. Pray take care of your health.

Text W MS ii. 406–7   *End. by W* L. M. April

To[3] Lady Mar[4] *3 Aug.* [*1716*]

Rotterdam, Friday Aug't 3. O.S.[5]

I flatter my selfe (dear Sister) that I shall give you some pleasure in letting you know that I am safely past the Sea, thô we had the ill fortune of a storm. We were perswaded by the Captain of our Yatcht to set out in a calm, and he pretended that there was nothing so easy as to tide it over,

Administration 1716, f. 90). Mrs. Cocks had two sons; LM probably means the elder, James Cocks (1685–1750), M.P.

[1] Perhaps Joseph Banks at Scofton, where W could stop to break his journey from Wharncliffe to London.

[2] Robert Benson (1676–1731), 1st Baron Bingley, had been appointed Ambassador Extraordinary to Spain in May 1714, but did not go, presumably because of Queen Anne's death (*DNB*; D. B. Horn, *Brit. Dipl. Rep. 1689–1789*, 1932, p. 131). His servants' liveries would thus be for sale.

[3] Here begin LM's famous Turkish Embassy Letters (discussed above,

pp. xiv–xvii). Instead of giving names, LM headed the letters with initials or titles. These have been expanded whenever possible.

[4] In MS 'To the Countesse of ——'.

[5] On Wednesday, 1 Aug., W left London for his embassy (HMC *Polwarth MSS*, i, 1911, pp. 49, 52), and the next day embarked at Gravesend for Holland (*Weekly Journal, or British Gazetteer*, 4 Aug. 1716). The date which LM wrote is inaccurate, and this is true of many other Embassy letters. But since her dates are at least approximate they have been retained, corrected in the footnotes whenever possible.

but after 2 days slowly moving, the Wind blew so hard that none of the Sailors could keep their feet, and we were all Sunday night toss'd very handsomely. I never saw a Man more frighted than the Captain. For my part I have been so lucky neither to suffer from Fear or sea sickness, thô I confess I was so impatient to see my selfe once more upon dry land, that I would not stay till the Yatcht could get to Rotterdam, but went in the long boat to Helver Sluyse where we hir'd Voitures to carry us to the Brill.

I was charm'd with the neatness of this little Town, but my arival at Rotterdam presented me a new scene of Pleasure. All the streets are pav'd with broad stones, and before the meanest artificers' doors, seats of various colour'd marbles, and so neatly kept that I'll assure you I walk'd allmost all over the Town Yesterday, incognito, in my slippers without receiving one spot of Dirt, and you may see the Dutch maids washing the Pavement of the street with more aplication than ours do our bed chambers.[1] The Town seems so full of people with such busie faces, all in motion, that I can hardly fancy that it is not some celebrated fair, but I see 'tis every day the same. 'Tis certain no Town can be more advantagiously situated for Commerce. Here are 7 large Canals on which the merchant ships come up to the very doors of their Houses. The shops and warehouses are of a surprizing neatness and Magnificence, fill'd with an incredible Quantity of fine Merchandize, and so much cheaper than what we see in England, I have much ado to perswade my selfe I am still so near it. Here is neither Dirt nor Beggary to be seen. One is not shock'd with those loathsome Cripples so common in London, nor teiz'd with the Importunitys of idle Fellows and Wenches that chuse to be nasty and lazy. The common Servants and little shop Women here are more nicely clean than most of our Ladys, and the great variety of neat dresses (every Woman dressing her Head after her own Fashion) is an additional pleasure in seeing the Town.

You see hitherto, Dear Sister, I make no complaints, and

[1] Other travellers remarked that the streets were so clean that women could walk about in their slippers (Maximilien Misson, *Voyage d'Italie*, ed. 1743, i. 4; Edward Brown, *An Account of Several Travels Through a Great Part of Germany*, 1677, p. 3). The servants of each house were 'obliged every day to wash and rub the pavement before their door' (Nugent, i. 43).

if I continue to like travelling as well as I do at present, I shall not repent my project. It will go a great way in makeing me satisfy'd with it if it affords me oppertunitys of entertaining you, but it is not from Holland that you must expect a disinterested offer. I can write enough in the stile of Rotterdam to tell you plainly, in one word, I expect Returns of all the London News.[1] You see I have allready learnt to make a good Bargain, and that it is not for nothing I will so much as tell you that I am Your Affectionate Sister.

Text H MS 253, pp. 1–4

To [Jane Smith][2] 5 *Aug.* [*1716*]

Hague, Aug't 5. O.S.

I make haste to tell you, dear Madam, that after all the dreadfull fatigues you threaten'd me with, I am hitherto very well pleas'd with my Journey. We take care to make such short stages every day, I rather fancy my selfe upon partys of Pleasure than upon the road, and sure nothing can be more agreable than travelling in Holland. The whole Country appears a large Garden, the roads all well pav'd, shaded on each side with rows of Trees and border'd with large Canals full of Boats passing and repassing. Every 20 paces gives you the prospect of some villa and every 4 hours a large Town, so surprizingly neat, I am sure you would be charm'd with them. The Place I am now at is certainly one of the finest Villages in the World. Here are several Squares finely built, and (what I think a particular Beauty) set with thick large Trees. The Voorhout is at the same time the Hide-Park and the Mall of the people of Quality, for they take the air in it both on foot and in Coaches.[3] There are shops for Wafers, cool Liquors, etc. I have been to see several

[1] Lady Mar had remained in London after her husband, a leader of the Jacobite rebellion of 1715, fled to France.

[2] In MS 'Mrs. S'. Almost certainly Jane (d. 1730), da. of John Smith, Speaker of the House of Commons 1705–8. She was an early friend of LM's

(Stuart, p. 57), and since 1715 had been Maid of Honour to the Princess of Wales. She is listed as a correspondent in LM's 'Heads' of actual letters for 1 April 1717 (see below, p. 345).

[3] The Voorhout is similarly described by Nugent (i. 110).

of the most celebrated Gardens, but I will not teize you with their Descriptions.

I dare swear you think my Letter allready long enough, but I must not conclude without begging your pardon for not obeying your commands in sending the Lace you order'd me. Upon my word, I can yet find none that is not dearer than you may buy it in London. If You want any Indian Goods, here are great Variety of Pennorths and I shall follow your orders with great pleasure and exactness, being, Dear Madam, etc.

Text H MS 253, pp. 4–7

To [Sarah Chiswell][1] *13 Aug.* [*1716*]

Nimeguen, Aug't 13 O.S.

I am extreamly sorry, my dear S[arah], that your fears of disobliging your Relations and their fears for your Health and safety has hinder'd me the happyness of your Company, and you the pleasure of a diverting Journey. I receive some degree of Mortification from every agreable novelty or pleasing prospect by the Refflexion of your having so un-luckily miss'd the same pleasure, which I know it would have given you. If you were with me in this Town you would be ready to expect to receive visits from your Nottingham freinds. No 2 places were ever more ressembling; one has but to give the Maese[2] the name of the Trent and there is no distinguishing the prospects: the Houses, like those of Nottingham, built one above another and intermixd in the same manner with Trees and Gardens. The Tower they call Julius Caesar's has the same situation with Nottingham Castle, and I can't help fancying I see from it the Trent field, Adboulton, etc., places so well known to us. 'Tis true the fortifications make a considerable difference. All the learned in the art of war bestow great Commendations on them. For my part that know nothing of the matter, I shall content my selfe with telling you tis a very pritty walk on the

[1] In MS 'To Mrs. S. C.'—a friend who had occasionally stayed with LM   at Thoresby (see above, p. 114, n. 4).   [2] Actually the Waal.

Ramparts, on which there is a Tower very deservedly call'd
the Belvidere, where people go to drink Coffee, Tea, etc.,
and enjoy one of the finest prospects in the World. The
Publick walks have no great Beauty but the thick shade of
the Trees, but I must not forget to take notice of the Bridge,
which appear'd very Surprizing to me. Tis large enough to
hold hundreds of Men with Horses and Carriages. They
give the value of an English two pence to get upon it and
then away they go, bridge and all, to the other side of the
river, with so slow a motion, one is hardly sensible of any
at all.

I was yesterday at the French church and star'd very
much at their manner of Service. The Parson claps on a
broad brim'd hat in the first place, which gave him entirely
the air of what de'e call him, in Bartholomew Fair,[1] which
he kept up by extrodinary antick Gestures and talking much
such stuff as tother preach'd to the puppets. However, the
Congregation seem'd to receive it with great Devotion, and
I was inform'd by some of his flock that he is a person of
particular fame among 'em. I beleive you are by this time
as much tir'd of my Account of him as I was with his
sermon, but I'm sure your brother[2] will excuse a digression
in favour of the Church of England. You know, speaking
disrespectfully of Calvinists is the same thing as speaking
honourably of the Church.

Adeiu, my Dear S[arah]. Allways remember me and be
assur'd I can never forget you.

Text H MS 253, pp. 7–11

To Lady —— *16 Aug.* [*1716*]

Collen [Cologne], Aug't 16. O.S.
If my Lady —— could have any Notion of the Fatigues
that I have suffer'd this last 2 days, I am sure she would own

---

[1] Lanthorn Leatherhead in Ben Jonson's *Bartholomew Fair*, 1614, Act V, Scene iv.

[2] Probably brother-in-law, Humphrey Perkins (*c.* 1646–*c.* 1717), Rector of Holme Pierrepont (near Thoresby) 1680–1717; he m. (1697) as his second wife Ann Cheswell (J. Venn, *Alumni Cantab. to 1751*, iii. 347).

it a great proofe of regard that I now sit down to write to her. We hir'd Horses from Nimeguen hither, not having the conveniency of the post, and found but very indifferent accomodation at Reinberg, our first stage, but that was nothing to what I suffer'd yesterday. We were in hopes to reach Collen. Our horses tir'd at Stamel 3 hours from it, where I was forc'd to pass the night in my Cloths in a room not at all better than a Hovel, for thô I have my own bed, I had no mind to undress where the wind came in from a thousand places. We left this wretched lodging at day break and about 6 this morning came safe here, where I got immediately into bed and slept so well for 3 hours that I found my selfe perfectly recover'd and have had Spirits enough to go see all that is curious in the Town, that is to say, the churches, for here is nothing else worth seeing,[1] tho it is a very large Town, but most part of it old built.

The Jesuits' church is the neatest,[2] which was shew'd me in a very complaisant Manner by a handsome young Jesuit, who, not knowing who I was, took a Liberty in his complements and railerys which very much diverted me. Having never before seen any thing of that nature, I could not enough admire the magnificence of the altars, the rich Images of the Saints (all massy silver) and the enchasures of the Relicks, thô I could not help murmuring in my heart at that profusion of pearls, Diamonds and Rubys bestow'd on the adornment of rotten teeth, dirty rags, etc.[3] I own that I had wickedness enough to covet St. Ursula's pearl necklace, thô perhaps it was no wickedness at all, an Image not being certainly one's Neighbour; but I went yet farther and wish'd even she her selfe converted into dressing plate, and a great St. Christopher I imagin'd would have look'd very well in a Cistern. These were my pious refflexions, thô I was very well satisfy'd to see, pil'd up to the Honnour of

[1] Cologne was styled by other travellers the Rome or the Holy City of Germany (Edward Brown, *Account of Travels Through Germany*, 1677, p. 42; Nugent, ii. 320).

[2] This church is described by Brown (p. 40) as 'well built and stored with rich Copes, Altar-pieces, and other Ornaments'.

[3] The rich decorations were also observed by Maximilien Misson (*Voyage d'Italie*, ed. 1743, i. 54–56). In her ridicule of religious relics here and elsewhere (e.g. 20 Oct. [1755]) LM shared an attitude common among English travellers of her time (W. E. Mead, *The Grand Tour in the Eighteenth Century*, 1914, pp. 111–12).

our Nation, the Skulls of the 11,000 Virgins.[1] I have seen some Hundreds of Relicks here of no less consequence, but I will not imitate the common stile of Travellers so far as to give you a list of 'em, being perswaded that you have no manner of curiosity for the Titles given to Jaw bones and bits of worm eaten wood.

—Adeiu. I am just going to supper where I shall drink your Health in an admirable sort of Lorrain Wine, which I am sure is the same you call Burgundy in London.

Text H MS 253, pp. 11–14

To Lady Bristol[2] *22 Aug.* [*1716*]

Nieurenburg, Aug't 22. O.S.

After 5 days travelling post, I am sure I could sit down to write on no other Occassion but to tell my dear Lady [Bristol] that I have not forgot her obliging command of sending her some account of my travells. I have allready past a large part of Germany. I have seen all that is remarkable in Collen, Frankfort, Wurtzburg, and this place, and tis impossible not to observe the difference between the free Towns and those under the Government of absolute Princes (as all the little Sovereigns of Germany are). In the first there appears an air of Commerce and Plenty. The streets are well built and full of people neatly and plainly dress'd, the shops loaded with Merchandize, and the commonalty clean and cheerfull.[3] In the other, a sort of shabby finery, a Number of dirty people of Quality tawder'd out, Narrow nasty streets out of repair, wretchedly thin of Inhabitants, and above halfe of the common sort asking alms. I can't help

[1] St. Ursula's tomb and the 'Tomb of divers of the Eleven thousand Virgins, martyred by the *Huns*' are mentioned by Brown (p. 40) and Misson (i. 54–56), but Nugent (ii. 320) points out that 'this story is exploded by some of the *Roman* catholic writers themselves, who have shewn the source whence this error is derived'. Legend also credited them with British origin.

[2] In MS 'To the Countesse of B'. Before her husband's elevation to an earldom (in 1714), she had been Lady Hervey (see above, p. 75, n. 2).

[3] The superiority of Nuremberg, a free Imperial city since 1552, was noted by other travellers, e.g. Brown (p. 61).

fancying one under the figure of a handsome clean Dutch Citizen's wife and the other like a poor Town Lady of Pleasure, painted and riban'd out in her Head dress, with tarnish'd silver lac'd shoes, and a ragged under petticoat, a miserable mixture of Vice and poverty.

They have sumptuary Laws in this Town which distinguish their Rank by their dress and prevents that Excesse which ruins so many other Citys, and has a more agreable Effect to the Eye of a Stranger than our fashions. I think after the ArchBishop of Cambray having declar'd for them,[1] I need not be asham'd to own that I wish these Laws were in force in other parts of the World. When one considers impartialy the Merit of a rich suit of cloaths in most places, the respect and the smiles of favour that it procures, not to speak of the Envy and the sighs that it occassions (which is very often the principal charm to the Wearer), one is forc'd to confesse that there is need of an uncommon understanding to resist the temptation of pleasing freinds and mortifying Rivals, and that it is natural to young people to fall into a Folly which betrays them to that want of Money which is the Source of a thousand basenesses. What Numbers of Men have begun the world with generous Inclinations, that have afterwards been the Instruments of bringing misery on a whole people! led by a vain expence into Debts that they could clear no other way but by the forfeit of their Honnour, and which they would never have contracted if the respect the Many pay to Habits was fix'd by Law only to a particular colour, or cut of plain cloth! These Refflexions draw after them others that are too melancholy.

I will make haste to put 'em out of your head by the farce of Relicks with which I have been entertain'd in all the Romish churches. The Lutherans are not quite free from those follys. I have seen here in the principal Church a large piece of the Cross set in Jewels, and the point of a Spear which they told me very gravely was the same that pierce'd the side of Our Saviour. But I was particularly diverted in a little Roman Catholic church which is permitted here,[2]

[1] François de la Mothe Fénelon (1651–1715), Archbishop of Cambrai, expressed himself against luxury in two works: *Traité de l'éducation des filles* (1687) and *Télémaque* (1699).

[2] This, the only Roman Catholic church in the Protestant city, belonged to the Teutonic Order (Nugent, ii. 296).

where the professors of that Religion are not very rich and consequently cannot adorn their Images in so rich a manner as their Neighbours, but not to be quite destitute of all finery, they have dress'd up an Image of our Saviour over the Altar in a fair full bottom'd wig, very well powder'd.[1] I imagine I see your Ladyship stare at this article of which you very much doubt the veracity, but upon my word I have not yet made use of the privelege of a Traveller, and my whole account is writ with the same plain Sincerity of Heart with which I assure you that I am, dear Madam, Your Ladyship's etc.

Text H MS 253, pp. 15–20

To [Anne] Thistlethwayte[2] *30 Aug.* [*1716*]

Ratisbon,[3] Aug't 30th O.S.

I had the pleasure of receiving yours but the day before I left London. I give you a thousand thanks for your good wishes, and have such an Opinion of their Efficacy I am perswaded that I owe (in part) to them the good Luck of having proceeded so far in my long Journey without any ill Accident, for I do not reckon it any being stopp'd a few days in this Town by a Cold, since it has not only given me an Oppertunity of seeing all that is curious in it, but of makeing some acquaintance with the Ladys, who have all been to see me with great civility, particularly Madam ——, the wife of our King's Envoy from Hanover.[4] She has

[1] In Cologne Maximilien Misson had seen (in 1687) 'un Crucifix qui porte la perruque' (*Voyage d'Italie*, ed. 1743, i. 56).

[2] In MS 'Mrs. T'. In the Embassy letter of 4 Jan. [1718], the name Thistlethwayte is struck out and 'Mrs. T' put at the head. Moy Thomas further identifies her as probably Anne (b. 1669) of Winterslow, near West Dean, Wilts. (1861, i. 232, n. 1). But no evidence survives to support this assumption. Anne had two sisters—Mary (b. 1663) and Catherine (1666–1746)—and a

sister-in-law Mary Pelham Thistlethwayte (m. 1683, d. 1720) (R. C. Hoare, *History of Modern Wilts.*, 1822–44, V, i. 46); any of these could also have been the person addressed.

[3] English name of Regensburg, the seat of the Holy Roman Empire, where the Imperial Diet met regularly after 1663.

[4] Rudolf Johann, Freiherr von Wrisberg, envoy from Hanover to the Imperial Diet 1714–26 (F. Hausmann, *Repertorium der diplomatischen Vertreter*, 1936–50, ii. 175).

carry'd me to all the assemblys and I have been magnificently entertain'd at her House, which is one of the finest here. You know that all the Nobility of this place are Envoys from different States. Here are a great Number of them, and they might passe their time agreably enough if they were less delicate on the point of Ceremony; but instead of joyning in the design of makeing the Town as pleasant to one another as they can and improving their little Societys, they amuse themselves no other way than with perpetual Quarrels, which they take care to eternize by leaving them to their Successors, and an Envoy to Ratisbon receives regularly halfe a dozen Quarrels amongst the perquisites of his employment.

You may be sure the Ladys are not wanting on their side in cherishing and improving these important piques, which divides the Town allmost into as many partys as there are familys, and they chuse rather to suffer the mortification of siting almost alone on their assembly Nights than to recede one jot from their pretentions. I have not been here above a Week and yet I have heard from allmost every one of 'em the whole History of their wrongs and dreadfull complaints of the Injustice of their Neighbours in hopes to draw me to their Party, but I think it very prudent to remain Neuter, thô if I was to stay amongst them there would be no possibillity of continuing so, their Quarrels running so high they will not be civil to those that visit their Adversarys. The Foundation of these everlasting Disputes turns entirely upon place and the title of Excellency, which they all pretend to, and what is very hard, will give it to nobody. For my part, I could not forbear advising them (for the public good) to give the Title of Excellency to every body, which would include the receiving it from every body, but the very mention of such a dishonnourable peace was receiv'd with as much indignation as Mrs. Blackacre did the motion of a Reference,[1] and I begun to think my selfe ill-natur'd to offer to take from 'em, in a Town where there is so few diversions, so entertaining an Amusement. I know that my peaceable disposition allready gives me a very ill

---

[1] In William Wycherley's *The Plain Dealer*, 1677, Act III, Mrs. Blackacre scorns a 'reference'— that a dispute be settled by a Master in Chancery.

figure, and that 'tis publickly whisper'd as a piece of impertinent pride in me that I have hitherto been saucily civil to every body, as if I thought no body good enough to quarrel with.[1] I should be oblig'd to change my behaviour if I did not intend to persue my Journey in a few days.

I have been to see the churches here and had the permission of touching the Relicks, which was never suffer'd in places where I was not known. I had by this privelege the oppertunity of makeing an observation, which I don't doubt might have been made in all the other churches, that the Emeralds and Rubys that they show round their Relicks and Images are most of them false, thô they tell you that many of the Crosses and Madonas set round with them stones have been the Gifts of the Emperors and other great princes, and I don't doubt but they were at first Jewels of Value, but the good fathers have found it convenient to apply them to other uses and the people are just as well satisfy'd with bits of Glass. Amongst these Relicks they show'd me a prodigious claw set in Gold which they call'd the claw of a Griffin, and I could not forbear asking the reverend Priest that shew'd it, whither the Griffin was a Saint. This Question almost put him beside his Gravity, but he answer'd, they only kept it as a curiosity. But I was very much scandaliz'd at a large Silver Image of the Trinity where the Father is represented under the figure of a decrepid old Man with a Beard down to his knees and a Triple crown on his head, holding in his arms the Son fix'd on the Crosse, and the Holy Ghost in the shape of a Dove hov'ring over him.——

Madame ——[2] is come this minute to call me to the assembly, and forces me to tell you very aprubtly [*sic*] that I am ever yours.

Text H MS 253, pp. 21–28

[1] 'Your post at Ratisbon is full of ceremony,' a British envoy was warned later in the century. 'You cannot spit out of the window without offending the head or paraphernalia of an *Excellence*. You are all so, that Ceremonial there is looked on as essential and subject to contests' (quoted in D. B. Horn, *The British Diplomatic Service 1689–1789*, 1961, p. 24).

[2] Evidently Mme von Wrisberg (in MS *Mme* is followed by *de*, which is struck out), the wife of the Hanoverian envoy.

To Lady Mar *8 Sept.* [*1716*]

Vienna, September 8 O.S.

I am now (my dear sister) safely arriv'd at Vienna[1] and I thank God have not at all suffer'd in my Health, nor (what is dearer to me) in that of my Child, by all our Fatigues. We travell'd by Water from Ratisbon, a Journey perfectly agreable, down the Danube in one of those little vessels that they very properly call wooden Houses, having in them all the conveniencys of a Palace, stoves in the chambers, Kitchins, etc.[2] They are row'd by 12 men each, and move with an incredible swiftness that in the same day you have the pleasure of a vast variety of Prospects, and within a few Hours space of time one has the different diversion of seeing a Populous City adorn'd with magnificent Palaces, and the most romantic Solitudes which appear distant from the commerce of Mankind, the Banks of the Danube being charmingly diversify'd with woods, rocks, Mountains cover'd with Vines, Fields of Corn, large Citys, and ruins of Ancient Castles. I saw the great Towns of Passaw and Lintz, famous for the retreat of the Imperial Court when Vienna was beseig'd.[3]

This Town, which has the Honnour of being the Emperor's Residence, did not at all answer my Ideas of it, being much lesse than I expected to find it. The streets are very close and so narrow one cannot observe the fine fronts of the Palaces, thô many of them very well deserve observation, being truly magnificent, all built of fine white stone and excessive high. The Town being so much too little for the number of the people that desire to live in it, the Builders seem to have projected to repair that misfortune by claping one Town on the Top of another, most of the houses being of 5 and some of them of 6 storys. You may easily imagine that

---

[1] W and his party had arrived in Vienna on 3 Sept. O.S. (dispatch of 16 Sept. 1716 [N.S.], SP 97/23).

[2] The journey by water from Ratisbon to Vienna was a route recommended for comfort and speed (Nugent, ii. 274).

[3] In 1683, when the Turkish army reached the walls of Vienna, Emperor Leopold I and his court fled the city until the Turks were driven back by the King of Poland's army.

the streets being so narrow, the upper rooms are extream Dark, and what is an inconveniency much more intolerable in my Opinion, there is no house that has so few as 5 or 6 familys in it. The Apartments of the greatest Ladys and even of the Ministers of state are divided but by a Partition from that of a Tailor or a shoe-maker, and I know no body that has above 2 floors in any house, one for their own use, and one higher for their servants. Those that have houses of their own, let out the rest of them to whoever will take 'em; thus the great stairs (which are all of stone) are as common and as dirty as the street. 'Tis true when you have once travell'd through them, nothing can be more surprizingly magnificent than the Apartments. They are commonly a suitte of 8 or 10 large rooms, all inlaid, the doors and windows richly carv'd and Gilt, and the furniture such as is seldom seen in the Palaces of sovereign Princes in other Countrys: the Hangings the finest Tapestry of Brussells, prodigious large looking glasses in silver frames, fine Japan Tables, the Beds, Chairs, Canopys and window Curtains of the richest Genoa Damask or Velvet, allmost cover'd with gold Lace or Embrodiery—the whole made Gay by Pictures and vast Jars of Japan china, and almost in every room large Lustres of rock chrystal.

I have already had the Honour of being invited to Dinner by several of the first people of Quality,[1] and I must do them the Justice to say the good taste and Magnificence of their Tables very well answers to that of their Furniture. I have been more than once entertain'd with 50 dishes of meat, all serv'd in silver and well dress'd, the desert proportionable, serv'd in the finest china; but the variety and richnesse of their wines is what appears the most surprizing. The constant way is to lay a list of their names upon the plates of the Guests along with the napkins, and I have counted several times to the number of 18 different sorts, all exquisite in their kinds. I was yesterday at Count Schonbourn's, the vice chancellor's Garden, where I was invited to Dinner, and

[1] On 23/12 Sept. the French Ambassador, comte du Luc, remarked that 'Milord Montagu et sa femme fournissons [*sic*] aux conversations de la Cour et de la Ville'; on 30/19 Sept. that they 'se produisent dans les assemblées pour se faire connoitre et suivre le train de Vivre de ce pais' (Ministère des Affaires Étrangères, Autriche, vol. 116, ff. 199, 219).

I must own that I never saw a place so perfectly delightfull as the Fauxbourgs of Vienna. It is very large and almost wholly compos'd of delicious Palaces; and if the Emperor found it proper to permit the Gates of the Town to be laid open that the Fauxbourgs might be joyn'd to it, he would have one of the largest and best built Citys of Europe. Count Schonbourne's Villa is one of the most magnificent, the Furniture all rich brocards, so well fancy'd and fited up, nothing can look more Gay and Splendid, not to speak of a Gallery full of raritys of Coral, mother of Pearl, etc., and through out the whole House a profusion of Gilding, Carving, fine paintings, the most beautifull Porcelane, statues of Alablaster and Ivory, and vast Orange and Lemon Trees in Gilt Pots. The Dinner was perfectly fine and well-order'd and made still more agreable by the Good humour of the Count.[1] I have not yet been at Court, being forc'd to stay for my Gown, without which there is no waiting on the Empresse, thô I am not without a great Impatience to see a Beauty that has been the admiration of so many different Nations.[2] When I have had that Honnour I will not fail to let you know my real thoughts, allways takeing a particular pleasure in communicating them to my dear Sister.

Text H MS 253, pp. 28–35

To [Sarah Chiswell] *8 Sept. 1716*

[*A spurious letter, printed 1770 in* The London Museum of Politics, Miscellanies and Literature, *i. 39–40*]

[1] Friedrich Karl, Count von Schönborn (1674–1746), the *arbiter elegantiarum* of Viennese Court society, whose palace was the centre of social life (Hugo Hantsch, *Reichsvizekanzler Friedrich Karl v. Schönborn 1674–1746*, 1929, pp. 347–8; Bruno Grimschitz, *Hildebrandt*, 1959, plates 47 to 52 for pictures of his *Gartenpalast*). His affability and magnificence are praised by Karl Ludwig Pöllnitz in his *Lettres et Mémoires* (i. 271). (These important memoirs, though they pretend to cover the period 1729–33, are really based on Pöllnitz's travels during the period 1710–23—W. D. Robson-Scott, *German Travellers in England 1400–1800*, 1953, p. 127.)

[2] For the Empress, see below, pp. 265–6.]

To Alexander Pope[1] *14 Sept.* [*1716*]

Vienna, Sept. 14th O.S.

Perhaps you'l laugh at me for thanking you very gravely for all the obliging concern you express for me. 'Tis certain that I may, if I please, take the fine things you say to me for wit and railery, and it may be it would be takeing them right, but I never in my Life was halfe so well dispos'd to beleive you in earnest, and that distance which makes the continuation of your Freindship improbable has very much encreas'd my Faith for it,[2] and I find that I have (as well as the rest of my sex), whatever face I set on't, a strong disposition to beleive in miracles. Don't fancy, however, that I am infected by the air of these popish Countrys, thô I have so far wander'd from the Discipline of the Church of England to have been last Sunday at the Opera, which was perform'd in the Garden of the Favorita,[3] and I was so much pleas'd with it, I have not yet repented my seeing it[4] Nothing of that kind ever was more Magnificent, and I can easily beleive what I am told, that the Decorations and habits cost the Emperour £30,000 Sterling. The Stage was built over a very large

<hr />

[1] In MS 'To Mr. P'. This is the first mention in LM's letters of the poet whose friendship and later hatred was to make her notorious. They were apparently acquainted by the summer of 1715; and after she left for Constantinople, if not before, his friendship turned to fervid gallantry (Halsband, *LM*, pp. 48–49, 57–58). From Holland she had written him a short letter telling him that she had escaped being sea-sick; he mentions this in his own letter of 20 Aug. (*Corr.* i. 356).

[2] Pope thanked her for her favour 'in taking what I writ to you in the serious manner it was meant'; and again: 'You touch me very sensibly, in saying you think so well of my *friendship* . . .' (*Corr.* i. 383, 389). There are occasionally similar correlations between Pope's letters, which are the actual ones sent to LM, and her compiled ones to him or

to other correspondents. For example, he writes: 'The Shrines and Reliques you tell me of . . .' (10 Nov. 1716, *Corr.* i. 368); she deals with this topic in Embassy letters addressed to other correspondents but not to him. A further indication of the difference between her actual letters and Embassy ones: 'I beg you will put dates to your letters,' she writes (*Corr.* i. 385); almost all of her Embassy letters, including those to him, are precisely if inaccurately dated.

[3] The Favorita palace—the Theresianum of modern Vienna—had gardens which were, in Nugent's opinion, 'pretty large, but otherwise mean enough' (ii. 209).

[4] Pope refers to her 'Sunday-opera' in his letter of 10 Nov. (*Corr.* i. 368), which shows that she had also described it in a letter actually sent to him.

Canal, and at the beginning of the 2nd Act divided into 2 parts, discovering the Water, on which there immediately came from different parts 2 fleets of little gilded vessels that gave the representation of a Naval fight. It is not easy to imagine the beauty of this Scene, which I took particular Notice of, but all the rest were perfectly fine in their kind. The story of the Opera is the Enchantments of Alcina,[1] which gives Oppertunity for a great variety of Machines and changes of the Scenes, which are perform'd with a surprizing swiftnesse. The Theatre is so large that 'tis hard to carry the Eye to the End of it, and the Habits in the utmost magnificence to the number of 108. No house could hold such large Decorations, but the Ladys all siting in the open air exposes them to great Inconveniencys, for there is but one canopy for the Imperial Family, and the first night it was represented, a shower of rain happening, the Opera was broke off and the company crouded away in such confusion, I was allmost squeez'd to Death.[2]

But if their Operas are thus delightfull, their comedys are in as high a degree ridiculous. They have but one Playhouse, where I had the curiosity to go to a German Comedy,[3] and was very glad it happen'd to be the story of Amphitrion; that subject having been allready handled by a Latin, French and English Poet, I was curious to see what an Austrian Author would make of it.[4] I understood enough of the language to comprehend the greatest part of it, and besides I took with me a Lady that had the Goodness to explain to

[1] *Angelica Vincitrice di Alcina* by Johann Josef Fux, the libretto by Pietro Pariati. LM's description of its elaborate scenery and staging is accurate (cf. J. H. van der Meer, *Johann Josef Fux als Opernkomponist*, 1961, i. 135–6, 147).

[2] The date of the premiere, given in van der Meer as 13 Sept. [N.S.] and in Grove's *Dict. of Music*, rev. ed. 1954, as 21 Sept., is incorrect. As stated in the Imperial Court records, the first performance of *Alcina* took place on Monday, 14/3 Sept. It was next given on the following Sunday, 20/9 Sept.—which must have been the uninterrupted

performance attended by LM (Hofzeremonialprotokoll, 1716, ff. 210, 214–15, Haus-, Hof-, und Staatsarchiv, Vienna). The opera is unmentioned in Alfred Loewenberg, *Annals of Opera 1597–1940*, rev. ed., 1955.

[3] The playhouse for comedy was under the direction of Joseph Anton Stranitzky (1676–1726), actor and impresario. It stood near the old Kärntner Tower (Hans Tietze, *Wien*, 1931, p. 258).

[4] By Plautus, Molière (1668), and Dryden (1690); the German version seen by LM, although sought by literary scholars, remains unidentified.

me every word.¹ The way is to take a Box which holds 4 for your selfe and company. The fix'd price is a gold Ducat.² I thought the House very low and dark, but I confess the comedy admirably recompens'd that deffect. I never laugh'd so much in my Life. It begun with Jupiter's falling in Love out of a peep hole in the clouds and ended with the Birth of Hercules; but what was most pleasant was the use Jupiter made of his metamorphose, for you no sooner saw him under the figure of Amphitrion, but instead of flying to Alcmena with the raptures Mr. Dryden puts into his mouth,³ he sends to Amphitrion's Tailor and cheats him of a lac'd Coat, and his Banker of a bag of money, a Jew of a Di'mond ring, and bespeaks a great Supper in his name; and the greatest part of the comedy turns upon poor Amphitrion's being tormented by these people for their debts, and Mercury uses Sosia in the same manner.⁴ But I could not easily pardon the Liberty the Poet has taken of Larding his play with not only indecent expressions, but such grosse Words as I don't think our Mob would suffer from a Mountebank, and the 2 Sosias very fairly let down their breeches in the direct view of the Boxes, which were full of people of the first Rank that seem'd very well pleas'd with their Entertainment, and they assur'd me this was a celebrated Piece. I shall conclude my Letter with this remarkable Relation very well worthy the serious consideration of Mr. Colleir.⁵ I won't trouble you with farewell complements, which I think generally as impertinent as Curtchys [*sic*] at leaving the room when the visit has been too long allready.

Text H MS 253, pp. 36–42

¹ Soon after LM moved to London in 1715 she began to learn German (see above, p. 245, n. 1). But when visiting Blankenburg (see below, p. 290) she claimed not to understand the language.

² The ducat was equivalent to eight shillings (Nugent, ii. 60).

³ O let me live for ever on these Lips!
   The Nectar of the Gods to these is tasteless.
   I swear, that were I *Jupiter*, this Night

I wou'd renounce my Heav'n to be *Amphitryon*.
   (*Amphitryon*, 2nd ed., 1694, p. 8).

⁴ Just as Jupiter impersonates Amphitryon, so Mercury impersonates Amphitryon's servant Sosia.

⁵ Jeremy Collier in his *Short View of the Immorality and Profaneness of the English Stage* (1698) attacked the Restoration playwrights, Dryden among them.

To Lady Mar *14 Sept.* [*1716*]

Vienna, Sept. 14 O.S.

Thô I have so lately trouble'd you (dear Sister) with a long letter, yet I will keep my promise in giving you an Account of my first going to Court.

In order to that ceremony, I was squeez'd up in a Gown and adorn'd with a Gorget and the other implements thereunto belonging: a dresse very inconvenient, but which certainly shews the neck and shape to great advantage. I cannot forbear in this place giving you some description of the Fashions here, which are more monstrous and contrary to all common sense and reason than tis possible for you to imagine. They build certain fabricks of Gause on their heads about a yard high consisting of 3 or 4 storys fortify'd with numberless yards of heavy riband. The foundation of this structure is a thing they call a Bourlé, which is exactly of the same shape and kind, but about 4 times as big, as those rolls our prudent milk maids make use of to fix their Pails upon. This machine they cover with their own Hair, which they mix with a great deal of false, it being a particular beauty to have their heads too large to go into a moderate Tub. Their Hair is prodigiously powder'd to conceal the mixture, and set out with 3 or 4 rows of Bodkins, wonderfully large, that stick 2 or 3 inches from their Hair, made of Diamonds, Pearls, red, green and yellow stones, that it certainly requires as much art and Experience to carry the Load upright as to dance upon May Day with the Girland. Their whalebone petticoats out-do ours by several yards Circumference and cover some Acres of Ground. You may easily suppose how much this extrodinary Dresse sets off and improves the natural Uglyness with which God Allmighty has been pleas'd to endow them all generally. Even the Lovely Empresse her selfe is oblig'd to comply in some degree with these absurd Fashions, which they would not quit for all the World.

I had a private Audience (according to ceremony) of halfe an hour and then all the other Ladys were permitted to come make their Court. I was perfectly charm'd with the Empresse.[1]

[1] Elisabeth Christine (1691–1750), da. of Ludwig Rudolf, Duke of Bruns-wick-Wolfenbüttel, m. (1708) Charles VI (Isenburg, i. 18).

I can-not, however, tell you that her features are regular.
Her Eyes are not large but have a lively look full of sweetness, her complexion the finest I ever saw, her nose and
forehead well made, but her mouth has ten thousand charms
that touch the Soul. When she smiles tis with a beauty and
sweetnesse that forces adoration.[1] She has a vast Quantity
of fine fair Hair, but then her Person! One must speak of it
poetically to do it rigid Justice; all that the Poets have said of
the mein of Juno, the air of Venus, come not up to the truth.
The Graces move with her; the famous statue of Medicis
was not form'd with more delicate proportions;[2] nothing
can be added to the beauty of her neck and hands. Till I saw
them I did not beleive there were any in Nature so perfect;
and I was allmost sorry that my rank here did not permit me
to kisse them, but they are kiss'd sufficiently, for every body
that waits on her pays that homage at their entrance and
when they take leave.[3] When the Ladys were come in, she
sat down to Quinze.[4] I could not play at a Game I had never
seen before, and she order'd me a seat at her right hand and
had the Goodnesse to talk to me very much with that Grace
so natural to her. I expected every moment when the Men
were to come in to pay their Court, but this drawing room
is very different from that of England. No Man enters it
but the old Grand Master, who comes in to advertise the
Empress of the Approach of the Emperor. His Imperial
Majesty did me the Honnour of speaking to me in a very
obliging manner, but he never speaks to any of the other
Ladys and the whole passes with a Gravity and air of ceremony that has something very formal in it.[5] The Empresse
Amalia, Dowager of the late Emperour Joseph, came this

[1] She was reputed one of the most
beautiful and charming women of her
time (A. von Gleichen-Russwurm, *Das
galante Europa: Geselligkeit der grossen
Welt 1600–1789*, 1919, pp. 269–70;
E. Vehse, *Memoirs of the Court, Aristocracy, and Diplomacy of Austria*, transl.
F. Demmler, 1856, ii. 113–14).

[2] Many years later, in Florence, LM
saw the original Venus di Medici (see
letter of 3 Sept. [1740], ii. 203).

[3] The court ceremonials were extremely formal and elaborate; visitors

presented to the Emperor and Empress
did them reverence after the Spanish
fashion, by kissing their hands (von
Gleichen-Russwurm, p. 107).

[4] A card game. This is the first use of
the word recorded in English (*OED*).

[5] Charles VI (1685–1740) had succeeded his brother Joseph I in 1711. He
was of a stern and melancholy expression; 'Spanish *grandezza* and starched
pomposity never for a moment lost
their hold upon him. . . . No one ever
saw him laugh' (Vehse, ii. 105, 111).

Evening to wait on the reigning Empresse, follow'd by the 2 Arch Dutchesses, her daughters, who are very agreable young Princesses.[1] Their Imperial Majestys rise and go to meet her at the door of the room, after which she is seated in an arm'd chair next the Empresse, and in the same Manner at Supper, and there the Men have the permission of paying their Court. The Arch Dutchesses sit on chairs with backs without arms. The Table is entirely serv'd and all the dishes set on by the Empresse's Maids of honnour, which are 12 young Ladys of the first Quality. They have no salary but their chambers at Court where they live in a sort of confinement, not being suffer'd to go to the Assemblys or public places in Town except in complement to the Wedding of a Sister Maid, whom the Empress allways presents with her picture set in Diamonds. The 3 first of them are call'd Ladys of the key, and wear gold keys by their sides, but what I find most pleasant is the custom which obliges them as long as they live after they have left the Empresse's Service to make her some present every Year on the day of her feast. Her majesty is serv'd by no marry'd Woman but the Grand Maitresse, who is gennerally a Widow of the first Quality, allways very old, and is at the same time Groom of the stole and Mother of the Maids. The dressers are not at all in the figure they pretend to in England, being look'd upon no otherwise than as downright chamber maids.

I had audience the next Day of the Empresse Mother, a Princesse of great Virtue and Goodnesse, but who piques her selfe so much on a violent devotion, she is perpetually performing extrodinary acts of pennance without having ever done any thing to deserve them.[2] She has the same Number of maids of Honnour, whom she suffers to go in Colours, but she her selfe never quits her mourning, and sure nothing can

---

[1] Wilhelmine Amalie (1673–1742), da. of Johann Friedrich, Duke of Brunswick-Lüneburg, m. (1699) Joseph I (1678–1711). Their daughters were Marie Josefa (1699–1757) and Marie Amalie (1701–56) (Isenburg, i. 18).

[2] Eleonore Magdalene (1655–1720), da. of Prince-Elector Philipp Wilhelm von der Pfalz, 3rd wife of Leopold I (1640–1705). She had been brought up with the austerity of an anchorite, and after her marriage 'kept a severe register of her thoughts and actions, condemned herself to stigmas for real or imaginary faults' (W. Coxe, *Hist. of the House of Austria*, 3rd ed., 1847, ii. 520).

be more dismal than the mournings here, even for a Brother. There is not the least bit of linnen to be seen: all-black crape in stead of it, the neck, ears and side of the face cover'd with a plaited piece of the same stuff; and the face that peeps out in the midst of it looks as if it were pillory'd. The Widows wear over and above, a crape forehead Cloth, and in this solemn weed go to all the public places of Diversion without scruple.

The next day I was to wait on the Empresse Amalia, who is now at her Palace of retirement halfe a mile from the Town. I had there the pleasure of seeing a Diversion wholly new to me, but which is the common Amusement of this Court. The Empress her selfe was seated on a little Throne at the end of a fine Alley in her Garden, and on each side of her rang'd 2 partys of her Ladys of honnour with other young Ladys of Quality, headed by the 2 young Arch Dutchesses, all dress'd in their Hair, full of Jewels, with fine light Guns in their Hands, and at proper distances were plac'd 3 oval Pictures which were the Marks to be shot at. The first was that of a Cupid filling a Bumper of Burgundy, and the motto, 'tis easy to be valiant here; the 2nd, a Fortune holding a Garland in her hand, the motto, for her whom fortune favours; the 3rd was a sword with a lawrel wreath on the point, the Motto, here is no shame to the Vanquish'd. Near the Empresse was a Gilded Trophy wreath'd with Flowers and made of little Crooks on which were hung rich Turkish Handkercheifs, Tippets, ribands, Laces etc. for the small prizes. The Empresse gave the first with her own hand, which was a fine ruby ring set round with di'monds, in a Gold Snuff box. There was for the 2nd a little Cupid set with brilliants, and besides these a set of fine china for a tea table enchas'd in Gold, Japan Trunks, fans, and many Galantrys of the same nature. All the men of Quality at Vienna were Spectators, but only the Ladys had permission to shoot, and the Arch Dutchesse Amalia carry'd off the first prize. I was very well pleas'd with having seen this Entertainment, and I don't know but it might make as good a figure as the prize shooting in the Æneid if I could write as well as Virgil.[1] This is the favourite pleasure of the

---

[1] *Aeneid*, v. 485–544. As early as April 1710 W wrote to her, 'Your own Poet Virgil. . . .' (W MS i. 82); and when the French Ambassador to

Emperour, and there is rarely a week without some feast
of this kind, which makes the young Ladys skilfull enough
to defend a fort, and they laugh'd very much to see me afraid
to handle a Gun.¹

My dear Sister, you will easily pardon an abrupt conclusion. I beleive by this time you are ready to fear I would
never conclude at all.

Text H MS 253, pp. 43–54

To Lady R[ich]² *20 Sept.* [*1716*]

Vienna, Sept. 20 O.S.

I am extreamly pleas'd, but not at all surpriz'd, at the
long delightfull Letter you have had the goodnesse to send
me. I know that you can think of an absent Freind even in
the midst of a Court, and that you love to oblige where you
can have no view of a Return, and I expect from you that
you should love me and think of me when you don't see me.

I have compassion for the Mortifications that you tell me
befall our little Freind, and I pity her much more since I
know that they are only owing to the barbarous Customs of
our Country. Upon my word, if she was here she would
have no other fault but being something too young for the
Fashion, and she has nothing to do but to transplant hither
about 7 years hence to be again a young and blooming

Turkey met her, it seemed to him that
she knew Virgil and Horace by heart
(13 April 1717, Ministère des Affaires
Étrangères, Constantinople, vol. 57,
f. 151).

¹ The *Wienerisches Diarium* (Sept.–
Oct., *passim*) frequently reports such
contests (*Cränzl-Schieszen*) in the garden
of the Favorita. Thomas Coke (later
Earl of Leicester), when he visited
Vienna the following year, remarked
that the emperor 'diverts himself every
afternoon by shooting at a white mark,
which he has also made the Empress and
Ladys of the Court use themselves to'
(C. W. James, *Chief Justice Coke: His*

Family & Descendants at Holkham, 1929,
p. 205).

² In MS 'To the Lady R'. Elizabeth
(1692–1773), eldest daughter of Col.
Edward Griffith, m. (*c.* 1710) Sir
Robert Rich (*DNB*). In July Pope and
LM had written her a joint letter of
which only his half survives (Pope,
Corr. i. 345–6). Their opinion of her
may be gauged by LM's anecdote
(Stuart, p. 100) of her giddy vanity in
pretending to be young—which this
letter curiously foretells—and by Pope's
tribute to her immorality in 'The Court
Ballad' of 1717 (*Minor Poems*, ed.
N. Ault and J. Butt, 1954, p. 182).

Beauty. I can assure you that wrinkles or a small stoop in the shoulders, nay, Gray Hair it selfe, is no objection to the makeing new conquests. I know you can't easily figure to your selfe a young Fellow of five and twenty ogling my Lady Suff[olk] with passion, or pressing to lead the Countesse of O[xfor]d from an Opera,[1] but such are the sights I see every day and I dont perceive any body surprizd at 'em but my selfe. A Woman till 5 and thirty is only look'd upon as a raw Girl and can possibly make no noise in the World till about forty. I don't know what your Ladyship may think of this matter, but tis a considerable comfort to me to know there is upon Earth such a paradise for old Women, and I am content to be insignificant at present in the design of returning when I am fit to appear no where else.

I cannot help lamenting upon this Occassion the pittifull case of so many good English Ladys long since retir'd to pruderie and rattafia, whom, if their stars had luckily conducted them hither, would still shine in the first rank of Beautys; and then that perplexing word Reputation has quite another meaning here than what you give it at London, and getting a Lover is so far from loseing, that 'tis properly geting reputation, Ladys being much more respected in regard to the rank of their Lovers than that of their Husbands. But what you'l think very odd, the 2 sects that divide our whole nation of Petticoats are utterly unknown. Here are neither Coquets nor Prudes. No woman dares appear coquet enough to encourrage 2 lovers at a time, and I have not seen any such Prudes as to pretend fidelity to their Husbands, who are certainly the best-natur'd set of people in the World, and they look upon their Wives' Galants as favourably as Men do upon their Deputys that take the troublesome part of their busynesse off of their hands, thô they have not the less to do, for they are gennerally deputys in another place themselves. In one word, 'tis the establish'd custom for every Lady to have 2 Husbands, one that bears the Name, and another that performs the Dutys;

---

[1] Elderly widows: probably Mary (c. 1650–1721), da. of Rev. Ambrose Upton, m. (1691) 5th Earl of Suffolk (1627–1709); and Diana (d. 1719), da. of George Kirke, m. (1673) 20th Earl of Oxford (1627–1703).

and these engagements are so well known, that it would be a down right affront and publickly resented if you invited a Woman of Quality to dinner without at the same time inviteing her 2 attendants of Lover and Husband, between whom she allways sits in state with great Gravity. These sub-marriages gennerally last 20 year together, and the Lady often commands the poor Lover's estate even to the utter ruin of his family, thô they are as seldom begun by any passion as other matches. But a Man makes but an ill figure that is not in some commerce of this Nature, and a Woman looks out for a Lover as soon as she's marry'd as part of her Equipage, without which she could not be gentile; and the first article of the Treaty is establishing the pension, which remains to the Lady thô the Galant should prove inconstant, and this chargable point of honnour I look upon as the real foundation of so many wonderfull instances of Constancy. I realy know several Women of the first Quality whose pensions are as well known as their Anual Rents, and yet no body esteems them the lesse. On the contrary, their Discretion would be call'd in Question if they should be suspected to be mistresses for nothing, and a great part of their Emulation consists in trying who shall get most; and having no intrigue at all is so far a disgrace that I'll assure you a Lady who is very much my freind here told me but yesterday how much I was oblig'd to her for justifying my conduct in a conversation on my Subject, where it was publickly asserted that I could not possibly have common sense that had been about Town above a Fortnight and had made no steps towards commenceing an Amour. My freind pleaded for me that my stay was uncertain and she beleiv'd that was the cause of my seeming stupidity, and this was all she could find to say in my Justification.

But one of the pleasantest adventures I ever met in my life was last night and which will give you a just Idea after what delicate manner the Belle-Passions are manag'd in this Country. I was at the Assembly of the Countesse of ——, and the Young Count of —— led me down stairs, and he ask'd me how long I intended to stay here. I made answer that my stay depended on the Emperour and it was not in my power to determine it. Well Madam (said he), whither your time here is to be long or short, I think you ought to pass it agreably, and to that end you must engage in a little affair of the Heart.—My Heart, answer'd I gravely enough, does not engage very easily, and I have no design of parting with it.—I see, Madam (said he sighing), by the ill nature of that answer, that I am not to hope for it, which is a great mortification to me that am charm'd with you; but however, I am still devoted to your service, and since I am not worthy of entertaining you my selfe, do me the Honnour of leting me know who you like best amongst us and I'll engage to manage the affair entirely to your satisfaction.—You may Judge in what manner I should have receiv'd this complement in my own Country, but I was well enough acquainted with the way of this to know that he realy intended me an obligation, and thank'd him with a grave Curtsie for his Zeal to serve me and only assur'd him that I had no Occassion to make use of it.[1] Thus you see, my Dear, Galantry and good breeding are as different in different Climates as Morality and Religion.[2] Who have the rightest notions of both we shall never know till the Day of Judgment, for which great Day of Éclaircissement I own there is very little impatience in your etc.

Text H MS 253, pp. 55–65

To Mrs. ⟨T——l⟩[3] *26 Sept.* [*1716*]

Vienna, Sept. 26. O.S.

I never was more agreably surpriz'd than by your obliging Letter. 'Tis a particular mark of my Esteem that I tell you

[1] In his letter of 10 Nov. (*Corr.* i. 368), Pope commented on her account of Viennese gallantry, which she must have sent to him in an actual letter.

[2] When John Moore travelled to Vienna half a century later, during the puritanical reign of Maria Theresa, he verified LM's description of sub-marriages: 'I do not imagine they are common at present, in all the latitude of her description. But it is not uncommon for married ladies here to avow the greatest degree of friendship and attachment to men who are not their husbands, and to live with them in great intimacy, without hurting their reputation, or being suspected, even by their own sex, of having deviated from the laws of modesty' (*A View of Society and Manners in France, Switzerland, and Germany*, 1779, ii. 339).

[3] Dallaway (1803, ii. 8) and Moy

so, and I can assure you that if I lov'd you one Grain less
than I do, I should have been very sorry to see it, as diverting
as it is. The mortal Aversion I have to writeing makes me
tremble at the thoughts of a new Correspondant,[1] and I
beleive I disoblig'd no lesse than a dozen of my London
Acquaintance by refusing to hear from them, thô I did
verily think they intended to send me very entertaining
Letters; but I had rather lose the pleasure of reading several
witty things than be forc'd to write many stupid ones. Yet
in spite of these considerations, I am charm'd with this
proofe of your freindship and beg a continuation of the
same Goodnesse, thô I fear the dullness of this will make you
immediately repent of it.

It is not from Austria that one can write with vivacity, and
I am already infected with the Phlegm of the Country. Even
their Amours and their Quarrels are carry'd on with a surprizing temper, and they are never lively but upon points of
ceremony. There, I own, they shew all their passions; and tis
not long since 2 Coaches meeting in a narrow street at night,
the Ladys in them, not being able to adjust the Ceremonial
of which should go back, sat there with equal Galantry till 2
in the morning, and were both so fully determin'd to dye upon
the spot rather than yeild in a point of that importance
that the street would never have been clear'd till their Deaths
if the Emperor had not sent his Guards to part 'em; and even
then they refus'd to stir till the Expedient was found out of
takeing them both out in chairs exactly at the same moment,
after which it was with some difficulty the pas was decided
between the 2 Coachmen, no lesse tenacious of their Rank
than the Ladys. Nay, this passion is so omnipotent in the
Breasts of the Women that even their Husbands never dye
but they are ready to break their Hearts because that fatal
hour puts an end to their Rank, no Widows having any place
at Vienna.

The Men are not much lesse touch'd with this Point of
Honnour, and they do not only scorn to marry but to make
love to any Woman of a Family not as illustrious as their

Thomas (1861, i. 246) have assumed this
to be Mrs. Thistlethwayte, but it is
clearly unlike any other heading.

[1] Further proof that the correspondent is not Mrs. Thistlethwayte, to whom
LM had addressed the letter of 30 Aug.

own, and the pedigree is much more consider'd by 'em than either the complexion or features of their Mistrisses. Happy are the shee's that can number amongst their Ancestors Counts of the Empire. They have neither occassion for Beauty, money, or good Conduct to get them Lovers and Husbands. 'Tis true, as to money, 'tis seldom any advantage to the Man they marry. The Laws of Austria confine a Woman's portion not to exceed 2,000 florins, about £200 English, and whatever they have beside remains in their own possesion and disposal.[1] Thus here are many Ladys much richer than their Husbands, who are however oblig'd to allow them pin money agreable to their Quality, and I attribute to this considerable branch of prerogative the Liberty that they take upon other Occassions.

I am sure you, that know my lazyness and extreme indifference on this subject, will pity me Entangle'd amongst all these Ceremonys, which are wonderfull burdensome to me, thô I am the Envy of the whole Town, having, by their own Customs, the Pas before them all. But they revenge upon the poor Envoys this Great respect shew'd to Ambassadors, using them with a contempt that (with all my Indifference) I should be very uneasy to suffer. Upon days of Ceremony they have no Entrance at Court, and on other days must content themselves with walking after every Soul and being the very last taken Notice of—but I must write a Volume to let you know all the Ceremonys, and I have allready said too much on so dull a subject, which, however, employs the whole care of the people here.[2] I need not, after this, tell you how agreably the time slides away with me. You know as well as I do the taste of your etc.

Text H MS 253, pp. 65–71

---

[1] By Austrian law although a husband could administer his wife's property he could not take it over. Dowries were limited to 1,000 florins for a *nobilis*, and 3,000 for a *comes* if his own estate was 300,000 (A. Ogonowski, *Oesterreichisches Ehegüterrecht*, 1880, pp. 91, 93, n. 1).

[2] LM's descriptions of the coach incident, gallantry, and the elaborate court dress and ceremony are quoted by A. von Gleichen-Russwurm (*Das galante Europa: Geselligkeit der grossen Welt 1600–1789*, 1919, pp. 271–2).

To Lady X—— *1 Oct.* [*1716*]

Vienna, Oct. 1. O.S.

You desire me, Madam, to send you some account of the Customs here and at the same time a description of Vienna. I am allways willing to obey your Commands, but I must upon this Occasion desire you to take the Will for the deed. If I should undertake to tell you all the particulars in which the manner here differs from ours, I must write a whole Quire of the dullest stuff that ever was read or printed without being read.

Their Dresse agrees with the French or English in no one article but wearing Petticoats, and they have many fashions peculiar to themselves, as that 'tis indecent for a Widow ever to wear Green or Rose colour, but all the other gayest colours at her own Discretion. The assemblys here are the only regular diversion, the Operas being allways at Court and commonly on some particular Occasion. Madam Rabutin has th'assembly constantly every night at her House[1] and the other Ladys whenever they have a fancy to display the magnificence of their apartments or oblige a freind by complementing them on the day of their Saint; they declare that on such a day the assembly shall be at their House in Honnour of the Feast of the Count or Countesse such a one. These days are call'd Days of Gallá, and all the Freinds or Relations of the Lady whose Saint it is, are oblig'd to appear in their best Cloths and all their Jewells. The Mistrisse of the House takes no particular notice of any body, nor returns any body's visit, and whoever pleases may go without the formality of being presented. The company are entertain'd with ice in several forms, Winter and Summer. Afterwards they divide into partys of Ombre, piquet or conversation, all games of Hazard being forbid. I saw 'tother day the Gallá for Count Altheim,

---

[1] Dorothea Elisabeth (1645–1725), da. of Philipp Ludwig, Duke of Holstein, m. (1682) as her 2nd husband Ludwig, Count von Rabutin (Isenburg, i. 90). Pöllnitz called her house the rendezvous of all people of the first rank (i. 268).

the Emperor's Favourite,[1] and never in my Life saw so many fine Cloths ill fancy'd. They embroder the richest gold Stuffs, and provided they can make their cloths expensive enough, that is all the taste they shew in them. On other days the general Dress is a scarf and what you please under it.

But now I am speaking of Vienna I am sure you expect I should say something of the Convents. They are of all sorts and sizes, but I am best pleas'd with that of St. Lawrence,[2] where the Ease and neatness they seem to live with appears to me much more edifying than those stricter orders where perpetual pennance and nastynesse must breed discontent and wretchednesse. The Nuns are all of Quality; I think there is to the Number of 50. They have each of them a little cell perfectly clean, the walls cover'd with pictures, more or less fine according to their Quality. A long white stone Gallery runs by all of 'em, furnish'd with the pictures of Exemplary Sisters; the chappel extreme neat and richly adorn'd. But I could not forbear laughing at their shewing me a wooden head of our Saviour which they assur'd me spoke during the Seige of Vienna, and as a proofe of it, bid me remark his mouth which had been open ever since. Nothing can be more becoming than the dress of these Nuns. It is a fine white camlet, the sleeves turn'd up with fine white callico, and their head dress and [   ][3] the same, only a small vail of black Crape that falls behind. They have a lower sort of serving Nuns that wait on them as their chamber maids. They receive all visits of Women and play at Ombre in their chambers with permission of the Abbesse, which is very easy to be obtain'd. I never saw an old Woman so good natur'd. She is near fourscore and yet shews very little sign of decay, being still lively and cheerfull.[4] She caress'd me as if I had been her daughter, giving me some pritty things of her own work

---

[1] Michael Johann III, Count von Althann (1679–1722), Privy Councillor, Grand Master of the Horse. On 1 Oct./ 20 Sept. he had returned from the military front in Hungary (*Wienerisches Diarium*, 30 Sept.–2 Oct. 1716).
[2] The Laurenzerinnenklöster, of the Augustinian order, built in 1327 on the old Fleischmarkt (LM, *Reisebriefe*, transl. and ed. H. H. Blumenthal, 1931).
[3] The MS has a blank space here.
[4] From 1700 to 1723 the Abbess was Maria Regina Erenberger, a convert (Theodor Wiedemann, *Geschichte der Frauenklöster St. Laurenz & Maria Magdalena*, 1883, pp. 73–74).

and sweetmeats in Abundance. The Grate is not one of the
most rigid. It is not very hard to put a head thrô and I don't
doubt but a Man a little more slender than ordinary might
squeeze in his whole person. The young Count of Salmes[1]
came to the Grate while I was there, and the Abbesse gave
him her Hand to kisse.

But I was surpriz'd to find here the only beautifull young
Woman I have seen at Vienna, and not only beautifull but
Genteel, witty and agreable, of a Great Family, and who had
been the admiration of the Town. I could not forbear shewing my surprize at seeing a Nun like her.[2] She made me a
thousand obliging complements and desir'd me to come
often. It will be an infinite pleasure to me (said she sighing)
to see you, but I avoid with the greatest care seeing any of my
former Acquaintance, and whenever they come to our Convent I lock my selfe in my Cell.—I observ'd tears come into
her Eyes, which touch'd me extremely, and I begun to talk
to her in that strain of tender pity she inspir'd me with, but
she would not own to me that she is not perfectly happy. I
have since endeavor'd to learn the real cause of her retirement
without being able to get any account but that every body was
surpriz'd at it and no body guess'd the Reason. I have been
several times to see her, but it gives me too much melancholy
to see so agreable a young Creature bury'd alive, and I am
not surpriz'd that Nuns have so often inspir'd violent passions, the pity one naturally feels for them when they seem
worthy of another Destiny makeing an easy way for yet more
tender sentiments; and I never in my Life had so little charity
for the Roman Catholic Religion as since I see the misery it
occasions so many poor unhappy Women, and the grosse
superstition of the common people who are, some or other of
'em, day and night off'ring bits of candle to the wooden
figures that are set up almost in every street. The processions
I see very often are a pageantry as offensive and apparently
contradictory to all common sense as the Pagods of China.
God knows whither it be the womanly spirit of Contradiction

[1] Franz Wilhelm, Count von Salm (1672–1734), equerry to the Dowager Empress Wilhelmine Amalie, had three sons; this must be the eldest, Carl Anton (1697–1755) (Isenburg, iii. 149).

[2] Possibly Josepha, Baroness von Gallenfels, who had entered in 1713 (Wiedemann, p. 74).

that works in me, but there never before was so much Zeal against popery in the Heart of, Dear Madam, etc.

Text H MS 253, pp. 72–81

To Mr. —— *10 Oct.* [*1716*]

Vienna, Oct. 10. O.S.

I deserve not at all the reproaches you make me. If I have been some time without answering your Letter, it is not that I don't know how many thanks are due to you for it, or that I am stupid enough to prefer any amusements to the pleasure of hearing from you; but after the proffessions of esteem you have so obligeingly made me, I cannot help delaying as long as I can showing you that you are mistaken; and if you are sincere when you say you expect to be extremely entertain'd by my Letters, I ought to be mortify'd at the disapointment that I am sure you will receive when you hear from me, thô I have done my best endeavors to find out something worth writeing to you.

I have seen every thing that is to be seen with a very diligent Curiosity. Here are some fine Villas, particularly the late Prince of Lictenstein's, but the statues are all modern and the pictures not of the first hands.[1] 'Tis true the Emperor has some of great Value. I was Yesterday to see that repository which they call his Treasure, where they seem to have been more diligent in amassing a Great Quantity of things than in the choice of them. I spent above 5 hours there and yet there were very few things that stop'd me long to consider 'em, but the number is prodigious, being a very long Gallery fill'd on both sides and 5 large rooms. There are a vast Quantity of paintings amongst which are many fine Miniatures, but the most valuable pictures are a few of Corregio, those of Titian being at the Favorita. The Cabinet of Jewells did not appear to me so rich as I expected to see it. They

---

[1] Johann Adam, Prince von Liechtenstein (1656–1712) (Isenburg, i. 176). His palace, in the Italian style, was considered by Pöllnitz to be as large and magnificent as that of Savoy, and worth seeing for its paintings (i. 264).

shew'd me there a cup about the size of a tea-dish of one entire Emerald, which they had so particular a respect for, only the Emperor has the privelege of touching it. There is a large cabinet full of curiositys of Clock work, only one of which I thought worth observing. That was a Crawfish with all the motions so natural it was hard to distinguish it from the Life. The next cabinet was a large Collection of Agates, some of them extreme beautifull and of an uncommon size, and several vases of Lapis Lazuli. I was surpriz'd to see the Cabinet of Medals so poorly furnish'd; I did not remark one of any value, and they are kept in a most ridiculous disorder.[1] As to the antiques, very few of 'em deserv'd that name. Upon my saying they were modern, I could not forbear laughing at the answer of the profound Antiquary that shew'd 'em, that they were ancient enough, for to his knowlege they had been there this 40 year. But the next Cabinet diverted me yet better, being nothing else but a parcel of wax babys and Toys in Ivory, very well worthy to be presented children of 5 year old. 2 of the Rooms were wholly fill'd with relicks of all kinds set in Jewells, amongst which I was desir'd to observe a crucifix that they assur'd me had spoke very wisely to the Emperor Leopold.[2] I won't trouble you with the catalogue of the rest of the Lumber, but I must not forget to mention a small piece of Loadstone that held up an Anchor of Steel too heavy for me to lift. This is what I thought most curious in the whole Treasure. There are some few heads of Ancient Statues, but several of them defac'd by modern Additions.[3]

I foresee that you will be very little satisfy'd with this Letter, and I dare hardly ask you to be good natur'd enough to charge the dullness of it on the barreness of the Subject, and overlook the Stupidity of Your etc.

Text H MS 253, pp. 82–87

[1] Actually Charles VI, an ardent numismatist, built up a magnificent collection. Blumenthal (transl. cit.) conjectures that LM visited it at an unpropitious moment.

[2] Blumenthal surmises that LM meant the crucifix of Ferdinand II, father of Leopold I.

[3] The 'treasures', including many which LM mentions, are listed and described in Edward Brown, *Account of Travels Through Germany*, 1677, pp. 95–100.

To Lady Mar *17 Nov.* [*1716*]

O.S. Nov. 17, Prague

I hope my dear Sister wants no new proofe of my Sincere affection for her, but I'm sure if you did, I could not give you a stronger than writeing at this time, after 3 days, or more properly speaking 3 nights and days, hard post travelling.[1]

The Kingdom of Bohemia is the most desart of any I have seen in Germany; the Villages so poor and the post houses so miserable, clean straw and fair Water are blessings not allways to be found and better Accommodation not to be hop'd. Thô I carry'd my own bed with me, I could not sometimes find a place to set it up in, and I rather chose to travel all night, as cold as it is, wrap'd up in my furs, than go into the common Stoves, which are fill'd with a mixture of all sort of ill Scents.

This Town was once the Royal seat of the Bohemian Kings, and is still the Capital of the Kingdom. There are yet some remains of its former Splendour, being one of the Largest Towns in Germany, but for the most part old built and thinly inhabited, which makes the Houses very cheap; and those people of Quality who can-not easily bear the Expence of Vienna chuse to reside here, where they have assemblys, Music, and all other diversions (those of a Court excepted) at very moderate rates, all things being here in great Abundance, especially the best wild fowl I ever tasted.[2] I have allready been visited by some of the most considerable Ladys whose Relations I knew at Vienna. They are dress'd after the Fashions there, as people at Exeter imitate those of London. That is, their Imitation is more excessive than the

---

[1] W's main diplomatic task was to mediate in the war between Austria and Turkey, and help to arrange a peace treaty. But instead of going from Vienna to Belgrade, he set out—on 24/13 Nov. —for Hanover, where the King was in residence (Schaub to Townshend, 25 Nov. 1716 [N.S.], SP 80/33). There he

was to receive further instructions and credentials (Stanyan to Townshend, 9 Dec. 1716 [N.S.], SP 80/34; his instructions, dated Dec. 1716, are W MS vii. 121–2).

[2] Both Pöllnitz (i. 244) and Nugent (ii. 256) praise the pheasants and ortolans as particularly good eating.

Original, and 'tis not easy to describe what extrodinary figures they make. The person is so much lost between Head dress and Petticoat, they have as much occassion to write upon their backs, This is a Woman, for the information of Travellers, as ever sign post painter had to write, This is a bear.[1]

I will not forget to write to you again from Dresden and Lypsic, being much more solicitous to content your Curiosity than to indulge my own repose. I am etc.

Text H MS 253, pp. 88–91

To Lady Mar *21 Nov.* [*1716*]

Nov. 21, O.S., Lypsic[2]

I beleive (dear Sister) you will easily forgive my not writeing to you from Dresden as I promis'd, when I tell you that I never went out of my Chaise from Prague to that Place. You may imagine how heartily I was tir'd with 24 hours post travelling without sleep or refreshment (for I can never sleep in a Coach However fatigu'd). We pass'd by moonshine the frightfull Precipices that divide Bohemia from Saxony, at the bottom of which runs the River Elbe, but I cannot say that I had reason to fear drowning in it, being perfectly convinc'd that in case of a Tumble it was utterly impossible to come alive to the bottom. In many places the road is so narrow that I could not discern an inch of Space between the wheels and the precipice; yet I was so good a Wife not to wake Mr. [Wortley], who was fast asleep by my side, to make him share in my fears, since the danger was unavoidable, till I perceiv'd, by the bright light of the moon, our Postillions nodding on horseback while the Horses were on a full Gallop, and I thought it very convenient to call out to desire 'em to look where they were going. My calling wak'd Mr. W[ortley] and he was much more surpriz'd than my

---

[1] A reference to an anecdote in the *Tatler* No. 18 (21 May 1709).
[2] On 9 Dec./28 Nov. W was reported as having 'passed lately' through Leipzig on his way to Hanover (*Daily Courant*, 12 Dec. 1716).

selfe at the Scituation we were in, and assur'd me that he had pass'd the Alps 5 times in different places without ever having done a road so dangerous.¹ I have been told since, tis common to find the bodys of Travellers in the Elbe, but thank God that was not our Destiny and we came Safe to Dresden, so much tir'd with fear and fatigue, it was not possible for me to compose my selfe to write. After passing these dreadfull Rocks, Dresden appear'd to me a Wonderfull Agreable Scituation in a fine large Plain on the banks of the Elbe. I was very glad to stay there a day to rest my selfe.²

The Town is the neatest I have seen in Germany. Most of the Houses are new built, the Elector's Palace very handsome, and his repository full of Curiositys of Different kinds with a Collection of Medals very much esteem'd.³ Sir [Richard Vernon], our King's Envoy, came to see me here,⁴ and Madame de L[orme], whom I knew in London when her Husband was Minister to the King of Poland there.⁵ She offer'd me all things in her power to entertain me and brought some Ladys with her whom she presented to me. The Saxon Ladys ressemble the Austrian no more than the Chinese those of London. They are very genteely dress'd after the French and English modes, and have gennerally pritty faces, but the most determin'd Minaudieres in the whole world. They would think it a mortal sin against good breeding if they either spoke or mov'd in a natural manner. They all affect a little soft Lisp and a pritty pitty pat step, which female frailtys ought, however, to be forgiven 'em

¹ W had made the Grand Tour from 1700 to 1703.

² After Nathaniel Wraxall travelled the same road in 1777 he wrote: 'I . . . crossed the Mountains which divide Saxony from Bohemia, with the greatest Difficulty, among Precipices which overhang the Elbe, and thro' continual Snows. I found Lady Wortley Montagu's Description, tho' written 60 Years ago, literally verified' (Eliz. Montagu, *Letters 1762–1800*, ed. R. Blunt, 1923, ii. 40).

³ Augustus the Strong (1670–1733), Elector of Saxony (1694), King of Poland (1697). His palace with its collections and curiosities is described

by Nugent (ii. 262–3).

⁴ Vernon (1678–1725) was British Envoy Extraordinary at Dresden 1715–18. Although from Oct. to 19/8 Dec. 1716 Vernon was in Hanover, and not in Dresden (D. B. Horn, *Brit. Dipl. Rep. 1689–1789*, 1932, p. 89), where LM claims he visited her, she did actually see him a month later in Dresden, when she again passed through it *en route* from Hanover to Vienna (see below, p. 291, n. 1).

⁵ Charles Pierre de Lorme, Resident of Saxony to London 1710–14 (F. Hausmann, *Repertorium der diplomatischen Vertreter*, 1936–50, i. 455).

in favour of their civility and good nature to strangers, which
I have a great deal of reason to praise.[1]

The Countesse of Cozelle[2] is kept prisoner in a melancholy castle some Leagues from hence, and I cannot forbear
telling you what I have heard of her, because it seems to me
very extrodinary, thô I foresee I shall swell my Letter to the
size of a pacquet. She was Mistrisse to the King of Poland
(Elector of Saxony) with so absolute a dominion over him
that never any Lady had had so much power in that Court.
They tell a pleasant story of his majesty's first declaration of
Love, which he made in a visit to her, bringing in one hand
a bag of 100,000 Crowns, and in the other a Horse Shoe,
which he snap'd in sunder before her face, leaving her to
draw consequences from such remarkable proofes of
Strength and Liberality. I know not which charm'd her,
but she consented to leave her Husband to give her selfe up
to him entirely, being divorc'd publickly in such a manner
as (by their Law) permits either party to marry again. God
knows whither it was at this time or in some other fond fit,
but 'tis certain the King had the weakness to make her a
formal contract of marriage, which thô it could signify
nothing during the Life of the Queen,[3] pleas'd her so well
that she could not be contented without telling all people
she saw of it and giving her selfe the airs of a Queen.

Men endure every thing while they are in Love, but when
the Excess of passion was cool'd by long possession, His
Majesty begun to refflect on the ill consequences of leaving
such a paper in her hands, and desir'd to have it restor'd to
him. She rather chose to endure all the most violent Effects of
his Anger than give it up; and thô she is one of the richest
and most avaricious Ladys of her Country, she has refus'd
the offer of the continuation of a large pension and the security of a vast Summ of Money she has amass'd, and has at last
provok'd the King to confine her person where she endures
all the terrors of a strait imprisonment and remains still
inflexible either to Threats or promises, thô her violent
passions has brought her into fits, which 'tis suppos'd will

[1] Pöllnitz's opinion of Saxon ladies
is similar to LM's (i. 153–4).
[2] See next page, n. 1.

[3] Eberhardine (1671–1727), da. of
Elector of Brandenburg, m. (1693)
Augustus.

soon put an end to her Life.[1] I cannot forbear having some compassion for a Woman that suffers for a point of Honnour, however mistaken, especially in a country where points of Honnour are not over scrupulously observ'd amongst Ladys.

I could have wish'd Mr. W[ortley]'s busyness had permitted a longer stay at Dresden. Perhaps I am partial to a Town where they professe the Protestant Religion, but every thing seem'd to me with quite another air of Politenesse than I have found in other places. Lypsic, where I am at present, is a Town very considerable for its Trade, and I take this Oppertunity of buying pages' Liverys, Gold stuffs for my selfe, etc.,[2] all things of that kind being at least double the price at Vienna, partly because of the excessive customs and partly the want of Genius and Industry in the people, who make no one sort of thing there, and the Ladys are oblig'd to send even for their shoes out of Saxony. The Fair here is one of the most considerable in Germany, and the resort of all the people of Quality as well as the Merchants.[3] This is a fortify'd Town, but I avoid ever mentioning fortifications, being sensible that I know not how to speak of 'em. I am the more easy under my ignorance when I refflect that I am sure you'l willingly forgive the Omission, for if I made you the most exact description of all the Ravlins and Bastions I see in my travells, I dare swear you would ask me, What is a Ravlin? and what is a Bastion?

Adeiu, my dear Sister.

Text H MS 253, pp. 91–102

[1] Anna Constanze von Brockdorf (1680–1765) m. (1699) Adolf Magnus, Count von Hoym; in 1700 she became mistress to Augustus, who created her Countess von Cosel in 1706. Except for the detail of the King's bending a horseshoe, LM's narrative is substantially that given by Pöllnitz in *La Saxe Galante, or The Amorous Adventures and Intrigues of Frederick-Augustus II,* 1750.

[2] '*Leipsic* has considerable manufactures of its own, as in stuffs, gold and silver lace . . .' (Nugent, ii. 229). The liveries bought in England, probably from Lord Bingley (see above, p. 248),

were being sent out to Constantinople by ship. In Leipzig W evidently did not buy enough liveries, for when he reached Adrianople he had new ones made (dispatch from [?] to [?Stanhope], Pera of Constantinople, March 1717, SP 97/24). His bill to the Secretary of State included charges 'for liveries for all my livery servants, those I had on the ship not being arrived' (Constantinople, 19 July 1717, Tickell MS owned by Sir Eustace F. Tickell).

[3] 'The king of *Poland* comes generally to the fair, which draws a vast concourse of nobility' (Nugent, ii. 228).

To the Countess of ——[1] *23* Nov. [*1716*]

O.S. Nov. 23, Brunswic

I am just come to Brunswick, a very old Town, but which has the advantage of being the capital of the Duke of Wolfumbutel's Dominions, a family (not to speak of its ancient Honnours) illustrious by having its younger Branch on the Throne of England, and having given 2 Empresses to Germany.[2] I have not forgot to drink your health here in Mum, which I think very well deserves its reputation of being the best in the world.[3]

This Letter is the 3rd I have writ to you during my Journey, and I declare to you that if you do not send me immediately a full and true Account of all the changes and chances amongst our London Acquaintance, I will not write you any description of Hannover (where I hope to be to night), thô I know you have more Curiosity to hear of that place than of any other.

Text H MS 253, pp. 102–3

To Lady Bristol *25* Nov. [*1716*]

Hannover, Nov. 25. O.S.

I receiv'd your Ladyship's but the day before I left Vienna, thô by the date I ought to have had it much sooner, but nothing was ever worse regulated than the post in most parts of Germany. I can assure you the pacquet at Prague was ty'd behind my Chaise and in that manner convey'd to Dresden. The secrets of halfe the country were at my Mercy

---

[1] Although Dallaway (1803, ii. 33) and Moy Thomas (1861, i. 257) address this letter to Lady Mar, I am sceptical for two reasons: it lacks LM's customary affectionate phrase 'dear Sister', and she had already addressed five Embassy letters to Lady Mar, not two (as this letter states).

[2] King George I and the consorts of Joseph I and Charles VI (Isenburg, i. 72, 74).

[3] The chief trade of Brunswick, besides leather tanning, was 'brewing *mum* from a malt made of barley, with a small mixture of wheat, well hopped' (Nugent, ii. 243).

if I had had any curiosity for 'em. I would not longer delay my thanks for yours, thô the number of my Acquaintance here and my Duty of attending at Court leaves me hardly any time to dispose of. I am extreamly pleas'd that I can tell you without either flattery or partiality that our young Prince[1] has all the Accomplishments that tis possible to have at his Age, with an Air of Sprightlynesse and understanding, and something so very engaging and easy in his behaviour, that he needs not the advantage of his rank to appear charming. I had the honnour of a long conversation with him last night before the King came in. His Governour[2] retir'd on purpose (as he told me afterwards) that I might make some judgment of his Genius by hearing him speak without constraint, and I was surpriz'd at the quicknesse and politenesse that appear'd in every thing he said, joyn'd to a person perfectly agreable and the fine fair Hair of the Princesse.[3]

This Town is neither large nor handsome, but the Palace capable of holding a greater Court than that of St. James's, and the King has had the goodnesse to appoint us a Lodging in one part of it, without which we should be very ill Accomodated; for the vast number of English crouds the Town so much, tis very good Luck to be able to get one sorry room in a miserable Tavern. I din'd to day with the Portugueze Ambassador,[4] who thinks himselfe very happy to have 2 wretched Parlors in an Inn.

I have now made the Tour of Germany and cannot help observing a considerable difference between travelling here and in England. One sees none of those fine Seats of Noblemen that are so common amongst us, nor any thing like a Country Gentleman's house, thô they have many Scituations perfectly fine; but the whole people are divided into Absolute Sovereignitys, where all the riches and magnificence are at Court, or Communitys of Merchants, such as Neiurenbourg and Francfort, where they live allways in Town for the Convenience of Trade. The King's company of French

---

[1] Frederick Louis (1707–51), eldest son of the Prince of Wales.

[2] His tutor was Jean Hanet, a Frenchman (*Cal. of Treasury Papers 1720–28*, ed. J. Redington, 1889, p. 65).

[3] His mother, the Princess of Wales.

[4] Dom Luis da Cunha (1662–1740), Portuguese Ambassador to England 1697–1710 and 1715–18. (F. Hausmann, *Repertorium der diplomatischen Vertreter*, 1936–50, i. 429, 483). He had accompanied the King to Hanover.

Comedians play here every night.¹ They are very well dress'd and some of them not ill actors. His Majesty dines and sups constantly in Public. The Court is very numerous and his affability and goodnesse makes it one of the most agreable places in the World to, Dear Madam, Your Ladyship's etc.²

Text H MS 253, pp. 104–8

To Lady R[ich] *1 Dec.* [*1716*]

Hanover, Dec. 1. O.S.

I am very glad, my dear Lady R[ich], that you have been so well pleas'd, as you tell me, at the report of my returning to England, thô, like other Pleasures, I can assure you it has no real foundation. I hope you know me enough to take my word against any report concerning my selfe. Tis true, as to Distance of place, I am much nearer London than I was some weeks ago, but as to the Thoughts of a Return, I never was farther off in my Life. I own I could, with great Joy, indulge the pleasing hopes of seeing you and the very few others that share my Esteem, but while Mr. [Wortley] is determin'd to proceed in his design, I am determin'd to follow him.—I am running on upon my own affairs; that is to say, I am going to write very dully as most people do when they write of themselves.

¹ 'The opera-house, as well as the theatre for the *French* comedians, both within the palace, are ancient but commodious' (Nugent, ii. 239).

² LM's favour at Court was patriotically observed by Lady Cowper's father: 'Her *Ladyship* is mighty gay and airy, and occasions a great deal of Discourse. Since her Arrival the *King* has took but little Notice of any other Lady, not even of Madame *Kielmansegg* [one of his mistresses], which the Ladies of *Hanover* don't relish very well' (Mary, Countess Cowper, *Diary*, ed. S. Cowper, 2nd ed., 1865, p. 195). On 7 Dec. Count von Bothmer, Hanoverian Representative in London, wrote to Jean de Robethon, the King's secretary: 'Je sais que le sejour de nos Ambassadeurs sera court à Hannover. Mylady Wortley Montagu ne s'y sera pas attendu. Elle aura composer le Carneval à Hannover. Je suis faché qu'elle a fait son si penible voyage pour un si court sejour. Vous devriés la ramener icy au lieu de la faire aller à Constantinople. Don Louis retournera sans doute à la Haye et en suite icy; je vous prie de luy faire ma recommendation et à Mr. et à Mylady Wortley Montagu aussi s'ils sont encor à Hannover' (BM Stowe MS 229, ff. 329–30).

I will make haste to change the disagreable Subject by telling you that I am now got into the Region of Beauty. All the Woman here have litterally rosy cheeks, snowy Foreheads and bosoms, jet Eyebrows, and scarlet lips, to which they generally add Coal black Hair. These perfections never leave them till the hour of their Death and have a very fine Effect by Candlelight, but I could wish they were handsome with a little more variety. They ressemble one another as much as Mrs. Salmon's court of Great Brittain,[1] and are in as much danger of melting away by too near approaching the Fire, which they for that reason carefully avoid, thô 'tis now such excessive cold weather, that I beleive they suffer extremely by that piece of selfe denial. The Snow is allready very deep and people begin to slide about in their Traineaus. This is a favourite diversion all over Germany. They are little machines fix'd upon a sledge that hold a Lady and a Gent-[leman] and drawn by one Horse. The Gentleman has the Honnour of driving and they move with a prodigious swiftness. The Lady, the Horse and the Traineau are all as fine as they can be made, and when there are many of 'em together, 'tis a very agreable shew. At Vienna, where all pieces of Magnificence are carry'd to Excesse, there are sometimes Traineaus that cost 5 or £600 English.[2]

The Duke of Wolfumbutel[3] is now at this Court. You know he is nearly related to our King, and Uncle to the reigning Empresse, who is (I beleive) the most Beautifull Queen upon Earth. She is now with child, which is all the consolation of the Imperial Court for the losse of the Arch Duke.[4] I took my leave of her the day before I left Vienna, and she begun to speak to me with so much greife and tenderness of the death of that young Prince, I had much ado to withhold my tears.[5] You know that I am not at all partial to people for their Titles, but I own that I love that charming

---

[1] Mrs. Salmon's waxwork exhibition, in Fleet Street, is mentioned in the *Spectator*, Nos. 28 and 31.

[2] 'The nobility ... endeavour to outvie one another in the splendor and magnificence of their equipage' (Nugent, ii. 207).

[3] August Wilhelm (1662–1731), Duke of Brunswick-Wolfenbüttel, succ.

1714 (Isenburg, i. 72).

[4] Archduke Leopold, born April 1716, had died on 4 Nov. Maria Theresa was born in May of the following year.

[5] The French Ambassador described the Empress as so overcome with sorrow that her health was endangered (7 Nov. 1716, Ministère des Affaires Étrangères, Autriche, vol. 117, f. 103).

Princesse (if I may use so familiar an Expression) and if I did not, I should have been very much mov'd at the Tragical end of an only Son born after being so long desir'd and at length kill'd by want of good managment, weaning him in the beginning of the Winter.

Adeiu, my dear Lady R[ich]. Continu to write to me, and beleive none of your Goodness is lost upon Your etc.

Text H MS 253, pp. 109–14

To Lady Mar *17 Dec.* [*1716*]

Blankenburg, Dec. 17. O.S.

I receiv'd yours (Dear Sister) the very day I left Hanover. You may easily imagine I was then in too great a Hurry to answer it, but you see I take the first opertunity of doing my selfe that pleasure. I came here the 15th very late at night, after a terrible journey in the worst roads and weather that ever poor Travellers suffer'd. I have taken this little fatigue meerly to oblige the reigning Empresse and carry a message from her Imperial Majesty to the Dutchesse of Blankenburg, her mother, who is a Princesse of great Addresse and good breeding, and may be still call'd a fine Woman.[1] It was so late when I came to this Town, I did not think it proper to disturb the Duke and D[uche]sse with the news of my arival and took up my quarters in a miserable inn;[2] but as soon as I had sent my Complement to their Highnesses, they immediately sent me their own Coach and 6 Horses, which had, however, enough to do to draw us up the very high Hill on which the Castle is situated. The Dutchesse is extreamly obliging to me and this little Court is not without its Diversions.[3] The Duke taillys at Basset every Night; and the Dutchesse tells me that she is so well

---

[1] Christine Luise (1671–1747), da. of Prince Albert von Oettingen, m. (1690) Ludwig Rudolph (1671–1735), Duke of Blankenburg (1707), brother to the Duke of Brunswick-Wolfenbüttel, whom he succeeded 1731 (Isenburg, i. 72).

[2] Pöllnitz thought the town small, and the houses ill built and inconvenient (i. 108).

[3] Pöllnitz has only pleasant things to say of Blankenburg's rulers and their delight in entertaining foreigners at their court (i. 104–5).

pleas'd with my Company, I should find it very difficult to steal time to write if she was not now at church, where I cannot wait on her, not understanding the Language enough to pay my Devotions in it.

You will not forgive me if I do not say something of Hannover. I cannot tell you that the Town is either large or magnificent. The Opera House, which was built by the late Elector,[1] is much finer than that of Vienna. I was very sorry the ill Weather did not permit me to see Hern-hausen in all its beauty, but in spite of the snow I thought the Gardens very fine. I was particularly surpriz'd at the vast Number of Orange Trees, much larger than any I have ever seen in England, thô this climate is certainly colder. But I had more reason to wonder that night at the King's Table. There was brought to him from a Gentleman of this Country 2 large Baskets full of ripe Oranges and Lemons of different sorts, many of which were quite new to me, and what I thought worth all the rest, 2 ripe Ananas's, which to my taste are a fruit perfectly delicious. You know they are naturally the Growth of Brasil, and I could not imagine how they could come there but by Enchantment. Upon Enquiry I learnt that they have brought their Stoves to such perfection, they lengthen the Summer as long as they please, giveing to every plant the degree of heat it would receive from the Sun in its native Soil. The Effect is very near the same. I am surpriz'd we do not practise in England so usefull an Invention. This refflection naturally leads me to consider our obstinancy in shakeing with cold 6 months in the year rather than make use of Stoves, which are certainly one of the greatest conveniencys of Life; and so far from spoiling the form of a Room, they add very much to the magnificence of it when they are painted and gilt as at Vienna, or at Dresden where they are often in the shapes of China Jars, Statues, or fine Cabinets, so naturally represented they are not to be distinguish'd. If ever I return, in defiance to the Fashion you shall certainly see one in the chamber of, Dear Sister, etc.

---

[1] Built inside the palace, 1688–9, by Ernst August I (1629–98), it was one of the largest and handsomest houses of the time (Georg Schnath, 'Die Ge- schichte des Leinesschlosses 1636–1943', *Hannoversche Geschichtblätter*, ix, 1956, pp. 54, 57).

I will write often, since you desire it, but I must beg you
to be a little more particular in yours. You fancy me at
40 miles distance and forget that after so long an Absence
I cant understand hints.[1]

Text H MS 253, pp. 115–20

To Lady ——— *1 Jan. 1717*[2]

Vienna, Jan. 1. 1717 O.S.

I have just receiv'd here at Vienna your Ladyship's complement on my return to England, sent me from Hanover.
You see, Madam, all things that are asserted with confidence
are not absolutely true and that you have no sort of reason
to complain of me for makeing my design'd return a mystery
to you when you say all the World are inform'd of it. You
may tell all the World in my Name that they are never so
well inform'd of my affairs as I am my selfe, and that I am
very positive I am at this time at Vienna, where the Carnival
is begun and all sort of diversions in perpetual practise
except that of masqueing, which is never permitted during
a War with the Turks. The Balls are in publick places, where
the Men pay a Gold Ducat at Entrance, but the Ladys
nothing. I am told that these houses get sometimes a 1,000
Ducats on a Night. They are very Magnificently furnish'd,
and the Music good if they had not that detestable Custom
of mixing hunting horns with it that allmost deafen the
company, but that noise is so agreable here they never make
a consort without 'em. The Ball allways concludes with
English country dances to the number of 30 or 40 couple,

[1] After leaving Blankenburg LM and W continued by way of Dresden, where they arrived 1 Jan. 1717/21 Dec. 1716 —when Sir Richard Vernon, British Envoy, reported: 'This morning between seven and eight a clock Mr. Wortley Mountague and Lady Mary arrivd here Post from Hanover, and were so presst to return soon to Vienna, that they continud their journey towards that place in less then two hours after' (to Townshend, 1 Jan. 1717, SP 88/24).

[2] W and LM reached Vienna on 7 Jan. 1717/27 Dec. 1716; the British Ambassador to Vienna also reported that W 'talks of setting out for Belgrade in a little time, but cannot yet fix a Day for his Departure' (Stanyan to Townshend, 9 Jan. 1717 N.S., SP 80/34).

and so ill danc'd that there is very little pleasure in 'em. They
know but halfe a dozen, and they have danc'd them over and
over this 50 year. I would fain have taught them some new
ones, but I found it would be some months labour to make
them comprehend 'em.

Last night there was an Italian Comedy acted at Court.
The Scenes were pritty, but the comedy it selfe such intolerable low farce without either wit or humour, that I was
surpriz'd how all the Court could sit there attentively for
4 hours together. No Women are suffer'd to act on the stage,
and the men dress'd like 'em were such aukard figures they
very much added to the ridicule of the Spectacle. What
compleated the Diversion was the Excessive cold, which was
so great I thought I should have dy'd there. It is now the
very Extremity of the Winter here. The Danube is entirely
frozen, and the Weather not to be supported without stoves
and furs, but, however, the air so clear allmost every body
is well, and colds not halfe so common as in England, and
I am perswaded there cannot be a purer air, nor more whole-
some than that of Vienna. The plenty and excellence of all
sort of provisions is greater here than in any place I was ever
in, and 'tis not very expensive to keep a splendid Table.[1]
Tis realy a pleasure to passe through the markets and see the
Abundance of what we should think raritys of Fowls and
Venisons that are daily brought in from Hungary and
Bohemia. They want nothing but shell fish, and are so fond
of Oysters they have 'em sent from Venice and eat 'em
very greedily, stink or not stink.[2]

Thus I obey your commands, Madam, in giving you an
account of Vienna, tho I know you will not be satisfy'd with
it. You chide me for my Lazynesse in not telling you a
thousand agreable and surprizing things that you say you
are sure I have seen and heard. Upon my word, Madam,
'tis my regard to Truth and not Lazynesse that I do not
entertain you with as many prodigys as other Travellers use
to divert their Readers with. I might easily pick up wonders

---

[1] 'There is no place in the world
where people live more luxuriously than
at *Vienna*. Their chief diversion is
feasting and carousing, on which occasions they are extreamly well served with
wine and eatables' (Nugent, ii. 208).

[2] Nugent also writes of oysters im-
ported from Venice but not of their
stink (ii. 210).

in every Town I pass through, or tell you a long series of Popish miracles, but I cannot fancy that there is any thing new in letting you know that preists can lye and the mob beleive all over the World. Then, as for news that you are so inquisitive about, how can it be entertaining to you that dont know the people, that the Prince of —— has forsaken the Countesse of ——? or that the Princesse such a one has an Intrigue with Count such a one? Would you have me write novelles like the Countesse of D'Aunois?[1] and is it not better to tell you a plain Truth, that I am etc.

Text H MS 253, pp. 121–7

To [Lady Bristol] *1 Jan. 1717*

[*A spurious letter, printed in* The London Museum of Politics, Miscellanies, and Literature, *1770, i. 245–6*]

To the Abbé Conti *2 Jan. 1717*

[*A spurious letter, printed 1767, pp. 14–23; 1861, i. 264–7*]

To Lady Mar *16 Jan. 1717*

Vienna, Jan. 16. 1717 O.S.

I am now, dear Sister, to take leave of you for a long time and of Vienna for ever, designing to morrow to begin my Journey[2] through Hungary in spite of the excessive Cold and deep snows which are enough to damp a greater Courage than I am mistriss of, but my principle of passive Obedience carrys me throû every thing. I have had my Audiences of leave of the Empresses. His imperial Majesty was pleas'd

---

1 Marie Catherine d'Aulnoy (*c.* 1650–1705), author of historical romances (e.g. *Mémoires de la cour d'Espagne*, 1692) as well as fairy tales.

2 On 16 Jan. O.S. W and his party left Vienna for Turkey, intending to reach Peterwardein in eight days (Stan-

yan to Methuen, 27 Jan. 1717 [N.S.], SP 80/34). The Emperor had given him the choice of going by land through Hungary or by sea from Leghorn (W's dispatch, 21 Oct. 1716, SP 97/23), and he chose the former, undoubtedly for its greater speed.

to be present when I waited on the Reigning Empress, and after a very obliging Conversation both their imperial Majestys invited me to take Vienna in my road back, but I have no thoughts of enduring over again so great a fatigue.

I deliver'd a Letter to the Empress from the D[uche]sse of Blankenburg. I staid but few days at that court, thô her Highnesse press'd me very much to stay, and when I left her engag'd me to write to her. I writ you a long letter from thence which I hope you have receiv'd,[1] thô you don't mention it, but I beleive I forgot to tell you one Curiosity in all the German Courts, which I cannot forbear takeing Notice of. All the Princes keep favourite Dwarfs.[2] The Emperour and Empresse have 2 of these little monsters as ugly as Devils, especially the Female, but all bedaw'd with Di'monds and stands at her majesty's Elbow in all public places. The Duke of Wolfumbutel has one and the D[uche]sse of Blankenburg is not without hers, but indeed the most proportionable I ever saw. I am told the King of Denmark[3] has so far improv'd upon this fashion that his Dwarf is his cheife Minister. I can assign no reason for their fondness for these pieces of deformity but the opinion that all Absolute Princes have that 'tis below them to converse with the rest of Mankind; and not to be quite alone they are forc'd to seek their companions amongst the refuse of Human Nature, these Creatures being the only part of their Court priveleg'd to talk freely to 'em.

I am at present confin'd to my chamber by a sore throat,[4] and am realy glad of the Excuse to avoid seeing people that I love well enough to be very much mortify'd when I think I am going to part with them for ever. 'Tis true the Austrians are not commonly the most polite people in the World or the most agreable, but Vienna is inhabited by all Nations, and I had form'd to my selfe a little Society of such as were perfectly to my own taste, and thô the Number was not very great, I could never pick up in any other place such a

---

[1] The Embassy letter of 17 Dec. [1716] from Blankenburg is addressed to Lady Mar.

[2] The Elector of Saxony maintained dwarfs from 1700 to 1733 (Enid Welsford, *The Fool*, 1935, p. 190).

[3] Frederick IV (1671–1730).

[4] In his letter of 3 Feb. 1717 O.S. Pope writes: 'What you say of your illness. . . .' (*Corr.* i. 389). LM must have mentioned it to him in an actual letter.

number of reasonable, agreable people. We were allmost allways together, and you know I have ever been of Opinion that a chosen conversation compos'd of a few that one esteems is the greatest happynesse of Life.¹ Here are some Spaniards of both Sexes that have all the Vivacity and Generosity of Sentiments anciently ascrib'd to their Nation, and could I beleive the whole Kingdom were like them, I should wish nothing more than to end my days there.

The Ladys of my acquaintance have so much goodness for me, they cry whenever they see me, since I am determin'd to undertake this Journey, and indeed I am not very easy when I reflect on what I am going to suffer. Allmost every body I see frights me with some new Difficulty. Prince Eugene² has been so good to say all things he could to perswade me to stay till the Danube is thaw'd that I may have the conveniency of going by Water, assuring me that the Houses in Hungary are such as are no defence against the Weather and that I shall be oblig'd to travel 3 or 4 days between Buda and Esseek without finding any house at all, through desart plains cover'd with Snow, where the cold is so violent many have been kill'd by it. I own these Terrors have made a very deep impression on my mind because I beleive he tells me things truly as they are, and no body can be better inform'd of them. Now I have nam'd that Great Man I am sure you expect I should say something particular of him, having the advantage of seeing him very often, but I am as unwilling to speak of him at Vienna as I should be to talk of Hercules in the Court of Omphale if I had seen him there.³ I don't know what comfort other people find in considering the

¹ 'Lady Mary is pretty much the subject of conversation here,' Stanyan wrote to Lord Stair, Ambassador at Paris. 'She sticks to her English modes and manners, which exposes her a little to the railleries of the Vienna ladies. She replies with a good deal of wit, and is engaged in a sort of petty war; but they all own she is a witty woman, if not a well-dressed one' (John Murray Graham, *Annals and Corr. of the Earls of Stair*, 1875, ii. 35–36).

² Prince Eugene of Savoy (1663–1736), famous Austrian general. In Jan.–March 1712, on a visit to England, he had been extravagantly entertained by the leading Whigs (*Wentworth Papers*, pp. 247, 258, 260), but LM had apparently not met him there.

³ In comparing Prince Eugene to Hercules, dressed as a woman and set to feminine tasks at the court of the Lydian Queen, LM probably refers to the Prince's reputation as a Mars without a Venus. The exact meaning of her innuendo is still a matter of historical doubt Nicholas Henderson, *Prince Eugene of Savoy*, 1964, pp. 238-9).

Weaknesses of Great men because it brings them nearer to their own Level,[1] but 'tis allways a mortification to me to observe that there is no perfection in Humanity. The young Prince of Portugal is the admiration of the whole Court. He is handsome and Polite with a great vivacity. All the officers tell wonders of his Galantry the last Campaign. He is lodg'd at Court with all the honnours due to his rank.[2]

Adeiu, Dear Sister. This is the last Account you will have from me of Vienna. If I survive my Journey you shall hear from me again. I can say with great truth in the words of Moneses, I have long learnt to hold my selfe at nothing,[3] but when I think of the fatigue my poor infant must suffer, I have all a mother's fondness in my Eyes and all her tender passions in my Heart.

P.S. I have writ a letter[4] to my Lady —— that I beleive she won't like, and upon cooler refflexion, I think I had done better to have let it alone, but I was downright peevish at all her Questions and her ridiculous imagination that I have certainly seen abundance of wonders that I keep to my selfe out of meer malice. She is angry that I won't lie like other travellers. I verily beleive she expects I should tell her of the Anthropophagi [and] men whose heads grow below their shoulders. However, pray say something to pacify her.

Text H MS 253, pp. 128–37

To Alexander Pope *16 Jan.* [*1717*]

Vienna, Jan. 16. O.S.

I have not time to answer your Letter, being in all the hurry of preparing for my Journey, but I think I ought to

    1 LM here agrees with the opinion in the *Tatler* No. 92 (see above, p. 19, n. 1).

    2 Dom Manuel of Braganza (1697–1766), son of Pedro II and brother of the reigning João V, had joined the Austrian army against his brother's

orders in the spring of 1716, and fought with conspicuous bravery at the Battle of Peterwardein (Isenburg, ii. 55; *Encicl. Portugesa*, xiv. 169–70).

    3 Prince Moneses says this in Nicholas Rowe's *Tamerlane* (1702), Act I, Scene i.

    4 The preceding Embassy letter.

bid Adeiu to my freinds with the same Solemnity as if I was
going to mount a breach, at least if I am to beleive the
Information of the people here, who denounce all sort of
Terrors to me; and indeed the Weather is at present such as
very few ever set out in. I am threaten'd at the same time
with being froze to death, bury'd in the Snow, and taken by
the Tartars who ravage that part of Hungary I am to passe.[1]
'Tis true we shall have a considerable Escorte, so that possibly
I may be diverted with a new Scene by finding my selfe in the
midst of a Battle. How my Adventures will conclude I leave
entirely to Providence; if comically, you shall hear of 'em.

Pray be so good to tell Mr. ——[2] I have receiv'd his
Letter. Make him my Adeius. If I live I will answer it.
The same complement to my Lady R[ich].

Text H MS 253, pp. 137–8

To Lady Mar *30 Jan.* [*1717*]

Peterwaradin,[3] Jan. 30. O.S.

At length (dear Sister) I am safely arriv'd with all my
family in good health at Peterwaradin, having suffer'd little
from the rigour of the Season (against which we were well
provided by Furs) and found every where (by the care of
sending before) such tolerable Accomodation, I can hardly
forbear laughing when I recollect all the frightfull ideas that
were given me of this Journey, which were wholly owing
to the tenderness of my Vienna Freinds and their desire of
keeping me with 'em for this Winter. Perhaps it will not
be disagreable to give you a short Journal of my Journey,[4]

[1] On 3 Feb. 1717 O.S. Pope replied
to a letter from LM related to this
Embassy one: he was 'grievously
afflicted' by the news of her dangerous
journey; 'It is no figure of speech when
I tell you, that those Mountains of
Snow, and Woods layd in ashes you
describe, are what I could wish to
traverse with you' (*Corr.* i. 389).

[2] Probably William Congreve, an
intimate friend of Pope's, and one of
LM's correspondents while she was on
the Embassy (Pope, *Corr.* i. 357, 370,
385, 405). She sent her promised answer
to him on 1 April 1717 (p. 346 below).

[3] Peterwardein (now Petrovaradin,
Yugoslavia) was a famous fortress-town
ceded by the Turks to the Austrians in
the Peace of Carlowitz (1699). In the
current war Prince Eugene had defended
it successfully in Aug. 1716.

[4] Unlike any other Embassy letter
this one seems to be almost wholly
copied from a day-by-day journal.

being through a Country entirely unknown to you, and very little pass'd even by the Hungarians themselves who generally chuse to take the conveniency of going down the Danube. We have had the blessing of being favour'd by finer weather than is common at this time of the year, thô the Snow was so deep we were oblig'd to have our Coaches fix'd upon Traineaus, which move so swift and so easily 'tis by far the most agreable manner of travelling post.

We came to Raab[1] the 2nd day from Vienna on the 17 instant[2] where Mr. [Wortley], sending word of our Arival to the Governour, we had the best house in the Town provided for us, the Garison put under Arms, a Guard order'd at our door, and all other Honnours paid to us, the Governour and officers immediately waiting on Mr. [Wortley] to know if there was any thing to be done for his service. The Bishop of Temeswar[3] came to visit us with great civillity, earnestly pressing us to dine with him the next day, which we refusing, as being resolv'd to persue our Journey, he sent us several Baskets of Winter fruit and a great variety of fine Hungarian Wines with a young Hind just kill'd. This is a Prelate of great Power in this Country, of the Ancient family of Nadasti, so considerable for many ages in this Kingdom. He is a very polite, agreable, cheerfull Old Man, wearing the Hungarian habit, with a Venerable white Beard down to his Girdle.

Raab is a strong Town, well garrison'd and fortify'd, and was a long time the frontier Town between the Turkish and German Empires. It has its name from the river Rab, on which it is scituated just on its meeting with the Danube in an open champian Country. It was first taken by the Turks under the command of Bassa Sinan[4] in the reign of Sultan Amurath the 3rd, 1594. The Governour, being suppos'd to have betraid it, was afterwards beheaded by the Emperor's command. The Counts of Swartzenburg and Palfi retook it by surprize 1598,[5] since which time it has remain'd

[1] Now Győr, Hungary.

[2] In her letter of 16 Jan. she stated that she was leaving Vienna on the 17th (see above, p. 293 and n. 2).

[3] Ladislaus, Count Nádasdy (d. 1730), since 1710 Bishop of Csanád

(Conrad Eubel, *Hierarchia Catholica*, 1901–58, v. 177).

[4] Kodja Sinan Pasha (d. 1596) (*Encycl. of Islam*, iv. 432–3).

[5] These facts are related in Edward Brown's *Brief Account of some Travels*

in the hands of the Germans, thô the Turks once more attempted to gain it by stratagem, 1642.[1] The Cathedral is large and well built, which is all that I saw remarkable in the Town.

Leaving Comora on the other side the river, we went the 18th to Nosmuhl, a small village where, however, we made shift to find tolerable accomodation. We continu'd 2 days travelling between this place and Buda, through the finest plains in the world, as even as if they were pav'd, and extreme fruitfull, but for the most part desert and uncultivated, laid waste by the long war between the Turk and Emperour, and the more cruel civil War occassion'd by the barbarous persecution of the protestant Religion by the Emperour Leopold. That Prince has left behind him the character of an extrodinary Piety and was naturally of a mild mercifull temper, but putting his conscience into the hands of a Jesuit, he was more cruel and treacherous to his poor Hungarian Subjects than ever the Turk has been to the Christians, breaking without scrupule his Coronation oath and his faith solemnly given in many public Treatys.[2] Indeed, nothing can be more melancholy than travelling through Hungary, refflecting on the former flourishing state of that Kingdom and seeing such a noble spot of Earth allmost uninhabited.[3]

This is also the present circumstances of Buda (where we arriv'd very early the 22nd),[4] once the royal seat of the Hungarian Kings, where their Palace was reckon'd one of the most beautifull Buildings of the Age, now wholly destroy'd,[5] no part of the Town having been repair'd since

in Hungaria . . ., 1673, p. 26. The Austrian governor, Ferdinand, Count zu Hardegg (1549–95), was executed in Vienna for his treachery; the Imperial generals who recaptured the town were Adolf, Count von Schwarzenberg (1547–1600), and Nikolaus II, Count Palffy (1552–1600).

[1] The (unsuccessful) stratagem is related in Richard Knolles (*Turkish History*, cont. by Paul Rycaut, 6th ed. 1687, ii. 53): Turkish soldiers, disguised as peasants, brought into the town carts of hay in which other soldiers

were hidden.

[2] LM's account is from Rycaut (*History of the Turks*, 1700, pp. 18–21). The religious impartiality of Leopold I is defended by Albert Lefaivre (*Les Magyars*, 1902, ii. 2–3, 92–94).

[3] This description is confirmed by H. Marczali, who cites LM (*Hungary in the Eighteenth Century*, 1910, p. 199).

[4] W arrived at Buda on 21 Jan. O.S., and the same day continued his journey toward Belgrade (*London Gazette*, 12–16 Feb. 1717).

[5] Immediately after describing Buda,

the last seige but the fortifications and the Castle, which is
the present residence of the Governour, General Ragule, an
Officer of great Merit. He came immediately to see us and
carry'd us in his Coach to his House, where I was receiv'd
by his Lady with all possible Civillity and magnificently
entertain'd.[1] This City is situate upon a little Hill on the
South side of the Danube,[2] the Castle being much Higher
than the Town, from whence the Prospect is very noble.
Without the walls lye a vast number of little Houses, or
rather huts, that they call the Rascian [Serbian] Town, being
alltogether inhabited by that people. The Governour assur'd
me it would furnish 12,000 fighting men. These Towns
look very odd; their Houses stand in rows, many 1,000s of
them so close together they appear at a little distance like
odd fashion'd thatch'd Tents. They consist, every one of
them, of one hovel above and another under ground; these
are their Summer and Winter apartments.

Buda was first taken by Solyman the Magnificent, 1526,
and lost the following year to Ferdinand I, King of Bohemia.
Solyman regain'd it, 1529, by the Treachery of the Garrison, and voluntarily gave it into the hand of King John of
Hungary, after whose death, his son being an Infant,[3] Ferdinand laid seige to it, and the Queen Mother was forc'd to
call Solyman to her aid, who rais'd the Seige but left a
Turkish Garrison in the Town and commanded her to
remove her court from thence, which she was forc'd to
submit to, 1541. It resisted afterwards the Seiges laid to it
by the Marquis of Brandenbourg, 1542; the Count of
Swartzenburg, 1598; General Rosworm, 1602; and of the
Duke of Lorrain,[4] commander of the Emperour's forces,

Rycaut writes of nearby Vicegrade:
'This place hath been so considerable in
former times, that it was the Residence
of the Hungarian Kings, of which there
remain great Ruins to this day of
sumptuous and magnificent Palaces'
(*History*, 1700, p. 140).

[1] Maximilian Ludwig Regal (d.
1717), Count von Kranichsfeld, m.
(1709) Eleanore Christiana, Countess
von Metternich. He was killed six
months later in the Siege of Belgrade
(LM, *Reisebriefe*, transl. and ed. H. H.

Blumenthal, 1931).

[2] West side.

[3] John I Zapolya (1487–1540), King
of Hungary, m. (1539) Isabella (1519–
59), da. of Sigismund I, King of Poland;
their son was John Sigismund Zapolya
(1540–71).

[4] Joachim II, Elector of Brandenburg (1505–71) (Isenburg, i. 62); Her-
mann Christof, Count von Russworm
(1565–1605) (*ADB*); Charles IV, Duke
of Lorraine (1643–90) (Isenburg, i. 14).

1684, to whom it yeilded, 1686, after an obstinate defence, Apti Bassa, the Governour,[1] being kill'd fighting in the breach with a Roman Bravery. The loss of this Town was so important and so much resented by the Turks, it occasion'd the deposing of their Emperour Mahomet the 4th the year following.[2]

We did not proceed on our Journey till the 23rd, passing through Adam and Fodowar,[3] both considerable Towns when in the hands of the Turks. They are now quite ruin'd; only the remains of some Turkish Towers shew something of what they have been. This part of the Country is very much overgrown with wood, and so little frequented tis incredible what vast numbers of wild Fowl we saw, who often live here to a good old age

And, undisturb'd by Guns, in quiet Sleep.

We came the 25th to Mohatch and were shew'd the field near it where Lewis, the young King of Hungary, lost his Army and his Life, being drown'd in a ditch, trying to fly from Balybeus, the General of Solyman the Magnificent.[4] This Battle open'd the first passage for the Turks into the heart of Hungary. I don't name to you the little villages of which I can say nothing remarkable, but I'll assure you I have allways found a warm stove and great plenty, particularly of Wild Boar, Ven'son, and all kind of Gibier.[5] The few people that inhabit Hungary live easily enough. They have no money, but the woods and plains afford them provision in great Abundance. They were order'd to give us all things necessary, even what horses we pleas'd to demand, Gratis, but Mr. W[ortley] would not oppress the poor country people by makeing use of this order, and allways paid them the full worth of what we had from 'em. They were so surpriz'd at this unexpected Generosity, which they are very little us'd to, they allways press'd upon us at parting a dozen of fat Pheasants or something of that sort, for a present. Their dress is very primitive, being only a

[1] Abd al-Rahman Pasha (*Encycl. of Islam*, i. 1284).

[2] Many of these facts, including dates, are given in Rycaut, *History*, 1700, pp. 218–19; LM copied them—as she admits at the end of her letter (p. 303).

[3] Mentioned by Brown as Adom and Fodwar (p. 35).

[4] This episode in 1526 is related in Knolles, i. 405–6.

[5] Brown also remarks on the abundance of wild fowl near 'Mohatz' (p. 12).

plain sheep's skin without other dressing than being dry'd in the Sun, and a cap and boots of the same Stuff. You may imagine this lasts them for many Winters, and thus they have very little Occasion for money.

The 26th we pass'd over the frozen Danube with all our Equipage and Carriages. We met on the other side General Veterani,[1] who invited us with great civility to pass the night at a little castle of his a few miles off, assuring us we should have a very hard day's Journey to reach Esseek, which we found but too true, the Woods being scarce passable, and very dangerous from the vast quantity of wolves that herd in them. We came, however, safe thô late to Esseck, where we staid a day to dispatch a Courier with Letters to the Bassa of Belgrade,[2] and I took the oppertunity of seeing the Town, which is not very large but fair built and well fortify'd. This was a Town of great Trade, very rich and populous when in the hands of the Turks. It is scituated on the Drave, which runs into the Danube. The Bridge was esteem'd one of the most extrodinary in the World, being 8,000 paces long and all built of Oak, which was burn't and the City laid in ashes by Count Lesley, 1685,[3] but again repair'd and fortify'd by the Turks, who however abandonn'd it, 1687, and General Dunnewalt[4] took possession of it for the Emperor, in whose hands it has remaind ever since, and is esteem'd one of the Bulwarks of Hungary.

The 28th we went to Bocowar, a very large Rascian Town, all built after the manner I have describ'd to you. We were met there by Collonel ———, who would not suffer us to go any where but to his Quarters, where I found his Wife, a very agreable Hungarian Lady, and his Neice and Daughter, 2 pritty young Women, crouded in 3 or 4 Rascian Houses cast into one and made as neat and convenient as those places

---

[1] Julius Franz, Count Veterani (1666–1736) (Blumenthal).

[2] W informed Stanyan that they had arrived at Esseg—now Osijek, Yugoslavia—on 4 Feb./24 Jan. 'after having been seaven hours on the road in going the last post, which is a double one. The snow was very deep between Buda and this place . . . least an extraordinary accident shoud happen I am advised to pass over the Ice two posts from hence and again at Peterwaradin' (SP 80/34).

[3] Jacob, Count von Leslie (d. 1685). LM's account of Esseg and its bridge is almost verbatim from Rycaut (*History*, 1700, pp. 171–2).

[4] Johann Heinrich, Count von Dünewalt (1620–91), Austrian Cavalry General.

were capable of being made. The Hungarian Ladys are much handsomer than those of Austria. All the Vienna Beautys are of that Country; they are gennerally very fair and well shap'd. Their dress I think extreme becoming. This Lady was in a Gown of Scarlet velvet, lin'd and fac'd with Sables, made exact to her shape and the skirt falling to her feet. The sleeves are strait to their arms and the stays button'd before with 2 rows of little Buttons of gold, pearl or di'monds. On their heads they wear a cap embrodier'd with a Tassel of Gold that hangs low on one side, lin'd with sable or some other fine fur. They gave us a handsome Dinner, and I thought their conversation very polite and agreable. They would accompany us part of our way.

The 29th we arriv'd here, where we were met by the Commandant at the head of all the officers of the Garrison. We are lodg'd in the best Apartment of the Governour's house and entertain'd in a very splendid manner by the Emperor's order. We wait here till all points are adjusted concerning our reception on the Turkish frontiers. Mr. [Wortley]'s Coureir, which he sent from Esseck, return'd this morning with the Bassa's answer in a purse of scarlet Satin, which the Interpreter here has translated. 'Tis to promise him to be honnourably receiv'd, and desires him to appoint where he would be met by the Turkish convoy. He has dispatch'd the Coureir back naming Betsko, a village in the midway between Peterwaradin and Belgrade. We shall stay here till we receive the answer.[1] Thus, dear Sister, I have given you a very particular and, I'm afraid you'l think, a tedious account of this part of my travels. It was not an affectation of shewing my reading that has made me tell you some little scraps of the history of the Towns I have pass'd through. I have allways avoided any thing of that kind when I spoke of places which I beleiv'd you knew the story of as well as my selfe, but Hungary being a part of the World that I beleive quite new to you, I thought you might read with some pleasure an Account of it which I have been very solicitous to get from the best hands.[2] However, if you

---

[1] Also in W's dispatch of 9 Feb. 1717 (SP 97/24; printed in 1861, i. 276, n. 1).
[2] LM's library in 1739 contained a copy of Rycaut's *History of the Turks* (Wh MS 135)—the book from which she quotes so extensively in this letter.

don't like it, tis in your power to forbear reading it. I am,
Dear Sister, etc.

I am promis'd to have this letter carefully sent to Vienna.

Text H MS 253, pp. 139–58

To Alexander Pope *12 Feb.* [*1717*]

Belgrade, Feb. 12 O.S.

I did verily intend to write you a long letter from Peterwaradin,[1] where I expected to stay 3 or 4 days, but the
Bassa here was in such haste to see us, he dispatch'd our
Coureir back (which Mr. [Wortley] had sent to know the
time he would send the convoy to meet us) without suffering
him to pull off his boots. My Letters were not thought
important enough to stop our Journey, and we left Peterwaradin the next day, being waited on by the cheife officers
of the Garison and a considerable convoy of Germans and
Rascians.[2] The Emperor has several regiments of these
people, but to say truth, they are rather plunderers than
soldeirs, having no pay and being oblig'd to furnish their
own Arms and horses. They rather look like Vagabond
Gypsies or stout beggars than regular Troops. I can't forbear speaking a word of this race of Creatures, who are very
numerous all over Hungary. They have a Patriarch of their
own at Grand Cairo and are realy of the Greek Church,[3]
but their extreme Ignorance gives their Preists occasion to
impose several new notions upon 'em. These fellows, leting
their Hair and beards grow inviolate, make exactly the
figure of the Indian Bramins. They are Heirs General to all
the money of the Laity, for which in return they give 'em

1 LM did in fact write to Pope from
here, as he acknowledged in June (*Corr.*
i. 407).

2 LM and W had left on 31 Jan. O.S.
(*London Gazette*, 5–9 March 1717).
Their escort consisted of 100 foot
soldiers, 50 grenadiers, and 50 hussars
(*Wienerisches Diarium*, 27 Feb.–2 March)

—but the *Gazette* reports 300 men.

3 The independent Patriarchate of
the Serbian church was re-established
at Peć (Yugoslavia) in 1557. Its
Patriarch at this time was Moisije
Rajović (d. 1730) (Ladislas Hadrovics,
*Le Peuple serbe et son église sous la
domination turque*, 1947, pp. 49, 149).

PLATE 5

Lady Mary Wortley Montagu in Turkish Dress
From a painting attributed to Charles Philips

formal passports sign'd and seal'd for Heaven, and the Wives and Children only inherit the houses and cattle. In most other points they follow the Greek Rites.

This little digression has intterupted my telling you we pass'd over the feilds of Carlowitz, where the last great Victory was obtaind by Prince Eugene over the Turks.[1] The marks of that Glorious bloody day are yet recent, the feild being strew'd with the Skulls and Carcases of unbury'd Men, Horses and Camels. I could not look without horror on such numbers of mangled humane bodys, and refflect on the Injustice of War, that makes murther not only necessary but meritorious. Nothing seems to me a plainer proofe of the irrationality of Mankind (whatever fine claims we pretend to Reason) than the rage with which they contest for a small spot of Ground, when such vast parts of fruitfull Earth lye quite uninhabited. 'Tis true, Custom has now made it unavoidable, but can there be a greater demonstration of want of reason than a Custom being firmly establish'd so plainly contrary to the Interest of Man in General? I am a good deal inclin'd to beleive Mr. Hobbs that the State of Nature is a State of War,[2] but thence I conclude Humane Nature not rational, if the word reason means common sense, as I suppose it does. I have a great many admirable arguments to support this refflexion, but I won't trouble you with 'em but return in a plain stile to the History of my travels.

We were met at Betsko (a village in the midway between Belgrade and Peterwaradin) by an Aga of the Janizarys with a body of Turks exceeding the Germans by 100 men, thô the Bassa had engag'd to send exactly the same Number.[3] You may judge by this of their fears. I am realy perswaded that they hardly thought the odds of one 100 men set them even with the Germans. However, I was very uneasy till they were parted, fearing some quarrel might arise notwithstanding the parole given.

[1] At the Battle of Zenta (1697), where the Grand Vizier, four viziers, and 30,000 Turks fell (*Encycl. of Islam*, iv. 1226). The Peace of Carlowitz (1699) followed.

[2] A paraphrase from the *Leviathan* by Thomas Hobbes, 1651, pp. 62, 64.

[3] The *London Gazette* (5–9 March 1717) states that the governor of Belgrade sent a guard of 300; and this is confirmed in a dispatch from the Venetian Ambassador in Vienna (27 Feb. 1717, Archivio di Stato, Venice).

We came late to Belgrade,[1] the deep snows makeing the ascent to it very difficult. It seems a strong City, fortify'd on the east side by the Danube and on the south by the River Save, and was formerly the Barrier of Hungary. It was first taken by Solyman [the] Magnificent and since by the Emperour's forces led by the Elector of Bavaria,[2] who held it only 2 year, it being retaken by the Grand Vizier,[3] and is now fortify'd with the utmost care and skill the Turks are capable of, and strengthen'd by a very numerous Garison of their bravest Janizarys commanded by a Bassa Seraskier (i.e. General). This last expression is not very just, for to say truth the Seraskier is commanded by the Janizarys, who have an absolute Authority here, not much unlike a Rebellion, which you may judge of by the following story, which at the same time will give you an Idea of the admirable Intteligence of the Governour of Peterwaradin, thô so few hours distant.

We were told by him at Peterwaradin that the Garison and Inhabitants of Belgrade were so weary of the war, they had kill'd their Bassa about 2 months ago in a Mutiny because he had suffer'd him selfe to be prevaild upon by a bribe of 5 purses (£500 sterling) to give permission to the Tartars to ravage the German Frontiers. We were very well pleas'd to hear of such favourable dispositions in the people, but when we came hither we found the Governour had been ill inform'd, and this the real truth of the story. The late Bassa fell under the displeasure of his soldeirs for no other reason but restraining their Incursions on the Germans. They took it into their heads from that mildnesse, he was of intteligence with the Enemy, and sent such information to the Grand Signor[4] at Adrianople, but redress not coming quick from thence, they assembled them selves in a tumultuous manner and by force dragg'd their Bassa before the Cady and Mufti, and there demanded Justice in a mutinous way; one crying out, why he protected the infidels? another, why he squeez'd them of their Money? that easily guessing their purpose, he

---

[1] On 16/5 Feb. (*Daily Courant*, 7 March 1717).
[2] Solyman captured Belgrade in 1521, and the Elector of Bavaria (Maximilian II, 1662–1726) in 1688.
[3] Köprülüzade Mustafa Pasha (1637–

91), Grand Vizier 1689–91, captured Belgrade in 1690 (*Encycl. of Islam*, ii. 1061).
[4] The Sultan, Ahmed III (1673–1736).

calmly reply'd to them that they ask'd him too many questions; he had but one Life, which must answer for all. They immediately fell upon him with their Scimitars (without waiting the sentence of their Heads of the Law) and in a few moments cut him in peices. The present Bassa has not dar'd to punish the murder. On the Contrary, he affected to applaud the Actors of it as brave fellows that knew how to do them selves Justice.[1] He takes all pretences of throwing money amongst the Garison and suffers them to make little Excursions into Hungary, where they Burn some poor Rascian Houses. You may imagine I cannot be very easy in a Town which is realy under the Government of an insolent Soldiery. We expected to be immediately dismiss'd after a night's lodging here, but the Bassa detains us till he receives orders from Adrianople, which may possibly be a month a coming.

In the mean time we are lodg'd in one of the best Houses, belonging to a very considerable Man amongst 'em, and have a whole Chamber of Janizarys to guard us. My only diversion is the Conversation of our Host, Achmet-Beg, a title something like that of Count in Germany. His father was a great Bassa and he has been educated in the most polite Eastern Learning, being perfectly skill'd in the Arabic and Persian Languages, and is an extrodinary Scribe, which they call Effendi. This accomplishment makes way to the greatest preferments, but he has had the good sense to prefer an easy, quiet, secure life to all the dangerous Honnours of the Port. He sups with us every night and drinks wine very freely. You cannot imagine how much he is delighted with the Liberty of converseing with me. He has explain'd to me many peices of Arabian Poetry, which I observ'd are in numbers not unlike ours, gennerally alternate verse, and of a very musical sound. Their expressions of Love are very passionate and lively. I am so much pleas'd with them, I realy beleive I should learn to read Arabic if I was to stay here a few months. He has a very good Library of their Books of all kinds and, as he tells me, spends the greatest part of his Life there. I pass for a great Scholar with him by relateing to him some of the Persian Tales, which I find are

[1] W's explanation, sent to London on 10 April 1717, is similar (SP 97/24).

Genuine.[1] At first he beleiv'd I understood Persian. I have
frequent disputes with him concerning the difference of our
Customs, particularly the confinements of Women. He
assures me there is nothing at all in it; only, says he, we have
the advantage that when our Wives cheat us, no body knows
it.[2] He has wit and is more polite than many Christian men
of Quality. I am very much entertain'd with him. He has
had the Curiosity to make one of our servants set him an
Alphabet of our Letters and can allready write a good Roman
hand; but these amusements do not hinder my wishing
heartily to be out of this place, thô the Weather is colder
than I beleiv'd it ever was any where but in Greenland. We
have a very large stove constantly kept hot and yet the Windows of the room are frozen on the inside. God knows when
I may have an opertunity of sending this Letter, but I have
writ it in the discharge of my own Conscience,[3] and you
cannot now reproach me that one of yours can make ten
of mine.

Text H MS 253, pp. 158–72

To Mrs. Frances Hewet[4] *1 April 1717*

Adrianople,[5] April 1, 1717.[6]
I dare say my dear Mrs. Hewet thinks me the most stupid
thing alive, to neglect so agreeable a correspondence; but it

[1] François Pétis de la Croix, who
published *Les Milles et un jours, contes
persanes* (1710–12), wrote in his preface
that he had heard them from a dervish;
but according to scholarly opinion the
tales existed in Persian and Turkish
writing, though no specific manuscript
source is known (ed. A. Loiseleur-
Deslongchamps, 1843, p. 2). LM's
library in 1739 contained a copy of
'Mille et un Jour [*sic*]' in 2 volumes
(Wh MS 135).

[2] Here LM introduces her favourite
paradox of Islam: that the subjection
of women has given them greater freedom than those in the West. She develops
the idea more fully in later letters.

[3] LM made this promise in an actual
letter sent to Pope, for he later repeated
her phrase (*Corr.* i. 383).

[4] This is an actual letter sent by LM
during the Embassy; it does not have
any counterpart in her compilation of
Embassy Letters. The MS letter was
sold at Sotheby's on 4 Nov. 1898, lot
181. Several sentences quoted there differ
significantly from the printed text only
as noted below.

[5] A dispatch from W states that his
party arrived in Adrianople on 24/13
March (10 April 1717, SP 97/24).

[6] Among LM's MS is a document
endorsed by W: 'Heads of LM's Letters
From Turky' (W MS vii. 124–5; see

has hitherto been utterly out of my power to continue it. I have been hurried up and down, without intermission, these last eight months, wholly[1] taken up either in going post, or unavoidable court attendance. You know very well how little leisure it is possible to find on either of those employments. I like travelling extremely, and have had no reason to complain of having had too little of it, having now gone through all the Turkish dominions in Europe, not to reckon my journeys through Hungary, Bohemia, and the whole tour of Germany; but those are trifles to this last. I cannot, however, (thank God,) complain of having suffered by fatigue, either in my own health or that of my family. My son never was better in his life. This country is certainly one of the finest in the world; hitherto all I see is so new to me, it is like a fresh[2] scene of an opera every day. I will not tire you with descriptions of places or manners, which perhaps you have no curiosity for; but only desire you would be so good as to let me hear as oft as you can, (which can be no other than very seldom,) what passes on your side of the globe. Before you can receive this, you must consider all things as six months old, which now appear new to me. There will be a great field for you to write, if your charity extends so far, as it will be entirely disinterested and free from ostentation, (it not being possible for me here to boast of your letters,) and it will be very beneficial to your precious soul, which I pray Heaven to put into your head to consider and practise accordingly.

M. W. M.

Text 1805, v. 256–7

above, p. xv). On it she had listed various of her correspondents, with summaries of the letters she sent them. That to 'M. H[t]' dated 18 April matches this letter: 'I like travelling. Hurryd up and down. Long Journeys, new scenes every day. Desire her to write, a charity beneficial to her own soul.'

1 'My time has been wholly . . . (Sotheby Catalogue).

2 'first' instead of 'fresh' (Sotheby Catalogue).

To the Princess of Wales[1] *1 April* [*1717*]

Adrianople, Ap. 1. O.S.[2]

I have now, Madame, past a Journey that has not been undertaken by any Christian since the Time of the Greek Emperours, and I shall not regret all the fatigues I have suffer'd in it if it gives me an opertunity of Amuseing your Royal Highness by an Account of places utterly unknown amongst us, the Emperor's Ambassadors and those few English that have come hither, allways going on the Danube to Nicopolis;[3] but that River was now frozen, and Mr. [Wortley] so zealous for the service of his Majesty he would not defer his Journey to wait for the Conveniency of that passage.[4] We cross'd the Desarts of Servia allmost quite overgrown with Wood, thô a Country naturally fertile and the Inhabitants industrious, but the Oppression of the peasants is so great they are forc'd to abandonn their Houses and neglect their Tillage, all they have being a prey to the Janizarys whenever they please to seize upon it. We had a guard of 500 of 'em, and I was allmost in tears every day to see their insolencies in the poor villages through which we pass'd.

After 7 days travelling through thick Woods we came to Nissa, once the Capital of Servia, situate in a fine Plain on the river Nissava, in a very good Air, and so fruitfull a Soil that the great plenty is hardly credible. I was certainly assur'd that the Quantity of Wine last vintage was so

---

[1] In MS: 'To Her R. H. the P'. For LM's earlier relations with Princess Caroline, see Halsband, *LM*, pp. 50, 52–53.

[2] Under this date the 'Heads of LM's Letters From Turky' lists one to the 'P. of W.': 'Description Sophia. Phill[ippopolis]. Country fine. Oppression. Liberty. In her hand to read or throw away.' The topics, though rearranged, match this Embassy letter.

[3] LM exaggerates; Christians had made the journey by land—as early as the 16th century, when the Imperial

Ambassador, Ogier de Busbecq, had travelled by land from Belgrade to Adrianople (*Turkish Letters*, transl. E. S. Forster, 1927, pp. 12–13, 15–24).

[4] W gave a different account: that by the time he could depart from Belgrade the Danube was unfrozen and he 'might have gone in a great deal lesse time and very conveniently by the river without lying in those miserable Houses upon the Confines,' but the Pasha refused him an escort without express orders; and rather than stay there any longer he set out by land (10 April 1717, SP 97/24).

prodigious they were forc'd to dig holes in the Earth to put it in, not having Vessells enough in the Town to hold it. The happyness of this Plenty is Scarse perceiv'd by the oppress'd people. I saw here a new Occasion for my compassion, the wretches that had provided 20 Waggons for our Baggage from Belgrade hither for a certain hire, being all sent back without payment, some of their Horses lam'd and others kill'd without any satisfaction made for 'em. The poor fellows came round the House weeping and tearing their Hair and beards in the most pitifull manner without geting any thing but drubs from the insolent Soldeirs. I cannot express to your Royal Highness how much I was mov'd at this Scene. I would have paid them the money out of my own pocket with all my Heart, but it had been only giving so much to the Aga, who would have taken it from them without any remorse.

After 4 days journey from this place over the Mountains we came to Sophia, scituate in a large beautifull Plain on the river Isca, surrounded with distant mountains. 'Tis hardly possible to see a more agreable Landschape. The City it selfe is very large and extremely populous. Here are Hot baths, very famous for their Medicinal Virtues. 4 days Journey from hence we arriv'd at Philipopoli, after having pass'd the ridges between the Mountains of Hæmus and Rhodophe, which are allways cover'd with Snow. This Town is scituate on a riseing Ground near the River Hebrus[1] and is allmost wholly inhabited by Greeks. Here are still some ancient Christian churches. They have a Bishop, and several of the richest Greeks live here, but they are forc'd to conceal their Wealth with great care, the appearance of Poverty (which includes part of its inconveniencys) being all their Security against feeling it in Earnest. The Country from hence to Adrianople is the finest in the World. Vines grow wild on all the Hills, and the perpetual Spring they enjoy makes every thing look gay and flourishing, but this Climate, as happy as it seems, can never be prefer'd to England with all its Snows and frosts, while we are bless'd with an easy Government under a King who makes his own Happyness consist in the Liberty of his people, and chooses rather to be

[1] LM wrote of these places in an actual letter to Conti (see above, p. xvi).

look'd upon as their Father than their Master.—This Theme would carry me very far, and I am sensible that I have allready tir'd out your Royal Highness's patience, but my Letter is in your Hands, and you may make it as short as you please by throwing it into the fire when you are weary of reading it.

I am, Madam, with the greatest respect etc.

Text H MS 253, pp. 172–8

To Lady —— 1 *April* [1717]

Adrianople, Ap. 1. O.S.

I am now got into a new World where every thing I see appears to me a change of Scene, and I write to your Lady-ship with some content of mind, hoping at least that you will find the charm of Novelty in my Letters and no longer reproach me that I tell you nothing extrodinary. I won't trouble you with a Relation of our tedious Journey, but I must not omit what I saw remarkable at Sophia, one of the most beautifull Towns in the Turkish Empire and famous for its Hot Baths that are resorted to both for diversion and health. I stop'd here one day on purpose to see them. Designing to go incognito, I hir'd a Turkish Coach. These Voitures are not at all like ours, but much more convenient for the Country, the heat being so great that Glasses would be very troublesome. They are made a good deal in the manner of the Dutch Coaches, haveing wooden Lattices painted and gilded, the inside being painted with baskets and nosegays of Flowers, entermix'd commonly with little poetical mottos. They are cover'd all over with scarlet cloth, lin'd with silk and very often richly embrodier'd and fring'd. This covering entirely hides the persons in them, but may be thrown back at pleasure and the Ladys peep through the Lattices. They hold 4 people very conveniently, seated on cushions, but not rais'd.

In one of these cover'd Waggons I went to the Bagnio about 10 a clock. It was allready full of Women. It is built of Stone in the shape of a Dome with no Windows but in the

Roofe, which gives Light enough. There was 5 of these domes joyn'd together, the outmost being less than the rest and serving only as a hall where the portress stood at the door. Ladys of Quality gennerally give this Woman the value of a crown or 10 shillings, and I did not forget that ceremony. The next room is a very large one, pav'd with Marble, and all round it rais'd 2 Sofas of marble, one above another. There were 4 fountains of cold Water in this room, falling first into marble Basins and then running on the floor in little channels made for that purpose, which carry'd the streams into the next room, something less than this, with the same sort of marble sofas, but so hot with steams of sulphur proceeding from the baths joyning to it, twas impossible to stay there with one's Cloths on. The 2 other domes were the hot baths, one of which had cocks of cold Water turning into it to temper it to what degree of warmth the bathers have a mind to.

I was in my travelling Habit, which is a rideing dress, and certainly appear'd very extrodinary to them, yet there was not one of 'em that shew'd the least surprize or impertinent Curiosity, but receiv'd me with all the obliging civillity possible. I know no European Court where the Ladys would have behav'd them selves in so polite a manner to a stranger.

I beleive in the whole there were 200 Women[1] and yet none of those disdainfull smiles or satyric whispers that never fail in our assemblys when any body appears that is not dress'd exactly in fashion. They repeated over and over to me, Uzelle, pek uzelle, which is nothing but, charming, very charming. The first sofas were cover'd with Cushions and rich Carpets, on which sat the Ladys, and on the 2nd their slaves behind 'em, but without any distinction of rank by their dress, all being in the state of nature, that is, in plain English, stark naked, without any Beauty or deffect conceal'd, yet there was not the least wanton smile or immodest Gesture amongst 'em.[2] They Walk'd and mov'd with the

---

[1] The famous painting by Ingres of 'Le Bain Turc' (1862), now in the Louvre, shows the influence of LM's sensuous descriptions. Ingres copied into a notebook several passages from this letter, beginning here, using his copy of a French translation of the 1805 edition (Norman Schlenoff, *Ingres, ses sources littéraires*, 1956, pp. 281–3).

[2] Dumont's description of the baths is similar to LM's except for his statement that the women 'take care to cover

same majestic Grace which Milton describes of our General Mother.[1] There were many amongst them as exactly proportion'd as ever any Goddess was drawn by the pencil of Guido or Titian, and most of their skins shineingly white, only adorn'd by their Beautifull Hair divided into many tresses hanging on their shoulders, braided either with pearl or riband, perfectly representing the figures of the Graces. I was here convinc'd of the Truth of a Refflexion that I had often made, that if twas the fashion to go naked, the face would be hardly observ'd. I perceiv'd that the Ladys with the finest skins and most delicate shapes had the greatest share of my admiration, thô their faces were sometimes less beautifull than those of their companions. To tell you the truth, I had wickedness enough to wish secretly that Mr. Gervase could have been there invisible.[2] I fancy it would have very much improv'd his art to see so many fine Women naked in different postures, some in conversation, some working, others drinking Coffee or sherbet, and many negligently lying on their Cushions while their slaves (generally pritty Girls of 17 or 18) were employ'd in braiding their hair in several pritty manners. In short, tis the Women's coffée house, where all the news of the Town is told, Scandal invented, etc. They gennerally take this Diversion once a week, and stay there at least 4 or 5 hours without geting cold by immediate coming out of the hot bath into the cool room, which was very surprizing to me. The Lady that seem'd the most considerable amongst them entreated me to sit by her and would fain have undress'd me for the bath. I excus'd my selfe with some difficulty, they being all so earnest in perswading me. I was at last forc'd to open my skirt and shew them my stays, which satisfy'd 'em very well, for I saw they beleiv'd I was so lock'd up in that machine that it was not in my own power to open it, which contrivance they attributed to my Husband.[3] I was charm'd with their Civillity and

their Distinguishing Parts with a Cloth wrapt about their Belly, and tied on the Back' (p. 274).

[1] *Paradise Lost*, iv. 304–18.

[2] Charles Jervas (1675?–1739), portrait painter and friend of the London wits. In 1710 he had painted LM dressed as a shepherdess (frontispiece in Halsband, *LM*).

[3] In 1741, when LM met Joseph Spence in Rome, she related this episode, and quoted the lady's remark that 'the Husbands in England were much worse than in the East; for that they ty'd up

Beauty and should have been very glad to pass more time with them, but Mr. W[ortley] resolving to persue his Journey the next morning early, I was in haste to see the ruins of Justinian's church, which did not afford me so agreable a prospect as I had left, being little more than a heap of stones.

Adeiu, Madam. I am sure I have now entertaind you with an Account of such a sight as you never saw in your Life and what no book of travells could inform you of.[1] 'Tis no less than Death for a Man to be found in one of these places.[2]

Text H MS 253, pp. 179–89

To the Abbé Conti[3] *1 April* [*1717*][4]

Adrianople, Ap. 1. O.S.

You see that I am very exact in keeping the promise you engag'd me to make, but I know not whither your Curiosity will be satisfy'd with the Accounts I shall give you, thô I can assure you that the desire I have to oblige you to the utmost of my power has made me very diligent in my enquirys and observations. Tis certain we have but very imperfect relations of the manners and Religion of these people, this part of the World being seldom visited but by merchants who mind little but their own Affairs, or Travellers who make too short a stay to be able to report any thing exactly of their own knowledge. The Turks are too proud to converse familiarly with merchants etc., who can only

their Wives in little Boxes, of the shape of their bodies' (MS Eg 2234, f. 250; cf. Spence, *Anecdotes*, ed. J. M. Osborn, 1966, § LM 22).

[1] This same year Joseph de Tournefort, who visited Turkey in 1700, published his *Relation d'un voyage du Levant*, where he wrote: 'Les femmes Turques, sur le rapport de nos Françoises de Constantinople et de Smyrne qui les voyent au bain avec beaucoup de liberté, sont en général belles et bien faites' (ii. 93).

[2] Hill, who describes the beauty of the women's faces, confirms this statement (pp. 50, 110).

[3] In MS: 'To the Abbot ——'. The Abbé Antonio Conti (1677–1749), savant and *littérateur*. In 1715 he had visited England, where he was received at Court. From March 1717 to March 1718 he was again in England (Conti, *Prose e poesie*, 1739–56, ii. 23 ff.).

[4] Under this date in the 'Heads of LM's Letters From Turky' is one to 'Ab. C.': 'New world. Journey by land. Description of Phil[ippopolis], Hebrus. Paulines. Women's ignorance. Arnounts. Poetry Arab:. Courts. Tranquillity. Truth. Secresie.' The summary describes an actual letter to Conti (pp. xv–xvi above). She wrote to him in French.

pick up some confus'd informations which are generally false, and they can give no better an Account of the ways here than a French refugée lodging in a Garret in Greek street[1] could write of the Court of England. The Journey we have made from Belgrade hither by Land cannot possibly be pass'd by any out of a Public character. The desart Woods of Servia are the common refuge of Theeves who rob 50 in a company, that we had need of all our Guards to secure us, and the villages so poor that only force could extort from them necessary provisions. Indeed, the Janizarys had no mercy on their poverty, killing all the poultry and sheep they could find without asking who they belong'd to, while the wretched owners durst not put in their claim for fear of being beaten. Lambs just fall'n, Geese and Turkeys big with Egg: all masacre'd without distinction. I fancy'd I heard the complaints of Mœlibeus for the Hope of his flock.[2] When the Bassas travel 'tis yet worse. Those Oppressors are not content with eating all that is to be eaten belonging to the peasants; after they have cram'd themselves and their numerous retinue, they have impudence to exact what they call Teeth-money, a contribution for the use of their teeth, worn with doing them the Honnour of devouring their meat. This is a litteral known Truth,[3] however extravagant it seems, and such is the natural corruption of a Military Government, their Religion not allowing of this barbarity no more than ours does.

I had the advantage of lodging 3 weeks at Belgrade with a principal Effendi, that is to say, a Scholar. This set of men are equally capable of preferments in the Law or the Church, those 2 Sciences being cast into one, a Lawyer and a preist being the same word.[4] They are the only men realy considerable in the Empire; all the profitable Employments and church revenues are in their hands. The Grand Signor, thô general Heir to his people, never presumes to touch their lands or money, which goes in an untterupted succession

---

[1] After the revocation of the Edict of Nantes (1685) many French Protestants fled to England. Greek Street is in Soho, where many of them settled.

[2] In Virgil's first *Eclogue*.

[3] This had been noted by an earlier

English traveller (G. F. Abbott, *Under the Turk in Constantinople. A Record of Sir John Finch's Embassy 1674–1681*, 1920, p. 91).

[4] Cadi, or judge in religious law.

to their Children. 'Tis true they lose this privelege by accepting a place at Court or the Title of Bassa, but there are few examples of such fools amongst 'em. You may easily judge the power of these men who have engross'd all the Learning and allmost all the Wealth of the Empire. Tis they that are the real Authors, thô the Souldiers are the Actors of Revolutions. They depos'd the late Sultan Mustapha,[1] and their power is so well known 'tis the Emperor's interest to flatter them. This is a long digression.

I was going to tell you that an intimate daily conversation with the Effendi Achmet-Beg gave me opertunity of knowing their Religion and morals in a more particular manner than perhaps any Christian ever did. I explain'd to him the difference between the Religion of England and Rome, and he was pleas'd to hear there were Christians that did not worship images or adore the Virgin Mary. The ridicule of Transubstantiation appear'd very strong to him. Upon comparing our Creeds together, I am convinc'd that if our freind Dr. [Clarke] had free Liberty of preaching here, it would be very easy to perswade the Generallity to Christianity, whose Notions are allready little different from his.[2] Mr. Wh[iston] would make a very good apostle here.[3] I don't doubt but his Zeal will be much fir'd if you communicate this account to him, but tell him he must first have the Gift of tongues before he could possibly be of any use.

Mahometism is divided into as many Sects as Christianity, and the first institution as much neglected and obscur'd by interpretations. I cannot here forbear refflecting on the natural Inclination of Mankind to make Mysterys and Noveltys. The Zeidi, Kadari, Jabari, etc. put me in mind of the Catholic, Lutheran, Calvinist, etc., and are equally zealous against one Another.[4] But the most prevailing

[1] Mustafa II (1664–1703), brother of the reigning Sultan, had been deposed in 1703 by authority of the *ulema* [learned scholars] (*Encycl. of Islam*, iii. 760).

[2] Dr. Samuel Clarke, a mild deist and controversialist who remained in the Church. LM had asked him to recommend a chaplain for the Embassy (see above, p. 247).

[3] William Whiston (1667–1752), of even more extreme unorthodoxy, and an intimate friend of Dr. Clarke.

[4] Hill describes the various sects of Islam (chap. viii). The three mentioned by LM are Al-Zaidīya, Kadarīya, and Djabarīya (*Encycl. of Islam*, iv. 1196–8, ii. 605–6, i. 985). She made the same comparison in her actual letter to Conti (see above, p. xvi).

Opinion, if you search into the Secret of the Effendis, is plain Deism,[1] but this is kept from the people, who are amus'd with a thousand Different notions according to the different interests of their Preachers. There are very few amongst them (Achmet Beg deny'd there were any) so absurd as to set up for Wit by declaring they beleive no God at all. Sir Paul Rycaut is mistaken (as he commonly is) in calling the Sect Muserin (i.e. the secret with us) Atheists, they being Deists, and their impiety consists in makeing a Jest of their Prophet.[2] Achmet Beg did not own to me that he was of this opinion, but made no scruple of deviateing from some part of Mahomet's Law by drinking Wine with the same freedom we did. When I ask'd him how he came to allow himselfe that Liberty, he made Answer, all the Creatures of God were good and design'd for the use of Man; however, that the prohibition of Wine was a very wise maxim and meant for the common people, being the Source of all disorders amongst them, but that the Prophet never design'd to confine those that knew how to use it with moderation; however, scandal ought to be avoided, and that he never drank it in public. This is the general way of thinking amongst them, and very few forbear drinking wine that are able to afford it.[3]

He assur'd me that if I understood Arabic I should be very well pleas'd with reading the Alcoran, which is so far from the nonsense we charge it with, tis the purest morality deliver'd in the very best Language. I have since heard impartial Christians speak of it in the same manner, and I don't doubt but all our translations are from Copys got from the Greek Preists, who would not fail to falsify it with the extremity of Malice.[4] No body of Men ever were more ignorant and

---

[1] A similar comparison with Deism had been made by Leibnitz in 1706 ('Observation générale de la religion arabe', *Opera Omnia*, ed. 1768, v. 479).

[2] Paul Rycaut (1628–1700) had been secretary to the Turkish Embassy of the Earl of Winchilsea from 1661 for about six years. In *The Present State of the Ottoman Empire* (1668), chaps. ix–xii, he deals with Islamic sects, describing the 'Muserin' as atheists who absolutely deny the existence of a Deity (p. 129). Actually, the fundamental doctrine of

Al-Mutazila was a 'state intermediate between belief and scepticism' (*Encycl. of Islam*, iii. 787).

[3] Other travel-writers remarked on the widespread drinking, e.g. Dumont (p. 254), Hill (p. 43).

[4] Before George Sale's translation of the Koran in 1734, based on the Arab text, the only full translation in any modern language was an inaccurate French version of 1649; this was translated into English the same year (*DNB sub* Sale).

more corrupt, yet they differ so little from the Romish
Church, I confess there is nothing gives me a greater ab-
horrence of the cruelty of your Clergy than the barbarous
persecutions of 'em whenever they have been their masters,
for no other reason than not acknowledging the Pope. The
dissenting in that one article has got them the Titles of
Heretics, Schismatics, and, what is worse, the same treatment. I found at Phillipopolis a Sect of Christians that call
themselves Paulines.[1] They show an old Church where they
say St. Paul preach'd, and he is the favourite saint after the
same manner as St. Peter is at Rome; neither do they forget
to give him the same preference over the rest of the Apostles.

But of all the Religions I have seen, the Arnounts seem
to me the most particular. They are natives of Arnountlick,
the Ancient Macedonia, and still retain something of the
Courrage and Hardyness, thô they have lost the name of
Macedonians, being the best militia in the Turkish Empire
and the only check upon the Janizarys. They are foot
Souldeirs. We had a guard of them, releiv'd in every considerable Town we pass'd. They are all cloth'd and arm'd
at their own expence, gennerally lusty Young fellows,
dress'd in clean white coarse Cloth, carrying Guns of a
prodigious length, which they run with on their shoulders as
if they did not feel the weight of 'em, the Leader singing
a sort of rude Tune, not unpleasant, and the rest makeing up
the Chorus. These people, living between Christians and
Mahometans and not being skill'd in controversie, declare
that they are utterly unable to judge which Religion is best;
but to be certain of not entirely rejecting the Truth, they
very prudently follow both, and go to the Mosque on fridays
and the Church on Sundays, saying for their excuse, that
at the day of Judgment they are sure of protection from the
True Prophet, but which that is they are not able to determine in this World.[2] I beleive there is no other race of Mankind have so modest an opinion of their own capacity. These
are the remarks I have made on the diversity of Religions

---

[1] A dualistic, heretical sect, many of
whom lived in Philippopoli. They were
maltreated by the Moslems, and de-
spised by the Greek Orthodox.

[2] In her French letter to Conti LM
makes a similar remark. The sect is
treated in the *Encycl. of Islam, sub*
Arnawutluk.

I have seen. I don't ask your pardon for the Liberty I have taken in speaking of the Roman. I know you equally condemn the Quackery of all Churches as much as you revere the sacred Truths in which we both agree.

You will expect I should say something to you of the Antiquitys of this Country, but there are few remains of Ancient Greece. We pass'd near the peice of an Arch which is commonly call'd Trajan's Gate,[1] as supposing he made it to shut up the passage over the mountains between Sophia and Phillipopoli, but I rather beleive it the remains of some Triumphal Arch (thô I could not see any inscription), for if that passage had been shut up there are many others that would serve for the march of an Army; and notwithstanding the story of Baldwin, Earl of Flanders, being overthrown in these straits after he had won Constantinople,[2] I don't fancy the Germans would find them selves stopp'd by them. 'Tis true the road is now made (with great Industry) as commodious as possible for the march of the Turkish Army. There is not one ditch or Puddle between this place and Belgrade that has not a large strong bridge of Planks built over it, but the Precipices were not so terrible as I had heard them represented.

At the foot of these mountains we lay at the little village of Kiskoi, wholly inhabited by Christians, as all the peasants of Bulgaria are. Their Houses are nothing but little Huts rais'd of Dirt bak'd in the Sun, and they leave them and fly into the mountains some months before the march of the Turkish army, who would else entirely ruin them by driving away their whole flocks. This precaution secures them in a sort of plenty, for such vast Tracts of land lying in common they have Liberty of sowing what they please, and are generally very industrious Husbandmen. I drank here several sorts of delicious Wine. The Women dress themselves in a great variety of colour'd Glass beads, and are not ugly but of tawny Complexions. I have now told you all that is worth telling you (and perhaps more) relateing to my Journey.

---

[1] A Roman defence against barbarian tribes from Dacia (*Handbook for Travellers in the Ionian Islands, Greece, Turkey* . . ., pub. Murray: 1840, p. 217).

[2] Baldwin I (d. 1205), Count of Flanders, Emperor of Constantinople (1204), was overthrown by a Greek revolt in Thrace.

When I am at Constantinople I'll try to pick up some
curiositys and then you shall hear again from etc.

Text H MS 253, pp. 189–207

To Lady Bristol *1 April* [*1717*]

Adrianople, Ap. 1 O.S.[1]

As I never can forget the smallest of your Ladyship's
commands, my first busynesse here has been to enquire
after the Stuffs you order'd me to look for, without being
able to find what you would like. The difference of the dress
here and at London is so great, the same sort of things are not
proper for Caftans and Manteaûs. However, I will not give
over my search, but renew it again at Constantinople, thô
I have reason to beleive there is nothing finer than what is to
be found here, being the present residence of the Court.[2]

The Grand Signor's eldest daughter was marry'd some
few days before I came, and upon that Occassion the Turkish
Ladys display all their magnificence. The Bride was conducted to her Husband's House in very great Splendour.
She is Widow of the late Vizier who was kill'd at Peterwaradin, thô that ought rather to be call'd a contract than
a Marriage, not having ever liv'd with him. However, the
greatest part of his Wealth is hers. He had the permission of
visiting her in the Seraglio and, being one of the Handsomest Men in the Empire, had very much engag'd her
affections. When she saw this 2nd Husband, who is at least
50, she could not forbear bursting into Tears. He is a Man
of Merit and the declar'd Favourite of the Sultan, which they
call Mosayp, but that is not enough to make him pleasing
in the Eyes of a Girl of 13.[3]

[1] Among the 'Heads' of letters for
this date is one to 'L. B¹': 'Stuffs.
Absolute Government here. Army.
Malice and censure of w[ome]n.' The
first three topics are treated in this
Embassy letter.
[2] After two centuries of seclusion
within the Grand Seraglio in Con-

stantinople, the Sultans preferred the
freer life of Adrianople, where they
enjoyed game preserves and immense
gardens; they had virtually transferred
their capital there (Barnette Miller,
Beyond the Sublime Porte, 1931, pp. 115–
16).

[3] The marriage took place on 20

The Government here is entirely in the hands of the Army, and the Grand Signor with all his absolute power as much a slave as any of his Subjects, and trembles at a Janizary's frown. Here is, indeed, a much greater appearance of Subjection than amongst us. A minister of state is not spoke to but upon the Knee. Should a refflexion on his conduct be dropp'd in a Coffee-House (for they have spys every where) the House would be raz'd to the Ground and perhaps the whole Company put to the Torture. No Huzzaing Mobs, senseless Pamphlets and Tavern disputes about Politics:

> A Consequential ill that Freedom draws,
> A Bad Effect but from a Noble Cause,[1]

none of our harmless calling names; but when a Minister here displeases the people, in 3 hours time he is dragg'd even from his Master's arms. They cut off his hands, head and feet, and throw them before the palace Gate with all the respect in the World, while that Sultan (to whom they all profess an unlimited Adoration) sits trembling in his Apartment, and dare neither defend nor revenge his favourite. This is the blessed Condition of the most Absolute Monarch upon Earth, who owns noe Law but his Will. I cannot help wishing (in the Loyalty of my heart) that the Parliament would send hither a Ship Load of your passive Obedient Men that they might see A[r]bitrary Government in its clearest, strongest Light,[2] where tis hard to Judge whither

Feb. 1717 [N.S.], more than a month before LM's arrival (on 24/13 March). The first husband of Princess Fatma (1704–33) had been Ali Pasha (*c.* 1667–1716); her second was Ibrahim Pasha (*c.* 1666–1730) (A. D. Alderson, *Structure of the Ottoman Dynasty*, 1956, Table XLI). Thus both husbands were about the same age. W's account is less sentimental: 'The Mosaip, it is certain, has very earnestly pressed for an order to consummate his marriage with the Grand Signior's daughter, who is the widow of the late Vizier, and is now in this favourite's house. It is refused him, as it is said the Grand Signior declares this is not a proper time for the rejoicings that are usually made at this Court

upon such an occasion, and that he chose him for his son-in-law to take care of his affairs' (10 April 1717, SP 97/24, quoted 1861, i. 293, n. 1; a French translation of this dispatch, evidently intended for the King, is among the Tickell MS).

[1] In a poem on Sir Robert Walpole, probably written in the 1730's, LM repeats this verse, changing 'that Freedom' to 'good-nature' (1861, ii. 484).

[2] The High Anglican Tories held to the doctrine of Passive Obedience. Like LM, Aubry de La Mottraye observed that the Turkish 'Bashaw is taught by his religion "strict Passive Obedience"' (*Travels through Europe, Asia . . .*, 1723–32, i. 232).

the prince, people or Ministers are most miserable. I could make many refflexions on this Subject, but I know, Madam, your own good sense has allready furnish'd you with better than I am capable of.

I went yesterday with the French Ambassadresse[1] to see the Grand Signor in his passage to the Mosque. He was preceded by a Numerous Guard of Janizarys with vast white Feathers on their Heads, Spahys and Bostangées; these are the foot and Horse Guard and the Royal Gardiners, which are a very considerable body of men, dress'd in different habits of fine, lively Colours that at a distance they appear'd like a parterre of Tulips;[2] after them, the Aga of the Janizarys in a Robe of Purple velvet lin'd with silver Tissue, his Horse led by 2 slaves richly dress'd; next him the Kuzlir Aga (your Ladyship knows this is the cheife Guardian of the seraglio Ladys) in a deep yellow Cloth (which suited very well to his black face) lin'd with Sables; and last his Sublimity him selfe in Green lin'd with the Fur of a black Muscovite fox, which is suppos'd worth £1,000 Sterling, mounted on a fine Horse with Furniture embrodier'd with Jewells. 6 more Horses richly furnish'd were led after him, and 2 of his Principal Courtiers bore, one his Gold and the other his Silver Coffée Pot, on a staff. Another carry'd a Silver stool on his head for him to sit on. It would be too tedious to tell your Ladyship the various dresses and Turbants (by which their Rank is distinguish'd) but they were all extreme rich and gay to the number of some thousands, that perhaps there cannot be seen a more beautifull Procession. The Sultan appear'd to us a Handsome Man of about 40, with a very gracefull air but something severe in his Countenance, his Eyes very full and black.[3] He happen'd to stop

---

[1] Madeleine-Françoise de Gontaut-Biron (1698–1739), da. of duc de Biron, later Marshal of France, m. (Nov. 1715) Jean-Louis d'Usson, marquis de Bonnac or Bonac (1672–1738), who had been awarded the Turkish Embassy in May 1716. They had arrived in Adrianople, by way of Constantinople, on 12/1 Jan. 1717 (Charles Schefer, *Mémoire historique sur l'ambassade de France à Constantinople par le marquis de Bonnac*, 1894,

pp. xx–xxi, xxxi).

[2] An apt metaphor for what has been called the Age of the Tulip because of the Sultan's passionate love of that flower.

[3] W's predecessor had described him as 'exceedingly covetous, haughty, and ambitious . . . hasty, violent and cruel, but variable and unsteady' (Robert Sutton, *Despatches*, ed. A. N. Kurat, 1953, p. 2).

under the Window where we stood and (I suppose being told who we were) look'd upon us very attentively that we had full Leisure to consider him, and the French Ambassadresse agreed with me as to his good Mien.

I see that Lady very often. She is young and her conversation would be a great releife to me if I could perswade her to live without those forms and ceremonys that make Life formal and tiresome, but she is so delighted with her Guards, her 24 footmen, Gentleman Ushers, etc., that she would rather die than make me a visit without 'em, not to reckon a Coach full of attending Damsels yclep'd maids of Honour.¹ What vexes me is that as long as she will visit with this troublesome Equipage, I am oblig'd to do the same. However, our mutual interest makes us much together.² I went with her 'tother day all round the Town in an open Gilt chariot with our joynt train of Attendants, preceded by our Guards, who might have summon'd the people to see what they never had seen, nor ever would see again, 2 young Christian Ambassadresses never yet having been in this Country at the same time nor, I beleive, ever will again. Your Ladyship may easily imagine that we drew a vast croud of Spectators, but all silent as Death. If any of them had taken the Libertys of our Mob upon any strange sight, our Janizarys had made no scrupule of falling on 'em with their Scimetars without danger for so doing, being above Law. Yet these People have some good qualitys. They are very Zealous and faithfull where they serve, and look upon it as their busyness to fight for you upon all Occasions, of which I had a very pleasant instance in a village on this side Phillipopolis, where we were met by our Domestic Guard. I happen'd to bespeak pigeons for my Supper, upon which one of my Janizarys went immediately to the Cady (the cheife civil officer of the Town) and order'd him to send in some dozens. The poor Man answer'd

¹ Customarily the French ambassador's house was the rendezvous of polite society, and provided luxurious hospitality and elaborate entertainment (Albert Vandal, *Une Ambassade française en Orient sous Louis XV*, 1887, p. 38).

² The French Ambassador hoped that his young wife would profit from LM's instruction; he wrote: 'elle n'apprendra point le latin de madame de Montaigu mais je voudrois fort qu'elle apprît d'elle les bonnes maximes qu'elle a sur ses propres affaires' (23 April 1717, Ministère des Affaires Étrangères, Constantinople, vol. 57, f. 153).

that he had allready sent about but could get none. My Janizary, in the height of his Zeal for my service, immediately lock'd him up prisoner in his room, telling him he deserv'd Death for his impudence in offering to excuse his not obeying my command, but out of respect to me he would not punish him but by my order, and accordingly came very gravely to me to ask what should be done to him, adding by way of Complement that, if I pleas'd, he would bring me his head.[1] This may give some idea of the unlimited power of these fellows, who are all sworn Brothers and bound to revenge the injurys done to one another, whither at Cairo, Aleppo, or any part of the World; and this inviolable League makes them so powerfull, the greatest Man at the Court never speaks to them but in a flattering Tone, and in Assia any Man that is rich is forc'd to enroll himselfe a Janizary to secure his Estate.—But I have allready said enough and I dare swear, dear Madam, that by this time 'tis a very comfortable refflection to you that there is no possibillity of your receiving such a tedious Letter but once in 6 months. 'Tis that consideration has given me the assurance to entertain you so long and will, I hope, plead the Excuse of, Dear Madam, etc.[2]

Text H MS 253, pp. 208–21

To Lady Mar *1 April* [*1717*]

Adrianople, Ap. 1. O.S.[3]

I wish to God (dear Sister) that you was as regular in letting me have the pleasure of knowing what passes on your

[1] Baron François de Tott ridicules LM's anecdote as an example of how travellers unacquainted with the language can err; he conjectures that the Janizary thought her request so absurd that he impatiently offered her the head of the Cadi instead, a joke her interpreter failed to transmit (*Mémoires sur les Turcs et les Tartares*, 1784, i. xxvii–xxxi).

[2] On 9 Oct./28 Sept. 1717 Addison

forwarded to W a letter for LM from 'Lady Hervey' (*Letters*, ed. W. Graham, 1941, p. 378), which was probably an answer to an actual counterpart of this Embassy letter. (Addison absent-mindedly forgot that Lady Hervey had become Lady Bristol in 1714.)

[3] Among the 'Heads' of letters for this date is one to 'S. M^r' [Sister (Lady) Mar]: 'Hope she'l be glad to hear I am wel. French Ambassadresse and

side of the Globe as I am carefull in endeavouring to amuse
you by the Account of all I see that I think you care to hear
of. You content your selfe with telling me over and over
that the Town is very dull. It may possibly be dull to you
when every day does not present you with something new,
but for me that am in arrear at least 2 months news, all that
seems very stale with you would be fresh and sweet here;
pray let me into more particulars. I will try to awaken your
Gratitude by giving you a full and true Relation of the
Noveltys of this Place, none of which would surprize you
more than a sight of my person as I am now in my Turkish
Habit, thô I beleive you would be of my Opinion that 'tis
admirably becoming. I intend to send you my Picture; in
the mean time accept of it here.

The first peice of my dresse is a pair of drawers, very full,
that reach to my shoes and conceal the legs more modestly
than your Petticoats. They are of a thin rose colour damask
brocaded with silver flowers, my shoes of white kid Leather
embrodier'd with Gold. Over this hangs my Smock of a fine
white silk Gause edg'd with Embrodiery. This smock has
wide sleeves hanging halfe way down the Arm and is clos'd
at the Neck with a diamond button, but the shape and colour
of the bosom very well to be distinguish'd through it. The
Antery is a wastcoat made close to the shape, of white and
Gold Damask, with very long sleeves falling back and
fring'd with deep Gold fringe, and should have Diamond or
pearl Buttons. My Caftan of the same stuff with my Drawers
is a robe exactly fited to my shape and reaching to my feet,
with very long strait falling sleeves. Over this is the Girdle
of about 4 fingers broad, which all that can afford have entirely of Diamonds or other precious stones. Those that will
not be at that expence have it of exquisite Embrodiery on
Satin, but it must be fasten'd before with a clasp of Di'monds.
The Curdée is a loose Robe they throw off or put on according to the Weather, being of a rich Brocade (mine is green
and Gold) either lin'd with Ermine or Sables; the sleeves

Ambassador pomp. Cavalcade thro the
Town. Court to me. Description of
Dress. Jew Ladys.' (The last two topics
are treated in this Embassy letter.) An
actual letter to Lady Mar reached London at the end of Aug. through the
Secretary of State, and was forwarded
to her at her house in Whitehall (HMC
Stuart Papers, v, 1912, pp. 25–26).

PLATE 6

here, they generally shape their 228
Eyebrows, & ye Greeks & Turks have
a custom of putting round their Eyes
on ye inside a black Tincture, yt at a distance,
or by candle-light adds very
much to ye Blackness of ym. I fancy
many of our Ladys would be overjoyd
to know ye secret, but tis too visible
by day. they dye their Nails rose
colour, I own I cannot enough
accustom my selfe to ye fashion, to
find any Beauty in it. as to their
Morality or good conduct, I can
say like Arlequin, tis just as tis
wth you, & the Turkish Ladys
don't commit one sin the less for
not being Christians. now I am a

Page of the Turkish Embassy Letters, dated 1 April [1717]
Harrowby MSS, vol. 253, p. 228

reach very little below the Shoulders. The Headress is compos'd of a Cap call'd Talpock, which is in winter of fine velvet embrodier'd with pearls or Di'monds and in summer of a light shineing silver stuff. This is fix'd on one side of the Head, hanging a little way down with a Gold Tassel and bound on either with a circle of Di'monds (as I have seen several) or a rich embrodier'd Handkercheif. On the other side of the Head the Hair is laid flat, and here the Ladys are at Liberty to shew their fancys, some putting Flowers, others a plume of Heron's feathers, and, in short, what they please, but the most general fashion is a large Bouquet of Jewels made like natural flowers, that is, the buds of Pearl, the roses of different colour'd Rubys, the Jess'mines of Di'monds, Jonquils of Topazes, etc., so well set and enammell'd tis hard to imagine any thing of that kind so beautifull. The Hair hangs at its full length behind, divided into tresses braided with pearl or riband, which is allways in great Quantity.

I never saw in my Life so many fine heads of hair. I have counted 110 of these tresses of one Ladys, all natural; but it must be own'd that every Beauty is more common here than with us. 'Tis surprizing to see a young Woman that is not very handsome. They have naturally the most beautifull complexions in the World and generally large black Eyes. I can assure you with great Truth that the Court of England (thô I beleive it the fairest in Christendom) cannot shew so many Beautys as are under our Protection here. They generally shape their Eyebrows, and the Greeks and Turks have a custom of putting round their Eyes on the inside a black Tincture that, at a distance or by Candle-light, adds very much to the Blackness of them. I fancy many of our Ladys would be overjoy'd to know this Secret, but tis too visible by day. They dye their Nails rose colour; I own I cannot enough accustom my selfe to this fashion to find any Beauty in it.

As to their Morality or good Conduct, I can say like Arlequin, 'tis just as 'tis with you,[1] and the Turkish Ladys don't commit one Sin the less for not being Christians. Now

---

[1] In Aphra Behn's *The Emperor of the Moon*, 1687, Harlequin announces that morality there is no different from that on earth (Act III, Scene i).

I am a little acquainted with their ways, I cannot forbear admiring either the exemplary discretion or extreme Stupidity of all the writers that have given accounts of 'em.[1] Tis very easy to see they have more Liberty than we have, no Woman of what rank so ever being permitted to go in the streets without 2 muslins, one that covers her face all but her Eyes and another that hides the whole dress of her head and hangs halfe way down her back; and their Shapes are wholly conceal'd by a thing they call a Ferigée, which no Woman of any sort appears without. This has strait sleeves that reaches to their fingers ends and it laps all round 'em, not unlike a rideing hood. In Winter 'tis of Cloth, and in Summer, plain stuff or silk. You may guess how effectually this disguises them, that there is no distinguishing the great Lady from her Slave, and 'tis impossible for the most jealous Husband to know his Wife when he meets her, and no Man dare either touch or follow a Woman in the Street.

This perpetual Masquerade gives them entire Liberty of following their Inclinations without danger of Discovery.[2] The most usual method of Intrigue is to send an Appointment to the Lover to meet the Lady at a Jew's shop, which are as notoriously convenient as our Indian Houses, and yet even those that don't make that use of 'em do not scruple to go to buy Pennorths and tumble over rich Goods, which are cheiffly to be found amongst that sort of people.[3] The Great Ladys seldom let their Gallants know who they are, and 'tis so difficult to find it out that they can very seldom guess at her name they have corresponded with above halfe a year together. You may easily imagine the number of faithfull Wives very small in a country where they have nothing to fear from their Lovers' Indiscretion, since we see so many that have the courrage to expose them selves to that in this

---

[1] Hill (p. 97) and Dumont (p. 268), for example, assert that Turkish women were strictly confined and kept from men. But Joseph de Tournefort (*Relation d'un voyage du Levant*, 1717, ii. 95) observed that though adultery was a fatal crime, most women arranged their intrigues undetected.

[2] Other travellers agree that women's

convenient dress assisted them in conducting their love affairs (—— Du Loir, *Voyages*, 1654, p. 185; Robert Withers, *A Description of the Grand Signor's Seraglio . . .*, 1650, p. 200).

[3] Jews were active as go-betweens, and Jewesses especially because they had entrée into harems (Du Loir, p. 179; Tournefort, i. 473–4).

World and all the threaten'd Punishment of the next, which
is never preach'd to the Turkish Damsels. Neither have they
much to apprehend from the resentment of their Husbands,
those Ladys that are rich having all their money in their own
hands, which they take with 'em upon a divorce with an
addition which he is oblig'd to give 'em.[1] Upon the Whole,
I look upon the Turkish Women as the only free people in
the Empire. The very Divan pays a respect to 'em, and the
Grand Signor himselfe, when a Bassa is executed, never
violates the priveleges of the Haram (or Women's apartment) which remains unsearch'd entire to the Widow. They
are Queens of their slaves, which the Husband has no permission so much as to look upon, except it be an old Woman
or 2 that his Lady chuses. 'Tis true their Law permits them
4 Wives, but there is no Instance of a Man of Quality that
makes use of this Liberty, or of a Woman of Rank that would
suffer it.[2] When a Husband happens to be inconstant (as
those things will happen) he keeps his mistrisse in a House
apart and visits her as privately as he can, just as tis with you.
Amongst all the great men here I only know the Tefterdar
(i.e. Treasurer) that keeps a number of she slaves for his own
use (that is, on his own side of the House, for a slave once
given to serve a Lady is entirely at her disposal) and he is
spoke of as a Libertine, or what we should call a Rake, and
his Wife won't see him, thô she continues to live in his
house.[3]

Thus you see, dear Sister, the manners of Mankind doe

[1] LM's account is similar to that of
Paul Rycaut (*Present State of the Ottoman Empire*, 1668, p. 156) and of
Tournefort (ii. 89). But Du Loir (p. 176)
states that if a husband repudiates his
wife with good cause he gives her
nothing.

[2] This is corroborated by Aubry de
La Mottraye (*Travels through Europe,
Asia . . .*, 1723–32, i. 250).

[3] In a private letter to Addison, who
was appointed Secretary of State in
April 1717, W closely parallels several
of LM's observations: 'The men of
Consideration among the Turks appear
in their conversation as much civilized

as any I have met with in Italy and are
not unlike the Italians in their Carriage.
Those that are in good credit have but
one wife. She has commonly several
slaves, which the Husband does not see;
if he does it makes an intire breach with
the wife. But they frequently keep
women at private places. The wives who
go abroad with their faces hid are
thought to take as much liberty as they
do in Italy. The Privilege of having
more wives than one is very rarely made
use of unless by those that travel into
distant Countries' (22 Aug. 1717,
Tickell MS).

not differ so widely as our voyage Writers would make us beleive. Perhaps it would be more entertaining to add a few surprizing customs of my own Invention, but nothing seems to me so agreable as truth, and I beleive nothing so acceptable to you. I conclude with repeating the great Truth of my being, Dear Sister, etc.

Text H MS 253, pp. 221–35

To Alexander Pope *1 April* [*1717*]

Adrianople, Ap. 1. O.S.[1]

I dare say You expect at least something very new in this Letter after I have gone a Journey not undertaken by any Christian of some 100 years. The most remarkable Accident that happen'd to me was my being very near overturn'd into the Hebrus; and if I had much regard for the Glorys that one's Name enjoys after Death I should certainly be sorry for having miss'd the romantic conclusion of swimming down the same River in which the Musical Head of Orpheus repeated verses so many ages since.

> ——Caput a cervice revulsum,
> Gurgite cum medio portans Oeagrius Hebrus
> Volveret, Euridicen vox ipsa, et frigida lingua,
> Ah! Miseram Euridicen! anima fugiente vocabat,
> Euridicen toto referebant flumine ripæ.[2]

Who knows but some of your bright Wits might have found it a subject affording many poetical Turns, and have told the World in a Heroic Elegy that

> As equal were our Souls, so equal were our fates?

[1] Among the 'Heads' of letters for this date is one to 'M. Pp:': 'A Journey not pass'd since the G[reek] E[mperors]. Like to be overturn'd in the Hebrus. Comparison to Orpheus. Romantic situation the Fashion. T[urkish] Women have intrigues. Write to Mr. C[ongreve] very oft, hear very seldom.' Several of these topics are treated in Embassy Letters of this date.

[2] '... [while] Oeagrian Hebrus swept and rolled in mid-current that head, plucked from its [marble] neck, the bare voice and death-cold tongue, with fleeting breath, called Eurydice—ah, hapless Eurydice! "Eurydice" the banks re-echoed, all adown the stream' (Virgil, *Georgics*, iv. 523–7, transl. Loeb Library). LM quoted this also in an actual letter to Conti (see above, p. xvi).

I dispair of ever having so many fine things said of me as so extrodinary a Death would have given Occasion for.[1]

I am at this present writeing in a House situate on the banks of the Hebrus, which runs under my Chamber Window. My Garden is full of Tall Cypress Trees, upon the branches of which several Couple of true Turtles are saying soft things to one another from Morning till night. How naturally do boughs and vows come into my head at this minute! And must not you confess to my praise that tis more than an ordinary Discretion that can resist the wicked Suggestions of Poetry in a place where Truth for once furnishes all the Ideas of Pastorall? The Summer is allready far advanc'd in this part of the World, and for some miles round Adrianople the whole ground is laid out in Gardens, and the Banks of the River set with Rows of Fruit trees, under which all the most considerable Turks divert them selves every Evening; not with walking, that is not one of their Pleasures, but a set party of 'em chuse out a green spot where the Shade is very thick, and there they spread a carpet on which they sit drinking their Coffée and generally attended by some slave with a fine voice or that plays on some instrument. Every 20 paces you may see one of these little companys listening to the dashing of the river, and this taste is so universal that the very Gardiners are not without it. I have often seen them and their children siting on the banks and playing on a rural Instrument perfectly answering the description of the Ancient Fistula, being compos'd of unequal reeds, with a simple but agreable softness in the Sound. Mr. Adison might here make the Experiment he speaks of in his travells, there not being one instrument of music among the Greek or Roman statues that is not to be found in the hands of the people of this country.[2] The young Lads gennerally divert themselves with makeing Girlands for their favourite Lambs, which I have often seen painted and adorn'd with flowers, lying at their feet while

---

[1] These ideas helped inspire Pope with sentiments that went into his 'Elegy to the Memory of an Unfortunate Lady' (*The Rape of the Lock and Other Poems*, ed. G. Tillotson, 3rd ed.,

1962, p. 354).
[2] *Remarks on Several Parts of Italy, &c.* (1705), *Misc. Works*, ed. A. C. Guthkelch, 1914, ii. 147.

they sung or play'd. It is not that they ever read Romances, but these are the Ancient Amusements here, and as natural to them as Cudgel playing and football to our British Swains, the softness and warmth of the Climate forbiding all rough Exercises, which were never so much as heard of amongst 'em, and naturally inspiring a Lazyness and aversion to Labour, which the great Plenty indulges. These Gardiners are the only happy race of Country people in Turkey. They furnish all the City with Fruit and herbs, and seem to live very easily. They are most of 'em Greeks and have little Houses in the midst of their Gardens where their Wives and daughters take a Liberty not permitted in the Town: I mean, to go unvail'd. These Wenches are very neat and handsome, and pass their time at their Looms under the shade of their Trees. I no longer look upon Theocritus as a Romantic Writer; he has only given a plain image of the Way of Life amongst the Peasants of his Country, which before oppresion had reduc'd them to want, were I suppose all employ'd as the better sort of 'em are now. I don't doubt had he been born a Briton his Idylliums had been fill'd with Descriptions of Thrashing and churning, both which are unknown here, the Corn being all trod out by Oxen, and Butter (I speak it with sorrow) unheard of.

I read over your Homer[1] here with an infinite Pleasure, and find several little passages explain'd that I did not before entirely comprehend the Beauty of, many of the customs and much of the dress then in fashion being yet retain'd; and I don't wonder to find more remains here of an Age so distant than is to be found in any other Country, the Turks not takeing that pains to introduce their own Manners as has been generally practis'd by other nations that imagine themselves more polite. It would be too tedious to you to point out all the passages that relate to the present customs, but I can assure you that the Princesses and great Ladys pass their time at their Looms embrodiering Veils and Robes, surrounded by their Maids, which are allways very numerous, in the same Manner as we find Andromache and Helen describ'd. The description of the belt of Menelaüs exactly ressembles those that are now worn by the great

[1] The second volume of Pope's translation of the *Iliad* (March 1716).

Men, fasten'd before with broad Golden Clasps and embrodier'd round with rich work. The Snowy Veil that Helen
throws over her face is still fashionable; and I never see (as
I do very often) halfe a dozen old Bashaws with their reverend Beards siting basking in the Sun, but I recollect Good
King Priam and his Councellors. Their manner of danceing
is certainly the same that Diana is sung to have danc'd by
Eurotas.[1] The great Lady still Leads the dance and is follow'd
by a troop of young Girls who imitate her steps, and if she
sings, make up the Chorus. The Tunes are extreme Gay
and Lively, yet with something in 'em wonderfull soft. The
steps are vary'd according to the Pleasure of her that leads
the dance, but allways in exact time and infinitly more Agreable than any of our Dances, at least in my Opinion. I sometimes make one in the Train, but am not skilfull enough
to lead. These are Grecian Dances, the Turkish being very
different.

I should have told you in the first place that the Eastern
Manners give a great light into many scripture passages that
appear odd to us, their Phrases being commonly what we
should call Scripture Language. The vulgar Turk is very
different from what is spoke at Court or amongst the people
of figure, who allways mix so much Arabic and Persian in
their discourse that it may very well be call'd another Language; and 'tis as ridiculous to make use of the expressions
commonly us'd, in speaking to a Great Man or a Lady, as it
would be to talk broad Yorkshire or Sommerset shire in the
drawing-room. Besides this distinction they have what they
call the Sublime, that is, a stile proper for Poetry, and which
is the exact scripture stile. I beleive you would be pleas'd to
see a genuine example of this, and I am very glad I have it in
my power to satisfy your Curiosity by sending you a faithfull
copy of the Verses that Ibrahim Bassa, the reigning favourite, has made for the young Princesse, his contracted Wife,
whom he is not yet permitted to visit without Wittnesses,
thô she is gone home to his House. He is a Man of Wit and

---

[1] In Homer (*Odyssey*, vi) Artemis
and her nymphs dance on Erymanthus,
a mountain which gives its name to a
river. But LM puts the scene beside
another river in the Peloponnesus. In
June, Pope reminded her of her 'great
Eclaircissements upon many passages in
Homer' (*Corr.* i. 406).

Learning, but whither or no he is capable of writing good
verse himselfe,[1] you may be sure that on such an Occasion
he would not want the Assistance of the best Poets in the
Empire.[2] Thus the verses may be look'd upon as a Sample of
their finest Poetry, and I don't doubt you'l be of my Mind
that it is most wonderfully ressembling the Song of Solomon,
which was also address'd to a Royal Bride.[3]

Turkish Verses address'd to the Sultana, Eldest daughter of
S[ultan] Achmet 3rd

Stanza 1st

1 V. The Nightingale now wanders in the Vines,
   Her Passion is to seek Roses.

2 I went down to admire the beauty of the Vines,
   The sweetness of your charms has ravish'd my Soul.

3 Your Eyes are black and Lovely
   But wild and disdainfull as those of a Stag.

Stanza 2nd

1 The wish'd possession is delaid from day to day,
   The cruel Sultan Achmet will not permit me to see those
     cheeks more vermillion than roses.

2 I dare not snatch one of your kisses,
   The sweetness of your charms has ravish'd my Soul.

3 Your Eyes are black and lovely
   But wild and disdainfull as those of a Stag.

Stanza 3rd

1 The wretched Bassa Ibrahim sighs in these verses,
   One Dart from your Eyes has pierc'd through my Heart.

2 Ah, when will the Hour of possession arrive?
   Must I yet wait a long time?
   The sweetnesse of your charms has ravish'd my soul.

3 Ah Sultana stag-ey'd, an Angel amongst angels,
   I desire and my desire remains unsatisfy'd.
   Can you take delight to prey upon my heart?

[1] Ibraham Pasha (see above, p. 321, n. 3) was actually a very accomplished writer (*Encycl. of Islam*, ii. 442).

[2] The best known was Ahmad Nadim (d. 1730), patronized by Ibra-him Pasha (ibid. iii. 809–10).

[3] LM's opinion is quoted and corroborated by Thomas Harmer in his *Outlines of a New Commentary on Solomon's Song*, 1768, pp. xi–xvi.

Stanza 4th

1   My crys peirce the Heavens,
My Eyes are without sleep;
Turn to me, Sultana, let me gaze on thy beauty.

2   Adeiu, I go down to the Grave;
If you call me I return.
My Heart is hot as Sulphur; sigh and it will flame.

3   Crown of my Life, fair light of my Eyes, my Sultana, my
Princesse,
I rub my face against the Earth, I am drown'd in scalding
Tears—I rave!
Have you no Compassion? Will you not turn to look upon
me?

I have taken abundance of pains to get these Verses in a litteral Translation, and if you were acquainted with my Interpreters, I might spare my selfe the trouble of assuring you that they have receiv'd no poetical Touches from their hands. In my opinion (allowing for the inevitable faults of a prose Translation into a Language so very different) there is a good deal of Beauty in them. The Epithet of Stag-Ey'd (thô the Sound is not very agreable in English) pleases me extremely,[1] and is, I think, a very lively image of the Fire and indifference in his mistrisse's Eyes. Monsieur Boileau has very justly observ'd, we are never to judge of the Elevation of an Expression in an Ancient Author by the Sound it carrys with us, which may be extremely fine with them, at the same time it looks low or uncouth to us.[2] You are so well acquainted with Homer, you cannot but have observ'd the same thing, and you must have the same Indulgence for all Oriental Poetry. The repetitions at the End of the 2 first stanzas are meant for a sort of chorus and agreable to the ancient manner of Writeing. The Music of the verses apparently changes in the 3rd stanza where the Burden is alter'd,

[1] Sir William Jones in discussing compound epithets peculiar to Arabic languages mentions that this one— literally *a fawn* and *the eye*—is imperfectly translated by LM (*A Grammar of the Persian Language*, ed. S. Lee, 1828, pp. 74–75).

[2] Boileau writes: '. . . prendrons-nous le parti d'accuser Homère et Virgile de bassesse, pour n'avoir pas préveû que ces termes, quoy que si nobles et si doux à l'oreille, en leur langue, seroient *bas* et grossiers estant traduits un jour en François ?' ('Réflexions critiques. Sur quelques passages du Rhéteur Longin,' *Dialogues . . . Œuvres diverses*, ed. C.-H. Boudhors, 1942, p. 106).

and I think he very artfully seems more passionate at the conclusion as 'tis natural for people to warm themselves by their own discourse, especially on a Subject where the Heart is concern'd, and is far more touching than our modern custom of concluding a Song of passion with a Turn which is inconsistent with it. The 1st Verse is a description of the Season of the Year, all the Country being now full of Nightingales, whose Amours with Roses is an Arabian fable[1] as well known here as any part of Ovid amongst us, and is much the same thing as if an English poem should begin by saying: Now Philomela sings—Or what if I turn'd the whole into the stile of English Poetry to see how twould look?

Stanza 1

Now Philomel renews her tender strain,
Indulging all the night her pleasing Pain.
I sought the Groves to hear the Wanton sing,
There saw a face more beauteous than the Spring.
Your large stag's-eyes where 1,000 glorys play,
As bright, as Lively, but as wild as they.

2

In vain I'm promis'd such a heavenly prize,
Ah, Cruel Sultan who delays my Joys!
While pierceing charms transfix my amorous Heart
I dare not snatch one kiss to ease the smart.
Those Eyes like etc.

3

Your wretched Lover in these lines complains,
From those dear Beautys rise his killing pains.
When will the Hour of wish'd-for Bliss arrive?
Must I wait longer? Can I wait and live?
Ah, bright Sultana! Maid divinely fair!
Can you unpitying see the pain I bear?

Stanza 4th

The Heavens relenting hear my peircing Crys,
I loath the Light and Sleep forsakes my Eyes.
Turn thee, Sultana, ere thy Lover dyes.

---

[1] In Persian and Turkish poetry, the nightingale is consumed with un- requited love for the rose; hence its unceasing song (*Encycl. of Islam*, i. 785).

> Sinking to Earth, I sigh the last Adeiu—
> Call me, my Goddesse, and my Life renew.
> My Queen! my Angel! my fond Heart's desire,
> I rave—my bosom burns with Heavenly fire.
> Pity that Passion which thy charms inspire.

I have taken the Liberty in the 2nd verse of following what I suppose is the true Sense of the Author, thô not litterally express'd. By saying he went down to admire the beauty of the Vines and her charms ravish'd his Soul, I understand by this a poetical fiction of having first seen her in a Garden where he was admiring the beauty of the Spring; but I could not forbear retaining the comparison of her Eyes to those of a Stag, thô perhaps the novelty of it may give it a burlesque sound in our Language. I cannot determine upon the whole how well I have succeeded in the Translation. Neither do I think our English proper to express such violence of passion, which is very seldom felt amongst us; and we want those compound words which are very frequent and strong in the Turkish Language.—You see I am pritty far gone in Oriental Learning, and to say truth I study very hard.[1] I wish my studys may give me occasion of entertaining your curiosity, which will be the utmost advantage hop'd from it by etc.[2]

Text H MS 253, pp. 235–56

To [Sarah Chiswell] *1 April* [*1717*]

Adrianople, Ap. 1. O.S.

In my Opinion, dear S[arah], I ought rather to quarrel with you for not answering my Nimeguen Letter of Aug't

[1] Her library contained (in 1739) *A Grammar of the Turkish Language* by Thomas Vaughan, 1709 (Wh MS 135); she wrote out exercises in Turkish translation (MS Commonplace Book, ff. 18–20, Fisher Library, University of Sydney); and among her MS, in a different hand, are notes in Turkish and Italian of vocabulary and grammar (W MS vii. 270–83).

[2] That LM did send such an actual letter to Pope is evident from his remark: 'I extreamly regret the loss of your Oriental Learning, for that letter I never had, but am heartily glad you kept a Copy' (*Corr.* i. 470)

till December, than to excuse my not writeing again till now. I am sure there is on my side a very good Excuse for Silence, having gone such tiresome Land Journeys, thô I don't find the conclusion of 'em so bad as you seem to imagine. I am very easy here and not in the Solitude you fancy me; the great Quantity of Greek, French, English and Italians that are under our Protection make their court to me from Morning till Night, and I'll assure you are many of 'em very fine Ladys, for there is no possibillity for a Christian to live easily under this Government but by the protection of an Ambassador, and the richer they are the greater their Danger.

Those dreadfull Storys you have heard of the plague have very little foundation in Truth. I own I have much ado to reconcile my selfe to the Sound of a Word which has allways given me such terrible Ideas, thô I am convinc'd there is little more in it than a fever, as a proofe of which we past through 2 or 3 Towns most violently infected. In the very next house where we lay, in one of 'em, 2 persons dy'd of it. Luckily for me I was so well deceiv'd that I knew nothing of the matter, and I was made beleive that our 2nd Cook who fell ill there had only a great cold. However, we left our Doctor to take care of him, and yesterday they both arriv'd here in good Health and I am now let into the Secret that he has had the Plague.[1] There are many that 'scape of it, neither is the air ever infected. I am perswaded it would be as easy to root it out here as out of Italy and France, but it does so little mischeife, they are not very solicitous about it and are content to suffer this distemper instead of our Variety, which they are utterly unacquainted with.

A propos of Distempers, I am going to tell you a thing that I am sure will make you wish your selfe here. The Small Pox so fatal and so general amongst us[2] is here entirely harmless by the invention of engrafting (which is the term they give it). There is a set of old Women who make it their business to perform the Operation. Every Autumn in the month of September, when the great Heat is abated, people

[1] In his dispatch of 10 April 1717 [31 March O.S.] W wrote that when he set out from Belgrade 'notwithstanding I was inform'd there was nothing of the Plague in the road, it was in my family before I got to Nissa' (SP 97/24).

[2] In Dec. 1715 LM had been stricken with smallpox, but unexpectedly recovered (Halsband, *LM*, pp. 51–52).

send to one another to know if any of their family has a mind
to have the small pox. They make partys for this purpose,
and when they are met (commonly 15 or 16 together) the old
Woman comes with a nutshell full of the matter of the best
sort of small-pox and asks what veins you please to have
open'd. She immediately rips open that you offer to her with
a large needle (which gives you no more pain than a common
scratch) and puts into the vein as much venom as can lye
upon the head of her needle, and after binds up the little
wound with a hollow bit of shell, and in this manner opens
4 or 5 veins. The Grecians have commonly the superstition
of opening one in the Middle of the forehead, in each arm
and on the breast to mark the sign of the cross, but this has
a very ill Effect, all these wounds leaving little Scars, and is
not done by those that are not superstitious, who chuse to
have them in the legs or that part of the arm that is conceal'd. The children or young patients play together all the
rest of the day and are in perfect health till the 8th. Then the
fever begins to seize 'em and they keep their beds 2 days,
very seldom 3. They have very rarely above 20 or 30 in their
faces, which never mark, and in 8 days time they are as well
as before their illness. Where they are wounded there
remains running sores during the Distemper, which I don't
doubt is a great releife to it. Every year thousands undergo
this Operation, and the French Ambassador says pleasantly
that they take the Small pox here by way of diversion as
they take the Waters in other Countrys. There is no example of any one that has dy'd in it, and you may beleive
I am very well satisfy'd of the safety of the Experiment
since I intend to try it on my dear little Son.[1] I am Patriot
enough to take pains to bring this usefull invention into
fashion in England, and I should not fail to write to some
of our Doctors very particularly about it if I knew any one
of 'em that I thought had Virtue enough to destroy such
a considerable branch of their Revenue for the good of
Mankind, but that Distemper is too beneficial to them
not to expose to all their Resentment the hardy wight
that should undertake to put an end to it. Perhaps if I live
to return I may, however, have courrage to war with 'em.

[1] She did so in March of the next year (see below, p. 392).

Upon this Occasion, admire the Heroism in the Heart of your Freind, etc.[1]

Text H MS 253, pp. 256–65

To [Anne] Thistlethwayte *1 April* [*1717*]

Adrianople, Ap. 1. O.S.

I can now tell Dear Mrs. T[histlethwayte] that I am safely arriv'd at the End of my very long Journey. I will not tire you with the account of the many fatigues I have suffer'd. You would rather hear something of what I see here, and a Letter out of Turkey that has nothing extrodinary in it would be as great a Disapointment as my visiters will receive at London if I return thither without any raritys to shew them. What shall I tell you of? You never saw Camels in your Life and perhaps the Description of them will appear new to you. I can assure you the first sight of 'em was very much so to me, and thô I have seen hundreds of pictures of those Animals, I never saw any that was ressembling enough to give me a true Idea of 'em. I am going to make a bold Observation, and possibly a false one, because nobody has ever made it before me, but I do take them to be of the Stag-kind; their Legs, bodys and Necks are exactly shap'd like them and their Colour very near the same. 'Tis true they are much larger, being a great deal higher than a horse, and so swift that after the defeat of Peterwaradin, they far out-run the swiftest horses and brought the first news of the loss of the battle to Belgrade. They are never thoroughly tam'd. The drivers take care to tye them one to another with strong ropes, 50 in a string, led by an Ass on which the driver rides. I have seen 300 in one Caravan. They carry the 3rd part more than any Horse, but 'tis a particular Art to load them because of the bunch on their backs. They seem to me very ugly Creatures, their heads being ill form'd and disproportion'd to their bodys. They carry all the burdens,

---

[1] LM's activity in pioneering smallpox inoculation is treated in Halsband, *LM*, pp. 80–81, 104–5, 109–12; and in Genevieve Miller, *The Adoption of Inoculation for Smallpox in England and France*, 1957, pp. 45–69 *passim*.

and the Beasts destin'd to the Plough are Buffolos, an Animal
you are also unacquainted with. They are larger and more
clumsey than an Oxe. They have short black Horns close to
their heads, which grow turning backwards. They say this
horn looks very beautifull when tis well polish'd. They are all
black with very short hair on their Hides and extreme little
white Eyes that make them look like Devils. The Country
people dye their Tails and the Hair of their foreheads red
by way of Ornament. Horses are not put here to any
Laborious Work, nor are they at all fit for it. They are beautifull and full of spirit, but generally little and not so strong
as the breed of Colder Countrys, very gentle with all their
vivacity, swift and sure footed. I have a little white favourite
that I would not part with on any terms. He prances under
me with so much fire you would think that I had a great
deal of courrage to dare Mount him, yet I'll assure you I
never rid a Horse in my life so much at my command.[1] My
Side Saddle is the first was ever seen in this part of the World
and gaz'd at with as much wonder as the ship of Columbus
was in America. Here are some birds held in a sort of religious Reverence and for that reason Multiply prodigiously:
Turtles on the Account of their Innocency, and Storks because they are suppos'd to make every Winter the Pilgrimage
to Mecha.[2] To say truth, they are the happiest Subjects
under the Turkish Government, and are so sensible of their
priveleges they walk the streets without fear and gennerally
build in the low parts of Houses. Happy are those that are so
distinguish'd; the vulgar Turks are perfectly perswaded
that they will not be that year either attack'd by Fire or
Pestilence. I have the happyness of one of their Sacred nests
just under my chamber Window.

Now I am talking of my Chamber I remember the description of the houses here would be as new to you as any
of the Birds or beasts. I suppose you have read in most of our
Accounts of Turkey that their Houses are the most miserable pieces of building in the World. I can speak very

[1] LM was an enthusiastic rider all
her life. When she left Constantinople
a year later, four of the Ambassador's
horses—probably Arabians, like the
one she describes here—were put on the
ship (Master's log, *Preston*, PRO Ad
52/254).

[2] The Turkish reverence for birds is
noted by Dumont (p. 254).

learnedly on that Subject, having been in so many of 'em, and I assure you tis no such thing. We are now lodg'd in a Palace belonging to the Grand Signor. I realy think the Manner of building here very agreable and proper for the Country. 'Tis true they are not at all solicitous to beautify the outsides of their houses, and they are gennerally built of Wood, which I own is the cause of many inconveniencys, but this is not to be charg'd on the ill taste of the people but the Oppression of the Government. Every House upon the death of its Master is at the Grand Signor's disposal, and therefore No Man cares to make a great Expence which he is not sure his family will be the better for. All their design is to build a House commodious and that will last their Lives, and are very indifferent if it falls down the Year after. Every house, great and small, is divided into 2 distinct parts which only joyn together by a narrow passage. The first House has a large Court before it and open Gallerys all round it, which is to me a thing very agreable. This Gallery leads to all the chambers, which are commonly large and with 2 rows of windows, the 1st being of painted Glass. They seldom build above 2 storys, each of which has such Gallerys. The Stairs are broad and not often above 30 steps. This is the House belonging to the Lord and the adjoyning one is call'd the Haram, that is, the Ladys' apartment, for the name of Seraglio is peculiar to the Grand Signor's. It has also a Gallery running round it towards the Garden to which all the Windows are Turn'd, and the same number of Chambers as the other, but more gay and splendid both in painting and furniture. The 2nd row of Windows are very low, with grates like those of Convents.

The rooms are all spread with Persian Carpets and rais'd at one end of 'em (my chamber is rais'd at both ends) about 2 foot. This is the Sopha and is laid with a richer sort of Carpet, and all round it a sort of Couch rais'd halfe a foot, cover'd with rich Silk according to the fancy or magnificence of the Owner. Mine is of Scarlet Cloath with a gold fringe. Round this are plac'd, standing against the Wall, 2 rows of Cushions, the first very large and the next little ones, and here the Turks display their greatest Magnificence. They are gennerally Brocade or embrodiery of Gold Wire upon

Satin. Nothing can look more gay and splendid. These seats
are so convenient and easy I shall never endure Chairs as
long as I live. The rooms are low, which I think no fault, the
Ceiling allways of Wood, gennerally inlaid, or painted and
Gilded. They use no hangings, the rooms being all wainscoated with Cedar set off with silver nails or painted with
Flowers, which open in many places with folding doors and
serve for Cabinets, I think more conveniently than ours.
Between the Windows are little Arches to set pots of perfume or baskets of Flowers, but what pleases me best is the
fashion of having marble Fountains in the lower part of the
room which throws up several spouts of Water, giving at
the same time an agreable Coolness and a pleasant dashing
sound falling from one basin to another. Some of these
fountains are very Magnificent. Each House has a Bagnio,
which is gennerally 2 or 3 little rooms leaded on the Top,
pav'd with Marble, with basins, Cocks of Water and all
conveniencys for either hot or cold baths. You will perhaps
be surpriz'd at an Account so different from what you have
been entertaind with by the common Voyage-writers who
are very fond of speaking of what they don't know. It must
be under a very particular character or on some Extrodinary
Occassion when a Christian is admitted into the House of a
Man of Quality, and their Harams are allways forbidden
Ground. Thus they can only speak of the outside, which
makes no great Appearance; and the Women's Apartments
are all built backward, remov'd from sight, and have no
other prospect than the Gardens, which are enclos'd with
very high Walls. There is none of our Parterres in them but
they are planted with high Trees, which give an agreable
shade and, to my fancy, a pleasing view. In the midst of the
Garden is the Chiosk, that is, a large Room, commonly
beautify'd with a fine fountain in the midst of it. It is rais'd
9 or 10 steps and enclos'd with Gilded Lattices, round which
Vines, jess'mines and Honey suckles twineing make a sort
of Green Wall. Large Trees are planted round this place,
which is the Scene of their greatest Pleasures, and where the
Ladys spend most of their Hours, employ'd by their Music
or Embrodiery. In the public Gardens there are public
chiosks where people go that are not so well accommodated

at home, and drink their Coffée, sherbet, etc. Neither are they ignorant of a More Durable Manner of building. Their Mosques are all of free Stone, and the Publick Hans or Inns extremely Magnificent, many of 'em takeing up a large square, built round with shops under stone Arches, where poor Artificers are lodg'd Gratis. They have allways a Mosque joyning to them, and the body of the Han is a most noble Hall, capable of holding 3 or 400 persons, the Court extreme spacious, and Cloisters round it that give it the air of our Colleges.¹ I own I think these foundations a more reasonable piece of charity than the founding of Convents.—I think I have now told you a great deal for once. If you don't like my choice of subjects, tell me what you would have me write upon. There is nobody more desirous to entertain you than, Dear Mrs. T[histlethwayte], etc.

Text H MS 253, pp. 266–80

'Heads of Letters' *1 April 1717*

Ap. 1, 1717

Countesse of Wackerbarth²
    I shant forget her tho I cant hope to see her.

Miss Griff:³
    Desire to continu to hear from her. No news. Fine Country.

S. G. [Sister (Lady) Gower]
    Hope she will [be] glad to hear we [are] all well. Compliments.

Ab. C. [Abbé Conti: *printed above, p. 315, n. 4*]⁴

¹ The hans are described in Dumont (pp. 160–1) and Hill (p. 132).
² Caterina Balbiano (1670–1719) m. (1707) August Christoph, Count von Wackerbarth, Field-Marshal of the King of Poland and his Ambassador to Vienna 1712–18 (F. Hausmann, *Repertorium der diplomatischen Vertreter*, 1936–50, ii. 332). Pöllnitz refers to her reputation as a clever woman (i. 146).
³ Probably this is Anne Griffith (d. 1719), Lady Rich's sister, who m. (*c.* 1718) William Stanhope, later 1st Earl of Harrington.
⁴ The actual letter is discussed above, pp. xv–xvi.

Mad^me Ki.[Kielmannsegge][1]
I won't tell how oft I have writ, I will think she
remembers me.[2] Balm of Mecca. Potargo.[3] Greek no
Slaves. Magnificence and dress of Turks. Bagnio Civillity.
French Ambassadresse. Ceremony. Pomp. Court to me.
Fine weather. One letter to serve for many. Nothing to
recompence. My picture.

L B^l [Lady Bristol: *printed above, p. 321, n. 1*]

L. R^h [Lady Rich]
She won't forget me. L[ady]G[odolphi]n.[4] Desire her
to write.[5] Mine will be dull. G[rand] S[ignor] handsome.
Sultana marry'd to the F[avourite]. Turkish verses.
Women not lock'd up. French Emb[assadress] and me in
several H[are]ms.

L. C^n [Lord Cadogan][6]
Not heard from him. Horse. Gratitude better ft
[? fortune] than exp[ecte]d.

M. Pp: [Pope: *printed above, p. 330, n. 1*]

Mrs. S^h [Smith][7]
Never heard from her. Dont suspect her F[riend]-
s[hi]p. Hope she'l be glad to hear I am wel.

[1] Sophia Charlotte von Platen (1675–
1725) m. (1701) Johann Adolf, Freiherr
von Kielmannsegge (d. 1717) *Familien-
Chronik . . . Kielmansegg*, ed. E. Kielmansegg, 1910, table III B). She was
one of George I's two mistresses resident
in England. LM later portrayed her
as having 'a greater vivacity in conversation than ever I knew in a German
of either sex. She loved reading, and
had a taste of all polite learning. Her
humour was easy and sociable. Her constitution inclined her to gallantry. She
was well bred and amusing in company'
('Account of George I', 1861, i. 128).

[2] On 28 Sept. 1717 [O.S.] Addison
forwarded to W a letter for LM from
Madame Kielmannsegge (*Letters*, ed.
W. Graham, 1941, p. 378).

[3] Botargo—a relish made of the roe

of the mullet or tunny (*OED*).

[4] Probably Henrietta Churchill
(1681–1733), wife of the 2nd Earl of
Godolphin and later Duchess of Marlborough in succession to her father. She
was Congreve's mistress (Kathleen M.
Lynch, *A Congreve Gallery*, 1951, p. 61).

[5] In June Pope forwarded to LM
letters from Lady Rich and from Congreve (*Corr.* i. 405).

[6] Probably William Cadogan (1672–
1726), Baron, later 1st Earl. He had
been an officer in Marlborough's army
and commander of a famous regiment
of cavalry. From 1716 to 1721 he served
as Ambassador to Holland.

[7] Probably the correspondent to
whom LM addressed the Embassy letter
from the Hague (see above, p. 250).

my F[ather (Duke of Kingston)]
    Letters miscarry. Places alike. Small pox. Dutys.[1]

S. M[r] [Sister (Lady) Mar: *printed above, p. 325, n. 3*]

P. of W. [Princess of Wales: *printed above, p. 310, n. 2*]

M. C[e] [Congreve]
    Forget all things but E[nglan]d. Cir[cassian] Slaves
not to be depended on. Ladys free. Healthy climate.
Fond of hearing. Omit no Occ[asion] remember my
f[riend]s. Where Orp[heus] etc.

H. V. [Henrietta Vernon][2]
    Answerd hers soon, never fail doing it. Sir R[ichard]
V[ernon]. D[?]n pritty. Desire to hear from her. L[ady]
B[?]ly. Dress becoming.

D. B. W. [Duchess of Brunswick-Wolfenbüttel][3]
    Commanded me to write. Descr[iption] Ad[rianople].
Serv[ian] desart. G[rand] S[ignor] handsome. His
D[aughter] marryd. Verses on her. Magnificence of Ladys,
not less sinners for not being Christians. Hope A. D. bn
in Victory.[4] Empress reign.

M. B[r] [Bothmer][5]
    3 letters since I heard.[6] Importunity. Projects. Very
weary. Ladys free.

Text W MS vii. 124   *End. by* W Heads of LM's Letters From Turky

---

1 LM mentions a letter from her father, perhaps a reply to this one, in her letter to W on 9 April [1718]. In 1715 her father had been created Duke of Kingston-upon-Hull.

2 Henrietta, da. of Sir Thomas Vernon, co-heiress of her brother, Sir Richard Vernon, British Envoy in Dresden.

3 Elisabeth von Holstein-Norburg (1683–1767), m. as 3rd wife (1710) August Wilhelm, Duke of Brunswick-Wolfenbüttel (Isenburg, i. 72). The Austrian Empress was his niece.

4 Probably 'Hope Archduke will be born in Victory'. The infant Archduke had died in the previous autumn; the Empress was about to bear another child—whose sex and good fortune LM tactfully foretells. But the child, born in May, was a girl (Maria Theresa); and the next victory was the Battle of Belgrade in Aug. 1717.

5 Johann Caspar, Count von Bothmer (1656–1732) (*ADB*). As Hanoverian agent in London, he was one of the King's two counsellors who almost entirely guided the inexperienced monarch (Basil Williams, *The Whig Supremacy*, 2nd ed., 1962, p. 153).

6 In a letter to LM, Charles Chevallier, a clerk in the Treasury, reported that he had received two packets of letters from her dated 1 April 1717, one

To Lady Mar *18 April* [*1717*]

Adrianople, Ap. 18. O.S.

I writ to you (dear Sister) and all my other English Correspondants by the last Ship, and only Heaven can tell when I shall have another Oppertunity of sending to you, but I cannot forbear writeing, thô perhaps my Letter may lie upon my hands this 2 Months. To confess the Truth my head is so full of my Entertainment yesterday that 'tis absolutely necessary for my own repose to give it some vent. Without farther preface I will then begin my Story.

I was invited to dine with the Grand Vizier's Lady and twas with a great deal of pleasure I prepar'd my selfe for an Entertainment which was never given before to any Christian. I thought I should very little satisfy her Curiosity (which I did not doubt was a considerable Motive to the Invitation) by going in a Dress she was us'd to see, and therefore dress'd my selfe in the Court habit of Vienna, which is much more Magnificent than ours. However, I chose to go incognito to avoid any disputes about Ceremony, and went in a Turkish coach only attended by my Woman that held up my Train and the Greek Lady who was my interpretress. I was met at the Court door by her black Eunuch, who help'd me out of the Coach with great Respect and conducted me through several rooms where Her She Slaves, finely dress'd, were rang'd on each side. In the innermost, I found the Lady siting on her Sofa in a Sable vest. She advanc'd to meet me and presented me halfe a dozen of her freinds with great Civillity. She seem'd a very good Woman, near 50 year old. I was surpriz'd to observe so little Magnificence in her House, the furniture being all very moderate, and except the Habits and Number of her Slaves nothing about her that appear'd expensive. She guess'd at my thoughts and told me that she was no longer of an Age to spend either her time or Money

by land and the other by sea, which arrived in London about three weeks apart. In the slower packet was one for Bothmer which LM asked Chevallier to deliver in person at Hampton Court

(4 Sept. 1717, W MS iv. 168). This suggests that LM dated so many letters on 1 April because they were dispatched on that day, as is corroborated by the opening sentence of her letter on 18 April.

in Superfluitys, that her whole expence was in charity and her Employment praying to God. There was no Affectation in this Speech; both she and her Husband are entirely given up to Devotion.[1] He never looks upon any other Woman, and what is much more extrodinary touches no bribes, notwithstanding the Example of all his Predecessors. He is so scrupulous in this point, he would not accept Mr. W[ortley]'s present till he had been assur'd over and over twas a settle'd perquisite of his place at the Entrance of every Ambassador.[2]

She entertain'd me with all kind of Civillity till Dinner came in, which was serv'd one Dish at a time, to a vast Number, all finely dress'd after their manner, which I do not think so bad as you have perhaps heard it represented. I am a very good Judge of their eating, having liv'd 3 weeks in the house of an Effendi at Belgrade who gave us very magnificent dinners dress'd by his own Cooks, which the first week pleas'd me extremely, but I own I then begun to grow weary of it and desir'd my own Cook might add a dish or 2 after our manner, but I attribute this to Custom. I am very much enclin'd to beleive an Indian that had never tasted of either would prefer their Cookery to ours. Their Sauces are very high, all the roast very much done. They use a great deal of rich Spice. The Soop is serv'd for the last dish, and they have at least as great Variety of ragoûts as we have. I was very sorry I could not eat of as many as the good Lady would have had me, who was very earnest in serving me of every thing. The Treat concluded with Coffée and perfumes, which is a high mark of respect. 2 slaves kneeling cens'd my Hair, Cloaths, and handkercheif.[3] After this Ceremony she commanded her Slaves to play and dance, which they did with their Guitars in their hands, and she excus'd to me their want of skill, saying she took no care to accomplish them in

---

[1] The Grand Vizier at this time was Arnand Khalil Pasha (*c.* 1655–1733), an Albanian, who had been in office since Aug. 1716. He was a mild, pious man (*Encyl. of Islam*, ii. 890).

[2] The French Ambassador had presented a magnificent clock, a chiming watch in a gold case, and cloth of gold and silver (Charles Schefer, *Mémoire historique sur l'ambassade de France à Constantinople par le marquis de Bonnac*, 1894, p. xxxii).

[3] Ingres copied the preceding two sentences, in French translation, into his notebooks (see above, p. 313, n. 1).

that art. I return'd her thanks and soon after took my Leave.

I was conducted back in the same Manner I enter'd, and would have gone strait to my own House, but the Greek Lady with me earnestly solicited me to visit the Kahya's Lady, saying he was the 2nd Officer in the Empire and ought indeed to be look'd upon as the first, the Grand Vizier having only the name while he exercis'd the authority. I had found so little diversion in this Haram that I had no mind to go into Another, but her importunity prevail'd with me, and I am extreme glad that I was so complaisant. All things here were with quite another Air than at the Grand Vizier's, and the very house confess'd the difference between an Old Devote and a young Beauty. It was nicely clean and magnificent. I was met at the door by 2 black Eunuchs who led me through a long Gallery between 2 ranks of beautifull young Girls with their Hair finely plaited almost hanging to their Feet, all dress'd in fine light damasks brocaded with silver. I was sorry that Decency did not permit me to stop to consider them nearer, but that Thought was lost upon my Entrance into a Large room, or rather Pavilion, built round with gilded sashes which were most of 'em thrown up; and the Trees planted near them gave an agreable Shade which hinder'd the Sun from being troublesome, the Jess'mins and Honey suckles that twisted round their Trunks sheding a soft perfume encreas'd by a white Marble fountain playing sweet Water in the Lower part of the room, which fell into 3 or 4 basons with a pleasing sound. The Roof was painted with all sort of Flowers falling out of gilded baskets that seem'd tumbling down.

On a sofa rais'd 3 steps and cover'd with fine Persian carpets sat the Kahya's Lady, leaning on cushions of white Satin embrodier'd, and at her feet sat 2 young Girls, the eldest about 12 year old, lovely as Angels, dress'd perfectly rich and allmost cover'd with Jewells. But they were hardly seen near the fair Fatima (for that is her Name), so much her beauty effac'd every thing. I have seen all that has been call'd lovely either in England or Germany, and must own that I never saw any thing so gloriously Beautifull, nor can I recollect a face that would have been taken notice of near hers. She stood up to receive me, saluteing me after their fashion, putting her hand upon her Heart with a sweetness full of Majesty that no Court breeding could ever give. She order'd Cushions to be given me and took care to place me in the Corner, which is the place of Honnour. I confesse, thô the Greek Lady had before given me a great Opinion of her beauty I was so struck with Admiration that I could not for some time speak to her, being wholly taken up in gazing. That surprizing Harmony of features! that charming result of the whole! that exact proportion of Body! that lovely bloom of Complexion unsully'd by art! the unutterable Enchantment of her Smile! But her Eyes! large and black with all the soft languishment of the bleu! every turn of her face discovering some new charm! After my first surprize was over, I endeavor'd by nicely examining her face to find out some imperfection, without any fruit of my search but being clearly convinc'd of the Error of that vulgar notion, that a face perfectly regular would not be agreable, Nature having done for her with more successe what Apelles[1] is said to have essay'd, by a Collection of the most exact features to form a perfect Face; and to that a behaviour so full of Grace and sweetness, such easy motions, with an Air so majestic yet free from Stiffness or affectation that I am perswaded could she be suddenly transported upon the most polite Throne of Europe, nobody would think her other than born and bred to be a Queen, thô educated in a Country we call barbarous. To say all in a Word, our most celebrated English Beautys would vanish near her.

She was dress'd in a Caftan of Gold brocade flowerd with Silver, very well fited to her Shape and shewing to advantage the beauty of her Bosom, only shaded by the Thin Gause of her shift. Her drawers were pale pink, Green and silver; her Slippers white, finely embrodier'd; her lovely Arms adorn'd with bracelets of Diamonds, and her broad Girdle set round with Diamonds; upon her Head a rich Turkish Handkercheif of pink and Silver, her own fine black Hair hanging a great length in various Tresses, and on one side of her Head some bodkins of Jewells. I am afraid you will accuse me of extravagance in this Description. I think I have

---

[1] The most celebrated Greek painter.

read somewhere that Women allways speak in rapture when they speak of Beauty, but I can't imagine why they should not be allow'd to do so. I rather think it Virtue to be able to admire without any Mixture of desire or Envy. The Gravest Writers have spoke with great warmth of some celebrated Pictures and Statues. The Workmanship of Heaven certainly excells all our weak Imitations, and I think has a much better claim to our Praise. For me, I am not asham'd to own I took more pleasure in looking on the beauteous Fatima than the finest piece of Sculpture could have given me. She told me the 2 Girls at her feet were her Daughters, thô she appear'd too young to be their Mother.

Her fair Maids were rang'd below the Sofa to the number of 20, and put me in Mind of the pictures of the ancient Nymphs. I did not think all Nature could have furnish'd such a Scene of Beauty. She made them a sign to play and dance. 4 of them immediately begun to play some soft airs on Instruments between a Lute and a Guitarr, which they accompany'd with their voices while the others danc'd by turns. This Dance was very different from what I had seen before. Nothing could be more artfull or more proper to raise certain Ideas, the Tunes so soft, the motions so Languishing, accompany'd with pauses and dying Eyes, halfe falling back and then recovering themselves in so artfull a Manner that I am very possitive the coldest and most rigid Prude upon Earth could not have look'd upon them without thinking of something not to be spoke of. I suppose you may have read that the Turks have no Music but what is shocking to the Ears,[1] but this account is from those who never heard any but what is play'd in the streets, and is just as reasonable as if a Foreigner should take his Ideas of the English Music from the bladder and string, and marrow bones and cleavers. I can assure you that the Music is extremely pathetic. 'Tis true I am enclin'd to prefer the Italian, But perhaps I am partial. I am acquainted with a Greek Lady who sings better than Mrs. Robinson,[2] and is very well skill'd in both, who gives the preference to the Turkish. Tis certain they have very fine Natural voices; these were very agreable.

[1] Hill, pp. 72–73.
[2] Anastasia Robinson (d. 1755),   *prima donna* of the London stage from 1714 to 1724.

When the Dance was over 4 fair slaves came into the room with silver Censors in their hands and perfum'd the air with Amber, Aloes wood and other rich Scents. After this they serv'd me coffée upon their knees in the finest Japan china with soûcoupes of Silver Gilt. The lovely Fatima entertain'd me all this time in the most polite agreable Manner, calling me often Uzelle Sultanam, or the beautifull Sultana, and desiring my Freindship with the best Grace in the World, lamenting that she could not entertain me in my own Language. When I took my Leave 2 Maids brought in a fine Silver basket of Embrodier'd Handkercheifs. She begg'd I would wear the richest for her sake, and gave the others to my Woman and Interpretress. I retir'd through the same Ceremonys as before, and could not help fancying I had been some time in Mahomet's Paradice, so much I was charm'd with what I had seen. I know not how the relation of it appears to you. I wish it may give you part of my pleasure, for I would have my dear Sister share in all the Diversions of etc.

Text H MS 253, pp. 281–99

'Heads of Letters' *18 April 1717*

Ap. 18, 1717

M. H^t [Mrs. Hewet: *printed above, p. 308, n. 6*]

M. T^t [Mrs. Thistlethwayte]
   Hope she judges too rightly of my heart to beleiv my silence can proceed from neglect. Hurry. All my family safe and well. Tenderly concernd for her. Mrs. ⟨ ?S⟩ hard fortune. No Distance can make me less hers.

Mrs. W^t [West]¹
   All well. Country much better than I expected. Complements.

---

¹ Probably Elizabeth (d. 1748), da.   West (*DNB sub* West; *London Mag.*, of Bishop Burnet, m. (1714) Richard   1748, p. 42).

Mrs. C[1] [Chiswell]

Pomp. Country agreable. No particulars. Homage.

L. D. D. [Lady Dowager Denbigh][1]

Hope her Goodness wil make her glad to hear I am wel. Family safe. Wish her Her health and Life.

Mr. W. F. [William Feilding][2]

Hope he'l be pleas'd to hear we're al wel. About my Money.[3]

M. Sch. [Mlle Schulenburg][4]

I don't know where she is.[5] If she has a mind to hav long leters from me, always at her service.

Text W MS vii. 124 *End. by W* Heads of LM's Letters From Turky

To the Abbé Conti *17 May* [*1717*]

Adrianople, May 17. O.S.

I am going to leave Adrianople, and I would not do it without giving some Account of all that is curious in it, which I have taken a great deal of pains to see. I will not trouble you with wise dissertations whither or no this is the same City that was anciently Orestesit or Oreste,[6] which you know better than I do. It is now call'd from the Emperour Adrian,[7] and was the first European seat of the Turkish

[1] LM's step-grandmother (see above, p. 228, n. 1).

[2] LM's uncle the Hon. William Feilding (d. 1723), Groom of the Bedchamber to the King and M.P. for Castle Rising. She sent this letter through Charles Chevallier, who on 4 Sept. 1717 acknowledged receiving and delivering it (W MS iv. 168).

[3] She had loaned her uncle £1,550, and now apparently asks him to return it, which he did with interest (see below, pp. 391, 393).

[4] Melusina von der Schulenburg (see her letter to LM, p. 245 above) had been created Duchess of Munster in the Irish Peerage on 18 July 1716. Since she was 'very angry at her not being an English

dutchesse' (R. Walpole to Stanhope, 10 Aug./30 July 1716 in William Coxe, *Memoirs of* . . . *Sir Robert Walpole*, 1798, ii. 59), LM may have been considerate in disregarding the Irish title.

[5] The Duchess, George I's favourite mistress, may have accompanied him to Hanover in July 1716; if so, LM is asking whether she has returned to England with him (in Jan. 1717).

[6] G. F. Gemelli Careri writes: '. . . Orestesit, Oreste, or Viscudama in former times, now in our language Adrianople, from the Emperor' (A. and J. Churchill, *Voyages*, 1704, iv. 59).

[7] The Emperor Hadrian (A.D. 76–138) enlarged and renamed the city.

Empire and has been the favourite Residence of many
Sultans. Mahomet the 4th, the father, and Mustapha, the
Brother of the reigning Emperour, were so fond of it that
they wholly abandonn'd Constantinople, which Humour so
far exasperated the Janizarys, it was a considerable Motive
to the Rebellions which depos'd them.[1] Yet this Man seems
to Love to keep his Court here. I can give no reason for this
Partiality. Tis true the Situation is fine and the Country all
round very beautifull, but the air is extreme bad and the
Seraglio it selfe is not free from the ill effect of it. The Town
is said to be 8 mile in compass; I suppose they reckon in the
Gardens. There are some good Houses in it; I mean large
ones, for the Architecture of their Palaces never makes any
great shew. It is now very full of people, but they are most of
them such as follow the Court or Camp, and when they are
remov'd, I am told, 'tis no populous City. The River Maritza
(anciently the Hebrus) on which it is situated is dry'd up
every Summer, which contributes very much to make it
unwholsome. It is now a very pleasant Stream; there are 2
noble bridges built over it. I had the Curiosity to go to see
the Exchange in my Turkish dress, which is disguise sufficient, yet I own I was not very easy when I saw it crowded
with Janizarys, but they dare not be rude to a Woman, and
made way for me with as much respect as if I had been in
my own figure. It is halfe a Mile in Length, the roofe
arch'd, and kept extremely neat. It holds 365 shops furnish'd with all sort of rich Goods expos'd to sale in the same
Manner as at the New Exchange in London,[2] but the pavement kept much neater, and the shops all so clean they
seem'd just new painted. Idle people of all sorts walk here
for their Diversion or amuse themselves with drinking coffee
or sherbet, which is cry'd about as Oranges and Sweetmeats
are in our Playhouses.

I observ'd most of the rich Tradesmen were Jews. That

[1] Mehmed IV (1642–93) was the
father, and Mustafa II the brother of
the reigning Ahmed III. According to
A. D. Alderson (*Structure of the Ottoman Dynasty*, 1956, p. 76) they were
deposed by the Viziers for military
failures; according to the *Encycl. of*
Islam (iii. 660–1, 760) their preferring
Adrianople made them lose favour.

[2] The New Exchange, 'a kind of
bazaar on the south side of the Strand',
became popular during the Restoration for its many shops (H. B. Wheatley,
London Past and Present, 1891, ii. 581).

people are in Incredible Power in this country.[1] They have
many priveleges above the natural Turks themselves, and
have form'd a very considerable common wealth here, being
judg'd by their own Laws, and have drawn the whole Trade
of the Empire into their Hands, partly by the firm Union
amongst themselves, and prevailing on the Idle temper and
want of Industry of the Turks. Every Bassa has his Jew who
is his Homme d'Affaires. He is let into all his secrets and
does all his busyness. No bargain is made, no bribe receiv'd,
no Merchandize dispos'd of but what passes through their
Hands. They are the Physicians, the Stewards, and the
Interpreters of all the Great Men. You may Judge how
advantageous this is to a people who never fail to make use
of the smallest advantages. They have found the secret of
makeing themselves so necessary, they are certain of the
protection of the Court whatever Ministry is in power. Even
the English, French and Italian Merchants, who are sensible
of their artifices, are however forc'd to trust their affairs to
their Negotiation, nothing of Trade being manag'd without
'em, and the meanest amongst them is too important to be
disoblig'd since the whole body take care of his Interests with
as much Vigour as they would those of the most considerable
of their Members. They are many of 'em vastly rich, but
take care to make little public shew of it, thô they live in their
Houses in the utmost Luxury and Magnificence. This
copious subject has drawn me from my Description of the
Exchange founded by Ali Bassa, whose name it bears.[2] Near
it is the Shershi, a street of a mile in Length, full of shops
of all kind of fine Merchandize but excessive dear, nothing
being made here. It is cover'd on the Top with boards to keep
out the rain, that Merchants may meet conveniently in all
Weathers. The Bisisten near it is another Exchange, built
upon Pillars, where all sort of horse furniture is sold; glittering every where with Gold, rich Embrodiery and Jewels,
[it] makes a very agreable shew.

From this place I went in my Turkish Coach to the Camp,

[1] Others travellers remarked on the
power of the Jews, who controlled
banking and trade in the Levant
(Dumont, p. 300; Aubry de La Mottraye, *Travels through Europe, Asia . . .*,
1723–32, i. 153).
[2] Ali Pasha, the Grand Vizier killed
at the Battle of Peterwardein in Aug.
1716 (see above, p. 321, n. 3).

which is to move in a few days to the frontiers. The Sultan is allready gone to his Tents, and all his Court. The Appearance of them is indeed very Magnificent. Those of the great Men are rather like palaces than Tents, takeing up a great Compass of Ground and being divided into a vast number of Apartments.[1] They are all of Green, and the Bassas of 3 Tails have those Ensigns of their power plac'd in a very conspicuous manner before their Tents,[2] which are adorn'd on the Top with Gilded Balls, more or less according to their different Ranks. The Ladys go in their Coaches to see this camp as eagerly as ours did to that of Hide Park,[3] but 'tis easy to observe that the Soldeirs do not begin the Campaign with any great cheerfullness. The War is a general Greivance upon the people but particularly hard upon the Tradesmen.

Now the Grand Signor is resolv'd to lead his Army in Person, every company of 'em is oblig'd upon this Occassion to make a present according to their Abillity. I took the pains of rising at 6 in the Morning to see that Ceremony, which did not however begin till 8. The Grand Signor was at the Seraglio Window to see the procession, which pass'd through all the principal Streets. It was preceded by an Effendi mounted on a Camel richly furnish'd, reading aloud the Alcoran, finely Bound, laid upon a Cushion. He was surrounded by a parcel of Boys in white, singing some verses of it, follow'd by a Man dress'd in Green Boughs representing a Clean Husband Man sowing Seed· After him several reapers with Garlands of Ears of Corn, as Ceres is pictur'd, with Scythes in their hands seeming to Mow; Then a little Machine drawn by Oxen, in which was a Windmill and boys employ'd in grinding corn, follow'd by another Machine drawn by Buffolos carrying an Oven and 2 more Boys, one employ'd in kneading the bread, and another in drawing it out of the Oven. These boys threw little Cakes on both sides amongst the Croud, and were follow'd by the whole

---

[1] The sumptuous luxury of the tents is described by Hill, p. 28.

[2] Pashas were of three grades, distinguished by the number of horsetails (1, 2, or 3) which they were entitled to display as symbols of authority.

[3] In July 1715, during the Jacobite rebellion, Pope wrote to the Blount sisters about the encampment of soldiers in Hyde Park, and concluded: 'The sight of so many thousand gallant Fellows . . . may possibly invite your Curiosity to this place' (*Corr.* i. 308).

Company of Bakers marching on foot, 2 and 2, in their best Cloaths, with Cakes, Loaves, pastys, and pies of all sorts on their heads; and after them 2 Buffoons or Jack puddings with their faces and Cloaths smear'd with Meal, who diverted the Mob with their Antick Gestures. In the same Manner follow'd all the Companys of Trade in their Empire, the nobler sort, such as Jewellers, Mercers, etc., finely Mounted, and many of the Pageants that represented their Trades perfectly Magnificent; amongst which the Furriers made one of the best Figures, being a very large Machine set round with the Skins of Ermins, Foxes, etc., so well stuff'd the Animals seem'd to be alive, follow'd by Music and dancers. I beleive they were, upon the whole, at least 20,000 Men, all ready to follow his highness if he commanded them.[1]

The rear was clos'd by the Volunteers, who came to beg the Honnour of dying in his Service. This part of the shew seem'd to me so barbarous I remov'd from the Window upon the first appearance of it. They were all naked to the Middle, their Arms peirc'd throû with Arrows left sticking in 'em, others had 'em sticking in their heads, the blood trickling down their faces, and some slash'd their arms with sharp knives, makeing the blood spout out upon those that stood near; and this is look'd upon as an Expression of their Zeal for Glory.[2] I am told that some make use of it to advance their Love, and when they are near the Window where their Mistriss stands (all the Women in Town being vail'd to see this Spectacle) they stick another Arrow for her sake, who gives some sign of Approbation and Encourragment to this Galantry. The whole shew lasted near 8 hours, to my great sorrow, who was heartily tir'd, thô I was in the House of the Widow of the Capitan Bassa (Admiral), who refresh'd me with Coffée, Sweetmeats, Sherbet, etc., with all possible Civillity.

I went 2 days after to see the Mosque of Sultan Selim the

---

[1] Such a procession, to the camp outside Constantinople in 1715, is briefly described by Paul Lucas, who singles out as the most spectacular 'les Foureurs, les Tireurs d'Or, & les Tailleurs' (*Troisième Voyage*, 1719, i. 107–8).

[2] Sieur Du Loir tells (in 1640) how the soldiers in a military procession demonstrated their affection for the Sultan by piercing their temples with arrows and their arms with muskets (*Voyages*, 1654, p. 127).

1st, which is a Building very well worth the Curiosity of a Traveller.[1] I was dress'd in my Turkish habit and admitted without Scrupule, thô I beleive they guess'd who I was, by the Extreme Officiousness of the door keeper to shew me every part of it. It is situated very advantageously in the Midst of the city and in the highest part, makeing a very Noble Show. The first Court has 4 Gates and the innermost 3. They are both of them surrounded with cloisters with Marble pillars of the Ionic order, finely polish'd and of very lively Colours, the whole pavement being white Marble, the roofe of the Cloisters being divided into several Cupelos or Domes, leaded, with Gilt Balls on the Top, in the midst of each Court fine Fountains of white Marble, before the Great Gate of the Mosque a Portico with green Marble Pillars.

It has 5 Gates, the body of the Mosque being one prodigious Dome. I understand so little of Architecture I dare not pretend to speak of the proportions; it seem'd to me very regular. This I am sure of, it is vastly high; and I thought it the noblest building I ever saw. It had 2 rows of marble Gallerys on Pillars with marble Balustres, the pavement marble Cover'd with Persian Carpets; and in my Opinion it is a great addition to its beauty that it is not divided into pues and encumber'd with forms and benches like our churches, nor the Pillars (which are most of 'em red and white marble) disfigur'd by the little tawdry images and pictures that give the Roman Catholic churches the air of Toy shops. The walls seem'd to me inlaid with such very lively colours in small flowers, I could not imagine what stones had been made use of; but going nearer, I saw they were crusted with Japan China which has a very beautifull Effect. In the midst hung a vast Lamp of Silver gilt, besides which I do verily beleive there was at least 2,000 of a lesser size. This must look very glorious when they are all lighted, but that being at Night no Women are suffer'd to enter. Under the large lamp is a great pulpit of carv'd wood gilt and just by it a fountain to wash, which you know is an Essential part of their devotion. In one Corner is a little Gallery enclos'd with Gilded Lattices for the

---

[1] LM means the Mosque of Selim II, built 1568–74, the most celebrated   building in Adrianople (*Encycl. of Islam*, ii. 3).

Grand Signor; at the upper End, a large Niche very like
an Altar, rais'd 2 steps, cover'd with Gold Brocade, and
standing before it 2 silver Gilt Candlesticks the Height of
a Man and in them white Wax Candles as thick as a man's
waste. The outside of the Mosque is adorn'd with 4 Towers
vastly high, gilt on the Top, from whence the Imaums call
the people to prayers. I had the curiosity to go up one of
them, which is contriv'd so artfully as to give Surprize to all
that see it. There is but one door, which leads to 3 different
stair cases going to the 3 different storys of the Tower in
such a Manner that 3 priests may ascend rounding without
ever meeting each other, a contrivance very much admir'd.
Behind the Mosque is an Exchange full of shops where poor
Artificers are lodg'd Gratis. I saw several Dervises at their
prayers here. They are dress'd in a plain peice of Woolen
with their arms bare and a Woolen Cap on their heads like
a high crown'd Hat without brims.[1] I went to see some other
Mosques built much after the same Manner, but not comparable in point of Magnificence to this I have describ'd,
which is infinitely beyond any Church in Germany or England. I won't talk of other Countrys I have not seen. The
Seraglio does not seem a very Magnificent palace, but the
Gardens very large, plentifully supply'd with Water, and
full of Trees, which is all I know of 'em, having never been
in them.

I tell you nothing of the Order of Mr. W[ortley's] entry
and his Audience.[2] Those things are allways the same and
have been so often describ'd, I won't trouble you with the
repetition.[3] The Young Prince, about 11 year old, sits near
his Father when he gives Audience. He is a handsome boy,
but probably will not immediately succeed the Sultan, there
being 2 Sons of Sultan Mustapha (his eldest brother) remaining, the Eldest about 20 year old, on whom the hopes
of the people are fix'd.[4] This reign has been bloody and

---

[1] LM gives a fuller account of the
dervishes in her letter of 10 April 1718
(pp. 402–3 below).

[2] W had his audience with the Grand
Vizier on 11 April/31 March and with
the Sultan on 18/7 April (*London
Gazette*, 4–8 June 1717).

[3] The ceremony had been described
by, among others, Dumont (pp. 168–
74), George Sandys (*Travels*, 7th ed.,
1673, p. 58), and Du Loir (pp. 87–88).

[4] The young Prince was Süleyman
(1710–32), then nearly seven years old
(Alderson, Table XLI). Bonnac, the

avaritious. I am apt to beleive they are very impatient to see the End of it. I am, Sir, your etc.

I will write to you again from Constantinople.

Text H MS 253, pp. 299–319

To the Abbé Conti *29 May* [*1717*]

Constantinople, May 29. O.S.

I have had the advantage of very fine weather all my Journey, and the Summer being now in its beauty, I enjoy'd the pleasure of fine prospects; and the meadows being full of all sort of Garden flowers and sweet herbs, my Berlin perfum'd the air as it press'd 'em. The Grand Signor furnish'd us with 30 cover'd Waggons for our Baggage and 5 Coaches of the Country for my Women. We found the Road full of the great Spahys and their Equipages, coming out of Assia to the War. They allways travel with tents, but I chose to lye in Houses all the way. I will not trouble you with the names of the Villages we pass'd in which there was nothing remarkable, but at Ciorlu[1] we were lodg'd in a Conac, or little Seraglio, built for the use of the Grand Signor when he goes this road. I had the curiosity to veiw all the Apartments destin'd for the Ladys of his Court. They were in the midst of a thick grove of Trees, made fresh by fountains, but I was surpriz'd to see the Walls almost cover'd with little distichs of Turkish verse writ with pencils. I made my Interpreter explain them to me and I found several of them very well turn'd, thô I easily beleiv'd him that they lost much of their Beauty in the Translation. One runs litterally thus in English:

French Ambassador, also observed him at an audience with the Sultan, and thought him 'doué d'une physionomie assez agréable' (Charles Schefer, *Mémoire historique sur l'ambassade de France à Constantinople par le marquis de Bonnac*, 1894, p. xxxiii). Mustafa II's two sons who did become sultans were Mahmud I (1696–1754) and Osman III (1699–1757); a third son, overlooked by LM, was Hasan (1699–1733) (Alderson, Tables XL, XLII).

[1] Mentioned also by John Covel, who travelled the same route in the opposite direction in the 1670's ('Extracts from the Diaries,' *Early Voyages and Travels in the Levant*, ed. J. T. Bent, Hakluyt Soc., vol. 87, 1893, p. 180).

> We come into this World, we lodge, and we depart;
> He never goes that's lodgd within my Heart.

The rest of our Journey was through fine painted Meadows by the side of the sea of Marmora, the ancient Propontis. We lay the next night at Selivrea, anciently a noble Town. It is now a very good sea port, and neatly built enough, and has a bridge of 32 Arches.[1] Here is a famous ancient Greek church.[2] I had given one of my Coaches to a Greek Lady who desir'd the Conveniency of travelling with me. She design'd to pay her Devotions and I was glad of the Oppertunity of going with her. I found it an ill built place, set out with the same sort of Ornaments but less rich than the Roman Catholic Churches. They shew'd me a saint's body, where I threw a piece of Money, and a Picture of the Virgin Mary drawn by the hand of St. Luke, very little to the Credit of his painting, but, however, the finest Madona of Italy is not more famous for her Miracles.[3] The Greeks have the most monstrous taste in their pictures, which for more finery are allways drawn upon a gold Ground. You may imagine what a good air this has, but they have no notion either of shade or proportion. They have a Bishop here, who officiated in his purple Robe, and sent me a Candle almost as big as my selfe for a present when I was at my Lodging.

We lay the next Night at a Town call'd Büjük Cekmege or Great bridge, and the night following at Kujük Cekmege, little Bridge, in a very pleasant Lodging, formerly a Monastery of Dervises, having before it a large Court encompass'd with marble Cloisters with a good Fountain in the middle.[4] The prospect from this place and the Gardens round it are the most agreable I have seen, and shews that Monks of all Religions know how to chuse their

---

[1] Covel also counted 32 arches in the 'very fair stone bridge' (ibid.).

[2] Richard Pococke also observed an old Greek church 'adorned with Mosaic of the middle ages' (*Description of the East*, 1743–5, II, ii. 139).

[3] Covel was shown the images reputed to have been painted by saints (*Some Account of the Present Greek Church*,

1722, p. 374).

[4] Covel describes the lodging thus: 'There is a pretty large court . . . one story high, with cloysters and little chambers (with chimneys) round about, and a fountain in the middest. All passengers carry their own beds, or mats, or quilts to sleep on and set on. . . .' (*Early Voyages*, p. 175).

Retirements. Tis now belonging to a Hogia or School-master, who teaches boys here; and asking him to shew me his own Apartment I was surprizd to see him point to a tall Cypress Tree in the Garden, on the Top of which was a place for a bed for himselfe, and a little lower, one for his wife and 2 Children, who slept there every Night. I was so much diverted with the fancy I resolv'd to examine his Nest nearer, but after going up 50 steps, I found I had still 50 to go and then I must climb from Branch to branch with some hazard of my Neck. I thought it the best way to come down again.

We arriv'd the next Evening at Constantinople,[1] but I can yet tell you very little of it, all my time having been taken up with receiving visits, which are at least a very good Enter-tainment to the Eyes, the young Women being all Beautys and their beauty highly improv'd by the good taste of their dress. Our Palace is in Pera, which is no more a suburb of Constantinople than Westminster is a suburb to London. All the Ambassadors are lodg'd very near each other. One part of our House shews us the Port, the City and the Seraglio, and the distant hills of Assia, perhaps all together the most beautifull Prospect in the World. A certain French Author[2] says that Constantinople is twice as large as Paris. Mr. W[ortley] is unwilling to own 'tis bigger than London, thô I confess it appears to me to be so, but I don't beleive tis so populous. The burying feilds about it are certainly much larger than the whole City. 'Tis surprizing what a vast deal of Land is lost this way in Turkey. Sometimes I have seen burying places of several miles belonging to very inconsider-able Villages which were formerly great Towns and retain no other mark of their Ancient Grandeur. On no Occasion they remove a stone that serves for a Monument. Some of them are costly enough, being of very fine marble. They set up a pillar with a carv'd Turbant on the Top of it to the memory of a Man, and as the Turbants by their different shapes shew the Quality or profession, tis in a manner putting up the arms of the deceas'd; besides, the pillar commonly bears a large inscription in Gold Letters. The Ladys have a simple Pillar without other Ornament, except those that dye

[1] On 28 May O.S. (Tickell MS).   [2] Dumont, p. 147.

unmarry'd, who have a Rose on the Top of it. The Sepulchres of particular familys are raild in and planted round with Trees. Those of the Sultans and some great Men have lamps constantly burning in them.

When I spoke of their Religion I forgot to mention 2 particularitys, one of which I had read of, but it seem'd so odd to me I could not beleive it. Yet tis certainly true that when a Man has divorc'd his wife in the most solemn manner, he can take her again upon no other Terms than permitting Another Man to pass a night with her, and there are some Examples of those that have submitted to this Law rather than not have back their Beloved.[1] The other point of Doctrine is very extrodinary: any Woman that dyes unmarry'd is look'd upon to dye in a state of reprobation. To confirm this beleife, they reason that the End of the Creation of Woman is to encrease and Multiply,[2] and she is only properly employ'd in the Works of her calling when she is bringing children or takeing care of 'em, which are all the Virtues that God expects from her; and indeed their way of Life, which shuts them out of all public commerce, does not permit them any other. Our Vulgar Notion that they do not own Women to have any Souls is a mistake.[3] Tis true they say they are not of so elevated a kind and therefore must not hope to be admitted into the paradise apointed for the Men, who are to be entertain'd by Celestial Beautys; but there is a place of Happyness destin'd for Souls of the Inferior Order, where all good Women are to be in Eternal bliss.[4] Many of 'em are very superstitious and will not remain Widows 10 days for fear of dying in the reprobate state of a useless

[1] Although this was true, as other travellers including Paul Rycaut observed (*Present State of the Ottoman Empire*, 1668, p. 156), Joseph de Tournefort writes that the husband usually chose a friend whose tactful continence he could rely on (*Relation d'un voyage du Levant*, 1717, ii. 89).

[2] Here LM echoes Hill: ' "Encrease and Multiply" is considered a very good and necessary maxim by the Turkish nation' (p. 98).

[3] Its popular expression can be seen in George Farquhar's *The Beaux'*

Stratagem (1707), where the rebellious Mrs. Sullen says: 'Were I born an humble Turk, where women have no soul nor property, there I must sit contented' (Act IV, Scene i).

[4] Jean de Thévenot (*Travels into the Levant*, transl. 1687, i. 56) states that they do not enjoy any Paradise. LM's version is similar to Robert Withers's that 'women also shall come into heaven, but shall be in a place far inferior to men, and be less glorified' (*A Description of the Grand Signor's Seraglio . . .*, 1650, p. 173).

Creature.[1] But those that like their Liberty and are not slaves to their Religion content themselves with marrying when they are afraid of dying. This is a piece of Theology very different from that which teaches nothing to be more acceptable to God than a vow of perpetual Virginity. Which Divinity is most rational I leave you to determine.

I have allready made some progress in a Collection of Greek Medals. Here are several profess'd antiquarys who are ready to serve any body that desires them, but you can't imagine how they stare in my Face when I enquire about 'em, as if no body was permitted to seek after Medals till they were grown a piece of antiquity them selves. I have got some very valuable of the Macedonian Kings, particularly one of Perseus, so lively I fancy I can see all his ill Qualitys in his face.[2] I have a Porphyry Head finely cut of the true Greek Sculpture, but who it represents is to be guess'd at by the Learned when I return, for you are not to suppose these antiquarys (who are all Greeks) know any thing. Their Trade is only to sell. They have Correspondants at Aleppo, Grand Cairo, in Arabia, and Palestine, who send them all they can find, and very often great heaps that are only fit to melt into pans and Kettles. They get the best price they can for any of 'em, without knowing those that are valuable from those that are not. Those that pretend to skill generally find out the image of some Saint in the Medals of the Greek Citys. One of them, shewing me the figure of a Pallas with a victory in her hand on a reverse, assur'd me it was the Virgin holding a Crucifix. The same Man offer'd me the head of a Socrates on a Sardonix, and to enhance the value gave him the Title of St. Augustin. I have bespoke a Mummy, which I hope will come safe to my hands, notwithstanding the misfortune that befell a very fine one design'd for the King of Sweden.[3] He gave a great Price for it, and the Turks

---

[1] LM's theology is wrong: matrimony does not affect the spiritual fate of Muslim women; and a widow is forbidden to remarry for a period of four months and ten nights (*Koran*, Surah 2 : 234; G. F. Gemelli Careri in A. and J. Churchill, *Voyages*, 1704, iv. 94).

[2] After having his brother murdered, Perseus, last king of the Macedonians, reigned from 179 to 168 B.C.

[3] Charles XII (1682–1718), who after being defeated in 1709 remained near Adrianople until 1714 as a 'guest' of the Turks.

took it into their heads that he must certainly have some considerable project depending upon't. They fancy'd it the body of God knows who, and that the Fate of their Empire mystically depended on the Conservation of it. Some old prophecys were remember'd upon this Occasion, and the Mummy committed prisoner to the 7 Towers,[1] where it has remain'd under close Confinement ever since. I dare not try my Interest in so considerable a point as the release of it, but I hope mine will pass without Examination.—I can tell you nothing more at present of this famous City. When I have look'd a little about me you shall hear from me again. I am, Sir, etc.

Text H MS 253, pp. 320–35

To Alexander Pope *17 June* [*1717*]

Belgrade Village,[2] June 17. O.S.[3]

I hope before this time you have receiv'd 2 or 3 of my letters. I had Yours but yesterday, thô dated the 3rd of Feb., in which You Suppose me to be dead and bury'd.[4] I have already let you know that I am Still alive, but to say Truth I look upon my present Circumstances to be exactly the Same with those of departed Spirits. The Heats of Constantinople have driven me to this place which perfectly answers the Description of the Elysian fields. I am in the

---

[1] An ancient castle, on the south-east side of Constantinople, used to safeguard state prisoners (Hill, p. 146).

[2] W wrote to Addison on 18 July O.S. 'We pass our time chiefly at a Country house ten miles from Constantinople, this being the Plague season, tho there is little of it this year' (Tickell MS). The village is described by Edmund Chishull (*Travels in Turkey . . .*, 1747, p. 43) and by James Dallaway (*Constantinople*, 1797, p. 147). One hundred years later John Hobhouse identified the site of LM's 'mansion . . . an object of curiosity to every traveller' (*A Journey through Albania . . . to Con-*

stantinople, 2nd ed., 1813, ii. 861).

[3] Among the 'Heads' of LM's letters under the date 1 Aug. 1717 is one addressed to Pope, and summarized only as 'Copyd at length'. This Embassy letter of 17 June is, in fact, not in her holograph—as all the preceding ones are—but in the hand of a copyist. Pope answered her actual letter in [Oct. 1717] (*Corr.* i. 439–42).

[4] Pope had imagined her as dead but not buried—unless she took that to be his meaning in: 'may you appear to distant Worlds like a Sun that is sunk out of the sight of our Hemisphere, to gladden the other' (*Corr.* i. 389).

Midle of a Wood consisting chiefly of fruit Trees, water'd by a Vast number of Fountains famous for the Excellency of their water, and divided into many Shady Walks upon short grass, that seems to me Artificial but I am assur'd is the pure work of Nature, within View of the Black Sea, from whence we perpetually enjoy the Refreshment of cool breezes that makes us insensible of the heat of the Summer. The Village is wholly Inhabited by the richest amongst the Christians, who meet every night at a fountain 40 paces from my house to Sing and dance, the Beauty and dress of the women exactly resembling the Ideas of the Ancient Nymphs as they are given us by the representations of the Poets and Painters. But what perswades me more fully of my Decease is the Situation of my own Mind, the profound Ignorance I am in of what passes amongst the Living, which only comes to me by chance, and the great Calmness with which I receive it. Yet I have still a hankering after my friends and Acquaintance left in the World, according to the Authority of that Admirable Author,

> That ⟨Spirits⟩ departed are wondrous kind
> To friends and Relations left behind,
>   Which no body can deny,

of which Solemn Truth I am a dead Instance. I think Virgil is of the Same Opinion, That in Human Souls There will still be some remains of Human Passions.

> —Curæ non ipsâ in Morte relinquunt;[1]

and 'tis very necessary to make a perfect Elyzium that there shou'd be a River Lethe, which I am not So happy to find. To Say Truth, I am Sometimes very weary of this Singing and dancing and Sunshine, and wish for the Smoak and Impertinencies in which You toil, thô I endeavour to perswade my Self that I live in a more agreeable Variety than You do, and that Monday Seting of partridges, Tuesday reading English, Wednesday Studying the Turkish Language (in which, by the way, I am already very learned), Thursday Classical Authors, Friday spent in Writing, Saturday at my Needle, and Sunday admitting of Visits and hearing Musick, is a better way of disposing the Week than Monday at the

---

[1] 'Even in death the pangs leave them not' (*Aeneid,* vi. 444, transl. Loeb Library).

Drawing Room, Tuesday Lady Mohun's,[1] Wednesday the Opera, Thursday the Play, Friday Mrs. Chetwynd's,[2] etc.: a perpetual round of hearing the same Scandal and seeing the same follies acted over and over, which here affect me no more than they do other dead people. I can now hear of displeasing things with Pity and without Indignation. The Reflection on the great Gulph between You and Me cools all News that comes hither. I can neither be sensibly touch'd with Joy or Grief when I consider that possibly the Cause of either is remov'd befor the Letter comes to my hands; but (as I said before) this Indolence does not extend to my few friendships. I am still warmly sensible of Yours and Mr. C⟨ongreve's⟩[3] and desire to live in your remembrances, thô dead to all the World beside.

Text H MS 253, pp. 336–8

To Lady ——— *17 June* [*1717*]

Belgrade Village, June 17. O.S.

I heartily beg your Ladyship's pardon, but I realy could not forbear laughing heartily at your Letter and the Commissions you are pleas'd to honnour me with. You desire me to buy you a Greek slave who is to be mistrisse of a thousand good Qualitys. The Greeks are subjects and not slaves. Those who are to be bought in that manner are either such as are taken in War or stole by the Tartars from Russia, Circassia or Georgia, and are such miserable, aukard, poor Wretches, you would not think any of 'em worthy to be your House-maid. 'Tis true that many thousands were taken in the Morea, but they have been most of them redeem'd by the charitable Contributions of the Christians or ransom'd by their own Relations at Venice. The fine slaves that wait

[1] Elizabeth Lawrence (d. 1725), widow of Col. Edward Griffith, and mother of Lady Rich, m. (before March 1711) 4th Baron Mohun, killed in 1712 in the famous duel with the Duke of Hamilton.

[2] The house of Mrs. Chetwynd (see above, p. 75, n. 2) was noted as a gossip-centre. 'Now Mrs. Chetwynde's out of town I have no opportunity to learn any Lady's news' (Craggs to Newcastle, 15 July 1714, Add. MS 32, 686, ff. 16–17: also John Hervey, *Letter-Books*, 1894, i. 326, 352).

[3] Struck out by LM.

upon the great Ladys, or serve the Pleasures of the great Men, are all bought at the age of 8 or 9 year old and educated with great care to accomplish 'em in singing, danceing, Embrodiery, etc. They are commonly Circassians, and their Patron never sells them except it is as a Punishment for some very great fault. If ever they grow weary of 'em, they either present them to a freind or give them their freedoms. Those that are expos'd to sale at the Markets are allways either guilty of some Crime or so entirely worthless that they are of no use at all. I am afraid you'l doubt the Truth of this Account, which I own is very different from our common Notions in England, but it is not less truth for all that.

Your whole Letter is full of mistakes from one end to 'tother. I see you have taken your Ideas of Turkey from that worthy author Dumont, who has writ with equal ignorance and confidence.[1] Tis a particular pleasure to me here to read the voyages to the Levant, which are generally so far remov'd from Truth and so full of Absurditys I am very well diverted with 'em. They never fail giving you an Account of the Women, which 'tis certain they never saw, and talking very wisely of the Genius of the Men, into whose Company they are never admitted, and very often describe Mosques, which they dare not peep into. The Turks are very proud, and will not converse with a Stranger they are not assur'd is considerable in his own Country. I speak of the Men of Distinction, for as to the Ordinary Fellows, you may imagine what Ideas their Conversation can give of the general Genius of the people.

As to the Balm of Mecha, I will certainly send you some, but it is not so easily got as you suppose it, and I cannot in Conscience advise you to make use of it.[2] I know not how it comes to have such universal Applause. All the Ladys of my acquaintance at London and Vienna have begg'd me to send Pots of it to them. I have had a present of a small Quantity (which I'll assure you is very valuable) of the best sort, and

---

[1] Jean Dumont (d. 1726), French historian; his *Nouveau Voyage au Levant* (1694) was translated into English in 1696.

[2] For the fabulous Balm of Mecca, whose formula was a secret of the Sultans, see H. F. M. Prescott, *Once to Sinai*, 1958, pp. 119–22.

with great joy apply'd it to my face, expecting some wonderfull Effect to my advantage. The next morning the change
indeed was wonderfull; my face was swell'd to a very extrodinary size and all over as red as my Lady ⟨?⟩'s. It remain'd
in this lamentable state 3 days, during which you may be
sure I pass'd my time very ill. I beleiv'd it would never be
otherwise, and to add to my Mortification Mr. W[ortley]
reproach'd my indiscretion without ceasing. However, my
Face is since in statu quo. Nay, I am told by the Ladys
here that tis much mended by the operation, which I confess
I cannot perceive in my Looking Glasse. Indeed, if one was
to form an opinion of this Balm from their faces, one should
think very well of it. They all make use of it and have the
loveliest bloom in the world. For my part, I never intend to
endure the pain of it again;—let my Complexion take its
natural course and decay in its own due time. I have very
little Esteem for med'cines of this Nature; but do as you
please, Madam, only remember before you use it that your
face will not be such as you'l care to shew in the drawing
room for some days after.

If one was to beleive the Women in this Country, there
is a surer way of makeing one's selfe belov'd than by becoming handsome, thô you know that's our Method. But they
pretend to the knowledge of secrets that by way of Enchantment gives them the Entire Empire over whom they please.
For me, that am not very apt to beleive in Wonders, I cannot
find faith for this. I disputed the point last night with a Lady
who realy talks very sensibly on any other Subject, but she
was downright angry with me that she did not perceive she
had perswaded me of the Truth of 40 storys she told me of
this kind, and at last mention'd several ridiculous marriages
that there could be no other reason assign'd for. I assur'd
her that in England, where we were entirely ignorant of all
Magic, where the Climate is not halfe so warm nor the
Women halfe so handsome, we were not without our ridiculous Marriages; and that we did not look upon it as any thing
supernatural when a Man plaid the fool for the sake of a
Woman. But my Arguments could not convince her against
(as she said) her certain knowledge, thô she added that she
scrupul'd makeing use of Charms her selfe, but that she could

do it whenever she pleas'd and, staring in my face, said (with a very learned air) that no Enchantments would have their Effect upon me, and that there were Some people exempt from their power, but very few. You may imagine how I laugh'd at this discourse, but all the Women here are of the Same Opinion. They don't pretend to any Commerce with the Devil, but that there are certain Compositions to inspire Love. If one could send over a ship Load of them I fancy it would be a very quick way of raising an Estate. What would not some Ladys of our acquaintance give for such Merchandize?

Adeiu my dear Lady——, I cannot conclude my Letter with a subject that affords more delightfull scenes to Imagination. I leave you to figure to your selfe the extreme Court that will be made to me at my return if My travells should furnish me with such a usefull piece of Learning. I am, Dear Madam, etc.

Text H MS 253, pp. 339–49

'Heads of Letters' *1 Aug. 1717*[1]

Aug't 1, 1717

Mr. Pp [Pope]
　　Copyd at length.[2]
Mr. C. [Congreve]
　　Predestination.

Text W MS vii. 124   *End. by W* Heads of LM's Letters From Turky

[1] During the next five months there are neither Embassy letters nor 'Heads of Letters'. LM remained in Constantinople when W left, on 12 Sept. O.S., for the Sultan's camp (Hefferman to [Addison], Sophia, 7 Oct. 1717 O.S., SP 97/24). While carrying on his diplomatic negotiations he was notified by Addison, writing with extreme tact from London on 28 Sept. O.S., that the King had ordered his recall (*Letters*, ed. W. Graham, 1941, pp. 376–8). (In August the decisive victory of the Austrians in capturing Belgrade had made it clear—except to W—that any attempt at mediation should recognize their superior bargaining position. For details of his negotiations, see Halsband, *LM*, pp. 76–79.)

[2] Her Embassy letter to Pope, dated 17 June [1717] (p. 365 above), was indeed 'copied at length' into the MS of the Embassy Letters.

To Alexander Pope *1 Sept. 1717*

[A spurious letter, printed 1767, pp. 24–36; 1861, i. 336–9]

To [Anne] Thistlethwayte[1] *4 Jan.* [*1718*]

Pera of Constantinople, Jan. 4.

I am Infinitely oblig'd to you, Dear Mrs. T⟨histle-thwayte⟩,[2] for your entertaining Letter. You are the only One of my Correspondants that have Judg'd right enough to think I wou'd gladly be inform'd of the News amongst you. All the rest of 'em tell me (almost in the same words) that they Suppose I know everything. Why they are pleas'd to Suppose in this manner, I can guess no reason except they are perswaded that the breed of Mahomet's Pigeon still Subsists in this Countrey and that I receive Supernatural Intelligence.[3] I wish I could return Your goodness with Some diverting Accounts from hence, but I know not what part of the Scenes here wou'd gratify Your Curiosity or whether You have any Curiosity at all for things so far distant. To say the truth, I am at this present writing not very much turn'd for the recollection of what is diverting, my head being wholly fill'd with the preparations necessary for the Encrease of my family, which I expect every day.[4] You may

---

[1] Only the heading 'To Mrs. T' and the date and place are in LM's autograph; the letter itself is in the same copyist's hand as the Embassy letter addressed to Pope and dated 17 June [1717]. The 'Heads of Letters' dated 8 Jan. 1718 includes one to Mrs. T: 'Copyd at length'. Thus, like the copyist's letter to Pope, the actual letter evidently bore a later date than its Embassy counterpart—perhaps the date when it was sent off.

[2] The copyist had written out the name Thistlethwayte but except for the initial letter it is struck out, probably by LM.

[3] 'The Story of the *Pidgeon*, which is said to have been taught by *Mahomet*

to pick Corn out of his Ear, and which the *Vulgar* took to be the Whispers of the *Holy Ghost*, hath no better Foundation, that ever I could learn than a *Castle* . . . in the Air' (Joseph Pitts, *A Faithful Account of the Religion and Manners of the Mahometans*, 1704, 4th ed. 1738, pp. x–xi). This legend was cited by Pope in his 1743 *Dunciad* (iv. 364).

[4] A daughter, the future Countess of Bute (d. 1794), was born on 19 Jan. and christened Mary ('Pedigree of John Stuart, Baron Cardiff 1776', MS of Marquess of Bute). The French Ambassador and his wife stood as godparents (letters from Mme de Bonnac, 20 Sept. 1719, 28 April 1720, W MS iv. 155–6).

easily guess at my uneasie Situation; but I am, however, in some degree comforted by the glory that accrues to me from it, and a reflection on the contempt I shou'd otherwise fall under.

You won't know what to make of this Speech, but in this country 'tis more despicable to be marry'd and not fruitfull, than 'tis with us to be fruitfull befor Marriage. They have a Notion that whenever a woman leaves off bringing children, 'tis because she is too old for that business, whatever her face sayes to the contrary, and this Opinion makes the Ladys here so ready to make proofs of their Youth (which is as necessary in order to be a receiv'd Beauty as it is to shew the proofs of Nobility to be admited Knight of Malta) that they do not content themselves with using the natural means, but fly to all sort of Quackerys to avoid the Scandall of being past Child bearing and often kill themselves by 'em. Without any exaggeration, all the women of my Acquaintance that have been marry'd 10 year have 12 or 13 children, and the Old ones boast of having had 5 and Twenty or 30 a peice and are respected according to the Number they have produc'd. When they are with Child, 'tis their common expression to say they hope God will be so mercifull to 'em to send two this time, and when I have ask'd them Sometimes how they expected to provide for such a Flock as they desire, They answer that the Plague will certainly kill half of 'em; which, indeed, generally happens without much concern to the Parents, who are Satisfy'd with the Vanity of having brought forth so plentifully. The French Ambassadress is forc'd to comply with this fashion as well as my Self. She has not been here much above a year and has Lain in Once[1] and is big again. What is most wonderfull is the Exemption they seem to enjoy from the Curse entail'd on the Sex. They See all Company the day of their Delivery and at the fortnight's end return Visits, set out in their Jewells and new Cloaths. I wish I may find the Influence of the Climate in this particular, but I fear I shall continue an English woman in that Affair as well as I do in my dread of fire and Plague, which are two things very Little fear'd here, most families having had their houses burnt down Once or

---

[1] François-Armand de Bonnac (d. 1782) was born on 7 Dec. 1716.

twice, occasion'd by their extraordinary way of warming themselves, which is neither by Chimneys nor Stoves, but a certain Machine call'd a Tendour, the height of two foot, in the form of a Table, cover'd with a fine carpet or Embroidery. This is made only of wood, and they put into it a Small Quantity of hot ashes and sit with their legs under the Carpet. At this table they work, read, and very often Sleep; and if they chance to dream, kick down the Tendour and the hot ashes commonly Sets the house on fire. There was 500 houses burnt in this manner about a fortnight ago, and I have Seen Several of the Owners Since who seem not at all mov'd at so common a Misfortune. They put their goods into a Bark and see their houses burn with great Philosophy, their Persons being very seldom endanger'd, having no stairs to descend.

But having entertain'd you with things I don't Like, 'tis but just I should tell you Something that pleases me. The Climate is Delightfull in the extreamest degree. I am now siting, this present 4th of January, with the windows open, enjoying the warm Shine of the Sun,[1] while you are freezing over a Sad Sea-coal fire; and my chamber [is] Set out with Carnations, Roses and Jonquils, fresh from my Garden. I am also charm'd with many points of the Turkish Law, to our shame be it Spoken, better design'd and better executed than Ours, particularly the punishment of convicted Lyars (Tryumphant Criminals in our countrey, God knows). They are burnt in the forehead with a hot Iron, being prov'd the Authors of any Notorious falsehood.[2] How many white foreheads shou'd we see Disfigur'd? How many fine Gentlemen wou'd be forc'd to wear their Wigs as low as their Eyebrows? were this Law in practice with us. I shou'd go on to tell you many other parts of Justice, but I must Send for my Midwife.

Text H MS 253, pp. 350–3

[1] LM expressed these feelings in her 'Verses Written in the Chiosk of the British Palace at Pera', dated Jan. 1718, and printed without her consent in 1720 (1861, ii. 449–51; Halsband, *LM*, p. 80; letter of 4 Sept. [1758]).

[2] Also in Sieur Du Loir, *Voyages*, 1654, p. 81.

'Heads of Letters' 8 Jan. 1718

Jan. 8, 1718

Mr. C. [Congreve]
Why he lets Pp [Pope] make Lampoons.¹ B[isho]ps facetious.

Mr. P. [Pope]
Thanks for his works.² Reception of my last letter.³

Mrs. T. [Thistlethwayte]
Copyd at length.⁴

Text W MS vii. 125   *End. by W* Heads of LM's Letters From Turky

To the Abbé Conti⁵ [*Feb. 1718*]

Je suis charmée de votre obligeante Lettre, Monsieur; & vous voyez par ce grand papier, que j'ay dessein de repondre

¹ LM may be referring to 'The Court Ballad', published 31 Jan. 1717 (Pope, *Minor Poems*, ed. N. Ault and J. Butt, 1954, pp. 180–4) or to the prose satire *The Plot Discover'd*, published at the end of 1717 (G. Sherburn, *Early Career of Pope*, 1934, pp. 199–200).

² LM is thanking Pope for the first volume of his *Works* and the third volume of his *Iliad* translation, both published in June 1717. He had asked her: 'How may I send a large Bundle to you?' and later, in [June 1717]: 'I send you . . . the third volume of the Iliad, and as many other things as fill a wooden box directed to Mr Wortley. Among the rest, you have all I am worth, that is, my Workes: There are a few things in them but what you have already seen, except the Epistle of Eloisa to Abelard; in which you will find one passage, that I can't tell whether to wish you should understand, or not?' (*Corr.* i. 385, 407). (He refers to the concluding eight lines of the

'Epistle'. For a discussion of this literary point see Pope, *The Rape of the Lock and Other Poems*, ed. G. Tillotson, 3rd ed., 1962, pp. 311–12; and Halsband, *LM*, pp. 75–76.)

³ That of 17 June [1717] (pp. 365–7).

⁴ This is the Embassy letter dated 4 Jan. [1718].

⁵ This letter, which is not in the MS of the Embassy Letters, is apparently genuine. It is probably the one referred to by Nicolas-François Rémond (see below, p. 395); hence its date. The letter survives only as printed, with its translation: *The Genuine Copy of a Letter Written From Constantinople by an English Lady, who was lately in Turkey, and who is no less distinguish'd by her Wit than by her Quality; To a Venetian Nobleman, one of the prime Virtuosi of the Age* (London, 1719). A so-called second edition—a new impression with 'The Second Edition' added to the title page—was also issued. The exact circumstances of its printing are mysterious.

exactement à toutes vos questions, du moins si mon François me le permet. Car comme c'est une langue que je ne sçai pas à fonds, je crains fort que je seray obligée de finir bientot, faute d'expressions. Souvenez vous donc, que j'ecris dans une langue qui m'est etrangere, & croyez bonnement que toutes les impertinences & les fadaizes, qui partiront de ma plume, ne viennent que de mon incapacité à pouvoir exprimer ce que je pense, mais nullement de stupidité ou d'une legereté naturelle.

Ces conditions ainsi faites & stipulées, je vous dirai d'abord que vous avez une idée juste de l'*Alcoran*, dont les Prêtres Grecs (la plus grande canaille de l'univers) font des contes ridicules, qu'ils ont inventé à plaisir, pour decrier la Loy de *Mahomet*; pour la condamner, dis-je, sans aucun examen; car ils ne veulent pas seulement que le peuple la lise: craignant, que s'il commençoit une fois à decouvrir ses defauts, il ne s'arretât pas là; mais qu'il pourroit bien encore faire usage de son discernement, à l'égard de leurs propres fictions & de leurs legendes. En effet, rien ne se ressemble mieux, que les fables des Grecs & celles des Mahometans. Ces derniers ont une multitude de Saints, aux tombeaux desquels il se fait des miracles, selon eux, tous les jours; & les relations de la vie de ces bienheureux *Musulmans*, ne sont gueres moins farcies d'extravagances, que les Romans spirituels des *Papas* Grecs.

Quant à votre seconde demande, je vous diray que c'est une chose certainement fausse, quoique communément crue parmi nous, que *Mahomet* exclut les femmes de toute participation à une vie future & bienheureuse. Il etoit trop galant homme & aimoit trop le beau Sexe, pour le traiter d'une maniere si barbare. Au contraire, il promet un trèsbeau Paradis aux femmes Turques. Il dit, à la verité, que ce sera un Paradis separé de celuy de leurs Maris: mais je crois

Rémond later remarked sarcastically that the letter had been printed through Conti's indiscretion (see below, p. 449). Another friend of Conti's, who was shown an earlier French letter LM had sent, praised its style as 'aise, badin et enjoüé' and its turn of phrase, clarity, and orthography (see above, p. xvi).

The translation of the 1719 letter was reprinted in the *Gentleman's Mag.*, 1766, pp. 299–301, and the *Annual Register*, 1766, pp. 216–18; and from these, probably, it was lifted for the *Additional Volume* of LM's letters, 1767, pp. 64–78 —the only authentic letter among the spurious ones. The translation is given below, pp. 454–7.

que la pluspart n'en seront pas moins contentes pour cela;
& que le regret de cette separation, ne leur rendra pas ce
Paradis moins agreable. Au reste, les vertus que *Mahomet*
exige des femmes, pour leur procurer la jouïssance de la
felicité future, c'est de ne pas vivre d'un maniere qui les
rende inutiles sur la terre; mais de s'occuper, autant qu'il
est possible, à faire des petits *Musulmans*. Les Vierges que
meurent Vierges, & les Veuves qui ne se remarient point,
mourant dans un peché damnable, sont exclues du Paradis.
Car les femmes, dit-il, n'etant capables ni d'affaires d'Etat,
ni d'essuier les fatigues de la Guerre, Dieu ne leur donne pas
le soin de gouverner ni de reformer le monde; mais il les
charge (employ qui n'est pas moins honorable) de multiplier
la race humaine: & celles, qui, par malice ou par paresse, ne
s'occupent point à porter ou à elever des enfans, ne remplis-
sent pas le devoir de leur vocation, & sont rebelles aux ordres
de Dieu. Voilà des Maximes terriblement contraires à vos
Couvents. Que deviendront vos *Saintes Catherines*, *Thereses*,
Claires, & toute la bande de vos pieuses *Vierges & Veuves?*
lesquelles, etant jugées par ce Systeme de vertu, sont des
infames, qui ont passé toute leur vie dans un libertinage
effroyable.

Je ne sçai ce que vous penserez d'une doctrine si extraordinaire à notre egard: mais je puis vous assurer, Monsieur,
que les Turcs ne sont point si ignorants en matiere de Politique, de Philosophie, ou meme de Galanterie, que nous le
croyons. Il est vrai, que la Discipline militaire, telle qu'elle
est pratiquée presentement dans la Chretienté, ne les accom-
mode point. Une longue Paix les a plongez dans une paresse
universelle. Contents de leur etat, & accoutumez à un luxe
sans bornes, ils sont devenus grands ennemis de toute sorte
de fatigues. Mais, en recompense, les Sciences fleurissent
chez eux. Les *Effendis*, (ce mot veut dire les Sçavans) sont
fort dignes de ce nom. Ils n'ont pas plus de foy pour l'Inspiration de *Mahomet*, que pour l'Infaillibilité du *Pape*. Ils
font profession ouverte de *Deisme* entre eux, ou avec ceux
en qui ils ont de la confiance; & ne parlent jamais de leur
Loy, que comme d'une Institution politique, que les personnes sages doivent observer à present, quoiqu'introduite
au commencement par des Politiques & des Enthousiastes.

Il me semble (si je m'en souviens bien) que je vous ay deja ecrit, que nous avons logé à Belgrade chez un grand *Effendi*, fort riche, homme d'esprit, de sçavoir, & d'une humeur fort agreable. Nous fumes environ un mois dans sa maison, & il mangeoit toujours avec nous, buvant du vin sans scrupule. Comme je le raillai un peu là-dessus, il me repondit en souriant, que toutes les creatures du monde ont été faites pour le plaisir de l'homme; & que Dieu n'auroit pas laissé croitre la vigne, s'il y avoit du peché à en gouter le jus: mais que cependant la Loy qui en defendoit l'usage au vulgaire, etoit fort sage; parce que ces sortes de gens n'ont pas assez d'esprit, pour s'en servir avec moderation. Cet *Effendi* n'ignoroit pas les differens partis, qui regnent chez nous: il paroissoit meme avoir quelque connoissance de nos disputes de Religion & de nos Ecrivains; & je fus surprise de luy entendre demander, entre autres choses, *comment se portoit Monsieur Toland*.[1]

Mon papier, tout grand qu'il est, va finir. Pour ne pas aller plus loin que ses bornes, il faut que je saute des *Religions* aux *Tulipes*, dont vous me demandez des nouvelles. Leur Melange fait des Effets surprenants. Mais ce qu'on voit de plus surprenant, c'est l'experience dont vous parlez concernant les Animaux, & qu'on fait ici tous les jours. Les fauxbourgs de Pera, Jophana [*sic*], & Galata, sont des collections d'Etrangers de touts les Pays de l'univers. Ils se sont si souvent entre-mariés, que cela forme des races les plus bizarres du monde. Il n'y a pas une seule famille de Natifs, qui se puisse vanter de n'etre point melée. On voit fort souvent une personne, dont le pere est né Grec, la mere Italienne, le grand-pere François, la grand'mere Armenienne, & les Ancêtres Anglois, Russiens, Asiatiques, &c.

Ce mêlange fait naitre des creatures plus extraordinaires, que vous ne sçauriez imaginer; aussi n'ay-je pu jamais douter, qu'il ne se trouvât des especes d'hommes toutes differentes: puisque les blancs, les noirs velus & à longue chevelure, les Chinois & les Tartares aux petits yeux, les Brasiliens sans barbe, & (pour n'en pas nommer d'avantage)

[1] John Toland (1670–1722), deist writer. The previous four paragraphs treat of topics similar to those in the Embassy Letters of 1 April and 29 May [1717], both addressed to Conti.

les Nova-zembliens avec leur peau jaune & huileuse, ont des differences aussi specifiques sous le meme genre, que les levriers, les mâtins, les epagneuls, les *Bull-dogs*, ou la race de ma petite *Diane*, s'il m'est permis de me servir de cette comparaison. Or comme les differents melanges de ces derniers animaux produisent des Mêtifs: de meme les hommes ont aussi les leurs, divisés & subdivisés en des especes infinies. Nous en avons ici des preuves tous les jours, comme je vous l'ay dit auparavant. On remarque quelque fois dans le meme animal la fausseté Grecque, la meffiance Italienne, l'arrogance Espagnole, le caquet François; & tout d'un coup il luy vient des accès d'un serieux Anglois, tirant un peu sur l'hebeté, que plusieurs d'entre nous ont herité de la stupidité de nos ancetres Saxons.

Mais la famille qui me charme le plus, c'est celle qui provient de la bizarre conjonction d'un male Hollandois avec une femelle Grecque. Comme ce sont des Natures extremement opposées, c'est un plaisir de remarquer, comment les atomes differents se font une guerre perpetuelle dans les enfants, meme jusque dans leur figure externe. Ils ont les grands yeux noirs du païs, avec la chair grasse, blanche, poissoneuse de Hollande, & un air vif raïé de stupidité. Ils montrent en meme temps cet amour pour la depense, si universel parmi les Grecs, & un penchant vers la frugalité Hollandoise. Pour en donner un exemple, les filles se ruinent pour se parer la tête de Bijoux, mais elles n'ont pas le cœur d'acheter des souliers, je veux dire des patouches neuves, leurs piés etant ordinairement dans un etat bien pietre. Pratique bien opposée à celle de nos Angloises, qui, pour faire voir la propreté de leur chaussure, & nullement pour montrer autre chose, sont si passionement amourachées de leurs *Hoop-pettycoats*. J'aurois bien d'autres particularités à vous communiquer, mais je suis au bout de mon Papier & de mon François.

Text: Genuine Copy of a Letter Written From Constantinople by an English Lady, 1719, pp. 8–12

'Heads of Letters' *1 March* [*1718*]

March 1.

Mrs. Wᵗ [West]
   Complements.

S. Mʳ [Sister (Lady) Mar]
   A short letter.¹

Mr. C. [Congreve]
   A Note.

Mr. P. [Pope]
   The world here Romantic. Women differ from ours.
Unaffected. Lazy Life.

Text W MS vii. 125   *End. by* W Heads of LM's Letters From Turky

To Lady Mar *10 March* [*1718*]

Pera of Constantinople, March 10. O.S.

I have not writ to you (Dear Sister) these many Months,
a great piece of selfe-denial, but I knew not where to direct
or what part of the world you were in.² I have receiv'd no
letter from you since your short note of April last in which
you tell me that you are on the point of leaving England and
promise me a Direction for the place you stay in, but I have
in vain expected it till now, and now I only learn from the
Gazette that you are return'd, which induces me to venture
this Letter to your House at London.³ I had rather ten of
my Letters should be lost than you imagine I don't write
and I think tis hard fortune if one in ten don't reach you.
However, I am resolv'd to keep the Copys as testimonys of

¹ An Embassy letter to Lady Mar dated 10 March follows but it is long.

² Lady Mar had gone to the Continent in April 1717 to visit her husband —attainted for his part in the Jacobite rebellion—and had returned to their house in London on 15 Oct. 1717 (HMC *Stuart Papers*, iv, 1910, p. 220; *Post Boy*, 17–19 Oct. 1717).

³ In the Privy Gardens of Whitehall. In Feb. 1717 it had been granted to her for 31 years by the King, with her uncle Lord Cheyne as trustee (PRO Chancery Inquisitions, C 211, E 16).

my Inclination to give you (to the utmost of my power) all the Diverting part of my travells while you are exempt from all the fatigues and inconveniencys.[1]

In the first place I wish you joy of your Niece, for I was brought to bed of a daughter 5 weeks ago.[2] I don't mention this as one of my diverting adventures, thô I must own that it is not halfe so mortifying here as in England, there being as much difference as there is between a little cold in the head, which sometimes happens here, and the Consumptive Coughs so common in London. No body keeps their house a Month for lying-in, and I am not so fond of any of our Customs to retain them when they are not necessary. I return'd my visits at 3 weeks end, and about 4 days ago cross'd the Sea which divides this place from Constantinople to make a new one, where I had the good fortune to pick up many Curiositys.

I went to see the Sultana Hafife,[3] favourite of the last Emperour Mustapha, who, you know (or perhaps you don't know) was depos'd by his brother, the reigning Sultan, and dy'd a few weeks after, being poison'd, as it was gennerally beleiv'd.[4] This Lady was immediately after his death saluted with an Absolute order to leave the Seraglio and chuse her selfe a Husband from the great Men at the Port. I suppose you imagine her overjoy'd at this proposal.—Quite Contrary; these Women, who are call'd and esteem them selves Queens, look upon this Liberty as the greatest disgrace and affront that can happen to them. She threw her selfe at the Sultan's feet and begg'd him to poniard her rather than use his brother's Widow with that contempt. She represented to him in agonys of Sorrow that she was priveleg'd from this misfortune by having brought 5 Princes into the Ottoman family, but all the boys being dead and only one Girl surviving, this excuse was not receiv'd and she compell'd to make her choice.[5] She chose Bekir Effendi, then Secretary

---

[1] Here is one explanation for LM's compilation of the Embassy Letters.

[2] See above, p. 371, n. 4.

[3] Hafise (b. *c.* 1683)—whose name is clearly misspelled by LM.

[4] Mustafa II was deposed in Aug. 1703, and died four months later—of dropsy (A. D. Alderson, *Structure of the Ottoman Dynasty*, 1956, Table XL and p. 110).

[5] Her sons had been born in 1698, 1699, 1702, and (twins) 1703. For the position of widowed ladies of the harem, see Alderson, pp. 81–82.

of State,[1] and above fourscore year old, to convince the World
that she firmly intended to keep the vow she had made of
never suffering a 2nd Husband to approach her bed, and
since she must honnour some subject so far as to be call'd
his Wife she would chuse him as a mark of her Gratitude,
since it was he that had presented her at the Age of 10 year
old to her lost Lord. But she has never permitted him to pay
her one visit, thô it is now 15 year she has been in his house,
where she passes her time in unintterupted Mourning with a
constancy very little known in Christendom, especially in a
widow of 21, for she is now but 36. She has no black Eunuchs
for her Guard, her Husband being oblig'd to respect her as
a Queen and not enquire at all into what is done in her apartment, where I was led into a large room, with a Sofa the
whole length of it, adorn'd with white Marble Pillars like a
ruelle, cover'd with pale bleu figur'd velvet on a silver Ground,
with Cushions of the same, where I was desir'd to repose till
the Sultana appear'd, who had contriv'd this manner of
reception to avoid riseing up at my Entrance, thô she made
me an Inclination of her head when I ris up to her. I was
very glad to observe a Lady that had been distinguish'd by
the favour of an Emperour to whom Beautys were every day
presented from all parts of the World. But she did not seem
to me to have ever been halfe so beautifull as the fair Fatima
I saw at Adrianople,[2] thô she had the remains of a fine face
more decay'd by Sorrow than time.

But her dress was something so surprizingly rich I cannot
forbear describing it to you. She wore a vest call'd Dualma,
and which differs from a Caftan by longer sleeves, and folding
over at the bottom. It was of purple Cloth strait to her shape
and thick set, on each side down to her feet and round the
sleeves, with pearls of the best water, of the same size as their
buttons commonly are. You must not suppose I mean as
large as those of my Lord —— but about the bigness of a pea;
and to these buttons, large loops of Diamonds in the form
of those gold loops so common upon birth-day Coats. This
habit was ty'd at the waste with 2 large tassells of smaller

---

[1] Ebubekir Efendi (d. 1723), Reis-ül
Küttab, i.e. Minister for Foreign Affairs
(Alderson, Table XL).

[2] Described in the Embassy letter
to Lady Mar dated 18 April [1717]
(pp. 349–51 above).

pearl, and round the arms embrodier'd with large Diamonds; her shift fasten'd at the bosom with a great Diamond shap'd like a Lozenge; her Girdle as broad as the broadest English Riband entirely cover'd with Di'monds. Round her neck she wore 3 chains which reach'd to her knees, one of large Pearl at the bottom of which hung a fine colour'd Emerald as big as a Turkey Egg, another consisting of 200 Emeralds close joyn'd together, of the most lively Green, perfectly match'd, every one as large as a halfe Crown piece and as thick as 3 Crown pieces, and another of small Emeralds perfectly round. But her Earrings eclips'd all the rest; they were 2 Diamonds shap'd exactly like pears, as large as a big hazle nut. Round her Talpoche she had 4 strings of Pearl, the whitest and most perfect in the world, at least enough to make 4 necklaces every one as large as the Dutchesse of Marlbrô's,[1] and of the same size, fasten'd with 2 roses consisting of a large ruby for the middle stone, and round them 20 drops of clean di'monds to each. Besides this, her headdress was cover'd with bodkins of Emeralds and di'monds. She wore large Di'mond bracelets and had 5 rings on her fingers, all single Di'monds, (except Mr. Pit's)[2] the largest I ever saw in my Life. Tis for Jewellers to compute the value of these things, but according to the common Estimation of Jewels in our part of the world, her whole dress must be worth above £100 thousand sterling. This I am very sure of, that no European Queen has halfe the Quantity, and the Empresse's jewels (thô very fine) would look very mean near hers.

She gave me a Dinner of 50 dishes of meat, which (after their fashion) was plac'd on the table but one at a time, and was extreamly tedious, but the magnificence of her table answer'd very well to that of her dress. The Knives were of Gold, the hafts set with di'monds, but the piece of Luxury that greiv'd my Eyes was the Table cloth and napkins, which

---

[1] Sarah Jennings (1660–1744) m. (1678) John Churchill, later 1st Duke of Marlborough. A catalogue of her jewels in 1718 lists a large necklace of 39 pearls (Frank Chancellor, *Sarah Churchill*, 1932, p. 290). She bequeathed it to her daughter the Duchess of Montagu (A. L. Rowse, *The Early Churchills*, 1956, p. 412).

[2] Thomas Pitt (1653–1726), owner of an enormous diamond, which he took to France in 1717 to sell to the Regent.

were all Tiffany embrodier'd with silks and Gold in the finest
manner in natural flowers. It was with the utmost regret that
I made use of these costly Napkins, as finely wrought as the
finest handkercheifs that ever came out of this Country. You
may be sure that they were entirely spoilt before Dinner was
over. The Sherbet (which is the Liquor they drink at meals)
was serv'd in China Bowls, but the covers and salvers, massy
Gold. After Dinner water was brought in a Gold bason and
towels of the same kind of the napkins, which I very unwillingly wip'd my hands upon, and Coffée was serv'd in
China with Gold soûcoupes.

The Sultana seem'd in very good humour, and talk'd to me
with the utmost Civillity. I did not omit this oppertunity
of learning all that I possibly could of the Seraglio, which is
so entirely unknown amongst us. She assur'd me that the
story of the Sultan's throwing a Handkercheif is altogether
fabulous,[1] and the manner upon that occasion no other but
that he sends the Kuslir Aga to signify to the Lady the
honnour he intends her. She is immediately complemented
upon it by the others, and led to the bath where she is
perfum'd and dress'd in the most magnificent and becoming
Manner. The Emperor precedes his visit by a Royal present
and then comes into her apartment. Neither is there any
such thing as her creeping in at the bed's feet.[2] She said that
the first he made choice of was always after the first in rank,
and not the Mother of the eldest Son, as other writers would
make us beleive. Sometimes the Sultan diverts him selfe in
the Company of all his Ladies, who stand in a circle round
him, and she confess'd that they were ready to dye with
Jealousie and envy of the happy She that he distinguish'd by
any appearance of preference. But this seem'd to me neither
better nor worse than the Circles in most Courts where the
Glance of the Monarch is watch'd and every Smile waited

[1] One account by Paul Rycaut, who
writes of the Grand Signor and his
women: '. . . the Damsels being ranged
in order by the Mother of the Maids, he
throws his handkerchief to her, where
his eye and fancy best directs, it being
a token of her election to his bed' (*Present State of the Ottoman Empire*, 1668,
p. 39). Authorities still differ as to the
accuracy of this story: of the most
recent ones, Alderson denies it (p. 80,
n. 1) and Norman Penzer supports it
(*The Harem*, 1937, pp. 180–2).
[2] Hill, who discounts the handkerchief story, mentions this manner of
entering the bed (pp. 164, 166).

for with impatience and envy'd by those that cannot obtain it.

She never mention'd the Sultan without tears in her Eyes, yet she seem'd very fond of the discourse. My past happyness (said she) appears a dream to me, yet I cannot forget that I was belov'd by the greatest and most Lovely of Mankind. I was chose from all the rest to make all his campaigns with him. I would not survive him if I was not passionately fond of the Princesse, my Daughter, yet all my tenderness for her was hardly enough to make me preserve my Life when I lost him. I pass'd a whole twelvemonth without seeing the light. Time has soften'd my Dispair, yet I now pass some days every week in tears devoted to the Memory of my Sultan.—There was no affectation in these words. It was easy to see she was in a deep Melancholy, thô her good humour made her willing to divert me.

She ask'd me to walk in her Garden, and one of her slaves immediately brought her a Pellice of rich Brocade lin'd with Sables. I waited on her into the Garden, which had nothing in it remarkable but the fountains, and from thence she shew'd me all her apartments. In her bed chamber her Toilet was display'd, consisting of 2 looking Glasses, the frames cover'd with pearls, and her night Talpoche set with bodkins of Jewels, and near it 3 vests of fine Sables, every one of which is at least worth 1,000 Dollars, £200 English money. I don't doubt these rich habits were purposely plac'd in sight, but they seem'd negligently thrown on the sofa. When I took my leave of her I was complemented with perfumes as at the Grand Vizier's, and presented with a very fine Embrodier'd Handkercheif. Her slaves were to the number of 30, besides 10 little ones, the eldest not above 7 year old. These were the most beautifull Girls I ever saw, all richly drest; and I observ'd that the Sultana took a great deal of pleasure in these lovely Children, which is a vast Expence, for there is not a handsome Girl of that age to be bought under £100 sterling. They wore little Girlands of Flowers, and their own hair braided, which was all their head dress, but their habits all of Gold stuffs. These serv'd her Coffée kneeling, brought water when she wash'd, etc. Tis a great part of the busyness of the older slaves to take care of these Girls, to learn them to embrodier and serve them as carefully as if they were children of the family.

Now do I fancy that you imagine I have entertain'd you all this while with a relation that has (at least) receiv'd many Embellishments from my hand. This is but too like (says you) the Arabian tales;[1] these embrodier'd Napkins, and a jewel as large as a Turkey's egg!—You forget, dear Sister, those very tales were writ by an Author of this Country and (excepting the Enchantments) are a real representation of the manners here. We Travellers are in very hard circumstances. If we say nothing but what has been said before us, we are dull and we have observ'd nothing. If we tell any thing new, we are laugh'd at as fabulous and Romantic, not allowing for the difference of ranks, which afford difference of company, more Curiosity, or the changes of customs that happen every 20 year in every Country. But people judge of Travellers exactly with the same Candour, good Nature, and impartiallity they judge of their Neighbours upon all Occasions. For my part, if I live to return amongst You, I am so well acquainted with the Morals of all my dear freinds and acquaintance, that I am resolv'd to tell them nothing at all, to avoid the Imputation (which their charity would certainly incline them to) of my telling too much. But I depend upon your knowing me enough to beleive whatever I seriously assert for truth, thô I give you leave to be surpriz'd at an account so new to you. But what would you say if I told you that I have been in a Haram where the winter Apartment was wainscoted with inlaid work of Mother of Pearl, Ivory of different Colours and olive wood, exactly like the little Boxes you have seen brought out of this Country; and those rooms design'd for Summer, the walls all crusted with Japan china, the roofs gilt, and the floors spread with the finest Persian carpets. Yet there is nothing more true; such is the Palace of my Lovely freind, the fair Fatima, who I was acquainted with at Adrianople. I went to visit her Yesterday, and (if possible) she appear'd to me handsomer than before. She met me at the door of her Chamber, and, giving me her hand with the best Grace in the World: You Christian

---

[1] *Les Mille et une nuits, contes arabes*, transl. Antoine Galland, 1704– 17. LM owned (in 1739) this book in ten volumes (Wh MS 135).

Ladys (said she with a smile that made her as handsome as an Angel) have the reputation of Inconstancy, and I did not expect, whatever goodness you express'd for me at Adrianople, that I should ever see you again; but I am now convince'd that I have realy the happyness of pleasing you, and if you knew how I speak of you amongst our Ladys, You would be assur'd that you do me justice if you think me your freind.—She plac'd me in the Corner of the Sofa, and I spent the afternoon in her conversation with the greatest pleasure in the World.

The Sultana Hafife is what one would naturally expect to find a Turkish Lady, willing to oblige, but not knowing how to go about it, and tis easy to see in her Manner that she has liv'd excluded from the World.[1] But Fatima has all the politeness and good breeding of a court, with an air that inspires at once Respect and tenderness; and now I understand her Language, I find her Wit as engaging as her Beauty. She is very curious after the manners of other countrys and has not that partiality for her own, so common to little minds. A Greek that I carry'd with me who had never seen her before (nor could have been admitted now if she had not been in my Train) shew'd that Surprize at her Beauty and manner which is unavoidable at the first sight, and said to me in Italian: This is no Turkish Lady; she is certainly some Christian. Fatima guess'd she spoke of her, and ask'd what she said. I would not have told, thinking she would have been no better pleas'd with the Complement than one of our Court Beautys to be told she had the air of a Turk. But the Greek Lady told it her and she smil'd, saying: It is not the first time I have heard so. My Mother was a Poloneze taken at the Seige of Caminiec,[2] and my father us'd to rally me, saying he beleiv'd his Christian Wife had found some Christian Gallant, for I had not the Air of a

---

[1] In a French essay on the subject of marriage, LM reported a conversation with a lady of high rank in Constantinople, who contrasted the seclusion of Turkish wives with the exposure of Western ones ('Sur la Maxime de M. de Rochefoucault, qu'il y a des mariages commodes, mais point de délicieux',

1861, ii. 427). LM made a similar observation to Joseph Spence (*Anecdotes*, ed. J. M. Osborn, 1966, LM § 22).

[2] Camieniec, a strong fortress of the Poles on the Turkish frontier, was captured by Mehmed IV in 1672 (*Encycl. of Islam*, i. 827).

Turkish Girl. I assur'd her that if all the Turkish Ladys were like her, it was absolutely necessary to confine them from public view for the repose of Mankind, and proceeded to tell her what a noise such a face as hers would make in London or Paris. I can't beleive you (reply'd she agreably); if Beauty was so much valu'd in your Country as you say, they would never have suffer'd you to leave it.

Perhaps (dear Sister) you laugh at my Vanity in repeating this complement, but I only do it as I think it very well turn'd and give it you as an instance of the Spirit of her Conversation. Her House was Magnificently furnish'd and very well fancy'd, her winter rooms being furnish'd with figur'd velvet on gold Grounds, and those for summer with fine Indian quilting embrodier'd with Gold. The Houses of the great Turkish Ladys are kept clean with as much nicety as those in Holland. This was situated in a high part of the Town, and from the windows of her Summer Apartment we had the Prospect of the Sea and the Islands and the Assian Mountains.—My Letter is insensibly grown so long, I am asham'd of it. This is a very bad Symptom. Tis well if I don't degenerate in a downright story teller. It may be our Proverb that knowledge is no burden,[1] may be true as to one's selfe, but knowing too much is very apt to make us troublesome to other people.

Text H MS 253, pp. 354–72

To Lady ——— *16 March* [*1718*]

Pera, Constantinople, March 16. O.S.

I am extremely pleas'd (my dear Lady)[2] that you have at length found a commission for me that I can answer without disapointing your expectation, thô I must tell you that it is not so easy as perhaps you think it, and that if my Curiosity had not been more diligent than any other stranger's has

---

[1] Knowledge is no burthen' (*Out-landish Proverbs* by George Herbert, 1640; in Gurney Benham, *Book of Quotations*, ed. [1949], p. 1311).

[2] The opening sentence of this letter clearly refers to the same anonymous lady to whom the Embassy letter of 17 June [1717] is addressed (p. 367).

ever yet been, I must have answer'd you with an excuse, as I was forc'd to do when you desir'd me to buy you a Greek slave. I have got for you, as you desire, a Turkish Love-letter, which I have put in a little Box, and order'd the Captain of the Smyrniote to deliver it to you with this letter.[1] The Translation of it is litterally as follows. The first piece you should pull out of the purse is a little Pearl, which is in Turkish call'd ingi, and should be understood in this manner:

Pearl	Sensin Uzellerin gingi
Ingi	Fairest of the young.
Caremfil	Caremfilsen cararen Yok
a clove	conge gulsun timarin yok
	Benseny chok tan severim
	Senin benden haberin Yok
	You are as slender as this clove;
	You are an unblown Rose;
	I have long lov'd you, and you have not known it.
Pul	derdime derman bul
a Jonquil	Have pity on my passion.
Kihat	Biîlerum sahat sahat
paper	I faint every hour.
ermut	ver bize bir umut
pear	Give me some hope.
sabun	Derdinden oldum Zabun
soap	I am sick with Love.
chemur	ben oliyim size umur
coal	May I die, and all my years be yours!
Gul	ben aglarum sen gul
a Rose	May you be pleas'd, and all your sorrows mine!
hazir	Oliîm sana Yazir
a straw	Suffer me to be your slave.

---

[1] The merchantman *Smyrniote*, commanded by Captain Nathaniel Clark, arrived at Smyrna from England on 24 Feb. 1718 O.S. and stopped there again on 16 April on her way home (SP 105/335, f. 355; SP 105/339, f. 266). Hence she must have been in Constantinople in mid-March. In Oct. she reached England 'richly laden from Turkey' (*Weekly Journal and Sat. Post*, 18 Oct. 1718).

Jo ha	ustune bulunmaz Paha
cloth	Your Price is not to be found.
tartsin	sen ghel ben chekeim senin hargin
cinamon	But my Fortune ⟨Estate⟩ is yours.
Gira	esking-ilen oldum Ghira
a match	I burn, I burn, my flame consumes me.
Sirma	uzunu benden ayirma
Gold thread	Don't turn away your face.
Satch	Bazmazun tatch
Hair	Crown of my Head.
Uzum	Benim iki Guzum
Grape	My Eyes.
tel	uluyorum tez ghel
Gold wire	I die—come quickly.

And by way of postscript:

biber	Bize bir dogru haber
pepper	Send me an Answer.[1]

You see this letter is all verses, and I can assure you there is as much fancy shewn in the choice of them as in the most study'd expressions of our Letters, there being (I beleive) a million of verses design'd for this use. There is no colour, no flower, no weed, no fruit, herb, pebble, or feather that has not a verse belonging to it; and you may quarrel, reproach, or send Letters of passion, freindship, or Civillity, or even of news, without ever inking your fingers.[2]

---

[1] In her previous letter LM states that she now understands Turkish. She translated these verses, with others, in a more literal form in a Commonplace Book (ff. 18–20, MS in Fisher Library, University of Sydney). Her vocabulary and orthography are given here verbatim. For an accurate version of these Turkish lines and translation, see Appendix II below (pp. 464–5).

[2] Dumont describes a similar love letter as 'nothing but bits of Charcoal, *Scarlet Cloth, Saffron, Ashes*, and such like Trash, wrapt up in a Piece of Paper' (p. 268). Aubry de La Mottraye, who appends examples of this kind of verse, explains: 'Fruit, Flowers, and Gold & Silver Thread, or Silk of divers Colours, . . . have each of them their particular Meaning explain'd by certain *Turkish* verses, which the young Girls learn by Tradition of one another' (*Travels through Europe, Asia . . .*, 1723–32; i. 254; ii. 72).

I fancy you are now wondering at my profound Learning, but alas, dear Madam, I am allmost falln into the misfortune so common to the Ambitious: while they are employ'd on distant, insignificant Conquests abroad, a Rebellion starts up at home. I am in great danger of loseing my English. I find it is not halfe so easy to me to write in it as it was a twelve-month ago. I am forc'd to study for expressions, and must leave off all other Languages and try to learn my Mother tongue. Humane understanding is as much limited as humane Power or humane strength. The Memory can retain but a certain Number of Images, and tis as impossible for one Humane Creature to be perfect master of ten different Languages as to have in perfect subjection ten different Kingdoms, or to fight against ten Men at a time. I am afraid I shall at last know none as I should do. I live in a place that very well represents the Tower of Babel; in Pera they speak Turkish, Greek, Hebrew, Armenian, Arabic, Persian, Russian, Sclavonian, Walachian, German, Dutch, French, English, Italian, Hungarian; and, what is worse, there is ten of these Languages spoke in my own family. My Grooms are Arabs; my footmen French, English and Germans; my Nurse an Armenian; my Housemaids Russians; halfe a dozen other servants Greeks; my steward an Italian; my Janizarys Turks,[1] that I live in the perpetual hearing of this medley of Sounds, which produces a very extrodinary Effect upon the people that are born here. They learn all these Languages at the same time and without knowing any of 'em well enough to write or read in it. There is very few men, women or children here that have not the same compass of words in 5 or 6 of 'em. I know my selfe several infants of 3 or 4 year old that speak Italian, French, Greek, Turkish, and Russian, which last they learn of their Nurses, who are gennerally of that Country. This seems allmost incredible to you, and is (in my Mind) one of the most curious things in this Country, and takes off very much from the Merit of our Ladys who set up for such extrodinary Geniuses upon the credit of some superficial knowledge of French and Italian. As I prefer English to all the rest, I am extremely

---

[1] For the numerous household staff, see A. C. Wood's 'The English Embassy at Constantinople 1660–1762' (*Eng. Hist. Rev.*, xl, 1925, pp. 538–41).

mortify'd at the daily decay of it in my head, where I'll assure you (with greife of heart) it is reduce'd to such a small number of Words, I cannot recollect any tolerable phrase to conclude my Letter, and am forc'd to tell your Ladyship very bluntly that I am Your faithfull humble Servant.

Text H MS 253, pp. 373–9

To Wortley *23 March* [*1718*][1]

March 23. Sunday

This day news is come of the Grey-hound's safe arrival at Smyrna.[2] It has brought the minister for this place,[3] and my money that was in my uncle's hands.[4] The Captain has writ that he met the Preston Man of War at Cadiz having orders for Barbary and did not propose for this part of the world till July at soonest.[5] The Dutch Madam is a perfect mad woman.[6] I sent a Jeweller to her to offer her the money for her pearls and she would not take it, which she is very

[1] On this day W arrived in Adrianople from Sophia to take leave of the Sultan's Court (W to Addison, 4 April 1718, SP 97/24).

[2] The *Greyhound*, commanded by Captain Richard Stratton, left London in Nov. 1717 and on 7 or 8 March 1718 arrived at Smyrna (15 Nov. 1717, SP 105/116; SP 105/335, f. 355).

[3] Thomas Andrews was appointed chaplain on 27 Nov. 1717 to succeed William Crosse (Levant Comp. to Stanyan, SP 105/116). But on 26 March 1718, even before he reached Constantinople, he was transferred at his own request to Aleppo (Levant Comp. to Andrews, SP 105/116). He was perhaps Thomas Andrewes (b. 1688) (J. Venn, *Alumni Cantab. to 1751*, i. 31).

[4] On 18 April 1717 LM had written to her uncle William Feilding about her loan to him [of £1,550] ('Heads of Letters', p. 353 above). She was informed by Charles Chevallier, on 4 Sept. 1717, that it had been repaid with interest of

£35. 5s. 11d., and that the most advantageous way of remitting it would be to buy Spanish dollars or pieces of eight (for £1,600) through Sir John Williams, who would then send the money from Spain (W MS iv. 168–9).

[5] The *Preston* was a newly built warship, commissioned in Nov. 1717; she set sail for Constantinople in Jan. 1718 to bring the Ambassador to London (*Weekly Journal*, 7 Dec. 1717, 11 Jan. 1718). She reached Cadiz Bay on 27 Jan. (remaining there until 11 March), Tripoli—in the Barbary states—on 9 May, and Constantinople on 19 June (Captain's log, PRO Ad 51/4296: all dates O.S.).

[6] Catharina de Bourg m. (1713) Count Jacob Colyer (1657–1725), Dutch Ambassador to Turkey 1688–1725 (*Nieuw Nederlandsch Biog. Woordenboek*, 1911–37, iv. 448; F. Hausmann, *Repertorium der diplomatischen Vertreter*, 1936–50, ii. 249).

much in the right, for they are worth more; but tis very strange she should get a good bargain and complain of it. But she cheats the Ambassador. Her own vanity caus'd the discovery of her secret, which I kept very faithfully, and now he is (I suppose) angry at her laying her money out in Ornaments. She would make him beleive she did it to oblige me, and would seem glad to get rid of 'em, at the same time she won't part with them.

The Boy was engrafted last Tusday, and is at this time singing and playing and very impatient for his supper.[1] I pray God my next may give as good an Account of him. I suppose you know the allowance the King has made the Company on this Occasion.[2] I think you may with more justice insist on your Extrodinarys which has never, yet been refus'd neither Sir R. Sutton nor no other Ambassador.[3]

I cannot engraft the Girl; her Nurse has not had the small Pox.

Text Wh MS 507[4]   *Address* To His Excellency Wortley Montagu Ambassador at the Port   *End. by W* L. M. 23 Mar. 1717/8 The ship Greyhound is arrived at Smyrna and has brought the money that was in her Unkles hands

[1] Edward Wortley Montagu, jun., was inoculated on 18 March O.S. by the Embassy surgeon, Charles Maitland (1668–1748), who described the operation in his *Account of Inoculating the Small Pox*, 1722, 2nd ed. 1723, pp. 7–8 (quoted in Halsband, *LM*, pp. 80–81). In an Embassy letter of 1 April [1717] (p. 337 above) LM had described inoculation in detail; and Dr. Emanuel Timoni, whom W engaged in Constantinople as his family physician (W to Addison, 26 Aug. 1717, SP 97/24), had submitted a description of the operation to the Royal Society in 1714 (printed in its *Transactions*, xxix. 72–82).

[2] W had entered into the customary articles of agreement to stay at least five years, but since the King had recalled him so abruptly the Levant Company —who claimed the right to choose ambassadors to Turkey—asked for compensation of not less than £4,000

(Levant Comp. to Onslow, 8 Oct. 1717, SP 105/116). They were granted exactly that sum in Dec. 1717 (*Cal. of Treasury Papers 1714–19*, ed. J. Redington, 1883, p. 413).

[3] Sir Robert Sutton (1671–1746) had been Ambassador 1701–16. W's efforts to be paid for his 'extraordinaries' were unceasing—in letters to the Levant Company, to Addison (e.g. 18 and 19 July, 26 Aug. 1717, Tickell MS), and even as late as 1747 in a memorial prepared for submission to George II (Halsband, *LM*, p. 94). Actually, the Levant Company, when informing him of his recall, allowed him £500 for his expenses, the same amount they had allowed Sutton for his return (7 Nov. 1717, SP 105/116).

[4] Sold on 22 Jan. 1828 at Southgate's Auction Rooms to William Upcott. Part of it had been published in facsimile in 1803 (i. facing p. 36); hence its separation from the W MS.

To Wortley *1 April* [*1718*]

Ap. 1.

Your Son is as well as can be expected, and I hope past all manner of danger. The ship that has brought my Pieces of 8 is safe arriv'd in the Port. 'Tis directed to Mr. Lethuilere,[1] and therefore I thought him the properest person to apply to, to take care of my Money that is on board, and sent for him and desir'd him to keep it in his warehouse, giving me a note for the receit of it. He tells me that they are now lower than ever, this place being over stock'd with them, and that he has himselfe 16,000 lying dead upon his hands, but I know all that he says is not to be litterally depended on. However, having receivd at the same time a letter from Sir John Williams in which he offers to pay me back my 1,600 livres in England,[2] I don't know whither I had not best accept of it, and should be glad to have your advice, who understand busyness better than I do. You have made me no answer to my Question whither you can carry Goods from hence custom free. In that case I could turn every Dollar into 4 shillings. I beg you would write particularly on this Subject as soon as possible because Sir John Williams desires a speedy answer to his offer.

[*Postscript*] Pray send me my Letters.

Text W MS i. 309–10 *Address* To His Excellency Wortley Montagu Ambassador at the Port. *End. by* W L. M. 1 April 1718. Her money sent by her unkle is come. Asks whether she had best take money for it in England or buy goods.

To Wortley *9 April* [*1718*]

I have Mr. Barker's note[3] for the 2,000 Dollars. I have not mention'd to any body whatever your design of going sooner

[1] John Lethieullier (1667–1737), Turkey merchant. In 1720 he became treasurer of the Levant Company in Constantinople (SP 105/164, f. 28).

[2] Sir John Williams, knight (1713) and Alderman, was 'at the Head of the

Turkey Trade' at his death in 1743 (*Gentleman's Mag.*, p. 274).

[3] Edward Barker (d. 1747), treasurer of the Levant Company in Constantinople (13 March 1717, SP 105/116; *London Mag.*, 1747, p. 580).

than by the Man of War, but it has been writ to several
people from Adrianople.[1] I was ask'd, and made answer (as
I allways do upon your affairs) that I knew nothing of it.
I perceive by my F[ather]'s Letter that he is desirous to be
well with us, and am very clearly of Opinion (if my opinion
is of any weight with you) that you should write him a civil
Letter. The birth of your Daughter is a proper occasion,
and you may date your Letter as if writ during my Lying in.
I know him perfectly well, and am very sure such a triffleing
respect would make a great Impression upon him. You need
not apprehend my expresing any great Joy for our return.
I hope tis less shocking to you[2] than to me, who have realy
suffer'd in my health by the uneasyness it has given me,
thô I take care to conceal it here as much as I can. Your Son
is very well; I cannot forbear telling you so, thô you do not
so much as ask after him.

Ap. 9.

Pray send me my other Letters.

I hear the F[rench] A[mbassador]'s busyness at Adrianople
is to buy the Holy Land,[3] and that there is a 1,000 purses[4]
offer'd for it, which is to pass throû his hands. I beleive he
neglects no oppertunity.

I sent for Mr. Leithuilier 2 days ago to speak to him
concerning my pieces of 8, and he made me abundance of
Complements and offers of service, saying that if you would
leave your money consign'd to him and have patience to

[1] W's plans for returning to England
were in flux. On 3 March 1718 O.S. he
informed Abraham Stanyan, his successor as ambassador, that he would
embark as soon as the man-of-war
arrived; but on 1 July O.S. Stanyan
wrote to James Craggs, Secretary of
State, that before news of the ship's
arrival at Smyrna had come, W 'was
resolved to return by Land, and I sent
him Passes for that Purpose, so that
I cannot yet determine which way he
will determine to go' (SP 97/24).

[2] W rationalized his diplomatic
failure and his disappointment by draft-
ing two essays, dated 1718, entitled
'Fame' and 'Losses' (W MS vii. 126–9).
On 21 July his diplomatic mission was

successfully accomplished by Robert
Sutton as British mediator in the Treaty
of Passarowitz.

[3] Bonnac's actual business was to
arrange for the repair of the cupola of
the Church of the Holy Sepulchre in
Jerusalem, which honour—like the edifice
itself—was claimed by both the Greek and
the Roman Churches. His diplomatic instructions in May 1716 had specifically
charged him with this mission (Charles
Schefer, *Mémoire historique sur l'ambassade de France à Constantinople par le
marquis de Bonnac*, 1894, pp. xxii, 167).

[4] A *purse* was valued (in 1753) at
500 dollars, with 4 shillings to the
dollar, i.e. £100 (*OED*).

wait for it, he would engage to send it home at 4 shillings or 4 shillings 6 pence a dollar. I told him I would write word to you of it. I suppose you'l than⟨k him⟩, but tis very proper to think more than once of acce⟨pting it⟩. You bid me prepare for our Journey, without saying in what manner. If you mean any thing of money Matters, pray be particular in your orders about them.

Here is some table gilt plate offer'd to me for the weight. It is not fine Silver but makes the same shew. If you think you shall want any thing of that kind, it may be a pennorth.

Text W MS i. 307–8   *Address* To His Excellency Wortley Montagu Ambassador at the Port   *End. by W* 9 April 1718. Mr. Lethieullier spoke to her of her Ps of 8/8

From Nicolas-François Rémond[1] *20/9 April 1718*

Si vous aimez les choses extraordinaires cette lettre ne vous deplaira pas. Je n'ai jamais eu l'honneur de vous voir et vraisemblablement je ne l'aurai jamais, cependant je vous ecris sans pouvoir m'en empescher. Monsieur l'abbé C[onti], qui est particulierrement de mes amis, m'a confié une lettre que vous lui avez ecritte de Constantinople.[2] Je l'ai lu; je l'ai relu cent fois; je l'ai copié et je ne la quitte ni jour ni nuit. Voyez ma vanité; sur cette seule lettre j'ai cru connoistre la singularité de vostre caractere et les agremens infinis de vostre esprit. Depuis ce jour là je ne puis plus parler aux femmes les plus spirituelles de cette cour, *tædet quotidianarum harum formarum*;[3] et si j'avois une maitresse je crois que je serois assez honnete homme pour la quitter. Ce que je fais ressemble un peu à ces inspirations subites dont parle Homere, et vous ne savez peutestre pas qu'on peut encore moins resister à celles de cette divinité qu'à celles de Minerve. Ou en suis

---

[1] Born 1676, a brother of the mathematician Pierre Rémond de Montmort (1678–1719) and of the littérateur Toussaint Rémond de Saint-Mard (1682–1757). He was *conseiller* in the Parlement de Paris in 1699, *premier conseiller* to the duc d'Orléans in 1705, and *introducteur des ambassadeurs* June 1719 to Dec. 1723 (Saint-Simon, *Mémoires*, ed. A. de Boislisle, 1879–1930, xxix. 262, n. 4). (He later mentions to LM his position as *introducteur*: W MS iv. 219.) Contemporary diarists charac-

terize him as ridiculous, unattractive, and pretentious, extremely clever and unscrupulous in ingratiating himself with people to further his fortune (Saint-Simon, ed. G. Truc, 1954–61, v. 156–7, 228; vi. 302–3; Mathieu Marais, *Journal*, ed. M. de Lescure, 1863, i. 503). This letter is translated on p. 457 below.

[2] Probably that on pp. 374–8 above.

[3] 'I am sick of your everyday beauties' (Terence, *The Eunuch*, II, iii, 6; transl. Loeb Library).

je, puisque dans mon egarement je cherche la justification d'un procedé si extraordinaire dans la theologie Payenne? Je n'ecoute plus vostre ami sur Monsieur Newton; je ne lui parle que de M[ilady] M[arie], et j'en aime moins Sharper[1] avec qui je suis tendrement uni depuis qu'il est en ce pays.[2] Si j'estois beau et aimable je crois que je serois allé m'embarquer à Marseille, et vous auriez été bien surprise de voir un disciple de Socrate venir se jetter à vos pieds dans ces promenades que vous faittes le long de cette riviere sous des ciprés et des orangers. Mais quelque philosophe que vous soyez je doute que la beauté de l'ame tint lieu auprès de vous des charmes de la figure, et je crains que vous ne m'eussiez renvoié à Madame de B[onnac]. J'ai toujours suivi mes sentimens plustost que ma raison et jusqu'à cette heure je ne m'en suis jamais mal trouvé. Voici la plus forte preuve que j'en donnerai de ma vie. Vous allez me croire le plus grand fou du monde; je veux bien en courre le risque si vous estes aussi aimable que vostre lettre.

à Paris ce 20 d'Avril 1718

Text W MS iv. 212–13   *End. by W* R.

To Lady Bristol[3] [*10 April 1718*]

At length I have heard, for the 1st time,[4] from My Dear Lady B⟨ristol, this present 10th of April 1718. Yet⟩[5] I am perswaded You have had the goodness to writ[e] before, but I have had the ill fortune to Lose your letters. Since my Last I have stay'd quietly at Constantinople, a City that I ought in Conscience to give Your Ladyship a right Notion of, Since I know You can have none but what is Partial and mistaken from the writings of Travellers. 'Tis certain there

[1] Apparently Lord Stair, British Ambassador in Paris. LM had used this nickname in her *Court Poems* (1716) to refer to him (Halsband, *LM*, pp. 49–50).

[2] According to Saint-Simon, Rémond was Stair's tool, used to further the Ambassador's political intrigues (ed. Truc, v. 157). Except for the spring of 1717, Stair had been in Paris since Jan. 1715 (D. B. Horn, *Brit. Dipl. Rep. 1689–1789*, 1932, p. 15).

[3] Only the superscription 'Letter 42 / To the Countesse of B' is in LM's hand; the letter itself is in the hand of the same copyist as the other two copied letters (to Pope, 17 June [1717]; to Mrs.

Thistlethwayte, 4 Jan. [1718]). That this letter had an actual counterpart is evident from Lady Bristol's remark to her husband on 31 July 1718: 'I think I am like Lady M. Wortley, who has wrote me four sheets of paper from Constantinople; I wish I coud send it' (John Hervey, *Letter-Books*, 1894, ii. 66).

[4] LM contradicts her earlier acknowledgement that she had received in Vienna a letter from Lady Bristol (see above, p. 285).

[5] These words, though struck out by LM, can still be deciphered.

are many people that pass years here in Pera without having ever seen it, and yet they all pretend to describe it.

Pera, Tophana and Galata, wholly inhabited by Frank Christians (and which together make the appearance of a very fine Town), are divided from it by the Sea, which is not above half so broad as the broadest part of the Thames, but the Christian men are loath to hazard the adventures they Sometimes meet with amongst the Levents or Seamen (worse Monsters than our Watermen), and the Women must cover their faces to go there, which they have a perfect aversion to do. 'Tis true they wear Vails in Pera, but they are Such as only Serve to Shew their Beauty to more advantage, and which would not be permitted in Constantinople. Those reasons deter almost every Creature from Seeing it, and the French Ambassadresse will return to France (I believe) without ever having been there. You'l wonder, Madam, to hear me add that I have been there very often. The asmak, or Turkish vail, is become not only very easy but agreeable to me, and if it was not, I would be content to endure some inconveniency to content a passion so powerfull with me as Curiosity; and indeed the pleasure of going in a Barge to Chelsea is not comparable to that of rowing upon the Canal of the Sea here, where for 20 miles together down the Bosphorus the most Beautifull variety of Prospects present themselves. The Asian Side is cover'd with fruit trees, villages and the most delightfull Landschapes in nature. On the European stands Constantinople, situate on Seven Hills. The unequal heights make it seem as Large again as it is (tho' one of the Largest Citys in the world), Shewing an agreeable mixture of Gardens, Pine and Cypress trees, Palaces, Mosques and publick buildings, rais'd one above another with as much Beauty and appearance of Symetry as your Ladyship ever saw in a Cabinet adorn'd by the most skilfull hands, Jars shewing themselves above Jars, mix'd with Canisters, babys and Candlesticks. This is a very odd Comparison, but it gives me an exact Image of the thing.[1]

I have taken care to see as much of the Seraglio as is

[1] This passage was probably what impressed Byron as 'the very view / Which charm'd the charming Mary Montagu' (*Don Juan*, v. 3).

to be seen. It is on a point of Land runing into the Sea: a Palace of prodigious extent, but very irregular; The Gardens a large Compass of ground full of high Cypress trees, which is all I know of them; The buildings all of white Stone, leaded on Top, with Gilded Turrets and Spires, which look very magnificent, and indeed I beleive there is no Christian King's Palace half so Large. There are 6 Large Courts in it all built round and set with trees, having Gallerys of Stone: one of these for the Guard, another for the Slaves, another for the Officers of the Kitchin, another for the Stables, the 5th for the Divan, The 6th for the Apartment destin'd for Audiences. On the Ladys' side there is at least as many more, with distinct Courts belonging to their Eunuchs and Attendants, their Kitchins, etc.[1]

The next remarkable Structure is that of St. Sophia, which 'tis very difficult to see. I was forc'd to send three times to the Caimaicam (the Governour of the Town), and he assembl'd the Chief Effendis or heads of the Law and inquir'd of the Mufti whether it was Lawfull to permit it. They pass'd some days in this Important Debate, but I insisting on my request, permission was granted. I can't be inform'd why the Turks are more delicate on the Subject of this Mosque than any of the others, where what Christian pleases may enter without Scruple.[2] I fancy they imagine that having been once consecrated, people on pretence of Curiosity might prophane it with prayers, particularly to those Saints who are still very visible in Mosaick work, and no other way defac'd but by the decays of time,[3] for 'tis absolutely false what is so universally asserted, that the

[1] A full, detailed description of the Seraglio is given in Norman Penzer, *The Harem*, 1937, chap. iii–v.

[2] Permission for Christians to visit Saint Sophia, though expressly forbidden, was sometimes granted, according to Dumont (p. 154). More specifically, it was usually granted to ambassadors (Jean Otter, *Voyage en Turquie et en Perse*, 1748, i. 25). Hence LM's visit, as related in this letter, is plausible. In 1741, she told Joseph Spence a fantastic tale of how she had disguised herself as a Turk, and accompanied by the

similarly disguised Princess of Transylvania had risked her life to visit the mosque (Eg MS. 2234, f. 249; in Halsband, *LM*, pp. 82–83).

[3] Travellers disagreed as to whether the images were defaced by the Turks. Their varying accounts are gathered in Cyril Mango, *The Mosaics of St. Sophia at Istanbul*, 1962, Appendix II. In addition, see Sandys, *Travels*, 7th ed., 1673 (p. 25); *Nouvelle Description de la ville de Constantinople*, 1721 (pp. 17–18); Richard Pococke, *Description of the East*, 1743–5 (II, ii. 129).

Turks defac'd all the Images that they found in the City. The Dome of St. Sophia is said to be 113 foot Diameter, built upon Arches, Sustain'd by vast pillars of Marble, the pavement and Stair-case Marble. There is 2 rows of Gallerys Supported with pillars of particollour'd Marble, and the whole roof Mosaic work, part of which decays very fast and drops down. They presented me a handfull of it. The Composition Seems to me a Sort of glass or that Paste with which they make counterfit Jewells.[1] They Shew here the Tomb of the Emperour Constantine,[2] for which they have a great Veneration. This is a dull, imperfect description of this celebrated building, but I understand Architecture so Little that I am affraid of talking Nonsense in endeavouring to speak of it particularly.

Perhaps I am in the wrong, but some Turkish Mosques please me better. That of Sultan Soliman[3] is an Exact Square with 4 fine Towers on the Angles, in the midst a Noble Cupulo supported with beautifull Marble Pillars, Two lesser at the ends Supported in the Same manner, The Pavement and Gallery round the Mosque of Marble. Under the great Cupulo is a fountain adorn'd with Such fine collour'd pillars I can hardly think them natural Marble. On one Side is the Pulpit of white Marble, and on the other the little Gallery for the Grand Signor. A fine Stair case leads to it and it is built up with gilded Lattices. At the upper end is a sort of Altar where the name of God is written, and before it stands 2 Candlesticks as high as a man, with wax candles as thick as 3 Flambeaux. The Pavement is Spread with fine Carpets and the Mosque illuminated with a vast number of Lamps. The Court leading to it is very Spacious, with Gallerys of Marble with green Coloums, cover'd with 28 leaded Cupulos on 2 sides, and a fine fountain of 3 basins in the midst of it. This Description may serve for all the Mosques in Constantinople; the Model is exactly the same, and they

[1] A century later an observer noted that 'the mosaic of the dome is constantly falling from its cement, and is found to consist of small cubes about the size of playing-dice, of various-coloured glass, which the imaums collect and sell . . .' (Robert Walsh, *Constantinople and the Scenery of the Seven* *Churches of Asia Minor*, First Series, [*c.* 1839], i. 47).

[2] Guides tell strange tales. None of the Imperial tombs is or ever was in Saint Sophia.

[3] Described by G. F. Gemelli Careri in A. and J. Churchill, *Voyages*, 1704 (iv. 78).

only differ in Largeness and richness of Materials. That of the Validé is the Largest of all, built entirely of Marble, the most prodigious and (I think) the most beautifull Structure I ever saw, be it spoke to the honour of our Sex, for it was founded by the Mother[1] of Mahomet the 4th; (between friends) St. Paul's Church would make a pitifull figure near it, as any of our Squares would do near the Atlerdan [sic] or Place of Horses, *At* signifying a horse in Turkish.

This was the Hyppodrome in the Reign of the Greek Emperors. In the midst of it is a brazen Column of three Serpents twisted together with their mouths gapeing. 'Tis impossible to learn why so odd a Pillar was erected; the Greeks can tell nothing but fabulous Legends when they are ask'd the meaning of it, and there is no Sign of its having ever had any Inscription.[2] At the upper End is an Obelisk of porphyry, probably brought from Egypt, the Hierogly-phics all very entire, which I look upon as meer Ancient Puns. It is plac'd on 4 little brazen Pillars upon a Pedestal of Square free stone full of Figures in bas reliefe on two sides, one Square representing a Battle, another an Assembly. The others have Inscriptions in Greek and Latin. The last I took in my pocket book and is Literally:

> Difficilis quondam Dominis parere serenis
> Iussus et extinctis palmam portare Tyrannis
> Omnia Theodosio cedunt, sobolique perreni.[3]

[1] Hadice Turhan (1627–82), Valide Sultan (Princess-mother), favourite of Sultan Ibrahim (1615–48) (A. D. Alderson, *Structure of the Ottoman Dynasty*, 1956, Table XXXVII). Dumont considered it the most beautiful mosque he had ever seen (p. 157).

[2] The serpent column in the At-meydan had been brought from Delphi, but its exact significance to the Turks was disputed by travel writers: Edmund Chishull (*Travels in Turkey* . . ., 1747, pp. 40, 45), Sieur Du Loir (*Voyages*, 1654, pp. 53–54), and Dumont (p. 151). LM describes it as intact, as does Robert de Dreux (*Voyage en Turquie et en Grèce* . . . *1665–1669*, ed. H. Pernot, 1925, p. 50); other travellers noted that

one or more of the heads had been broken off. Aaron Hill may provide the solution for this puzzle: that one of the heads had fallen off but was then fastened 'by some Ingenious Artist' (p. 138). The serpent column did bear an inscription, and had been brought from Delphi, where it had been topped by a golden tripod (E. L. Hicks and G. F. Hill, *Greek Hist. Inscriptions*, rev. ed., 1901, pp. 22–25).

[3] The inscription continues:

> Ter denis sic victus ego domitusque diebus
> Iudice sub Proclo superas elatus ad auras.

(Of lords serene a stubborn subject

PLATE 7

Lady M-y W-r-t-l-y M-nt-g-e
The Female Traveller
In the Turkish Dress.

Let Men who glory in their better sense,
Read, hear, and learn Humility from hence;
No more let them Superior Wisdom boast,
They can but epual M-nt-g-e at most.

Engraving of Lady Mary Wortley Montagu as
'The Female Traveller'

Your Lord will interpret these lines.[1] Don't fancy they are a Love Letter to him. All the Figures have their heads on, and I cannot forbear reflecting again on the Impudence of Authors who all Say they have not, but I dare swear the greatest part of them never saw them, but took the report from the Greeks, who resist with incredible fortitude the conviction of their own eyes whenever they have invented Lyes to the Dishonnour of their Enemys. Were you to ask them, there is nothing worth seeing in Constantinople but Sancta Sophia, tho' there are several larger Mosques. That of Sultan Achmet[2] has that of particular, its gates are of brass. In all these Mosques there are little Chappels where are the Tombs of the Founders and their families, with Vast Candles burning before them.

The Exchanges are all Noble Buildings, full of fine Alleys, the greatest part Supported with pillars, and kept wonderfully neat.[3] Every Trade has their distinct Alley, the Merchandize dispos'd in the same order as in the New Exchange at London. The Bisisten, or Jewellers' Quarter, shews so much Riches, Such a Vast quantity of Diamonds and all kind of precious Stones, that they dazle the Sight. The Embroiderers' is also very glittering, and people walk here as much for Diversion as busyness. The Markets are most of them handsome Squares, and admirably well provided, perhaps better than in any other part of the World. I know You'l expect I should say something particular of that of the Slaves, and you will Imagine me half a Turk when I don't speak of it with the same horror other Christians have done before me, but I cannot forbear applauding the Humanity of the Turks to those Creatures. They are never ill us'd and

once, bidden to bear the palm to tyrants also that have met their doom—all yields to Theodosius and his undying issue—so conquered I in thrice ten days and tamed, was under Proclus' judgeship raised to the skies above.) Chishull (p. 41) could read only four lines, the fifth being covered in the ground; he copied the hidden fifth line from Sandys, who gives the entire inscription (p. 27). Both the inscription and the translation are given in

Preliminary Report upon the Excavations Carried Out in the Hippodrome of Constantinople in 1927 on Behalf of the British Academy, 1928, pp. 43–44.

[1] In his letters John Hervey (1665–1751), 1st Earl of Bristol, frequently quotes Latin tags (Hervey, *Letter-Books*, 1894, *passim*).

[2] 'For beauty, it exceeds *S. Sophia*' (G. F. Gemelli Careri, p. 76).

[3] Described by Hill (p. 142) and Dumont (p. 149).

their Slavery is in my Opinion no worse than Servitude all over the world. 'Tis true they have no wages, but they give them yearly Cloaths to a higher Value than our Salarys to any ordinary Servant. But You'l object Men buy women with an Eye to Evil. In my opinion they are bought and sold as publickly and more infamously in all our Christian great Citys. I must add to the Description of Constantinople that the Historical Pillar is no more, dropp'd down about 2 year befor I came.[1] I have seen no other footsteps of Antiquity, except the Aquæducts,[2] which are So Vast that I am apt to believe they are yet ancienter than the Greek Empire, tho' the Turks have clapp'd in Some stones with Turkish Inscriptions to give their Nation the honnour of so great a Work, but the Deceit is easily discover'd.

The other publick Buildings are the Hans and Monasterys, the first very large and numerous, The 2nd few in number and not at all Magnificent. I had the Curiosity to visit one of them and observe the Devotions of the Dervises, which are as Whimsical as any in Rome. These fellows have permission to marry, but are confin'd to an odd Habit, which is only a peice of Coarse white cloath wrapp'd about 'em, with their Legs and Arms naked. Their Order has few other rules, except that of performing their Fantastic rites every Tuesday and Friday, which is in this manner. They meet together in a Large Hall, where they all Stand with their Eyes fix'd on the Ground and their Arms across, while the Imaum, or preacher, reads part of the Alcoran from a Pulpit plac'd in the midst; and when he has done, 8 or 10 of them make a Melancholly Consort with their Pipes, which are no unmusical Instruments. Then he reads again and makes a Short exposition on what he has read, after which they Sing and play till their Superiour (the only one of them dress'd in green) rises and begins a sort of Solemn dance. They all stand about him in a regular figure; and while Some play, the others tye their robe (which is very wide) fast round their Wasts and begin to turn round with an Amazing Swiftness and yet with great regard to the Musick, moving Slower or

---

[1] Actually in 1695, after having been weakened by earthquakes and fire (1861, i. 358, n. 1).

[2] That of Valentinian, 34 miles in length, was praised by Hill (p. 146).

faster as the Tune is plaid. This lasts above an hour without any of them shewing the least appearance of Giddyness, which is not to be wonder'd at when it is consider'd they are all us'd to it from Infancy, most of them being devoted to this way of life from their Birth, and Sons of Dervises. There turn'd amongst them Some little Dervises of 6 or 7 years old who seem'd no more disorder'd by that exercise than the others. At the end of the Ceremony they shout out: There is no other God but God, and Mahomet is his prophet; after which they kiss the Superiour's hand and retire. The whole is perform'd with the most Solemn Gravity. Nothing can be more Austere than the form of these people. They never raise their Eyes and seem devoted to Contemplation, And as ridiculous as this is in Description, there is Something touching in the Air of Submission and mortification they assume. —This Letter is of a horrible length, but you may burn it when you have read enough.

⟨Mr. Wortley is not yet here,[1] but I may assure your Ladyship in his name of the respect he has for you. I give humble service to My Lord Bristol and Mr. Hervey.⟩[2]

Text H MS 253, pp. 380–97

To Madame ——— [*April 1718*][3]

Je suis si aise de vous retrouver, Ma chere Madame, que je ne puis plus me plaindre de vous avoir perduë; & le plaisir que me donne cette lettre que je viens de recevoir aujourd'huy, me fait entierement oublier les inquietudes de dix mois passez.

L'Oisiveté est la mere des vices (comme vous sçavez)

[1] W was still in Adrianople as late as 30 April/11 May, when he wrote to Craggs (SP 97/24); he was expected to depart for Constantinople four or five days later (Stanyan to Craggs, 29 April 1718 O.S., SP 97/24).

[2] The postscript was struck out by LM. John Hervey (1696–1743), later Baron Hervey, was Bristol's second son. He became one of LM's intimate friends.

[3] Madame de Bonnac teased LM: 'si j'en crois une Lettre imprimée dans le Mercure galand du mois d'octobre de l'année passée, on pretend que les femmes n'ont d'autre plaisir dans ce pais cy que d'y faire des enfans. Si vous connoissés, par hazard, l'auteur de cette lettre, he vous prie, madame, de l'avertir qu'il y peut encore ajouter un article sur mon sujet, puis que Je viens d'accoucher d'un troisieme garcon,' LM evidently expressed annoyance at its publication (20 Sept. 1719, 28 April 1720, W MS iv. 154, 156).

LM's letter, now ascribed for the first time, is translated on p. 458 below.

& n'ayant rien de meilleur à faire, j'ai fait une fille.¹ Je sçai que vous m'allez dire que j'ai fort mal fait; mais, si vous aviez été à ma place, je crois (Dieu me pardonne) que vous en auriez fait deux ou trois. Dans ce païs ci, il est tout aussi necessaire de faire voir des preuves de jeunesse, pour être reçûë parmi les beautez, que de montrer des preuves de Noblesse pour être reçû parmi les Chevaliers de Malte.² J'etois très fâchée de cette necessité; mais, remarquant qu'on me regardoit avec un grand air de mépris, je me suis mise enfin à la mode, & je suis accouchée comme les autres. Pour cette raison là, entre une infinité d'autres, je voudrois de tout mon coeur hâter mon retour, parce que je suis obligée absolument d'acoucher tous les ans, tant que je resterai ici. L'Ambassadrice de France s'en est donné à coeur joye; elle est accouchée & est encore grosse. Les Dames du païs n'estiment les femmes, que selon la quantité de leurs productions; & j'ai peine à leur persuader que c'est une excuse legitime d'être trois mois sans grossesse, parce que mon Mari est à cent lieuës de moi.

Je fais tous les jours des voeux pour revoir mon Roy, ma patrie, & mes amis. Je suis fort diligente de tout voir; je parle passablement la langue, & j'ai eu l'avantage de faire amitié avec des Dames Turques, & de leur être agreable; & je puis me vanter d'être la premiere étrangere qui ait jamais eu ce plaisir. J'ai visité une Sultane veuve du feu Empereur; & par ce moyen, je suis instruite de tout le manege du Serail; elle m'a assuré que l'histoire du Mouchoir si bien crûë chez nous, n'a pas un mot de vrai.³

J'ai attrapé un billet doux Turc que je vous porterai, & qui est veritablement si curieux, que je ne puis assez admirer la stupidité des Voyageurs de n'en avoir pas encore aporté en Europe.⁴ Ma chere Madame, Dieu vous donne (en phrase Turque) le plaisir qui vous contenteroit, & à moi celui de vous revoir.

Text 'Lettre De Me . . . à Me . . . écrite de Constantinople', *Le Nouveau Mercure* [*Galant*], Oct. 1718, pp. 98–99⁵

¹ Mary, b. 19 Jan. 1718.

² LM repeats this observation and comparison in her letter to Mrs. Thistlethwayte of 4 Jan. [1718] (p. 372 above).

³ LM gives a fuller account of this visit in her letter to Lady Mar of 10 March [1718] (pp. 380-5 above).

⁴ LM describes such a 'billet doux' in her letter of 16 March [1718] (pp. 388-9 above).

⁵ Discussed by the Editor in *Philological Quart.*, xliv, 1965, pp. 180-3.

To the Countesse of —— [*May 1718*][1]

⟨Your Lady ship may be assur'd I receiv'd yours with very
great pleasure. I am very glad to hear that our freinds are in
good Health, particularly Mr. Congreve, who I heard was
ill of the Gout.⟩[2] I am now prepareing to leave Constantinople, and perhaps you will accuse me of Hipocricy when I
tell you 'tis with regret, but I am us'd to the air and have
learnt the Language. I am easy here, and as much as I love
travelling, I tremble at the inconveniencys attending so great
a Journey with a numerous family and a little Infant hanging
at the breast. However, I endeavour upon this Occasion to
do as I have hitherto done in all the odd turns of my Life,
turn 'em, if I can, to my Diversion. In order to this, I ramble
every day, wrap'd up in my ferigé and asmak, about Constantinople and amuse my selfe with seeing all that is curious
in it. I know you'l expect this declaration should be follow'd
with some account of what I have seen, but I am in no
humour to copy what has been writ so often over. To what
purpose should I tell you that Constantinople was the
Ancient Bizantium; that tis at present the Conquest of a
race of people suppos'd Scythians; that there is 5 or 6,000
Mosques in it; that Sancta Sophia was founded by Justinian,
etc? I'll assure you tis not want of learning that I forbear
writeing all these bright things. I could also, with little
trouble, turn over Knolles and Sir Paul Rycaut to give you
a list of Turkish Emperours,[3] but I will not tell you what you
may find in every Author that has writ of this Country.

I am more enclin'd, out of a true female spirit of Contradiction, to tell you the falsehood of a great part of what you
find in authors; as, for example, the admirable Mr. Hill,
who so gravely asserts that he saw in Sancta Sophia a sweating Pillar very Balsamic for disorder'd heads. There is not
the least tradition of any such matter, and I suppose it was

[1] The letter bears no date; from its
position in the MS this one is probable.
[2] The two sentences between brackets
were struck out by LM. Pope had
mentioned Congreve's 'fitts of the
Gout' in a letter to her the previous
autumn (*Corr.* i. 442).
[3] Richard Knolles (1550?–1610),
historian of the Turks, published his
work in 1603; Paul Rycaut wrote a continuation of it, the final volume published 1700. LM used both as sources.

reveal'd to him in Vision during his wonderfull stay in the Egyptian Catacombs, for I am sure he never heard of any such miracle here.[1] Tis also very pleasant to observe how tenderly he and all his Brethren Voyage-writers lament the miserable confinement of the Turkish Ladys, who are (perhaps) freer than any Ladys in the universe, and are the only Women in the world that lead a life of unintterupted pleasure,[2] exempt from cares, their whole time being spent in visiting, bathing, or the agreable Amusement of spending Money and inventing new fashions. A Husband would be thought mad that exacted any degree of Œconomy from his wife, whose expences are no way limited but by her own fancy. Tis his busyness to get Money and hers to spend it, and this noble prerogative extends it selfe to the very meanest of the Sex. Here is a fellow that carrys embrodier'd handkercheifs upon his back to sell, as miserable a figure as you may suppose such a mean dealer, yet I'll assure you his wife scorns to wear any thing less than cloath of Gold, has her Ermin Furs, and a very handsome set of Jewells for her head. They go abroad when and where they please. Tis true they have no public places but the Bagnios, and there can only be seen by their own Sex; however, that is a Diversion they take great pleasure in.

I was 3 days ago at one of the finest in the Town and had the oppertunity of seeing a Turkish Bride receiv'd there and all the ceremonys us'd on that Occasion, which made me recollect the Epithilamium of Helen by Theocritus,[3] and it seems to me that the same Customs have continu'd ever since. All the she-freinds, Relations and acquaintance of the 2 familys newly ally'd meet at the Bagnio. Several others go out of Curiosity, and I beleive there was that day at least 200 Women. Those that were or had been marry'd, place'd themselves round the room on the marble Sofas, but the Virgins very hastily threw off their cloaths and appear'd

[1] Hill writes of the sweating column (p. 138) and the Egyptian catacombs (pp. 263–71). His considerable shortcomings as a travel writer are noticed by Terence Spencer (*Fair Greece, Sad Relic*, 1954, pp. 142–5). The sweating column is, however, also mentioned in 1599 by George Douse (1861, i. 361, n. i) and in 1610 by George Sandys (*Travels*, 7th ed., 1673, p. 25).

[2] LM treats this topic more fully in her letter to Lady Mar, 1 April [1717] (pp. 327–9 above).

[3] *Idyllium* xviii.

without other Ornament or covering than their own long hair braided with pearl or Riband. 2 of them met the bride at the door, conducted by her Mother and another grave relation. She was a Beautifull Maid of about 17, very richly drest and shineing with Jewells, but was presently reduce'd by them to the state of nature. 2 others fill'd silver gilt pots with perfume and begun the procession, the rest following in pairs to the number of 30. The Leaders sung an Epithilamium answer'd by the others in chorus, and the 2 last led the fair Bride, her Eyes fix'd on the ground with a charming affectation of Modesty. In this order they march'd round the 3 large rooms of the bagnio. Tis not easy to represent to you the Beauty of this sight, most of them being well proportion'd and white skin'd, all of them perfectly smooth and polish'd by the frequent use of Bathing. After having made their tour, the bride was again led to every Matron round the rooms, who saluted her with a compliment and a present, some of Jewells, others pieces of stuff, Handkercheifs, or little Galantrys of that nature, which she thank'd them for by kissing their hands.[1]

I was very well pleas'd with having seen this ceremony, and you may beleive me that the Turkish Ladys have at least as much wit and Civillity, nay, Liberty, as Ladys Amongst us. Tis true the same customs that give them so many oppertunitys of gratifying their evil Inclinations (if they have any) also puts it very fully in the power of their Husbands to revenge them if they are discover'd, and I don't doubt but they suffer sometimes for their Indiscretions in a very severe manner. About 2 months ago there was found at day break not very far from my House the bleeding body of a young woman, naked, only wrapp'd in a coarse sheet, with 2 wounds with a knife, one in her side and another in her Breast. She was not yet quite cold, and so surprizingly Beautifull that there were very few men in Pera that did not go to look upon her, but it was not possible for any body to know her, no woman's face being known. She was suppos'd to be brought in dead of night from the Constantinople side

---

[1] Most of the above paragraph was copied by Ingres (in French translation) into his notebooks; it influenced his painting, 'Le Bain Turc' (see above, p. 313, n. 1).

and laid there. Very little enquiry was made about the Mur-
derer, and the corps privately bury'd without noise.[1] Murder
is never persu'd by the King's officers as with us. Tis the
busyness of the next Relations to revenge the dead Person;
and if they like better to compound the matter for Money (as
they generally do) there is no more said of it.[2] One would
imagine this deffect in their Government should make such
Tragedys very frequent, yet they are extreamly rare, which is
enough to prove the people not naturally cruel, neither do I
think in many other particulars they deserve the barbarous
character we give them.

    I am well acquainted with a Christian Woman of Quality
who made it her choice to live with a Turkish Husband, and
is a very agreable sensible Lady. Her story is so extrodinary
I cannot forbear relateing it, but I promise you it shall be in
as few words as I can possibly express it. She is a Spaniard,
and was at Naples with her family when that Kingdom was
part of the Spanish Dominion. Coming from thence in a
Feloucca, accompany'd by her Brother, they were attack'd
by the Turkish Admiral, boarded and taken; and now, how
shall I modestly tell you the rest of her Adventure? The
same Accident happen'd to her that happen'd to the fair
Lucretia so many Years before her, but she was too good
a Christian to kill her selfe as that heathenish Roman did.
The Admiral was so much charm'd with the Beauty and
long-suffering of the Fair Captive that as his first complement he gave immediate Liberty to her Brother and attendants, who made haste to Spain and in a few months sent the
sumn of £4,000 sterling as a Ransom for his sister. The
Turk took the Money, which he presented to her, and told
her she was at Liberty, but the Lady very discreetly weigh'd
the different treatment she was likely to find in her native
Country. Her Catholic Relations, as the kindest thing they
could do for her in her present Circumstances, would certainly confine her to a Nunnery for the rest of her Days. Her
Infidel Lover was very handsome, very tender, fond of her,

---

[1] This is corroborated by Thomas
Thornton at the end of the century:
'I have frequently heard, during my
residence in Pera, of atrocities such as
Lady M. W. Montagu mentions' (*The
Present State of Turkey*, 1809, ii. 291).
  [2] 'Money clears the most barbarous
Malefactor' (Dumont, p. 239).

and lavish'd at her feet all the Turkish Magnificence. She answer'd him very resolutely that her Liberty was not so precious to her as her Honnour, that he could no way restore that but by marrying her. She desir'd him to accept the Ransom as her Portion and give her the satisfaction of knowing no Man could boast of her favours without being her Husband. The Admiral was transported at this kind offer and sent back the Money to her Relations, saying he was too happy in her Possession. He marry'd her and never took any other wife, and (as she says her selfe) she never had any reason to repent the choice she made. He left her some years after one of the richest widows in Constantinople, but there is no remaining honnourably a single woman, and that consideration has oblig'd her to marry the present Capitan Bassa (i.e. Admiral), his Successor.[1] I am afraid you'l think that my Freind fell in love with her Ravisher, but I am willing to take her word for it that she acted wholly on principles of Honnour, thô I think she might be reasonably touch'd at his Generosity, which is very often found amongst the Turks of Rank.

Tis a degree of Generosity to tell the Truth, and tis very rare that any Turk will assert a solemn falsehood.[2] I don't speak of the lowest sort, for as there is a great deal of Ignorance, there is very little virtue amongst them; and false Wittnesses are much cheaper than in Christendom, those wretches not being punish'd (even when they are publickly detected) with the rigour they ought to be. Now I am speaking of their Law, I don't know whither I have ever mention'd to you one custom peculiar to this Country. I mean Adoption, very common amongst the Turks and yet more amongst the Greeks and Armenians. Not having it in their power to give their Estates to a Freind or distant Relation to avoid its falling into the Grand Signor's treasury, when they are not likely to have Children of their own they chuse

---

[1] The hero of LM's romantic tale was probably Ibrahim Pasha, who held office as Lord Admiral from 1706 to 1709 (when Naples was a Spanish possession) and again from Feb. 1717 to Feb. 1718. His successor was Süleyman Kodja, who held office until 1721

(Joseph von Hammer, *Geschichte des osmanischen Reiches*, 1827–35, vii. 624).

[2] She had discussed lying in her letter of 4 Jan. [1718] (p. 373 above). Hill (p. 79) also comments on the Turks' truthfulness.

some pritty child of either sex amongst the meanest people, and carry the child and its parents before the cady, and there declare they receive it for their Heir. The Parents at the same time renounce all future claim to it, a writeing is drawn and wittness'd, and a child thus adopted cannot be disinherited. Yet I have seen some common Beggars that have refus'd to part with their children in this manner to some of the richest amongst the Greeks; so powerfull is the instinctive fondness natural to Parents! thô the adopting Fathers are generally very tender to these children of their Souls, as they call them. I own this custom pleases me much better than our absurd following our Name. Methinks tis much more reasonable to make happy and rich an infant whom I educate after my own manner, brought up (in the Turkish Phrase) upon my knees, and who has learnt to look upon me with a filial respect, than to give an Estate to a creature without other Merit or relation to me than by a few Letters. Yet this is an Absurdity we see frequently practis'd.

Now I have mention'd the Armenians, perhaps it will be agreable to tell you something of that Nation, with which I am sure you are utterly unacquainted. I will not trouble you with the Geographicall account of the Situation of their country, which you may see in the Map, or a Relation of their Ancient greatness, which you may read in the Roman History. They are now subject to the Turks, and, being very industrious in trade, and encreasing and multiplying, are dispers'd in great numbers through all the Turkish Dominions. They were (as they say) converted to the Christian Religion by St. Gregory, and are (perhaps) the devoutest Christians in the whole world. The cheife precepts of their Preists enjoyn the strict keeping of their Lents, which are at least 7 months in every year and are not to be dispens'd with on the most emergent necessity.[1] No occasion whatever can excuse them if they touch any thing more than meer herbs or Roots (without oil) and plain dry Bread. This is their Lenten diet. Mr. W[ortley] has one of his Interpreters of this nation, and the poor fellow was brought so low with the

[1] Other travel-writers remarked on this rigorous fasting (Hill, p. 186; Dumont, pp. 294–5; Paul Rycaut, *Present State of the Greek and Armenian Churches*, 1679, p. 415).

Severity of his fasts that his Life was dispair'd of, yet neither his master's commands or the Doctor's intreatys (who declar'd nothing else could save his life) were powerfull enough to prevail with him to take 2 or 3 spoonfulls of Broth. Excepting this, which may rather be call'd custom than an Article of Faith, I see very little in their Religion different from ours. Tis true they seem to encline very much to Mr. Wh[iston]'s doctrine;[1] neither do I think the Greek church very distant from it, since tis certain the insisting on the Holy Spirit only proceeding from the Father is makeing a plain subordination in the Son. But the Armenians have no notion of Transubstantiation, whatever Account Sir Paul Rycaut gives of them (which account I am apt to beleive was design'd to complement our Court in 1679),[2] and they have a great horror for those amongst them that change to the Roman Religion.

What is most extrodinary in their Customs is their Matrimony, a Ceremony I beleive unparrellell'd all over the world. They are allways promis'd very young, but the espous'd never see one another till 3 days after their Marriage. The Bride is carry'd to church with a cap on her head in the fashion of a large Trencher, and over it a red silken vail which covers her all over to her feet. The Preist asks the Bridegroom whither he is contented to marry that woman, be she deaf, be she blind? These are the litteral words, to which having answer'd yes, she is led home to his house accompany'd with all the freinds and Relations on both sides, singing and danceing, and is plac'd on a cushion in the corner of the Sofa, but Her vail never lifted up, not even by her husband, till she has been 3 days marry'd.[3] There is something so odd and monstrous in these ways that I could not beleive them till I had enquir'd of several Armenians my

[1] William Whiston (see above, p. 317) upheld the Arian doctrine that Christ was not of the same essence or substance with God.

[2] 'They hold Transubstantiation as do the *Papists*, from whom the Priests readily accepted of such a Doctrine as tends to their Honour and Profit' (Rycaut, in his book on the Greek and Armenian Churches 'Written at the Command of his Majesty [Charles II],' p. 433). This controversial point of comparative theology is discussed in Spencer (pp. 95–101).

[3] Sandys (p. 69), Rycaut (p. 312), and Joseph de Tournefort (*Relation d'un voyage du Levant*, 1717, ii. 415–17) give slightly differing accounts of Armenian marriage customs.

selfe who all assur'd me of the truth of them, particularly one young fellow who wept when he spoke of it, being promis'd by his Mother to a Girl that he must marry in this manner, thô he protested to me he had rather dye than submit to this slavery, having allready figur'd his Bride to himselfe with all the Deformitys in Nature.

I fancy I see you bless your selfe at this terrible Relation. I cannot conclude my letter with a more surprizing story, yet tis as seriously true as that I am, Dear Sister,[1] your etc.

Text H MS 253, pp. 398–415

To the Abbé Conti *19 May 1718*

Constantinople, May 19, 1718

I am extremely pleas'd with hearing from You, and my vanity (the darling frailty of Humankind) not a little flatter'd by the uncommon questions you ask me, thô I am utterly incapable of answering them, and indeed were I as good a Mathematician as Euclid himselfe, it requires an age's stay to make just observations on the air and vapours.

I have not been yet a full Year here and am on the point of removing; such is my rambling Destiny. This will surprize you, and can surprize no body so much as my selfe. Perhaps You will accuse me of Lazyness or Dullness, or both together, that can leave this place without giving you some account of the Turkish Court. I can only tell you that if you please to read Sir Paul Rycaut You will there find a full and true Account of the Viziers, the Beglerbeys, the civil and spiritual Government, the officers of the Seraglio, etc., things that tis very easy to procure lists of and therefore may be depended on, thô other Storys, God knows—I say no more—every body is at liberty to write their own Remarks. The manners of people may change or some of them escape the observation of travellers, but 'tis not the same of the Government, and for that reason, since I can tell you nothing new

---

[1] This is an 'editorial' addition made by LM in transcribing the letter, for the opening two sentences, which she had struck out, make it clear that her sister was not the recipient.

I will tell nothing of it. In the same silence shall be pass'd over the Arsenal and 7 Towers; and for Mosques I have allready describ'd one of the noblest to you very particularly;[1] but I cannot forbear takeing notice to you of a mistake of Gemelli (thô I honnour him in a much higher degree than any other voyage-writer).[2] He says that there is noe remains of Calcedon.[3] This is certainly a mistake. I was there yesterday and went cross the canal in my Galley, the sea being very narrow between that city and Constantinople. 'Tis still a large Town, and has several Mosques in it. The Christians still call it Calcedonia, and the Turks give it a name I forgot, but which is only a corruption of the same word.[4] I suppose this an Errour of his Guide, which his short stay hinder'd him from rectifying, for I have (in other matters) a very just Esteem for his veracity.

Nothing can be pleasanter than the Canal, and the Turks are so well acquainted with its beautys, all their Pleasure-seats are built on its banks, where they have at the same time the most beautifull Prospects in Europe and Assia. There are near one another some hundreds of Magnificent Palaces. Humane Grandeur being here yet more unstable than any where else, 'tis common for the Heirs of a great three-tail'd Bassa not to be rich enough to keep in repair the House he built; thus in a few years they all fall to Ruin. I was yesterday to see that of the late Grand Vizier who was kill'd at Peter-waradin. It was built to receive his Royal Bride, daughter of the present Sultan, but he did not live to see her there.[5] I have a great mind to describe it to you, but I check that Inclination, knowing very well that I cannot give you, with my best description, such an Idea of it as I ought. It is situated on one of the most delightfull parts of the Canal, with a fine wood on the side of a Hill behind it. The extent of it is prodigious; the Guardian assur'd me there is 800

---

[1] In the letter addressed from Adrianople the previous year on 17 May (pp. 357–9 above).

[2] Giovanni Francesco Gemelli Careri (1651–1725), a Neapolitan doctor of civil law. The veracity of his travel-writings has been disputed.

[3] 'After Dinner, I went over in a Boat to *Asia*, to see the Remains of the Antient *Calcedon*, where Landing, I found no thing to prove there had been such a City, but the fair Ground it stood on' (in A. and J. Churchill, *Voyages*, 1704, iv. 82).

[4] In modern Turkish Kadıköy.

[5] LM related this pathetic incident in her letter to Lady Bristol on 1 April [1717] (p. 321 above).

Rooms in it. I will not answer for that number since I did not count them, but tis certain the number is very large and the whole adorn'd with a profusion of marble, gilding, and the most exquisite painting of fruit and flowers. The Windows are all sash'd with the finest cristaline Glass brought from England, and all the expensive Magnificence that you can suppose in a Palace founded by a vain young Luxurious Man with the wealth of a vast Empire at his Command. But noe part of it pleas'd me better than the Apartments destin'd for the Bagnios. There are 2 exactly built in the same Manner, answering to one Another; the Baths, fountains and pavements all of white marble, the roofes gilt, and the walls cover'd with Japan china; but adjoyning to them 2 Rooms, the upper part of which is divided into a sofa; in the 4 corners falls of water from the very Roofe, from shell to shell of white marble to the lower end of the room, where it falls into a large Basin surrounded with pipes that throw up the water as high as the room. The walls are in the nature of Lattices and on the outside of them vines and woodbines planted that form a sort of green Tapestry and give an agreable obscurity to these delightfull chambers. I should go on and let you into some of the other Apartments (all worthy your curiosity), but tis yet harder to describe a Turkish palace than any other, being built entirely irregular. There is nothing can be properly call'd front or wings, and thô such a confusion is (I think) pleasing to the sight, yet it would be very unintteligible in a Letter. I shall only add that the chamber destin'd for the Sultan, when he visits his daughter, is wainscoated with mother of Pearl fasten'd with Emeralds like nails; there are others of mother of Pearl and olive wood inlaid, and several of Japan China. The Gallerys (which are numerous and very large) are adorn'd with Jars of Flowers and Porcellane dishes of Fruit of all sorts, so well done in Plaister and colour'd in so lively a manner that it has an enchanting Effect. The Garden is suitable to the House, where Arbours, fountains, and walks are thrown together in an agreable Confusion. There is no Ornament wanting except that of Statues.

Thus you see, Sir, these people are not so unpolish'd as we represent them. Tis true their Magnificence is of a different taste from ours, and perhaps of a better. I am allmost of opinion they have a right notion of Life; while they consume it in Music, Gardens, Wine, and delicate eating, while we are tormenting our brains with some Scheme of Politics or studying some Science to which we can never attain, or if we do, cannot perswade people to set that value upon it we do our selves. 'Tis certain what we feel and see is properly (if any thing is properly) our own; but the good of Fame, the Folly of praise, hardly purchas'd, and when obtain'd—poor Recompence for loss of time and health! We dye, or grow old and decrepid, before we can reap the fruit of our Labours. Considering what short liv'd, weak Animals Men are, is there any study so beneficial as the study of present pleasure? I dare not persue this theme; perhaps I have allready said too much, but I depend upon the true knowledge you have of my heart. I don't expect from you the insipid Railerys I should suffer from another in answer to this letter. You know how to divide the Idea of Pleasure from that of Vice, and they are only mingle'd in the heads of Fools—but I allow you to laugh at me for the sensual declaration that I had rather be a rich Effendi with all his ignorance, than Sir Isaac Newton with all his knowledge. I am, Sir, etc.

Text H MS 253, pp. 416–24

To the Abbé Conti[1] *31 July* [*1718*]

Tunis, July 31 O.S.[2]

I left Constantinople the 6th of the last month,[3] and this is the first port from whence I could send a Letter, thô I have often wish'd for the oppertunity that I might impart some

[1] The MS shows that LM had first addressed this letter 'To the Countesse of ——' and had inserted 'My dear Sister' into the body, but she then struck these words out. Conti was a far more suitable recipient for such a virtuoso letter. Furthermore, she begins her next letter (28 Aug.), addressed to her sister, with the statement that she had written to Conti from Tunis.

[2] This date is accurate; from 29 July to 2 Aug. O.S. the *Preston* was anchored near Tunis (Captain's log, PRO Ad 51/4296).

[3] The *Preston* had left Constantinople on the afternoon of 5 July (ibid.).

of the Pleasure I have found in this voyage through the most agreable part of the world, where every Scene presents me some poetical Idea.[1]

> Warm'd with Poetic Transport I survey
> Th' Immortal Islands, and the well known Sea,
> For here so oft the Muse her harp has strung
> That not a Mountain rears his head unsung.

I beg your pardon for this Sally, and will (if I can) continu the rest of my Account in plain prose. The 2nd day after we set sail, we pass'd Gallipolis, a fair City, situate in the Bay of Chersonessus and much respected by the Turks, being the first Town they took in Europe. At 5 the next morning we anchor'd in the Hellespont between the Castles of Sestos and Abydos, now call'd the Dardanelli.[2] There is now 2 little ancient castles, but of no strength, being commanded by a rising ground behind them which, I confess, I should never have taken notice of if I had not heard it observ'd by our Captain and officers,[3] my Imagination being wholly employ'd by the Tragick story that you are well acquainted with:

> The swimming lover and the nightly Bride,
> How Hero lov'd, and how Leander dy'd.

Verse again! I am certainly infected by the Poetical air I have pass'd through. That of Abydos is undoubtedly very Amorous, since that soft passion betraid the castle into the hands of the Turks in the reign of Orchanes, who beseig'd it. The Governour's Daughter, imagining to have seen her

---

[1] LM's preparations for her voyage through a classical landscape may have been similar to Addison's, who wrote: 'Before I entered on my voyage I took care to refresh my memory among the Classic Authors, . . . to examine these several Descriptions, as it were, upon the spot, and to compare the natural face of the country with the Landskips that the Poets have given us of it' (*Remarks on Several Parts of Italy, &c.*, 1705, in *Misc. Works*, ed. A. C. Guthkelch, 1914, ii. 18). LM's library in 1739 contained 'Addison's Travels' (Wh MS 135). The second couplet of her verse comes from Addison's *Letter from Italy* (1703), in *Misc. Works*, i. 51.

[2] On 7 July the *Preston* anchored off Gallipoli, two miles from shore on the Asia side, and the Ambassador—accompanied no doubt by LM—'went a shore to a small tour on curiosity' (Master's log, PRO Ad 52/254).

[3] The *Preston*'s captain was Robert Johnson (d. 1723) (John Charnock, *Biographia Navalis*, 1795, iii. 400). The master was Walter Morrison; the lieutenant, Charles Cotterell (d. 1754) (National Maritime Museum, Greenwich; Charnock, iv. 140).

future husband in a dream (thô I don't find she had either slept upon bride Cake or kept St. Agnes' Fast) fancy'd she afterwards saw the dear figure in the form of one of her Beseigers and, being willing to obey her Destiny, toss'd a note to him over the Wall with the offer of her person and the delivery of the castle. He show'd it to his General, who consented to try the Sincerity of her Intentions and withdrew his army, ordering the Young Man to return with a select body of Men at midnight. She admitted him at the appointed hour; he destroy'd the Garrison, took her Father prisoner, and made her his Wife.[1] This Town is in Assia, first founded by the Milesians. Sestos is in Europe and was once the principal City in Chersonessus.[2] Since I have seen this streight, I find nothing improbable in the adventure of Leander or very wonderfull in the Bridge of Boats of Xerxes.[3] Tis so narrow, 'tis not surprizing a young Lover should attempt to swim it or an Ambitious King try to pass his Army over it. But then tis so subject to storms, 'tis no wonder the Lover perish'd and the Bridge was broken. From hence we had a full view of Mount Ida,

> Where Juno once carres'd her Amorous Jove
> And the World's Master lay subdu'd by Love.

Not many leagues sail from hence I saw the point of land where poor old Hecuba was bury'd,[4] and about a league from that place is Cape Janizary, the famous promontory of Sigæum, where we anchor'd; and my Curiosity supply'd me with strength to climb to the top of it to see the place where Achilles was bury'd and where Alexander ran naked round his Tomb in his honnour,[5] which, no doubt, was a great comfort to his Ghost. I saw there the ruins of a very large City, and found a Stone on which Mr. W[ortley] plainly

---

[1] This tale, in the reign of Orhan (1324–60), is recounted in George Sandys (*Travels*, 7th ed., 1673, p. 20) —where, however, the heroine does not become the wife of the victorious Turk.

[2] This sentence is paraphrased from Sandys, p. 20.

[3] This story, originally in Herodotus (*Histories*, Loeb Library, iii. 436–51), is repeated by Sandys (p. 20) and other travellers.

[4] On the European side, opposite Rhodius, Richard Chandler saw the '*Barrow of Hecuba* . . . still very conspicuous' (*Travels in Asia Minor*, 2nd ed., 1776, p. 13).

[5] This is related by Sandys (p. 15); its origin is Diodorus Siculus (*Bibliothèque historique*, transl. 1834–8, v. 195).

distinguish'd the words of Sigæon polin. We order'd this
on board the Ship[1] but were show'd others much more
curious by a Greek Preist, thô a very ignorant Fellow that
could give no tolerable Account of any thing. On each side
the door of his little Church lies a large stone about ten foot
long each, 5 in breadth, and 3 in Thickness. That on the right
is very fine white marble, the side of it beautifully carv'd in
bas Releif. It represents a woman who seems to be design'd
for some Deity siting on a Chair with a footstool, and before
her another woman weeping and presenting to her a Young
Child that she has in her Arms, follow'd by a procession of
women with Children in the same manner. This is certainly
part of a very ancient Tomb, but I dare not pretend to give
the true Explanation of it.[2] On the Stone on the left side is
a very fair Inscription, which I am sure I took off very
exactly, but the Greek is too Ancient for Mr. W[ortley]'s
interpretation. This is the exact Copy. [*Here follow eleven
double lines of Greek, apparently copied in another hand.*]
I am very sorry not to have the Original[3] in my possession,
which might have been purchas'd of the poor Inhabitants
for a small sumn of Money, but our Captain assur'd us that

[1] This marble, according to Chandler (p. 37), lay in the precincts of the Temple of Minerva on the Acropolis of Sigeum, then occupied by a 'mean church'. After transporting it to England, W kept the marble in his London house, where Scipione Maffei, the Veronese antiquary, inspected it in 1736 (LM's letter of 24 July [1755]). By W's direction, it was presented to Trinity College, Cambridge, after his death (*Annual Register for 1766*, p. 81). It is treated in P. P. Dobree's 'Greek Inscriptions . . . of Trinity College, Cambridge' (*Classical Journal*, xxx, 1824, pp. 137–8); in *Corpus Incriptionum Graecarum*, ed. A. Böckh (ii, 1843, No. 3595); and in Adolf Michaelis's *Ancient Marbles in Great Britain* (transl. C. A. M. Fennell, 1882, p. 269). It can be seen today set in the wall at the entrance to Trinity College Library.

[2] The explanation, as given by Chandler (p. 36), is that 'The Greeks were accustomed to consign their infants to the tutelar care of some deity; the midwife, dressed in white, with her feet bare, carrying the child to be presented on the fifth day after its birth . . .' The carving itself is depicted in Chandler's *Ionian Antiquities*, i, 1769, p. 1.

[3] This, the most famous Sigean inscription, one of the oldest known examples of Greek palaeography, is now among the Elgin marbles in the BM. It is reproduced in Edmund Chishull's *Antiquitates Asiaticae . . .*, 1728 (facing p. 4), in Richard Knight's *Greek Alphabet*, 1791 (plate ii), and in Gisela Richter's *Archaic Attic Gravestones*, 1944 (photograph, fig. 36). After her return to England LM loaned the Embassy Letters MS to the 8th Earl of Pembroke, collector of classical statues and medals, and he was so impressed by this inscription that he called on her to discuss it (2 letters from Lady Pembroke to LM, [?1725], W MS iv. 208–11; 1861, ii. 11–13).

without having Machines made on purpose, twas impossible
to bear it to the Sea Side, and when it was there his long
Boat would not be large enough to hold it.[1]

The ruins of this great City is now inhabited by poor
Greek peasants who wear the Sciote habit, the women being
in short petticoats fastend by straps round their shoulders
and large Smock sleeves of white Linnen, with neat shoes and
stockings, and on their heads a large piece of Muslin which
falls in large folds on their shoulders. One of my Country-
men, Mr. Sands (whose book I do not doubt you have read,
as one of the best of its kind), speaking of these ruins,
supposes them to have been the foundation of a City begun
by Constantine before his building at Byzantium,[2] but I
see no good reason for that Imagination and am apt to beleive
them much more Ancient. We saw very plainly from this
promontory the River Simois rolling from Mount Ida and
runing through a very spacious valley. It is now a considerable River and calld Simores, joyn'd in the vale by the
Scamander, which appear'd a small stream halfe choak'd with
Mud, but is perhaps large in the winter. This was Xanthus
amongst the Gods, as Homer tells us,[3] and tis by that
heavenly Name the Nymph Oenone invokes it in her epistle
to Paris.[4] The Trojan Virgins us'd to offer their first favours
to it by the name of Scamander, till the adventure which
Monsieur de La Fontaine has told so agreably abolish'd that
heathenish Ceremony.[5] When the stream is mingle'd with
the Simois, they run together to the Sea.

All that is now left of Troy is the ground on which it
stood, for I am firmly perswaded whatever pieces of Antiquity may be found round it are much more modern, and I

[1] The stone's dimensions, exaggerated by LM, are actually about 7′ 6″ long, 1′ 7″ wide, and 10½″ thick (Richter, p. 21). A later ambassador, Lord Elgin, succeeded in transporting to England this '. . . monument which several ambassadors from Christian Powers to the Porte, and even Louis XIV in the height of his power, had ineffectually endeavoured to obtain. Lord Elgin found it forming a seat or couch at the door of a Greek chapel . . .' ([William Richard Hamilton], *Memorandum on the Subject of the Earl of Elgin's Pursuits in Greece*, 2nd ed., 1815, p. 35).

[2] Sandys, p. 15.

[3] *Iliad*, xxi. 136, 145.

[4] Ovid, *Heroides*, v.

[5] The 'adventure' of an ingenuous maiden duped by a man masquerading as a river god is told by La Fontaine in 'Le Fleuve Scamandre' (*Œuvres*, ed. H. Régnier, 1883–97, vi. 12–23). LM's library in 1739 contained a copy of his *contes* (Wh MS 135). The story is also related by Sandys (p. 17).

think Strabo says the same thing.[1] However, there is some pleasure in seeing the valley where I imagin'd the famous Duel of Menelaus and Paris had been fought,[2] and where the greatest City in the world was situate; and tis certainly the noblest Situation that can be found for the head of a great Empire, much to be prefer'd to that of Constantinople, the harbour here being allways convenient for Ships from all parts of the world and that of Constantinople inaccessible allmost 6 months in the year while the North Wind reigns. North of the promontory of Sigæum we saw that of Rhœteum, fam'd for the sepulchre of Ajax.[3] While I view'd these celebrated Fields and Rivers, I admir'd the exact Geography of Homer, whom I had in my hand.[4] Allmost every Epithet he gives to a Mountain or plain is still just for it, and I spent several hours in as agreable Cogitations as ever Don Quixote had on Mount Montesinos.[5] We saild that night to the shore where tis vulgarly reported Troy stood[6] and I took the pains of rising at 2 in the morning to view cooly those Ruins which are commonly shew'd to strangers and which the Turks call eski-Stamboul, i.e. old Constantinople.[7] For that reason, as well as some others, I conjecture them to be the remains of that city begun by Constantine. I hir'd an Ass (the only voiture to be had there) that I might go some miles into the Country and take a tour round the Ancient Walls, which are of a vast extent. We found the remains of a castle on a Hill and another in a valley, several broken Pillars, and 2 pedestals from which I took these Latin Inscriptions.

[1] 'But no trace of the ancient city survives' (*Geography*, transl. Loeb Library, vi. 74–75).

[2] *Iliad*, iii. 351–86.

[3] LM paraphrases Sandys: 'Rhœtum, celebrated for the Sepulchre of *Ajax*, and his statue . . .' (p. 17).

[4] Henry F. Tozer writes: 'The plain of Troy has been a battle-field, not only of heroes, but of scholars and geographers, and the works which have been written on the subject form a literature to themselves' (*Researches in the Highlands of Turkey*, 1869, i. 22). LM's account is put into the context of contemporary scholarly opinion by T. J. B.

Spencer in 'Robert Wood and the Problem of Troy', *Journal of Warburg and Courtauld Inst.*, xx, 1957, pp. 85–86.

[5] LM means the *cave* of Montesinos, where Don Quixote passes about an hour so enchanted by his visions that when he is drawn up he thinks he has spent three days there.

[6] On 8 July, when the *Preston* anchored in Troy Bay: 'This morning our Embassadore went ashore to view the ruins of Troye' (Master's log).

[7] These ruins, carefully described by James Dallaway (*Constantinople*, 1797, pp. 326–7), were those of Alexandria Troas.

[*Here follow the two inscriptions of nine and twelve lines.*][1]
I do not doubt but the remains of a temple near this place
are the ruins of one dedicated to Augustus, and I know not
why Mr. Sands calls it a Christian Temple,[2] since the
Romans certainly built hereabouts. Here are many tombs
of fine Marble and vast pieces of Granite, which are daily
lessen'd by the prodigious Balls that the Turks make from
them for their Canon.

We pass'd that Evening the Isle of Tenedos, once under
the patronage of Apollo, as he gave it in himselfe in the
particular of his Estate when he courted Daphne.[3] It is but
10 mile in circuit, but in those days very rich and well
people'd, still famous for its excellent Wine. I say nothing of
Tenes, from whom it was call'd,[4] but naming Mytilene where
we pass'd next, I can-not forbear mentioning Lesbos, where
Sapho sung and Pittacus reign'd,[5] famous for the Birth of
Alcæus, Theophrastus, and Arion, those masters in Poetry,
Philosophy, and Music. This was one of the last Islands that
remain'd in the Christian Dominion after the conquest of
Constantinople by the Turks.[6] But need I talk to you of
Catucuseno[7] etc.? princes that you are as well acquainted
with as I am. Twas with regret I saw us sail swift from this
Island into the Egean Sea, now the Archipelago, leaving
Scio (the ancient Chios) on the left, which is the richest and
most populous of these Islands, fruitfull in cotton, corn and
silk, planted with groves of Orange and Lemon trees, and the
Arvisian Mountain still celebrated for the nectar that Virgil
mentions.[8] Here is the best manufacture of silks in all
Turkey. The Town is well built, the women famous for their
Beauty, and shew their faces as in Christendom. There are

---

[1] These inscriptions are accurately
given in *Corpus Inscript. Lat.*, ed. T.
Mommsen, iii, 1873, p. 74, no. 386;
for LM's version see 1861, i. 378–9.

[2] Sandys, p. 18.

[3] Ovid, *Metamorphoses*, i. 516.

[4] Sandys, who estimates the peri-
meter of the island as 10 miles, also
gives the origin of its name from Tenes,
son of Cycnus, who reigned in a city
of Troas (p. 15).

[5] Pittacus (*c.* 650–570 B.C.), one of

the Seven Sages of Greece, reigned on
Lesbos for about ten years.

[6] Mitylene was the capital of Lesbos,
and subsequently the name of the
island—which came under Turkish
control in 1462.

[7] Of the Cantacuzene family, John V
(*c.* 1293–1383) ruled the Eastern Roman
Empire during its decline.

[8] *Eclogues*, v. 71: 'I will pour from
goblets the fresh nectar of Chian wine'
(transl. Loeb Library).

many rich familys, thô they confine their magnificence to the inside of their houses to avoid the Jealousie of the Turks, who have a Bassa here. However, they enjoy a reasonable Liberty and indulge the genius of their Country,

> And eat and sing and dance away their time,
> Fresh as their Groves, and happy as their Clime.

Their Chains hang lightly on them,[1] thô 'tis not long since they were impos'd, not being under the Turk till 1566; but perhaps 'tis as easy to obey the Grand Signor as the state of Genoa, to whom they were sold by the Greek Emperor. But I forget my selfe in these historical touches, which are very impertinent when I write to you.[2]

Passing the strait between the Island of Andros and Achaia (now Libadia) we saw the Promontory of Sunium (now call'd Cape Colonna), where are yet standing the vast pillars of a Temple of Minerva.[3] This venerable sight made me think with double regret on a Beautifull Temple of Theseus, which I am assur'd was allmost entire at Athens till the last Campaign in the Morea, that the Turks fill'd it with Powder and it was accidentally blown up.[4] You may beleive I had a great mind to land on the fam'd Peloponessus, thô it were only to look on the Rivers of Asopus, Peneus, Inachus, and Eurotas, the Feilds of Arcadia and other Scenes of ancient Mythology. But instead of demy Gods and heros, I was credibly inform'd 'tis now over run by Robbers, and that I should run a great risque of falling into their hands by

[1] In spite of her full description of the island and its carefree inhabitants, LM did not stop there; she writes of sailing past it swiftly, and the *Preston*'s log bears this out. Aaron Hill describes its neat buildings, handsome and gay women, and its produce (pp. 208–9); and Sandys its merry life (p. 11). See also Terence Spencer, *Fair Greece, Sad Relic*, 1954, pp. 165–6.

[2] Rycaut (*History of the Turks*, 1700, p. 526) states that the Greeks of the island preferred Turkish rule to Italian, as LM implies; and this opinion is supported by modern historians (e.g. William Miller, *Eng. Hist. Rev.*, xxx, 1915, pp. 431–2). One of LM's 'historical touches' is inexact: John V,

Eastern Roman Emperor, did not sell Chios to Genoa; in 1348 he merely proposed that Genoa, which had seized the island two years before, should pay an annual tribute, and although the stipulation was accepted it was never carried out (George Finlay, *History of Greece*, ed. H. F. Tozer, 1877, iii. 453).

[3] Chandler also calls this ruin the Temple of Minerva (*Travels in Asia Minor*, 2nd ed., 1776, p. 9), but recent excavations have proved it to be of Poseidon (Isabel H. Grinnell, *Greek Temples*, 1943, pp. 38–39).

[4] The Parthenon was partially wrecked by a bomb when the Venetians besieged Athens in 1687.

undertakeing such a Journey through a desart country, for which, however, I have so much respect I have much ado to hinder my selfe from troubling you with its whole history from the foundation of Mycana and Corinth to the last campaign there. But I check that inclination as I did that of landing, and saild quietly by Cape Angelo,[1] once Malea, where I saw no remains of the famous temple of Apollo.[2] We came that evening in sight of Candia. It is very Mountainous; we easily distinguish'd that of Ida. We have Virgil's authority here was 100 Citys,

Centum urbes habitant magnas,[3]

the cheife of them, Gnossus, the scene of Monstrous Passions.[4] Metellus first conquer'd this birth place of his Jupiter.[5] It fell afterwards into the hands of ———. I am runing on to the very seige of Candia,[6] and I am so angry at my selfe that I will pass by all the other Islands with this general refflection, that 'tis impossible to imagine any thing more agreable than this Journey would have been between 2 and 3,000 years since, when, after drinking a dish of tea with Sapho, I might have gone the same evening to visit the temple of Homer in Chios,[7] and have pass'd this voyage in takeing plans of magnificent Temples, delineateing the miracles of Statuarys and converseing with the most polite and most gay of humankind. Alas! Art is extinct here. The wonders of Nature alone remain, and 'twas with vast pleasure I observ'd that of Mount Ætna, whose Flame appears very bright in the night many Leagues off at Sea,[8] and fills the

---

[1] The *Preston* passed Cape Angelo at noon on 11 July (Captain's log).

[2] Mentioned by Pausanias in his *Description of Greece* (III, xxiii, 2).

[3] *Aeneid*, iii. 106.

[4] LM refers to the legend connected with the birth of the Cretan Minotaur and his feasting on Athenian youths and maidens until he was slain by Theseus.

[5] This Roman general conquered Crete 67 B.C., where according to the early legend Zeus was born.

[6] The city of Candia was besieged by the Turks from 1648 to 1669 before it surrendered.

[7] On Chios, generally considered to have been the birthplace of Homer, stood a temple dedicated to Apollo (*Atlas of the Classical World*, ed. A. A. van der Heyden and H. H. Scullard, 1960, Map 18). Or LM may mean a sanctuary of Cybele commonly called the School of Homer, mentioned by Jean de Thévenot (*Travels into the Levant*, transl. A. Lovell, 1687, p. 96) and by Richard Pococke (*Description of the East*, 1743–5, II, ii. 6 and plate xxxvii).

[8] Mount Etna was sighted to the north-west by the *Preston* on 21 July.

head with a thousand Conjectures. However, I honnour Philosophy too much to imagine it could turn that of Empedocles, and Lucian shall never make me beleive such a scandal of a man of whom Lucretius says

—vix humana vide[a]tur stirpe creatus.[1]

We pass'd Trinacria without hearing any of the Syrens that Homer describes, and being neither thrown on Scylla nor Charibdis came safe to Malta,[2] first call'd Melita from the abundance of Honey. It is a whole Rock cover'd with very little Earth. The Grand Master lives here in the state of a Sovereign Prince,[3] but his strength at Sea [is] now very small. The fortifications are reckon'd the best in the world, all cut in the solid Rock with Infinite Expence and Labour. Off of this Island we were toss'd by a severe storm, and very glad after 8 days to be able to put into Porta Farine on the Africk shore, where our Ship now rides.[4]

We were met here by the English Consul who resides at Tunis.[5] I readily accepted of the offer of his House there for some days, being very curious to see this part of the world and particularly the ruines of Carthage. I set out in his chaise at 9 at night; the moon being at full, I saw the prospect of the Country allmost as well as I could have done by day light,

[1] Lucian, who frequently mentions Empedocles' suicide in the crater of Mount Etna, did not invent that legend; he merely added to it the cause—melancholy—that drove the philosopher to self-destruction (Joseph Bidez, *La Biographie d'Empédocle*, 1844, p. 89). Lucretius had praised Empedocles with this quoted line: 'he seems hardly to be born of mortal stock' (*De Rerum Natura*, i. 733, transl. Loeb Library).

[2] After passing Cape Passaro, the southeast tip of Sicily (Trinacria), on 22 July, the *Preston* reached Malta the next day at noon (Captain's log). LM, still concerned with Homeric parallels, has followed the tradition putting the Sirens on Trinacria instead of the mainland (*Atlas of the Classical World*, Map 10); and since the *Preston* did not pass through the Straits of Messina she had nothing to fear from Scylla or Charybdis.

[3] The Grand Master of the Order of St. John from 1697 to 1720 was Ramon Perellos y Roccaful (C.-É. Engel, *L'Ordre de Malte en Méditerranée*, 1957, p. 323).

[4] Actually the *Preston*, after meeting fresh gales and hazy weather on 26 July (two days after leaving Malta), anchored at Porto Farina for 29-31 July, and in the Bay of Carthage on 1 Aug. in a moderate gale and fair weather (Captain's log).

[5] Richard Lawrence had been consul since 1711 (*Cal. of Treas. Papers 1708–14*, ed. J. Redington, 1879, pp. 261–2). He reported the *Preston*'s arrival on 9 Aug. N.S. [29 July O.S.], and supplied the ship with water and provisions, but he says nothing of the Ambassador's visit ashore (to Craggs, 23 Aug. 1718 N.S., SP 71/27). The ship remained there until 2 Aug.—for four days, allowing LM ample time for sightseeing.

and the heat of the Sun is now so intolerable, tis impossible
to travel at any other time. The soil is for the most part
sandy, but every where fruitful in Date, olive and fig trees,
which grow without art, yet afford the most delicious fruit
in the world. Their vineyards and melon feilds are enclos'd
by hedges of that plant we call the Indian Fig,[1] which is an
admirable Fence, no wild Beast being able to pass it. It grows
a great height, very thick, and the spikes or thorns are as long
and sharp as Bodkins. It bears a fruit much eaten by the
peasants and which has no ill taste. It being now the season
of the Turkish Ramadan (or Lent) and all here professing,
at least, the Mahometan Religion, they fast till the going
down of the Sun and spend the night in feasting. We saw
under the Trees in many places Companys of the country
people, eating, singing, and danceing to their wild music.
They are not quite black, but all mullattos, and the most
frightfull Creatures that can appear in a Human figure.
They are allmost naked, only wearing a piece of coarse serge
wrap'd about them, but the women have their Arms to their
very shoulders and their Necks and faces adorn'd with
Flowers, Stars and various sort of figures impress'd by Gun-
powder; a considerable addition to their natural Deformity,
which is, however, esteem'd very Ornamental amongst them,
and I beleive they suffer a good deal of pain by it. About
6 mile from Tunis we saw the remains of that noble Aquæ
duct which carry'd the water to Carthage over several high
Mountains the length of 40 mile. There is still many arches
entire. We spent 2 hours veiwing it with great attention, and
Mr. W[ortley] assur'd me that of Rome is very much inferior
to it.[2] The stones are of a prodigious size and yet all polish'd
and so exactly fited to each other, very little Cement has
been made use of to joyn them. Yet they may probably stand
1,000 years longer if Art is not us'd to pull them down.

Soon after day break I arriv'd at Tunis, a Town fairly
built of a very white stone, but quite without Gardens, which
(they say) were all destroy'd and their fine Groves cut down

---

[1] LM was one of the first to use this
term for the prickly pear (*OED*).

[2] The aqueduct to Carthage was of
Roman rather than Punic origin
(J. Toutain, *Les Cités romaines de la*

Tunisie, 1896, p. 73). It is described
with admiration similar to LM's by
Thomas Shaw (*Travels, or Observations
Relating to Several Parts of Barbary
and the Levant*, 1738, p. 153).

when the Turks first took it. None haveing been planted since, the dry sand gives a very disagreable prospect to the Eye, and the want of shade contributing to the natural heat of the Climate, renders it so excessive I have much ado to support it. 'Tis true here is every noon the refreshment of the Sea breeze, without which it would be impossible to live, but no fresh water but what is preserv'd in the Cisterns of the rains that fall in the Month of September. The women in the Town go vail'd from head to foot under a black Crape, and, being mix'd with a breed of Renegades, are said to be many of them fair and handsome. This city was beseig'd 1270 by Lewis, King of France,[1] who dy'd under the walls of it of a Pestilential Fever. After his death, Philip, his Son, and our Prince Edward, son of Henry the 3rd, rais'd the Seige on honnourable Conditions.[2] It remain'd under its natural African Kings till betray'd into the hands of Barberussa, admiral of Solyman the magnificent. The Emperor Charles the 5th expell'd Barberussa, but it was recover'd by the Turk under the Conduct of Sinan Bassa in the reign of Selim the 2nd.[3] From that time till now it has remain'd tributary to the Grand Signor, govern'd by a Bey, who suffers the name of Subject to the Turk, but has renounc'd the Subjection, being absolute and very seldom paying any tribute. The Great City of Bagdat is at this time in the same Circumstance, and the Grand Signor connives at the losse of these dominions for fear of losing even the Titles of them.

I went very early yesterday morning (after one night's repose) to see the ruins of Carthage. I was, however, halfe broil'd in the Sun, and overjoy'd to be led into one of the subterrean Apartments, which they call'd the stables of the Elephants, but which I cannot beleive were ever design'd for that use.[4] I found in many of them broken pieces of Columns of fine marble and some of Porphyry. I cannot think

---

[1] Louis IX the Holy (1214–70).

[2] Philip III the Strong (1245–85), Edward I (1239–1307), Henry III (1207–72).

[3] Tunis, captured in 1534 by Barbarossa (Khair al-Din, *c.* 1483–1546), was taken in 1535 by Charles V, and retaken in 1574 by Kodja Sinan Pasha (*Encycl. of Islam*, ii. 871–3, iv. 432–3).

[4] Strabo had mentioned elephant stables in Carthage (*Geography*, Loeb Library, viii. 184–5), but they have not been found. What LM saw were probably cisterns or reservoirs; they were identified as such by Shaw (p. 151) and Nathan Davis (*Carthage and her Remains*, 1861, pp. 362–4).

any body would take the insignificant pains of carrying them thither, and I cannot imagine such fine pillars were design'd for the Ornament of a stable. I am apt to beleive they were summer apartments under their Palaces, which the heat of the climate render'd Necessary. They are now us'd as Granarys by the country people. While I sat here, from the Town of tents not far off many of the women flock'd in to see me and we were equally entertain'd with veiwing one another. Their posture in siting, the colour of their skin, their lank black Hair falling on each side their faces, their features and the shape of their Limbs, differ so little from their own country people, the Baboons, tis hard to fancy them a distinct race, and I could not help thinking there had been some ancient alliances between them. When I was a little refresh'd by rest and some milk and exquisite fruit they brought me, I went up the little Hill where once stood the castle of Birsa,[1] and from whence I had a distinct view of the situation of the Famous City of Carthage, which stood on an isthmus, the sea coming on each side of it. 'Tis now a marshy Ground on one side where there is salt ponds. Strabo calls Carthage 40 mile in circuit.[2] There is now no remains of it but what I have describ'd, and the history of it too well known to want my Abridgement of it.

You see that I think you esteem Obedience more than Compliments. I have answer'd your Letter by giving you the accounts you desir'd and have reserv'd my thanks to the conclusion. I intend to leave this place to morrow and continu my Journey through Italy and France.[3] In one of those places I hope to tell You by word of mouth that I am your humble servant.

Text H MS 253, pp. 426–54

[1] Strabo (loc. cit.) calls the acropolis of Carthage 'Byrsa'.

[2] Ibid., 182–3.

[3] The *Preston* weighed anchor 2 Aug. The Captain sailed for Naples, reported the Consul, but if the wind should prove contrary he would proceed 'for Leghorn or else for Toulon where the Embassadore designs to disimbark and proceed homewards by Land' (Lawrence to Craggs, 23 Aug. 1718 N.S., SP 71/27).

To Lady Mar *28 Aug.* [*1718*]

Genoa,[1] Aug. 28.[2]

I beg your pardon (my dear Sister) that I did not write to you from Tunis (the only Oppertunity I have had since I left Constantinople), but the heat there was so excessive and the Light so bad for the sight, I was halfe blind by writeing one letter to the Abbot [Conti] and durst not go on to write many others I had design'd, nor, indeed, could I have entertain'd you very well out of that barbarous Country. I am now surrounded with Objects of pleasure, and so much charm'd with the Beautys of Italy, I should think it a kind of Ingratitude not to offer a little praise in return for the Diversion I have had here. I am in the house of Mrs. D'avenant[3] at St. Pierre l'Arene[4] and should be very unjust not to allow her a share of that Praise I speak of, since her good humour and good Company has very much contributed to render this place agreable to me. Genoa is Situate in a very fine bay, and being built on a rising Hill, intermix'd with Gardens and beautify'd with the most excellent Architecture, gives a very fine prospect off at Sea, thô it lost much of its Beauty in my Eyes, having been accustom'd to that of Constantinople. The Genoese were once Masters of several Islands in the Archipelago and all that part of Constantinople which is now call'd Galata. Their betraying the Christian Cause by facilitating the takeing of Constantinople by the

---

[1] From Tunis the *Preston* had sailed north, past Sardinia and Elba, to Leghorn, and stopped there for two days before continuing to Genoa, arriving there on 15 Aug. (Captain's log). Although W would have preferred to disembark at Toulon, the prevailing calm persuaded him to leave the ship in Genoa on the 17th with LM and 'parts of his Family' (Captain Johnson to J. Burchett, 21 Aug. 1718, PRO Ad 1/1982). Their son remained aboard the *Preston* (*Daily Courant*, 23, 27 Sept. 1718) on a slower journey to England, and finally reached London the following Jan.

[2] This date is close to the actual one, for W and his party had to perform quarantine for ten days (Johnson's letter in previous note).

[3] Frances (d. after 1725), da. of Villiers Bathurst, m. (before 1713) Henry Molins Davenant (R. C. Hoare, *History of Modern Wilts.*, 1822–44, V, ii. 86). Davenant was British Envoy to Genoa 1714–22 (D. B. Horn, *Brit. Dipl. Rep. 1689–1789*, 1932, p. 74).

[4] San Pietro d'Arena was the fashionable suburb where the houses were extraordinarily beautiful and grand (Maximilien Misson, *Voyage d'Italie*, ed. 1743, iii. 159).

Turk,[1] deserv'd what has since happen'd to them, the loss of all their Conquest on that side to those Infidels. They are at present far from Rich, and dispis'd by the French since their Doge was forc'd by the late King to go in person to Paris to ask pardon for such a triffle as the Arms of France over the house of the Envoy being spatter'd with Dung in the Night (I suppose) by some of the Spanish Faction, which still makes up the Majority here, thô they dare not openly declare it.[2]

The Ladys affect the French habit and are more gentile than those they imitate. I do not doubt but the Custom of Tetis beys has very much improv'd their airs.[3] I know not whither you have ever heard of those animals. Upon my Word, nothing but my own Eyes could have convinc'd [me] there were any such upon Earth. The fashion begun here and is now receiv'd all over Italy, where the Husbands are not such terrible Creatures as we represent them. There are none among them such Brutes to pretend to find fault with a Custom so well establish'd and so politically founded, since I am assur'd here that it was an Expedient first found out by the Senate to put an end to those family Hatreds which tore their state to pieces, and to find Employment for those young Men who were forc'd to cut one another's throats pour passer le temps, and it has succeeded so well that since the Institution of Tetis beys there has been nothing but peace and good humour amongst them. These are Gentlemen that devote themselves to the service of a particular Lady (I mean a marry'd one, for the virgins are all invisible, confin'd to convents). They are oblig'd to wait on her to all public places, the Plays, Operas, and Assemblys (which are call'd here conversations), where they wait behind her Chair, take care of her fan and Gloves if she plays, have the privelege

---

[1] When Mehmed II besieged Constantinople in 1453 the Genoese allowed him to evade the naval barrier by carrying his light boats across Galata and into the Golden Horn (Steven Runciman, *The Fall of Constantinople 1453*, 1965 pp. 105–9).

[2] The insult, in 1684, was revenged by the French bombardment of Genoa. In May of the following year, the Doge —Francesco Imperiale Lercaro (1628–

1712)—accompanied by four Senators submitted an apology to Louis XIV at Versailles (Carlo Varese, *Storia della repubblica di Genova . . .*, 1835–8, vii. 128–9; Émile Vincens, *Hist. de Gênes*, 1843, iii. 226–7).

[3] The custom of *cicisbeismo*, frequently described by later eighteenth-century travellers, is fully treated in Luigi Valmaggi, *I Cicisbei* (1927).

of Whispers, etc. When she goes out they serve her instead of Lacquys, gravely trotting by her Chair. 'Tis their busyness to present against any Day of public appearance, not forgetting that of her Name. In short, they are to spend all their time and Money in her service who rewards them according to her Inclination (for Oppertunity they want none), but the husband is not to have the Impudence to suppose 'tis any other than pure platonic Freindship. 'Tis true they endeavour to give her a 'tetis bey of their own chusing, but when the Lady happens not to be of the same taste (as that often happens) she never fails to bring it about to have one of her own fancy. In former times one Beauty us'd to have 8 or 10 of these humble admirers, but those days of Plenty and Humility are no more; men grow more scarce and sawcy, and every Lady is forc'd to content her selfe with one at a time. You see the Glorious Liberty of a Republic, or more properly an Aristocracy, the common people being here as errant slaves as the French, but the old nobles pay little respect to the Doge, who is but 2 years in his office, and at that very time his Wife assumes no Rank above another Noble Lady. 'Tis true the Family of Andrea Doria (that great Man who restor'd them that Liberty they enjoy) has some particular priveleges; when the Senate found it necessary to put a stop to the Luxury of Dress, forbidding the wear of Jewels and Brocades, they left them at Liberity [*sic*] to make what expence they pleas'd. I look'd with great pleasure on the Statu of that Hero which is in the Court belonging to the House of Duke Doria.[1]

This puts me in Mind of their Palaces, which I can never describe as I ought. Is it not enough that I say they are most of them of the design of Palladio? The street call'd Strada Nova here is perhaps the most beautifull line of Building in the World. I must particularly mention the vast palace of Durazzo, those of 2 Balbi joyn'd together by a Magnificent [colonade],[2] that of the Imperiali at this village of St. Pierre

[1] In the garden of the Doria Palace stood a gigantic statue of the naval hero (1466–1560) 'with the symbols of *Neptune*, drawn in a triumphal carr by three stately horses; and all this group is cut out of one block of marble, together with the other parts and embellishments of the whole fountain' (J. G. Keysler, *Travels through Germany . . .*, transl. 1756, i. 379).

[2] Inserted by LM's first editor in 1763; a blank space in MS.

l'Arene, and another of the Doria. The perfection of architure and the utmost profusion of rich furniture is to be seen here, dispos'd with most elegant taste and lavish magnificence, but I am charm'd with nothing so much as the Collection of Pictures by the Pencils of Raphael, Paulo Veronese, Titian, Carache [Carracci], Michael Angelo, Guido and Corregio, which 2 I mention last as my particular favourites. I own I can find no pleasure in objects of Horror, and in my Opinion the more naturaly a Crucifix is represented the more disagreable it is. These, my beloved Painters, shew nature and shew it in the most charming Light. I was particularly pleas'd with a Lucretia in the House of Balbi. The expressive Beauty of that Face and Bosome gives all the passion of Pity and admiration that could be rais'd in the Soul by the finest poem on that Subject. A Cleopatra of the same hand deserves to be mention'd, and I should say more of her if Lucretia had not first engag'd my Eyes.[1] Here are also some inestimable Ancient Bustos. The Church of St. Lawrence is all Black and white Marble, where is kept that famous plate of a single Emerald, which is not now permitted to be handle'd, since a Plot which (they say) was discover'd to throw it on the pavement and break it, a childish piece of Malice which they ascribe to the King of Sicily, to be reveng'd for their refusing to sell it to him.[2] The Church of the Anunciata is finely lin'd with Marble, the Pillars of red and white marble, that of St. Ambrose very much adorn'd by the Jesuits; but I confess all those Churches appeard so mean to

[1] The 'Cleopatra' and 'Lucretia' by Guido Reni are noticed by J. Northall (*Travels through Italy*, 1766, p. 46) who thought the pictures in the Balbi Palace the noblest collection in Genoa. Edward Gibbon praised the same two pictures (*Journey from Genoa to Rome, 1764*, ed. G. A. Bonnard, 1961, p. 69). (LM's critique is unmentioned in G. C. Cavalli and C. Gnudi, *Guido Reni*, 1955.)

[2] Aubry de La Mottraye (*Travels through Europe, Asia . . .*, 1723–32, i. 60) could give no reason for the prohibition against handling the emerald —which, Keysler noted with scepticism, was said to be a present from the Queen of Sheba to Solomon (i. 383). By hearsay, John Breval describes it as very closely guarded, and produced only for princes or at lowest ambassadors (*Remarks on Several Parts of Europe*, 1738, i. 279). When Lady Miller saw it in 1770 she scornfully dismissed it as a gross deception (*Letters from Italy*, 2nd ed., 1777, i. 217). During the Napoleonic wars it was taken to Paris, where it was analysed as glass-paste (LM, *Reisebriefe*, transl. and ed. H. H. Blumenthal, 1931). In LM's own day a great tome was devoted to the history of this gem (Fra Gaetano de S. Teresa, *Il Catino di smeraldo orientale . . .*, Genoa, 1726).

me after that of Sancta Sophia, I can hardly do them the
Honnour of writeing down their Names; but I hope You'l
own I have made good use of my time in seeing so much,
since 'tis not many days that we have been out of the Quar-
aintaine from which no body is exempt coming from the
Levant; but ours was very much shorten'd and very agreably
pass'd in Mrs. Davenant's Company in the village of St.
Pierre l'Arene, about a mile from Genoa in a house built by
Palladio, so well design'd and so nobly proportion'd 'twas
a pleasure to walk in it. We were visited here only in the
company of a noble Genoese Commission'd to see we did not
touch one Another. I shall stay here some days longer and
could allmost wish it for all my Life, but mine (I fear) is not
destin'd to so much tranquillity.[1]

Text H MS 253, pp. 455–63

To Lady [Mar][2] *12 Sept.* [*1718*]

Turin, Sept. 12. O.S.

I came in 2 days from Genoa through fine roads to this
place. I have allready seen what is shew'd to strangers in the
Town, which indeed is not worth a very particular description, and I have not respect enough for the holy Handkercheif
to speak long of it.[3] The Church is handsome and so is the
King's Palace, but I have lately seen such perfection of
Architecture I did not give much of my attention to these
pieces. The Town it selfe is fairly built, situate in a fine plain
on the banks of the Po. At a little distance from it we saw
the Palaces of La Venerie and La Valentin, both very agreable retreats.[4] We were lodg'd in the Piazza Royale, which is

[1] Here ends the first volume of the
Embassy Letters MS.

[2] With this letter LM began the
second volume of her transcription,
heading it 'Copys of Letters', with a new
series of numbers. The first letter is
addressed to 'the Countesse of ——'.

[3] The *Sudarium* or Holy Shroud of
Turin, for which a special chapel had
been built (described by Maximilien

Misson, *Voyage d'Italie*, ed. 1743, iii.
172–3), was supposed to preserve the
marks of blood and sweat from the body
of Christ (*Catholic Encycl.*, xiii. 762–3).
The *London Gazette* in 1722 translated
Santo Sudario as 'Holy Handkerchief'
(*OED sub* Handkerchief).

[4] The Venaria was a hunting lodge
built by Charles Emanuel II (1634–75),
and the Valentino a palace in French

one of the noblest Squares I ever saw, with a fine Portico of white stone quite round it. We were immediately visited by the Chevalier——, whom you knew in England, who with great Civillity begg'd to introduce us at Court,[1] which is now kept at Rivoli about a League from Turin. I went thither yesterday, and had the honnour of waiting on the Queen,[2] being presented to her by her first Lady of Honnour. I found her Majesty in a magnificent apartment, with a train of handsome Ladys all dres'd in Gowns, amongst which it was easy to distinguish the fair Princesse of Carignan.[3] The Queen entertain'd me with a world of sweetness and affabillity and seem'd mistrisse of a great share of good Sense. She did not forget to put me in Mind of her English blood,[4] and added that she allwaies felt in her selfe a particular Inclination to love the English. I return'd her Civillity by giving her the title of Majesty as often as I could, which perhaps she will not have the comfort of hearing many months longer.[5] The King has a great vivacity in his Eyes, and the young Prince of Piedmont is a very handsome Youth,[6] but the great Devotion which this Court is at present falln into does not permit any of those Entertainments proper for his age. Processions and Masses are all the Magnificences in fashion here, and Galantry so criminal that the poor Count of ——, who was our acquaintance at London, is very seriously disgrac'd for some small overtures he presum'd to make to a

Renaissance style begun by Victor Amadeus I (1587–1637) in 1633 for his French wife (Amy Vitelleschi, *Romance of Savoy*, 1905, i. 172, 186; Isenburg, ii. 113).

[1] England had no diplomatic representative to Savoy at this time; hence the Wortley Montagus could not be presented by a British ambassador.

[2] Anne (1669–1728), da. of Philip I, Duke of Orleans, m. (1684) Victor Amadeus II (1666–1732), Duke of Savoy (1675) and King of Sicily (1713).

[3] Maria Anna (1690–1766), da. of Victor Amadeus II, m. (1714) the Prince of Carignan. The King's natural daughter, legitimated in 1701, she was noted for her beauty and intelligence (Pöllnitz, v. 188; J. G. Keysler, *Travels*

through Germany ..., transl. 1756, i. 216).

[4] Her mother was Henrietta, da. of Charles I.

[5] Victor Amadeus had been awarded the kingdom of Sicily by the Treaty of Utrecht in 1713, but the island had been invaded by Spain during the summer of 1718.

[6] LM seems to be dazzled by royalty. Although the late Prince of Piedmont (d. 1715) had been handsome, intelligent, and charming, his brother Charles Emanuel III (1701–73) was ugly, hunchbacked, and clumsy of understanding (Domenico Carutti, *Storia del regno di Vittorio Amadeo II*, 1863, p. 487; Vitelleschi, ii. 473). In 1729, however, Keysler observed him in a more favourable light (i. 214).

Maid of Honnour. I intend to set out to morrow to pass those dreadfull Alps, so much talk'd of. If I come alive to the bottom you shall hear of me.

Text H MS 254, pp. 1–3

To [Anne] Thistlethwayte *Sept.* [*1718*]

Lyons, Sept. 25. O.S.[1]

I receiv'd at my arrival here both your obliging letters, and from many of my other Freinds, design'd to Constantinople and sent me from Marseilles hither, our merchant there knowing we were upon our return.

I am surpriz'd to hear my Sister [Mar] has left England.[2] I suppose what I writ to her from Turin will be lost, and where to direct I know not, having no account of her affairs from her own hand. For my own part, I am confin'd to my chamber, having kept my Bed till yesterday ever since the 17th that I came to this Town, where I have had so terrible a fever I beleiv'd for some time that all my Journeys were ended here, and I do not at all wonder that such fatigues as I have pass'd should have such an Effect. The 1st day's journey, from Turin to Novalese, is through a very fine Country, beautifully planted, and enrich'd by art and nature. The next day we begun to ascend Mount Cenis, being carri'd in little seats of twisted Osiers fix'd upon Poles, on men's shoulders, our chaises taken to pieces and laid upon Mules.[3] The prodigious Prospect of Mountains cover'd with Eternal Snow, Clouds hanging far below our feet, and the vast cascades tumbling down the Rocks with a confus'd roaring, would have been solemnly entertaining to me if I

[1] This date is clearly inaccurate since LM arrived in Paris on 18 Sept. O.S.

[2] Lady Mar planned to leave London for Paris on 8 Sept. O.S., and reached Boulogne on the 12th (HMC *Stuart Papers*, vii, 1923, p. 287; *Stuart Papers at Windsor*, ed. A. and H. Taylor, [1939], p. 49).

[3] Other travellers exclaimed over the dangers of passing Mont Cenis, e.g. in 1716 George Berkeley (*Corr. with Sir John Percival*, ed. B. Rand, 1914, p. 160) and in 1739 Horace Walpole (*Corr.*, ed. W. S. Lewis *et al.*, xiii, 1948, p. 189) and Thomas Gray (*Corr.*, ed. P. Toynbee and L. Whibley, 1935, i. 126).

had suffer'd less from the extreme cold that reigns here, but the misty rain, which falls perpetually, penetrated even the thick fur I was wrap'd in, and I was halfe dead with cold before we got to the foot of the Mountain, which was not till 2 hours after twas dark. This Hill has a spacious plain on the top of it, and a fine lake there, but the Descent is so steep and slippery, 'tis surprizing to see these chairmen go so steadily as they do, yet I was not halfe so much afraid of breaking my Neck as I was of falling sick, and the Event has show'd that I plac'd my fears in the right place. The other mountains are now all passable for a chaise, and very fruitfull in vines and Pastures; amongst them is a breed of the finest Goats in the World. Aiguebellet is the last, and soon after we enter'd Pont Beauvoisin, the frontier Town of France, whose bridge parts this Kingdom and the Dominion of Savoy. The same night we arriv'd late at this Town, where I have had nothing to do but to take care of my Health. I think my selfe allready out of any danger, and am determin'd that the Sore throat, which still remains, shall not confine me long. I am impatient to see the Antiquitys of this famous City and more Impatient to continu my Journey to Paris, from whence I hope to write you a more diverting Letter than tis possible for me to do now, with a mind weaken'd by sickness, a head muddled with Spleen, from a sorry Inn, and a Chamber cram'd with the mortifying objects of Apothecarys' viols and Bottles.

Text H MS 254, pp. 5–8

To Alexander Pope *Sept.* [*1718*]

Lyons, Sept. 28. O.S. [*sic*]

I receiv'd yours here and should thank you for the pleasure you express for my return,[1] but I can hardly forbear being angry at you for rejoyceing at what displeases me so much. You will think this but an odd compliment on my side. I'll

---

[1] Pope's letter (*Corr.* i. 469–71), dated [1718] by Sherburn, can more definitely be placed in the summer because of his conclusion: 'you are now come into the region of Posts, and under the Care of Secretaries'.

assure you 'tis not from Insensibillity of the Joy of seeing my Freinds, but when I consider that I must at the same time see and hear a thousand disagreable impertinents, that I must receive and pay visits, make curtsies, and assist at tea tables where I shall be halfe kill'd with Questions; on the other part, that I am a creature that cannot serve any body but with insignificant good wishes, and that my presence is not a necessary good to any one Member of my Native Country, I think I might much better have stay'd where ease and Quiet made up the happyness of my Indolent Life.—I should certainly be melancholy if I persu'd this theam one line farther. I will rather fill the remainder of this paper with the Inscriptions on the tables of Brass that are plac'd on each side the Town house here.

[*Here follow 39 lines of Latin inscription in capitals.*]

I cannot take the pains with the 2nd Table I have done with the first. You may easily imagine it in the same character and pointed after the same Manner. These are the Words.

[*Here follow 40 lines of Latin inscription.*][1]

I was also shew'd without the gate of St. Justinus[2] some remains of a Roman aqua duct,[3] and behind the monastery of St. Mary's there is the Ruins of the Imperial Palace where the Emperor Claudius was born and where Severus liv'd.[4] The great Cathedral of St. John is a good Gothic building, and its Clock much admir'd by the Germans.[5] In one of the most conspicuous parts of the Town is the late King's statue set up, trampling upon Mankind.[6] I can't

[1] The brass tablets record the patent from the Emperor Claudius to the inhabitants of Lyons, bestowing on them the privileges of Roman citizens (Dumont, pp. 36–37). The inscription was recommended by Gilbert Burnet as 'one of the noblest Antiquities in the World' (*Some Letters Containing an Account of ... Switzerland, Italy, &c.*, 1686, p. 4); it is given in *Corpus Inscript. Lat.*, ed. T. Mommsen, vol. xiii, part 1, 1899, pp. 232–5, no. 1668; for LM's version see 1861, i. 391–3).

[2] St. Justus, Bishop of Lyons (374–81).

[3] The aqueducts of Mark Antony, built entirely of square stone (Nugent, iv. 164–5).

[4] Before becoming emperor, Lucius Septimius Severus (146–211) was governor of the Gallic province whose capital was Lyons.

[5] The clock is described by Dumont (p. 35).

[6] A large equestrian statue of Louis XIV in copper, on a pedestal of white marble, stood in the Place de Louis le Grand (Edward Wright, *Some Observations Made in Travelling through France, 1720–1722*, ed. 1764, i. 12). It

forbear saying one word here of the French Statues (for I never intend to mention any more of them) with their gilded full bottom'd wigs. If their King had intended to express, in one Image, Ignorance, Ill taste, and Vanity, his Sculpturers could have made no other figure to represent the odd mixture of an old Beau who had a mind to be a Hero, with a Bushel of curl'd hair on his head and a gilt Truncheon in his hand. The French have been so volumnious [*sic*] on the history of this Town I need say nothing of it. The Houses are tolerably well built, and the Belle Cour well planted, from whence is seen the celebrated joyning of the Soane and Rhone.

> Ubi Rhodanus ingens amne praerapido fluit,
> Ararque dubitans quo suos fluctus agat.[1]

I have had time to see every thing with great leisure, having been confin'd several days to this Town by a swelling in my Throat, the remains of a fever occasion'd by a cold I got in the Damps of the Alps. The Doctors here (who are charm'd with a new customer) threaten me with all sorts of Distempers if I dare to leave them till this swelling is quite vanishe'd; but I, that know the Obstinancy of it, think it just as possible to continu my way to Paris with it as to go about the streets of Lyons, and am determin'd to persue my Journey to morrow in spite of Doctors, Apothecarys, and sore throats. When you see Lady R[ich], tell her I have receiv'd her letter and will answer it from Paris, beleiving that the place she would most willingly hear of.

Text H MS 254, pp. 9–20

was by Marc Chabry (1660–1727) (Natalis Rondot, *Les Sculpteurs de Lyon du quatorzième au dix-huitième siècle,* 1884, p. 55).

[1] Hence, mighty Rhone, thy rapid torrents flow,

And Arar, much in doubt which way to go.
(Seneca, *Apocolocyntosis,* 7; transl. Loeb Library, pp. 384–5.) LM substitutes *fluctus* for *cursus,* without changing the meaning significantly.

To Lady [Rich] [*Sept. 1718*]

Paris, Oct. 10 O.S.[1]

I cannot give my dear Lady R[ich] a better proofe of the pleasure I have in writeing to her than chusing to do it in this Seat of various Amusements, where I am acablée with visits, and those so full of vivacity and Compliment that 'tis full employment to hearken whither one answers or not. The French Ambassadresse at Constantinople has a very considerable and numerous Family here, who all come to see me and are never weary of makeing enquirys.[2] The air of Paris has allready had a good Effect on me, for I was never in better health, thô I have been extreme ill all the road from Lyons to this place. You may judge how agreable the Journey has been to me, which did not need that addition to make me dislike it. I think nothing so terrible as Objects of misery, except one had the God like attribute of being capable to redress them, and all the Country villages of France shews nothing else. While the post horses are chang'd, the whole town comes out to beg, with such miserable starv'd faces and thin, tatter'd Cloaths, they need no other Eloquence to perswade [one of] the wretchedness of their Condition.

This is all the French Magnificence till you come to Fontainebleau. There you begin to think the Kingdom rich when you are show'd 1,500 rooms in the King's hunting Palace. The Apartments of the royal Family are very large and richly gilt, but I saw nothing in the Architecture or Painting worth remembring. The Long Gallery, built by Henry the 4th, has prospects of all the King's houses on its walls,[3] design'd after the taste of those times, but appears now very mean. The Park is indeed finely wooded and water'd, the trees well grown and planted, and in the fish ponds are kept tame Carp, said to be some of them 80 years

---

[1] W arrived in Paris on 18 Sept. O.S. (Stair to Earl Stanhope, 29 Sept. 1718, SP 78/162).

[2] The marquise de Bonnac was a daughter of the duc de Biron; of his twenty-six offspring, fourteen survived

childhood. Mme de Bonnac later wrote to LM of 'des discours que vous aviés tenu sur mon Sujet a Paris' (20 Sept. 1719, W MS iv. 154).

[3] It is mentioned with admiration by Nugent (iv. 138).

of age. The late King pass'd some months every year at
this Seat, and all the rocks round it, by the pious Sentences
inscrib'd on them, show the Devotion in fashion at his
Court, which I beleive dy'd with him; at least, I see no
exterior marks of it at Paris, where all people's thoughts seem
to be on present Diversion. The fair of St. Lawrence is now
in Season.[1] You may be sure I have been carry'd thither, and
think it much better dispos'd than ours of Bartholemew.
The shops being all set in rows so regularly well lighted,
they made up a very agreable Spectacle. But I was not at all
satisfy'd with the Grosseirté of their Arlequin, no more than
with their Music at the Opera, which was abominable grate-
ing after being us'd to that of Italy. Their House is a
Booth compar'd to that of the Haymarket,[2] and the playhouse not so neat as that in Lincoln's Inn Feilds;[3] but then
it must be own'd to their praise, their Tragedians are much
beyond any of ours. I should hardly alow Mrs. O[ldfield][4]
a better place than to be confidante to La [Desmares]. I have
seen the Tragedy of Bajazet so well represented,[5] I think
our best actors can be only said to speak, but these to feel;
and tis certainly infinitely more moving to see a man appear
unhappy than to hear him say that he is so, with a jolly face
and a stupid smirk in his countenance.—A propos of coun-
tenances, I must tell you something of the French Ladies.
I have seen all the Beauties, and such (I can't help makeing
use of the coarse word) Nauseous——, so fantasticaly absurd
in their dress! so monstrously unnatural in their paint! their

[1] The fair was held from the end of
June to the last day of September.

[2] The Paris opera at this time was
housed in the Palais-Royal, on the rue
Saint-Honoré. The only performance
during LM's visit to Paris was that of
9 Oct./28 Sept., the premiere of André
Campra's opera-ballet *Les Âges* (J.-G.
Prod'homme, *L'Opéra 1669-1925*, 1925,
pp. 55, 73). The opera house in the
Haymarket, London, built by Vanbrugh, opened in 1705.

[3] The Comédie Française had played
since 1689 in a theatre in St-Germain-
des-Prés, a semi-circular hall which
could hold about 2,000 spectators (H. C.
Lancaster, *French Tragedy . . . 1715-*

1774, 1950, p. 4). The theatre rebuilt in
Lincoln's Inn Fields had opened in
1714.

[4] Anne Oldfield (1683-1730), leading
actress at Drury Lane, played in both
comedy and tragedy.

[5] Racine's *Bajazet*, whose Turkish
subject was so appropriate to LM,
played at the Comédie Française during
the week she was in Paris—on 2, 4, 6,
and 8 Oct. N.S. (Lancaster, *Trans.
Amer. Philos. Soc.*, New Series, xli,
1951, p. 659). Charlotte Desmares (*c.*
1682-1753) played Roxane, and Ad-
rienne Lecouvreur the young Atalide
(Archives of the Comédie Française).

Hair cut short and curl'd round their faces, loaded with powder that makes it look like white wool, and on their cheeks to their Chins, unmercifully laid on, a shineing red japan that glistens in a most flameing manner, that they seem to have no ressemblance to Humane faces, and I am apt to beleive took the first hint of their dress from a fair sheep newly raddled. 'Tis with pleasure I recollect my dear pritty Country women, and if I was writeing to any body else I should say that these grotesque Dawbers give me still a higher esteem of the natural charms of dear Lady R[ich]'s auborne hair and the lively colours of her unsully'd Complexion.

I have met the Abbé [Conti] here, who desires me to make his compliments to you.

Text H MS 254, pp. 21–26

To [Anne] Thistlethwayte [*Sept. 1718*]

Paris, Oct. 16th O.S. [*sic*]

You see I am just to my Word in writeing to you from Paris, where I was very much surpriz'd to meet my Sister [Mar];[1] I need not add, very much pleas'd. She as little expected to see me as I her (having not receiv'd my late Letters), and this meeting would shine under the hand of Mr. de Scuderie,[2] but I shall not imitate his style so far as to tell you how often we embrac'd, how she enquir'd by what odd chance I return'd from Constantinople? And I answer'd her by asking what adventure brought her to Paris?[3] To shorten the story, all Questions and answers and exclamations and compliments being over, we agreed upon running about together[4] and have seen Versailles, Trianon,

---

[1] Lady Mar arrived in Paris on 1 Oct./20 Sept., and she too was surprised to meet her sister (HMC *Stuart Papers*, vii, 1923, p. 351).

[2] Georges de Scudéry (1601–67), brother of the famous *romancière*, and himself a writer of extravagant plays.

[3] Lady Mar was on her way to Italy to join her husband, who with the Pretender and his court had been ex-

pelled from France. Jacobite gossip accused her of being a spy sent over by her Whig father and the King (HMC *Stuart Papers*, vii, 547).

[4] 'I sit twice a day for my picture,' Lady Mar wrote to her husband on 2 Oct./21 Sept., 'and pass the rest of my time with my sister, when I can get free of a hundred people. . . .' (ibid., 351–2).

Marli and St. Cloûd. We had an order for the Waters to play for our Diversion, and I was follow'd thither by all the English at Paris. I own Versailles appear'd to me rather vast than Beautifull, and after have[ing] seen the exact proportions of the Italian buildings, I thought the irregularity of it shocking.[1] The King's Cabinet of Antiques and Medals is indeed very richly furnish'd.[2] Amongst that Collection none pleas'd me so well as the Apotheosis of Germanicus on a large Agate, which is one of the most delicate pieces of the kind that I remember to have seen.[3] I observ'd some Ancient Statues of great Value, but the nauseous Flattery and tawdry Pencil of Le Brun are equally disgusting in the Gallery.[4] I will not pretend to describe to you the great Apartment, the vast variety of Fountains, the Theatre, the Grove of Æsop's Fables, etc., all which you may read very amply particulariz'd in some of the French Authors that have been paid for those descriptions.[5] Trianon in its littleness pleas'd me better than Versailles, Marli better than either of them, and St. Cloud best of all, having the advantage of the Seine running at the Bottom of the Gardens. The great Cascade etc. You may find in the foresaid Books, if you have any Curiosity to know the exact number of the Statues and how many foot they cast up the Water. We saw the King's Pictures in the magnificent house of the D[uc] D'Antin, who has the care of preserving them till his Majesty is of age. There is not many, but of the best hands. I look'd with great pleasure on the Arch Angel of Raphael, where the Sentiments

---

[1] John Breval explains that the incongruity of the old part of the building gives 'a sensible Shock to an Eye that is accustom'd to Harmony' (*Remarks on Several Parts of Europe*, 1738, ii. 309).

[2] 'There is not in all *Europe* a richer cabinet than the king's at *Versailles*' (Nugent, iv. 107).

[3] Nugent describes it as the 'finest agate in *Europe*, being of three colours, and four or five inches in diameter, representing the figure of a naked emperor, carried on the back of an eagle, and crowned with victory' (iv. 115). It was identified as portraying Germanicus only in 1717, and is now in the Louvre (Anatole Chabouillet, *Catalogue . . . des*

camées et pierres gravées de la bibliothèque impériale, [1858], p. 35).

[4] Charles Le Brun (1619–90). Breval calls the painting 'less remarkable for the Goodness of the Performance, than the Vanity of the Subjects' (ii. 31.1).

[5] These lead fountain-statues of Aesop's fabulous characters had been designed by Le Nôtre in 1673 (A. Pérate, *Versailles*, 1927, p. 62). They are elaborately described in Charles Perrault's *Labyrinte de Versailles*, 1677; 2nd ed. [1682]. In her own library in 1739 LM had a copy of Mlle de Scudéry's *Promenade de Versailles*, 1669 (Wh MS 135), but this informal dialogue is a general eulogy rather than a guide book.

of Superior beings are as well express'd as in Milton.¹ You
won't forgive me if I say nothing of the Thuilleries, much
finer than our Mall, and the Cour more Agreable than our
Hide Park, the high trees giving shade in the hottest
season.² At the Louvre I had the oppertunity of seeing the
King, accompany'd by the D[uke] Regent. He is tall and well
shap'd, but has not the Air of holding the Crown so many
years as his Grandfather.³ And now I am speaking of the
Court, I must say I saw nothing in France that delighted
me so much as to see an Englishman (at least a Briton)
absolute at Paris. I mean Mr. L[aw],⁴ who treats their Dukes
and Peers extremely de haut en bas, and is treated by them
with the utmost Submission and respect. Poor Souls! This
refflection on their abject slavery puts me in mind of the
Place des Victoires,⁵ but I will not take up your time and my
own with such Descriptions, which are too numerous. In
General, I think Paris has the advantage of London in the
neat pavement of the streets, and the regular lighting of
them at nights,⁶ the proportion of the streets, the houses
being all built of Stone, and most of those belonging to people
of Quality beautify'd by Gardens; but we certainly may
boast of a Town very near twice as Large, and when I have
said that, I know nothing else we surpass it in. I shall not
continu here long. If you have any thing to command me

---

¹ Louis-Antoine de Gondrin, duc
d'Antin (1665–1736), had been Super-
intendent of Works for the Crown since
1716. His house was filled not only with
his own magnificent furniture but with
tapestries and pictures of great value
belonging to the King, including a
'Saint Michael' by Raphael (Nugent,
iv. 64). The picture, now in the Louvre,
is described in *Raphael*, Phaidon ed.,
1948, p. 27.
² The Cour de la Mayne, 'three alleys
of great length ranging with the Seine,
planted with high trees' was thought
inferior to Hyde Park by Martin
Lister (*Account of Paris at the Close of
the 17th Century*, ed. G. Henning,
[1823], p. 150).
³ Louis XV, eight years old at this
time, had succeeded his great-grand-

father (1715), whose nephew Philippe
duc d'Orléans (1674–1723) acted as
regent.
⁴ John Law (1671–1729), Scottish
financial wizard who organized the Mississippi Scheme, the French speculative
venture.
⁵ Here stood a tremendous gilt-
bronze statue of Louis XIV on a white
marble pedestal with a captive slave in
bronze at each corner (Nugent, iv.
73–74).
⁶ Lister describes the Paris streets as
paved with square stones, eight to ten
inches thick, and well lit all through the
winter; whereas in London the lights
were extinguished when the moon was
up, whether or not it was obscured
(pp. 32, 48).

during my short stay, write soon, and I shall take pleasure in obeying you.

Text H MS 254, pp. 27–31

To Alexander Pope [*Paris, no date*]

[*A spurious letter, printed 1767, pp. 56–63; 1861, i. 398–400*]

To the Abbé Conti *Sept.* [*1718*]

Dover, Oct. 31. O.S.[1]

I am willing to take your word for it that I shall realy oblige you by letting you know as soon as possible my safe passage over the water. I arriv'd this morning at Dover after being toss'd a whole night in the pacquet Boat in so violent a manner that the master, considering the weakness of his Vessel, thought it prudent to remove the mail, and gave us notice of the Danger. We call'd a little fisher boat, which could hardly make up to us, while all the people on board us were crying to Heaven, and 'tis hard to imagine one's selfe in a scene of greater Horror than on such an occasion; and yet, shall I own it to you? thô I was not at all willing to be drown'd, I could not forbear being entertain'd at the double distress of a fellow passenger. She was an English Lady that I had met at Calais, who desir'd me to let her go over with me in my Cabin. She had bought a fine point head which she was contriving to conceal from the custom house Officers.[2] When the wind grew high and our little vessel crack'd, she fell very heartily to her prayers and thought wholly of her soul; when it seem'd to abate, she return'd to the worldly

---

[1] This date is about a month off, for LM arrived in London on 2 Oct. (*St. James's Eve. Post*, 2–4 Oct. 1718).

[2] A later traveller tells how English customs officers found contraband Flanders lace concealed in the breeches of a French ship's captain and beneath the petticoats of his mother and sisters (César de Saussure, *A Foreign View of England in the Reigns of George I & George II*, transl. and ed. van Muyden, 1902, pp. 33–34).

care of her head dress, and address'd her selfe to me—Dear
madam, will you take care of this point? if it should be lost
—Ah Lord! we shall all be lost! Lord have mercy on my
Soul—pray, madam, take care of this head dress.—This easy
transition from her soul to her head dress, and the alternate
Agonys that both gave her, made it hard to determine which
she thought of greatest value.[1] But, however, the scene was
not so diverting but I was glad to get rid of it and be thrown
into the little boat, thô with some hazard of breaking my
neck. It brought me safe hither, and I cannot help looking
with partial Eyes on my Native Land. That partiality was
certainly given us by Nature to prevent Rambling, the Effect
of an Ambitious thirst after knowledge which we are not
form'd to Enjoy. All we get by it is a fruitless Desire of
mixing the different pleasures and conveniencies which are
given to Different parts of the World and cannot meet in
any one of them. After having read all that is to be found in
the Languages I am mistriss of, and having decaid my sight
by midnight studys, I envy the easy peace of mind of a ruddy
milk maid who, undisturb'd by doubt, hears the Sermon with
humility every Sunday, having not confus'd the sentiments
of Natural Duty in her head by the vain Enquirys of the
Schools, who may be more Learned, yet after all must remain
as ignorant. And, after having seen part of Asia and Africa
and allmost made the tour of Europe, I think the honest
English Squire more happy who verily beleives the Greek
wines less delicious than March beer, that the African fruits
have not so fine a flavour as golden Pipins, and the Becá-
figúas of Italy are not so well tasted as a rump of Beef, and
that, in short, there is no perfect Enjoyment of this Life out
of Old England. I pray God I may think so for the rest of
my Life, and since I must be contented with our scanty
allowance of Daylight, that I may forget the enlivening Sun
of Constantinople.

Text H MS 254, pp. 33–36

[1] When LM loaned the MS of these
letters to Lord Pembroke he observed,
as his wife wrote, 'that your Ladyship
had the art of making common circumstances agreable, as the ladie's care
of her lace in the storm, etc.' ([?1725],
W MS iv. 208).

To Alexander Pope [*Sept. 1718*]

Dover, Nov. 1 [*sic*]

I have this minute receiv'd a Letter of yours sent me from Paris.[1] I beleive and hope I shall very soon see both you and Mr. Congreve, but as I am here in an Inn where we stay to regulate our March to London, bag and Baggage, I shall employ some of my Leisure time in answering that part of yours that seems to require an Answer.

I must Applaud your good nature in supposing that your pastoral Lovers (vulgarly call'd Haymakers) would have liv'd in everlasting joy and Harmony if the Lightening had not interrupted their scheme of Happyness.[2] I see no reason to imagine that John Heughs[3] and Sarah Drew were either wiser or more virtuous than their Neighbours. That a Well set man of 25 should have a fancy to marry a brown woman of eighteen is nothing marvellous, and I cannot help thinking that had they marry'd, their lives would have pass'd in the common Tract with their Fellow Parishioners. His endeavoring to shield her from the storm was a natural Action and what he would have certainly done for his Horse if he had been in the same situation. Neither am I of Opinion that their sudden Death was a reward of their mutual Virtue. You know the Jews were reprov'd for thinking a village destroy'd by Fire more wicked than those that had escap'd the Thunder. Time and chance happen to all men. Since you desire me to try my skill in an Epitaph, I think the following lines perhaps more just, thô not so poetical as yours:[4]

[1] Pope's letter, dated 1 Sept. (*Corr.* i. 493–6), had apparently been sent to Italy and then forwarded.

[2] In his letter Pope had related the pathetic tale, which he also sent to other friends, of how two rustic lovers seeking shelter during a thunder-storm had been killed by lightning; and he added two epitaphs on the unfortunate pair. (He also treated the incident with a bawdy couplet, but did not send this to LM.)

All three epitaphs are in his *Minor Poems*, ed. N. Ault and J. Butt, 1954, pp. 197–201.)

[3] Instead of 'Hewet', the name given by Pope.

[4] 'I like neither,' Pope had written to her of his two epitaphs, 'but wish you had been in England to have done this office better. . . .' (*Corr.* i. 495). Now in England, LM obliges.

Here lyes John Hughs and Sarah Drew;
Perhaps you'l say, what's that to you?
Believe me, Freind, much may be said
On this poor Couple that are dead.
On Sunday next they should have marry'd,
But see how oddly things are carry'd.
On Thursday last it rain'd and Lighten'd;
These tender Lovers sadly frighten'd
Shelter'd beneath the cocking Hay
In Hopes to pass the storm away.
But the bold Thunder found them out
(Commission'd for that end no Doubt)
And seizing on their trembling Breath,
Consign'd them to the Shades of Death.
Who knows if 'twas not kindly done?
For had they seen the next Year's Sun
A Beaten Wife and Cuckold Swain
Had jointly curs'd the marriage chain.
Now they are happy in their Doom
For P[ope] has wrote upon their Tomb.

I confess these sentiments are not altogether so Heroic as yours, but I hope you will forgive them in favor of the two last lines. You see how much I esteem the Honour you have done them, thô I am not very impatient to have the same and had rather continue to be your stupid living Humble Servant than be celebrated by all the Pens in Europe.

I would write to Mr. C[ongreve] but suppose you will read this to him if he enquires after me.

Text H MS 254, pp. 37–40

From Nicolas-François Rémond[1] [*1719*]

Que je suis eloigné de me plaindre de vous! Je ne me plains que du malheur de ma destinée qui me tient eloigné de tout ce que j'aime en ce monde. Vos manieres sont si nobles et si douces que je ne puis rien imaginer de plus aimable, et la reconnoissance dont vous me flattez remplit mon ame de charme et de felicité. Mais je vous assure que je ne crois pas estre amoureux de vous, et ce qui me le persuade

---

[1] See above, p. 395. He and LM must have met face to face in Paris. These excerpts from his letters are translated on pp. 459–63 below.

c'est le fonds de tendre amitié que j'ai pour vostre personne. [*Passage omitted*] Quand je lis le Phedrus de Platon[1] ces liaisons foibles et vulgaires qu'on appele amitiez ne me semblent rien au prix de l'amour que ce tendre philosophe (c'est ainsi que vous le nommez) appele une espece de fureur divine et dont il fait une description pleine de cette meme fureur. Ne vous effrayez point d'un nom si aimable. Je ne l'entens que d'une amitié parfaite, que d'un gout qui en exclut tout autre, et que d'une certaine habitude de n'estre rempli que d'un seul objet. Si l'amour est autre chose je vous rassure en vous declarant que je n'en ai point pour Mil[ady] M[arie]. [*Passage omitted*] Comptez que vous verrez toujours le fonds de mon ame, et je suis sur d'y gagner. Ne vous effrayez donc point du voiage que vous ferez ici. Je ne suis pas assez heureux pour que vous en soyez allarmée; il ne sera dangereux que pour moi. [*Passage omitted*]

Adieu. Pensez quelque fois à moi et soyez assurée qu'aucune femme n'a jamais été aimée autant que je vous aime.

Text W MS iv. 223–4   *End. by* W R.

From Nicolas-François Rémond [*Dec. 1719*]

Vostre ecrit est tres spirituel, mais ce n'est pas une lettre. Je suis fort baissé auprès de vous. La singularité de l'impression que vous avez faitte sur mon ame ne vous amuse plus, et vous estes deja rebutée d'un commerce de quelques mois, qui sont des siècles pour vous. Il faut donc faire taire l'amant et que le pedant reponde à vostre dissertation. [*Passage omitted*] Je me contente pour moi de la liberté Angloise, et si dieu me prete vie, je vous ferai de beaux vers blancs, et vous dirai sans rime mais avec bien de la raison que je suis tous les jours plus charmé de vostre esprit et de la maniere dont vous l'avez scu cultiver. Je sens deja que *i love* a toute une autre efficace que *j'aime*; et donnant une honnete liberté à mon esprit, au lieu de dire en tremblant *je vous aime* je dirai sans craindre *i love you My Lady at all my heart.* [*Passage omitted*] Madame la comtesse de Stafford[2] va chez vous pour y demander son douaire, et elle y va conduite par un Paladin nommé Milord Peterboroug.[3] Elle est anciennement et particulierement de ma connoissance, fort peu francoise et d'un caractere qui n'est pas

[1] Rémond was called 'le Grec' by his contemporaries.

[2] Claude-Charlotte de Gramont (d. 1739), m. (1694) 10th Earl of Stafford, and separated from him after a year. He had died on 27 April 1719.

[3] Charles Mordaunt (c. 1658–1735), 3rd Earl of Peterborough, military hero. He arrived at Dover from the Continent on 22 Jan. 1720 (*Weekly Packet*, 30 Jan. 1720).

commun. Elle a beaucoup de curiosité pour vous. Vous me direz ce que vous en pensez.

Text W MS iv. 214–15   *End. by W* Remond

From Nicolas-François Rémond [*c. 12/1 Feb. 1720*]

Je serois bien indigne des bontez dont vous m'honnorez si je n'en avois pas toute la reconnoissance imaginable. Cette amitié qui vous fait descendre jusqu'au detail de mes affaires domestiques, ces conseils que vous me donnez pour assurer ma petite fortune chancelante, enfin cet interest que vous daignez prendre à ce que vous croiez pouvoir contribuer au bonheur de ma vie — tout cela est si adorable que je me crois par un simple sentiment de bienveillance d'une personne de vostre merite, le plus riche et le plus heureux de tous les hommes. Cependant pour ne vous pas deplaire, et sans oser vous faire des remerciemens, puisque vous m'ordonnez de compter sur vous (je me livre avec facilité et avec douceur à un plaisir si charmant) je vas vous repondre avec une naïveté dont vous serez contente.

Si j'estois le maistre de ma destinée, ne croiez pas que je pusse imaginer autre chose que de passer ma vie auprès de vous, à ne voir et à n'adorer que Mil[ady] M[arie]. Oui, je prefererois d'estre l'été à Thuydenham[1] et l'hyver à Kinsington,[2] sans connoistre ni la ville ni la cour, à estre Regent de France sans vous. [*Passage omitted*] Je vous ecris cette lettre ou plustost ce factum pendant que toute la cour est aux Thuilleries et qu'on fait le mariage de Mlle de Valois.[3] Mes gens me disent qu'elle est toute en pleurs. Nos princesses sont elevées d'une façon à ne se trouver lieu nulle part. Je suis sur que l'abbé C[onti] n'aura pas manqué ce spectacle. C'est un bon enfant qui sait beaucoup de philosophie. [*Passage omitted*]

Text W MS iv. 220, 222   *End. by W* R.

[1] Twickenham (the Dutch spelling was current in France). In June 1719, W had rented a house in this village from Sir Godfrey Kneller (Pope, *Corr.* ii. 6–7, 12).

[2] LM actually had a town house in Covent Garden.

[3] Charlotte-Aglaé d'Orléans, demoiselle de Valois, daughter of the Regent, was formally betrothed (11 Feb. 1720 N.S.), and married (12 Feb.) to the Prince of Modena (Saint-Simon, *Mémoires,* ed. G. Truc, 1954–61, vi. 525–6).

From Nicolas-François Rémond *26/15 Feb.* [*1720*]

Il s'est tenu une assemblée generale à la banque. Pour moi, je suis demeuré au coin de mon feu à lire Properce et à penser à mes amours, et je vous l'avoue quoique vous vous mocquiez souvent en moi de ce que vous admirez dans Platon mesme malgré la severité de sa morale. [*Passage omitted*] Je crois que M[ilord] St[air] vous sera bientost rendu.[1] Il a joué ici un grand rosle et je ne sais si le Roy d'Angleterre le pourra recompenser selon ses merites, quoiqu'il soit un grand Roy. Je serai faché de ne le plus voir, et je l'aime assez pour souhaiter qu'il parte. [*Passage omitted*] Pour remplir ma lettre de toute sorte de choses, je vous dirai qu'en cherchant quelques papiers j'ai trouvé la traduction francoise de la premiere partie de la preface de vostre ami M. Poppe sur Homere.[2] Je l'ai relue avec un grand plaisir. Je voudrois qu'il la fit traduire en latin entiere avec ses notes; ce seroit un ouvrage utile et agreable. Les gens qui pensent bien sont rares et je les aime beaucoup. [*Passage omitted*]

ce Lundi 26 de fevrier

Text W MS iv. 218–19   *End. by W* Mr Remond from Paris before he came into England.

From Nicolas-François Rémond [*March 1720*]

Je suis etonné, Madame, de vostre long silence. Est ce la cour ou la philosophie qui vous detourne? Peutestre que mes lettres vous importunent, pendant que les vostres font un des grands plaisirs de ma vie. Au moins ne me l'avouez point pour que je ne sois pas obligé de me corriger. Presque toutes les femmes de ce pays cy m'ennuient et me font penser aux ⟨c⟩harmes de vostre conversation à laquelle je ne trouve rien qui ressemble. Si j'estois aussi indiscret que l'abbé Conti[3] je gagnerois autant à faire ⟨i⟩mprimer vos lettres que j'ai gagné aux actions du Missisipi, et rien ne flatteroit tant ma pedanterie qu'un

---

[1] Lord Stair, Ambassador in Paris since 1715, was recalled early in 1720, and arrived in London in June (*Political State of Great Britain*, xix, 1720, p. 665).

[2] *Traduction de la première partie de la préface de l'Homère anglois de Mon-* *sieur Pope,* [1719] (E. Audra, *Les Traductions françaises de Pope 1717–1825,* 1931, no. 3).

[3] Referring to the printed letter of [Feb. 1718] (pp. 374–8 above).

commerce si delicieux avec une personne aussi distinguée que vous. [*Passage omitted*] Je souhaite quelquefois d'estre en Angleterre pour que vous daigniez prendre soing de mon pauvre esprit; nous lirions Homere avec Mr. Poppe, et vous nous y feriez remarquer des beautez qui lui echapent à lui mesme. C'est vous louer dignement apres ce que j'ai recu de lui. Je crois n'avoir que ce moien la pour apprendre l'Anglois que je voudrois savoir. Miledye Stair,[1] qui parle francois assez aisement, devroit m'encourager, mais j'ai la teste beaucoup plus libertine qu'une dame si raisonnable, et mortelle ennemie de toute grammaire. Vous la reverrez bientost avec son epoux, homme de grand merite et que j'aimerai toute ma vie. Pour vous j'ai deja eu l'honneur de vous inviter a venir passer l'été ici; j'irois en Angleterre si je le pourois. [*Passage omitted*] Il ne faut pas finir sans dire un petit mot des actions. Elles vont comme il plait au dieu, et ce dieu est Monsieur Law.[2] Pour moi, je suis toujours plein de confiance parce que c'est un estat de parresse et de tranquilité. [*Passage omitted*]

Text W MS iv. 225–6   *End. by* W Mr Remond has got by the Misisippi, from Paris before he came to England.

To Catherine Lady Gower[3] [*June 1720*]

Madam

If I had undertaken this business 3 days sooner, it had certainly been done; however, my Freind gives me very good hopes of it, the D[irectors] being inclin'd to do all things to oblige me. To morrow I shall know his positive answer and will send your Ladyship word, but I must beg you, Madam, to assure me of the Summ of £500, being determin'd that I will take no part of it my selfe, and I have

---

[1] Eleanor Campbell (d. 1759), da. of 2nd Earl of Loudoun, m. (1708) Lord Stair.

[2] When Rémond had bought the post of *introducteur des ambassadeurs*, John Law had loaned him more than half the purchase price ([A. Boppe, *Les Introducteurs des ambassadeurs 1585-1900*, 1901, p. 54; Philippe de Dangeau, *Journal*, ed. F. de Conches, 1860, xviii. 14, 61).

[3] Catherine Manners (1675–1723), da. of 1st Duke of Rutland, m. (1692) John, later 1st Baron Gower. The formal tone of LM's letter indicates that it is addressed to the Dowager Lady Gower and not to LM's sister Evelyn. It is true that the junior Lady Gower extravagantly played and lost in the South Sea Bubble (GEC *Peerage*), but so did everybody else.

desir'd £5,000 stock.¹ I am, Madam, with Inclination and respect, your Ladyship's most humble Servant,

M. Wortley Mon[tagu].

Text MS owned by the Duke of Sutherland *Address* To The Rt Honble The Lady Gower

From Nicolas-François Rémond² [*July 1720*]

Me refuserez vous toujours vos conseils avec opiniatreté et parce que vous haissez (à ce que tout le monde dit a Paris) la France et tous les Francois? Faut il qu'un pauvre diable ruiné du Missisipi de France ne puisse pas profiter de vos lumieres—vous qui estes le conseil de tous les gens les plus eclairez? Je suis parti fort riche de Paris et, par les nouvelles que m'a apporté Mylord Stair, je suis tres pauvre.³ Mais ce n'est pas de quoi il s'agit. On m'a donné des souscriptions pour deux mille livres; que feray je? Faut il recevoir un profit present mediocre ou coure des risques dans l'esperance d'un plus grand?⁴ Je meurs d'envie de causer avec vous sur tout cela, mais il est tres difficile de vous voir.⁵ En attendant je chercherai de l'argent pour n'estre pas raié de la liste. Je vous demande un entretien car je n'entens rien à tout cela, et je suis plus porte à avoir confiance en vous qu'en personne, malgré vos rigueurs.

Text W MS iv. 216 *End. by W* Mr Remond. Ruined by the Misissippi. Writ in London.

¹ When the books for the third subscription of South Sea stock were opened, on 15 June 1720, only ten per cent. was asked for, with the next instalment not due for more than a year (John Carswell, *The South Sea Bubble*, 1960, p. 159).

² As *introducteur des ambassadeurs*, a post he had purchased in 1719, Rémond was to have accompanied the duc de la Force to the English Court to congratulate George I on his reconciliation with the Prince of Wales. On 11 June N.S. Mathieu Marais noted that the embassy had been cancelled, but that Rémond had already sailed from Calais (*Journal*, ed. M. de Lescure, 1863, i. 283). He was actually in England by 19 May, when he dined at Lady Cowper's; and on 4 July he supped at Madame Kielmannsegge's (Mary, Countess Cowper, *Diary*, ed. S. Cowper, 2nd ed., 1865, pp. 167, 174).

³ The Mississippi Scheme collapsed in May 1720.

⁴ LM evidently advised him to sell, and at a very handsome profit, as can be seen in the copies of two documents, one signed by George Middleton, the goldsmith-banker, and the other by Lord Stair, both dated 12 Aug. 1720, in which Rémond sold his £2,000 worth of South Sea stock to Stair for £2,840 (Stair MS at Lochinch Castle, vol. 24, 1719–1732).

⁵ Rémond had complained to a friend in London: 'Dittes, je vous prie, a Mil[ady] M[arie] Qu'elle n'aime que les absens. Il y a bientost quinze jours que je suis a Londres et je ne l'ai vue qu'une fois à un soupé ou elle ne dit pas un mot' (to Alverez, W MS iv. 227).

To James Craggs[1] *18 July* [*1720*]

When I have so much reason to return you thanks for
your last favour, I am asham'd to trouble you for another.
You are so often importun'd in this manner I hope you
know how to forgive it, thô to say truth I do think it very
impertinent in me to desire you to put my Name in your
next List of Subscribers to the S.S. stock for what Summ you
please.[2] I am, Sir, Your oblig'd humble Servant,
July 18.   M. Wortley Montagu.

Text MS owned by Sir Eustace F. Tickell   *End. by* [?*Tickell*[3]] Lady
Mary Wortley Answered

From James Craggs *28 July 1720*

Cockpit,[4] July 28, 1720.

Madam,

I will not fail to insert your Ladyship's name in my list for the next
South Sea subscription, though I am not sure whether the directors
will receive another from me.[5] I am, with the greatest respect, Madam,
Your Ladyship's Most obedient humble Servant,

J. Craggs.

Text 1803, i. 41[6]   *Address* To the Honorable the Lady Mary
Wortley Montagu, at Twickenham.

[1] James Craggs the younger (1686–1721) was at this time Secretary of State. For an anecdote about him and LM at Court, see Stuart, pp. 76–77.

[2] Craggs was very active in allocating stock in the third subscription, which had been exhausted at the end of June. On 27 July the directors of the South Sea Company resolved to open a fourth subscription, but limited it to holders of former subscriptions; and the books were not opened for it until 24 Aug. (Craggs to Sutton, 28 July 1720, SP 78/168; John Carswell, *The South Sea Bubble*, 1960, pp. 161, 175–6).

[3] Thomas Tickell (1686–1740), poet, had been appointed Under-Secretary of State in 1717 by his friend Addison, who

was succeeded a year later by Craggs.

[4] Familiar term for the Treasury, Whitehall.

[5] The directors meant this subscription, the fourth, to be a City one, for they had found the nobility better at promising than at paying instalments (Carswell, p. 176). The subscription was finally opened on St. Bartholomew's Day (24 Aug.). On the 22nd, Pope, a neighbour at Twickenham, advised LM to buy South Sea stock because it would 'certainly rise in some weeks, or less' (*Corr.* ii. 52).

[6] Formerly Harrowby MS; sold at Sotheby's on 25 July 1903 as lot 571. In the catalogue it is dated 25 July 1720.

From Nicolas-François Rémond
4 Sept./24 Aug. [*1720*][1]

à Paris ce 4 de Septembre

Enfin me voici a Paris. [*Passage omitted*] Je ne regrette point le climat ni la societé d'Angleterre, mais bien la conversation de quelques personnes — surtout la vostre dont je n'ai joui que rarement, et que je mets au dessus de toutes les autres pour la vertu des sentimens aussi bien que pour la delicatesse de l'esprit. Je comptois que nous aurions un commerce plus vif et plus assidu, mais le mouvement des actions et le gout de la campagne vous occupent uniquement. [*Passage omitted*] Si vous venez jamais en France (en verité c'est un beau pays) vous serez plus contente de moi que je n'ai du estre content de vous. Tout cela n'est pas pour me plaindre; je sais que les dames Angloises sont incapables d'amitié et d'amour. Je ne me soucie gueres de la folie de l'un, mais je suis fort sensible à la douceur de l'autre. Je vous aimerai sans exiger de retour et vous serez pour moi le dieu des Epicuriens, adoré pour ses perfections. [*Passage omitted*] Avant que de finir je vous dirai que les bonnes tetes de ce pays cy n'ont pas grande opinion du succes de vostre compagnie du sud. Cela m'a fait penser à vous, si l'on pouvoit engager Mr. de M[ontagu] a realiser ores. J'appele realiser, acheter des terres ou avoir des guinées dans son coffre. Mais vous avez du bon sens et de la capacité l'un et l'autre. Je crois que vous ne pechez pas par temerité. Recevez seulment ce petit avis comme une preuve de mon attachement. [*Passage omitted*]

Text W MS iv. 229–30   *End. by* W Mr Remond After his return to Paris. His Loss by the Misisippi, and his Small gain in England. Advises to realise.

[1] This is evidently the last surviving letter from Rémond to LM. The unfortunate outcome of his visit, friendship, and investment is recounted in detail in LM's letters to Lady Mar the following year (vol. ii, 1–14).

Appendix I

TRANSLATION OF FRENCH
CORRESPONDENCE

From Baroness von der Schulenburg [*1715*]

I fear I have no words strong enough to assure you of the joy I felt in ⟨?⟩ that you ⟨have done me⟩ the honour of writing to me, assuring you that no one could be more grateful than I am for the goodness you show me, and that you will do me great pleasure and honour by coming here when you please. You can be well persuaded that the soonest will be the most agreeable to me; I thus flatter myself with having the honour very soon of being able to tell you in person how much I love you and how much I am, my dear madam, Your very humble and very obedient Servant,

M. de Schoulenbourg.

It is up to me to make many apologies for such a scribble, but as I am very busy I hope you will not look at it too closely.

Text (p. 245 above)

To the Abbé Conti [*Feb. 1718*]

I am charm'd, Sir, with your obliging Letter; and you may perceive, by the Largeness of my Paper, that I intend to give punctual Answers to all your Questions, at least if my *French* will permit me; for as it is a Language I do not understand to Perfection, so I much fear, that, for want of Expressions, I shall be quickly oblig'd to finish. Keep in Mind, therefore, that I am writing in a Foreign Language; and be sure to attribute all the Impertinences and Triflings dropping from my Pen, to the want of proper Words for declaring my Thoughts, but by no means to any Dullness or natural Levity.

These Conditions being thus agreed and settled, I begin with telling you, that you have a true Notion of the *Alcoran*, concerning which the *Greek Priests* (who are the greatest Scoundrels in the Universe) have invented out of their own Heads a Thousand ridiculous Stories, in order to decry the Law of *Mahomet*; to run it down, I say, without any Examination, or as much as letting the People read it: being afraid, that if once they begun to sift the Defects of the *Alcoran*, they might not stop there; but proceed to make use of their Judgment, about their own Legends and Fictions. In effect there's nothing so like as the Fables of the *Greeks* and of the *Mahometans*: And the last have Multitudes of Saints, at whose Tombs Miracles are by them said to be daily perform'd; nor are the Accounts of the Lives of those blessed *Mussulmans* much less stuff'd with Extravagancies, than the Spiritual Romances of the *Greek Papas*.

As to your next Enquiry, I assure you 'tis certainly false, though commonly believ'd in our Parts of the World, that *Mahomet* excludes Women from any Share in a future happy State. He was too much a Gentleman, and lov'd the Fair Sex too well, to use 'em so barbarously. On the contrary, he promises a very fine Paradise to the *Turkish* Women. He says indeed, that this Paradise will be a separate Place from that of their Husbands: But I fancy the most Part of 'em won't like it the worse for that; and that the Regret of this Separation will not render their Paradise the less agreeable. It remains to tell you, that the Virtues which *Mahomet* requires of the Women, to merit the Enjoyment of future Happiness, are: Not to live in such a Manner as to become useless to the World; but to employ themselves, as much as possible, in making little *Musselmans*. The Virgins who dye Virgins, and the Widows who marry not again, dying in mortal Sin, are excluded out of Paradise. For Women, says he, not being capable to manage Affairs of State, nor to support the Fatigues of War, God has not order'd them to govern or reform the World; but he has entrusted them with an Office which is not less honourable, even that of multiplying human Race: And such as, out of Malice or Laziness, do not make it their Business to bear or to breed Children, fulfil not the Duty of their Vocation, and rebel against the Commands of God. Here are Maxims for you, prodigiously contrary to those of your *Convents*. What will become of your Saint *Catharines*, your Saint *Theresas*, your Saint *Claras*, and the whole Bead-roll of your *holy Virgins and Widows?* who, if they are to be judged by this System of Virtue, will be found to have been infamous Creatures, that past their whole Lives in a most abominable Libertinism.

I know not what your Thoughts may be concerning a Doctrine so extraordinary with respect to us: but I can truly inform you, Sir, that the *Turks* are not so ignorant, as we fancy 'em to be, in Matters of

Politicks, or Philosophy, or even of Gallantry. 'Tis true, that Military Discipline, such as now practis'd in *Christendom*, does not mightily sute them. A long Peace has plung'd them into an universal Sloth. Content with their Condition, and accustom'd to boundless Luxury, they are become great Enemies to all manner of Fatigues. But, to make Amends, the Sciences flourish among them. The *Effendis* (which is to say, the Learned) do very well deserve this Name: They have no more Faith in the Inspiration of *Mahomet*, than in the Infallibility of the *Pope*. They make a frank Profession of *Deism* among themselves, or to those they can trust: and never speak of their Law but as of a politick Institution, fit now to be observ'd by wise Men, however at first introduc'd by Politicians and Enthusiasts.

If I remember right, I think I have told you in some former Letter, that at *Belgrade* we lodg'd with a great and rich *Effendi*, a Man of Wit and Learning, and of a very agreeable Humour. We were in his House about a Month, and he did constantly eat with us, drinking Wine without any Scruple. As I rally'd him a little on this Subject, he answer'd me smiling, that all the Creatures in the World were made for the Pleasure of Man; and that God would not have let the Vine grow, were it a Sin to taste of its Juice: But that nevertheless the Law, which forbids the Use of it to the Vulgar, was very wise; because such sort of Folks have not Sense enough to take it with Moderation. This *Effendi* appear'd no Stranger to the Parties that prevail among us: Nay, he seem'd to have some Knowledge of our Religious Disputes, and even of our Writers; and I was surpriz'd to hear him ask, among other Things, *How Mr.* Toland *did?*

My Paper, large as it is, draws towards an End. That I may not go beyond its Limits, I must leap from Religions to Tulips, concerning which you also ask me News. Their Mixture produces surprizing Effects. But what is to be observ'd most surprizing, is the Experiment of which you speak concerning Animals, and which is try'd here every Day. The Suburbs of *Pera*, *J[T]ophana*, and *Galata*, are Collections of Strangers from all Countries of the Universe. They have so often intermarry'd, that this forms several Races of People, the oddest imaginable. There's not one single Family of Natives that can value it self on being unmixt. You frequently see a Person, whose Father was born a *Grecian*, the Mother an *Italian*, the Grandfather a *French-man*, the Grandmother an *Armenian*, and their Ancestors *English*, *Muscovites*, *Asiaticks*, etc.

This Mixture produces Creatures more extraordinary than you can imagine. Nor could I ever doubt but there were several different Species of Men: Since the *Whites*, the Woolly and the Long-hair'd *Blacks*, the Small-ey'd *Tartars* and *Chinese*, the Beardless *Brasilians*, and (to name no more) the Oily-skinn'd Yellow *Nova-Zemblians*, have as specifick Differences under the same general Kind; as Greyhounds, Mastiffs, Spaniels, Bull-dogs, or the Race of my little *Diana*, if no Body is offended at the Comparison. Now as the various intermixing of these latter Animals causes Mungrels, so Mankind have their Mungrels too, divided and subdivided into endless Sorts. We have daily Proofs of it here, as I told you before. In the same Animal is not seldom remark'd the *Greek* Perfidiousness, the *Italian* Diffidence, the *Spanish* Arrogance, the *French* Loquacity, and all of a sudden he's seiz'd with a Fit of *English* Thoughtfulness, bordering a little upon Dulness, which many of us have inherited from the Stupidity of our *Saxon* Progenitors.

But the Family which charms me most, is that which proceeds from the fantastical Conjunction of a *Dutch* Male with a *Greek* Female. As these are Natures opposite in Extremes, 'tis a Pleasure to observe how the differing Atoms are perpetually jarring together in the Children, even so as to produce Effects visible in their external Form. They have the large black Eyes of the Country, with the fat, white, fishy Flesh of *Holland*, and a lively Air streak'd with Dulness. At one and the same Time they shew that Love of Expensiveness, so universal among the *Greeks*, and an Inclination to the *Dutch* Frugality. To give an Example of this, Young Women ruin themselves to purchase Jewels for adorning their Heads, while they have not the Heart to buy new Shoes, or rather Slippers, for their Feet, which are commonly in a tatter'd Condition: a thing so contrary to the Taste of our *English Women*, that it is for shewing how neatly their Feet are drest, and for shewing this only, they are so passionately enamour'd with their Hoop-pettycoats. I have abundance of other Singularities to communicate to you, but I am at the End both of my *French* and my Paper.

Text 1719 edition, pp. 3–7 (p. 374 above)

From Nicolas-François Rémond *20/9 April 1718*

If you like unusual things, this letter won't displease you. I have never had the honour of seeing you and probably never shall, nevertheless I cannot stop myself from writing to you. The Abbé C[onti], who is one of my particular friends, has entrusted me with a letter which you wrote to him from Constantinople. I have read it; I have re-read it a hundred times; I have copied it and I never lay it aside day or night. Consider my vanity: from that letter alone I believe I understand the singularity of your character and the infinite charms of your mind. Since that day I can no longer speak to the most intelligent ladies of this court, 'I am sick of your everyday beauties'; and if I had a mistress I believe that I should be honourable enough to leave her. What I am doing is a little like those sudden inspirations of which Homer speaks, and perhaps you do not know that it is even less possible to resist those of that deity than those of Minerva. How far gone must I be, since in my distraction I seek justification in Pagan theology for such extraordinary behaviour? I no longer listen to your friend about Mr. Newton; I speak to him only about M[y Lady] M[ary], and I am less fond of Sharper, with whom I have been on affectionate terms since he came to this country. If I were handsome and pleasing I believe that I would have gone to embark at Marseilles, and you would have been very much surprised to see a disciple of Socrates come and throw himself at your feet on those walks that you take beside that river beneath cypresses and orange-trees. But however philosophical you may be, I doubt that beauty of soul can hold its own in your opinion with physical charms, and I fear you might have relegated me to Madame de B[onnac]. I have always followed my emotions rather than my reason, and until now I have never been mistaken. Here is the strongest proof of it that I shall give in my life. You will think me the greatest fool in the world. I am very willing to run the risk if you are as amiable as your letter.

Paris, 20 April 1718

Text (p. 395 above)

To Madame —— [*April 1718*]

I am so glad to find you again, My dear Madam, that I cannot complain any more of having lost you; and the pleasure given me by that letter which I have just received today, makes me forget completely the uneasiness of the past ten months.

Idleness is the mother of vices (as you know) and having nothing better to do, I have produced a daughter. I know you will tell me that I have done very badly; but, if you had been in my place, I believe (God forgive me) that you would have produced two or three. In this country, it is just as necessary to show proofs of youth, to be recognized among beauties, as it is to show proofs of Nobility to be admitted among the Knights of Malta. I was very angry at this necessity; but, noticing that people looked at me with a great air of contempt, I finally complied with the fashion, and I lay in like the others. For that reason, among innumerable others, I wish with all my heart to hasten my return, because I am absolutely obliged to lie in every year, as long as I remain here. The French Ambassadress has complied to her heart's content; she has lain in and is big again. The Ladies of the country respect women only for the number of their offspring; I can hardly convince them that I have a legitimate excuse for being three months without pregnancy, because my Husband is a hundred leagues away from me.

I pray every day to see my King, my country, and my friends again. I take great pains to see everything; I speak the language passably, and I have had the advantage of forming friendships with Turkish Ladies, and of their liking me; and I can boast of being the first foreigner ever to have had that pleasure. I have visited a Sultana, widow of the late Emperor; and by this means I have learned all about the intrigue of the Seraglio; she assured me that the story of the Handkerchief, so firmly believed among us, has not a syllable of truth.

I have got hold of a Turkish love-letter which I will bring you, and which is truly so curious, that I cannot sufficiently marvel at the stupidity of Travellers in not having brought any back to Europe before. My dear Madam, may God give you (in the Turkish phrase) whatever pleasure would make you happy, and to me that of seeing you again.

Text (p. 403 above)

From Nicolas-François Rémond [*1719*]

How far I am from complaining of you! I complain only of the unhappiness of my destiny which keeps me separated from all that I love in this world. Your manners are so noble and so kind that I can imagine nothing sweeter, and the gratitude with which you flatter me fills my soul with delight and felicity. But I assure you that I do not believe myself in love with you, and what convinces me of it is the depth of tender friendship which I have for your person. [*Passage omitted*] When I read the Phaedrus of Plato those faint and common connections which are called friendships seem to me nothing compared with the love which that tender philosopher (that is what you call him) terms a kind of divine passion, and of which he gives a description full of that same passion. Do not be afraid of so delightful a name. I understand by it only a perfect friendship, a liking which excludes all others, and a particular habit of being occupied only with one single object.

459

If love is anything else, I reassure you by declaring that I have none at all for My Lady M[ary]. [*Passage omitted*] Believe that you will always see the depths of my heart, and I am certain to be the gainer for it. Do not alarm yourself at all, then, about the journey that you are going to make here. I am not fortunate enough for you to be alarmed; it will be dangerous only for me. [*Passage omitted*]

Farewell. Think of me sometimes, and be assured that no woman has ever been loved as much as I love you.

Text (p. 446 above)

From Nicolas-François Rémond [*Dec. 1719*]

Your writing is very witty, but it isn't a letter. I am very much sunk in your estimation. The oddness of the impression that you have made on my heart no longer amuses you, and you are already disgusted with a relationship of a few months, which seem to you centuries. The lover, then, must be silenced, and the pedant reply to your dissertation. [*Passage omitted*] For my part I am satisfied with English liberty, and if God gives me time, I will write beautiful blank verse to you, and tell you without rhyme but with plenty of reason that I am every day more charmed by your wit and by the way you have found to excercise it. I perceive already that *I love* has quite a different force from *j'aime*; and giving my heart an honourable freedom, instead of saying quiveringly *je vous aime*, I shall say fearlessly *I love you My Lady at all my heart*. [*Passage omitted*] The Countess of Stafford is going to your country to claim her jointure, and she goes there escorted by a Paladin named My Lord Peterborough. She is an old and special friend of mine, not very French, and of an unusual character. She is most curious about you. You must tell me what you think of her.

Text (p. 447 above)

From Nicolas-François Rémond [*c. 12/1 Feb. 1720*]

I should be quite unworthy of the favours with which you honour me if I didn't feel all conceivable gratitude for them. That friendship which makes you condescend even to the details of my domestic affairs, that advice you give me to guarantee my little tottering fortune, finally that interest you deign to take in what you feel can contribute to the felicity of my life—all this is so charming that I believe myself, simply by an expression of favour from a person of your merit, the richest and happiest of all men. Yet in order not to displease you, and without daring to thank you, since you bid me rely on you (I devote myself readily and sweetly to so charming a pleasure) I am going to reply with a candour that will satisfy you. If I were master of my destiny, don't think that I could imagine anything else than spending my life by your side, seeing and adoring only My Lady M[ary]. Yes, I should prefer being at Twickenham in the summer and Kensington in the winter, without knowing either the town or the court, to being Regent of France without you. [*Passage omitted*] I am writing you this letter or rather this memorandum while all the court is at the Tuileries and the marriage of Mlle de Valois is being celebrated. My servants tell me she is all in tears. Our princesses are brought up in such a way as to find no place for themselves anywhere. I am sure the Abbé C[onti] will not have missed this show. He's a good fellow who knows lots of philosophy. [*Passage omitted*]

Text (p. 448 above)

From Nicolas-François Rémond 26/15 Feb. [1720]

A general meeting has been held at the bank. I myself stayed in my chimney-corner reading Propertius and thinking of love, and I admit it to you although you often ridicule in me what you admire in Plato even in spite of the austerity of his ethics. [*Passage omitted*] I believe that Lord Stair will soon be restored to you. He has played a great part here, and I don't know if the King of England will be able to reward him according to his deserts, great King though he be. I shall be sorry not to see him any more, and I love him well enough to wish him to go. [*Passage omitted*] To fill my letter with all sorts of things, I will tell you that in searching for some papers I found the French translation of the first part of your friend Mr. Pope's preface to Homer. I read it again with great pleasure. I wish he would have the whole work translated into Latin with his notes; it would be a useful and pleasing work. People who think well are rare and I appreciate them greatly. [*Passage omitted*]

Monday, 26 February

Text (p. 449 above)

461

From Nicolas-François Rémond [*March 1720*]

I am astonished, Madam, at your long silence. Is it the court or philosophy that distracts you? Perhaps my letters annoy you, while yours form one of the great pleasures of my life. At least do not admit it to me, so that I may not be compelled to reform. Almost all the ladies of this country bore me, and make me think of the charms of your conversation, whose equal I cannot find. If I were as indiscreet as the Abbé C[onti], I should make as much money by having your letters printed as I have from the Mississippi stock, and nothing would flatter my pedantry as much as so delightful a connection with a person as distinguished as you. [*Passage omitted*] I sometimes wish to be in England, so that you might condescend to take care of my poor wit; we should read Homer with Mr. Pope, and you would point out to us beauties in it which escape even him. That is giving you worthy praise, considering what I have heard of him. I believe I have only that means of learning English, which I should like to know. My Lady Stair, who speaks French fairly fluently, should encourage me, but I have a mind far more emancipated than such a sensible lady, and a mortal enemy to all grammar. You will soon see her again with her husband, a man of great merit whom I shall love all my life. As for you, I have already had the honour of inviting you to come and spend the summer here; I should go to England if I could. [*Passage omitted*]
    I must not end without saying a brief word about the stocks. They go as the deity pleases, and that deity is Mr. Law. For myself, I am always full of confidence because that is a state of laziness and tranquillity.

Text (p. 449 above)

From Nicolas-François Rémond [*July 1720*]

Will you always stubbornly refuse me your advice because (as everyone says in Paris) you hate France and all the French? Must a poor devil ruined by the French Mississippi be unable to benefit by your knowledge—you who are the adviser of all the most enlightened people? I left Paris very rich and, according to the news my Lord Stair brought me, I am very poor. But that's not the point. I have been given subscriptions for two thousand pounds; what shall I do? Should I accept an immediate modest profit, or run risks in the hope of a larger one? I am dying to talk to you about all this, but it is very difficult to see you. While waiting I shall try to find some money, so as not to be struck off the list. I beg you for an interview because I don't understand anything about all this, and I am more inclined to have faith in you than in anyone, in spite of your harshness.

Text (p. 451 above)

From Nicolas-François Rémond *4 Sept./24 Aug. 1720*

Paris, 4 September .
Here I am at last in Paris. [*Passage omitted*] I don't regret the climate or the society of England at all, but I do very much the conversation of a few people—especially yours, which I enjoyed only seldom, and which I place above all the rest for the loftiness of your sentiments as much as for the refinement of your wit. I anticipated our having a livelier and steadier friendship, but the fluctuation of stocks and your taste for the country take up all your time. [*Passage omitted*] If ever you come to France (it really is a beautiful country) you shall be more satisfied with me than I have had cause to be with you. All this is not a complaint; I know that English ladies are incapable of friendship and of love. I care very little for the folly of the one, but I am strongly susceptible to the sweetness of the other. I will love you without exacting any return, and you shall be for me the god of the Epicureans, adored for his perfections. [*Passage omitted*] Before concluding I shall tell you that the good brains of this country have no great expectation of the success of your South [Sea] Company. This made me think of you, [and] whether Mr. Montagu could be persuaded to realise straight away. I call it realising, to buy land or to have money in your purse. But you both have common sense and judgement. I don't think you err through recklessness. Only receive this little hint as a proof of my attachment. [*Passage omitted*]

Text (p. 453 above)

Appendix II

TURKISH VERSE[1] IN EMBASSY LETTER[2]

Inci	Sensin güzellerin inci(si).
Pearl	You are the pearl of the beauties (fairest of the fair maidens).
Karanfil	Karanfilsin, kararın yok.
	Konca gülsün, tımarın yok.
	Ben seni çoktan severim.
	Senin benden haberin yok.
Carnation[3]	You are the carnation inconstant.
	You are the budding rose inattentive.
	I have long loved you.
	You have had no word (of it) from me.
Ful(ya)	Derdime derman bul.
Jonquil	Find the remedy for my passion.
Kâğıt	Bayılırım saat saat.
Paper	I faint hourly.
Armut	Ver bize bir umut.
Pear	Give me some hope.
Sabun	Derdinden oldum zabun.
Soap	I am weak with passion for you.
Kömür	Ben olayım size ömür.
Coal, charcoal	Let me live for you.
Gül	Ben ağlarım. Sen gül.
Rose	I weep. You laugh.

[1] Both the Turkish and translation have been checked by Mrs. Mary Lou Green.

[2] See above, pp. 388-9.

[3] 'Clove', LM's translation, is a secondary meaning of *karanfil*.

Hasır	Olayım sana asir.
Straw mat	Let me be your slave.
Çuha	Üstüne bulunmaz paha.
Cloth	Your price is not to be found.
Tarçın	Sen gel. Ben çekeyim harcın(ı).
Cinnamon	Come. Let me bear your expenses.
Çıra	Aşkın ilen oldum çıra.
Torch	I have become a torch with your passion.
Sırma	Yüzünü benden ayırma.
Gold thread	Turn not your face from me.
Saç	Başımızın taç.
Hair	Crown of my head.
Üzüm	Benim iki gözüm.
Grape	My two eyes.
Tel	Ölüyörüm. Tez gel.
Silver or	I am dying. Come quickly.
gold wire	
Biber	Bize bir doğru haber.
Pepper	(Send) me a true answer.

Appendix III

MARY ASTELL'S PREFACE[1] TO THE EMBASSY LETTERS

The Travels of an English Lady in Europe, Asia and Affrica

> Let the *Male-Authors* with an envious eye
> Praise coldly, that they may the more decry:
> *Women* (at least I speak the Sense of some)
> This little Spirit of Rivalship o'recome.
> I read with transport, and with Joy I greet
> A Genius so Sublime and so Complete,
> And gladly lay my Laurels at her Feet.
>
> M[ary] A[stell]

To the Reader.

I was going, like common Editors, to advertise the Reader of the Beautys and Excellencys of the Work laid before him; to tell him that the Illustrious Author had oppertunitys that other Travellers, whatever their Quality or Curiosity may be, cannot obtain, and a Genius capable of making the best Improvement of every oppertunity. But if the Reader, after perusing *one Letter* only, has not discernment to distinguish that natural Elegance, that delicacy of Sentiment and Observation, that easy gracefulness and lovely Simplicity (which is the Perfection of Writing) in which these *Letters* exceed all that has appear'd in this kind, or almost in any other, let him lay the Book down and leave it to those who have.

The noble Author had the goodness to lend me her M.S. to satisfy my Curiosity in some enquirys I made concerning her Travels. And when I had it in my hands, how was it possible to part with it! I once had the Vanity to hope I might acquaint the Public that it ow'd this invaluable Treasure to my Importunitys. But alas! The most Ingenious Author has condemn'd it to obscurity during her Life, and

[1] See above, p. xvii.

466

Conviction, as well as Deference, obliges me to yeild to her Reasons. However, if these *Letters* appear hereafter, when I am in my Grave, let *this* attend them in testimony to Posterity, that among her Contemporarys *one Woman*, at least, was just to her Merit.

There is not any thing so excellent but some will carp at it, and the rather because of its excellency. But to such Hypercritics, I shall only say,   *   *   *   *   *   *   *   *

*   *   *   *   *   *   *   *   *   *

I confess I am malicious enough to desire that the World shou'd see to how much better purpose the LADYS Travel than their LORDS, and that whilst it is surfeited with Male Travels, all in the same Tone and stuft with the same Trifles, a *Lady* has the skill to strike out a New Path and to embellish a worn-out Subject with variety of fresh and elegant Entertainment. For besides that Vivacity and Spirit which enliven every part and that inimitable Beauty which spreds thro the whole, besides that Purity of Style for which it may justly be accounted the Standard of the *English* Tongue, the Reader will find a more true and accurate Account of the Customs and Manners of the several Nations with whom the Lady Convers'd than he can in any other Author. But as her Ladyship's penetration discovers the inmost follys of the heart, so the candor of her Temper passes over them with an air of pity rather than reproach, treating with the politeness of a Court and gentleness of a Lady what the severity of her Judgment cannot but Condemn.

In short, let her own Sex at least do her Justice; Lay aside diabolical Envy and its Brother Malice with all their accursed Company, Sly Whispering, cruel backbiting, spiteful detraction, and the rest of that hideous crew, which I hope are very falsely said to attend the *Tea Table*, being more apt to think they haunt those Public Places where Virtuous Women never come. Let the Men malign one another, if they think fit, and strive to pul down Merit when they cannot equal it. Let us be better natur'd than to give way to any unkind or disrespectful thought of so bright an Ornament of our Sex, merely because she has better Sense. For I doubt not but our hearts will tell us that this is the Real and unpardonable Offence, whatever may be pretended. Let us be better Christians than to look upon her with an evil eye, only because the Giver of all good Gifts has entrusted and adorn'd her with the most excellent Talents. Rather let us freely own the Superiority of this Sublime Genius as I do in the sincerity of my Soul, pleas'd that a *Woman* Triumphs, and proud to follow in her Train. Let us offer her the *Palm* which is justly her due, and if we pretend to any Laurels, lay them willingly at her Feet.

Dec. 18th 1724.   M[ary] A[stell]

Charm'd into Love of what obscures my *Fame,*⎫
If I had Wit, I'de celebrate Her Name,   ⎬
And all the Beautys of her Mind proclaim;   ⎭
Till Malice deafned with the mighty sound,
Its ill-concerted Calumnys confound,
Let fall the Mask, and with pale Envy meet
To ask, and find, their Pardon at Her *Feet*.

You see, Madam, how I lay every thing at your Feet. As the Tautology shews the poverty of my Genius, it likewise shews the extent of your Empire over my Imagination.

May 31. 1725

Text H MS 254